KARL MARX

Theories of Surplus Value

PART II

LAWRENCE & WISHART LONDON

1969

Translated by Renate Simpson
Copyright © Lawrence & Wishart, 1969
SBN 85315 194 6

KARL MARX

THEORIES OF SURPLUS-VALUE

Volume IV of *Capital*

PART II

PROGRESS PUBLISHERS

Moscow 1968

TRANSLATED FROM THE GERMAN
EDITED BY S. RYAZANSKAYA

К. МАРКС

ТЕОРИИ ПРИБАВОЧНОЙ СТОИМОСТИ

(IV том «Капитала»)

Часть II

На английском языке

First printing 1968

Printed in the Union of Soviet Socialist Republics

PUBLISHERS' NOTE

This translation has been made from Karl Marx, *Theorien über den Mehrwert*, Teil 2, Dietz Verlag, Berlin, 1959. The arrangement of the material and the notes correspond on the whole to the Russian edition of Marx-Engels, *Complete Works*, Vol. 26, Part II, Moscow, 1963, prepared by the Institute of Marxism-Leninism in Moscow, where the manuscript of the work is kept.

It has been attempted to keep the translation as closely as possible to the original. When, for the sake of clarity, it has been found necessary to insert a few words these are enclosed in square brackets. In order to avoid confusion, the square brackets occasionally used by Marx in the manuscript have been replaced either by pointed brackets ⟨ ⟩ or, when the passages enclosed were longer, by braces { }.

Quotations from French and German authors are given in English in the text and are reproduced in the original language in the Appendix. In the case of British writers cited by Marx from a French source, the original English version appears in the text and the French translation used by Marx in the Appendix. Where an omission in a passage quoted has not been indicated by Marx, the ellipsis is enclosed in square brackets. Other discrepancies between the quotations as recorded by Marx and as they appear in the original source, are mentioned in footnotes. Words underlined by Marx, both in his own writing and in the extracts quoted by him, are set in italics, as are also titles of publications and foreign words customarily italicised (words underscored by two lines are set in spaced italics). Chapter and section headings correspond in general to those of the Russian edition. Headings set in square brackets have been provided by the Institute of Marxism-Leninism in Moscow on the basis of formulations used by Marx in the chapter or section in question.

The numbers of Marx's notebooks are indicated by Roman numerals, those of the manuscript pages by Arabic numerals, which are separated from the text by vertical lines. As a rule these numbers are printed only at the beginning of the relevant portion of the manuscript, but where passages have been transposed the number of the manuscript page (and, when there is a change to another notebook, also the number of the notebook) is shown both at the beginning of the passage (e.g. ||XII-659|) and also at the end (e.g. |XII-659||).

CONTENTS

[CHAPTER VIII]

HERR RODBERTUS. NEW THEORY OF RENT. (DIGRESSION)[1]

[1. Excess Surplus-Value in Agriculture. Agriculture Develops Slower Than Industry under Conditions of Capitalism]

||X-445| *Herr Rodbertus. Dritter Brief an von Kirchmann von Rodbertus. Widerlegung der Ricardoschen Lehre von der Grundrente und Begründung einer neuen Rententheorie*, Berlin, 1851.

The following remark has to be made beforehand: supposing the necessary wage is equal to 10 hours, then this is most easily explained in the following manner. If 10 hours' labour (i.e., a sum of money equal to 10 hours) enabled the agricultural labourer, on an average, to purchase all the necessary means of subsistence, agricultural, industrial products, etc., then this is the average wage for unskilled labour. We are thus concerned here with the *value* of his daily product which must fall to his share. In the first place this value exists in the form of the *commodity* which he produces, i.e., [in] a certain *quantity of this commodity*, in exchange for which, after deducting what he himself consumes of the commodity (if he [does consume any of it]), he can procure for himself the necessary means of subsistence. Not only the *use-value* which he himself produces, but industry, agriculture, etc., thus come into the estimation of his necessary "income". But this is inherent in the concept of *commodity*. He produces a commodity, not merely a product. We need therefore waste no words about this.

Herr Rodbertus first investigates the situation in a country where there is *no separation* between land ownership and ownership of capital. And here he comes to the important conclusion that rent (by which he means the entire *surplus-value*) is simply equal to the unpaid labour or the quantity of products which it represents.

In the first instance it is noteworthy that Rodbertus only takes into account the growth of *relative* surplus-value, i.e., the growth of surplus-value in so far as it arises out of the growing productivity of labour and not the growth of surplus-value derived from the prolongation of the working-day itself. All absolute surplus-value is of course relative in one respect. Labour must be sufficiently productive for the worker not to require all his time to keep himself alive. But from this point the distinction comes into force. Incidentally, if originally labour is but little productive, the needs are also extremely simple (as with slaves) and the masters themselves do not live much better than the servants. The relative productivity of labour necessary before a profit-monger, a parasite, can come into being is very small. If we find a high rate of profit though labour is as yet very unproductive, and machinery, division of labour etc., are not used, then this is the case only under the following circumstances; either as in India, partly because the requirements of the worker are extremely small and he is depressed even below his modest needs, but partly also because low productivity of labour is identical with a relatively small fixed capital in proportion to the share of capital which is spent on wages or, and this comes to the same thing, with a relatively high proportion of capital laid out in wages in relation to the total capital; or finally, because labour-time is excessively long. The latter is the case in countries (such as Austria etc.) where the capitalist mode of production is already in existence but which have to compete with far more developed countries. Wages can be low here partly because the requirements of the worker are less developed, partly because agricultural products are cheaper or—this amounts to the same thing as far as the capitalist is concerned—because they have less value in terms of money. Hence the quantity of the product of, say, 10 hours' labour, which must go to the worker as necessary wages, is small. If, however, he works 17 hours instead of 12 then this can make up [for the low productivity of labour]. In any case because in a given country the value of labour is falling relatively to its productivity, it must not be imagined that wages in different countries are inversely proportional to the productivity of labour. In fact exactly the opposite is the case. The more productive one country is relative to another in the world market,

the higher will be its wages as compared with the other. In England, not only nominal wages but [also] real wages are higher than on the continent. The worker eats more meat; he satisfies more needs. This, however, only applies to the industrial worker and not the agricultural labourer. But in proportion to the productivity of the English workers their wages are not higher [than the wages paid in other countries].

Quite apart from the variation in rent according to the fertility of the land, the very existence of rent—i.e., the modern form of landed property—is feasible because the average wage of the agricultural labourer is below that of the industrial worker. Since, to start with, by tradition (as the farmer turns capitalist before capitalists turn farmers) the capitalist passed on part of his gain to the landlord, he compensated himself by forcing wages down below their level. With the labourers' desertion of the land, wages had to rise and they did rise. But hardly has this pressure become evident, when machinery etc. is introduced and the land once more boasts a (relative) surplus population. (Vide England.) Surplus-value can be increased, without the extension of labour-time or the development of the productive power of labour, by forcing wages below their traditional level. And indeed this is the case wherever agricultural production is carried on by capitalist methods. Where it cannot be achieved by means of machinery, it is done by turning the land over to sheep grazing. Here then we already have a *potential basis* of ||446| rent since, *in fact*, the agricultural labourer's wage does not equal the average wage. This rent would be feasible quite independent of the *price* of the product, which is equal to its value.

Ricardo is also aware of the second type of rent increase, which arises from a greater product sold at the same price, but he does not take it into account, since he measures rent per quarter and not per acre. He would not say that rent has risen (and *in this way* rent can rise with falling prices) because 20 quarters [at] 2s. is more than 10 [quarters at] 2s. or 10 quarters [at] 3s.

Incidentally, however the phenomenon of rent may be explained, the *significant difference* between agriculture and industry remains, in that in the latter, excess surplus-value is created by cheaper production, in the former, by dearer production. If the average price of 1 lb. of yarn is 2s. and I can produce it for 1s. then, in order to gain an increased market for it, I will necessarily sell [it] for 1s. 6d. [or] at any rate below 2s. And

what is more, this is absolutely necessary, for cheaper production presupposes production on a larger scale. So, compared with
before, I am now glutting the market. I must sell *more* than
before. Although 1 lb. of yarn costs only 1s. this is only the
case if I now produce, say, 10,000 lbs. as against my previous
8,000 lbs. The low cost is only achieved because fixed capital is
spread over 10,000 lbs. If I were to sell only 8,000 lbs., the
depreciation of the machines alone would raise the price per lb.
by one-fifth, i.e., 20 per cent. So I sell at below 2s. in order to be
able to sell 10,000 lbs. In doing so, I am still making an excess
profit of 6d., i.e., of 50 per cent on the value of my product which
is 1s. and already includes the normal profit. In any case, I am
hereby forcing down the market-price with the result that the
consumer gets the product more cheaply. But in agriculture I
sell at 2s. since, if I had sufficient fertile land, the less fertile
would not be cultivated. If the area of fertile land were enlarged,
or the fertility [of the] poorer soil so improved that I could satisfy
demand, then this game would end. Not only does Ricardo not
deny this, but he expressly calls attention to it.

Thus if we admit that the varying fertility of the land accounts
not for rent itself, but only for the differences in rent, there
remains the law that while in industry, on an average, excess
profit arises from the lowering of the price of the product, in
agriculture the relative size of rent is determined not only by the
relative raising of the price (raising the price of the product of
fertile land above its value) but by selling the cheaper product at
the cost of the dearer. This is, however, as I have already
demonstrated (Proudhon)[2], merely the law of competition, which
does not emanate from the "soil" but from "capitalist production" itself.

Furthermore, Ricardo would be right in another respect, except
that, in the manner of the economists, he turns a historical
phenomenon into an eternal law. This historical phenomenon is
the relatively faster development of manufacture (in fact the
truly bourgeois branch of industry) as against agriculture. The
latter has become more productive but not in the same ratio as
industry. Whereas in manufacture productivity has increased
tenfold, in agriculture it has, perhaps, doubled. Agriculture has
therefore become *relatively* less productive, although absolutely
more productive. This only proves the very queer development
of bourgeois production and its inherent contradictions. It does
not, however, invalidate the proposition that agriculture becomes

relatively less productive and hence, compared with the value of the industrial product, the value of the agricultural product rises and with it also rent. That in the course of development of capitalist production, agricultural labour has become relatively less productive than industrial labour only means that the productivity of agriculture has not developed with the same speed and to the same degree.

Suppose the relation of industry A to industry B is as 1:1. Originally agriculture [was] more productive because not only natural forces but also a machine created by nature play a part in agriculture; right from the start, the individual worker is working with a machine. Hence, in ancient times and in the Middle Ages agricultural products were relatively much cheaper than industrial products, which is obvious (see *Wade*)[3] from the ratio of the two within the average wage.

At the same time let $1° : 1°$ indicate the fertility of the two [branches of production]. Now if industry A becomes $10°$, [i.e.] its fertility increases tenfold while industry B merely increases threefold, becomes $3°$, then whereas the industries were previously as $1 : 1$ they are now as $10 : 3$ or as $1 : {}^3/_{10}$. The fertility of industry B has decreased relatively by ${}^7/_{10}$ although absolutely it has increased threefold. For the highest rent [it is] the same—relatively to industry—as if it had risen because the poorest land had become ${}^7/_{10}$ less fertile.

Now it does not by any means follow, as Ricardo supposes, that the rate of profit has fallen because wages have risen as a result of the relative increase in the price of agricultural products ||447|. For the average wage is not determined by the relative but by the absolute value of the products which enter into it. It does however follow that the rate of profit (really the rate of surplus-value) has not risen in the same ratio as the productive power of manufacturing industry, and this is due to agriculture (not the land) being relatively less productive. This is absolutely certain. The reduction in the necessary labour-time seems small compared with the progress in industry. This is evident from the fact that the agricultural products of countries like Russia etc. can beat those of England. The lower value of money in the wealthier countries (i.e., the low relative production costs of money in the wealthier countries) does not enter into it at all. For the question is, why it does not affect their industrial products in competition with poorer countries when it does affect their agricultural products. (Incidentally, this does not prove that

2*

poor countries produce more cheaply, that their agricultural labour is more productive. Even in the United States, the volume of corn at a given price has increased, as has recently been proved by statistical information, not however because the yield per acre has risen, but because more acres have come under cultivation. It cannot be said that the land is more productive where there is a great land mass and where large areas, superficially cultivated, yield a greater absolute product with the same amount of labour than much smaller areas in the more advanced country.)

The fact that *less productive* land is brought under cultivation does not necessarily prove that agriculture has become less productive. On the contrary, it may prove that it has become more productive; that the inferior land is being cultivated, not [only] because the price of the agricultural product has sufficiently risen to compensate for the capital investment, but also the converse, that the means of production have developed to such an extent that the unproductive land has become "productive" and capable of yielding not only the normal profit but also rent. Land which is fertile at a [given] stage of development of productive power may be unfertile for a lower developmental stage.

In agriculture, the extension of labour-time—i.e., the augmentation of absolute surplus-value—is only possible to a limited degree. One cannot work by gaslight on the land and so on. True, one can rise early in spring and summer. But this is offset by the shorter winter days when, in any case, only a relatively small amount of work can be accomplished. So in this respect *absolute surplus-value is greater in industry* so long as the normal working-day is not regulated by force of law. A second reason for a smaller amount of *surplus-value* being created in agriculture is the long period during which the product remains in the process of production without any labour being expended on it. With the exception of certain branches of agriculture such as stock-raising, sheep farming, etc., where the population is positively ousted from the land, the number of people employed relatively to the constant capital used, is still far greater—even in the most advanced large-scale agriculture—than in industry, or at least in the dominating branches of industry. Hence in this respect even if, for the above-mentioned reasons, the mass of surplus-value is relatively smaller than it [would be] with the employment of *the same* number of people in industry—this latter condition is partly offset again by the wage falling below its average level—the rate of profit can be greater than in industry. But if there are, in agriculture, any causes (we only indicate the above) which raise the rate of profit (not temporarily but on an average as compared with industry) then the mere existence of the landlord would cause this extra profit to consolidate itself and accrue to the landlord rather than enter into the formation of the general rate of profit.

[2. The Relationship of the Rate of Profit to the Rate of Surplus-Value. The Value of Agricultural Raw Material as an Element of Constant Capital in Agriculture]

In general terms the question to be answered with regard to Rodbertus is as follows:

The general form of capital advanced is:

Constant capital	*Variable capital*
Machinery—Raw materials	Labour-power

In general the two elements of constant capital are the instruments of labour and the subject of labour. The latter is not necessarily a commodity, a product of labour. It may therefore not exist as an *element of capital*, although it is invariably an *element in the labour-process*. Soil is the husbandman's raw material, the mine that of the miner, the water that of the fisherman and even the forest is that of the hunter.[4] In the most complete form of capital, however, these three elements of the labour-process also exist as three elements of capital, i.e., they are all commodities, use-values which have an exchange-value and are products of labour. In this case all three elements enter into the process of creating value, although machinery [enters into it] not to the extent to which it enters into the labour-process but only in so far as it is consumed.

The following question now arises: Can the absence of one of these elements in a particular branch of industry enhance the *rate of profit* (not the rate of surplus-value) in that industry? In general terms, the formula itself provides the answer:

The rate of profit equals the ratio of surplus-value to the total capital advanced.

Throughout this investigation it is assumed that the *rate of surplus-value*, i.e., the division of the value of the product between the capitalist and the worker, remains constant.

||448| The rate of surplus-value is $\frac{s}{v}$; the rate of profit is $\frac{s}{c+v}$. Since s', the rate of surplus-value, is given, v is given and $\frac{s}{v}$ is assumed to be a constant value. Therefore the magnitude of $\frac{s}{c+v}$ can only alter when $c + v$ changes and since v is given, this can only increase or decrease because c decreases or increases. And further, $\frac{s}{c+v}$ will increase or decrease not in the ratio of $c : v$ but according to c's relation to the sum of $c + v$. If c equals nought, then $\frac{s}{c+v}=\frac{s}{v}$. The rate of profit [would] in this case equal the rate of surplus-value and this is its highest possible amount, since no sort of *calculation* can alter the magnitude of s and v. Suppose $v = 100$ and $s = 50$, then $\frac{s}{v}=\frac{50}{100}=\frac{1}{2}=50$ per cent. If a constant capital of 100 were added, then the rate of profit [would be] $\frac{50}{100+100}=\frac{50}{200}=\frac{1}{4}=25$ per cent. The rate of profit would have decreased by half. If 150 c were added to 100 v then the rate of profit would be $\frac{50}{150+100}=\frac{50}{250}=\frac{1}{5}=20$ per cent. In the first instance, total capital equals v, i.e., equals variable capital, hence the rate of profit equals the rate of surplus-value. In the second instance, total capital equals $2 \times v$, hence the rate of profit is only half the rate of surplus-value. In the third instance total capital is $2\frac{1}{2} \times 100$, that is $2\frac{1}{2} \times v$, that is $\frac{5}{2} \times v$; v is now only $\frac{2}{5}$ of total capital. Surplus-value equals half of v, i.e., half of 100, hence is only half of $\frac{2}{5}$ of total capital, or $\frac{2}{10}$ of total capital. $\frac{250}{10} = 25$ and $\frac{2}{10}$ of $250 = 50$. But $\frac{2}{10} = 20$ per cent.

Hence to start with this much has been established. Provided v remains constant and $\frac{s}{v}$ too, then it is of no consequence how c is composed. If c has a certain magnitude, say 100, then it makes no difference whether it consists of 50 units of raw material and 50 of machinery or 10 of raw material and 90 of machinery, or no raw material and 100 machinery or the other way about. For the rate of profit is determined by the relationship $\frac{s}{c+v}$; the relative value of the various production elements contained in c is of no consequence here. For instance, in the production of coal the raw materials (after deducting coal itself which is used as an auxiliary material) may be reckoned as nought and the entire constant capital can be assumed to consist of machinery (including buildings and tools). On the other hand, with a tailor, machinery can be considered as nought and here the whole of constant capital resolves into raw materials (particularly where tailors running a large business do not as yet use sewing-machines and, on the other hand, even save buildings, as sometimes occurs nowadays in London, by employing their workers as outworkers. This is a *new phenomenon*, where the second *division of labour* reappears *in the form* of the first[5]). If the colliery owner employs 1,000 units of machinery and 1,000 units of labour and the tailor 1,000 of raw materials and 1,000 of labour, then with an equal rate of surplus-value, the rate of profit in both instances is the same. If [we] assume that surplus-value is 20 per cent, then the rate of profit would in both cases be 10 per cent, namely: $^{200}/_{2,000} = {}^2/_{20} = {}^1/_{10} = 10$ per cent. Hence there are only two instances in which the ratio between the component parts of c, i.e., raw materials and machinery, can affect the rate of profit: 1. If a change in this ratio modifies the absolute magnitude of c. 2. If the ratio between the component parts of c modifies the size of v. This would imply organic changes in production itself and not merely the tautologous statement that if a particular part of c accounts for a smaller portion, then the other must make up a larger portion of the total amount.

In the real bill of an English farmer, *wages* amount to £ 1,690, *manure* to £ 686, *seeds* to £ 150, *fodder for cows* to £ 100. Thus "raw material" comes to £ 936, which is more than half the amount spent on wages. (See F. W. Newman, *Lectures on Political Economy*, London, 1851, p. 166.)

"In *Flanders*" (in the *Belgian* areas) "*dung* and hay are in these parts imported from Holland" (for flax-growing, etc. In turn they export flax, *linseed*, etc.). "The refuse of the towns has therefore become[a] a matter of trade, and is regularly sold at high prices to Belgium.... At about twenty miles from Antwerp, up the Schelde, the reservoirs may be seen for the manure that is brought from Holland. The trade is managed by a company of capitalists and the[b] Dutch boats" etc. (*Banfield*).[6]

---

a Instead of "of the towns has therefore become" in the manuscript: "In Dutch towns is".—*Ed.*

b Instead of "and the" in the manuscript: "on".—*Ed.*

And so even manure, plain muck, has become merchandise, not to speak of bone-meal, guano, pottash etc. That the elements of production *are estimated* in terms of money is not merely due to the formal change in production. New materials are introduced into the soil and its old ones are sold for reasons of *production*. This is not merely a formal difference between the capitalist and the previous mode of production. The seed trade has risen in importance to the extent to which the importance of seed rotation has become recognised. Hence it would be ridiculous to say that no "raw material"—i.e., raw material as a commodity— enters into agriculture whether it be reproduced by agriculture itself or bought as a commodity, acquired from outside. It would be equally absurd to say that the machine employed by the engineer ||449| who constructs machines does not figure as an element of value in his capital.

A German peasant who year after year produces his own elements of production, seeds, manure etc., and, with his family, consumes part of his crops needs to spend money (as far as production itself is concerned) only on the purchase of a few tools for cultivating the land, and on wages. Let us assume that the value of all his expenses is 100 [half of this having to be paid out in money]. He consumes half [of the product] in kind (production costs [are also included here]). The other half he sells and he receives, say, 100. His gross income is thus 100 and if he relates this to his capital of 50 then it amounts to 100 per cent [profit]. If one-third of the 50 is deducted for rent and one-third for taxes ($33\frac{1}{3}$ in all) then he retains $16\frac{2}{3}$, calculated on 50 this is $33\frac{1}{3}$ per cent. But in fact he has only received $16\frac{2}{3}$ per cent [of the 100 he laid out originally]. The peasant has merely miscalculated and has cheated himself. The capitalist farmer does not make such errors.

Mathieu de Dombasle says in his *Annales agricoles* etc. 4 ième livraison, Paris 1828 that under the métairie contract (in [the province of] Berry, for example):

"the landlord supplies the land, the buildings and usually all or part of the livestock and the tools required for cultivation; the tenant for his part supplies his labour and nothing, or almost nothing else. The products of the land are shared in equal parts" (l.c., p. 301). "The tenants are as a rule submerged in dire poverty" (l.c., p. 302). "If the metayer, having laid out 1,000 francs, increases his gross product by 1,500 francs" (i.e., a gross gain of 500 francs) "he must pass half of it on to the landowner, retaining merely 750 and so loses 250 francs of his expenses" (l.c., p. 304). "Under the previous system of cultivation the expenses or costs of production were almost exclusively drawn in kind, from the products themselves, for the consumption of the animals and of the cultivator of the land and his family; hardly any cash was paid out. Only these particular circumstances could give rise to the belief that landowner and tenant could divide amongst themselves the whole of the harvest which had not been consumed during production. But this process is only applicable to this type of agriculture, namely, *low-level agriculture*. But when it is desired to raise that level, it is realised that this is only possible by making certain advances which have to be deducted from the gross product in order to be able to utilise them again in the following year. Hence this kind of division of the gross product becomes an insurmountable obstacle to any sort of improvement" (l.c., p. 307).

[3. Value and Average Price[7] in Agriculture. Absolute Rent]

[a) Equalisation of the Rate of Profit in Industry]

Herr Rodbertus seems to think that competition brings about a normal profit, or average profit or general rate of profit by reducing the commodities to their *real value*; i.e., that it regulates their price relationships in such a manner that the correlative quantities of labour-time contained in the various commodities are expressed in money or whatever else happens to be the measure of value. This is of course not brought about by the price of a commodity at any given moment being equal to its value nor does it have to be equal to its value. [According to Rodbertus, this is what happens:] For example the price of commodity A rises above its value and for a time remains, moreover, at this high level, or even continues to rise. The profit of [the capitalist who produces] A thus rises above the average profit in that he appropriates not only his own "unpaid" labour-time, but also a part of the unpaid labour-time which other capitalists have "produced". This has to be compensated by a fall in profit in one or other sphere of production provided the price of the other commodities in terms of money remains constant. If the commodity is a means of subsistence generally consumed by the worker, then it will depress the rate of profit in all other branches; if it enters as a constituent part into the constant capital, then it will force down the rate of profit in all those spheres of production where it forms an element in constant capital.

Finally, the commodity may neither be an element in any constant capital, nor form a *necessary* item in the workers' means of subsistence (for those commodities which the worker can choose to buy or abstain from buying, he consumes as a consumer in general and not as a worker) but it may be one of the consumer goods, an article for individual consumption in general. If, as such, it is consumed by the industrial capitalist himself, then the rise in its price in no way affects the amount of surplus-value or the rate of surplus-value. Now if the capitalist wanted to maintain his previous standard of consumption, then that part of profit (surplus-value) which he uses for individual consumption would rise in relation to that which he sinks into industrial reproduction. The latter would decrease. As a result of the price rise, or the rise in profit above its average rate, in A, the volume of profit in B, C, etc. would diminish within a certain space of time (which is also determined by reproduction). If article A was exclusively consumed by other than industrial capitalists, then they would consume more than before of commodity A as compared with commodities B, C, etc. The demand for commodities B, C, etc. would fall; their price would fall and, in this case, the price rise in A, or the rise in profit in A above the average rate, would have brought about a fall in the profit in B, C, etc. below the average rate by forcing down the money prices of B, C, etc. (in contrast to the previous instances where the money price of B, C, etc. ||450| remained constant). Capitals would migrate from B, C, etc., where the rate of profit has sunk below the [average] level, to A's sphere of production. This would apply particularly to a portion of the new capital which is continually entering the market and which would naturally tend to penetrate into the more profitable sphere A. Consequently, after some time, the price of article A would fall below its value and would continue to do so for a longer or shorter period, until the reverse movement set in again. The opposite process would take place in the spheres B, C, etc., partly as a result of the reduced supplies of articles B, C, etc., because of the exodus of capital, i.e., because of the organic changes taking place in these spheres of production themselves, and partly as a result of the changes which have occurred in A and which in turn are affecting B, C, etc. in the opposite direction.

Incidentally, it may well be that in this process—assuming the value of money to be constant—the money prices of B, C, etc., never regain their original level, although they may rise above the value of commodities B, C, etc. and hence the rate of profit in B, C, etc. may also rise above the general rate of profit. Improvements, inventions, greater economy in the means of production, etc. are introduced not at times when prices rise above their average level, but when they fall below it, i.e., when profit falls below its normal rate. Hence during the period of falling prices of B, C, etc., their *real value* may fall, in other words the minimum labour-time required for the production of these commodities may decrease. In this case, the commodity can only regain its former money price if the rise in its price over its value equals the margin, i.e., the difference between the price which expresses its new value and the price which expressed its higher former value. Here the *price* of the commodity would have changed the value of the commodity by affecting supply, and the costs of production.

The result of the above-mentioned movement: If we take the average of the increases and decreases in the price of the commodity above or below its value, or the period of equalisation of rises and falls—periods which are constantly repeated—then the *average price* is equal to the *value* of the commodity. The average profit in a particular sphere is therefore also equal to the general rate of profit; for although, in this sphere, profit rose above or fell below its old rate with the rise or fall in prices—or with the increase or decrease in costs of production while the price remained constant—on an average, over the period, the commodity was sold at its *value. Hence* the profit yielded is equal to the general rate of profit. This is Adam Smith's conception and, even more so, *Ricardo*'s, since the latter adheres more firmly to the real concept of value. Herr Rodbertus acquires it from them. And yet this conception is wrong.

What is the effect of the competition between capitals? The *average price* of the commodities during a period of equalisation is such that these prices yield the same profits to the producers of commodities in every sphere, for instance, 10 per cent. What else does this mean? That the price of each commodity stands at one-tenth above the price of the production costs, which the capitalist has incurred, i.e., the amount he has spent in order to produce the commodity. In general terms this just means that capitals of equal size yield equal profits, that the price of each commodity is one-tenth higher than the price of the capital advanced, consumed or represented in the commodity. It is however quite incorrect to say that capitals in the various spheres of production produce the same surplus-value in relation to their size, even if we assume that the absolute working-day is equally long in all spheres, i.e., if we assume a set rate of surplus-value. ⟨We leave aside here the possibility of one capitalist enforcing

longer working hours than another, and we assume a fixed
absolute working-day for all spheres. The variation in absolute
working-days is partly offset by the varying intensity of labour
etc., and partly these differences only signify arbitrary excess
profits, exceptional cases, etc.⟩

Bearing in mind the above assumption, the amount of surplus-
value produced by capitals of *equal* size varies *firstly* according
to the correlation of their organic components, i.e., of variable
and constant capital; *secondly* according to their period of circulation in so far as this is determined by the ratio of fixed capital
to circulating capital and also [by] the various periods of reproduction of the different sorts of fixed capital; *thirdly* according
to the duration of the actual period of production as distinct from
the duration of labour-time itself,[8] which again may lead to
substantial differences between the length of the production
period and circulation period. (The first of these correlations,
namely, that between constant and variable capital, can itself
spring from a great divergency of causes; it may, for example,
be purely formal so that the raw material worked up in one
sphere is dearer than that worked up in another, or it may result
from the varying productivity of labour, etc.)

Thus, if the commodities were sold at their values or if the
average prices of the commodities were equal to their values,
then the rate of profit in the various spheres would have to vary
a great deal. In one case it would be 50, in others 40, 30, 20, 10,
etc. Taking the total volume of commodities for a year in sphere
A, for instance, their value would be equal to the capital advanced
in them plus the unremunerated labour they contain. Ditto in
spheres B and C. But since A, B and C contain different amounts
of unpaid labour, for instance, A more than B and B more than
C, the commodities A might perhaps yield $3\,S$ ($S =$ surplus-value)
to their producers, $B = 2\,S$ and $C = S$. Since the rate of profit
is determined by the ratio of surplus-value to capital advanced,
and as on our assumption this is the same in A, B, C, etc., then
||451| if C is the capital advanced, the various rates of profit
will be $\dfrac{3S}{C}, \dfrac{2S}{C}, \dfrac{S}{C}$. Competition of capitals can therefore
only equalise the rates of profit, for instance in our example, by
making the rates of profit, equal to $\dfrac{2S}{C}, \dfrac{2S}{C}, \dfrac{2S}{C}$, in the
spheres A, B, C. A would sell his commodity at 1 S less and C
at 1 S more than its value. The average price in sphere A would

be below, and in sphere C would be above, the value of the commodities A and C.

As the example of B shows, it *can* in fact happen that the average price and the value of a commodity coincide. This occurs when the surplus-value created in sphere B itself equals the average profit; in other words, when the relationship of the various components of the capital in sphere B is the same as that which exists when the total sum of capitals, the capital of the capitalist class, is regarded as one *magnitude* on which the whole of surplus-value [is] calculated, irrespective of the sphere in which it has been created. In this aggregate capital the periods of turnover, etc. are equalised; one can, for instance, consider that the whole of this capital is turned over during one year. In that case every section of the *aggregate capital* would in accordance with its magnitude participate in the aggregate surplus-value and draw a corresponding part of it. And since every individual capital is to be regarded as shareholder in this aggregate capital, it would be correct to say *first* that its *rate of profit* is the same as that of all the others [because] capitals of the same size yield the same amount of profit; *secondly*, and this arises automatically from the first point, that the volume of profit depends on the size of the capital, on the number of shares the capitalist owns in that aggregate capital. Competition among capitals thus seeks to treat every capital as a share of the aggregate capital and correspondingly to regulate its participation in surplus-value and hence also in profit. Competition more or less succeeds in this by means of its equalisations (we shall not examine here the reason why it encounters particular obstacles in certain spheres). But in plain language this just means that the capitalists strive (and this striving is competition) to divide among themselves the quantity of unpaid labour—or the products of this quantity of labour—which they squeeze out of the working class, not according to the surplus-labour produced directly by a *particular* capital, but corresponding *firstly* to the relative portion of the aggregate capital which a particular capital represents and *secondly* according to the amount of surplus-labour produced by the aggregate capital. The capitalists, like hostile brothers,[9] divide among themselves the loot of other people's labour which they have appropriated so that on an average one receives the same amount of unpaid labour as another.

Competition achieves this equalisation by regulating average prices. These average prices themselves, however, are either above or below the value of the commodity so that no commodity yields a higher rate of profit than any other. It is therefore wrong to say that competition among capitals brings about a general rate of profit by equalising the prices of commodities to their values. On the contrary it does so *by converting the values of the commodities into average prices, in which a part of surplus-value is transferred from one commodity to another*, etc. The *value* of a commodity equals the quantity of paid and unpaid labour *contained* in it. The *average price* of a commodity equals the quantity of paid labour it *contains* (materialised or living) plus an average quota of unpaid labour. The latter does not depend on whether this amount was contained in the commodity itself or on whether more or less of it was embodied in the value of the commodity.

[b) Formulation of the Problem of Rent]

It is possible—I leave this over for a later inquiry which does not belong to the subject-matter of this book[10]—that certain spheres of production function under circumstances which work against a reduction in their values to average prices in the *above* sense, and do not permit competition to achieve this victory. If this were the case for instance with agricultural rent or rent from mines (there are rents which are altogether only explicable by monopoly conditions, for instance the water rent in Lombardy, and in parts of Asia, also house rent in so far as it represents rent from landed property) then it would follow that while the product of all industrial capitals is raised or lowered to the average price, the product of agriculture [would] equal its value, which would be above the average price. Might there be obstacles here, which cause more of the *surplus-value created* in this sphere of production to be appropriated as property of the sphere itself, than should be the case according to the laws of competition, more than it should receive according to the quota of capital invested in this branch of industry?

Supposing industrial capitals which are producing 10 or 20 or 30 per cent more surplus-value ||452| than industrial capitals of equal size in other spheres of production, not just temporarily, but because of the very nature of *their* spheres of production as opposed to others; supposing I say, they were able to hang on to this excess surplus-value in the face of competition and to prevent it from being included in the general accounts (distribution) which determine the general rate of profit, then, in this case, one could distinguish between two recipients in the spheres of production of these capitals, the one who would get the general rate of profit, and the other who would get the surplus exclusively inherent in this sphere. Every capitalist could pay, hand over, this excess to the privileged one, in order to invest his capital here, and he would retain for himself the general rate of profit, like every other capitalist, working under the same conditions. If this were the case in agriculture etc., then the splitting of *surplus-value* into *profit* and *rent* would by no means indicate that labour as such is actually more "productive" ([in the sense of production] of surplus-value) here than in manufacture. Hence [it would not be necessary] to ascribe any magic powers to the soil; this, moreover, is in any case absurd, since *value equals labour, therefore surplus-value cannot possibly equal soil* (although relative surplus-value may be due to the natural fertility of the soil, but under no circumstances could this result in a *higher price* for the products of the soil. Rather the opposite). Nor would it be necessary to have recourse to Ricardo's theory, which is disagreeably linked with the Malthusian trash, has repulsive consequences and, though in theory it is not especially opposed to my views on relative surplus-value, it deprives them of much of their practical significance.

Ricardo's point is this: Rent (for instance, in agriculture) can be nothing other than an excess above general profit where—as he presupposes—agriculture is run on capitalist lines, where [there] is [a] *farmer*. Whether that which the landlord receives is actually equal to this rent in the bourgeois-economic sense is quite irrelevant. It may be purely a deduction from wages (vide Ireland) or it may be partly derived from the reduction of the farmer's profit below the average level of profits. Which of these possible factors happens to be operative is of no consequence whatsoever. *Rent*, in the bourgeois system, only exists as a special, characteristic form of surplus-value in so far as it is an excess over and above (general) profit.

But how is this possible? The commodity wheat, like every other commodity, is [according to Ricardo] sold at its *value*, i.e., it is exchanged for other commodities in relation to the labour-time embodied in it. ⟨This is the first erroneous assumption which complicates the problem by posing it artificially. Only in exceptional circumstances are commodities exchanged at their value. Their *average prices* are determined in a different way.

See above.⟩ The farmer who grows wheat makes the same profit as all the other capitalists. This proves that, like all the others, he appropriates that portion of labour-time for which he has not paid his workers. Where, on top of this, does the rent come from? It must represent labour-time. Why should surplus-labour in agriculture resolve into profit and rent while in industry it is just profit? And, how is this possible at all, if the profit in agriculture equals the profit in every other sphere of production? ⟨Ricardo's faulty conception of profit and the way in which he confuses it with surplus-value have also a detrimental effect here. They make the whole thing more difficult for him.⟩

Ricardo solves this *difficulty* by assuming that *in principle* it is non-existent. ⟨This indeed is in principle *the only possibility* of overcoming any difficulty. But there are two ways of doing this. Either one shows that the contradiction to the principle is an *illusion* which arises from the development of the thing itself, or one *denies* the existence of the difficulty *at one point*, as Ricardo does, and then takes this as a starting-point from which one can proceed to explain its existence at some other stage.⟩

He assumes a point at which the farmer's capital, like every-one else's, only yields profit. ⟨This capital may be invested in a non-rent paying or individual farm, or in a non-rent paying part of the land of a farm. In fact it can be any capital which is employed in the cultivation of land that does not pay rent.⟩ This, moreover, is the starting-point, and it can also be expressed as follows: Originally the farmer's capital only pays profit, no rent ⟨although this *pseudo-historical* form is of no consequence and in other "laws" is common to all bourgeois economists⟩. It is no different from any other industrial capital. Rent only enters into it because the demand for grain rises and now, in contrast to other branches of industry, it becomes necessary to resort to "less" fertile ground. The farmer (the supposed original farmer) suffers, like any other industrial capitalist, in so far as he has to pay his workers more because of the rise in [the price of] food. But he gains because of the rise in price of his commodity above its value, firstly, to the extent to which the value of other com-modities which enter into his constant capital falls relatively to his commodity and so he buys them more cheaply, and secondly, in so far as he owns the surplus-value in the form of his dearer commodity. Thus this farmer's profit rises above the average rate of profit, which has, however, fallen. Hence another capitalist moves onto the less fertile land, No. II which, with this lower rate of profit, can supply produce at the price of I or perhaps even a little more cheaply. Be that as it may, we now have, once more, ||453| the normal situation on II, that surplus-value merely resolves itself into profit. But we have explained the rent for I by the existence of a twofold price of production: the production price of II [which] is simultaneously the market price of I. A temporary surplus gain has been [achieved], just as with the factory-made commodity which is produced under more favourable conditions. The price of corn, which in addition to profit comprises rent, in fact consists only of materialised labour, and is equal to its value; it is however equal not to the value embodied in itself, but to the value of II. It is impossible to have two market prices [side by side]. ⟨While Ricardo introduces farmer No. II because of the fall in the rate of profit, Stirling[11] introduces him because wages [have] *fallen* not risen following upon the price of corn. This fall in wages allows No. II to cultivate a piece [of land] No. II at the old rate of profit, although the soil is less fertile.⟩ Once the existence of rent has been established in this way, the rest follows easily. The *difference between rents* according to varying fertility, etc., of course remains correct. This does not necessarily imply that less and less fertile land has to come under cultivation.

So here we have Ricardo's theory. The higher price of corn, which yields an excess profit to I, does not yield even as much as the earlier rate of profit for II. It is thus clear that product II contains more value than product I, i.e., it is the product of more labour-time, it embodies a greater quantity of labour. Therefore more labour-time must be supplied to manufacture the same product—say, for instance, a quarter of wheat. And the rise in rent will be relative to this decreasing fertility of the land, or the growth in the quantity of labour which must be employed to produce, say, a quarter of wheat. Of course Ricardo would not talk of a "rise" in rent if there were just an increase in the number of quarters from which rent is paid, but only if the price of the *individual* quarter rose from say 30s. to 60s. True, he does sometimes forget that the *absolute volume of rent can grow with a reduced rate of rent, just as the absolute amount of profit can increase with a decreasing rate of profit.*

Others seek to by-pass this difficulty (*Carey* for instance) by directly denying its existence. Rent [they say] is only interest on the capital which, at an earlier stage, was incorporated in the land.[12] Therefore, again only a form of profit. Here then the very *existence of rent* is denied and so indeed *explained away*.

Others, for instance *Buchanan*, regard it just as a consequence of monopoly. See also *Hopkins*.[13] With them it is merely a *surcharge* above the *value*.

For Mr. *Opdyke*, a typical Yankee,* landed property or rent becomes "*the legalised reflection of the capital*".ᵃ [14]

With Ricardo the examination is rendered more difficult by the two false assumptions. ⟨Ricardo it is true was not the inventor of the theory of rent. West and Malthus had put it into print before him. The source, however, is *Anderson*. But what distinguished Ricardo is the way in which he links rent with his theory of value (although West did not entirely miss the real interconnection either). As his later polemic about rent with Ricardo shows, Malthus himself did not understand the theory he had adopted from Anderson.⟩ If we start from the correct principle that the value of commodities is determined by the labour-time necessary for their production (and that value in general is nothing other than materialised social labour-time) then it follows that the *average price* of commodities is determined by the labour-time required for their production. This conclusion would be the right one if it had been proved that *average price* equals *value*. But I show that just *because* the value of the commodity is determined by *labour-time*, the average price of the commodities (except in the *unique* case in which the so-called individual *rate of profit* in a particular sphere of production, i.e., the profit determined by the surplus-value yielded in this sphere of production itself, [is] equal to the average rate of profit on total capital) *can never* be equal to their value although this determination of the average price is only derived from the value which is based on labour-time.

In the first place, then, it follows that even commodities whose average price (if we disregard the value of constant capital) resolves only into wages and profit, in such a way that these stand at their normal rate, i.e., are average wages and average profit, can be sold above or below their own value. The fact that the commodity yields rent on top of profit ||454| does not prove

---

* ||486| ⟨As Opdyke calls landed property "the *legalised reflection of the capital*", so "*capital is the legalised reflection of other people's labour*".⟩ |486||

ᵃ Instead of "reflection of the capital" in the manuscript: "reflection of the value of capital".—*Ed.*

that the commodity is sold *above* its intrinsic value, any more
than the circumstance of the surplus-value of a commodity only
expressing itself in the category of normal profit proves that the
commodity is sold at its value. If a commodity can yield an
average rate of profit or *general rate of profit on capital* which is
below its own rate of profit determined by its real surplus-value,
then it follows that if on top of this average rate of profit commodities in a *particular sphere of production* yield a second
amount of surplus-value which carries a separate name, for instance, *rent,* then the sum of profit plus rent need not be higher
than the *surplus-value* contained in the commodity. Since profit
can be less than the intrinsic surplus-value of the commodity, or
the quantity of unpaid labour it embodies, profit plus rent need
not be larger than the intrinsic surplus-value of the commodity.

Why this occurs in a *particular* sphere of production as opposed
to other spheres has of course still to be explained. But the problem has been simplified. This commodity [the commodity yielding rent] differs from the others in the following way: In a number of these other commodities average price is *above* their
intrinsic value, but only in order to *raise* their rate of profit to
the level of the general rate. In another section of these other
commodities the average price stands at a level *below* their
intrinsic value, but only to the extent required to *reduce* their
rate of profit to concur with the general rate. Finally in a third
section of these other commodities, average price equals their
intrinsic value, but only *because* if sold at their *intrinsic* value
they yield the general rate of profit. But the commodity which
yields rent differs from all these three instances. Whatever the
circumstances, it is sold at a price which will yield *more than
average profit*—as determined by the general rate of profit on
capital.

Now the question arises, which, or how many, of these three
instances can occur. Supposing the *whole of the surplus-value
the commodity contains is realised* in its price. In that case, it
excludes the third instance, namely, those commodities whose
entire surplus-value is realised in their average price, because
they only yield ordinary profit. We may, therefore, dismiss this
one. Similarly, on *this* presupposition, we can exclude the first
instance, where the surplus-value realised in the price of the
commodity is *above* its intrinsic surplus-value. For it is assumed,
that "the surplus-value contained in it is realised" in its price.
This instance is thus analogous with case 2 of those commodities

3*

whose intrinsic surplus-value is higher than the surplus-value realised in their average price. As with these commodities the profit represents a form of this surplus-value—in this case profit on the capital employed—which has been reduced to the level of the general rate of profit. The *excess intrinsic surplus-value of the commodity over and above* this profit is, however, in contrast to *commodity 2*, also realised in these exceptional commodities, but accrues not to the owner of the capital, but to the owner of the land, the natural agent, the mine, etc.

Or [what happens if we assume that] the price is forced up to such a degree that it carries more than the *average rate of profit*? This is, for instance, the case with actual monopoly prices. *This assumption*—applied to every sphere of production where capital and labour may be freely employed [and] whose production, so far as the volume of capital employed is concerned, is subject to the general laws—would not only be a *petitio principii*, but would *directly contradict* the foundations of [economic] science and of capitalist production—the former being merely the theoretical expression of the latter. For such an assumption presupposes the very phenomenon which is to be explained, namely, that in a particular sphere of production, the price of a commodity *must* carry more than the general rate of profit, more than the average rate of profit, and to this end *must be sold above* its value. It presupposes that agricultural products are *excluded* from the general laws of value of commodities and of capitalist production. It, moreover, presupposes this, because the peculiar presence of rent side by side with profit *prima facie* makes it appear so. Hence this is absurd.

So there is nothing left but to assume that special circumstances exist in this particular sphere of production, which influence the situation and cause the prices of the commodities to realise [the whole] of their intrinsic surplus-value. This in contrast to [case] 2 of the other commodities, where only as much of their intrinsic surplus-value is realised by their prices as is yielded by the general rate of profit, where their average prices fall so far below their surplus-value that they only yield the general rate of profit, or in other words their average profit is no greater than that in all other spheres of production of capital.

In this way the problem has already become much simpler. It is no longer a question of explaining how it comes about that the price of a commodity yields rent as well as profit, thus *apparently* evading the general law of value and by raising its price above its *intrinsic surplus-value*, carrying *more than the general rate of profit* for a given capital. The question is why, in the process of equalisation of commodities at average prices, this particular commodity does not have to pass on to other commodities so much of its *intrinsic surplus-value* that it only yields the *average profit*, but is able to realise a portion of its own surplus-value which forms an excess *over and above* average profit; so that it is possible for a farmer, who invests capital in this sphere of production, to sell the commodity at prices which yield him the ordinary profit and at the same time enable him to pay the excess in surplus-value realised *over and above* this profit to a third person, the landlord.

||455| Put in this way, the very formulation of the problem carries its own solution.

[c) Private Ownership of the Land as a Necessary Condition for the Existence of Absolute Rent. Surplus-Value in Agriculture Resolves into Profit and Rent]

It is quite simply the *private ownership* of land, mines, water, etc. by certain people, which enables them to snatch, intercept and seize the *excess surplus-value over and above profit* (average profit, the rate of profit determined by the general rate of profit) contained in the commodities of these particular spheres of production, these particular fields of capital investment, and so to prevent it from entering into the general process by which the general rate of profit is formed. Moreover, some of this surplus-value is actually collected in every industrial enterprise, since rent for the land used (by factory buildings, workhouses etc.) figures in every instance, for even where the land is available free, no factories are built, except in the more or less populated areas with good means of communication.

Supposing the commodities produced by the poorest culti-vated land belonged to category 3, i.e., those commodities whose average price equals their value, in other words, the whole of their inherent surplus-value is realised in their price because only thus do they yield the ordinary profit; in this case the land would pay no rent and land ownership would be purely nominal. If a *payment* were made for the use of the land, then it would only prove that small capitalists, as is partly the case in England (see *Newman*),[15] are satisfied with making a profit *below* the aver-age. The same applies whenever the rate of rent is higher than the difference between the *inherent* surplus-value of a commodity and the *average profit*. There is even land whose cultivation at most suffices to pay wages, for, although here the labourer works for himself the whole of his working-day, his labour-time is longer than the socially *necessary* labour-time. It is so unproductive—relative to the generally prevailing productivity in *this* branch of work—that, although the man works for himself for 12 hours, he hardly produces as much as a worker under more favourable conditions of production does in 8 hours. This is the same relationship as that of the hand-loom weaver who competes with the power-loom. Although the product of this hand-loom weaver was equal to 12 hours of labour, it was only equal to 8 or less hours of socially *necessary* labour and his product therefore only [had] the value of 8 necessary labour hours. If in such an instance the cottager pays a rent then this is purely a deduction from his *necessary* wage and does not represent surplus-value, let alone an excess over and above average profit.

Assume that in a country like the United States, the number of competing farmers is as yet so small and the appropriation of land so much just a matter of form that everyone has the opportunity to invest his capital in land and the cultivation of the soil, without the permission of hitherto-existing owner-cultivators or farmers. In these circumstances it is possible over a considerable period—with the exception of that landed property which by its very situation in populated areas carries a monopoly—that the surplus-value which the farmer produces on top of average profit is not realised in the price of his product, but that he may have to share it with his brother capitalists in the same way as this is done with the surplus-value of all commodities which would give an excess profit, i.e., raise the rate of profit above the general rate, if their surplus-value were realised in their price. In this case the general rate of profit would rise, because wheat, etc., like other manufactured commodities, would be sold *below* its value. This selling *below* its value would not constitute an exception, but rather would prevent wheat from forming an exception to other commodities in the same category.

Secondly, assume that in a given country the land is all of a particular quality, so that if the whole of the surplus-value from the commodity were realised in its price, it would yield the usual profit on capital. In this case no rent would be paid. The absence of rent would in no way affect the general rate of profit, it would

neither raise it nor lower it, just as it is not influenced by the fact
that other non-agricultural products are to be found in this category. Since the commodities belong to this category just because
their *inherent surplus-value* equals the *average profit* [they] cannot alter the level of this profit, on the contrary they conform
with it and do not influence it at all, although it influences them.

Thirdly, assume that all the land consists of a particular type
of soil, but this is so poor that the capital employed in it is so
unproductive that its product belongs to that kind of commodity
whose surplus-value [lies] below average profit. Since wages
would rise everywhere as a result of the unproductiveness of
agriculture, surplus-value could in this case of course only be
higher where absolute labour-time can be prolonged, where the
raw material, such as iron, etc., is not the product of agriculture
or, further, where it [is] like cotton, silk etc., an imported article
and a product of more fertile soil. In this case, the price of the
[agricultural] commodity would include a surplus-value higher
than that inherent in it, to enable it to yield the usual profit. The
general rate of profit would consequently fall, despite the absence
of rent.

Or assume in *case 2*, that the soil is very unproductive. Then
surplus-value of this agricultural product, by its very equality
with average profit would show that the latter is altogether low
since in agriculture perhaps 11 of the 12 working hours are
required to produce just the wages, and the surplus-value only
equals 1 hour or less.

||456| These various examples illustrate the following:

In the first case, *the absence or lack of rent* is bound up with,
or concurs with, an *increased rate of profit*—as compared with
other countries where the phenomenon of rent has developed.

In the second case the lack or absence of rent does not affect
the rate of profit at all.

In the third case, compared with other countries where rent
exists, it is bound up with and indicative of a *low, a relatively
low*, general rate of profit.

It follows from this that the development of a particular rent
in itself has nothing to do with the *productivity of agricultural
labour,* since the absence or lack of rent can be associated with
a rising, falling or constant rate of profit.

The question here is not: Why is the *excess surplus-value above
average profit* retained in agriculture etc.? On the contrary, we
should rather ask: Why should the opposite take place here?

Surplus-value is nothing other than unpaid labour; the average or normal profit is nothing other than the quantity of unpaid labour which each capital of a given magnitude of value is supposed to realise. If we say that average profit is 10 per cent then this means nothing other than that a capital of 100 commands 10 units of unpaid labour; or 100 units of materialised labour command a tenth of their amount in *unpaid* labour. Thus *excess of surplus-value over average profit* implies that a commodity (its price or that part of its price which consists of surplus-value) contains a quantity of unpaid labour [which is] greater than the quantity of unpaid labour that forms average profit, which therefore in the average price of the commodities *forms the excess of their price over the costs of their production*. In each individual commodity the costs of production represent the capital advanced, and the excess over these production costs represents the *unpaid labour* which the advanced capital commands; hence the relationship of this excess in price over the costs of production shows the *rate* at which a given capital—employed in the production process of commodities—commands unpaid labour, irrespective of whether the unpaid labour contained in the commodity of the *particular* sphere of production is equal to this *rate* or not.

Now what forces the individual capitalist, for instance, to sell his commodity at an average price, which yields him only the average profit and makes him realise less unpaid labour than is in fact worked into his own commodity? This average price is *thrust* upon him; it is by no means the result of his own free will; he would prefer to sell the commodity *above* its value. It is forced upon him by the competition of other capitals. For every capital of the same size could also be rushed into A, the branch of production in which the relationship of unpaid labour to the invested capital, for instance, £ 100, is greater than in production spheres B, C, etc. whose products also satisfy a social need just as much as the commodities of production sphere A.

When there are spheres of production in which certain natural conditions of production, such as, for example, arable land, coal seams, iron mines, water falls, etc.—without which the production process cannot be carried out, without which commodities cannot be produced in this sphere—are in the hands of others than the proprietors or owners of the materialised labour, the capitalists, then this second type of *proprietor of the conditions of production* will say:

If I let you have this condition of production for your use,
then you will make your average profit; you will appropriate
the normal quantity of unpaid labour. But your production
yields an excess of surplus-value, of unpaid labour, above the
rate of profit. This excess you will not throw into the common
account, as is usual with you capitalists, but I am going to appropriate it myself. It belongs to me. This transaction should
suit you, because your capital yields you just the same in this
sphere of production as in any other and besides, this is a very
solid branch of production. Apart from the 10 per cent unpaid
labour which constitutes the average profit, your capital will
also provide a further 20 per cent of *additional* unpaid labour
here. This you will pay over to me and in order to do so, you
add 20 per cent unpaid labour to the price of the commodity, and
this you simply do not account for with the other capitalists.
Just as your ownership of one condition of production—capital,
materialised labour—enables you to appropriate a certain
quantity of unpaid labour from the workers, so my ownership of
the other condition of production, the land, etc., enables me to
intercept and divert away from you and the entire capitalist
class, that part of unpaid labour which is excessive to your
average profit. Your law will have it that under normal circumstances, capitals of equal size appropriate equal quantities of
unpaid labour and you capitalists can force each other ||457|
into this position by competition among yourselves. Well, I
happen to be applying this law to you. You are not to appropriate
any more of the unpaid labour of your workers than you could
with the same capital in any other sphere of production. But the
law has nothing to do with the excess of unpaid labour which
you have "produced" over the normal quota. Who is going to
prevent me from appropriating this "excess"? Why should I
act according to your custom and throw it into the common pot
of capital to be shared out among the capitalist class, so that
everyone should draw out a part of it in accordance with his
share in the aggregate capital? I am not a capitalist. The condition of production which I allow you to utilise is not materialised
labour but a natural phenomenon. Can you manufacture land or
water or mines or coal pits? Certainly not. The means of compulsion which can be applied to you in order to make you release
again a part of the surplus-labour you have managed to get hold
of does not exist for me. So out with it! The only thing your
brother capitalists can do is to compete against you, not against

me. If you pay me less excess profit than the difference between
the *surplus-time* you have made and the quota of surplus-labour
due to you according to the rule of capital, your brother capitalists will appear on the scene and by their competition will force
you to pay me fairly the *full amount* I have the power to squeeze
out of you.

The following problems should now be set forth: 1. The
transition from feudal landownership to a different form, commercial land rent, regulated by capitalist production, or, on the
other hand, the conversion of this feudal landed property into
free peasant property. 2. How rent comes into existence in
countries such as the United States, where originally land has
not been appropriated and where, at any rate in a formal sense,
the bourgeois mode of production prevails from the beginning.
3. The Asiatic forms of landownership still in existence. But all
this does not belong here.

According to this theory then, the private ownership of objects
of nature such as the land, water, mines etc., the ownership of
these conditions of production, this essential ingredient of production emanating from nature, is not a source from which flows
value, since value is only materialised labour. Neither is it the
source from which excess surplus-value flows, i.e., an excess of
unpaid labour over and above the unpaid labour contained in
profit. This ownership is, however, a source of revenue. It is a
claim, a means, which in the sphere of production that the property enters as a condition of production enables the owner to
appropriate that part of the unpaid labour squeezed out by the
capitalist which would otherwise be tossed into the general
capital fund as excess over normal profit. This ownership is a
means of obstructing the process which takes place in the rest of
the capitalist spheres of production, and of holding on to the
surplus-value created in this particular sphere, so that it is
divided between the capitalist and the landowner in that sphere
of production itself. In this way landed property, like capital,
constitutes a claim to unpaid labour, gratis labour. And just as
with capital, the worker's materialised labour appears as a power
over him, so with landed property, the circumstance which
enables the landowners to take part of the unpaid labour away
from the capitalists, makes landownership appear as a source
of value.

This then explains the existence of modern ground-rent. *With a
given capital investment*, the variation in the amount of rent is

only to be explained by the varying fertility of the land. The variation in the amount of rent, *given equal fertility*, can only be explained by the *varying amount of capital invested*. In the first case, rent rises because its rate increases in proportion to the capital employed (also according to the area of the land). In the second case, it rises because with the same or even with a different rate (if the second dose of capital is not equally productive) the amount of rent increases.

For this theory it is immaterial whether the least fertile land yields a rent or not. Further, it is by no means necessary for the fertility of agriculture to decline, although the diversity in productivity, if not artificially overcome (which is possible), is much greater than in similar spheres of industrial production. When we speak of greater or lesser fertility, we are still concerned with *the same* product. The relationship of the various products, one to another, is another question.

Rent as calculated on the land itself is the rental, the amount of rent. It can rise without an increase in the rate of rent. If the value of money remains unchanged, then the relative value of agricultural products can rise, not because agriculture is becoming less productive, but because, although its productivity is rising, it is rising slower than in industry. On the other hand, a rise in the money price of agricultural products, while the value of money remains the same, is only possible if their value rises, i.e., if agriculture becomes less productive (provided it is not caused by temporary pressure of demand upon supply as with other commodities).

In the cotton industry, the price of the raw material fell continuously with the development of the industry itself; the same applies to iron, etc., coal, etc. The growth of rent here was possible, not because its rate rose, but only because more capital was employed.

Ricardo is of the following opinion: The powers of nature, such as air, light, electricity, steam, water are gratis; the land is not, because it is limited. So already for this reason alone, agriculture is less productive than other industries. If the land were just as common, unappropriated, available in any quantities, as the other elements and powers of nature, then it would be much more productive.

||458| In the first place, if the land were so easily available, at everyone's free disposal, then a principal element *for the formation of capital* would be missing. A most important condition of

production and—apart from man himself and his labour—the only original condition of production could not be disposed of, could not be appropriated. It could not thus confront the worker as someone else's property and make him into a wage-labourer. The productivity of labour in Ricardo's sense, i.e., in the capitalist sense, the "producing" of someone else's unpaid labour would thus become impossible. And this would put an end to capitalist production altogether.

So far as the powers of nature indicated by Ricardo are concerned, it is true that these are partly to be had for nothing and do not cost the capitalist anything. Coal costs him something, but steam costs him nothing so long as he gets water gratis. But now, for example, let us take steam. The properties of steam always exist. Its industrial usefulness is a new scientific discovery which the capitalist has appropriated. As a consequence of this scientific discovery, the productivity of labour and with it relative surplus-value rose. In other words, the quantity of unpaid labour which the capitalist appropriated from a day's labour grew with the aid of steam. The difference between the productive power of steam and that of the soil is thus only that the one yields unpaid labour to the capitalist and the other to the landowner, who does not take it away from the worker, but from the capitalist. The capitalist is therefore so enthusiastic about this element "belonging to no one".

Only this much is correct: Assuming the capitalist mode of production, then the capitalist is not only a necessary functionary, but the dominating functionary in production. The landowner, on the other hand, is quite superfluous in this mode of production. Its only requirement is that land should *not* be common property, that it should confront the working class as a condition of production, *not belonging* to it, and the purpose is completely fulfilled if it becomes state-property, i.e., if the state draws the rent. The landowner, such an important functionary in production in the ancient world and in the Middle Ages, is a useless superfetation in the industrial world. The radical bourgeois (with an eye moreover to the suppression of all other taxes) therefore goes forward theoretically to a refutation of the private ownership of the land, which, in the form of state property, he would like to turn into the common property of the bourgeois class, of capital. But in practice he lacks the courage, since an attack on one form of property—a form of the private ownership of a condition of labour—might cast considerable doubts on the other form. Besides, the bourgeois has himself become an owner of land.

[4. Rodbertus's Thesis that in Agriculture Raw Materials Lack Value Is Fallacious]

Now to Herr Rodbertus.

According to Rodbertus, no raw material enters into agricultural calculations, because, so Rodbertus assures us, the German peasant does not reckon that seeds, feeding stuffs, etc. cost him anything. He does not count these as costs of production; in fact he *mis*calculates. In England, where the farmer has been doing his accounts correctly for more than 150 years, there should accordingly be *no* ground-rent. The conclusion therefore should not be the one drawn by Rodbertus, that the farmer pays a rent because his rate of profit is higher than in manufacture, but that he pays it because, as a result of a miscalculation, he is satisfied with a *lower* rate of profit. Dr. Quesnay, himself the son of a tenant farmer and closely acquainted with French farming, would not have received this idea kindly. [In his Tableau Economique], Quesnay includes the raw material which the tenant farmer needs, as one of the items in the annual outlay of 1,000 million, although the farmer reproduces it in kind.

Although hardly any fixed capital or machinery is to be found in one section of manufacture, in another section—the entire transport industry, the industry which produces change of location, [using] wagons, railways, ships, etc.—there is no raw material but only tools of production. Do such branches of industry yield a rent apart from profit? How does this branch of industry differ from, say, the mining industry? In both of them only machinery and auxiliary materials are used, such as coal for steamships and locomotives and mines, fodder for horses, etc. Why should the rate of profit be calculated differently in one sector than in the other? [Supposing] the advances to production which the peasant makes *in kind* are a fifth of the total capital he advances, to which we would then have to add four-fifths in advances for the purchase of machinery and labour-power, the total expenditure amounting to 150 quarters. If he then makes 10 per cent profit [this would be] equal to 15 quarters, i.e., the gross product would be 165 quarters. If he now deducted a fifth, equal to 30 quarters and calculated the 15 quarters only on 120, then he would have made a profit of 12$^1/_2$ per cent.

Alternatively, we could put it in this way: The value of his product, or his product, is equal to 165 quarters (£ 330). He reckons his advances to be 120 quarters (£ 240), 10 per cent on this equals 12 quarters (£ 24). But his gross product amounts to 165 quarters; from which thus 132 quarters are to be deducted, which leaves 33 quarters. But from these, 30 quarters are deducted in kind. This leaves an extra profit of 3 quarters (£ 6). His total profit is 15 quarters (£ 30) instead of 12 quarters (£ 24). So he can pay a rent of 3 quarters or £ 6 and *fancy* that he has made a profit of 10 per cent like every other capitalist. But this 10 per cent exists only in his imagination. In fact, he has made advances of 150 quarters, not of 120 quarters and on these, 10 per cent amounts to 15 quarters or £ 30. In fact he received 3 quarters too few, i.e., a quarter of the 12 quarters which he actually received ||459|, or a fifth of the total profit which he should have received, because he did not consider a fifth of his advances to be advances. Therefore, as soon as he learnt to calculate according to capitalist methods, he would cease to pay rent, which would merely amount to the difference between *his* rate of profit and the normal rate of profit.

In other words, the product of unpaid labour embodied in the 165 quarters amounts to 15 quarters, which equals £ 30, representing 30 labour weeks. Now if these 30 labour weeks or 15 quarters or £ 30 were calculated on the total advances of 150 quarters, then they would only form 10 per cent; if they were calculated only on 120 quarters, then they would represent a higher percentage, because 10 per cent on 120 quarters would be 12 quarters and 15 quarters are not 10 per cent of 120 quarters but 12$^1/_2$ per cent. In other words: Since the peasant did not include some of his advances in the account as a capitalist would have done, he calculates the accumulated surplus-labour on too small a portion of his advances. Hence it represents a higher rate of profit than in other branches of industry and can therefore yield a rent which is based solely on a miscalculation. The game would be over if the peasant realised that it is by no means necessary first to convert his advances into *real money*, i.e., to *sell* them, in order to assess them in money, and hence to regard them as commodities.

Without this mathematical error (which may be committed by a large number of German peasants but never by a capitalist farmer) Rodbertus's rent would be an impossibility. It only becomes possible *where* raw material enters into costs of production, but not where it *does not*. It only becomes feasible where the raw material enters [into production] *without* entering into the accounts. But it is not possible *where* it does not enter [into production], although Herr Rodbertus wants to derive his explanation of the existence of rent *not* from a *miscalculation*, but from the *absence* of a real item of expenditure.

Take the mining industry or the fisheries. Raw material does not figure in these, except as auxiliary material, which we can omit, since the use of machinery always implies (with very few exceptions) the consumption of auxiliary material, the food of the machine. Assuming that the general rate of profit is 10 per cent and £ 100 are laid out in machinery and wages; why should the profit on £ 100 amount to more than £ 10, because the £ 100 have not been expended on raw material, machinery and wages, but have been expended on raw material and wages only? If there is to be any sort of difference, this could only arise because in the *various instances*, the ratio of the values of constant capital and variable capital is in fact *different*. This varying ratio would result in varying surplus-value, even if the *rate* of surplus-value is taken to be constant. And if varying surplus-values are related to capitals of *equal size*, they must of course yield unequal profits. But on the other hand the general rate of profit means nothing other than the equalisation of these inequalities, abstraction from the organic components of capital and redistribution of surplus-value, so that capitals of equal size yield equal profits.

That the amount of surplus-value depends on the *size of the capital employed* does not hold good—according to the general laws of surplus-value—for capitals in *different* spheres of production, but for *different capitals* in *the same* sphere of production, in which it is assumed that the *organic* component parts of capital are in the same proportion. If one says for example: The volume of profit in *spinning* corresponds to the size of the capitals employed (which is also not quite correct, unless one adds that productivity is assumed to be *constant*), this in fact merely means that, given the rate of exploitation of the spinners, the total amount of exploitation depends on the number of exploited spinners. If, on the other hand, one says that the volume of profit in different branches of production corresponds to the size of the capitals employed, then this means that the rate of profit is the same for each capital of a given size, i.e., the volume of profit can only change with the size of this capital. In other words, the rate of profit is independent of the organic relationship of the components of a capital in a particular sphere of production; it is altogether independent of the amount of surplus-value which is realised in these particular spheres of production.

Mining production ought to be considered right from the start as belonging to industry and not to agriculture. Why? Because no product of the mine is used, in kind, as an element of production; no product of the mine enters in kind, straight from the mine, into the constant capital of the mining industry (the same applies to fishing and hunting, where the outlay consists to a still higher degree of the instruments of labour and wages or labour itself ||460|). In other words, because every production element in the mine—even if its raw material originates in the mine—not only alters its form, but becomes a commodity, i.e., it must be *bought*, before it can re-enter mining as an element of production. Coal forms the only exception to this. But it only appears as a means of production at a stage of development when the exploiter of the mine has graduated as a capitalist, who uses double entry book-keeping, in which he not only owes himself his advances, i.e., is a debtor against his own funds, but his own funds are debtors against themselves. Thus just here, where in fact no raw material figures in expenditure, capitalist accounting must prevail from the outset, making the illusion of the peasant impossible.

Now let us take manufacture itself, and in particular that section where all the elements of the labour-process are also elements in the process of the creation of value; i.e., where all the production elements enter into the production of the new commodity as items of expenditure, as use-values that have a value, as *commodities*. There is a considerable difference between the manufacturer who produces the first intermediate product and the second and all those that follow in the process towards the finished product. The raw material of the latter type of manufacturers enters the production process not only as a commodity, but is already a commodity of the second degree; it has already taken on a different form from the first commodity, which was a raw product in its natural form, it has already passed through a second phase of the production process. For example, the spinner: His raw material is cotton, a raw product which is already a commodity. The raw material of the weaver however is the yarn produced by the spinner; that of the printer or dyer is the woven fabric, the product of the weaver; and all these products, which reappear as raw materials in further phases of the process are at the same time commodities.[16] |460||

||461| We seem to have returned here to the question with which we have already been concerned on two other occasions, once when discussing John Stuart Mill,[17] and again during the general analysis of the relationship between constant capital and revenue.[18] The continual recurrence of this question shows that there is still a hitch somewhere. Really this belongs into Chapter III on profit.[19] But it fits in better here.

For example:

$$4{,}000 \text{ lbs. cotton equals } \pounds 100;$$
$$4{,}000 \text{ lbs. yarn equals } \pounds 200;$$
$$4{,}000 \text{ yards calico equals } \pounds 400.$$

On the basis of this assumption, 1 lb. cotton $=$ 6d., 1 lb. yarn $=$ 1s., 1 yard [calico] $=$ 2s.

Given a rate of profit of 10 per cent, then

A in $\pounds 100$, the outlay $= \pounds 90^{10}/_{11}$ and the profit $= \pounds 9^{1}/_{11}$
B in $\pounds 200$, the outlay $= \pounds 181^{9}/_{11}$ and the profit $= \pounds 18^{2}/_{11}$
C in $\pounds 400$, the outlay $= \pounds 363^{7}/_{11}$ and the profit $= \pounds 36^{4}/_{11}$

A $= cotton$ [the product of the] peasant (I); B $= yarn$ [the product of the] spinner (II), C $= woven$ $fabric$ [the product of the] weaver (III).

Under this assumption it does not matter whether A's $\pounds 90^{10}/_{11}$ itself includes a profit or not. It will not do so if it constitutes self-replacing constant capital. It is equally irrelevant for B, whether the $\pounds 100$ [the value of product A] includes profit or not, and ditto with C in relation to B.

The relationship of C (the cotton-grower) or I, of S (spinner) or II and of W (weaver) or III is as follows:

I) $Outlay = \pounds 90^{10}/_{11}$ $Profit = \pounds\, 9^{1}/_{11}$ $Total = \pounds 100$
II) $Outlay = \pounds 100$ (I) $+ \pounds 81^{9}/_{11}$ $Profit = \pounds 18^{2}/_{11}$ $Total = \pounds 200$
III) $Outlay = \pounds 200$ (II) $+ \pounds 163^{7}/_{11}$ $Profit = \pounds 36^{4}/_{11}$ $Total = \pounds 400$

The grand total equals 700.
Profit equals $\pounds 9^{1}/_{11} + \pounds 18^{2}/_{11} + \pounds 36^{4}/_{11}$ [$= \pounds 63^{7}/_{11}$]

Capital advanced in all three sections: $£90^{10}/_{11} + £181^9/_{11} + £363^7/_{11} =$
$$= £636^4/_{11}$$

Excess of 700 over $636^4/_{11} = 63^7/_{11}$. But [the ratio of]
$$63^7/_{11} : 636^4/_{11} \text{ is as } 10 : 100.$$

Continuing to analyse this rubbish, we obtain the following:

I) $Outlay = £90^{10}/_{11}$ $Profit = £9^1/_{11}$ $Total = £100$
II) $Outlay = £100$ (I) $+ £81^9/_{11}$ $Profit = 10 + £8^2/_{11}$ $Total = £200$
III) $Outlay = £200$ (II) $+ £163^7/_{11}$ $Profit = 20 + £16^4/_{11}$ $Total = £400$

I does not have to repay any profit, because it is assumed that his constant capital of $£ 90^{10}/_{11}$ does not include any profit, but represents purely constant capital. The entire product of I figures as constant capital in II's outlay. That part of constant capital which equals 100 yields a profit of $£ 9^1/_{11}$ to I. The entire product [of] II which amounts to 200, enters into III's outlay, and thus yields a profit of $£ 18^2/_{11}$. However, this does not in any way alter the fact that I's profit is not one iota larger than II's or III's, because the capital which he has to replace is smaller to the same degree and the profit corresponds to the volume of the capital, irrespective of the composition of the capital.

Now let us assume that III produces everything himself. Then the position *seems* to change, because his outlay now appears as follows:

$90^{10}/_{11}$ in the production of cotton; $181^9/_{11}$ in the production of yarn and $363^7/_{11}$ in the production of the woven fabric. He buys all three branches of production and must therefore continually employ a definite amount of constant capital in all three. If we now total this up we get: $90^{10}/_{11} + 181^9/_{11} + 363^7/_{11} = 636^4/_{11}$. 10 per cent of this is exactly $63^7/_{11}$, as above, only that one individual pockets the lot, whereas previously the $63^7/_{11}$ were shared among I, II and III.

||462| How did the wrong impression arise a little while ago?

But first, one other comment.

If from the 400, we deduct the profit of the weaver, which is included in it and which amounts to $36^4/_{11}$, then we are left with $400 - 36^4/_{11} = 363^7/_{11}$, his outlay. This outlay includes 200 paid out for yarn. Of these 200, $18^2/_{11}$ are the profit of the spinner. If we now deduct these $18^2/_{11}$ from the outlay of $363^7/_{11}$, we are left with $345^5/_{11}$. But the 200 which are returnable to the spinner, also contain $9^1/_{11}$ profit for the cotton-grower. If we deduct these from the $345^5/_{11}$, we are left with $336^4/_{11}$. And if we deduct these $336^4/_{11}$ from the 400—the total value of the woven fabric—then it becomes evident that it contains a profit of $63^7/_{11}$.

But a profit of $63^7/_{11}$ on $336^4/_{11}$ is equal to $18^{34}/_{37}$ per cent.

Previously we calculated these $63^7/_{11}$ on $636^4/_{11}$, and obtained a profit of 10 per cent. The excess of the total value of 700 over $636^4/_{11}$ was in fact $63^7/_{11}$.

According to the present calculation, therefore, $18^{34}/_{37}$ per cent would be made on 100 of this same capital, whereas according to the previous calculation only 10 per cent.

How does this tally?

Supposing I, II and III are one and the same person, but that this individual does not employ three capitals simultaneously, one in cotton-growing, one in spinning and one in weaving. Rather, as soon as he ceases to grow cotton, he begins to spin it and as soon as he has spun, he finishes with this and begins to weave.

Then his accounting would look like this:

He invests £ $90^{10}/_{11}$ in cotton-growing. From this he obtains 4,000 lbs. of cotton. In order to spin these he needs to lay out a further £ $81^9/_{11}$ in machinery, auxiliary materials and wages. With this he makes the 4,000 lbs. of yarn. Finally he weaves these into 4,000 yards which involves him in a further outlay of £ $163^7/_{11}$. If he now adds up his expenditure, the capital which he has advanced amounts to £ $90^{10}/_{11}$ + £ $81^9/_{11}$ + £ $163^7/_{11}$, i.e., £ $336^4/_{11}$. 10 per cent on this would be $33^7/_{11}$, because $336^4/_{11} : 33^7/_{11}$ is as 100 : 10. But £ $336^4/_{11}$ + £ $33^7/_{11}$ = £ 370. He would thus sell the 4,000 yards at £ 370 instead of at £ 400, i.e., at £ 30 less, i.e., at a price which is $7^1/_2$ per cent lower than before. If the value indeed were £ 400, he could thus sell at the usual profit of 10 per cent and in addition pay a rent of £ 30, because his rate of profit would not be $33^7/_{11}$ but $63^7/_{11}$ on his advances of $336^4/_{11}$, i.e., $18^{34}/_{37}$ per cent, as we saw earlier on. And this in fact appears to be the manner in which Herr Rodbertus makes out his calculation of rent.

What does the fallacy consist of? First of all it is evident that if spinning and weaving are combined, they should [according to Rodbertus] yield a rent, just as if spinning is combined with cultivation or if agriculture is carried on independently.

Evidently two different problems are involved here.

Firstly we are calculating the £ $63^7/_{11}$ only on one capital of £ $336^4/_{11}$, whereas we should be calculating it on three capitals of a total value of £ $636^4/_{11}$.

Secondly in the last capital, that of III, we are reckoning his outlay to be £ $336^4/_{11}$, instead of £ $363^7/_{11}$.

Let us go into these points separately.

Firstly: If III, II and I are united in one person, and if he spins up the entire product of his cotton harvest, then he does not use any part of this harvest at all to replace his agricultural capital. He does not employ part of his capital in ||463| cotton-growing—in expenditure on cotton-growing, seeds, wages, machinery—and another part in spinning, but he first puts a part of his capital into cotton-growing, then this part plus a second into spinning, and then the whole of these two first parts, now existing in the form of yarn, plus a third part, into weaving. Now when the fabric of 4,000 yards has been woven, how is he to replace its elements? While he was weaving he wasn't spinning, and he had no material from which to spin; while he was spinning he did not grow any cotton. Therefore his elements of production cannot be *replaced*. To help ourselves along, let us say: Well, the fellow sells the 4,000 yards and then "buys" yarn and the elements of cotton out of the £ 400. Where does this get us? To a position where we are in fact assuming that three capitals are simultaneously employed and engaged and laid out in production. But yarn cannot be bought unless it is available and in order to buy cotton it must be available as well. And so that they are available to replace the woven yarn and the spun cotton, simultaneously with the capital employed in weaving, capitals must be invested which are turned into cotton and yarn at the same time as the yarn is turned into woven fabric.

Thus, whether III combines all three branches of production or whether three producers share them, three capitals must be available simultaneously. If he wants to produce on *the same* scale, he cannot carry on spinning and cotton-growing with the same capital which he used for weaving. Every one of these capitals is engaged and their reciprocal replacement does not affect the problem under discussion. The replacement capitals are the constant capital which must be invested and operating in each of the three branches simultaneously. If the £ 400 contain a profit of £ $63^7/_{11}$, then this is only because besides his own profit of £ $36^4/_{11}$, we allow III to gather in the profit which he has to pay to II and I and which, according to the assumption, is realised in his commodity. But the profit was not made on his £ $363^7/_{11}$. The peasant made it on his additional £ $90^{10}/_{11}$ and the spinner on his £ $181^9/_{11}$. When he pockets the whole amount himself, he likewise has not made it on the £ $363^7/_{11}$ that he invested in weaving, but on this capital and on his two other capitals invested in spinning and cotton-growing.

Secondly: If we reckon III's outlay to be £ $336^4/_{11}$ instead of £ $363^7/_{11}$, then this arises from the following:

We take his outlay on cotton-growing to be only £ $90^{10}/_{11}$ instead of 100. But he needs the whole product and this equals £ 100 and not $90^{10}/_{11}$. It contains the profit of $9^1/_{11}$. Or else he would be employing a capital of £ $90^{10}/_{11}$ which would bring him *no profit*. His cotton-growing would yield him no profit but would just replace his expenditure of £ $90^{10}/_{11}$. In the same way, spinning would not bring him any profit, but the whole of the product would only replace his outlay.

In this case, his expenditure would indeed be reduced to $90^{10}/_{11} + 81^9/_{11} + 163^7/_{11} = 336^4/_{11}$. This would be the capital he has advanced. 10 per cent on this would be £ $33^7/_{11}$. And the value of the product would be £ 370. The value would not be one farthing higher because, according to the supposition, portions I and II have not brought in any profit. Accordingly III would have done much better to leave I and II well alone and to keep to the old method of production. For instead of the £ $63^7/_{11}$ which were previously at the disposal of I, II and III, III now has only £ $33^7/_{11}$ for himself whereas previously, when his fellows were alongside of him, he had £ $36^4/_{11}$. He would indeed be a very bad hand at business. He would only have saved an outlay of £ $9^1/_{11}$ in II because he had made no profit in I, and he would have saved an outlay of £ $18^2/_{11}$ in III, by not making a profit in II. The £ $90^{10}/_{11}$ in cotton-growing and the $81^9/_{11} + 90^{10}/_{11}$ in spinning would both have only replaced themselves. Only the third capital of $90^{10}/_{11} + 81^9/_{11} + 163^7/_{11}$ invested in weaving, would have yielded a profit of 10 per cent. This would mean that [£] 100 would yield 10 per cent profit in weaving, but not one farthing in spinning and cotton-growing. This would be very pleasant for III, so long as I and II are persons other than himself, but by no means so, if, in order *to save these petty profits and pocket them himself*, he has united these three branches of business in one and the same person, namely, his worthy self. The saving of advances for profit (or that component part of the ||464| constant capital of one capitalist which is profit for the others) arose therefore from the fact that [the products of] I and II contained no profits and that I and II performed no surplus-labour but regarded themselves merely as wage-labourers who only had to replace *their costs of production*, i.e., the outlay in constant capital and wages. Thus, in these circumstances—provided I and II were not prepared to work for III, since if they did, profit would go to *his* account—less labour would have been done in any case, and it would not matter to III whether the work for which he has to pay is only laid out in wages, or in wages and profit. This is all the same to him, in so far as he buys and pays for the product, the *commodity*.

Whether constant capital is wholly or partially replaced *in kind*, in other words, whether it is replaced by the producers of the commodity for which it serves as constant capital, is of no consequence. First of all, all constant capital must in the end be replaced in kind: machinery by machinery, raw material by raw material, auxiliary material by auxiliary material. In agriculture, constant capital may also enter as a *commodity*, i.e., be mediated directly by purchase and sale. In so far as organic substances enter into reproduction, the constant capital must of course be replaced by products of the same sphere of production. But it need not be replaced by the individual producers within this sphere of production. The more agriculture develops, the more all its elements enter into it as commodities, not just formally, but in actual fact. In other words, they come from outside, for instance, seeds, fertilisers, cattle, animal substances, etc., are the products of other producers. In industry, for example, the continual movement to and fro of iron into the machine shop and machines into the iron mines, is just as constant as is the movement of wheat from the granary to the land and from the land to the granary of the farmer. The products in agriculture are replaced directly. Iron cannot replace machines. But iron, to the value of the machine, replaces the machine for one [producer], and [the machine replaces] the iron for the other, in so far as the value of his machine is replaced by iron.

It is difficult to see what difference it is supposed to make to the rate of profit if the peasant, who lays out the £ $90^{10}/_{11}$ on a product of £ 100, were to compute that, for instance, he spends £ 20 on seeds etc., £ 20 on machinery etc., and £ $50^{10}/_{11}$ on wages. What he wants is a profit of 10 per cent on the total sum. The £ 20 of the product which he sets against seeds do not include any profit. Nevertheless, this is just as much £ 20 as the £ 20 in machinery, in which there may be a profit of 10 per cent, although this may be only formal. In actual fact the £ 20 in machinery, like the £ 20 in seeds, may not contain a single farthing of profit. This is the case if these £ 20 are merely a replacement for components of the machine builder's constant capital, which he draws from agriculture, for instance.

Just as it would be wrong to say that all machinery goes into agriculture as its constant capital, so it is incorrect to say that all raw material goes into manufacture. A very large part of it remains fixed in agriculture and only represents a reproduction of constant capital. Another part of it goes directly into revenue in the form of food and some of it, like fruit, fish, cattle etc., does not undergo a "manufacturing process" at all. It would therefore be incorrect to burden industry with the entire bill for all the raw materials "manufactured" by agriculture. Of course in those branches of manufacture where the raw material features as an advance, alongside wages and machinery, the capital advanced must be greater than in *those* branches of agriculture which supply the raw material used. It could also be assumed that if these branches of manufacture had their *own* rate of profit (different from the general rate) it would be smaller here than in agriculture because less labour is employed. For, with a given rate of surplus-value, more constant capital and less variable capital necessarily bring in a lower rate of profit. This, however, applies equally to certain branches of manufacture as against others and to certain branches of agriculture (in the economic sense) as against others. It is in fact least likely to occur in agriculture proper, because, although it supplies raw material to industry, it differentiates between raw materials, machinery and wages in its own expenditure account, but industry by no means pays agriculture for the *raw material*, i.e., for that part of constant capital which it replaces from within itself and not by exchange with industrial products.

[5. Wrong Assumptions in Rodbertus's Theory of Rent]

||465| Now to a brief resumé of Herr Rodbertus.

First he describes the situation as he imagines it, where the owner of the land is at the same time the capitalist and slave-owner. Then there comes a separation. That part of the "product of labour" which has been taken from the workers—the "one natural rent"—is now split up into "rent of land and capital gain" ([Rodbertus, *Sociale Briefe an von Kirchmann. Dritter Brief*, Berlin, 1851,] pp. 81-82). (Mr. *Hopkins*—see notebook[20]— explains this in even more simple and blunt terms.)

Then Herr Rodbertus divides the "raw product" and "manufactured product" (p. 89) between the landowner and the capitalist—*petitio principii*. One capitalist produces raw products and the other manufactured products. The landowner produces *nothing*, neither is he the "owner of raw products". That [i.e., that the landowner is the "owner of raw products"] is the conception of a German "landed proprietor" such as Herr Rodbertus is. In England, capitalist production began simultaneously in manufacture and in agriculture.

How a "rate of capital gain" (rate of profit) comes about, is explained by Herr Rodbertus purely from the fact that money now provides a "measure" of gain, making it possible to "express the relationship of gain to capital" (p. 94) and thus "supplying a standard gauge for the equalisation of capital gains" (p. 94). He has not even a remote idea that this *uniformity of profit is in contradiction* to the equality of rent and unpaid labour in each branch of production, and that therefore the values of commodities and the average prices must differ. This rate of profit also becomes the norm in agriculture because the "*return on property* cannot be calculated upon anything other than capital" (p. 95) and by far the "larger part of the national capital is employed" (p. 95) in manufacture. Not a word about the fact that with the advent of capitalist production, agriculture itself is revolutionised, not only in a formal sense but really, and the landowner is reduced to a mere receptacle, ceasing to fulfil any function in production. According to Rodbertus

"in manufacture, the *value of the entire product of agriculture* is included in the capital *as raw material*, whereas this cannot be the case in primary production" (p. 95).

The entire bit is *incorrect*.

Rodbertus now asks himself whether apart from the industrial profit, the profit on capital, there remains "a rent" for the raw product, and if so "for what reasons" (p. 96).

He even assumes

"that the raw product like the manufactured product exchanges according to its labour costs, that the value of the raw product is only equal to its labour cost" (p. 96).

True, as Rodbertus says, Ricardo also assumes this. But it is wrong, at least *prima facie*, since commodities do not exchange according to their values, but at average prices, which differ from their values, and this, moreover, is a consequence of the apparently contradictory law, the determination of the value of commodities by "labour-time". If the raw product carried a rent apart from and distinct from average profit, this would only be possible if the raw product were *not* sold at the average price and why this happens would then have to be explained. But let us see how Rodbertus operates.

"I have *assumed* that the rent" (the *surplus-value*, the unpaid labour-time) *"is distributed according to the v a l u e of the raw product and the manufactured product*, and that this value is determined by *labour costs"* (labour-time) (pp. 96-97).

To begin with we must examine this first *assumption*. In fact this just means that the *surplus-values* contained in the commodities are in the same proportion as their *values*, or, in other words, the *unpaid* labour *contained* in the commodities is proportionate to the total quantities of *labour* they *contain*. If the quantity of labour contained in the commodities A and B is as 3 : 1, then the unpaid labour—or surplus-values—contained in them is as 3 : 1. Nothing could be further from the truth. Given the necessary labour-time, for instance 10 hours, one commodity may be the product of 30 workers while the other is the product of 10. If the 30 workers only work 12 hours, then the surplus-value created by them [amounts to] 60 hours, which is 5 days (5×12), and if the 10 [others] work 16 hours a day, then the surplus-value created by them is also 60 hours. According to this, the value of product A would be $30 \times 12 = 120 \times 3 = 360$ [working hours] which is 30 working days ⟨12 hours are 1 working day⟩. And the value of commodity B would be equal to 160 working hours which is $13^{1}/_{3}$ working days. The *values* of commodities A and B [are as] 360 : 160, as 36 : 16, as 9 : 4, as 3 : $1^{1}/_{3}$. The surplus-values contained in the commodities, however, are as 60 : 60 = 1 : 1. They are equal, although the values are as $3 : 1^{1}/_{3}$.

||466| [Firstly] therefore, the surplus-values of the commodities are not proportionate to their values, if the absolute surplus-values, the extension of labour-time beyond the necessary labour, i.e., the *rates of surplus-value*, are different.

Secondly, assuming the rates of surplus-value to be the same, and leaving aside other factors connected with circulation and the reproductive process, then the surplus-values are not dependent on the relative quantities of labour contained in the two commodities, but on the proportion of the part of capital laid out in wages to the part which is laid out in constant capital, raw material and machinery. And this proportion can be entirely different with commodities of equal values, whether they be "agricultural products" or "products of manufacture", which in any case has nothing to do with this business, at least not on the face of it.

Rodbertus's first assumption, that, if the values of commodities are determined by labour-time, it follows that the quantities of unpaid labour *contained* in various commodities—or their surplus-values—are directly related to their values is therefore fundamentally wrong. It is therefore also incorrect to say that

"*rent* is distributed according to the *value* of the raw product and the manufactured product", if "this value is determined by *labour costs*" (pp. 96-97).

"Of course it follows from this that the size of these portions of rent is not determined by the *size of the capital on which the gain is calculated*, but by the *direct labour*, whether it be agricultural or manufacturing + that amount of labour which must be added on account of the wear and tear of tools and machines" (p. 97).

Wrong again. The volume of surplus-value (and in this case surplus-value is the *rent*, since rent is here regarded as the general term, as opposed to profit and ground-rent) depends only on the immediate labour involved and not on the depreciation of fixed capital. Just as it does not depend on the value of the raw material or indeed on any part of the constant capital.

The wear and tear does, of course, determine the rate at which fixed capital must be reproduced. (At the same time, its production depends on the formation of new capital, on the accumulation of capital.) But the surplus-labour which is performed in the production of fixed capital does not affect the sphere of production into which this fixed capital enters as such, any more than does the surplus-labour which goes into the production of, say, the raw materials. It is rather equally valid for all of them, agriculture, production of machines and manufacture, that their surplus-value is determined only by the amount of labour employed, if the rate of surplus-value is given, and, by the rate of surplus-value, if the amount of labour employed is given. Herr Rodbertus seeks to "drag in" wear and tear in order to chuck out "raw materials".

On the other hand, Herr Rodbertus maintains that the size of the rent can never be influenced by "that part of capital which consists of material value", since "for instance, the labour cost of wool as a raw material cannot affect the labour cost of a particular product such as yarn or fabric" (p. 97).

The labour-time which is required for spinning and weaving is as much, or rather as little, dependent on the labour-time— i.e., the *value*—of the machine, as it is on the labour-time which the raw material costs. Both machine and raw material enter into the labour process; neither of them enters into the process of creating surplus-value.

"On the other hand, the value of the primary product, or the material value, does figure as *capital outlay* in the capital upon which the owner has to calculate his gain, the part of the rent falling on the manufactured product. *But in agricultural capital this part of capital is missing.* Agriculture *does not require any material which is the product of a previous production, in fact it actually begins the production,* and in agriculture, that part of the property which is analogous with material, would be the land itself, which is however assumed to be without cost" (pp. 97-98).

This is the conception of the German peasant. In agriculture (excluding mining, fishing, hunting but *by no means stock-raising*) seeds, feeding stuffs, cattle, mineral fertilisers etc. form the material for manufacturing and this material ||467| is the product of *labour*. This *"outlay"* grows proportionately to the development of industrialised agriculture. All production—once we are no longer dealing with mere taking and appropriating—is reproduction and hence requires "the product of a previous production as material". Everything which is the result of production is at the same time a prerequisite of production. And the more large-scale agriculture develops the more it buys products of "a previous production" and sells its own. In agriculture these expenses feature as commodities in a formal sense—converted into commodities by being reckoned in money—as soon as the farmer becomes at all dependent on the sale of his product; as soon as the prices of various agricultural products (like hay for example) have established themselves, for division of the spheres of production takes place in agriculture as well. Queer things must be happening in the mind of a peasant if he reckons the quarter of wheat which he sells as *income*, but does not reckon the quarter which he puts into the soil as *expenditure*. Incidentally, Herr Rodbertus ought to try somewhere to "begin the production", for instance of flax or silk, without "products of a previous production". This is absolute nonsense.

And therefore also the rest of Rodbertus's conclusions:

"The two parts of capital that influence the *size* of the rent are thus common to agriculture and industry. The part of capital, however, that does not influence the size of the rent—but on which gain, i.e., the rent determined by those parts of capital, is also calculated—is to be found in industrial capital alone. According to the assumption, the value of the raw product like that of the manufactured product is dependent on labour cost and since rent accrues to the owners of the primary product and of the manufactured product proportionately to this value. Therefore *the rent yielded in raw material production and industrial production is relative to the quantities of labour which the respective product has cost, but the capitals employed in agriculture and in industry, on which the rent is distributed as gain*—namely in manufacture entirely, in agriculture according to the rate of gain prevailing *in manufacture*—are not in the same proportion as those quantities of labour and the rent determined by them. Although *an equal amount of rent accrues to the primary product and to the industrial product*, industrial capital is larger than agricultural capital by the entire value of the raw material it contains. Since the value of this raw material *augments the industrial capital on which the available rent is calculated as gain, but not the gain itself*, and thus simultaneously helps *to lower the rate of capital gain*, which also prevails in *agriculture*, there must necessarily be left over in agriculture a part of the rent accruing there which is not absorbed by the *calculation of gain based on this rate of gain*" (pp. 98-99).

First wrong proposition: *If* industrial products and agricultural products exchange according to their *values* (i.e., in relation to the labour-time required for their production), then they yield to their owners equal amounts of *surplus-value* or quantities of unpaid labour. Surplus-values *are not* proportional to values.

Second wrong proposition: Since Rodbertus presupposes *a rate of profit* (which he calls rate of capital gain) the supposition that commodities *exchange in the proportion of t h e i r   v a l u e s* is incorrect. One proposition excludes the other. For a (general) *rate of profit* to exist, the *values* of the commodities must have been *transformed into average prices* or must be in the process of transformation. The *particular rates of profit* which are formed in every sphere of production on the basis of the ratio of *surplus-value to capital advanced*, are equalised in this general rate. Why then not in agriculture? That is the question. But Rodbertus does not even formulate this question correctly, because *firstly* he presupposes that there is a general *rate of profit* and *secondly* he assumes that the *particular* rates of profit (hence also their differences) are *not* equalised and thus that commodities exchange at their *values*.

Third wrong proposition: *The value of the raw material does not enter into agriculture*. Rather here, the advances of seeds etc. are component parts of constant capital and are calculated *as such* by the farmer. To the same degree that agriculture becomes a mere branch of industry—i.e., that capitalist production is established on the land—||468| to the degree to which agricul-

ture produces for the market, produces *commodities*, articles
for sale and not for its own consumption—to the same degree it
calculates its outlay and regards each item of expenditure as a
commodity, whether it buys it from itself (i.e., from *production*)
or from a third person. The *elements of production* naturally
become commodities to the same extent as the *products* do, because, after all, these elements are those very same products.
Since wheat, hay, cattle, seeds of all kinds etc. are thus *sold* as
commodities—and, since this sale is the essential thing, not
their use as a means of subsistence—they also enter into production as *commodities* and the farmer would have to be a real
blockhead not to be able to use money as the unit of account.
This is, however, only the formal aspect of the calculation. But
simultaneously [the position] *develops* [in such a way] that the
farmer buys his *outlay*, seeds, cattle, fertilisers, mineral substances etc. while he sells his *receipts*, so that for the individual
farmer these advances are also advances in the formal sense in
that they are *bought commodities*. (They have always been commodities for him, component parts of his capital. And when he
has returned them, in kind, to production, he has regarded them
as *sold* to himself in his capacity as producer.) Moreover, this
takes place to the same extent as agriculture develops and the
final product is produced increasingly by industrial methods and
according to the capitalist mode of production.

It is therefore wrong to say that there is a part of capital which
enters into industry but *not* into agriculture.

Suppose then, according to *Rodbertus's (false) proposition*,
that the "portions of rent" (i.e., shares of surplus-value) yielded
by the agricultural product and the industrial product are given,
and that they are proportionate to the *values* of the agricultural
product and the industrial product. Supposing, in other words,
industrial products and agricultural products of *equal values*
yield equal *surplus-values* to their owners, i.e., contain *equal
quantities of unpaid labour*, then no disparity arises owing to *a*
part of capital entering into industry (for raw material) which
does not enter into agriculture, so that, for instance, the same
surplus-value would be calculated in industry on a capital
augmented by this amount and hence result in a smaller rate of
profit. For the same *item* of capital goes into agriculture. There
only remains the question of whether it does so *in the same
proportion*. But this brings us to *mere quantitative differences*
whereas Herr Rodbertus wants a "*qualitative*" difference. These

same *quantitative differences* occur between different *industrial* spheres of production. They compensate one another in the general rate of profit. Why not as between industry and agriculture (if there are such differences)? Since Herr Rodbertus allows agriculture to participate in the *general rate of profit,* why not in the process of its formation? But of course that would mean the end of his argument.

Fourth wrong proposition: It is wrong and arbitrary of Rodbertus to include *wear and tear of machinery* etc., that is an element of *constant capital*, in *variable capital*, that is, in the part of capital which creates surplus-value and in particular determines the rate of surplus-value, and at the same time, *not* to include raw material. He makes this *accounting error* in order to arrive at the result he wanted from the outset.

Fifth wrong proposition: If Herr Rodbertus wants to differentiate between agriculture and industry, then that *element of capital* which consists of fixed capital such as machinery and tools belongs entirely to *industry*. This element of capital, in so far as it becomes part of any capital, can only enter into *constant capital*; and can never increase *surplus-value* by a single farthing. On the other hand, as a *product of industry*, it is the result of a particular sphere of production. Its price, or the value which it forms within the whole of social capital, at the same time represents a *certain quantity of surplus-value* (just as is the case with raw material). Now it does enter into the agricultural product, but it stems from industry. If Herr Rodbertus reckons raw material to be an element of capital in industry which comes from outside, then he must charge machines, tools, vessels, buildings etc. as an element of capital in agriculture, which comes from outside. He [must] therefore say that industry comprises only wages and raw materials (because fixed capital, in so far as it is not raw materials, is a product of industry, its own product) whereas agriculture comprises only wages ||469| and machinery etc., i.e., fixed capital, because *raw material*, in so far as it is not embodied in tools etc., is the product of agriculture. It would then be necessary to examine how the absence of this "item" affects the account in industry.

Sixthly: It is quite true that mining, fishing, hunting, forestry (in so far as the trees have not been planted by man) etc., in short, the *extractive industries*—concerned with the extraction of raw material that is not *reproduced* in kind—use *no raw materials*, except *auxiliary materials*. This does *not* apply to agriculture.

But it is equally [true] that *the same* does hold good for a very large part of *industry*, namely the *transport industry*, in which *outlay* consists only of machinery, auxiliary materials and wages.

Finally, there are certainly other *branches of industry*, such as tailoring etc., which, relatively speaking, only absorb raw materials and wages, but no machinery, fixed capital etc.

In all these instances, the size of the *profit*, i.e., the *ratio of surplus-value* to *capital advanced*, would not depend on whether the advanced capital—after deduction of *variable capital, or the part of capital spent on wages*—consists of machinery or raw material or both, but it would depend on the magnitude of the capital advanced relative to the part of the capital spent on wages. Different rates of profit (apart from the modifications brought about by circulation) would thus exist in the different spheres of production, the result of their equalisation being the general rate of profit.

Rodbertus surmises that there is a difference between surplus-value and its special forms, in particular profit. But he misses the point because, right from the beginning, he is concerned with the explanation of a *particular* phenomenon (ground rent) and not [with] the establishment of a general law.

Reproduction occurs in all branches of production; but only in agriculture does this industrial reproduction coincide with natural reproduction. It does not do so in *extractive industry*. That is why, in the latter, the product does not in its natural form become an element in its own reproduction ⟨except in the form of auxiliary material⟩.

What distinguishes agriculture, stock-raising, etc. from other industries is, *firstly*, *not* the fact that a product becomes a means of production, since that happens to all industrial products which have not the definite form of individual means of subsistence. And even as such they become means of production of the *producer* who reproduces himself or maintains his labour-power by consuming them.

Secondly, the difference is *not* the fact that agricultural products enter into production as *commodities*, i.e., as component parts of capital; they go into production just as they come out of it. They emerge from it as commodities and they re-enter it as commodities. The commodity is both the prerequisite and the result of capitalist production.

Hence thirdly, there *only* [remains] the fact that they enter as their own means of production into the production process whose product they are. This is also the case with machinery. Machine builds machine. Coal helps to raise coal from the shaft. Coal transports coal etc. In agriculture this appears as a natural process, guided by man, although he also causes it to some extent. In the other industries it appears to be a direct effect of industry.

But Herr Rodbertus is on the wrong track altogether if he thinks that he must not allow *agricultural products* to enter into reproduction as *"commodities"* because of the peculiar way in which they enter it as "use-values" (technologically). He is evidently thinking of the time when agriculture was not as yet a trade, when only the *excess* of its production over what was consumed by the producer became a *commodity* and when even those products, in so far as they entered into production, were not regarded as *commodities*. This is a fundamental misunderstanding of the application of the capitalist mode of production to industry. For the capitalist mode of production, every product which has value—and is therefore in itself a *commodity*—also figures as a commodity in the accounts.

[6. Rodbertus's Lack of Understanding of the Relationship Between Average Price and Value in Industry and Agriculture. The Law of Average Prices]

Supposing, for example, that in the mining industry, the constant capital, which consists purely of machinery, amounts to £ 500 and that the capital laid out in wages also amounts to £ 500. Then, if the surplus-value is 40 per cent, i.e., £ 200, the profit [would be] 20 per cent. Thus:

Constant capital Machinery	Variable capital	Surplus-value
500	500	200

If the same variable capital were laid out in those branches of manufacture (or of agriculture) in which raw materials play a part, and furthermore, if the utilisation of this variable capital (i.e, the employment of this particular number of workers) required machinery etc., to the value of £ 500, then indeed a third element, the value of the raw materials, would have to be added, say again, £ 500. Hence in this case:

Constant capital			Variable capital	Surplus-value
Machinery	Raw materials			
500 $+$	500	$= 1,000$	500	200

The £ 200 would now have to be reckoned on £ 1,500 and would only be $13^1/_3$ per cent. This example would still apply, if in the first case the transport industry had been quoted as an illustration. On the other hand, the rate of profit would remain the same in the second case if machinery cost 100 and raw materials 400.

||470| What, therefore, Herr Rodbertus imagines is that in industry 100 are laid out in machinery, 100 in wages and x in raw materials, whereas in agriculture 100 are laid out in wages and 100 in machinery. The scheme would be like this:

I. Agriculture

Constant capital Machinery	Variable capital	Surplus-value	Rate of profit
100	100	50	$\frac{50}{200} = \frac{1}{4}$

II. Industry

Raw materials	Constant capital Machinery	Variable capital	Surplus-value	Rate of profit
x	$100 [= x + 100]$	100	50	$\frac{50}{200 + x}$

It must therefore be, at any rate, less than $1/_4$. Hence the rent in I.

Firstly then, this difference between agriculture and manufacture is *imaginary*, non-existent: it has *no bearing* on that form of rent which determines all others.

Secondly, Herr Rodbertus could find this difference between the rates of profit in any two individual branches of industry. The difference is dependent on the *proportion of constant capital to variable capital* and the proportion in turn may or may not be determined by the addition of raw materials. In those branches of industry which use raw materials as well as machinery, the value of the raw materials, i.e., the relative share which they form of the total capital, is of course very important, as I have shown earlier.[21] This has nothing to do with ground-rent.

"Only when the value of the raw product falls *below* the cost of labour is it possible that in agriculture too the whole *portion of rent accruing to the raw product is absorbed in the gain calculated on capital.* For then this portion of rent may be so reduced that although agricultural capital does not comprise the value of raw material, the ratio between these two is similar to that existing between the portion of rent accruing to the manufactured product and the manufacturing capital, although the latter contains the value of material. Hence only in those circumstances is it possible that in agriculture too, no rent is left over besides capital gain. But in so far as, in practice, as a rule, conditions gravitate towards the law that value equals labour cost, so, as a rule, ground-rent is also present. The absence of rent and the existence of nothing but capital gain, is not the original state of affairs, as Ricardo maintains, but only an exception" (p. 100).

Thus, continuing with the above example; but taking raw materials as £ 100, to have something tangible, we get:

I. Agriculture

Constant capital Machinery	Variable capital	Surplus-value	Value	Price	Profit
100	100	50	250	$233^1/_3$ [$33^1/_3$ =]	$16^2/_3$ per cent

II. Industry

Constant capital		Variable capital	Surplus-value	Value	Price	Profit
Raw materials	Machinery					
100	100	100	50	350	350	50 = $16^2/_3$ per cent

Here the rate of profit in agriculture and industry would be the same, therefore nothing would be left over for rent, because the agricultural product is sold at £ $16^2/_3$ *below* its *value*. Even if the example were as correct as it is false *for agriculture*, then the circumstance that the value of the raw product falls "*below* the cost of labour" would in any case only correspond to the law of *average prices*. Rather it needs to be explained *why* "*as an exception*" this is to a certain extent *not* the case in agriculture and why here the total surplus-value (or at least to a larger extent than in the other branches of industry, a *surplus* above the average rate of profit) *remains* in the price of the product of this particular branch of production and does not participate in the formation of the general rate of profit. It becomes evident here that Rodbertus does not understand what the (general) rate of profit and the average price are.

In order to make this *law* quite clear, and this is far more important than Rodbertus, we shall take five examples. We assume the rate of surplus-value to be the same throughout.

It is not at all necessary to compare commodities of *equal* value; they are to be compared only at *their value*. To simplify matters, the commodities compared here are taken as produced by capitals of equal size.

||471|

	Constant capital		Variable capital (wages)	Surplus-value	Rate of surplus-value	Profit	Rate of profit	Value of product
	Machinery	Raw materials						
I	100	700	200	100	50 per cent	100	10 per cent	1,100
II	500	100	400	200	50 per cent	200	20 per cent	1,200
III	50	350	600	300	50 per cent	300	30 per cent	1,300
IV	700	none	300	150	50 per cent	150	15 per cent	1,150
V	none	500	500	250	50 per cent	250	25 per cent	1,250

We have here, in the categories I, II, III, IV and V (five different spheres of production), commodities whose respective *values* are £ 1,100, £ 1,200, £ 1,300, £ 1,150 and £ 1,250. These are the money prices at which these commodities would exchange if they were exchanged according to their *values*. In all of them the capital advanced is of *the same* size, namely £ 1,000. If these commodities were exchanged at their values, then the rate of profit in I would be only 10 per cent; in II, twice as great, 20 per cent; in III, 30 per cent; in IV, 15 per cent; in V, 25 per cent. If we add up these particular rates of profit they come to 10 per cent+20 per cent+30 per cent+15 per cent+25 per cent, which is 100 per cent.

If we consider the entire capital advanced in all five spheres of production, then one portion of this (I) yields 10 per cent, another (II) 20 per cent etc. The average yielded by the total capital equals the average yielded by the five portions, and this is:

$$\frac{100 \text{ (the total sum of the rates of profit)}}{5 \quad \text{(the number of different rates of profit)}}$$

i.e., 20 per cent.

In fact we find that the £ 5,000 capital advanced in the five spheres yield a profit of 100+200+300+150+250=1,000; 1,000 on 5,000 is $^1/_5$ which is 20 per cent. Similarly: if we work out the *value of the total product*, it comes to £ 6,000 and the excess on the £ 5,000 capital advanced is £ 1,000, which is 20 per cent in relation to the *capital advanced*, that is $^1/_6$ or 16$^2/_3$ per cent *of the total product*. (This again is another calculation.) However, so that in fact each of the capitals advanced, i.e., I, II, III etc.—or what comes to the same thing, that capitals *of equal size*—should receive a part of the surplus-value yielded by the aggregate capital *only in proportion to their magnitude, i.e., only in proportion to the share they represent in the aggregate capital advanced*, each of them should get only 20 per cent profit and each must get this amount. ||472| But to make this possible, the products of the various spheres must in some cases be sold *above* their value and in other cases more or less *below* their value. In other words, the total surplus-value must be distributed among them not in the proportion in which it is made in the *particular* sphere of production, but in proportion to the *magnitude* of the capitals advanced. All must sell their product at £ 1,200, so that the excess of the value of the product over the capital advanced is $^1/_5$ of the latter, i.e., 20 per cent.

According to this apportionment:

	Value of product	Surplus-value	Average price	[Relation of average price to value]	Relation of profit to surplus-value in per cent	Calculated profit
I	1,100	100	1,200	Excess of average price over value 100	Excess of profit over surplus-value 100 per cent	200
II	1,200	200	1,200	Value equal to price 0	0	200
III	1,300	300	1,200	Decrease in average price below value 100	Decrease in profit below surplus-value $33^1/_3$ per cent	200
IV	1,150	150	1,200	Excess of price over value 50	Excess of profit over surplus-value $33^1/_3$ per cent	200
V	1,250	250	1,200	Excess of value over price 50	Excess of surplus-value over profit 25 per cent Decrease in profit below surplus-value 20 per cent	200

This shows that only in one instance (II) the average price equals the value of the commodity, because by coincidence, the *surplus-value* equals the *normal average profit of 200*. In all other instances a greater or a lesser amount of surplus-value is taken away from one [sphere] and given to another, etc.

What Herr Rodbertus had to explain was, why this [is] *not* the case in *agriculture*, hence [why] its commodities should be sold at their *value* and not their *average price*.

Competition brings about the equalisation of profits, i.e., the reduction of the *values* of the commodities to *average prices*. The individual capitalist, according to Mr. Malthus, expects an equal profit from every part of *his* capital[22]—which, in other words, means only that he regards each part of his captal (apart from its *organic* function) as an independent source of profit, that is how it *seems* to him. Similarly, in relation to the class of capitalists, every capitalist regards his *capital* as a source of profit *equal* in volume to that which is being made by every other capital of *equal size*. This means that each capital in a particular sphere of production is only regarded as *part of the aggregate capital which has been advanced to production* as a whole and demands its share in the total surplus-value, in the total amount of unpaid labour or labour products—in proportion to its size, its stock—in accordance to the proportion of the aggregate capital it constitutes. This *illusion* confirms for the capitalist—to whom everything in competition *appears* in reverse—and not only for him, but for some of his most devoted pharisees and scribes, that capital is a source of income *independent* of labour, since in fact the profit on capital in each particular sphere of production is by no means solely determined by the quantity of unpaid labour which it itself "*produces*" and throws into the pot of aggregate profits, from which the individual capitalists draw their quota in proportion to their shares in the total capital.

Hence Rodbertus's nonsense. Incidentally, in some branches of agriculture—such as stock-raising—the variable capital, i.e., that which is laid out in wages, is extraordinarily small compared with the constant part of capital.

"*Rent*, by its very nature, is always *ground-rent*" (p. 113).

Wrong. Rent is always paid to the landlord; that's all. However, if, as so often occurs in practice, it is partially or wholly a deduction from normal profit or a deduction from normal wages ⟨true surplus-value, i.e., profit plus rent, is never a *deduction f r o m* wages, but is that part of the product of the worker which remains *after deduction* of the wage *from* this product⟩ then from an economic point of view, it is not rent of land. In practice this is proved as soon as ||473| competition restores the normal wage and the normal profit.

Average prices, to which competition constantly tends to reduce the *values* of commodities, are thus achieved by constant *additions to* the *value* of the product of one sphere of production and *deductions from* the *value* of the product of another sphere —except in the case of II in the above table—in order to arrive at the *general rate of profit*. With the commodities of the particular sphere of production where the ratio of variable capital to the total sum of capital advanced ⟨assuming the rate of surplus-labour to be given⟩ corresponds to the average ratio of social capital—value equals average price; neither an *addition to* nor a *deduction from value* is therefore made. If, however, owing to special circumstances which we will not go into here, in certain spheres of production a *deduction* is not made from the value of the commodities (although it stands *above* the average price, not just temporarily but on an average) then this retention of the *entire surplus-value* in a particular sphere of production— although the *value* of the commodity is above the *average price* and therefore yields a rate of profit higher than the average—is to be regarded as a privilege of that sphere of production. What we are concerned with here and have to explain as a *peculiar feature*, as an *exception*, is not that the *average price* of commodities is reduced *below* their value—this [would be] a general phenomenon and a necessary prerequisite for equalisation—but why, in contrast to other commodities, certain commodities are sold *at* their value, above the average price.

The average price of a commodity equals its *cost of production* (the capital advanced in it, be it in wages, raw material, machinery or whatever else) plus average profit. Hence if, as in the above example, average profit is 20 per cent which is $^1/_5$, then the average price of each commodity is C (the capital advance) $+ \dfrac{P}{C}$ (the average rate of profit). If $C + \dfrac{P}{C}$ equals the *value* of this commodity, i.e., if S, the surplus-value created in this sphere of production, equals P, then the value of the commodity equals its average price. If $C + \dfrac{P}{C}$ is smaller than the *value* of the commodity, i.e., if the surplus-value S, created in this sphere, is larger than P, then the value of the commodity is *reduced* to its average price and part of its surplus-value is added on to the value of other commodities. Finally, if $C + \dfrac{P}{C}$ is greater than the *value* of the commodity, i.e., S is smaller than P, then the *value* of the commodity is raised to its average price and surplus-value created in other spheres of production is added to it.

Finally, should there be commodities which are sold at their value, although their value is greater than $C+\frac{P}{C}$, or whose value is at any rate not reduced to such an extent as to bring it down to the level of the normal average price $C+\frac{P}{C}$, then certain conditions must be operative, which put these commodities into an exceptional position. In this case the profit realised in these spheres of production stands *above* the general rate of profit. If the capitalist receives the general rate of profit here, the *landlord* can get the excess profit in the form of rent.

[7. Rodbertus's Erroneous Views Regarding the Factors Which Determine the Rate of Profit and the Rate of Rent]

What I call rate of profit and rate of interest or rate of rent, Rodbertus calls
"Level of Profit on Capital and Interest" (p. 113).

This level "depends on their ratio to capital.... In all civilised nations a capital of 100 is taken as a unit, which provides the standard measurement for the level to be calculated. Thus, the larger the figure that expresses the relation between the gain or interest falling to the capital of 100, in other words, the 'more per cent' a capital yields, the *higher* are profit and interest" (pp. 113-14).

"The level of *ground-rent and of rental* follows from their proportion to a particular piece of land" (p. 114).

This is bad. The rate of rent is, in the first place, to be calculated on the capital, i.e., as the *excess* of the *price of a commodity* over *its costs of production* and over that part of the *price* which forms the *profit*. Because it helps him to understand certain phenomena Herr Rodbertus makes the caculation with an acre or a morgen, the apparent form of the thing,||474| in which the intrinsic connection is lost. The rent yielded by an acre is the rental, the absolute amount of rent. *It may rise if the rate of rent remains the same or is even lowered.*

"The *level of the value of land* follows from the capitalisation of the rent of a particular piece of land. The greater the amount of capital derived from the capitalisation of the rent of a piece of land of a given area, the *higher* is the value of the land" (p. 114).

The word "level" is nonsense here. For to what does it express a relationship? That 10 per cent yields more than 20 is obvious; but the unit of measurement here is 100. Altogether the *"level of the value of land"* is the same general phrase as the *high* or *low level* of commodity prices in general.

Herr Rodbertus now wants to investigate:

"What then determines the level of capital profit and of ground-rent?" (p. 115)

[a) Rodbertus's First Thesis]

First of all he examines: What determines "the *level of rent in general*", i.e., what regulates the *rate of surplus-value?*

"I) With a given value of a product, or a product of a given quantity of labour or, which again amounts to the same thing, with a given national product, the level of rent in general bears an inverse relationship to the level of wages and a direct relationship to the level of productivity of labour in general. The lower the wages. the higher the rent; the higher the productivity of labour in general, the lower the wages and the higher the rent" (pp. 115-16).

The *"level"* of rent—the rate of surplus-value—says Rodbertus, depends upon the *"size* of this portion left over for rent" (p. 117), i.e., after deducting wages from the total product, in which *"that* part of the value of the product which serves as *replacement* of capital . . . can be disregarded" (p. 117).

This is good (I mean that in this consideration of surplus-value the constant part of capital is "disregarded").

The following is a somewhat peculiar notion:

"when wages fall, i.e., from now on form a smaller share of the total value of the product, the *aggregate* capital on which the *other part of rent"* (i.e., the industrial profit) "is to be calculated as profit, becomes smaller. Now it is, however, solely the ratio between the value that becomes capital profit or ground-rent, and the capital, or the land area on which it has to be *calculated* as such, which determines the *level* of profit and rent. Thus if wages allow a greater value to be left over for rent, a greater value is to be reckoned as profit and ground-rent, even with a *diminished capital* and the same area of land. The resulting ratio of both increases and, therefore, the two together, or rent in general, has risen.... It is assumed that the value of the product remains the same.... *Because the wage, which the labour costs, diminishes, the labour, which the product costs, does not necessarily diminish"* (pp. 117-18).

The last bit is good. But it is incorrect to say that when the variable capital that is laid out in wages decreases, the *constant capital* must diminish. In other words, it is not true that the *rate of profit* (the quite inappropriate reference to area of land etc. is omitted here) must rise because the *rate of sur-*

plus-value rises. For instance, wages fall because labour becomes more productive and in all cases this expresses itself
in more raw material being worked up by the same worker in
the same period of time; this part of constant capital therefore
grows, ditto machinery and its value. Hence the rate of profit
can fall with the reduction in wages. The *rate of profit* is
dependent on the *amout of surplus-value*, which is determined
not only by the rate of surplus-value, but also [by] the number
of workers employed.

Rodbertus correctly defines the necessary wage as equal to

"the *amount of necessary subsistence*, that is to a *fairly stable definite
quantity of material products* for a particular country and a particular
period" (p. 118).

||475| Herr Rodbertus then puts forward in a most *intricately
confused*, complicated and clumsy fashion, the propositions set
up by Ricardo on the inverse relationship of profit and wages
and the determination of this relationship by the productivity
of labour. The confusion arises partly because, instead of
taking labour-time as his measure, he foolishly takes *quantities
of product* and makes non-sensical differentiations between
"*level of the value of the product*" and "*magnitude of the value
of the product*".

By "*level of the value of the product*" this stripling means
nothing other than the relation of the product to the labour-time.
If *the same* amount of labour-time yields many products then
the *value of the product*, i.e., the value of separate portions of
the product is low, if the reverse, then the reverse. If one working-day yielded 100 lbs. yarn and later 200 lbs. then in the
second case the value of the yarn would be half what it was in
the first. In the first case its value is $1/100$ of a working-day; in
the second, the value of the lb. of yarn is $1/200$ of a working-day.
Since the worker receives the same amount of product, whether
its *value* be *high or low*, i.e., whether it contains more or less
labour, wages and profit move inversely, and wages take more
or less of the total product, according to the productivity of
labour. He expresses this in the following intricate sentences:

"...if the wage, as necessary subsistence, is a definite quantity of material
products, then, if the value of the product is high, the wage must have a
high value, if it is low, it must constitute a low value and, since the value
of the product available for distribution is assumed as constant, the wage
will absorb a large part if the value of the product is high, a small part of
it, if its value is low and finally, it will therefore leave either a large or a

small share of the value of the product for rent. But if one accepts the rule that the value of the product equals the quantity of labour which it cost, then the *level of the value of the product* is again determined *purely by the productivity of labour or the relationship* between the amount of product and the quantity of labour which is used for its production ... if the same quantity of labour brings forth more product, in other words, if productivity increases, then the same quantity of product contains less labour and conversely, if the same quantity of labour brings forth less product, in other words, if productivity decreases, then the same quantity of product contains more labour. But the *quantity of labour* determines the *value of the product* and the *relative value of a particular quantity of product* determines the *level of the value of the product....*" Hence "*the higher the productivity of labour in general, the higher*" must "be rent in general" (pp. 119-20).

But this is only correct if the product, for whose production the worker is employed, belongs to that species which—according to tradition or necessity—figures in his consumption as a means of subsistence. If this is not the case, then the productivity of this labour has no effect on the relative height of wages and of profit, or on the *amount of surplus-value* in general. *The same share in the value* of the total product falls to the worker as wages, irrespective of the number of products or the quantity of the product in which this share is expressed. The *division of the value* of the product in this case is not altered by any change in the productivity of labour.

[b) Rodbertus's Second Thesis]

"II) If with a given value of the product, the level of rent in general is given, then the level of ground-rent and of capital profit, bear an inverse relationship to one another, and also to the productivity of extractive labour and manufacturing labour respectively. The higher or lower the rent, the lower or higher the capital profit and vice versa; the higher or lower the productivity of extractive labour or of manufacturing labour, the lower or higher the rent or capital profit, and alternately also the higher or lower is the capital profit or rent" (p. 116).

First ([in thesis] I) we had the Ricardian [law] that wages and profit are related *inversely*.

Now the second Ricardian [law]—differently evolved or, rather, "made involved"— that profit and rent have an inverse relation.

It is obvious, that when a *given surplus-value* is divided between capitalist and landowner, then the larger the share of one, the smaller will be that of the other and vice versa. But Herr Rodbertus adds something of his own which requires closer examination.

In the first place, Herr Rodbertus regards it as a new discovery that *surplus-value in general* ⟨"the *value* of the product of labour which is in fact available for sharing out as rent"⟩, the entire *surplus-value* filched by the capitalist, "consists of the value of the raw product+the value of the manufactured product" (p. 120).

Herr Rodbertus first reiterates his "discovery" of the absence of "the value of the material" in ||476| agriculture. This time in the following flood of words:

"That portion of rent which accrues to the manufactured product and determines the rate of capital profit is reckoned as profit not only on the capital which is actually used for the production of this product but also on the whole of the raw product value which figures as *value* of the *material* in the capital fund of the manufacturer. On the other hand, as regards that portion of rent which accrues to the raw product and *from which the profit on the capital used in raw material production* is calculated *according to the given rate of profit in manufacture*" (yes! *given* rate of profit!) "leaving a remainder for ground-rent, such a material value is missing" (p. 121).

We repeat: quod non!

Assume that a *ground-rent exists*—which Herr Rodbertus has *not proved* and cannot prove by his method—that is to say, a certain portion of the surplus-value of the raw product falls to the landlord.

Further assume that: "the level of rent in general" (the *rate of surplus-value*) "in a particular value of the product is also given" (p. 121). This amounts to the following: For instance, in a commodity of £100, say half, £50, is unpaid labour; this then forms the fund from which all categories of surplus-value, rent, profit etc. are paid. Then it is quite evident that one shareholder in the £50 will draw the more, the less is drawn by the other and vice versa, or that profit and rent are inversely proportional. Now the question is, what determines the apportionment between the two?

In any case it remains true that the revenue of the manufacturer (be he agriculturist or industrialist) equals the surplus-value which he draws from the sale of his manufactured product (which he has pilfered from the workers in his sphere of production), and that rent of land (where it does not, as with the *waterfall* which is sold to the industrialist, stem directly from the *manufactured product*, which is also the case with rent for *houses* etc., since houses can hardly be termed *raw product*) only arises from the excess profit (that part of surplus-value which does not enter into the general rate of profit) which is

contained in the raw products and which the farmer pays over
to the landlord.

It is quite true that when the value of the raw product rises
[or falls], the rate of profit in those branches of industry which
use raw material will rise or fall inversely to the value of the
raw product. As I showed in a previous example, [23] if the value
of cotton doubles, then with a given wage and a given rate of
surplus-value, the rate of profit will fall. The same applies however to agriculture. If the harvest is poor and production is to be
continued on the same scale (we assume here that the commodities are sold at their *value*) then a greater part of the total
product or of its value would have to be returned to the soil
and after deducting wages, if these remain stationary, the
farmer's surplus-value would consist of a smaller quantity of
product, hence also a smaller quantity of value would be available for sharing out between him and the landlord. Although
the individual product would have a higher value than before,
not only the amount of product, but also the remaining *portion
of value* would be smaller. It would be a different matter if, as
a result of demand, the product rose *above* its value, and to such
an extent that a smaller quantity of product had a higher *price*
than a larger quantity of product did before. But this would be
contrary to our stipulation that the products are sold at their
value.

Let us assume the opposite. Supposing he cotton harvest is
twice as rich and that that part of it which is returned direct to
the soil, for instance as fertiliser and seed, costs less than before.
In this case the portion of value which is left for the cotton-
grower after deduction of wages is greater than before. The rate
of profit would rise here just as in the cotton industry. True,
in one yard of calico, the proportion of value formed by the raw
product would now be smaller than before and [that] formed by
the manufacturing process would be larger. Assume that calico
costs 2s. a yard when the value of the cotton it contains is 1s.
Now if cotton goes down from 1s. to 6d., (which, on the assumption that its *value* equals its price, is only possible because its
cultivation has become more productive) then the value of a
yard of calico is 18d. It has decreased by a quarter which is
25 per cent. But where the cotton-grower previously sold 100 lbs.
at 1s., he is now supposed to sell 200 at 6d. Previously the value
[was] 100s.; now too it is 100s. Although previously cotton
formed a greater proportion of the value of the product—and

the rate of surplus-value in cotton growing itself decreased simultaneously—the cotton-grower obtained only 50 yds. of calico
for his 100s. cotton at 1s. per lb.; now that the lb. [is sold] at
6d., he receives $66^2/_3$ yds. for his 100s.

On the assumption that the commodities are sold at their
value, it is wrong to say that the revenue of the producers who
take part in the production of the product is *necessarily* de-
pendent on the portion of value ||477| represented by their
products in the *total value* of the product.

Let the value of the total product of all manufactured commodities, including machinery, be £ 300 in one branch, 900 in
another and 1,800 in a third.

If it is true to say that the proportion in which the value of
the whole product is divided between the value of the raw
product and the value of the manufactured product determines
the proportion in which the surplus-value—the rent, as Rodbertus says—is divided into profit and ground-rent, then this
must also be true of different products in different spheres of
production where raw material and manufactured products
participate in varying proportions.

Suppose out of a value of £ 900, manufactured product accounts for £ 300 and raw material for £ 600, and that £ 1 equals
1 working-day. Furthermore, the *rate of surplus-value* is given
as, say, 2 hours on 10, with a normal working-day of 12 hours,
then the £ 300 [manufactured product] embodies 300 working-
days, and the £ 600 [raw product] twice as much, i.e., 2×300.
The amount of surplus-value in the one is 600 hours, in the other
1,200. This only means that, given the rate of surplus-value, its
volume depends on the number of workers or the number of
workers employed simultaneously. Furthermore, since it has
been *assumed* (not proved) that of the surplus-value which
enters into the value of the agricultural product a portion falls
to the landlord as rent, it would follow that in fact the *amount
of ground-rent* grows in the same proportion as the value of
the agricultural product compared with the "manufactured
product".

In the above example the ratio of the agricultural product
to the manufactured product is as 2:1, i.e., 600:300. Suppose [in
another case] it is as 300:600. Since the rent depends on the
surplus-value contained in the agricultural product, it is clear
that if this [amounts to] 1,200 hours in the first case as against
600 in the second, and if the rent constitutes a *certain* part of

this surplus-value, it must be greater in the first case than in the second. Or—the *larger the portion of value* which the agricultural product forms in the value of the total product, the larger will be its share in the *surplus-value of the whole product*, for every portion of the value of the product contains a certain portion of surplus-value and the larger the *share in the surplus-value of the whole product* which falls to the agricultural product, the larger will be the rent, since *rent* represents a definite proportion of the *surplus-value* of the agricultural product.

Let the rent be one-tenth of the agricultural surplus-value, then it is 120 [hours] if the value of the agricultural product is £ 600 out of the £ 900 and only 60 [hours] if it is £ 300. According to this, the *volume* of rent would in fact alter with the amount of the value of the agricultural product, hence also with the relative value of the agricultural product *in relation* to the manufactured product. But the *"level"* of the rent and of the profit—their rates—would have *absolutely nothing to do with it whatsoever*. In the first case the value of the product is £ 900 of which £ 300 is manufactured product and £ 600 agricultural product. Of this, 600 hours surplus-value accrue to the manufactured product and 1,200 to the agricultural product. Altogether 1,800 hours. Of these, 120 go to rent and 1,680 to profit. In the second case the value of the product is £ 900, of which £ 600 is manufactured product and £ 300 agricultural product. Thus 1,200 [hours] surplus-value for manufacture and 600 for agriculture. Altogether 1,800. Of this 60 go to rent and 1,200 to profit for manufacture and 540 for agriculture. Altogether 1,740. In the second case, the manufactured product is twice as great as the agricultural product (in terms of value). In the first case the position is reversed. In the second case the rent is 60, in the first it is 120. It has simply grown in the same proportion as the value of the agricultural product. As the volume of the latter increased so the volume of the rent increased. If we consider the total surplus-value, 1,800, then in the first case the rent is $1/15$ and in the second it is $1/30$.

If here with the increased *portion of value* that falls to agricultural product the *volume of rent* also rises and *with this, its volume*, increases its *proportional share in the total surplus-value*—i.e., the rate at which surplus-value accrues to rent also rises compared to that at which it accrues to profit—then this is only so, *because* Rodbertus assumes that rent participates *in the surplus-value of the agricultural product in a d e f i n i t e p r o-*

p o r t i o n. Indeed this must be so, if this fact is *given* or *presupposed.* But the fact itself by no means follows from the rubbish which Rodbertus pours forth about the "value of the material" and which I have already cited above *at the beginning of page* 476.[a]

But the *level* of the rent does not rise *in proportion* to the [surplus-value in the] product in which it participates, because now, as before, this [proportion is] one-tenth; its *volume* grows because the *product grows,* and because it grows in volume, without a rise in its "level", its "level" rises in comparison with the quantity of profit or the share of profit in the ||478| value of the total product. Because it is *presupposed* that a greater part of the value of the total product yields *rent,* i.e., a greater part of *surplus-value* is turned into rent, that part of surplus-value which is converted into rent is of course greater. This has absolutely nothing to do with the "value of the material". But that a

"*greater* rent" at the same time represents a "*higher* rent", "because the area or number of acres on which it is calculated remains the same and hence a greater amount of value falls to the individual acre" (p. 122)

is ridiculous. It amounts to measuring the "level" of rent by a "standard of measurement" that obviates the difficulties of the problem itself.

Since we do not know as yet what rent is, had we put the above example differently and had left the same *rate of profit* for the agricultural product as for the manufactured product, only adding on one-tenth for rent, which is really necessary since *the same* rate of profit is assumed, then the whole business would look different and become clearer.

	Manufactured product	Agricultural product	
I	£600 [7,200 hours]	£300 [3,600 hours]	1,200 [hours] surplus-value for manufacture, 600 for agriculture and 60 for rent. Altogether 1,860 [hours; of these] 1,800 for profit.
II	£300 [3,600 hours]	£600 [7,200 hours]	600 [hours] surplus-value for manufacture, 1,200 for agriculture and 120 for rent. Altogether 1,920 [hours; of these] 1,800 for profit.

a See this volume, p. 75.—*Ed.*

In case II the rent is twice that in I because the agricultural product, the share of the value of the product on which it sponges, has grown in proportion to the industrial product. The volume of profit remains the same in both cases, i.e., 1,800. In the first case [the rent] is $1/31$ of the total surplus-value, in the second case it is $1/16$.

If Rodbertus wants to charge the "value of the material" exclusively to industry, then above all, it should have been his duty to burden agriculture alone with that part of constant capital which consists of machinery, etc. This part of capital enters into agriculture as a product supplied to it by industry— as a "manufactured product", which forms the means of production for the "raw product".

Since we are dealing here with an account between two firms, so far as industry is concerned, that part of the value of the machinery which consists of "raw material" is already *debited* to it under the heading of "raw material" or "value of the material". We cannot therefore book this twice over. The other *portion of value of the machinery* used in manufacture, consists of added "manufacturing labour" (past and present) and this resolves into wages and profit (paid and unpaid labour). That part of capital which has been advanced here (apart from that contained in the raw material of the machines) therefore consists *only* of wages. Hence it increases not only the amount of capital advanced, but also the profit, the volume of surplus-value to be calculated upon this capital.

(The error usually made in such calculations is that, for instance, the wear and tear of the machinery or of the tools used is embodied in the machine itself, in its value and although, in the last analysis, this wear and tear can be reduced to *labour*— either labour contained in the raw material or that which transformed the raw material into machine, etc.—this *past labour* never again enters into profit or wages, but only acts as a produced condition of production (in so far as the necessary labour-time for reproduction does not alter) which, whatever its use-value in the labour-process, only figures as value of constant capital, in the process of creating surplus-value. This is of great importance and has already been explained in the course of my examination of the exchange of constant capital and revenue.[24] But apart from this, it needs to be further developed in the section on the accumulation of capital.)

So far as agriculture is concerned—that is, purely the production of raw products or so-called primary production—*in balancing the accounts between the firms "primary production" and "manufacture"* that part of the value of constant capital which represents machinery, tools, etc., can on no account be regarded in any other way than as an item which enters into agricultural capital without increasing its *surplus-value*. If, as a result of the employment of machinery etc., agricultural labour becomes more productive, the higher the price of this machinery etc., the smaller will be the increase in productivity. It is the use-value of the machinery and not its *value* which increases the productivity of agricultural labour or of any other sort of labour. Otherwise one might also say that the productivity of industrial labour is, in the first place, due to the presence of raw material and its properties. But again it is the use-value of the raw material, not its value, which constitutes a condition of production for industry. Its value, on the contrary, is a drawback. Thus what Herr Rodbertus says about the "value of the material" in respect to the industrial capital, is literally, ||479| *mutatis mutandis* valid for machinery etc.

"For instance the *labour costs* of a particular product, such as w h e a t or c o t t o n, cannot be affected by the labour costs of t h e p l o u g h o r g i n a s m a c h i n e s" (or the labour costs of a drainage canal or stable buildings). "On the other hand, the value of the m a c h i n e or the m a c h i n e v a l u e does figure in the amount of capital on which the owner has to calculate his gain, the rent that falls to the r a w p r o d u c t." (Cf. Rodbertus, p. 97.) [25]

In other words: That portion of the value of wheat and cotton representing the value of the wear and tear of the plough or gin, is not the result of the work of ploughing or of separating the cotton fibre from its seed, but the result of the labour which manufactured the plough and the gin. This component part of value goes into the agricultural product without being produced in agriculture. It only passes through agriculture, which uses it merely to replace ploughs and gins by buying new ones from the maker of machines.

The machines, tools, buildings and other manufactured products required in agriculture consist of two component parts: 1. the raw materials of these manufactured products [2. the labour added to the raw materials.] Although these raw materials are the product of agriculture, they are a part of its product which never enters into wages or into profit. Even if there were no capitalist, the farmer still could not chalk up this part of his product as wages for himself. He would in fact have to hand it over *gratis* to the machine manufacturer so that the latter would make him a machine from it and besides he would have to pay for the labour which is added to this raw material (equal to wages plus profit). This happens in reality. The machine maker buys the raw material but in purchasing the machine, agricultural producer must buy back the raw material. It is just as if he had not sold it at all, but had lent it to the machine maker to give it the form of the machine. Thus that portion of the value of the machinery employed *in agriculture* which resolves into raw material, although it is the product of agricultural labour and forms part of its value, belongs to production and not to the producer, it therefore figures in his expenses, like seed. The other part, however, represents the manufacturing labour embodied in the machinery and is a "product of manufacture" which enters into agriculture as a means of production, just as raw material enters as a means of production into industry.

Thus, if it is true that the firm "primary production" supplies the firm "manufacturing industry" with the "value of the material" which enters as an item into the capital of the industrialist, then it is no less true that the firm "manufacturing industry" supplies the firm "primary production" with the value of the machinery which enters wholly (*including that part which consists of raw material*) into the farmer's capital without this "component part of value" yielding him any surplus-value. This circumstance is a reason why the rate of profit *appears to be* smaller in "high agriculture", as the English call it, than in primitive agriculture, although the rate of surplus-value is greater.

At the same time this supplies Herr Ro̦dbertus with striking proof of how irrelevant it is to the nature of a *capital advance,* whether that portion of the product which is laid out in constant capital is replaced in kind and therefore only accounted for as a commodity—as money value—or whether it has really been alienated and has gone through the process of purchase and sale. Supposing the producer of raw materials handed over gratis to the machine builder the iron, copper, wood etc., embodied in his machine, so that the machine builder in selling him the machine would charge him for the added labour and the wear and tear of his own machine, then this machine would cost the agriculturist just as much as it costs him now and the same *component part of value* would figure as constant capital, as an advance, in his production. Just as it amounts to the same thing whether a farmer sells the whole of his harvest and buys seed from elsewhere with that portion of its value which represents seed (raw material) perhaps to effect a desirable change in the type of seed and to prevent degeneration by inbreeding— or whether he deducts this component part of value directly from his product and returns it to the soil.

But in order to arrive at his results, Herr Rodbertus misinterprets that part of constant capital which consists of machinery.

A second aspect that has to be examined in connection with [case] II of Herr Rodbertus is this: He speaks of the manufactured and agricultural products which make up the *revenue*, which is something quite different from those manufactured and agricultural products which make up the *total annual product*. Now supposing it were correct to say of the latter that after deducting the whole of that part of the agricultural capital which consists of machinery etc. ||480| and that part of the agricultural product which is returned direct to agricultural production, the proportion in which the *surplus-value* is distributed between farmer and manufacturer—and therefore also the proportion in which the surplus-value accruing to the farmer is distributed between himself and the landlord—must be determined by the share of manufacture and of agriculture in the total value of the products; then it is still highly questionable whether this is correct if we are speaking of those products which form the *common fund of revenue*. Revenue (we exclude here that part which is reconverted into *new* capital) consists of products which go into individual consumption and the question is, how much do the capitalists, farmers and landlords draw out of this pot. Is this quota determined by the share of manufacture and raw production in the *value* of the product that constitutes revenue? Or by the quotas in which the value of the total revenue is divisible into agricultural labour and manufacturing labour?

The mass of products which make up revenue, as I have demonstrated earlier,[26] does not contain any products that enter into production as instruments of labour (machinery), auxiliary material, semi-finished goods and the raw material of semi-finished goods, which form a part of the annual product of labour. Not only the *constant capital* of primary production is excluded but also the constant capital of the machine makers and the

6*

entire constant capital of the farmer and the capitalist which does *not* enter into the process of the creation of value though it enters into the labour-process. Furthermore, it excludes not only constant capital, but also the part of the unconsumable products that represents the *revenue* of their producers and enters into the capital of the producers of products consumable as revenue, for the replacement of their used up constant capital.

The *mass of products* on which the revenue is spent and which in fact represents that part of wealth which constitutes revenue, in terms of both *use-value* and *exchange-value*—this mass of products can, as I have demonstrated earlier,[27] be regarded as consisting only of *newly-added* (during the year) *labour*. Hence it can be resolved only into revenue, i.e., wages and profit (which again splits up into *profit, rent, taxes,* etc.), since not a single particle of it contains any of the value of the raw material which goes into production or of the wear and tear of the machinery which goes into production, in a word, it contains none of the value of the means of production. Leaving aside the derivative forms of revenue because they merely show that the owner of the revenue relinquishes his proportional share of the said products to another, be it for services etc. or debt etc.—let us consider this revenue and assume that wages form a third of it, profit a third and rent a third and that the value of the product is £ 90. Then each will be able to draw the equivalent of £ 30 worth of products from the whole amount.

Since the amount of products which forms the revenue consists only of *newly-added* (i.e., added during the year) labour, it seems very simple that if the product contains two-thirds agricultural labour and one-third manufacturing labour, then manufacturers and agriculturists will share the value in this proportion. One-third of the value would fall to the manufacturers and two-thirds to the agriculturists and the proportional amount of the surplus-value realised in manufacture and agriculture (the same rate of surplus-value is assumed in both) would correspond to these shares of manufacture and agriculture in the value of the total product. But rent again [would] grow in proportion to the farmer's volume of profit since it sits on it like a parasite. And yet this is wrong. Because a part of the value which consists of agricultural labour forms the *revenue* of the manufacturers of that fixed capital etc., which replaces the fixed capital worn out in agriculture. Thus the ratio between agricultural labour and manufacturing labour in the *component parts of value of those products which constitute the revenue*, in no way indicates the *ratio* in which the value of this mass of products or this mass of products itself is distributed between the manufacturers and the farmers, neither does it indicate the *ratio* in which manufacture and agriculture participate in total production.

Rodbertus goes on to say:

"But again it is only the productivity of labour in primary production or manufacture, which determines the relative level of the value of the primary product and manufactured product or their respective shares in the value of the total product. The value of the primary product will be the higher, the lower the productivity of labour in primary production and vice versa. In the same way, the value of the manufactured product will be the higher, the lower the productivity in manufacture and vice versa. Since a high value of the raw product effects a high ground-rent and low capital gain, and a high value of the manufactured product effects a high capital gain and low ground-rent, if the level of rent in general is given, the level of ground-rent and of capital gain must not only bear an inverse relationship to one another, but also to the productivity of their respective labour, that in primary production and that in manufacture" (p. 123).

If the productivity of two *different* spheres of production is to be compared, this can only be done relatively. In other words, one starts at any arbitrary point, for instance, when the values of hemp and linen, i.e., the correlative quantities of labour-time embodied in them, are as 1:3. If this ratio alters, then it is correct to say that the productivity of these different types of labour has altered. But it is wrong to say that because the labour-time required for the production of an ounce of gold ||481| equals three and that for a ton of iron also equals three, gold production is "less productive" than iron production.

The relative value of two commodities shows that the one costs more labour-time than the other; but one cannot say that because of this one branch is "more productive" than the other. This would only be correct if the labour-time were used for the production of *the same* use-values in both instances.

It would be entirely wrong to say that manufacture is three times as productive as agriculture if the value of the raw product is to that of the manufactured product as 3:1. Only if the ratio changes say to 4:1 or 3:2 or 2:1, i.e., when it rises or falls, could one say that the relative productivity in the two branches has altered.

[c) Rodbertus's Third Thesis]

III) "The *level of capital gain* is solely determined by the *level of the value of the product* in general and by the level of the value of the raw product and the manufactured product in particular; or by the productivity of labour in general and by the productivity of labour employed in the production of raw materials and of manufactured goods in particular. The *level* of ground-rent is, apart from this, also dependent on the *magnitude of the value of the product* or the *quantity of labour, or productive power*, which, with a *given state of productivity*, is used for production" (pp. 116-17).

In other words: The *rate of profit* depends solely on the *rate of surplus-value* and this is determined solely by the *productivity of labour*. On the other hand, given the productivity of labour, the *rate of ground-rent* also depends on the *amount* of labour (the number of workers) employed.

This assertion contains almost as many falsehoods as words.

Firstly the *rate of profit* is by no means solely determined by the *rate of surplus-value*. But more about this shortly. First of all, it is wrong to say that the *rate of surplus-value* depends solely on the productivity of labour. *Given the productivity* of labour, the rate of surplus-value alters according to the *length of the surplus labour-time*. Hence the rate of surplus-value depends not only on the productivity of labour but also on the *quantity* of labour employed because the quantity of *unpaid* labour can grow (while productivity remains constant) without the quantity of *paid* labour, i.e., that part of capital laid out in wages, growing. Surplus-value—absolute or relative (and Rodbertus only knows the latter from Ricardo)—cannot exist unless labour is at least sufficiently productive to leave over some surplus labour-time apart from that required for the worker's own reproduction. But assuming this to be the case, *with a given minimum productivity*, then the rate of surplus-value alters according to the length of surplus labour-time.

Firstly, therefore, it is *wrong* to say that because the rate of surplus-value is solely determined by the productivity of the labour exploited by capital, the rate of profit or the "*level* of capital gain" is so determined. *Secondly*: The *rate of surplus-value*—which, if the productivity of labour is given, alters with the *length* of the working-day and, with a given normal working-day, alters with the *productivity of labour*—is assumed to be *given. Surplus-value* itself will then vary according to the *number* of workers from whose every working-day a certain quantity of surplus-value is extorted, or according to the *volume* of variable capital expended on wages. The *rate of profit*, on the other hand, depends on the *ratio of this surplus-value* [to] the variable capital plus the constant capital. If the *rate of surplus-value is given*, the *amount of surplus-value* does indeed depend on the amount of variable capital, but the *level of profit*, the *rate of profit*, depends on the ratio of this surplus-value to the total capital advanced. In this case the rate of profit will thus be determined by the price of the raw material (if such exists in this branch of industry) and the value of machinery of a particular efficiency.

Hence what Rodbertus says is fundamentally wrong:

"Thus, as the amount of capital gain increases consequent upon the *increase in product value*, so also in the same proportion increases the amount of capital value on which the gain has to be reckoned, and the hitherto existing ratio between gain and capital is not altered at all by this increase in capital gain" (p. 125).

This is only valid if it [signifies] the *tautology* that: *given the rate of profit* ⟨very different from the rate of surplus-value and surplus-value itself⟩, *the amount of capital employed is immaterial*, precisely because the rate of profit is assumed to be *constant*. But as a rule the rate of profit can increase although the *productivity* of labour remains *constant*, or it can *fall* even though the productivity of labour rises and rises moreover in every department.

And now again the silly remark (pp. 125-26) about ground-rent, the assertion that the mere increase of rent raises its rate, because in every country it is calculated on the basis of an "unalterable number of acres" (p. 126). If the volume of profit grows (given the rate of profit), then the *amount* of capital from which it is drawn, grows. On the other hand, if rent increases, then [according to Rodbertus] only one factor changes, namely rent itself, while its standard of measurement, "the number of acres", remains unalterably fixed.

||482| "Hence rent can rise for a reason which enters into the economic development of society everywhere, namely the increase in labour used for production, in other words, the *increasing population*. This does not necessarily have to be followed by a *rise* in the raw product value since the drawing of rent from a *greater quantity* of primary product must already have this effect" (p. 127).

On p. 128, Rodbertus makes the strange discovery that even if the value of the raw product fell *below* its normal level, causing rent to disappear completely, it would be impossible *"for capital gain ever to amount to 100 per cent"* (i.e., if the commodity is sold at its value) "however high it may be, it must always amount to considerably less" (p. 128).

And why?

"Because it" (the capital gain) "is merely the result of the division of the value of the product. It must, accordingly, always be a *fraction* of this unit" (pp. 127-28).

This, Herr Rodbertus, depends entirely upon the nature of *your* calculation.

Let the constant capital advanced be 100, the wages advanced 50 and let the product of labour over and above this 50 be 150. We would then have the following calculation:

Constant capital	Variable capital	Surplus-value	Value	Cost of production	Profit	Per cent
100	50	150	300	150	150	100

The only requirement to produce this situation is that the worker should work for his master three quarters of his working-day, it is therefore assumed that one quarter of his labour-time suffices for his own reproduction. Of course, if Herr Rodbertus takes the total value of the product, which equals 300, and does not consider the excess it contains over the costs of production, but says that this *product* is to be divided between the capitalist and the worker, then in fact the capitalist's portion can only amount to a part of this product, even if it came to $^{999}/_{1,000}$. But the calculation is incorrect, or at least useless in almost every respect. If a person lays out 150 and makes 300 he is not in the habit of saying that he has made a profit of 50 per cent on the basis of reckoning the 150 on 300 instead of 150.

Assume, in the above example, that the worker has worked 12 hours, 3 for himself and 9 for the capitalist. Now let him work 15 hours, i.e., 3 for himself and 12 for the capitalist. Then, according to the former production ratio, an outlay of 25 on constant capital would have to be added (less in fact, because the outlay on machinery would not grow to the same degree as the quantity of labour). Thus:

Constant capital	Variable capital	Surplus-value	Value	Cost of production	Profit	Per cent
125	50	200	375	175	200	$114^2/_7$

Then Rodbertus comes up again with the growth of *"rent to infinity"*, firstly because he interprets its mere increase in volume as a rise, and therefore speaks of its rise when the same rate

of rent is paid on a larger amount of product. Secondly because
he calculates on "an acre" as his standard of measurement. Two
things which have nothing in common.

* * *

The following points can be dealt with quite briefly, since
they have nothing to do with my purpose.

The *"value of land"* is the *"capitalised ground-rent"*. Hence
this, its expression in terms of money, depends on the level of
the prevailing rate of interest. Capitalised at 4 per cent, it would
have to be multiplied by 25 (since 4 per cent is $1/25$ of 100); at
5 per cent by 20 (since 5 per cent is $1/20$ of 100). This would
amount to a difference in land value of 20 per cent (p. 131). Even
with a fall in the value of money, *ground-rent* and hence *the
value of land* would rise nominally, since—unlike the increase in
interest or profit (expressed in money)—the monetary expression
of capital does not rise evenly. The rent, however, which has
risen in terms of money has to be related "to the unchanged
number of acres of the piece of land" (p. 132).

Herr Rodbertus sums up his wisdom as applied to Europe
in this way:

1. "... with the European nations, the productivity of labour in general—
labour employed in primary production and manufacturing—has risen ...
as a result of which, the part of the national product used for wages has
diminished, the part left over for rent has increased ... so *rent in general
has risen*" (pp. 138-39).

2. "... the increase in productivity is *relatively greater* in manufacture
than in primary production ... an equal value of national product will
therefore at present yield a larger rent share to the raw product than to the
manufactured product. Therefore notwithstanding the rise in rent in general,
in fact only *ground-rent has risen while capital gain has fallen*" (p. 139).

Here Herr Rodbertus, just like Ricardo, explains the rise of
rent and the fall of the rate of profit one by the other; the fall
of one is equal to the rise of the other and the rise of the latter
is explained by the *relative unproductiveness* ||483| *of agri-
culture*. Indeed, Ricardo says somewhere quite expressly that it
is not a matter of absolute but of "relative" unproductiveness.[a]
But even if he had said the opposite, it would not comply with
the principle he establishes since *Anderson*, the original author
of the Ricardian concept, expressly declares that every piece of
land is capable of absolute improvement.

---

[a] See this volume, p. 336.—*Ed.*

If "surplus-value" (profit and rent) in general has risen then it is not merely possible that the rate of the total rent has fallen in proportion to constant capital, but it will have fallen because productivity has risen. Although the number of workers employed has grown, as has the rate at which they are exploited, the amount of capital expended on wages as a whole has fallen *relatively*, although it has risen absolutely; because the capital which as an advance—a product of the past—is set in motion by these workers and as a *prerequisite* of production forms an ever growing share of the total capital. Hence the rate of profit and rent taken together has fallen, although not only its volume (its absolute amount) has grown, but also the rate at which labour is being exploited has risen. This Herr Rodbertus cannot see, because for him constant capital is an invention of industry of which agriculture is ignorant.

But so far as the *relative* magnitude of profit and rent is concerned, it does not by any means follow that, because agriculture is relatively less productive than industry, the *rate of profit* has fallen absolutely. If, for instance, its relationship to rent was as 2:3 and is now as 1:3, then whereas previously it formed two-thirds of rent, it now forms only one-third, or previously [profit] formed two-fifths of the total surplus-value and now only a quarter, [or] previously $^8/_{20}$ and now only $^5/_{20}$; it would have fallen by $^3/_{20}$ or [by] 15 per cent.

Assume that the value of 1 lb. of cotton was 2s. It falls to 1s. 100 workers who previously span 100 lbs. in one day, now spin 300.

Previously, the outlay for 300 lbs. amounted to 600s.; now it is only 300s. Further, assume that in both cases machinery equals $^1/_{10}$, or 60s. Finally, previously 300 lbs. cost 300s. as an outlay for 300 workers, now only 100s. for 100 [workers]. Since the productivity of the workers "has increased", and we must suppose that they are paid here in their own product, assume that whereas previously the surplus-value was 20 per cent of wages, it is now 40.

Thus the cost of the 300 lbs. is:

in the first case:
Raw material 600, machinery 60, wages 300, surplus-value 60, altogether 1,020s.
in the second case:
Raw material 300, machinery 60, wages 100, surplus-value 40, altogether 500s.

In the first case: *The costs of production* 960, *profit* 60, *rate of profit* $6^1/_4$ [per cent].

In the second case: [*The costs of production*] 460, *profit* 40, *rate of profit* $8^{16}/_{23}$ [per cent].

Suppose the rent is a third of 1 lb., then in the first case it equals 200s., i.e., £ 10; in the second it is 100s. or £ 5. The rent has fallen here because the raw product has become cheaper by 50 per cent. But the whole of the product has become cheaper by more than 50 per cent. The industrial labour added in I [is to the value of the raw material] as $360:600=6:10=1:1^2/_3$; in II, as $140:300=1:2^1/_7$. Industrial labour has become relatively more productive than agricultural labour; yet in the first case the rate of profit is lower and the rent higher than in the second. In both cases rent amounts to one-third of raw materials.

Assume that the amount of raw materials in II doubles so that 600 lbs. are spun and the ratio would be:

II. 600 lbs. [cotton]=600s. raw material, 120s. machinery, 200s. wages, 80s. surplus-value. Altogether 920s. production costs, 80s. profit, rate of profit $8^{16}/_{23}$ per cent.

The rate of profit [has] risen compared with I. Rent would be just the same as in I. The 600 lbs. would cost only 1,000, whereas before they cost 2,040.

||484| It does not by any means follow from the relative dearness of the agricultural product that it yields a [higher] rent. However, if one assumes—as Rodbertus can be said to assume, since his so-called proof is absurd—that rent clings as a percentage on to every particle of value of the agricultural product, then indeed it follows that rent rises with the increasing dearness of agricultural produce.

"... as a result of the increased population, the value of the total national product has also grown to an extraordinary extent ... today, therefore, the nation draws *more* wages, *more* profit, *more* ground-rent ... furthermore, this *increased* amount of ground-rent has raised it, whereas the *increased* amount of wages and profit could not have a similar effect" (p. 139).

[8. The Kernel of Truth in the Law Distorted by Rodbertus]

Let us strip Herr Rodbertus of all nonsense (not to speak of such defective conceptions as I have detailed more fully above, for instance that the rate of surplus-value ("*level of rent*") can only rise when *labour* becomes *more productive*, i.e., the *over-looking* of *absolute surplus-value*, etc.);

namely the absurd conception that the "*value of the material*" does not form part of the expenditure in (capitalist) agriculture in the strict sense.

The *second* piece of nonsense: that he does not regard the *machinery* etc., the second part of the constant capital of agriculture and manufacture, as a "component part of value", which —just as the "value of the material"—does not arise from the labour of the sphere of production into which it enters as machinery, and upon which the profit made in each sphere of production is also calculated, even though the *value* of the machinery does not add a farthing to the profit, as little as the "value" of the material although both are means of production and as such enter into the labour process.

The *third* piece of nonsense: that he does not charge to agriculture the *entire* "value" of the "machinery" etc. which enters into it as an item of expenditure and that he does not regard that element of it which does not consist of raw material as a debit of agriculture to industry, which does not therefore belong to the expenditure of industry as a whole and in payment for which, a part of the raw material of agriculture must be supplied *gratis* to industry.

The *fourth* piece of nonsense: his belief that in addition to machinery and its auxiliary materials the "value of the material" enters into all branches of industry, whereas this is not the case in the entire transport industry any more than it is in the extractive industry.

The *fifth* piece of nonsense: that he does not see that although, besides variable capital, "raw material" does enter into many branches of manufacture (and this the more they supply finished produce for consumption) the other component part of constant capital disappears almost completely or is very small, incomparably smaller than in large-scale industry or agriculture.

The *sixth* piece of nonsense: that he confuses the average prices of commodities with their values.

Stripped of all this, which has allowed him to derive *his* explanation of rent from the farmer's *wrong calculation* and his own wrong calculation, so that rent would have to disappear to the extent to which the farmer *accurately calculates* the *outlay* he makes, then only the following assertion remains as the real kernel:

When the raw products are sold at their *values*, their value stands above the *average prices* of the other commodities   or above their *own average price*, this means their value is greater than the costs of production plus average profit, thus leaving an *excess profit* which constitutes *rent*. Furthermore, assuming the same *rate* of surplus-value, this means that the ratio of variable capital to constant capital is greater in primary production than it is, on an average, in those spheres of production which belong to industry (which does not prevent it from being higher in some branches of industry than it is in agriculture). Or, putting it into even more general terms: agriculture belongs to that class of industries, whose variable capital is greater proportionately to constant capital than in industry, on an average. Hence its surplus-value, calculated on its costs of production, must be higher than the average in the industrial spheres. Which means again, that its *particular* rate of profit stands above the *average rate of profit* or the *general rate of profit*. Which means again: when the rate of surplus-value is the same and the surplus-value itself is given, then the particular rate of profit in each sphere of production depends on the proportion of variable capital to constant capital in that particular sphere.

This would therefore only be an application of the law developed by me in a *general* form to a particular branch of industry.[a]

||485| Consequently:

1. One has to prove that agriculture belongs to those particular spheres of production whose *commodity values* are above their *average prices*, whose profit, so long as they appropriate it themselves and do not hand it over for the equalisation of the general rate of profit, thus stands above the *average profit*, yielding them, therefore, in addition to this, an *excess profit*. This point 1 appears certain to apply to agriculture on an average, because manual labour is still relatively dominant in it and it is characteristic of the bourgeois mode of production to develop manufacture more rapidly than agriculture. This is, however, a *historical* difference which can disappear. At the same time this implies that, on the whole, the means of production supplied by industry to agriculture fall in value, while the raw material which agriculture supplies to industry generally rises in value, the constant capital in a large part of manufacture has con-

---

a See this volume, pp. 66-71.—*Ed.*

sequently a proportionately greater value than that in agriculture. In the main, this will probably not apply to the extractive industry.

2. It is wrong to say, as Rodbertus does: If—according to the general law—the agricultural product is sold on an average at its *value* then it must yield an excess profit, *alias* rent; as though this selling of the commodity at its *value*, *above* its average price, were the general law of capitalist production. *On the contrary*, it must be shown why in primary production—*by way of exception* and *in contrast* to the *class of industrial products whose value similarly* stands *a b o v e* their average price—the values are *not* reduced to the average prices and therefore yield an excess profit, *alias* rent. This is to be explained simply by *property in land*. The equalisation takes place only between capitals, because only the action of capitals on one another has the force to assert the inherent laws of capital. In this respect, those who derive rent from *monopoly* are right. Just as it is the *monopoly* of capital alone that enables the capitalist to squeeze surplus-labour out of the worker, so the monopoly of land ownership enables the landed proprietor to squeeze that part of surplus-labour from the capitalist, which would form a constant *excess profit*. But those who derive rent from monopoly are mistaken when they imagine that monopoly enables the landed proprietor to force the *price of the commodity above its value*. On the contrary, it makes it possible to maintain the *value of the commodity above its average price*; to sell the commodity not *above*, but *at* its value.

Modified in this way, the proposition is correct. It explains the *existence of rent*, whereas Ricardo only explains the *existence of differential rents* and actually does not credit the *ownership of land* with any *economic* effect. Furthermore, it does away with the superstructure, which with Ricardo himself was anyhow only arbitrary and not necessary for his presentation, namely, that the agricultural industry becomes gradually less productive; it admits on the contrary that it becomes more productive. On the bourgeois basis however agriculture is *relatively less productive*, or slower to develop the productive power of labour, than industry. Ricardo is right when he derives his "excess surplus-value" not from greater productivity but from smaller productivity.

[9. Differential Rent and Absolute Rent in Their Reciprocal Relationship. Rent as an Historical Category. Smith's and Ricardo's Method of Research]

So far as the *difference in rents* is concerned, provided equal capital is invested in land areas of equal size, it is due to the *difference in natural fertility*, in the first place, specifically with regard to those products which supply bread, the chief nutriment; provided the land is of equal size and fertility, differences in rent arise from *unequal capital investment*. The first, *natural*, difference causes not only the difference in the size but also in the level or rate of rent, relatively to the capital which has been laid out. The second, *industrial difference*, only effects a *greater* rent in proportion to the volume of capital which has been laid out. Successive capital investments on the same land *may* also have different results. The existence of *different excess profits* or *different rents* on land of varying fertility does not distinguish agriculture from industry. What does distinguish it is that those excess profits in agriculture become permanent *fixtures*, because here they rest on a natural basis (which, it is true, *can* be to some extent levelled out). In industry, on the other hand—given the same average profit—these excess profits can only turn up *fleetingly* and they *only* appear because of a change-over to more productive machines and combinations of labour. In industry it is always the most recently added, *most productive* capital that yields an excess profit by *reducing* average prices. In agriculture excess profit *may* be the result, and *very often must* be the result, not of the absolute increase in fertility of the best fields, but the relative increase in their fertility, because *less productive* land is being cultivated. In industry the higher *relative* productiveness, the excess profit (which disappears), must *always* be due to the absolute increase in productiveness, or productivity, of the newly invested capital compared with the old. No capital can yield an *excess profit* in industry (we are not concerned here with a momentary rise in demand), *because* less productive capitals are *newly* entering into the branch of industry.

||486| It *can*, however, also happen in agriculture (and Ricardo admits this) that more fertile land—land which is either naturally more fertile or which becomes more fertile under newly developed advances in technique than the old land under

the old [conditions]—comes into use at a later stage and even throws a part of the old land *out of cultivation* (as in the mining industry and with colonial products), or forces it to turn to another *type* of agriculture which supplies a *different* product.

The fact that the *differences* in rents (excess profits) become more or less *fixed* distinguishes agriculture from industry. But the fact that the *market-price* is determined by the average conditions of production, thus raising the price of the product which is below this average, above its *price* and even above its *value*, this fact by no means arises from the land, but from *competition*, from *capitalist production*. Hence this is not a law of nature, but a social law.

This theory neither demands the payment of *rent* for the worst land, nor the *non*-payment of rent. Similarly, it is possible that a *lease rent* is paid where *no rent* is yielded, where only the ordinary profit is made, or where *not even this* is made. Here the landowner draws a rent although *economically none is available*.

Rent (excess profit) is paid only for the better (more fertile) land. Here rent "as such" does not exist. In such cases *excess profit*—just as the excess profit in industry—rarely becomes fixed in the form of rent (as in the *West of the United States of North America*).[28] |486||

||486| This is the case where, on the one hand, relatively great areas of disposable land have *not become private property* and, on the other, the natural fertility is so great that the values of the agricultural products are equal to (sometimes *below*) their *average prices*, despite the *scant development* of capitalist production and therefore the high proportion of variable capital to constant capital. If their values were higher, competition would reduce them to this level. It is however absurd to say, as for example Rodbertus does, that the state [appropriates the ground-rent because it] levies, for instance, a dollar or so per acre, a low, almost nominal price.[a] One could just as well say that the state imposes a "trade tax" on the pursuit of every branch of industry. In *this case* Ricardo's law exists. Rent exists only for relatively fertile land—although mostly not in a fixed but in a fluid state, like the excess profit in industry. The land that pays *no* rent does so, not because of its low fertility, but *because of its high fertility*. The better kinds of land pay rent, because they possess *more* than average fertility, as a result of their *relatively higher* fertility.

---

a See this volume, p. 156.—*Ed.*

But in countries *where landed property exists*, the same situation, namely that the last cultivated land pays *no rent*, may also occur for the *reverse* reasons. Supposing, for instance, that the *value* of the grain crops was so low (and that its low value was in no way connected with the payment of *rent*), that owing to the relatively low fertility of the last cultivated land the value of its crop were only equal to the *average price*, this means that, if the same amount of labour were expended here as on the land which carried a rent, the *number of quarters* would be so small (on the capital laid out), that with the average value of bread products, only the *average price* of wheat would be obtained.

||487| Supposing for example, that the last land which carries *rent* (and the land which carries the *smallest rent* represents *pure* rent; the others already differential rent) produces [with] a capital investment of £100, [a product] equal to £120 or 360 quarters of wheat at £$1/3$. In this case 3 quarters equal £1. Let £1 equal one week's labour. £100 are 100 weeks' labour and £120 are 120 weeks' labour. 1 quarter is $1/3$ of a week which is 2 days and of these 2 days or 24 hours (if the normal working-day is 12 hours) $1/5$, or $4^4/5$ hours, are unpaid labour which is equal to the surplus-value embodied in the quarter. 1 quarter equals £$1/3$ which is $6^2/3$s. or $6^6/9$s.

If the quarter is sold at its value and the average profit is 10 per cent then the *average price* of the 360 quarters would be £110 and the average price per quarter $6^1/9$s. The value would be £10 above the average price. And since the average profit is 10 per cent the rent would be equal to half the surplus-value, i.e., £10 or $5/9$s. per quarter. Better types of land, which would yield more quarters for the same outlay of 120 labour weeks (of which, however, only 100 are paid labour, be it materialised or living), would, at the price of $6^6/9$s. per quarter, yield a higher rent. But the worst cultivated land would yield a rent of £10 on a capital of £100 or of $5/9$s. per quarter of wheat.

Assume that a new piece of land is cultivated, which only yields 330 quarters with 120 labour weeks. If the value of 3 quarters is £1, then that of 330 quarters is £110. But 1 quarter would now be equal to 2 *days* and $2^2/11$ *hours*, while before it was equal to only two days. Previously, 1 quarter was equal to $6^6/9$s. or 1 quarter was equal to 6s. 8d.; now, since £1 equals 6 days, it is equal to 7s. 3d. $1^1/11$ farthing. To be sold at its *value* the quarter would now have to be sold at 7d. $1^1/11$ farthing more, at this price it would also yield the rent of $^5/_9$s. per quarter. The *value* of the wheat produced on the better land is here *below* the *value* of that produced on the worst land. If this worst land sells at the price per quarter of the next best or rent yielding land then it sells *below* its value but at its *average price*, i.e., the price at which it yields the normal profit of 10 per cent. It can therefore be cultivated and yield the normal average profit to the capitalist.

There are two situations in which the worst land would here yield a rent apart from profit.

Firstly if the *value* of the quarter of wheat were above $6^6/_9$s. (its *price* could be above $6^6/_9$s., i. e., above its value, as a result of demand; but this does not concern us here. The $6^6/_9$s., the price per quarter, which yielded a rent of £ 10 on the worst land cultivated previously, was equal to the *value* of the wheat grown on *this* land, which yields a non-differential rent), that is [if] the worst land previously cultivated and all others, while yielding *the same* rent, were proportionately less fertile, so that their value were higher *above* their average price and the average price of the other commodities. That the *new* worst land does *not* yield a rent is thus not due to its low fertility but to the *relatively high fertility* of the *other land*. As against the new type of land with the new capital investment, the worst, [previously] cultivated, rent-yielding land represents *rent in general*, the non-*differential* rent. And that its rent is not higher is due to the [high] *fertility* of the rent-yielding land.

Assume that there are three other classes of land besides the last rent-yielding land. Class II (that above I, the last rent-yielding land) carries a rent of one-fifth more because this land is one-fifth more fertile than class I; class III again one-fifth more because it is one-fifth more fertile than class II, and the same again in class IV because it is a fifth more fertile than class III. Since the rent in class I equals £ 10, it is $10+^1/_5=$£ 12 in class II, $12+^1/_5=$£$14^2/_5$ in class III and $14^2/_5+^1/_5=$£$17^7/_{25}$ in class IV.[29]

If IV's fertility were less, the rent of III-I inclusive ||488| would be greater and that of IV also greater absolutely (but would the proportion be the same?). This can be taken in two ways. *If I were more fertile then the rent of II, III, IV would be proportionately smaller.* On the other hand, I is to II, II is to III and III is to IV as the newly added, non-rent-yielding type of land is to I. The new type of land does not carry a rent because the *value* of the wheat from I is not above the average price [of that] from the new land. It would be above it if I were less fertile. Then the new land would likewise yield a rent. But the same applies to I. If II were more fertile then I would yield no rent or a smaller rent. And it is the same with II and III and with III and IV. Finally we have the reverse: The absolute fertility of IV determines the rent of III. If IV were yet more fertile, III, II, I would yield a smaller rent or no rent at all. Thus the rent yielded by I, the undifferentiated rent, is determined by the fertility of IV, just as the circumstance that the new land yields no rent is determined by the fertility of I. Accordingly, *Storch's law* is valid here, namely, that the rent of the *most fertile* land determines the rent of the last land to yield any rent at all, and therefore also the difference between the land which yields the undifferentiated rent and that which yields no rent at all.[30]

Hence the phenomenon that here the fifth class, the newly cultivated land I' (as opposed to I) yields *no rent*, is not to be ascribed to its *own lack of fertility*, but to its *relative* lack of fertility compared with I, therefore, to the relative fertility of I as compared with I'.

[*Secondly*] The value [of the product] of the rent-yielding types of land I, II, III, IV, that is 6s. 8d. per quarter (to make it more realistic, one could say *bushel* instead of quarter), equals the *average price* of I' and is *below* its own value. Now many intermediary stages are in fact possible. Supposing on a capital investment of £ 100, I' yielded any quantity of quarters between its real return of 330 bushels and the return of I which is 360 bushels, say 333, 340, 350 *up to* 360—x bushels. Then the value of the quarter at 6s. 8d. would be above the average price of I' (per bushel) and the last cultivated land would yield a rent. That it yields the *average profit* at all, it owes to the relatively low fertility of I, and therefore of I-IV. That it yields *no* rent, is due to the relatively high fertility of I and to its own relatively low fertility. The last cultivated land I' could yield a rent if the value of the bushel were *above* 6s. 8d., that is, if I, II, III, IV were less fertile, for then the value of the wheat would be greater. It could however also yield a rent if the value were given at 6s. 8d., i.e. if the fertility of I, II, III and IV were *the same*. This would be the case if it were more fertile itself, yielded more than 330 bushels and if the value of 6s. 8d. per bushel were *thus* above its *average price*; in other words, its

7*

average price would then be *below* 6s. 8d., and therefore *below* the value of the wheat grown on I, II, III, IV. If the value is above the average price, then there is an excess profit above the average profit, hence the possibility of a *rent*.

This shows: When comparing *different* spheres of production—for instance industry and agriculture—the fact that value is above average price indicates *lower productivity* in the sphere of production that yields the excess profit, the excess of value over the average price. In *the same* sphere, on the other hand, [it indicates] *greater productivity* of one capital in comparison with other capitals in the same sphere of production. In the above example, I yields a rent, only because in agriculture the proportion of variable capital to constant capital is greater than in industry, i.e., more new labour has to be added to the materialised labour—and because of the existence of landed property this excess of value *over* average price is not levelled out by competition between capitals. But that I yields a rent at all is due to the fact that the value of 6s. 8d. per bushel is not *below* its average price, and that its fertility is not so low that its own value rises above 6s. 8d. per bushel. Its *price* moreover is *not* determined by *its own value* but by the value of the wheat grown on II, III, IV or, to be precise, by that grown on II. Whether the *market-price* is merely equal to its *own average price* or stands above it, and whether its *value is above tts average price*, depends on its own productivity.

Hence Rodbertus's view that in agriculture every capital which yields the average profit *must* yield rent is wrong. This false conclusion follows from his ||489| false basis. He reasons like this: The capital in agriculture, for instance, yields £10. But because, in contrast to industry, *raw materials* do *not* enter into it, the £10 are reckoned on a smaller sum. They represent therefore more than 10 per cent. But the point is this: It is not the absence of raw materials (on the contrary, they do enter into agriculture proper; it wouldn't matter a straw if they *didn't* enter into it, provided *machinery* etc. increased proportionally) which raises the value of the agricultural products above the *average price* (their own and that of other commodities). Rather is this due to the higher proportion of variable to constant capital compared with that existing, not in *particular spheres* of industrial *production*, but *on an average* in industry as a whole. The magnitude of this *general* difference determines the amount and the existence of rent on No. I, the absolute, non-differential rent and hence the *smallest* rent. The price of wheat from I′, the newly cultivated land which does not yield a rent, is, however, *not* determined by the *value* of its own product, but by the value of I, and consequently by the average *market-price* of the wheat supplied by I, II, III and IV.

The privilege of agriculture (resulting from landed property), that it sells its product not at the *average price* but at its *value* if this value is *above* the average price, is by no means valid for products grown on different types of land as against one another, for products of different values produced within *the same* sphere of production. As against industrial products, they can only claim to be sold at their value. As against the other products of the same sphere, they are determined by the market-price, and it depends on the fertility of I whether the value—which equals the average market-price here—is sufficiently high or low, i.e., whether the fertility of I is sufficiently high or low, for I′, if it is sold at *this* value, to participate little, much or not at all in the general difference between the value and the average price of wheat. But, since Herr Rodbertus makes no distinction at all between values and average prices, and since he considers it to be a general law for all commodities, and not a privilege of agricultural products, that they are sold at *their* values—he must of course believe that the product of the least fertile land has also to be sold at *its* individual value. But it loses this privilege in competition with products of *the same* type.

Now it is possible for the average price of I′ to be above 6s. 8d. per bushel, the value of I. It can be assumed (although this is not quite correct), that for land I′ to be cultivated at all, demand must increase. The price of wheat from I must therefore rise *above* its *value*, above 6s. 8d., and indeed persistently so. In this case land I′ will be cultivated. If it can make the average profit at 6s. 8d. although its value is *above* 6s. 8d. and if it can satisfy demand, then the price will be reduced to 6s. 8d., since demand now again corresponds to supply, and so I must sell at 6s. 8d. again, ditto II, III, IV; hence also I′. If, on the other hand, the *average price* in I′ amounted to 7s. 8d. so that it could make the usual profit at this price only (which would be far below its individual value) and if the demand could not be otherwise satisfied, then the value of the bushel would have to consolidate itself at 7s. 8d. and the demand price of I would rise above its value. That of II, III, IV, which is already above *their* individual value, would rise even higher.

If, on the other hand, there were prospects of grain imports which would by no means permit of such a stabilisation, then I' could nevertheless be cultivated if small farmers were prepared to be satisfied with less than the average profit. This is constantly happening in both agriculture and industry. Rent could be paid in this case just as when I' yields the average profit, but it would merely be a deduction from the farmer's profit. If this could not be done either, then the landlord could lease the land to cottagers whose main concern, like that of the hand-loom weaver, is to get their wages out of it and to pay the surplus, large or small, to the landlord in the form of rent. As in the case of the hand-loom weaver, this surplus could even be a mere deduction, not from the product of labour, but from the *wages of labour*. In all these instances rent could be paid. In one case it would be a deduction from the capitalist's profit. In the other case, the landlord would appropriate the surplus-labour of the worker which would otherwise be appropriated by the capitalist. And in the final case he would live off the worker's wage as the capitalists are also often wont to do. But large-scale *capitalist production* is only possible where the last cultivated land yields at least the average profit, that is where the value of I enables I' to realise at least the average price.

One can see how the differentiation between *value* and *average price* surprisingly solves the question and shows that Ricardo and his opponents are right.[31]

||XI-490| If I, the land which yields absolute rent, were the only cultivated land, then it would sell the bushel of wheat at its *value*, at 6s. 8d. or $6^6/_9$s. and not reduce it to the average price of $6^1/_9$s. or 6s. $1^1/_3$d. If all land were of the same type and if the cultivated area increased tenfold, because demand grew, then since I yields a rent of £10 per £100, the rent would grow to £100, although only *a single type of land* existed. But its rate or level would not grow, neither compared with the *capital advanced* nor compared with the area of *land cultivated*. Ten times as many acres would be cultivated and ten times as much capital advanced. This would therefore merely be an augmentation of the *rental*, of the volume of rent, not of its level. The rate of profit would not fall; for the value and price of the agricultural products would remain the same. A capital which is ten times as large can naturally hand over a rent which is ten times larger than a capital which is one-tenth its size. On the other hand, if ten times as much capital were employed on the

same area of land with the same result, then the rate of rent compared with the capital laid out would have remained *the same*; it would have risen in proportion to the area of land, but would not have altered the rate of profit in any way.

Now supposing the cultivation of I became more productive, not because the land had altered but because more constant capital and less variable capital is being laid out, that is more capital is being spent on machinery, horses, mineral fertilisers etc. and less on wages; then the value of wheat would approach its average price and the average price of the industrial products, because the excess in the ratio of variable to constant capital would have decreased. In this case rent would fall and the rate of profit would remain unaltered. If the mode of production changed in such a way that the ratio of variable to constant capital became the same as the average ratio in industry, then the excess of value over the average price of wheat would disappear and with it rent, excess profit. Category I would no longer pay a rent, and landed property would have become nominal (in so far as the altered mode of production is not in fact accompanied by additional capital being embodied in the land, so that, on the termination of the lease, the owner might draw interest on a capital which he himself had not advanced; this is indeed a principal means by which landowners enrich themselves, and the dispute about tenantry-right in Ireland revolves around this very point). Now if, besides I, there also existed II, III, IV, in all of which this mode of production were applied, then they would still yield rents because of their greater natural fertility and the rent would be in proportion to the degree of their fertility. Category I would in this case have ceased to yield a rent and the rents of II, III, IV would have fallen accordingly, because the general ratio of productivity in agriculture had become equal to that prevailing in industry. The rent of II, III, IV would correspond with the Ricardian law; it would merely be equivalent to, and would *exist* only as an excess profit of more fertile compared to less fertile land, like similar excess profits in industry, except in the latter they lack the natural basis for consolidation.

The Ricardian law would prevail just the same, even if *landed property* were *non*-existent. With the abolition of landed property and the retention of capitalist production, this excess profit arising from the difference in fertility would remain. If the state appropriated the land and capitalist production continued, then rent from II, III, IV would be paid to the state, but rent as such would remain. If landed property became *people's property* then the whole basis of capitalist production would go, the foundation on which rests the confrontation of the worker by the conditions of labour as an independent force.

A question which is to be later examined in connection with rent: How is it possible for rent to rise in *value* and in *amount*, with more intensive cultivation, although the rate of rent falls in relation to the capital advanced? This is obviously only possible because the *amount of capital advanced* rises. If rent is $1/5$ and it becomes $1/10$, then $20 \times 1/5 = 4$ and $50 \times 1/10 = 5$. That's all. But if conditions of production in intensive cultivation became the same as those prevailing on an average in industry, instead of only *approximating* to them, then rent for the least fertile land would disappear and for the most fertile it would be reduced merely to the difference in the land. *Absolute* rent would no longer exist.

Now let us assume that, following upon a rise in demand, new land, II, were cultivated in addition to I. Category I pays the absolute rent, II would pay a differential rent, but the *price* of wheat (value for I, excess value for II) remains the same. The rate of profit, too, [is supposed] not to be affected. And so on till we come to IV. Thus the *level*, the rate of rent is also rising if we take the total capital laid out in I, II, III, IV. But the average rate of profit from II, III, IV would remain the same as that from I, which equals that in industry, the general rate of profit. Thus if ||491| we go on to more fertile land, the amount and rate of rent can grow, although the rate of profit remains unchanged and the price of wheat constant. The rise in level and amount of rent would be due to the growing productivity of the capital in II, III, IV, not to the diminishing productivity in I. But the growing productivity would not cause a rise in profits and a fall both in the price of the commodity and in wages, as happens necessarily in industry.

Supposing, however, the reverse process took place: from IV to III, II, I. Then the price would rise to 6s. 8d. at which it would still yield a rent of £10 on £100 on I. For the rent of wheat on IV [amounts to] £$17^7/_{25}$ on £100, of which, however, $7^7/_{25}$ are the excess of its price over the value of I. Category I gave 360 bushels at £100 (with a rent of £10 and the value of the *bushel at 6s. 8d.*). II—432 bushels. III—$518^2/_5$ bushels and IV—$622^2/_{25}$ bushels. But the price per bushel of 6s. 8d.

yielded IV an excess rent of $7^7/_{25}$ per 100. IV sells 3 bushels for £1 or $622^2/_{25}$ bushels at £$207^9/_{25}$. But its value is only £120, as in I; whatever is above this amount is excess of its price over its value.[32] IV would sell the bushel at its value or rather, [he would sell it at its value] if he sold it, at 3s. $10^8/_{27}$ d. and at this price he would have a rent of £10 on £100. The movement from IV to III, III to II and II to I, causes the price per bushel (and with it the rent) to rise until it eventually reaches 6s. 8d. with I, where this price now yields the same rent that it previously yielded with IV. The rate of profit would fall with the rise in price, partly owing to the rise in value of the means of subsistence and raw materials. The transition from IV to III could happen like this: Due to demand, the price of IV rises above its value, hence it yields not only rent but excess rent. Consequently III is cultivated which, with the normal average profit, is not supposed to yield a rent at this price. If the rate of profit has not fallen as a result of the rise in price of IV, but wages have, then III will yield the average profit. But due to the [additional] supply from III, wages should rise to their normal level again; [then] the rate of profit in III falls etc.

Thus the rate of profit falls with this downward movement on the *assumptions which we have made*, namely, that III cannot yield a rent at the price of IV and that III can only be cultivated at the old rate of profit because wages have momentarily fallen below their [normal] level.

Under these conditions [it is again possible for] the Ricardian law [to apply]. But not necessarily, even according to his interpretation. It is merely *possible* in certain circumstances. In reality the movements are contradictory.

This has disposed of the essence of the theory of rent.

With Herr Rodbertus, rent arises from eternal nature; at least of capitalist production, because of his "value of the material". In our view rent arises from an *historical difference* in the organic component parts of capital which may be partially ironed out and indeed disappear completely, with the development of agriculture. True, the difference in so far as it is merely due to variation in actual fertility of the land remains even if the *absolute* rent disappeared. But—quite apart from the possible ironing out of natural variations—*differential rent* is linked with the regulation of the market-price and therefore disappears along with the price and with capitalist production. There would remain only the fact that *land of varying fertility is cultivated by social labour* and, despite the difference in the amount of labour employed, labour can become more productive on all types of land. But the amount of labour used on the worse land would by no means result in more labour being paid for [the product] of the better land as now with the bourgeois. Rather would the labour saved on IV be used for the improvement of III and that saved from III for the improvement of II and finally that saved on II would be used to improve I. Thus the whole of the capital eaten up by the landowners would serve to equalise the labour used for the cultivation of the soil and to reduce the amount of labour in agriculture as a whole.

||492| {Adam Smith, as we saw above,[33] first correctly interprets value and the relation existing between profit, wages, etc. as component parts of this value, and then he proceeds the other way round, regards the prices of wages, profit and rent as antecedent factors and seeks to determine them independently, in order then to compose the *price of the commodity* out of them. The meaning of this change of approach is that first he grasps the problem in its *inner relationships*, and then in the *reverse form, as it appears in competition*. These two concepts of his run counter to one another in his work, naively, without his being aware of the contradiction. Ricardo, on the other hand, consciously *abstracts* from the form of competition, from the appearance of competition, in order to comprehend the *laws as such*. On the one hand he must be reproached for not going far enough, for not carrying his abstraction to completion, for instance, when he analyses the *value* of the commodity, he at once allows himself to be influenced by consideration of all kinds of concrete conditions. On the other hand one must reproach him for regarding the phenomenal form as *immediate and direct* proof or exposition of the general laws, and for failing to *interpret* it. In regard to the first, his abstraction is too incomplete; in regard to the second, it is formal abstraction which in itself is wrong.}

[10. Rate of Rent and Rate of Profit. Relation Between Productivity in Agriculture and in Industry in the Different Stages of Historical Development]

Now to return briefly to the remainder of Rodbertus.

"The *increase* in wages, capital gain and ground-rent respectively, which arises from the *increase* in the value of the national product can *raise* neither the wages nor the capital gain of the nation, since more wages are now distributed among more workers and a greater amount of capital gain accrues to capital increased in the same proportion; ground-rent, on the other hand, must *rise* since this always accrues to land *whose area has remained the same.* It is thus possible to explain satisfactorily the great *rise in land value*, which is nothing other than ground-rent capitalised at the normal rate of interest, without having to resort to a fall in productivity of agricultural labour, which is diametrically opposed to the idea of the perfectibility of human society and to all agricultural and statistical facts" (pp. 160-61).

First of all it should be noted that Ricardo [at whom this passage is aimed] *nowhere* seeks to explain the *"great rise in land value".* This is *no problem* at all for him. He says further, and Ricardo even noted this explicitly (see later in connection with Ricardo[a]), that—given the rate of rent—rent can *increase* with a constant value of corn or agricultural produce. This increase again presents no problem for him. The rise in the rental while the rate of rent remains the same, is no problem for him either. His problem lies in the rise in the *rate of rent*, i.e., rent in proportion to the agricultural capital advanced, and hence the rise in value not of the *amount* of agricultural produce, but the rise in the value, for example, of the quarter of wheat, i.e., of the same quantity of agricultural produce; in consequence of this the excess of its value over the average price increases and thereby also the excess of rent over the rate of profit. Herr Rodbertus here begs the Ricardian problem (to say nothing of his erroneous "value of the material").

The *rate of rent* can indeed rise relatively to the capital advanced, in other words, the relative value of the agricultural product can rise in proportion to the industrial product, even though agriculture is constantly becoming *more productive.* And this can happen for two reasons.

Firstly take the *above example*, the transition from I to II, III, IV, i.e., to ever more fertile land (but where the additional supply is not so great as to throw I out of cultivation or to reduce the difference between value and average price to such an extent that IV, III, II pay relatively lower rents and I no rent at all). If I's rent amounts to 10, II's to 20, III's to 30 and IV's to 40 and if £ 100 are invested in all four types of land, then I's rent would be $^1/_{10}$ or 10 per cent on the capital advanced, II's would be $^2/_{10}$ or 20 per cent, III's would be $^3/_{10}$ or 30 per cent and IV's rent would be $^4/_{10}$ or 40 per cent. Altogether £ 100 on 400 capital advanced, which gives an average rate of rent

---

a See this volume, p. 317.—*Ed.*

of $^{100}/_4$=25 per cent. Taking the entire capital invested in agriculture, the rent amounts now to 25 per cent. Had only the
cultivation of land I (the unfertile land) been extended, then
the rent would be 40 on 400, 10 per cent just as before, and it
would not have risen by 15 per cent. But in the first case (if
330 bushels resulted from an outlay of £100 on I) only *1,320*
bushels would have been produced at the price of 6s. 8d. per
bushel. In the second case [i.e., when all four classes of land are
cultivated], 1,500 bushels have been produced at the same
price. The same capital has been advanced in both cases.[34]

But the rise in the *level* of the rent here is only apparent. For
if we calculate the capital outlay in relation to the product, then
100 [would have been] needed in I to produce 330 and 400 to
produce *1,320* bushels. But now only 100+90+80+70, i.e.,
£340[35] are needed to produce 1,320 bushels. £90 in II produce
as much as 100 in I, 80 in III as much as 90 in II and 70 in IV
as much as 80 in III. The rate of rent [has] risen in II, III, IV,
compared with I.

If we take society as a whole, it means that a capital of 340
[was] employed to raise *the same* product, instead of a capital
of 400, that is 85 per cent [of the previous] capital.

||493| The 1,320 bushels [would] only be distributed, in a
different way from those in the first case. The farmer must hand
over as much on 90 as previously on 100, as much on 80 as
previously on 90 and as much on 70 as previously on 80. But the
capital outlay of 90, 80, 70, gives him just the same amount of
product as he previously obtained on 100. He hands over more,
not because he must employ more capital in order to supply
the same product, but because he employs less capital; not
because his capital has become less productive, but because
it has become more productive and he is still selling at the
price of I, as though he still required the same capital as before
in order to produce the same quantity of product.

[*Secondly.*] Apart from this rise in the *rate of rent*—which
corresponds to the uneven rise in excess profit in individual
branches of industry, though here it does not become fixed—
there is only one other possibility of the *rate of rent* rising
although the value of the product remains the same, that is,
labour does not become less productive. It occurs either when
productivity in agriculture remains *the same* as before but
productivity in industry rises and this rise expresses itself in
a fall in the rate of profit, in other words when the ratio of

variable to constant capital diminishes. Or, alternatively, when productivity is rising in agriculture as well though not at the same rate as in industry but at a lower rate. If productivity in agriculture rises as 1:2 and in industry as 1:4, then it is *relatively* the same as if it had remained at one in agriculture and had doubled in industry. In this case the ratio of variable capital to constant capital would be decreasing in industry twice as fast as in agriculture.

In both cases the rate of profit in industry would fall, and because it *fell* the *rate* of rent would rise. In the other instances the rate of profit does not fall absolutely (rather it remains *constant*) but it falls relatively to rent. It does so not because it *itself* is decreasing but because rent, the rate of rent in relation to the capital advanced, is rising.

Ricardo does not differentiate between these cases. Except in these cases (that is where the rate of profit, although constant, falls relatively because of the differential rents of the capital employed on the more fertile types of land or where the general ratio of constant to variable capital alters as a result of the increased productivity of industry and *hence* increases the excess of value of agricultural products above their average price) the rate of rent can only rise if the rate of profit falls without industry becoming more productive. This is, however, only possible if wages rise or if raw material rises in value as a result of the lower productivity of agriculture. In this case both the fall in the rate of profit and the rise in the level of rent are brought about by the same cause—the decrease in the productivity of agriculture and of the capital employed in agriculture. This is how Ricardo sees it. With the value of money *remaining the same*, this must then show itself in a rise in the *prices* of the raw products. If, as above, the rise is *relative*, then no change in the price of money can raise the money prices of agricultural products absolutely as compared with industrial products. If money fell by 50 per cent then 1 quarter which was previously worth £3 would now be worth £6, but 1 lb. yarn which was previously worth 1s. would now be worth 2s. The *absolute* rise in the money prices of agricultural products compared with industrial products can therefore never be explained by changes in [the value of] money.

On the whole it can be assumed that under the cruder, precapitalist mode of production, agriculture is *more productive* than industry, because nature assists here as a machine and an organism, whereas in industry the powers of nature are still almost entirely replaced by human action (as in the craft type of industry etc.). In the period of the stormy growth of capitalist production, productivity in industry develops rapidly as compared with agriculture, although its development *presupposes* that a significant change as between constant and variable capital *has* already taken place in agriculture, that is, a large number of people have been driven off the land. Later, productivity advances in both, although at an uneven pace. But when industry reaches a certain level the disproportion must diminish, in other words, productivity in agriculture must increase relatively more rapidly than in industry. This requires: 1. The replacement of the easy-going farmer by the businessman, the farming capitalist; transformation of the husbandman into a pure wage-labourer; large-scale agriculture, i.e., with concentrated capitals. 2. In particular however: Mechanics, the really scientific basis of large-scale industry, had reached a certain degree of perfection during the eighteenth century. The development of chemistry, geology and physiology, the sciences that *directly* form the specific basis of agriculture rather than of industry, ||494| does not take place till the nineteenth century and especially the later decades.

It is nonsense to talk of the greater or lesser productivity of two *different* branches of industry when merely comparing the values of their commodities. If, [in] 1800, the pound of cotton was 2s. and of yarn 4s., and if, in 1830, the value of cotton was 2s. or 18d. and that of yarn 3s. or 1s. 8d. then one might compare the proportion in which the productivity in both branches had grown—but only because the rate of 1800 is taken as the starting-point. On the other hand, because the pound of cotton is 2s. and that of yarn is 3, and hence the labour which produces the cotton is as great again as the [newly-added labour] of spinning, it would be absurd to say that the one is twice as productive as the other. Just as absurd as it would be to say that because canvas can be made more cheaply than the artist's painting on the canvas, the labour of the latter is less productive than that of the former.

Only the following is correct, even if it comprises the capitalist meaning of *productive*—productive of surplus-value along with the relative amounts of the product:

If, on an average, according to the conditions of production, £ 500 is needed in the form of raw material and machinery etc.

⟨at given values⟩ in order to employ 100 workers [whose wages] amount to £ 100 in the cotton industry, and, on the other hand, £ 150 is needed for raw materials and machinery in order to employ 100 workers [whose wages] amount to £ 100, in the cultivation of wheat, then the variable capital in I would form $1/6$ of the total capital of £ 600, and $1/5$ of the constant capital; in II, the variable capital would constitute $2/5$ of the total capital of £ 250 and $2/3$ of constant capital. Thus every £ 100 which is laid out in I can only contain £ $16^2/3$ variable capital and must contain £ $83^1/3$ constant capital; whereas in II it comprises £ 40 of variable capital and £ 60 of constant. In I, variable capital forms $1/6$ or $16^2/3$ per cent and in II, 40 per cent. Clearly the histories of prices are at present quite wretched. And they can be nothing but wretched until theory shows what needs to be examined. If the rate of surplus-value were given at, say, 20 per cent then the surplus-value in I would amount to £ $3^1/3$ (hence profit $3^1/3$ per cent). In II, however, £ 8 (hence profit 8 per cent). Labour in I would not be so productive as in II because it would be more productive (in other words, not so productive of surplus-value, because it is more productive of produce). Incidentally, it is cleary only possible to have a ratio of 1:$1/6$, for example, in the cotton industry, if a constant capital (this depends on the machines etc.) amounting to say £ 10,000 has been laid out, hence wages amounting to 2,000, making a total capital of 12,000. If only 6,000 were laid out, of which wages would be 1,000, then the machinery would be less productive etc. At 100 it could not be done at all. On the other hand it is possible that if £ 23,000 is laid out, the resulting increase in the efficiency of the machinery and other economies etc. are so great that the £ $19,166^2/3$ is not entirely allocated to constant capital, but that more raw material and the same amount of labour require *less* machinery etc. ([in terms of] value) which is assumed to cost £ 1,000 less than before. Then the ratio of variable to constant capital grows again, but only because the absolute [amount of] capital has grown. This is a check against the fall in the rate of profit. Two capitals of 12,000 would produce the same quantity of commodities as the one of 23,000, but firstly the commodities would be dearer since they required an outlay of £ 1,000 more, and secondly the rate of profit would be smaller because within the capital of £ 23,000, the variable capital is more than $1/6$ of the total capital, i.e., more than in the sum of the two capitals of £ 12,000. |494||

||494| (On the one hand, with the advance of industry, machinery becomes more effective and cheaper; hence, if only *the same quantity* of machinery were employed as in the past, this part of constant capital in agriculture would diminish; but the quantity of machinery grows faster than the reduction in its price, since this element is as yet little developed in agriculture. On the other hand, with the greater productivity of agriculture, the price of raw material—see cotton—falls, so that raw material does not increase as a component part of the process of creating value to the same degree as it increases as a component part of the labour-process.)[36] |494||

* * *

||494| Already *Petty* tells us that the Landlord of his time feared improvements in agriculture because they would cause the price of agricultural products and (the level of) rent to fall; ditto the *extension of the land* and the cultivation of previously unused land which is equivalent to an extension of the land. (In Holland this extension of the land is to be understood in an even more direct way.) He says:

"...that the draining of Fens, improving of Forests,[a] inclosing of Commons, Sowing of St. Foyne and Clovergrass, be grumbled against by Landlords, as the way to depress the Price of Victuals...." ([William Petty], "Political Arithmetick" [in: *Several Essays in Political Arithmetick*,] London, 1699, p. 230.)

("...the Rent of all England [...] Wales, and the Low-Lands of Scotland, be about Nine Millions per Annum....") (Ibid., p. 231.)

Petty fights this view and D'Avenant goes ||495| even further and shows how the *level of rent* may decrease while the amount of rent or the rental increases. He says:

"Rents may fall in some Places, and Counties, and yet the Land of the Nation" (he means value of the land) "improve all the while: As for Example, when Parks are dispark'd, and Forests, and Commons are taken in, and enclos'd; when Fen-Lands are drein'd, and when many Parts" (of the country) "are meliorated by Industry, and manuring[b] it must certainly depretiate that Ground which has been Improv'd to the full before, or[c] was capable of no

---

a In the manuscript: "woods".—*Ed.*

b In the manuscript: "manufacturing" instead of "manuring".—*Ed.*

c In the manuscript: "and" instead of "or".—*Ed.*

farther Improvement [...] the Rental[a] of private Men does thereby sink, yet the general Rental[b] of the Kingdom by such Improvements, at the same time rises." (Charles D'Avenant, *Discourses on the Publick Revenues, and on the Trade of England*, Part II, London, 1698, pp. 26-27.) "...fall in private Rents from 1666 to 1688 [...] but the Rise in the Kingdomes general Rental was greater in Proportion during that time, than in the preceeding Years, because the Improvements upon Land were greater and more universal, between those two Periods, than at any time before..." (l.c. p. 28).

It is also evident here, that the Englishman always regards the level of rent as rent related to capital and never to the *total land* in the kingdom (or to the acre in general, like Herr Rodbertus).

---

[a] In the manuscript: "income from rent" instead of "Rental".—*Ed.*
[b] In the manuscript: "rent" instead of "Rental".—*Ed.*

[CHAPTER IX]

NOTES ON THE HISTORY OF THE DISCOVERY OF THE SO-CALLED RICARDIAN LAW OF RENT. [SUPPLEMENTARY NOTES ON RODBERTUS] (DIGRESSION)

[1. The Discovery of the Law of Differential Rent by Anderson. Distortion of Anderson's Views by His Plagiarist, Malthus, in the Interests of the Landowners]

Anderson was a practical farmer. His first work, in which the nature of rent is discussed *in passing,* appeared in 1777,[37] at a time when, for a large section of the public, Sir James Steuart was still the leading economist, and while everyone's attention was focused on the *Wealth of Nations,* which had appeared a year earlier.[38] As against this, the work of the Scottish farmer, which had been occasioned by an immediate practical controversy and which did not *ex professo* deal with rent but only incidentally elucidated its nature, could not attract any attention. In this work, Anderson only dealt with rent accidentally, not *ex professo.* This theory of his appears again, in the same incidental fashion, in one or two of his collected essays which he himself published in three volumes under the title of: *Essays Relating to Agriculture and Rural Affairs,* 3 vols., Edinburgh, 1775-1796. Similarly in his *Recreations in Agriculture, Natural History, Arts,* etc., London (to be looked up in the British Museum) which were published in the years 1799 to 1802, all these writings are directly intended for farmers and agriculturists. [It would have been] different if Anderson had had an inkling of the importance of his find and had put it before the public separately, as an "Inquiry into the Nature of Rent", or if he had had the least bit of talent in trading his own ideas, as his fellow countryman, McCulloch, did so successfully with other people's. The reproductions of his theory which appeared in 1815 were published forthwith as independent *theoretical* inquiries into the nature of rent, as the very titles of the respective works of West and Malthus show:

Malthus: *An Inquiry into the Nature and Progress of Rent.* West: *Essay on the Application of Capital to Land.*

Furthermore, Malthus used the Andersonian theory of rent to give his population law, for the first time, both an economic and a real (natural-historical) basis, while the nonsense about geometrical and arithmetical progression borrowed from earlier writers, was a purely imaginary hypothesis. Mr. Malthus at once "improved" the matter. *Ricardo* even made this doctrine of rent, as he himself says in his preface,[39] one of the most important links in the whole system of political economy and—quite apart from the practical aspect—gave it an entirely new theoretical importance.

Ricardo evidently did not know Anderson since, in the preface to his *Principles of Political Economy,* he treats West and Malthus as the originators. Judging by the original manner in which he presents the law, *West* was possibly as little acquainted with Anderson as Tooke was with Steuart. With Mr. Malthus it is different. A close comparison of his writings shows that he knows and uses Anderson. He was in fact *plagiarist* by ||496| profession. One need only compare *the first edition* of his work on population[40] with the work of the Reverend Townsend[41] which I have quoted previously, to be convinced that he does not work him over as an independent producer, but copies him and paraphrases him like a slavish plagiarist, although he does *not mention him anywhere by name* and *conceals* his existence.

The manner in which Malthus used Anderson is characteristic. Anderson had defended premiums on exports of corn and duties on corn imports, not out of any interest for the landlords, but because he believed that this type of legislation "would *reduce* the average price of corn" and ensure an even development of the productive forces in agriculture. Malthus accepted this practical application of Anderson's because—being a staunch member of the Established Church of England—he was a professional sycophant of the landed aristocracy, whose rents, sinecures, squandering, heartlessness etc. he justified *economically.* Malthus defends the interests of the industrial bourgeoisie only in so far as these are identical with the interests of landed property, of the aristocracy, i.e., *against* the mass of the people, the proletariat. But where these interests diverge and are antagonistic to each other, he sides with the aristocracy against the bourgeoisie. Hence his defence of the "*unproductive* worker", over-consumption etc.

8*

Anderson, on the other hand, explained the difference between land which pays rent and that which does not, or between lands which pay varying rents, by the *relatively* low fertility of the land which bears *no* rent or a *smaller* rent compared with that which bears a rent or a greater rent. But he stated expressly that these degrees of relative productivity of *different* types of land, i.e., also the relatively low productivity of the worse types of land compared with the better, had absolutely nothing to do with the *absolute* productivity of agriculture. *On the contrary*, he stressed not only that the absolute productivity of *all* types of land could be constantly improved and must be improved with the progress in population, but he went further and asserted that the *differences* in *productivity* of various types of land can be progressively *reduced*. He said that the present degree of development of agriculture in England gives no indication at all of its *possibilities*. That is why he said that in one country the prices of corn may be high and rent low, while in another country the price of corn may be low and rent may be high, and this is in accordance with his principle, since the level and the existence of rents is in both countries determined by the *difference* between the fertile and the unfertile land, in neither of them by the absolute fertility; in each only by the degree of difference in fertility of the existing types of land, and not by the average fertility of these types of land. From this he concluded that the absolute fertility of agriculture has nothing to do with rent. Hence later, as we shall see below,[a] he declared himself a decided adversary of the Malthusian theory of population and it never dawned on him that his own theory of rent was to serve as the basis of this monstrosity. Anderson reasoned that the rise in corn prices in England between 1750 and 1801 as compared with the years 1700 to 1750 was by no means due to the cultivation of progressively less fertile types of land, but to the influence of legislation on agriculture during these two periods.

What then did Malthus do?

Instead of his (also plagiarised) chimera of the geometrical and arithmetical progression, which he retained as a "phrase", he made Anderson's theory the confirmation of his population theory. He retained Anderson's practical application of the theory in so far as it was in the interests of the landlords—this fact alone proves that he understood as little of the connection of

---

a See this volume, pp. 144-45.—*Ed.*

this theory with the system of bourgeois economy as Anderson himself. Without going into the counter-evidence which the discoverer of the theory put forward, he turned it against the proletariat. The theoretical and practical advance which could have been made from this theory was: theoretical—for the determination of the *value* of the commodity etc. and gaining an insight into the nature of landownership; practical—against the necessity of private ownership of the land, on the *basis of bourgeois production* and, more immediately, against all state regulations such as corn laws, which enhanced this ownership of land. These advances from Anderson's theory, Malthus left to Ricardo. The one practical conclusion which he drew from it was a defence of the protective tariffs which the landlords demanded in 1815— a sycophantic service for the aristocracy and a new *justification* for the poverty of the producers of wealth, a new apology for the exploiters of labour. In this respect it was a sycophantic service for the industrial capitalists.

Utter baseness is a distinctive trait of Malthus—a baseness which can only be indulged in by a parson ||497| who sees human suffering as the punishment for sin and who, in any case, needs a "vale of tears on earth", but who, at the same time, in view of the living he draws and aided by the dogma of predestination, finds it altogether advantageous to "sweeten" their sojourn in the vale of tears for the ruling classes. The "baseness" of this mind is also evident in his scientific work. *Firstly* in his shameless and mechanical *plagiarism*. *Secondly* in the *cautious*, not *radical*, conclusions which he draws from scientific premises.

[2. Ricardo's Fundamental Principle in Assessing Economic Phenomena Is the Development of the Productive Forces. Malthus Defends the Most Reactionary Elements of the Ruling Classes. Virtual Refutation of Malthus's Theory of Population by Darwin]

Ricardo, rightly for his time, regards the capitalist mode of production as the most advantageous for production in general, as the most advantageous for the creation of wealth. He wants *production for the sake of production* and this with *good reason*. To assert, as sentimental opponents of Ricardo's did, that production as such is not the object, is to forget that production for its own sake means nothing but the development of human productive forces, in other words the *development of the richness*

of human nature as an end in itself. To oppose the welfare of
the individual to this end, as Sismondi does, is to assert that the
development of the species must be *arrested* in order to safe-
guard the welfare of the individual, so that, for instance, no war
may be waged in which at all events some individuals perish.
(Sismondi is only right as against the economists who *conceal*
or deny this contradiction.) Apart from the barrenness of such
edifying reflections, they reveal a failure to understand the fact
that, although at first the development of the capacities of the
human species takes place at the cost of the majority of human
individuals and even classes, in the end it breaks through this
contradiction and coincides with the development of the individual; the higher development of individuality is thus only achieved
by a historical process during which individuals are sacrificed,
for the interests of the species in the human kingdom, as in the
animal and plant kingdoms, always assert themselves at the cost
of the interests of individuals, because these interests of the
species coincide only with the *interests of certain individuals*,
and it is this coincidence which constitutes the strength of these
privileged individuals.

Thus Ricardo's ruthlessness was not only *scientifically honest*
but also a *scientific necessity* from his point of view. But because
of this it is also quite immaterial to him whether the advance of
the productive forces slays landed property or workers. If this
progress devalues the capital of the industrial bourgeoisie it is
equally welcome to him. If the development of the productive
power of labour halves the value of the *existing* fixed capital,
what does it matter, says Ricardo. The productivity of human
labour has doubled. Thus here is *scientific honesty*. Ricardo's
conception is, on the whole, in the interests of the *industrial
bourgeoisie*, only *because*, and *in so far as*, their interests coincide with that of production or the productive development of
human labour. Where the bourgeoisie comes into conflict with
this, he is just as *ruthless* towards it as he is at other times
towards the proletariat and the aristocracy.

But *Malthus*! This wretch only draws such conclusions from
the given scientific premises (which he invariably *steals*), as
will be "*agreeable*" (useful) to the aristocracy against the bourgeoisie and to both *against* the proletariat. Hence he does not
want *production for the sake of production*, but only in so far
as it maintains or extends the *status quo*, and serves the interests
of the ruling classes.

Already his first work,[42] one of the most remarkable literary examples of the success of plagiarism at the cost of the original work, had the *practical* purpose to provide "economic" proof, in the interests of the *existing* English government and the *landed aristocracy*, that the tendency of the French Revolution and *its adherents in England* to perfect matters was utopian. In other words, it was a panegyric pamphlet for the existing conditions, against historical development and, furthermore, a justification of the war against revolutionary France.

His writings of 1815, on protective tariffs and rent,[43] were partly means to confirm the earlier apology of the poverty of the producers, in particular, however, to defend reactionary landed property against "enlightened", "liberal" and "progressive" capital, and especially to justify an intended *retrogressive step* in English legislation in the interests of the aristocracy against the industrial bourgeoisie.[44] Finally, ||498| his *Principles of Political Economy* directed *against* Ricardo had essentially the purpose of reducing the absolute demands of "industrial capital" and the laws under which its productivity develops, to the "desirable limits" "favourable" to the existing interests of the landed aristocracy, the "Established Church" (to which Malthus belonged), government pensioners and consumers of taxes. But when a man seeks to *accommodate* science to a viewpoint which is derived not from science itself (however erroneous it may be) but from *outside, from alien, external interests*, then I call him "*base*".

It is not a base action when Ricardo puts the proletariat on the same level as machinery or beasts of burden or commodities, because (from his point of view) their being purely machinery or beasts of burden is conducive to "production" or because they really are mere commodities in bourgeois production. This is stoic, objective, scientific. In so far as it does not involve *sinning* against his science, Ricardo is always a philanthropist, just as he was in *practice* too.

The parson Malthus, on the other hand, reduces the worker to a beast of burden for the sake of production and even condemns him to death from starvation and to celibacy. But when these same demands of production curtail the landlord's "rent" or threaten to encroach on the "tithes" of the Established Church, or on the interests of the "consumers of taxes"; and also when that part of the industrial bourgeoisie whose interests stand in the way of progress is being sacrificed to that part which represents the advance of production—and therefore whenever it is a question of the interests of the aristocracy against the bourgeoisie or of the conservative and stagnant bourgeoisie against the progressive—in all these instances "parson" Malthus does not sacrifice the particular interests to production but *seeks*, as far as he can, to sacrifice the demands of production to the particular interests of existing ruling classes or sections of classes. And to this end he *falsifies* his scientific conclusions. This is his *scientific* baseness, his sin against science, quite apart from his shameless and mechanical plagiarism. The scientific conclusions of Malthus are "*considerate*" towards the ruling classes in general and towards the reactionary elements of the ruling classes in particular; in other words he *falsifies* science for these interests. But his conclusions are *ruthless* as far as they concern the subjugated classes. He is not only *ruthless*; he *affects* ruthlessness; he takes a cynical pleasure in it and *exaggerates* his conclusions in so far as they are directed against the poor wretches, even *beyond* the point which would be scientifically justified from his point of view.*

The hatred of the English working classes for Malthus—the "*mountebank-parson*" as Cobbett *rudely* called him (Cobbett, though England's greatest *political* writer of this century, lacked the Leipzig professorial scholarship[45] and was a pronounced enemy of the "learned language")—was thus fully justified and the people's instinct was correct here, in that they felt he was no *man of science*, but a bought advocate of their opponents, a shameless sycophant of the ruling classes.

The inventor of an idea may exaggerate it in all honesty; when the plagiarist exaggerates it, he always makes "a business" of such an exaggeration.

Because the first edition of Malthus's work *On Population* contains not a single *new* scientific *word*, it is to be regarded purely as an obtrusive Capuchin's sermon, an Abraham a Santa Clara[46] version of the discoveries of Townsend, Steuart, Wallace, Herbert etc. Since in fact it only wants to impress by its *popular* form, *popular* hate rightly turns against it.

As compared to the wretched bourgeois economists who preach harmony, Malthus's only merit lies in his pointed emphasis on

---

* ||499| For instance, when Ricardo's theory (see above) convinces him that a rise in wages above their minimum does not raise the *value* of the commodities, he says so in a straightforward manner. Malthus wants to hold down wages so that the bourgeois may profit. |499||

the disharmonies, which, though none of them were *discovered* by him were all emphasised, amplified and publicised by him with complacent sacerdotal cynicism.

* * *

||499| *Charles Darwin*, in the introduction to his *On the Origin of Species by Means of Natural Selection, or the Preservation of Favoured Races in the Struggle for Life* (5th thousand), London, 1860, says the following:

"In the next chapter the *Struggle for Existence* amongst all organic beings throughout the world, which inevitably follows from the high geometrical ratio of their increase, will be treated of. This is the doctrine of *Malthus*, applied to the whole animal and vegetable kingdoms" (pp. 4-5).

In his splendid work, *Darwin* did not realise that by discovering the "geometrical" progression in the animal and plant kingdom, he *overthrew* Malthus's theory. Malthus's theory is based on the fact that he set Wallace's geometrical progression of man against the chimerical "*arithmetical*" progression of animals and plants. In Darwin's work, for instance on the extinction of species, we also find (quite apart from his fundamental principle) the detailed refutation, based on natural history, of the Malthusian theory. But in so far as Malthus's theory rests upon Anderson's theory of rent, it was refuted by *Anderson himself*.[47] |499||

[3. Roscher's Falsification of the History of Views on Ground-Rent. Examples of Ricardo's Scientific Impartiality. Rent from Capital Investment in Land and Rent from the Exploitation of Other Elements of Nature. The Twofold Influence of Competition]

||499| Anderson's first publication, in which he develops the theory of rent as a by-product, was a *practical* polemic, not on rent but on protection. It appeared in 1777 and its very title, *An Enquiry into the Nature of the Corn Laws, with a View to the New Corn Bill Proposed for Scotland,* Edinburgh, 1777, shows firstly, that it pursues a practical purpose, secondly, that it is related to an imminent act of legislation, in which the interests of the manufacturers and the landlords are diametrically opposed.

The law of 1773 (in England; to be looked up in McCulloch's *Catalogue*[48]), was due (so it appears) to be introduced into Scotland in 1777 (see in the Museum).

"The law of 1773 was constructed," says Anderson, with the "*avowed* intention of lowering the price of corn to our manufacturers, by encouraging the importation of corn from abroad[a] for the purpose of feeding[b] our own people at a cheaper rate." (James Anderson, *A Calm Investigation of the Circumstances that have led to the Present Scarcity of Grain in Britain*, London, 1801, p. 50.)

Thus Anderson's publication was a polemic on behalf of the interests of the agriculturists (protection) (inclusive of the landlords) against the interests of the manufacturers. And he published it "avowedly" as such a partisan piece of writing. The theory of rent comes in here only incidentally. In his later writings which are to a greater or lesser degree continuously concerned with this *battle of interests* he merely repeats the theory of rent once or twice in passing. He never pretends to a scientific interest in it and it does not even become an *independent* subject in his presentation. Accordingly one may judge the correctness of the following remarks of *Wilhelm Thukydides Roscher*[49] who was evidently *not* acquainted with Anderson's writings:

"Remarkable, how a doctrine, which in 1777 remained *almost* unnoticed, was immediately defended and attacked with the greatest interest in 1815 and the following years because it touched upon the contradiction between monied and landed interest which had meanwhile so sharply developed." (*Die Grundlagen der Nationalökonomie*, 3rd edition, 1858, pp. 297-98.)

This sentence contains as many falsehoods as words. *Firstly*, unlike West, Malthus and Ricardo, Anderson did not put forward his opinion as a *"doctrine"*. *Secondly*, it remained not *"almost"*, but *"entirely"* unnoticed. *Thirdly*, it first came in incidentally in a work whose s o l e purpose it was to deal with the contradiction between manufacturers and landlords—a contradiction which was considerably developed in 1777 and the work only "touched upon" this practical battle of interests and left "untouched" the general ||500| theory of political economy. *Fourthly*, in 1815 one of the reproducers of this theory, Malthus, expounded it just as much in support of the corn laws as Anderson had done. *The same* doctrine was used *in support* of landed

---

a In the manuscript: "encouragement of foreign importation", instead of "encouraging the importation of corn from abroad".—*Ed.*

b In the manuscript: "to place" instead of "for the purpose of feeding".—*Ed.*

property by its discoverer and [by] Malthus, but was turned *against* landed property by Ricardo. Thus, at most, one might say that some of those who put it forward were *defending* the interests of landed property while others who put it forward *fought those same* interests, but one could not say that this theory was attacked by the defenders of landed property in 1815 (for Malthus defended it *before Ricardo*), or that it was *defended* by the attackers of landed property (for Ricardo did not have to "defend" this theory against Malthus, since he himself regarded Malthus as one of its discoverers and as his own forerunner. He only had to "combat" the practical conclusions that were drawn by Malthus). *Fifthly*, the contradiction between "*monied*" and "*landed interest*", "touched upon" by Wilhelm Thukydides Roscher had, up to that moment, *absolutely nothing* to do either with Anderson's theory of rent or with its reproduction, defence and attack. As Wilhelm Thukydides could have gathered from John Stuart Mill (*Essays on Some Unsettled Questions of Political Economy*, London, 1844, pp. 109-10), by "monied class" the Englishman understands 1. the money-lenders; and 2. these money-lenders are people who either live altogether on interest or are *money-lenders by profession*, such as bankers, bill-brokers etc. Mill also observes that all these people who form the "monied class" are opposed to, or at any rate are distinct from, the "*producing class*" (by which Mill understands "industrial capitalists" besides the working men). Hence Wilhelm Thukydides should see that the interests of the "producing class", including the manufacturers, the industrial capitalists, and the interests of the monied class are two very different matters and that these classes are different classes. Furthermore, Wilhelm Thukydides should see that a battle between the industrial capitalists and the landlords was thus by no means a battle between the "*monied* interest" and the "*landed* interest". If Wilhelm Thukydides knew the history of the corn laws of 1815 and the struggle over these, then he would already have known from Cobbett that the borough-mongers (landed interest) and the loan-mongers (monied interest) combined against the industrial interest. But Cobbett is "crude". Furthermore, Wilhelm Thukydides should know from the history of 1815 to 1847 that in the battle over the corn laws, the majority of the monied interest and some even of the commercial interest (Liverpool for instance) were to be found amongst the *allies* of the landed interest against the manufacturing interest. |500||

||502| (At most Herr Roscher might have been surprised that
the same "doctrine" served *in favour* of "landed interest" in 1777
and *against* it in 1815 and that it caused a stir only *then*.[50] |502||

||500| If I were to elucidate in equal detail all similar gross fal-
sifications of history which Wilhelm Thukydides commits in his
literary historical notes, then I would have to write as fat a volume as his *Grundlagen*, and indeed, such a work would "not be
worth the paper it was written upon". But the harmful effects
which such learned ignorance as that of a Wilhelm Thukydides
can have on researchers in other fields of knowledge, can be seen
in the example of Herr *Adolf Bastian*. In his work *Der Mensch in
der Geschichte*, 1860, Vol. I, p. 374, Note, he quotes the above
sentence of Wilhelm Thukydides as documentary proof for a
"psychological" assertion. Incidentally, one cannot say of Bastian
that "*materiam superabat opus*".[a] Rather, in this case, the "opus"
does not master its own raw material. Besides, I have found out
through the few sciences which I "know", that Herr *Bastian* who
knows "*all*" sciences, very often relies on such authorities as Wilhelm Thukydides, which is in any case unavoidable in a "pan-
tologist".

||501| I hope I shall not be accused of "unkindness" towards
Wilhelm Thukydides. Note the "unkindness" with which this
pedant himself treats science! Anyhow, I have the same right to
speak of his "total untruths" as he has to speak in his self-satis-
fied and condescending manner of Ricardo's "half-truths".[51]
Furthermore, Wilhelm Thukydides is by no means "honest" in
his research and cataloguing. Anyone who is not "respectable"
does not exist for him historically either. For instance, Rodbertus
does not exist for him as a theoretician of rent because he is a
"communist". Besides, Wilhelm Thukydides is also inaccurate
when it comes to "respectable writers". For instance, Bailey
exists for McCulloch, who even regards his work as epoch-mak-
ing. For Wilhelm Thukydides he does not exist. If the *science*
||502| of political economy is to be furthered and popularised in
Germany, people like Rodbertus should found a journal which
would be open to all scholars (not pedants, prigs and vulgar-
isers) and whose main purpose it would be to demonstrate the
ignorance of the specialists in the science itself as well as in its
history. |502||

---

[a] "The work surpasses the material." (Ovid).

* * *

||501| Anderson was in no way concerned with any inquiry into the relationship of his theory of rent to the system of political economy. This is not in the least surprising, since his first book appeared one year after Adam Smith's *Wealth of Nations,* i.e., at a moment when the "system of political economy" was only first being consolidated, for Steuart's system too had only appeared a few years before. But so far as the material is concerned, which Anderson *examined, within the confines of the specific subject he was considering, this was decidedly more extensive than Ricardo's.* Just as in his theory of money, the reproduction of Hume's theory, Ricardo specifically only took into account the events from 1797 to 1809, so in the theory of rent, the reproduction of Anderson's theory, he considered only the economic phenomena relating to the rise in corn prices between 1800 and 1815.

* * *

The following paragraphs are very important because they clearly reflect Ricardo's character:

"I shall [...] greatly regret that *considerations for any particular class,* are allowed to check the progress of the wealth and population of the country." (David Ricardo, *An Essay on the Influence of a Low Price of Corn on the Profits of Stock,* second edition, London, 1815, p. 49.)

With free import of corn, *"land is abandoned"* (l.c., p. 46). In other words landed property is sacrificed to the development of production.

In connection with the free import of corn [he writes] however:

"That *some capital would be lost* cannot be disputed, but *is the possession or preservation of capital* the end, or the means? The means, undoubtedly. What we want is an *abundance of commodities"* (wealth in general) "and if it could be proved that by *the sacrifice of a part of our capital we should augment the annual produce* of those objects which contribute to our enjoyment and happiness we ought not [...] to repine *at the loss of a part of our capital."* (David Ricardo, *On Protection to Agriculture,* 4th ed., London, 1822, p. 60.)

Ricardo terms as *"our capital"* that capital which belongs neither to *us* nor to *him,* but which has been permanently invested in the land *by the capitalists.* But *we* signifies a cross-section of the nation. The increase in *"our"* wealth is the increase in *social* wealth, which is an end as such, irrespective of who are the participants in this wealth!

"To an individual with a capital of £20,000, whose profits were £2,000 per annum, it would be a matter quite indifferent whether his capital would employ a hundred or a thousand men, whether the commodity produced, sold for £10,000, or for £20,000, provided, in all cases, his profits were not diminished below £2,000. Is not the real interest of the nation similar? Provided its net real income, its rent and profits be the same, it is of no importance whether the nation consists of ten or of twelve millions of inhabitants." (David Ricardo, *On the Principles of Political Economy, and Taxation*, third edition, London, 1821, p. 416.)

Here the "proletariat" is sacrificed to wealth. In so far as it is irrelevant to the existence of wealth, its existence is a matter of indifference to wealth. Here mass—mass of human beings— is worth nothing. These three instances exemplify ||502| Ricardo's scientific impartiality.

* * *

{The element *in which* the capital employed in agriculture is invested, is *the soil (nature)* etc. Hence rent is here equal to the excess of the *value* of the product of labour created in this element, *over* its average price. If, on the other hand, an element of nature (or material) which is privately owned by an individual, is employed *in* another sphere of production whose (physical) basis it does not form, then the rent, if it only comes into being through the employment of this element, cannot consist in the excess of the *value* of this product over the average price, but only in the excess of the *general* average price of this product over its *own average price*. For instance, a waterfall may replace the steam-engine for a manufacturer and save him consumption of coal. While in possession of this waterfall, he would, for instance, constantly be selling yarn above its *average price* and making an excess profit. If the waterfall belongs to a landowner, this excess profit accrues to him as rent. In his book on rent, Mr. Hopkins observes that in Lancashire the waterfalls not only yield rent but, according to the degree of the natural motive power, they yield *differential rent*.[52] Here rent is purely the excess of the *average market-price* of the product over its *individual average price*.} |502||

* * *

||502| {In *competition* there are two distinct movements towards equalisation. Capitals *within* the same sphere of production equalise the prices of the commodities produced *within* this sphere to the same *market-price*, irrespective of the relationship

of the value of these commodities to this price. The *average market-price* should *equal* the *value* of the commodity, [were] it not for the equalisation between *different* spheres of production. As between these different spheres, competition equalises the values to the *average prices*, in so far as the reciprocal interaction of the capitals is not hampered, disrupted by a third element—landownership, etc.}

[4. Rodbertus's Error Regarding the Relation Between Value and Surplus-Value When the Costs of Production Rise]

Rodbertus is altogether mistaken when he thinks that because one commodity is *dearer* than another, thus realising more labour-time, it must therefore—given the same *rate of surplus-value or the equal exploitation of the workers* in *the different spheres*—also contain more *unpaid labour-time, surplus labour-time*. If *the same* labour yields 1 quarter on unfertile land and 3 on fertile (in a good or a bad year alike); if the same labour yields 1 oz of gold in land very rich in gold whereas in less rich or exhausted land it yields only $1/3$ oz; if the same labour-time which produces 1 lb. of wool spins 3 lb. of wool, then, to begin with, the values of the 1 quarter and the 3 quarters, of the 1 oz of gold and the $1/3$ oz, of the 1 lb. of wool and the 3 lbs. of woollen yarn (minus the value of the wool it contains) are of equal magnitude. They contain equal quantities of labour-time, therefore, according to the assumption, *equal quantities* of surplus labour-time. True, the quantity of surplus-labour embodied in the 1 quarter [grown on unfertile land] is greater, but then it is only 1 quarter whereas in the other case it is 3 quarters, or 1 lb. of wool whereas in the other case it is 3 lbs. of woollen yarn (minus the value of the material). The *volume* [of surplus-labour] is therefore the same, and the *proportional quantity of surplus-value*, comparing the individual commodities one with another, [is] also equal. According to the assumption, the amount of labour contained in the 1 quarter or the 1 lb. of wool, is the same as that contained in the 3 quarters or the 3 lbs. of yarn. The capital laid out in wages is therefore greater to exactly the same degree as the surplus-value. The 1 lb. of wool contains three times as much labour as the 1 lb. of yarn. Though the surplus-value is three times as great, the capital laid out in wages on which it is based is also three times as great. The proportion thus remains *the same*.

Rodbertus calculates quite wrongly here, or wrongly compares the capital laid out in *wages* with the ||503| greater or lesser *quantity* of commodities which these wages represent. But this calculation is completely wrong, if, as he *presupposes, wages* or the *rate of surplus-value* are *given*. The same *quantity of labour*, say, 12 hours, may result in x or $3x$ commodities. In one case, $1x$ commodities contain as much labour and surplus-labour as $3x$ in the other; but in *no* case would more than 1 working-day be spent and in no case would the rate of surplus-value be more than, say, $\frac{1}{5}$. In the first instance $\frac{1}{5}$ of the one x would be to x as in the second $\frac{1}{5}$ of the $3x$ would be to $3x$. And if we were to call each of the three x: x', x'', x''', then there would be $\frac{4}{5}$ paid and $\frac{1}{5}$ unpaid labour in each x', x'', x'''. It is quite right, on the other hand, that if *just as much commodity* were to be produced under the unproductive conditions as under *more productive*, the commodity would contain more labour and so also more surplus-labour. But then, proportionately, a greater capital would also have to be laid out. In order to produce $3x$, three times as much capital would have to be laid out (in wages) as is required to produce $1x$.

Now it is true that manufacture cannot work up more raw material than agriculture supplies. Thus, for instance, it cannot spin more pounds of wool than have been produced. If the productivity in wool spinning is trebled, then, provided the conditions of the production of wool remained *the same*, three times as much time as previously would have to be spent, three times as much capital would have to be expended on labour in wool production, whereas only *the same* amount of the spinners' labour-time would be required to spin up this trebled quantity of wool. But the *rate* [of surplus-value] would remain the same. The same spinning labour would have the same value as before and contain the same surplus-value. The wool-producing labour would have a trebled surplus-value but the labour embodied in it, or the capital advanced in wages, would accordingly have *trebled* as well. The three times greater surplus-value would thus be calculated on a three times greater capital. But *this is no reason* for saying that the rate of surplus-value is lower in spinning than in wool production. One would only say that the capital laid out in wages is three times as great in one as in the other (since it is assumed here that the changes in the spinning and in the production of wool are not due to any change in their constant capital).

It is necessary to make a distinction here. The same labour plus constant capital gives a smaller *output* in an unfavourable than a favourable season, in unproductive than in productive soil, in a poorer than in a richer mine. In the former case the *product* is thus dearer, contains *more* labour and more *surplus-labour* in *the same* number of products. But in the latter case, the *number* of these products is the greater. Furthermore, the *ratio* between paid and unpaid labour in each individual product in the two categories is not affected by this, for though the individual product contains less unpaid labour, according to the assumption, it also contains less paid labour in the same proportion. For it has been assumed here that there is no change in the proportions of the organic component parts of capital—of variable and constant capital. It is assumed that *the same amount of variable and constant capital* supplies *varying, greater or smaller, quantities of product* under varying conditions.

Herr Rodbertus appears to confuse this all the time, and as a matter of course to conclude from the mere increase in the price of the product that it contains a *greater surplus-value*. As to the *rate*, this is wrong even according to the assumption. As to the total, however, it is only right if more capital is advanced in one case than in the other, that means if as much is produced now of the dearer product as previously of the cheaper or if the increased quantity of the cheaper product (ʔs above with spinning) presupposes a correspondingly increased quantity of the dearer product.

[5. Ricardo's Denial of Absolute Rent—a Result of His Error in the Theory of Value]

||504| That rent, hence also the value of land, can rise, although the *rate of rent* remains the same or even decreases, that therefore the productivity of agriculture also increases—this Ricardo sometimes forgets, though he knows it. Anyhow, Anderson knows it and Petty and D'Avenant already knew it. That is not the question.

Ricardo abstracts from the *question of absolute rent* which he *denies on theoretical grounds* because he starts out from the *false* assumption that if the value of commodities is determined by labour-time, the *average prices of commodities must equal their values* (which is why he comes to the wrong practical conclusion, that competition from more fertile types of land must throw the

less fertile out of cultivation, even if they bore rent previously).
If *values* of commodities and *average prices* of commodities were
identical then absolute rent—i.e., rent on the worst cultivated
land or on that *originally* cultivated—would be equally impossible. What is the *average price* of the commodity? The total
capital (constant plus variable) laid out in its production plus the
labour-time contained in the average profit, say 10 per cent.
Supposing, that a capital produced a *higher value* than the *average price*, just because it was operating in a *particular* element,
an element of nature, say land, then the value of this commodity
would be *above* its value and this *excess value* would contradict
the conception of value being equal to a certain quantity of
labour-time. An element of nature, something heterogeneous
from social labour-time would be *creating* value. But this cannot
be. Hence capital invested in land pure and simple *cannot* bear
a *rent*. The worst land is land *pure and simple*. If the *better* land
bears a rent, then this only shows that the difference between the
individually necessary labour and that which is *socially necessary* becomes permanently established in agriculture because it has
a natural basis, whereas in industry it is constantly disappearing.

   Absolute rent cannot be permitted to exist, but only *differential
rent*. To admit the existence of absolute rent would be to admit
that *the same quantity of labour* (materialised, laid out in constant capital and bought with wages) creates *varying values* according to the element in which [the labour is expended] or according to the material which it works up. But if one admits this
diversity in value although in each sphere of production *the
same* amount of labour-time materialises itself in the product,
then one admits that *value is not determined by labour-time* but
by something heterogeneous. These different *magnitudes of value*
would invalidate the concept of value, they would invalidate the
proposition that the substance of value is social labour-time,
hence its differences can only be quantitative and these quantitative differences can only be equal to the differences in the
amounts of social labour-time applied.

   The maintenance of *value*—the determination not only of the
amount of value by the varying amount of labour-time, but also
of the substance of value by social labour—thus requires the
denial of absolute rent. The denial of absolute rent can, however,
be expressed in two ways.

   Firstly. The *worst* land cannot bear a rent. The rent from the
better types of land can be explained as arising from the market-

price which is the same for products which have been produced on more favourable types of land as for those which have been produced on less favourable. But the worst land *is land pure and simple*. It is not differentiated in itself. It differs from industrial capital investment only in that it is a *special* sphere of capital investment. If it bore a rent then this would arise from the fact that the *same quantity of labour* would produce *different values*, if applied in *different spheres of production;* this means that the quantity of labour in itself does not determine the value, and products which contain the same amount of labour are not equal [in terms of value].

||505| [*Secondly*.] Or one might say that the *land which was cultivated originally* must not bear rent. For what is the originally cultivated land? The land which is "originally" cultivated is neither better nor worse land; it is land pure and simple. Undifferentiated land. Originally, capital investment in agriculture can only differ from investment in industry because of the *spheres* in which these capitals are invested. But since equal quantities of labour are represented in *equal values*, there is absolutely no reason why the capital invested in land should yield a rent in addition to profit, unless *the same* quantity of labour applied in this *sphere* produced *a higher* value, so that the excess of this value over the value yielded in manufacture would produce an excess profit, equal to rent. But this would amount to saying that the land as such creates value, thus invalidating the concept of value itself.

The land which is cultivated *originally* therefore cannot *originally* bear a rent, if the whole theory of value is not to be discarded. Furthermore, this ties up very easily (*although not necessarily*, as Anderson shows) with the idea that *originally* people of course chose not the worst but rather the best land for cultivation. With the advance of civilisation and population, the land which originally bears no rent, does so at a later stage, because people are forced to descend to worse types of land and thus in this descent to Avernus, to ever worse land, rent must arise on the *originally cultivated, most fertile land*. And then, step by step, on the land which follows it, while the *worst land* which always represents simply land—the *particular* sphere of capital investment—*never* bears a rent. All this has a more or less logical coherence.

If, on the other hand, one knows that average prices and values are not identical, that the average price of a commodity may be either equal to its value or bigger or smaller, then the question, the problem itself, disappears and with it also the *hypotheses* for its solution. The only remaining question is why, in agriculture, the *value* of the *commodity,* or at any rate its *price*, is *above its average price* though not *above* its *value*. But this question no longer bears any relation to the fundamentals of the theory, the determination of value as such.

Ricardo knows of course that the *"relative* values" of commodities are modified according to the varying proportion of fixed capital and capital laid out in wages, which enter into their production. ⟨But these are not opposites; fixed capital and circulating capital are opposites, and circulating capital comprises not only wages but also raw materials and auxiliary materials. For example, the same ratio may exist between capital laid out in wages and fixed capital in the mining and fishing industries, as between that laid out in wages and in raw materials in tailoring.⟩ But Ricardo also knows that these relative values are equalised by competition. In fact he only makes the differentiation, so that *the same average profit* should result from these different capital investments. In other words these *relative* values of which he speaks are only the *average prices*. It does not even occur to him that *value* and *average price* are different. He only gets as far as their *identity*. Since however this identity *does not exist* when the ratio of the organic component parts of capital varies, he accepts it as an unexplained fact brought about by competition. Hence too, he does not come up against the question: Why do the values of agricultural products not equalise in average prices ||506|? On the contrary he assumes that *they do so* and poses the problem from that point of view.

It is quite incomprehensible why fellows à la Wilhelm Thukydides should be so ardently for Ricardo's theory of rent. From *their* point of view, Ricardo's "half truths", as Thukydides condescendingly calls them, lose their *whole* value.

For Ricardo the problem only exists because value is determined by labour-time. With those fellows this is not the case. According to Roscher, nature *as such* has value. See later.[53] In other words, he has absolutely no idea what value is. What prevents him therefore from allowing the *value of land* to enter into production costs from the outset and to form the rent; what prevents him from presupposing the value of land, i.e., rent, as an explanation for rent?

With these fellows, the phrase "production costs" is meaningless. We see this with Say. The value of the commodity is determined by the costs of production, capital, land, labour. But these are determined by demand and supply. In other words, no determination is taking place. Since the land performs "productive services", why should not the price of these "services" be determined by demand and supply, just as the services performed by labour or capital? And since the "land services" are in the possession of certain sellers, why should their article not have a market-price, in other words why should not rent exist as an element of price?

One can see how little reason Wilhelm Thukydides had for getting so well-meaningly "vexed" over the Ricardian theory.

[6. Ricardo's Thesis on the Constant Rise in Corn Prices. Table of Annual Average Prices of Corn from 1641 to 1859]

But apart from absolute rent, the following question remains for Ricardo:

The population grows and with it the demand for agricultural products. Therewith their price rises, as happens in similar cases in industry. But in industry, this rise in price ceases as soon as demand has become effective and brought about an increased supply of commodities. The product now falls to the old, or rather below the old, level of value. But in agriculture this *additional product* is thrown on to the market neither at the same price nor at a lower price. *It costs more* and effects a constant rise in market-prices and along with that, a raising of rent. How is this to be explained if not by the fact that ever less fertile types of land are being used, that ever more labour is required in order to produce the same product, that agriculture becomes progressively more sterile? Why, apart from the influence of the depreciation [of money], did agricultural products rise in England from 1797 to 1815 with the rapid development of the population? That they fell again later proves nothing. That supplies from foreign markets were cut off proves nothing. On the contrary. This in fact created the *right* conditions for demonstrating the effect of the law of rent as such. For it was the very cutting off of foreign supplies which forced the country to have recourse *to ever less fertile land*. This cannot be explained by an *absolute increase* in rent, because not only did the rental rise but also the rate of rent. The quarter of wheat, etc. rose in price.

It cannot be explained by *depreciation* because although this might well explain why, with greater productivity in industry, industrial products fell, hence why the relative price of agricultural products rose, it would not explain why *in addition to* this *relative rise*, the prices of agricultural products were continuously rising absolutely. Similarly, it cannot be explained as a *consequence* of the fall in the rate of profit. This would *never* explain a change in *prices*, but only a *change* in the distribution of value or of *price* between landlord, manufacturer and worker.

So far as *depreciation* is concerned, assume that £1 now equals £2. A quarter of wheat which was previously equal to £2 is now equal to £4. If the industrial product fell to $^1/_{10}$, and previously its value was 20s., then it would be now 2s. But these 2s. are now equal to 4s. True, depreciation could have something to do with this, the poor harvests as well.

||507| But quite apart from all this it can be assumed that, considering the *state of agriculture at that time, unfertile* land (for wheat) was being cultivated. The same land was later fertile, in that the rate of differential rents decreased, as is proved by the best barometer, namely, wheat prices.

The highest prices [occur in the years] 1800 and 1801 and 1811 and 1812; the first were years of poor growth, the second, [years] of the peak of depreciation. Similarly 1817 and 1818 were years of depreciation. But if these years are omitted, probably (to be checked up later) what was left would give the average price.

In comparing wheat prices etc. in different periods, it is at the same time important to compare the *amounts produced* at so much per quarter, because this shows to what extent the additional production of corn influences the price.

I
Average Wheat Prices

	Yearly average price	Highest price	Lowest price
1641-1649	60 s. $5^2/_3$ d.	[75 s. 6 d. (1645)]	[42 s. 8 d. (1646)]
1650-1659	45 s. $8^9/_{10}$ d.	68 s. 1 d. (1650)	23 s. 1 d. (1651)
1660-1669	44 s. 9 d.	65 s. 9 d. (1662)	32 s. 0d. (1666 & 1667)
1670-1679	44 s. $8^9/_{10}$ d.	61 s. 0d. (1674)	33 s. 0d. (1676)
1680-1689	35 s. $7^8/_{10}$ d.	41 s. 5 d. (1681)	22 s. 4 d. (1687)
1690-1699	50 s. $^4/_{10}$ d.	63 s. 1 d. (1695)	30 s. 2 d. (1691)

If we take the period *1650 to 1699* then the (yearly) average price for these 50 years is *44s. 2¹/₅ d.*

During the period (9 years) from 1641 to 1649, the highest yearly average price is 75s. 6d. for 1645, year of the revolution, then 71s. 1d. for 1649, 65s. 5d. for 1647 and the lowest price, 42s. 8d. for 1646.

II

	Yearly average price	The highest	and lowest
		prices in each decennial period	
1700-1709	35 s. ¹/₁₀ d.	69 s. 9 d. (1709)	25 s. 4 d. (1707)
1710-1719	43 s. 6⁷/₁₀ d.	69 s. 4 d. (1710)	31 s. 1 d. (1719)
1720-1729	37 s. 3⁷/₁₀ d.	48 s. 5 d. (1728)	30 s. 10 d. (1723)
1730-1739	31 s. 5⁵/₁₀ d.	58 s. 2 d. (1735)	23 s. 8 d. (1732)
1740-1749	31 s. 7⁹/₁₀ d.	45 s. 1 d. (1740)	22 s. 1 d. (1743& 1744)

Average price (yearly) for the 50 years [from] *1700 to 1749: 35s. 9²⁹/₅₀ d.*

‖508‖

III

	Yearly average price	The highest	and lowest
		prices in each decennial period	
1750-1759	36 s. 4⁵/₁₀ d.	53 s. 4 d. (1757)	28 s. 10 d. (1750)
1760-1769	40 s. 4⁹/₁₀ d.	53 s. 9 d. (1768)	26 s. 9 d. (1761)
1770-1779	45 s. 3²/₁₀ d.	52 s. 8 d. (1774)	33 s. 8 d. (1779)
1780-1789	46 s. 9²/₁₀ d.	52 s. 8 d. (1783)	35 s. 8 d. (1780)
1790-1799	57 s. 6⁵/₁₀ d.	78 s. 7 d. (1796)	43 s. 0d. (1792)

Yearly average for the 50 years [from] 1750 to 1799: 45s. 3¹³/₅₀ d.

IV

	Yearly average price	The highest	and lowest
		yearly average prices in each decennial period	
1800-1809	84 s. 8⁵/₁₀ d.	119 s. 6 d. (1801) 113 s. 10 d. (1800)	58 s. 10 d. (1803)
1810-1819	91 s. 4⁸/₁₀ d.	126 s. 6 d. (1812) 109 s. 9 d. (1813) 106 s. 5 d. (1810)	65 s. 7 d. (1815) 74 s. 4 d. (1814) 74 s. 6 d. (1819)
1820-1829	58 s. 9⁷/₁₀ d.	68 s. 6 d. (1825)	44 s. 7 d. (1822)
1830-1839	56 s. 8⁵/₁₀ d.	66 s. 4 d. (1831)	39 s. 4 d. (1835)
1840-1849	55 s. 11⁴/₁₀ d.	69 s. 5 d. (1847)	44 s. 6 d. (1849)
1850-1859	53 s. 4⁷/₁₀ d.	74 s. 9 d. (1855)	40 s. 4 d. (1850)

Yearly average for the 50 years [from] 1800 to 1849: 69s. 6⁹/₅₀ d.
Yearly average for the 60 years [from] 1800 to 1859: 66s. 9¹⁴/₁₅ d.

Hence yearly averages:

1641-1649	60 s.	$5^2/_3$ d.
1650-1699	44 s.	$2^1/_5$ d.
1700-1749	35 s.	$9^{29}/_{50}$ d.
1750-1799	45 s.	$3^{13}/_{50}$ d.
1800-1849	69 s.	$6^9/_{50}$ d.
1850-1859	53 s.	$4^7/_{10}$ d.

* * *

West says himself:

"...in an improved state of agriculture produce may be raised on the second or third quality of land at the little cost as it could under the old system upon the first quality." (Sir Edward West, *Price of Corn and Wages of Labour*, London, 1826, p. 98.)

[7. Hopkins's Conjecture about the Difference Between Absolute Rent and Differential Rent; Explanation of Rent by the Private Ownership of Land]

Hopkins grasps correctly the difference between *absolute* and *differential rent*:

"The principle of competition, which renders it impossible, that there should be two rates of profit in the same country [...], does [...] determine [...] their[a] [...] *relative rents...*" but not the *general average of rent*.[b] (Thomas Hopkins, *On Rent of Land, and Its Influence on Subsistence and Population...*, London, 1828, p. 30.)

||508a| *Hopkins* makes the following distinction between productive and unproductive labour or, as he says, between primary and secondary:

"If *all* labourers were employed for the same end, or object, as the diamond cutter and the opera singer, in a short time there would be no *wealth* to subsist them because *none of the wealth produced would then become capital*. If a considerable proportion were so employed, wages would be low; because, but a comparatively small part of what was produced would be used as capital;—but if only a few of the labourers were so employed, and, of course, nearly all were ploughmen, shoemakers, weavers, etc. [...], then much capital would be produced and wages *would*[c] be proportionally high" (l.c., pp. 84-85). "With the diamond cutter and the singer, must be classed all those who labour for the landlords, or annuitants, and who receive a part of their income as wages: all, in fact, whose labours *terminate* merely in

---

a In the manuscript: "the".—*Ed.*

b "but not the general average of rent" is a summary by Marx of the contents of the subsequent passages.—*Ed.*

c In the manuscript: "could".—*Ed.*

producing those things which gratify landlords and annuitants, and who receive in return for their labours, a part of the rent of the landlord, or of the income of the annuitant. These are all productive labourers, but all their labours are for the purpose of converting wealth which exists, in the shape of rents and annuities, into some other form, that shall, in that other form, more gratify the landlord and annuitant, and therefore they are *secondary* producers. All other labourers are *primary* producers" (l.c., p. 85.)

Diamonds and song are both congealed labour and can—like all commodities—be converted into *money* and *as money* into capital. But in this transformation of money into capital we must distinguish two things. All commodities can be converted into money and as money into capital, because in the form of *money* their use-value and their particular natural form become extinct. They are materialised labour in that social form in which it is exchangeable for any real labour, therefore convertible into any form of real labour. On the other hand, whether the commodities which are the product of labour can as such become elements of productive capital once again, depends on whether the nature of their use-values permits them to re-enter the process of production—be it as objective conditions of labour (tools and material) or as subjective conditions (means of subsistence of the worker), (in other words [as] elements of constant or of variable capital).

In Ireland, according to a moderate estimate and the census of 1821, the whole net produce which goes to the landlords, the government and the tythe-owners, amounts to £20³/₄ million, the whole wages, however, only to £14,114,000.[a]

"The cultivators" in Italy "generally paying from one-half to more than one-half of the produce as rent to the landlord, with moderate skill in agriculture, and a scanty supply of fixed capital. The greater part of the population is [...] composed of secondary producers and proprietors,[b] and generally the primary producers are a poor and degraded class" (l.c., pp. 101-02).

The same was the case in France under Louis XIV [XV and XVI]. According to Young, rent, tythes and taxes amounted to £140,905,304. Cultivation moreover was very poor. "The population of France, at this time, is stated to have been 26,363,074. Now" if there had been "six millions of labouring families (which is too high a figure), each family would have had to furnish annually, either directly or indirectly, an average of upwards of £23 of net wealth to the landlords, the church and the government."[c] According to Young, and taking into account various other factors, the labouring family "produced annually £42 10s.; £23 of which were paid away to others, and £19 10s. remained to subsist itself" (l.c., pp. 102-04).

---

[a] In this paragraph Marx reproduces in his own words the contents of a longer passage from Hopkins's book *On Rent of Land*, p. 94.—*Ed.*

[b] In the manuscript: "landlords".—*Ed.*

[c] This passage has been condensed by Marx.—*Ed.*

The Dependence of Population on Capital.

"The error of Mr. Malthus and his followers is to be found in the assumption, that a reduction of the labouring population would *not* be followed by a *correspondent reduction of capital!*" (l.c., p. 118.) "...Mr. Malthus" forgets "that this demand [for labourers is] limited by the *means of paying wages* and" that "these means do not arise spontaneously, but are always *previously created by labour*" (l.c., p. 122).

This conception of the *accumulation of capital* is correct. But the means can grow, i.e., the quantity of surplus produce or surplus-labour can grow, without a proportionate growth in the quantity of labour.

"It is somewhat extraordinary[a] that [there is] a strong inclination [...] to represent *net* wealth as *beneficial* to the labouring class, because it gives [...] *employment* though it is evidently ||509| not on account of being *net*, that it has that power, but because it is *wealth*,—that *which has been brought into existence by labour*: while, at the time,[b] an additional quantity of labour is represented as *injurious* to the labouring classes, though that labour produces three times as much as it consumes" (l.c., p. 126).

"If by the use of superior machines,[c] the whole primary produce could be raised from 200 to 250 or 300, while *net* wealth and profit took only 140, it is clear that there would remain as a fund for the wages of the primary producers 110 or 160 instead of 60" (l.c., p. 128).

"The condition of labourers is rendered *bad* either by crippling their productive power, or by taking from them what they have produced" (l.c., p. 129).

"No says Mr. Malthus, 'the *weight of your burthen* has nothing whatever to do with your distress; that arises solely there being *too many persons carrying it...*'" (l.c., p. 134).

"In the general principle, then, that *cost of production* regulates the exchangeable value of all commodities, *original materials* are not included; but the claim which the *owners* of these have upon produce, causes *rent* to enter into value..." (Thomas Hopkins, *Economical Enquiries Relative to the Laws Which Regulate Rent, Profit, Wages, and the Value of Money*, London, 1822, p. 11).

"*Rent*, or a charge for use, arises naturally out of *ownership*, or the establishment of a *r i g h t   o f   p r o p e r t y*" (l.c., p. 13).

"Any thing may yield a rent if possessed of the following qualities:—First,—It must exist in a degree of scarcity. Secondly,—It must have the power to aid labour in the great work of production" (l.c., p. 14). Of course one must not take the case "...where land... [is] so plentiful, *compared with the labour and stock to be employed upon it*", ⟨abundance and scarcity of land are of course *relative*, and are related to the disposable quantity of labour

---

a "It is somewhat extraordinary" is in the manuscript condensed to: "strange".—*Ed.*

b In the manuscript: "simultaneously" instead of "at the same time".—*Ed.*

c In the manuscript: "machinery".—*Ed.*

and capital) "that no charge for rent could be made, because it was not scarce" (l.c., p. 21).

"The landowner[a] [...] may obtain, in some countries 50 per cent [...], in others 10 per cent.[b] In some of the fertile regions of the East, man can subsist upon one-third of the produce of his labour employed upon the land; [...] but in parts of Switzerland and Norway, an exaction of 10 per cent might depopulate the country ... we see no *natural* bounds to the rent that may be exacted, but in the limited abilities of the payers..." (l.c., p. 31), and "where[c] inferior soils exist, *the competition of those inferior soils against the superior*" (l.c., pp. 33-34).

"There is much common land in England [...], the natural fertility of which is equal to what a large part *of the land now cultivated was, prior to its being taken into cultivation*; and yet *the expence of bringing such common lands into cultivation* is so great, *as to cause them not to yield the ordinary interest for the money expended in improving them,* leaving *nothing as rent for the natural fertility of the soil*: and this [...] with all the advantages of an immediate application of labour, aided by stock skilfully applied, and furnished with manufactures cheaply produced; added to the very important circumstance, of good roads being already formed in the neighbourhood[d]... the present land proprietors may be considered *the owners of all the accumulated labour which has for ages been expending,[e] in bringing the country to its present productive state*" (l.c., p. 35).

This is a very important circumstance in relation to rent, especially when the population suddenly grows significantly, as it did from 1780 to 1815, consequent upon the advance in industry, and hence a large portion of hitherto uncultivated land is *suddenly* brought into cultivation. The newly cultivated land may be as fertile as or even more fertile than old land was, *before centuries of cultivation* had accumulated in it. But what is demanded of the new land—if [this product] is *not* to be sold at a *dearer* price—is that its fertility must be equal *firstly* to the natural fertility of the cultivated ||510| land and *secondly* to the *artificial* fertility which has been engendered by cultivation, but which has now *become* its *natural fertility*. The newly cultivated land would thus have to be much more fertile than the old had been *before* its cultivation.

But it will be said:

---

[a] In the manuscript: "landlord".—*Ed.*

[b] Instead of "in others 10 per cent", in the manuscript: "in others not 10".—*Ed.*

[c] In the manuscript: "when".—*Ed.*

[d] Instead of "added to the very important circumstance, of good roads being already formed in the neighbourhood", in the manuscript: "in addition good roads in the neighbourhood, etc."—*Ed.*

[e] In the manuscript: "expendet".—*Ed.*

The fertility of the cultivated land originates in the first place from its natural fertility. Thus it depends on the natural condition of the newly cultivated land whether or not it possesses this fertility arising from and owing to nature. In either case it costs nothing. The other part of the fertility of cultivated land is an artificial product, owing to cultivation, the investment of capital. But this part of productivity involves costs of production which are repaid as interest on the fixed capital which has been sunk into the land. This part of rent is merely interest on the fixed capital tied up in the land. Hence it enters into the costs of production of the product of the previously cultivated land. Hence only the same capital needs to be thrown into the newly cultivated land for it to obtain this second part of fertility; and as with the first, the interest on the capital which has been employed to bring forth this fertility will enter into the price of the product. Why then should it not be possible to cultivate new land—unless it is more fertile—without the price of the product rising? If the natural fertility is the same, then the difference is brought about only by the capital invested and, in both cases alike, the interest on this capital enters into costs of production to the same extent.

However, this reasoning is wrong. A portion of the *costs* of bringing the land into cultivation etc. is no longer liable to be paid for, because, as *Ricardo* has already observed, the fertility thus created has partly coalesced with the *natural quality* of the soil (this applies to the costs of clearing, draining, levelling, the chemical change of the soil resulting from continued chemical processes etc.). Thus if [the product of] the newly cultivated land is to sell at the same price as [that of] the last cultivated land— the land must be sufficiently fertile for this *price* to cover that part of the costs of bringing it into cultivation which enters into its own costs of production but which has ceased to enter into the *costs* of the previously cultivated land, because it has coalesced with the natural fertility of the land.

"A *stream,* favourably situated, furnishes an instance of a rent being paid for an appropriated gift of nature, of as exclusive a kind as any that can be named. This is well understood in manufacturing districts, where considerable rents are paid for small streams of water, particularly if the fall is considerable. The power obtained from such streams being equal to that afforded by large steam-engines, it is as advantageous to use them, though subject to the payment of a heavy rent, as it is to expend large sums in the erection and working of steam-engines. Of streams, too, there are some larger, some smaller. Contiguity to the seat of manufacture is also an advantage which commands a higher rent. In the counties of York and Lancaster there is probably a much greater difference between the rents paid for the smallest and the largest streams of water, than there is between the rents paid for 50 of the least and 50 of the most fertile acres that are in common cultivation" (l.c., pp. 37-38).

[8. The Costs of Bringing Land into Cultivation. Periods of Rising and Periods of Falling Corn Prices (1641-1859)]

If we compare the average prices given earlier[a] and deduct firstly what is due to depreciation (1809-13) and secondly what is due to particularly bad seasons such as 1800 and 1801, then [we shall find] that a very important element is *the amount of new land* cultivated at a given moment or during a given period. A rise in price on the cultivated land here indicates a *growth in population* and hence an excess in price [as compared with costs]; on the other hand, the same increase in demand brings about the cultivation of fresh land. If *proportionately* the amount [of newly cultivated land] has greatly increased, then the rising price, and the *higher price,* in the early period merely shows that a large part of the *costs of bringing land into cultivation* enters into the additional quantity of food produced. If the price had not risen, this production [of additional food] would not have taken place. Its effect, a fall in price, can only come into evidence later, because the price of the recently created food comprises an element of the cost of production or price, that[b] has long become extinct in the older applications of capital to land, or in the older portions of cultivated soil. The difference would be even greater if, consequent upon the increased productivity of labour, the cost of appropriating soil to cultivation, had not greatly fallen, as compared to the costs of cultivation in former, bygone periods.

||511| The transformation of new land, whether more or equally or less fertile than old land, into such a state (and this state is given by the general rate of adaptation to culture prevailing on the existing land under cultivation) *as to make it* suitable for the application of capital and labour—under *the same conditions* under which capital and labour is employed on the average quantity of cultivated soil—this adaptation must be paid

---

[a] See this volume, pp. 134-36.—*Ed.*

[b] The following passages up to "...are cultivated" (p. 143) Marx wrote in English.—*Ed.*

for by the costs of converting waste land into cultivated land. This difference of cost must be borne by the newly cultivated land. If it does not enter into the price of its produce, there are only two cases possible, under which such a result can be realised. *Either* the produce of the newly cultivated land is not sold *at its real value*. Its price stands below its value, as is in fact the case with most of the land bearing no rent, because its price is not constituted by *its own value*, but by the value of the produce derived from more fertile soils. Or the newly cultivated land must be *so fertile*, that, if it was sold at its immanent, own value, according to the quantity of labour realised in it, it would be sold at a less price than the price of produce grown on the formerly cultivated soil.

If the difference between the *inherent value* [of its product] and the *market-price* settled by the value of the cultivated soil is such, that it *amounted for instance to* 5 per cent and if on the other hand the *interest*, entering into its costs of production on the part of the capital employed to bring it up to the level of productive ability common to the old soils, amounted also to 5 per cent, then the newly cultivated land would grow produce, which at the old market-price would be able to pay the usual wages, profits and rents. If the interest of the capital employed amounted to 4 per cent only while its degree of fertility exceeded 4 per cent, as compared to the older soils, the market-price, after the deduction of the 4 per cent interest for the capital employed to bring the new land into a "cultivable" state would leave a surplus, or it might be sold at a lower price than the *market-price settled by the value of the* least fruitful soil. Rents consequently would generally be lowered, together with the market-price of the produce.

Absolute rent is the excess of *value* over the *average price* of raw produce. *Differential rent* is the excess of the *market-price* of the produce grown on favoured soils over the *value* of their own produce.

If, therefore, the *price of raw produce* rises or remains constant in periods in which a relatively large part of the additional food, required by the increase of population, is produced on soil which from uncultivated state has been converted into a state of cultivation, this constancy or rise of prices does not prove that the fertility of the land has decreased, but only that it has not increased to such a degree as to counteract the fresh element of production—formed by the interest of capital applied with a view to bringing the uncultivated land to a level of the common conditions of production, under which the old soils—in a given state of development—are cultivated.

If the relative quantity of the newly cultivated soil is different in different periods, then even a *constant or rising price* does not prove that the new soil is unfertile or yields *less produce,* but only that an element of cost, which has become extinct in the old cultivated soils enters into the value of the products of the newly cultivated land. This new element of cost moreover remains, although under the new conditions of production, the costs of bringing new soil into cultivation have fallen considerably, compared with the costs of bringing the old soil from its *original, natural* state of fertility to its present state. It is therefore necessary to establish the *relative proportion* of enclosures during the different ||512| periods.[54]

The above list (pp. 507-08)[a] moreover shows:

That of the *decennial* periods examined,

the *period 1641-1649* reaches a *higher* level than any other decennial period up to 1860, with the exception of the decennial periods 1800-1809 and 1810-1819.

So far as the *fifty-year periods* are concerned, that of *1650-1699* is at a higher level than that of *1700-1749* and that of *1750-1799* higher than that of 1700-1749 and lower than that of 1800-1849 (or 1859).

Prices constantly fall in the period from 1810 to 1859, whereas in the period from 1750 to 1799, despite the lower average price over the 50 years, an upward movement [takes place]; the upward movement is just as consistent as the downward movement between 1810 and 1859.

In fact, compared with the period of 1641-1649, there is, on the whole, a continuous fall in decennial average prices, until this fall reaches its *peak* (*lowest point*) in the last two decennial periods of the first half of the 18th century.

From the middle of the eighteenth century onwards, an upward movement takes place. It commences from a price (36s. $4^5/_{10}$d. 1750-1759), which is lower than the 50 years average price of the second half of the seventeenth century and approximately corresponds [to or is] a little higher than the average price of the 50 year period 1700-1749 (35s. $9^{29}/_{50}$d.), the *first* half of the eighteenth century. This upward movement continues at an increasing pace in the two decennial periods 1800-1809 and 1810-

---

[a] See this volume, pp. 134-36.—*Ed.*

1819. In the latter it reaches its acme. From that point on, the consistent downward movement begins again. If we take the average of the period of rise from 1750 to 1819, then its average price (a little over 57s. per quarter) [is] equal to the starting-point of the period of fall from 1820 (namely a little over 58s. for the decennial period 1820-1829); just as the starting-point for the second half of the 18th century [equals] the average price of its first half.

Any mathematical example will show how individual circumstances, a poor harvest, depreciation of money, etc. can affect the average figure. For instance, 30+20+5+5+5=65. Average is 13, although the last three numbers here [are] always only equal to 5. As against this, 12+11+10+9+8[=50], average is 10, although, if one struck off the exceptional 30 and 20 in the first series, the average of any three years in [the] second [series] would be greater.

If one deducts the differential costs for the capital successively employed in bringing new land into cultivation, which for a certain period enters as an item into cost, then perhaps the prices of 1820-1859 [would be] lower than any of the earlier ones. And this to some extent may well be the notion in the heads of those fellows who explain rent as interest for fixed capital sunk into the soil.

[9. Anderson versus Malthus. Anderson's Definition of Rent. His Thesis of the Rising Productivity of Agriculture and Its Influence on Differential Rent]

Anderson says in:
A Calm Investigation of the Circumstances that have led to the Present Scarcity of Grain in Britain, London, 1801:

"From 1700 to 1750, there has been a regular [...] fall of price [...] from £2 18s. 1d. to £1 12s. 6d. per quarter of wheat; [...] from 1750 to 1800 [...] progressional rise [...] from £1 12s. 6d. to £5 10s. per quarter" (p. 11).

Thus, unlike West, Malthus, Ricardo, he did not one-sidedly consider the phenomenon of a rising scale of corn prices (from 1750 to 1813), but rather the double phenomenon, a whole century, of which the first half shows a constantly falling and the second half a constantly rising scale of corn prices. He says very definitely:

"...the population [...] was on the increase during the first half of this century[a] as well as the last" (l.c., p. 12).

He is a decided enemy of the theory of population[55] and says explicitly that the land is capable of increasing and perennial improvement.

"The soil can be *continuously improved* by chemical influences and cultivation" (l.c., p. 38).[56]

||513| "...under a judicious system of management, that productiveness[b] may be made to augment, from year to year, for a succession of time to which no limits can be assigned, till at last it may be made to attain a degree of productiveness, of which we cannot, perhaps, at this time conceive an idea" (l.c., pp. 35-36).

"... it may be with certainty said, that the present population is such a trifle compared to that" which this island can maintain, "as to be much below any degree of serious consideration" (l.c., p. 37).

"Wherever population increases [...], the produce of the country must be augmented along with it, unless *some moral influence is permitted to derange the economy of nature*" (l.c., p. 41).

The "theory of population" represents "the most pernicious prejudice" (l.c., p. 54). Anderson seeks to prove historically that the "productivity of agriculture" rises with a growing and falls with a declining population (l.c., pp. 55, 56, 60, 61 et seq.).

With a correct conception of *rent,* the first point to arise was of course that it does not originate from the land but from the *product of agriculture,* that is, from labour, from the *price of the product of labour,* for instance of wheat; in other words, from the *value* of the agricultural product, from the labour applied to the land, not from the land, and Anderson quite correctly emphasises this.

"It is not [...] the rent of the land that determines the price of its produce, but it is the price of that produce which determines the rent of the land, although the price of that produce is often highest in those countries where the rent of land is lowest."

⟨Rent has thus nothing to do with the *absolute* productivity of agriculture.⟩

"This seems to be a paradox that deserves to be explained. In every country there is a variety of soils, differing considerably from one another in point of fertility. These we shall at present suppose arranged into different classes, which we shall denote by the letters A, B, C, D, E, F etc., the class A comprehending the soils of the greatest fertility, and the other letters expressing

---

[a] In the manuscript: "the 18th century" instead of "this century".—*Ed.*
[b] In the manuscript: "the productivity of the soil" instead of "that productiveness".—*Ed.*

different classes of soils, gradually decreasing in fertility as you recede from
the first. Now, as *the expense of cultivating the least fertile soil is as great or
greater than that of the most fertile field*, it necessarily follows, that *if an
equal quantity of corn, the produce of each field, can be sold at the same
price*, the profit on cultivating the most fertile soil must be much greater
than that of cultivating the others"

⟨namely the excess of price over the expenses or the price of
the capital advanced⟩

"and as this" ⟨i.e., the profit⟩ "continues to decrease as the sterility increases,
it must at length *happen* that the *expense of cultivating* some of the inferior
classes will *equal the value of the whole produce.*" [James Anderson, *An
Enquiry into the Nature of the Corn Laws*, Edinburgh, 1777, pp. 45-48, quoted
from J. R. McCulloch, *The Literature of Political Economy*, London, 1845,
p. 69.]

The last field pays no rent. (This is cited from McCulloch, *The
Literature of Political Economy*, London, 1845. Does McCulloch
quote here from *An Enquiry into the Nature of the Corn Laws* or
from *Recreations in Agriculture, Natural History, Arts etc.*,
London, 1799-1802? This to be looked up at the Museum.)[57]

What Anderson calls *"value* of the whole produce" is evidently
nothing other than his conception of the *market-price* at which
the product is sold, whether it grows on better or on worse land.
With the more fertile types of land, this "price" (value) leaves
a greater or lesser excess over the expenses. This does not apply
to the last product. Here the *average price*—i.e., that formed by
the costs of production plus the average profit—coincides with
the market-price of the product. Hence it does not yield an excess
profit, which alone can constitute   rent. With Anderson, rent
equals the excess of the *market-price* of the product over its
average price. (The theory of value as yet does not worry
Anderson at all.) Thus if, as a result of the particularly low fertility of the land, the *average price* of the   product of this land
coincides with the *market-price* of the product, then there is no
excess and therefore no fund for the formation of rent. Anderson
does not say the last cultivated land *cannot bear a rent.* He only
says that if it "happens" that the expenses (the costs of production plus the average profit) are so great that the difference between the market-price of the product and its average price disappears, then rent also disappears and that this must be the case if
one descends ever further down the scale. Anderson says expressly that a definite *market-price equal* for equal quantities of
produce that have been produced under more favourable or less
favourable conditions of production, is the prerequisite for this

formation of rent. He says that a surplus profit or excess of profit from the better types of soil over that from the worse, necessarily follows "*if an equal quantity of corn,* the produce of *each* field, can be sold at *the same price*", i.e., if a general market-price is presupposed.

||514| Anderson by no means assumes, as might have appeared from the preceding passage, that different *degrees of fertility* are merely the product of nature. On the contrary the

"...infinite diversity of soils" arises partly from the fact that these "soils [...] may be so much altered from their original state by the modes of culture they have been formerly subjected to, by the manures..." etc. (*An Inquiry into the Causes that have hitherto Retarded the Advancement of Agriculture in Europe,* Edinburgh, 1779, p. 5).

On the one hand, the progress in the productivity of labour in general makes it easier to bring land into cultivation; on the other hand, cultivation increases the diversity of soils, in that the original fertility of land A which is cultivated and land B which is not, may have been the same if we deduct from A's fertility that part which, though it is now inherent in it, had previously been added *artificially.* Thus cultivation itself increases the diversity of natural fertility between cultivated and waste lands.

Anderson says expressly that that land for whose produce average price and market-price coincide, can pay *no* rent:

"Where there are two fields, the produce of which is nearly as above stated", namely the one yielding 12 bushels covering the costs, the other 20, "without requiring any *immediate outlay for their improvement,* the farmer would [...] pay even more rent than" 6 bushels for instance for the latter while [he would pay] none for the former. If "twelve bushels" are "just sufficient for the expense of cultivating [...] no rent whatever can be afforded for *cultivated* land that yields only twelve bushels" (James Anderson, *Essays Relating to Agriculture and Rural Affairs,* Vol. III, Edinburgh, 1796, pp. 107-09).

Then he immediately goes on to say:

"Yet it cannot be expected that, if the superior produce has been *immediately occasioned* by his own outlay of capital, and exertions of industry, he *can* pay nearly the same *proportion* of it as rent: but after the land has been *for some time in a permanent state of fertility to that degree,* though it even *originally derived that fertility* from his own industry, he will be content to pay such a proportion of rent as is here stated..." (l.c., pp. 109-10).

Supposing therefore the produce of the best cultivated land is 20 bushels per acre. Of this, according to the assumption, 12 bushels pay the expenses (advances plus average profit). Then it *can* pay 8 bushels as rent. Assume that the bushel is 5s., then

10*

8 bushels or 1 quarter are 40s. or £ 2 and 20 bushels are £ 5 $(2^1/_2$ quarters). Of these £ 5, 12 bushels or 60s. which is £ 3, is expenses. Then it pays a rent of £ 2 or 8 bushels. If the rate of profit is 10 per cent then of the £ 3 expenses, the outlay is $54^6/_{11}$s. and the profit is $5^5/_{11}$s. $(54^6/_{11} : 5^5/_{11} = 100 : 10)$. Now supposing, the farmer had to carry out various improvements on waste land, which is just as fertile as that yielding 20 bushels had been *originally*, in order to bring it into such a state of cultivation that would correspond to the general state of agriculture. Apart from the outlay of $54^6/_{11}$s. or, if we reckon the profit in with the expenses, apart from 60s., this may involve a further outlay of $36^4/_{11}$; then 10 per cent on this would be $3^7/_{11}$, and if the farmer always sold 20 bushels at 5s. he could pay a rent only after 10 years, only after the reproduction of his capital. From then on the artificially created fertility of the land would be reckoned as original and would fall to the landlord.

Although the newly cultivated land is as fertile as the best cultivated land was originally, the market-price and the average price for its product do nevertheless coincide now, because it contains an item of costs which is extinct in the best land, whose artificially created fertility and whose natural fertility coincide to a certain extent. But with the newly cultivated land, that part of fertility which is created artificially, by the application of capital, is still entirely distinct from the natural fertility of the land. The newly cultivated land can therefore pay *no rent* although its original fertility may be the same as that of the best cultivated land. After ten years, however, it could pay not only rent, but as much rent as the best type which was *cultivated* earlier. Thus Anderson comprehends both phenomena:

1. That the differential rent of the landlords is partly the result of the fertility which the farmer has given the land artificially.

2. That after a certain lapse of time, this artificial fertility appears as the original productivity of the soil itself, in that the soil itself has been transformed and the process by which this transformation has been accomplished, has disappeared and is no longer visible.

||515| If to-day I build a cotton mill for £ 100,000, I get a more efficient mill than my predecessor who set one up ten years ago. I do not pay for the difference between productivity in machine-building, building in general etc. of to-day and of ten years ago; on the contrary. It enables me to pay *less* for a mill of the same efficiency or only *the same* for a mill of higher efficiency. In ag-

riculture it is different. The difference between the original fertilities of the soils is magnified by that part of the so-called natural fertility of the soil which, in fact, has been once *produced* by men, but has now become incorporated in the soil and is no longer to be distinguished from its original fertility. Owing to the development of the productive power of labour in general, it costs less to raise uncultivated soil of the same original fertility to the *improved* level of fertility, than it cost to bring the original fertility of the cultivated soil to the apparently original fertility it now has, but some expenditure is still required to bring that equalisation about. The average price of the new product is consequently higher than that of the old, the difference between market-price and average price is thus smaller and may disappear completely. But supposing, in the above case, the newly cultivated soil is so fertile, that after the additional expense of 40s. (including profit) it yields 28 bushels instead of 20. In this case the farmer could pay a rent of 8 bushels or £ 2. And why? Because the newly cultivated soil yields 8 bushels more than the old, so that despite the higher average price, with the same market-price, it yields just as much in excess of the price. If it had involved no extra expense, its fertility would be double that of the old land. With this expense it is the same as that of the old land.

[10. The Untenability of the Rodbertian Critique of Ricardo's Theory of Rent. Rodbertus's Lack of Understanding of the Peculiarities of Capitalist Agriculture]

Now back to Rodbertus, definitively and for the last time.

"It" (Rodbertus's theory of rent) "explains all phenomena of wages and rent etc. ... by *a division of the labour product*, which necessarily occurs if two prerequisites, adequate productivity of labour and property in land and capital, are given. It explains that the adequate productivity of labour alone constitutes the *economic possibility of such a division*, in that this productivity gives to the value of the product so much actual content that in addition other people who do not work, can also live from it. And it explains that landed property and capital property alone constitute the *legal reality of such a division*, in that it forces the workers to *share their product* with the non-working proprietors of land and capital and, what is more, in such a proportion that they, the workers, only get so much of it as to enable them to live." (Rodbertus [*Sociale Briefe an von Kirchmann, Dritter Brief*, Berlin, 1851], pp. 156-57.)

Adam Smith sets forth this problem in two ways. [The first concept:] *Division of the product of labour* where this is regarded as given and he is in fact concerned with the *distribution of use-value*. This is also Herr Rodbertus's conception. It is also to be found with Ricardo who is all the more to be reproached on this account because he does not merely confine himself to general phrases but seriously tries to *determine the value by labour-time*. This conception is more or less, *mutatis mutandis,* applicable to all modes of production where the workers and the owners of the objective conditions of labour form different classes.

Smith's second conception, on the other hand, is characteristic of the capitalist mode of production. Hence it alone is a theoretically fruitful formula. For Smith here conceives of profit and rent as springing from the *surplus labour* which the worker adds to the subject of labour, apart from that portion of labour by which he only reproduces his own wage. This is the only correct standpoint where production rests solely on exchange-value. This concept comprises the process of development, whereas the first concept presupposes that *labour-time* is constant.

With Ricardo the one-sidedness arises also from the fact that in general he wants to show that the various economic categories or relationships *do not contradict the theory of value,* instead of on the contrary, *developing* them together with their apparent contradictions out of this basis or presenting the development of this basis itself.

||516| "You[a] know, that *all economists,* already from Adam Smith onwards, *split up the value of the product into wages, ground-rent and capital gain* and that therefore the idea of basing the incomes of the different classes and particularly also rent *on a division of the product* is nothing new." (Certainly not!) "Only the economists immediately go astray. All of them—not even excepting the Ricardian School—*first of all* commit the error of not regarding the *whole* product, the *entire* wealth, the *total national product* as the unit in which the workers, the landowners and the capitalists participate. On the contrary they regard the *division of the raw product* as a *particular division* in which *three participants* share, and the division of the manufactured product again as a particular division in which *only two* participants share. So these systems consider that the mere raw product and the mere manufactured product, each in itself, is a special kind of wealth which constitutes income" (l.c., p. 162).

First of all, by breaking down the *"whole* value of the product into wages, ground-rent and capital gain" [p. 162] and thus forgetting about constant capital which also forms a part of value, Adam Smith has in fact led *"astray"* all the later economists, in-

---

a von Kirchmann.—*Ed.*

cluding Ricardo and including Herr Rodbertus. As my exposition has shown, the lack of this differentiation made any scientific presentation quite impossible.[58] In this respect the Physiocrats were further advanced. Their *"avances primitives et annuelles"*[a] are defined as a part of the value of the annual product or as a part of the annual product itself, which is not resolved into wages, profit or rent, either for the nation or for the individual. According to the Physiocrats, the raw material of the agriculturists replaces the advances of the sterile class (the transformation of this raw material into machines of course devolves on the sterile class), while, on the other hand, the agriculturists replace a part of their own advances (seeds, cattle for breeding and draught animals, fertiliser etc.) from their product and get a part, machinery etc. replaced by the sterile class in exchange for raw material.

Secondly Herr Rodbertus errs in that he identifies *division of value* with *division of product*. The *"wealth which constitutes income"* has nothing directly to do with this *division of the value* of the product. That the portions of value which accrue, for instance, to the producers of yarn, and which are represented in certain quantities of gold, *exist* as agricultural and manufactured products of all kinds is equally well known to the economists as to Rodbertus. This is *taken for granted* because *commodities* are produced and not products for the immediate consumption of the producers themselves. Since the value which becomes available for distribution, i.e., the part of value which forms revenue, is created within each individual sphere of production, independently of the others—although, on account of the division of labour, it presupposes the others—Rodbertus takes a step backward and creates confusion, by not examining this creation of value on its own, but confusing it right from the start by asking what share of the available total product of the nation these component parts secure for their owners. With Rodbertus, division of the *value of the product* immediately becomes *division of use-values*. Because he foists this confusion upon the other economists, there arises the need for his corrective, i.e., the consideration of manufactured and raw products *en bloc*—a mode of procedure which is irrelevant to the creation of value, and hence wrong if it is to explain the latter.

---

[a] Original and annual advances.—*Ed.*

The only participants in the *value* of the manufactured product, in so far as it comprises revenue and in so far as the manufacturer does not pay a rent, be it for land on which the buildings stand or for waterfalls, etc., are the *capitalist and the wage-labourer*. The *value of the agricultural produce* is generally divided between three. This Herr Rodbertus also admits. The manner in which he explains this phenomenon does not in any way alter this fact. It is entirely in accord with the standpoint of capitalist production that the other economists, especially Ricardo, start from a *division into two,* between capitalist and wage-labourer, and only bring in the landowner who draws rent at a later stage, as a special excrescence. Capitalist production is based on the antithesis of two factors ||517|, materialised labour and living labour. Capitalist and wage-labourer are the sole functionaries and factors of production whose relationship and confrontation arise from the nature of the capitalist mode of production.

The circumstances under which the capitalist has in turn to share a part of the surplus-labour or surplus-value which he has captured, with a third, non-working person, are only of secondary importance. It is also a fact of production, that, after the part of the value which is equal to constant capital is deducted, the *entire surplus-value passes straight from the hands of the worker to those of the capitalist,* with the exception of that part of the value of the product which is paid out as wages. The capitalist confronts the worker as the *direct* owner of the entire surplus-value, in whatever manner he may later be sharing it with the money-lending capitalist, landowner etc. As James Mill observes,[59] production could therefore continue undisturbed if the landed proprietor disappeared and the state took his place. He—the private landowner—is not a necessary agent for capitalist production, although it does require that the land should belong to someone, so long as it is not the worker, but for instance, the state. Far from being an error on the part of Ricardo etc., this reduction of the classes participating directly in production, hence also in the value produced and then in the products in which this value is embodied, to *capitalists and wage-labourers,* and the *exclusion of the landowners* (who only enter *post festum,* as a result of conditions of ownership of natural forces that have *not grown out* of the capitalist mode of production but have been *passed on* to it) is rooted in the nature of the *capitalist mode of production*—as distinct from the feudal, ancient etc. This reduction is an adequate theoretical expression of the capitalist mode of production, and reveals its *differentia specifica*. Herr Rodbertus is still too much of an old Prussian "landed proprietor", to understand this. Furthermore, it can only be grasped and become self-evident when the capitalist has seized agriculture, and everywhere, as is generally the case in England, has taken charge of agriculture just as he has of industry, and has *excluded* the *landowner* from any direct participation in the production process. What Rodbertus regards as a "deviation", is, therefore, the right path, which however he does not understand because he is still engrossed in views that originated from the pre-capitalist mode of production.

"He too" (Ricardo) "does not divide the *finished* product among the parties concerned, but, like the other economists, regards the agricultural product as well as the manufactured product—as a separate product, which has to be divided" (l.c., p. 167).

Not the product, Herr Rodbertus, but the *value* of the product, and this is quite correct. Your "finished" product and its division have absolutely nothing to do with this division of value.

"He" (Ricardo) "regards capital property as given and *that even earlier* than landed property.... Thus he does not begin with the reasons for, but with the *fact* of the division of the product, and his entire theory is limited to the causes which determine and modify the *proportions of the shares....* The division of the product purely into *wages* and *capital gain* is for him the *original one* and originally also the only one" (l.c., p. 167).

This you fail to understand again, Herr Rodbertus. From the standpoint of capitalist production, *capital property* does in fact appear as the "original" because capitalist production is based on this sort of property and it is a factor of and fulfils a function in *capitalist production*; this does not hold good of landed property. The latter *appears* as derivative, because modern landed property is in fact *feudal* property, but transformed by the action of capital upon it; in its form as modern landed property it is therefore *derived from,* and the result of capitalist production. That Ricardo considers the position as it is and appears in modern society to be also the *historically* original situation (whereas you, instead of keeping to the modern form, cannot rid yourself of your memories of landownership) is a delusion from which the bourgeois economists suffer in respect of all bourgeois economic laws. They appear to them as "natural laws" and hence also as historically "primary".

||518| But Herr Rodbertus could already see from the very first sentence of his preface, that Ricardo, where it is not a ques-

tion of the *value* of the product, but of *the product itself,*
permits the *whole* of the "finished" product to be shared out.

"*The produce of the earth*—all that is derived from its surface by the
united application of labour, machinery, and capital, is divided among three
classes of the community; namely, the proprietor of the land, the owner of
the stock or capital necessary for its cultivation, and the labourers by whose
industry it is cultivated." (David Ricardo, *The Principles of Political Economy, and Taxation*, London, 1821, third edition, Preface, p. V.)

He continues forthwith:

"But in different stages of society, the proportions of the *whole produce*
of the earth which will be allotted to each of these classes, under the names
of rent, profit, and wages, will be essentially different" (l.c., p. V).

He is concerned here with the distribution of the "*whole produce*", not the manufactured product or the raw product. If
this "whole produce" is taken as given, these shares in the
"whole produce" are solely determined within each sphere of
production by the share which each shareholder has in the
"*value*" of his own product. This "value" is convertible into and
can be expressed in a certain proportional part of the "*whole
produce*". Ricardo only errs here, following Adam Smith, in that
he forgets that "the whole produce" is not divided into rent,
profit and wages, but that part of it "will be allotted" in the shape
of capital to one or some of these three classes.

"You might want to assert, that, just as *originally* the law of equal capital
gains would have had to depress raw product prices so far that ground-rent
would have to disappear only to be re-created as a result of a rise in prices
due to the difference between the yield of more fertile and less fertile land—
so, *to-day* the advantages of drawing rent besides the usual capital gain,
would induce the capitalist to spend capital on new cultivation and improvements until, due to the flooding of markets brought forth by this, prices
would fall sufficiently in order to make rents on the least favourable capital
investments disappear again. *In other words, this would be to assert that, so
far as the raw product is concerned, t h e l a w o f t h e e q u a l i s a t i o n
o f c a p i t a l g a i n s i n v a l i d a t e s t h e o t h e r l a w , t h a t t h e
v a l u e o f t h e p r o d u c t s i s g o v e r n e d b y l a b o u r c o s t s,* while
it is just *Ricardo*, who, in the first chapter of his work, uses the former to
prove the latter" (Rodbertus, l.c., p. 174).

Indeed, Herr Rodbertus! The law of the "*equalisation of capital
gains*" does not invalidate the law that the "*value*" of the products is governed by "labour costs". But it does invalidate Ricardo's assumption that the *average price* of the products equals
their "*value*". But there again, it is not the "raw product" whose
value is reduced to the average price, but *the other way about.*
Due to landed property, the "raw product" is distinguished by

the privilege that its value is *not* reduced to the average price. If, indeed, its *value* did decrease, which would be possible despite your "value of the material", to the level of the average price of the commodities, then rent would disappear. The types of land which possibly pay no rent to-day, pay none, because the *market-price* of raw products is for them equal to their own *average price*, and because the competition of more fertile types of land *deprives* them of the privilege of selling their product at *its* "value".

"Could it be true that *before* any cultivation takes place at all, capitalists already exist who receive a profit and invest their capital according to the law of profit equalisation?" (How very silly!) "... I admit, that if to-day an expedition from the civilised countries set out to a ||519| new, uncultivated land, an expedition in which the wealthier participants were equipped with supplies and tools—capital—from an old established culture and the poorer ones came along with a view to winning a high wage in the service of the former, then the capitalists would regard as their gain that which remains to them over and above the wages of the workers for they bring with them from their mother country things and ideas which have long been in existence there" (l.c., pp. 174-75).

Well, here you have it, Herr Rodbertus. Ricardo's whole conception is only appropriate to the presupposition that the capitalist mode of production is the predominant one. How he expresses this *presupposition,* whether he commits a historical *hysteron proteron* is irrelevant to the theory. The *presupposition* must be made, and it is therefore impossible to introduce, as you are doing, the peasant, who does not understand capitalist book-keeping and hence does not reckon seeds etc., as part of the capital advanced! The "absurdity" is introduced not by Ricardo but by Rodbertus, who assumes that capitalists and workers exist "*before* cultivation of the land" (l.c., p. 176).

"According to the Ricardian concept, cultivation of the land is supposed to begin ... only when ... capital has been created in a society and capital gain is known and paid" (l.c., p. 178).

What utter nonsense! Only when a capitalist has squeezed himself as farmer between the husbandman and the landed proprietor—be it that the old tenant has swindled his way into becoming a capitalist farmer, or that an industrialist has invested his capital in agriculture rather than in manufacture—only then begins, by no means "the cultivation of the land", but "capitalist" land cultivation which is very different, both in form and content, from the previous forms of cultivation.

"In every country the greater part of the land is already owned by someone long before it is cultivated; and certainly, long before a rate of capital profit has been established in industry" (l.c., p. 179).

To comprehend Ricardo's conception Rodbertus would have to be an Englishman instead of a Pomeranian landowner and would have to understand the history of the enclosure of commons and waste land. Rodbertus cites America. There the state sells the land

"in lots, first to the cultivators at a low price, it is true, but one which must *at all events* already represent a rent" (l.c., pp. 179-80).

By no means. This price does not constitute a ground-rent, any more than, say, a general trade tax constitutes a *trade rent* or in fact any tax constitutes a "rent".

"With regard to the cause of the rise under point b" (the increase in population or the increase in the *quantity of labour employed*) "I maintain, however, that rent has precedence over capital gain. The latter can *never* rise because, as a result of the increased value of the national product—if *productivity remains the same* but productive power increases (increased population)—*more* capital gain accrues to the nation, for this *greater* capital gain always accrues to a *capital* which is *greater* in the same *proportion*, the rate of profit therefore remains the same" (l.c., pp. 184-85).

This is wrong. The quantity of unpaid surplus-labour rises, for instance, if 3, 4, 5 hours surplus labour-time are worked instead of 2 hours. The volume of capital advanced does not grow [to the same extent] as the volume of this *unpaid* surplus-labour, firstly, because this further excess of surplus-labour is *not* paid for and so does not occasion a capital outlay; secondly, because the capital outlay for fixed capital does not grow in the same proportion as its utilisation in this instance. No more spindles etc. are required. True, they are used up more quickly but not in the same proportion in which their use *increases*. Thus, given the same productivity, profit grows here, because not only the surplus-value grows, but also the *rate of surplus-value*. In agriculture this is impracticable because of the natural conditions. On the other hand, *productivity* is easily altered with the increased outlay of capital. Although an absolutely large amount of capital is laid out, it is relatively not so big, due to economies in the conditions of production, quite apart from the division of labour and machinery. Thus the *rate of profit* could grow even if the surplus-value (not only *its rate*) remained the same.

||520| Rodbertus is positively wrong, and typically the Pomeranian landowner when he says:

"It is possible that in the course of these thirty years" (1800-1830) "*more* properties came into being through the parcelling out of land or *even through the cultivation of new land* and the increased rent was thus also divided among *more* landowners, but it was *not distributed over more acres in 1830 than in 1800*. Previously *the older properties* comprised the whole of the acreage of those newly separated or newly cultivated properties and the lower rent of 1800 was also *calculated* on them, and this influenced the level of English rent in general at that time just as much as the higher rent in 1830" (l.c., p. 186).

Worthy Pomeranian! Why do you always transfer your Prussian situation to England in a disparaging manner? The Englishman does not reckon that, if, as was the case (this to be looked up), three to four million acres were "enclosed" between 1800 and 1830, the rent on these four million acres[60] was calculated before 1830 as well and also in 1800. Rather they were waste land or commons which bore no rent and did not belong to anybody.

It has nothing to do with Ricardo if Rodbertus, like Carey (but in a different way), seeks to prove to Ricardo that for physical and other reasons, the "most fertile" land is usually not the first to be cultivated. The "most fertile" land is always the "most fertile" under the existing conditions of production.

A very large number of the objections which Rodbertus raises against Ricardo arise from the naïve manner in which he identifies the "Pomeranian" conditions of production with the "English". Ricardo presupposes capitalist production to which, where it is in fact carried out, as in England, corresponds the separation of the farming capitalist from the landlord. Rodbertus introduces circumstances which are in themselves alien to the capitalist mode of production, which has merely been built upon them. For instance, what Herr Rodbertus says about the position of economic centres in economic complexes applies perfectly to Pomerania but not to England, where the capitalist mode of production has become increasingly pre-eminent since the last third of the 16th century, where it has assimilated all the conditions and in different periods has progressively sent historical preconditions, villages, buildings and people, to the devil, in order to secure the "most productive" investment for capital.

What Rodbertus says about "capital investment" is equally wrong.

"Ricardo limits ground-rent to that which the landowner is paid for the use of the *original, natural and indestructible qualities of the land*. He thus wants to ensure that everything which would have to be ascribed to capital in the land which is already being cultivated, is deducted from rent. But it is clear that out of the yield from a piece of land he must never allot more to capital than the *full interest customary in a country*. For otherwise he would have to assume that there are two different rates of gain in the economic development of a country, one agricultural, which is greater than that prevailing in manufacture, and this latter. This assumption would overthrow his very system, which is based on the equality of the rate of gain" (l.c., pp. 215-16).

Again the notion of the Pomeranian landowner who gets money on tick in order to improve his property and who, for theoretical and practical reasons, only wants to pay the money-lender the "customary interest". But in England things are different. It is the farmer, the farming-capitalist, who lays out capital in order to improve the land. From this capital, just as from that which he lays out directly in production, he does not demand the customary interest but the *customary profit*. He does not lend the landowner any capital on which the latter is to pay the "customary" interest. He may borrow capital himself, or else he uses his own surplus capital so that it yields him the "customary" industrial profit, at least double the customary interest.

Incidentally, Ricardo knows what Anderson already knew and, into the bargain, expressly says that ||521| the productivity of the land thus engendered by capital, later coincides with its "natural" productivity, hence swells the rent. Rodbertus knows nothing of all this and therefore babbles away at random.

I have already given a correct explanation of modern landed property:

"Rent, in the Ricardian sense, is property in land in its bourgeois state; that is, feudal property which has become subject to the conditions of bourgeois production." (*Misère de la Philosophie*, Paris, 1847, p. 156.)[61]

Similarly I have already correctly observed:

"Ricardo, after postulating bourgeois production as necessary for determining rent, applies the conception of rent, nevertheless, to the landed property of all ages and all countries. This is an error common to all the economists who represent the bourgeois relations of production as eternal categories" (l.c., p. 160).[62]

I also pointed out correctly that "land as capital" could be increased like all other capitals:

"Land as capital can be *increased* just as much as all the other instruments of production. Nothing is added to its matter, to use M. Proudhon's language, but *the lands which serve as instruments of production are multiplied*. The very fact of applying further outlays of capital to land already transformed into means of production increases land as capital without adding anything to land as matter, that is, to the extent of the land" (l.c., p. 165).[63]

The difference between manufacture and agriculture which I pointed out at that time still remains correct:

"In the first place, one cannot, as in manufacturing industry, *multiply at will the instruments of production possessing the same degree of productivity*, that is, plots of land with the same degree of fertility. Then as population increases, land of an inferior quality begins to be exploited, or new outlays of capital, proportionately less productive than before, are made upon the same plot of land" (l.c., p. 157).[64]

Rodbertus says:

"But I must draw attention to yet another circumstance which, admittedly, much more gradually, but also far more generally, turns worse agricultural machines into better ones.[65] This is the *continued management* of a piece of land merely in accordance with a rational system, without making any special capital investment." ([*Sociale Briefe an von Kirchmann, Dritter Brief*], p. 222.)

Anderson already said cultivation improves the land. [Rodbertus continues.]

"You would have to prove that the working population engaged in agriculture had, in the course of time, increased to a greater degree than the production of food or even just compared with the rest of the population of a country. Only this could irrefutably show that increasing agricultural production also demands that progressively more labour is expended upon it. But it is just here that statistics contradict you" (l.c., p. 274). "Indeed, you will find that, [pretty well] as a rule, the denser the population of a country, the smaller will be the proportion of people engaged in agriculture.... The same phenomenon can be observed when the population of a country increases: that section which is. *not* engaged in agriculture will almost everywhere increase to a greater degree" (l.c., p. 275).

But this is partly because more arable land is turned over to cattle and sheep grazing, partly because with the higher stage of production—large-scale agriculture—labour becomes more productive. *But also,* and this is a circumstance which Herr Rodbertus overlooks entirely, because a greater part of the *non-agricultural population* assist in agriculture, supplying constant capital —which grows with the advance in cultivation—such as mineral fertilisers, seeds from other countries, machinery of every sort. According to Herr Rodbertus (l.c., p. 78):

"At present the agriculturist" (in Pomerania) "does not" (regard) "the feeding-stuffs for his draught animals as capital, if he has grown these in his own establishment...."
||522| "Capital in itself, or from an economic point of view, is a product which continues to be used for production.... But in respect of a particular gain which it is to yield, or from the point of view of *to-day's entrepreneurs,* it must appear as an '*outlay*' in order to be capital" (l.c., p. 77).

This concept of "outlay" however does not, as Rodbertus thinks, require that it is bought as a commodity. If instead of being *sold* as a commodity, a part of the product re-enters production, it does so as a *commodity*. It has previously been estimated as "money", this is easily done, since simultaneously all these "outlays", in agriculture too, are available on the market as "commodities": cattle, feeding-stuffs, fertilisers, corn for sowing, seeds of all kinds. But it seems that in "Pomerania" this is not reckoned as "outlay".

"The *value* of the particular results of these different sorts of work" (manufacture and primary production) "is not the income itself which accrues to their owner, but only the measure for its conversion into money. This particular income itself is a part of the social income, which is only produced by the combined labour in agriculture and manufacture, and its *elements* too are thus only produced by this combined effort" (l.c., p. 36).

This is quite irrelevant. The realisation of this *value* can only be its realisation in use-value. But we are not concerned with that. Furthermore, the *necessary wage* already implies how much value in the shape of agricultural and industrial products is contained in the means of subsistence the worker requires.

Done with

[CHAPTER X]

RICARDO'S AND ADAM SMITH'S THEORY OF COST-PRICE (REFUTATION)

[A. RICARDO'S THEORY OF COST-PRICE]

[1. Collapse of the Theory of the Physiocrats and the Further Development of the Theories of Rent]

With Anderson's thesis (partly also contained in Adam Smith's work): "It is not [...] the rent of the land that determines the *price* of its produce, but it is the *price* of that produce which determines the rent of the land..."[a] the doctrine of the Physiocrats was overthrown. The *price* of the agricultural produce, and neither this produce itself nor the land, had thus become the source of rent. This finished the notion that rent was the off-spring of the exceptional productivity of agriculture, which again was supposed to be the offspring of the special fertility of the soil. For, if *the same quantity of labour* was exerted in a particularly productive element and hence was itself exceptionally productive, then the result could only be that this labour manifested itself in a relatively *large* quantity of *products* and that the price of the individual product was therefore relatively low; but it could never have the opposite result, namely, that the *price* of its product was *higher* than that of other products containing the same quantity of labour and that this *price,* as distinct from that of other commodities, thus yielded a *rent, in addition to* profit and wages. (In his treatment of rent, *Adam Smith* to some extent returns to the physiocratic view, having previously refuted or at least rejected it by his original conception of rent as part of surplus-labour.)

Buchanan sums up this discarding of the physiocratic view in the following words:

---

[a] See this volume, p. 145.—*Ed.*

"The notion of agriculture yielding a produce, and a rent in consequence, because nature concurs with human industry in the process of cultivation, is a mere fancy. It is not from the produce, but from the price at which the produce is sold, that the rent is derived; and this price is got not because nature assists in the production, but because it is the price which suits the consumption to the supply." [David Buchanan in Adam Smith, *An Inquiry into the Nature and Causes of the Wealth of Nations*, Vol. II, Edinburgh, 1814, p. 55, note; quoted from David Ricardo, *On the Principles of Political Economy, and Taxation*, third edition, London, 1821, p. 66, note.]

After the rejection of this notion of the Physiocrats—which, however, was fully justified in its deeper sense, because they regarded rent as the only surplus, and capitalists and labourers together merely as the paid employees of the landlord—only the following viewpoints were possible.

||523| [Firstly:] The view that *rent* arises from the *monopoly price* of agricultural products, the monopoly price being due to the landowners possessing the *monopoly* of the land. According to this concept, the *price* of the agricultural product is constantly *above* its *value*. There is a *surcharge of price* and the law of the value of commodities is breached by the *monopoly* of landed property.

Rent arises out of the *monopoly price* of agricultural products, because supply is constantly *below* the level of demand or demand is constantly *above* the level of supply. But why does supply not rise to the *level* of demand? Why does not an *additional* supply equalise this relationship and thus, according to this theory, abolish *all* rent? In order to explain this, Malthus on the one hand takes refuge in the fiction that agricultural products provide themselves with direct consumers (about which more later, in connection with his row with Ricardo); on the other hand, in the Andersonian theory, that agriculture becomes less productive because the *additional supply* costs more labour. Hence, in so far as this view is not based on mere fiction, it coincides with the Ricardian theory. Here too, *price* stands a b o v e value, surcharge.

[Secondly:] *The Ricardian Theory: Absolute rent does not exist,* only a *differential rent*. Here too, the *price* of the agricultural products that bear rent is *above* their individual value, and in so far as rent exists at all, it does so through the *excess of the price of agricultural products over their value*. Only here this excess of price *over* value does not contradict the general theory of value (although the fact remains) because within each sphere of production the *value* of the commodities belonging to it is not

determined by the individual value of the commodity but by
its value as modified by the *general* conditions of production
of that sphere. Here, too, the price of the rent-bearing products
is a *monopoly price,* a monopoly however as it occurs in all
spheres of industry and only   becomes permanent in this one,
hence assuming the form of rent as distinct from excess profit.
Here too, it is an excess of *demand over supply* or, what amounts
to the same thing, that the additional demand cannot be satisfied
by an additional supply at *prices* corresponding to those of the
original supply, before its prices were forced up by the excess
of demand over supply. Here too, *rent comes into being* (differential rent) because of *excess of price over value*, [brought about
by] the rise of prices on the better land *above* the value of the
product, and this leads to the additional supply.

[Thirdly:] *Rent is merely interest on the capital sunk in the
land.*[a] This view has the following in common with the Ricardian, namely, that it denies the existence of *absolute rent*. It
must admit the existence of *differential rent,* when pieces of land
in which equal amounts of capital have been invested, yield rents
of varying size. Hence in fact, it amounts to the Ricardian view,
that certain land yields no *rent* and that where *actual* rent is
yielded, this is differential rent. But it is absolutely incapable of
explaining the rent of land in which *no* capital has been invested,
of waterfalls, mines etc. It was, in fact, nothing but an attempt
from a capitalist point of view, to save rent despite Ricardo—
under the name of *interest.*

Finally [fourthly]: Ricardo assumes that on the land which
does not bear a rent, the price of the product equals its value
because it equals the *average price*, i.e., capital outlay plus average profit. He thus wrongly assumes that the value of the commodity equals the average price of the commodity. If this wrong
assumption is dropped, then absolute rent becomes possible because the *value* of agricultural products, like that of a whole
large category of other commodities, stands *above* their average
price, but owing to landed property, the value of the agricultural
products, unlike that of these other commodities, is not levelled
out at the average price. Hence this view assumes, like the
monopoly theory, that property in land, as such, has something to
do with rent; it assumes differential rent along with Ricardo,
and finally it assumes that absolute rent by no means infringes
the law of value.

---

[a] See this volume, pp. 34, 140 and 144.—*Ed.*

[2. The Determination of Value by Labour-Time
—the Basis of Ricardo's Theory.
Despite Certain Deficiencies the Ricardian Mode
of Investigation Is a Necessary Stage in the Development
of Political Economy]

Ricardo starts out from the determination of the relative values (or exchangeable values) of commodities by "the *quantity of labour*". (We can examine later the various senses in which Ricardo uses the term value. This is the basis of Bailey's criticism and, at the same time, of Ricardo's *shortcomings*.) The character of this "labour" is not further examined. If two commodities are equivalents—or bear a *definite proportion* to each other or, which is the same thing, if their *magnitude differs* according to the ||524| *quantity of "labour"* which they contain—then it is obvious that regarded as exchange-values, their *substance* must be the same. Their substance is labour. That is why they are "values". Their magnitude varies, according to whether they contain more or less of this substance. But *Ricardo does not examine* the form—the peculiar characteristic of labour that creates exchange-value or manifests itself in exchange-values—the *nature* of this labour. Hence he does not grasp the connection of *this labour* with *money* or that it must assume the form of *money*. Hence he completely fails to grasp the connection between the determination of the exchange-value of the commodity by labour-time and the fact that the development of commodities necessarily leads to the formation of money. Hence his erroneous theory of money. Right from the start he is only concerned with the *magnitude of value,* i.e., the fact that the magnitudes of the values of the commodities are proportionate to the quantities of labour which are required for their production. Ricardo proceeds from here and he expressly names Adam Smith as his starting-point (Chapter I, Section I).

Ricardo's method is as follows: He begins with the determination of the magnitude of the value of the commodity by labour-time and then *examines* whether the other economic relations and categories *contradict* this determination of value or to what extent they modify it. The historical justification of this method of procedure, its scientific necessity in the history of economics, are evident at first sight, but so is, at the same time, its scientific inadequacy. This inadequacy not only shows itself in the method of presentation (in a formal sense) but leads to erroneous results because it omits some essential links and *directly* seeks to prove the congruity of the economic categories with one another.

Historically, this method of investigation was justified and necessary. Political economy had achieved a certain comprehensiveness with Adam Smith; to a certain extent he had covered the whole of its territory, so that Say was able to summarise it all in one textbook, superficially but quite systematically. The only investigations that were made in the period between Smith and Ricardo were ones of detail, on productive and unproductive labour, finance, theory of population, landed property and taxes. Smith himself moves with great naïveté in a perpetual contradiction. On the one hand he traces the intrinsic connection existing between economic categories or the obscure structure of the bourgeois economic system. On the other, he simultaneously sets forth the connection as it appears in the phenomena of competition and thus as it presents itself to the unscientific observer just as to him who is actually involved and interested in the process of bourgeois production. One of these conceptions fathoms the inner connection, the physiology, so to speak, of the bourgeois system, whereas the other takes the external phenomena of life, as they seem and appear and merely describes, catalogues, recounts and arranges them under formal definitions. With Smith both these methods of approach not only merrily run alongside one another, but also intermingle and constantly contradict one another. With him this is justifiable (with the exception of a few special investigations, [such as] that into money) since his task was indeed a twofold one. On the one hand he attempted to penetrate the inner physiology of bourgeois society but on the other, he partly tried to describe its externally apparent forms of life for the first time, to show its relations as they appear outwardly and partly he had even to find a nomenclature and corresponding mental concepts for these phenomena, i.e., to reproduce them for the first time in the language and [in the] thought process. The one task interests him as much as the other and since both proceed independently of one another, this results in completely contradictory ways of presentation: the one expresses the intrinsic connections more or less correctly, the other, with the same justification—and without any connection to the first method of approach—expresses the *apparent* connections without any internal relation. Adam Smith's successors, in so far as they do not represent the reaction against him of older and obsolete methods of approach, can pursue their particular investigations and observations undisturbedly and can always regard Adam Smith as their base, whether they follow the esoteric or the exoteric part of his work or whether, as is almost always the case, they jumble up the two. But at last Ricardo steps in and calls to science: Halt! The basis, the starting-point for the physiology of the bourgeois system—for the understanding of its internal organic coherence and life process—is the determination of *value by labour-time*. Ricardo starts with this and forces science to get out of the rut, to render an account of the extent to which the other categories—the relations of production and commerce—evolved and described by it, correspond to or contradict this basis, this starting-point; to elucidate how far a science which in fact only reflects and reproduces the manifest forms of the process, and therefore also how far these manifestations themselves, correspond to the basis on which the inner coherence, the actual physiology of bourgeois society rests or the basis which forms its starting-point; and in general, to examine how matters stand with the contradiction between the apparent and the actual movement of the system. This then is Ricardo's ||525| great historical significance for science. This is why the inane Say, Ricardo having cut the ground from right under his feet, gave vent to his anger in the phrase that "under the pretext of expanding it" (science) "it had been pushed into a vacuum".[66] Closely bound up with this scientific merit is the fact that Ricardo exposes and describes the economic contradiction between the classes—as shown by the intrinsic relations—and that consequently political economy perceives, discovers the root of the historical struggle and development. *Carey* (the passage to be looked up later) therefore denounces him as the father of communism.

"Mr. Ricardo's system is one of discords ... its whole tends to the production of *hostility among classes* and nations.... His book is the true manual of the demagogue, who seeks power by means of agrarianism, war, and plunder." (H. C. Carey, *The Past, the Present, and the Future*, Philadelphia, 1848, pp. 74-75.)

Thus it follows on the one hand that the Ricardian method of investigation is scientifically justified and has great historical value, on the other hand the scientific deficiencies of his procedure are clearly visible and will become more evident in what follows later.

Hence also the very peculiar and necessarily faulty architectonics of his work. The whole work consists of 32 chapters (in the third edition). Of this, 14 chapters deal with *taxes,* thus dealing only with the *application* of the theoretical principles.[67] The twentieth chapter, "Value and Riches, Their Distinctive Properties" is nothing but an examination of the difference between use-value and exchange-value, i.e., a supplement to the first chapter, "*On Value*". The twenty-fourth chapter "Doctrine of Adam Smith Concerning the Rent of Land", like the twenty-eighth chapter "On the Comparative Value of Gold, Corn and Labour..." and the thirty-second chapter "Mr. Malthus's Opinions on Rent" are mere supplements to, and in part a vindication of, Ricardo's rent theory, thus forming mere appendices to chapters II and III which deal with rent. The thirtieth chapter "On the Influence of Demand and Supply on Prices" is simply an appendix to the fourth chapter "On Natural and Market-Price." The nineteenth chapter, "On Sudden Changes in the Channels of Trade", forms a second appendix to this chapter. The thirty-first chapter, "On Machinery", is purely an appendix to the fifth and sixth chapters "On Wages" and "On Profits". The seventh chapter, "On Foreign Trade", and the twenty-fifth, "On Colonial Trade"—like the chapters on taxes—are mere applications of previously established principles. The twenty-first chapter "Effects of Accumulation on Profits and Interest" is an appendix to the chapters on rent, profits and wages. The twenty-sixth chapter "On Gross and Net Revenue" is an appendix to the chapters on wages, profits and rent. Finally, the twenty-seventh chapter "*On Currency and Banks*" stands quite apart from the rest of the work and merely consists of further explanations and in part modifications of views put forward in his earlier writings on money.

The Ricardian theory is therefore contained exclusively in the first six chapters of the work. It is in respect of this part of the work that I use the term faulty architectonics. The other part (with the exception of the section on money) consists of applications, elucidations and addenda which, by their very nature, are jumbled together and make no claim to being systematically arranged. But the faulty architectonics of the theoretical part (the first six chapters) is not accidental, rather it is the result of Ricardo's method of investigation itself and of the definite task which he set himself in his work. It expresses the scientific deficiencies of this method of investigation itself.

Chapter I is "*On Value*". It is subdivided into seven sections. The first section actually examines whether *wages contradict* the determination of the values of commodities by the labour-time they contain. In the third section Ricardo demonstrates that the entry of what I call constant capital into the value of the commodity does *not* contradict the determination of value and that the values of commodities are equally unaffected by the rise or fall in wages. The fourth section examines to what extent the determination of exchangeable values by labour-time is altered by the application of machinery and other fixed and durable capital, in so far as it enters into the total capital in varying proportions in different spheres of production. The fifth section examines how far a rise or fall in wages modifies the determination of values by labour-time, if capitals of unequal durability and varying periods of turnover are employed in different spheres of production. Thus one can see that in this first chapter not only are *commodities* assumed to exist—and when considering value as such, nothing further is required—but also wages, capital, profit, the general rate of profit and even, as we shall see, the various forms of capital as they arise from the process of circulation, and also the difference between "natural and market-price". This latter, moreover, plays a decisive role in the following chapters, Ch. II and Ch. III: "On Rent" and "On the Rent of Mines". In accordance with his method of investigation, the second chapter, *"On Rent"* ||526|—the third "On the Rent of Mines" is only a supplement to this—again opens with the question: Does landed property, and rent, *contradict* the determination of the value of commodities by labour-time?

This is how he opens the second chapter *"On Rent"*:

"It remains however to be considered, whether the appropriation of land, and the consequent creation of rent, will occasion any variation in the relative value of commodities, independently of the quantity of labour necessary to production" (*Principles of Political Economy*, third edition, London, 1821, p. 53).

In order to carry out this investigation, he introduces not only, *en passant,* the relationship of "market-price" and "real price" (monetary expression of value) but postulates the whole of capitalist production and his entire conception of the relationship between wages and profit. The fourth chapter "On Natural and Market-Price" and the fifth "On Wages" and the sixth "On Profits" are thus not only taken for granted, but fully developed in the first two chapters "On Value" and "On Rent" and in Chapter III as an appendix to II. The later three chapters, in so far as they bring any new *theoretical* points, fill in gaps here and there, and provide closer definitions, which for the most part should by rights have found their place in [chapters] I or II.

Thus the entire Ricardian contribution is contained in the first two chapters of his work. In these chapters, the developed relations of bourgeois production, and therefore also the developed categories of political economy, are confronted with their principle—the determination of value—and examined in order to determine the degree to which they directly correspond to this principle and the position regarding the apparent discrepancies which they introduce into the value relations of commodities. They contain the whole of his critique of hitherto existing political economy, the determined break with the contradiction that pervades Adam Smith's work with its esoteric and exoteric method of approach, and, at the same time, because of this critique, they produce some quite new and startling results. Hence the great theoretical satisfaction afforded by these first two chapters; for they provide with concise brevity a critique of the old, diffuse and meandering political economy, present the whole bourgeois system of economy as subject to one fundamental law, and extract the quintessence out of the divergency and diversity of the various phenomena. But this theoretical satisfaction afforded by these first two chapters because of their originality, unity of fundamental approach, simplicity, concentration, depth, novelty and comprehensiveness, is of necessity lost as the work proceeds. Here too, we are at times captivated by the originality of certain arguments. But as a whole, it gives rise to weariness and boredom. As the work proceeds, there is no further development. Where it does not consist of monotonous formal application of the same principles to various extraneous matters, or of polemical vindication of these principles, there is only repetition or amplification; at most one can occasionally find a striking chain of reasoning in the final sections.

In the critique of Ricardo, we have to separate what he himself failed to separate. [Firstly] his *theory of surplus-value,* which of course exists in his work, although he does not define *surplus-value* as distinct from its particular forms, profit, rent, interest. Secondly, his *theory of profit.* We shall begin with the latter, although it does not belong into this section, but into the historical appendix to *Section III.*[68]

[3. Ricardo's Confusion about the Question of "Absolute" and "Relative" Value. His Lack of Understanding of the Forms of Value]

Before we go on, just a few comments on how Ricardo confuses the definitions of "value". Bailey's polemic against him is based on this; it is however also important for us.

First of all Ricardo speaks of *"value in exchange"* (l. c., p. 1) and, like Adam Smith, defines it as *"the power of purchasing other goods"* (l.c., p. 1). This is exchange-value as it *appears* at first. Then, however, he proceeds to the real determination of value:

"It is the comparative quantity of commodities which labour will produce, that determines their present or past *relative value"* (l.c., p. 9).

"Relative value" here means nothing other than the exchangeable value as determined by labour-time. But *relative value* can also have another meaning, namely, if I express the exchange-value of a commodity in terms of the use-value of another, for instance the exchange-value of sugar in terms of the use-value of coffee.

"Two commodities vary in *relative value,* and we wish to know in which *the variation* has [...] taken place" (l.c., p. 9).

Which variation? Ricardo later also calls this "relative value" *"comparative value"* (p. 448 et seq.). We want to know in which commodity "the variation" has taken place. This means the variation of the "value" which was called "relative value" above. For instance, 1 pound of sugar equals 2 pounds of coffee. Later 1 pound of sugar equals 4 pounds of coffee. The "variation" which we want to know about is: whether the *"necessary labour-time"* has altered for sugar or for coffee, whether sugar costs twice as much labour-time as before or whether coffee costs half as much labour-time as before and which of these "variations" in the labour-time required for their respective production has called forth this variation in their *exchange relation.* This "relative or comparative value" of sugar and coffee—the ratio in which they exchange—is thus different from relative value in the first sense. In the first sense, the relative value of sugar is determined by the quantity of sugar which can be produced by a certain amount of labour-time ||527|. In the second case, the relative value of sugar [and coffee] expresses the ratio in which they are exchanged for one another and changes in this ratio can be the result of a change in the "relative value" in the first sense, in coffee or in sugar. The proportion in which they exchange for one another can remain *the same*, although their "relative values" in the first sense have altered. 1 lb. sugar can equal 2 lbs. coffee, as before, even though the labour-time for the production of sugar and of coffee has risen to double or has fallen to a half. *Variations* in their *comparative value*, that is, if the exchange-value of sugar is expressed in coffee, and vice versa, will only appear when the variations in their *relative value* in the first sense, i.e., the values determined by the quantity of labour, have *altered to a different extent*, when therefore *comparative* changes have occurred. Absolute changes, when they do not alter the original ratio, but are of equal magnitude and move in the same direction, will not call forth any variation in the comparative values—nor in the *money prices* of these commodities, since, if the value of money should change, it would do so equally for both [commodities]. Hence, whether the values of two commodities are expressed in their own reciprocal use-values or in their money price—representing both commodities in the form of the use-value of a third commodity—these *relative* or *comparative* values or prices are the same, and the changes in them must be distinguished from changes in their *relative values* in the first sense of the term, i.e., in so far as they only express the change in the labour-time required for their *own* production, and thus *realised in themselves*. The latter *relative value* thus appears as *"absolute value"* compared with relative values in the second sense, i.e., in the sense of actually representing the exchange-value of one commodity in terms of the use-value of the other or in money. That is why the term *"absolute value"* occurs in Ricardo's work, to denote "relative value" in the first sense.

If, in the above example, 1 lb. sugar costs the same amount of labour-time as before, then its "relative value" in the first sense has not altered. If, however, the labour cost of coffee has halved, then the value of sugar expressed in terms of coffee has altered, because the "relative value" of coffee, in the first sense, has altered. The relative values of sugar and coffee thus appear to be different from their "absolute values" and this difference becomes evident because the comparative value of sugar, for instance, has not altered in comparison with commodities whose absolute values have remained *unchanged*.

"The inquiry to which I wish to draw the reader's attention, relates to the effect of the *variations in the relative value of commodities*, and not in their *absolute value*" (l.c., p. 15).

At times Ricardo also calls this "absolute" value "real value" or simply *value* (for instance on p. 16).

See the whole of Bailey's polemic against Ricardo in:

A Critical Dissertation on the Nature, Measures and Causes of Value; chiefly in reference to the Writings of Mr. Ricardo and his Followers. By the Author of Essays on the Formation and Publication of Opinions, London, 1825. (See also his *A Letter to a Political Economist; occasioned by an article in the West-minster Review* etc., London, 1826.) [Bailey's polemic] partially revolves around these different instances of definitions of value, which are not explained by Ricardo but only occur de facto and are confused with one another, and Bailey sees in this only "contradictions". Secondly, [Bailey's polemic is directed] against "absolute value" or "real value" as distinct from *comparative value* (or relative value in the second sense).

In the first of the above-mentioned works, Bailey says:

"Instead of regarding value as a relation between two objects, they" (Ricardo and his followers) "consider it as a positive result produced by a definite quantity of labour." (Samuel Bailey, *A Critical Dissertation on the Nature, Measures and Causes of Value,* London, 1825, p. 30.)
They regard "value as something intrinsic and absolute" (l.c., p. 8).

The latter reproach arises from Ricardo's inadequate presentation, because he does not even examine the form of value—the particular form which labour assumes as the substance of value. He only examines the magnitudes of value, the quantities of this abstract, general and, in this form social, labour which engender differences in the *magnitudes of value* of commodities. Otherwise Bailey would have recognised that the relativity of the concept of value is by no means negated by the fact that all commodities, in so far as they are exchange-values, are only *relative* expressions of social labour-time and their relativity consists by no means solely of the ratio in which they exchange for one another, but of the ratio of all of them to this social labour which is their substance.

On the contrary, as we shall see, Ricardo is rather to be reproached for very often losing sight of this "real" or "absolute value" and only retaining "relative" and "comparative values".
||528| Thus:

[4.] Ricardo's Description of Profit, Rate of Profit, Average Prices etc.

[a) Ricardo's Confusion of Constant Capital with Fixed Capital and of Variable Capital with Circulating Capital. Erroneous Formulation of the Question of Variations in "Relative Values" and Their Causative Factors]

In Section III of the First Chapter Ricardo explains that the statement: the value of the commodity is determined by labour-time includes not only the labour directly employed on the commodity in the final labour process but also the labour-time contained in the raw material and the instruments of labour that are required for the production of the commodity. Thus it applies not only to the labour-time contained in the newly-added labour which has been bought, paid for by wages, but also to the labour-time contained in that part of the commodity which I call constant capital. Even the very heading of this Section III of Chapter I shows the deficiency of his exposition. It runs like that:

"Not only the labour applied immediately to commodities affect their value, but the labour also which is bestowed on the implements, tools, and buildings, with which such labour is assisted." (David Ricardo, *On the Principles of Political Economy, and Taxation*, third edition, London, 1821, p. 16.)

Raw material has been omitted here, yet the labour bestowed on raw material is surely just as different from "labour applied immediately to commodities" as the labour bestowed on "implements, tools and buildings". But Ricardo is already thinking of the next section. In Section III he assumes that *equal component parts of value* comprised in the instruments of labour employed enter into the production of the various commodities. In the next section he examines the modifications arising from the *varying proportions* in which fixed capital enters [into the commodities]. Hence Ricardo does not arrive at the concept of *constant capital,* one part of which consists of fixed capital and the other of circulating capital—raw material and auxiliary material—just as *circulating* capital not only includes variable capital but also raw material etc., and all means of subsistence which enter into *consumption in general,*[69] not only into the consumption of the workers.

The proportion in which constant capital enters into a commodity does not affect the *values* of the commodities, the relative quantities of labour contained in the commodities, but it does directly affect the different quantities of *surplus-value* or *sur-plus-labour* contained in commodities embodying equal amounts of labour-time. Hence this varying proportion gives rise to *average prices* that differ from values.

With regard to sections IV and V of Chapter I we have to note, first of all, that Ricardo does not examine a highly important matter which *directly* affects *the production of surplus-value,* namely, that in different spheres of production the same volume of capital contains different proportions of constant and variable capital. Instead, Ricardo concerns himself exclusively with the different forms of capital and the varying proportions in which the same capital assumes these various forms, in other words, [with] *different forms arising out of the process of the circulation of capital,* that is, fixed and circulating capital, capital which is fixed to a greater or lesser degree (i.e., fixed capital of varying durability) and unequal velocity of circulation or rates of turnover of capital. And the manner in which Ricardo carries out this investigation is the following: He presupposes *a general rate of profit* or an *average profit of equal magnitude* for different capital investments of equal magnitude, or for different spheres of production in which capitals of equal size are employed—or, which is the same thing, profit in proportion to the *size* of the capital employed in the various spheres of production. Instead of *postulating* this *general rate of profit,* Ricardo should rather have examined in how far its *existence* is in fact consistent with the determination of value by labour-time, and he would have found that instead of being consistent with it, *prima facie,* it *contradicts* it, and that its existence would therefore have to be explained through a number of intermediary stages, a procedure which is very different from merely including it under the law of value. He would then have gained an altogether different insight into the nature of profit and would not have identified it directly with surplus-value.

Having made *this presupposition* Ricardo then asks himself how will the rise or fall of wages affect the *"relative values",* when fixed and circulating capital are employed in different proportions? Or rather, *he imagines* that this is how he handles the question. In fact he deals with it quite differently, namely, as follows: He asks himself what effect the rise or fall of wages will have on the *respective profits* on capitals with different periods of turnover and containing different proportions of the various forms of capital. And here of course he finds that depending on the amount of fixed capital etc., a rise or fall of wages must have a very different effect on capitals, according to whether they contain a greater or lesser proportion of variable capital, i.e., capital which is laid out directly in wages. Thus in order to equalise again the profits in the different spheres of production ||529|, in other words, to re-establish the *general rate of profit*, the prices of the commodities—as distinct from their *values*—must be regulated in a different way. *Therefore,* he further concludes, these differences affect the "relative values" when wages rise or fall. He should have said on the contrary: Although these differences have nothing to do with the values as such, they do, through their varying effects on profits in the different spheres, give rise to average prices or, as we shall call them *cost-prices* which are different from the values themselves and are not directly determined by the values of the commodities but by the capital advanced for their production plus the average profit. Hence he should have said: These average *cost-prices* are different from the *values* of the commodities. Instead, he concludes that they are *identical* and with this *erroneous* premise he goes on to the consideration of rent.

Ricardo is also mistaken when he thinks that it is only [through] the three cases he examines that he discovers the "variations" in the "relative values" that occur independently of the labour-time contained in the commodities, that is in fact the difference between the cost-prices and the values of the commodities. He has already *assumed* this *difference,* in postulating a *general rate of profit*, thus presupposing that despite the varying ratios of the organic component parts of capitals, these yield a profit proportional to their *size*, whereas the surplus-value they yield is determined absolutely by the quantity of unpaid labour-time they absorb, and with a given wage this is entirely dependent on the volume of that part of capital which is laid out in wages, and not on the absolute size of the capital.

What he does in fact examine is this: supposing that cost-prices *differ* from the values of commodities—and the assumption of a *general rate of profit* presupposes this difference—how in turn are these cost-prices (which are now, for a change, called "relative values") themselves reciprocally modified, proportionately modified by the rise or fall of wages, taking also into account the varying proportions of the organic component parts of capital? If Ricardo had gone into this more deeply, he would have found that—owing to the diversity in the organic composition of capital which first manifests itself in the immediate production process as the difference between variable and constant capital and is later enlarged by differences arising from the circulation process—the mere existence of a *general rate of profit* necessitates *cost-prices* that differ from *values.* He would have found that, even if *wages* are assumed to *remain constant,* the difference exists and therefore is *quite independent* of the rise or fall in wages, thus he would have arrived at a new definition. He would also have seen how incomparably more important and decisive the understanding of this difference is for the whole theory, than his observations on the variation in *cost-prices* of commodities brought about by the rise or fall of wages. The result with which he contents himself—and that he is content accords with the whole manner in which he carries out his investigation—is as follows: Once the *variations in the cost-prices* (or, as he says, "relative values") of the commodities—in so far as they are due to changes, rises or falls, in wages when capital of different organic composition is invested in different spheres— are admitted and taken into consideration the law remains valid; that "the relative values" of the commodities are determined by labour-time does not *contradict* the law; for all other changes— changes that are not merely transitory—in the cost-prices of the commodities can only be explained by a change in the necessary labour-time required for their respective production.

On the other hand, it must be regarded as a great merit that Ricardo associates the differences in fixed and circulating capital with the varying periods of turnover of capital and that he deduces all these differences from the varying periods of *circulation,* i.e., in fact from the *circulation* or *reproduction period of capital.*

First of all, let us consider these differences themselves, as he presents them in Section IV (Chapter I) and then examine his views on how they act or bring about variations in the "relative values".

1. "In every state of society, the tools, implements, buildings, and machinery employed in different trades may be of *various degrees of durability,* and may require *different portions of labour to produce them*" (l.c., p. 25).

So far as the "different portions of labour to produce them" are concerned, this can imply—and here it seems to be Ricardo's sole point—that the less durable ones require *more* labour (recurring, directly applied labour), partly for their repair and partly for their reproduction; or it can also mean that machinery etc. of *the same degree of durability* may be more or less expensive, the product of more or less labour. This latter aspect, important for the proportion of variable to constant capital, is not relevant to Ricardo's consideration and therefore he does not take it up anywhere as a separate point.

||530| 2. "The proportions, too, in which the capital that is to support labour" (the variable capital), "and the capital that is invested in tools, machinery, and buildings" (fixed capital), "may be *variously combined*". Thus we have a "difference in the *degree of durability of fixed capital*, and this variety in the proportions in which *the two sorts of capital may be combined*" (l.c., p. 25).

It is at once evident why he is not interested in that part of constant capital which exists as raw material. The latter is itself part of circulating capital. A rise in wages does not cause *increased expenditure* on that part of capital which consists of machinery and does not need *to be replaced* but remains available; the rise, however, causes an increased outlay for that part which consists of *raw material*, since this has to be constantly replenished, hence also constantly reproduced.

"The food and clothing consumed by the labourer, the buildings in which he works, the implements with which his labour is assisted, are all of a *perishable nature*. There is however a vast difference in the time for which these different capitals will endure.... According as capital is rapidly perishable, and requires *to be frequently reproduced*, or is of slow consumption, it is classed under the heads of circulating, or of fixed capital" (l.c., p. 26).

Thus the difference between fixed and circulating capital is here reduced to the difference in the *time of reproduction* (which coincides with the period of circulation).

3. "It is also to be observed that the *circulating* capital may *circulate*, or be *returned to its employer*, in *very unequal times*. The *wheat bought by a farmer to sow** is comparatively a fixed capital to the wheat purchased by a baker to make into loaves. One leaves it in the ground, and can obtain no return for a year; the other can get it ground into flour, sell it as bread to his customers and have his capital free to renew the same, or commence any other employment in a week" (l.c., pp. 26-27).

On what does *this* difference in the circulation periods of different circulating capitals depend? [On the fact] that in one case, the same capital remains for a longer time in the *actual sphere of production*, though the *labour-process* does not continue. This applies, for instance, to wine which lies in the cellar to attain maturity, or to certain chemical processes in tanning, dyeing etc.

---

* Here Herr Rodbertus can see that in England seeds are "bought".

"Two trades then may employ *the same amount of capital*; but it may be very differently divided with respect to the portion which is fixed, and that which is circulating." (l.c., p. 27.)

4. "Again two manufacturers may employ the same amount of fixed, and the same amount of circulating capital; but the *durability of their fixed capitals*" (therefore also their period of reproduction) "may be very unequal. One may have steam-engines of the value of £10,000, the other, ships of the same value" (l.c., pp. 27-28).

"Different degrees of durability of ... capitals, or, which is the same thing ... *of the time which must elapse* before one set of commodities can be brought to market" (l.c., p. 30).

5. "It is hardly necessary to say, that commodities which have *the same quantity of labour bestowed on*[a] *their production,* will differ in exchangeable value, if they cannot be brought *to market in the same time*" (l.c., p. 34).

[Thus we have:] 1. A difference in the proportion of fixed to circulating capital. 2. A difference in the period of turnover of *circulating* capital as a result of a break in the labour-process while the production process continues. 3. A difference in the *durability* of fixed capital. 4. A difference in the relative period during which a commodity is altogether subjected to the labour-process (without any break in the labour-process or without any difference between production period and labour period[70]) before it can enter the actual circulation process. The last case is described by Ricardo as follows:

"Suppose I employ twenty men at an expense of £1,000 for a year in the production of a commodity, and at the end of the year I employ twenty men again for another year, at a further expense of £1,000 in finishing or perfecting the same commodity, and that I bring it to market at the end of two years, if *profits be 10 per cent,* my commodity must sell for £2,310; for I have employed £1,000 capital for one year, and £2,100 capital for one year more. Another man employs precisely the same quantity of labour, but he employs it all in the first year; he employs forty men at an expense of £2,000, and at the end of the first year he sells it with 10 per cent profit, or for £2,200. Here then are two commodities *having precisely the same quantity of labour bestowed on them,* one of which sells for £2,310—the other for £2,200" (l.c., p. 34).

||531| But how is a change in the *relative values* of these commodities brought about by this difference—whether in the degree of durability of fixed capital, or in the period of turnover of circulating capital, or in the proportions in which the two sorts of capital may be combined or, finally, in the time required by different commodities upon which the same quantity of labour is bestowed [to come on to the market]. Ricardo says in the first place, that

---

[a] In the manuscript: "upon".—*Ed.*

"*This difference* ... and [...] *variety in the proportions*" etc. "*introduce another cause*, besides the greater or less quantity of labour necessary to produce commodities, for the variations in their relative value—*this cause is the rise or fall in the value of labour*" (l.c., pp. 25-26).

And how is this proved?

"A rise in the wages of labour cannot fail to affect unequally, *commodities* produced under such different circumstances" (l.c., p. 27).

Namely when capitals of *equal size* are employed in *different* industries, and one capital consists chiefly of fixed capital and contains only a small amount of capital "employed in the support of labour" (l.c., p. 27), whereas in the other capital the proportions are exactly the reverse. To begin with, it is nonsense to say that the "commodities" are affected. He means their *values*. But how far are the values affected by these circumstances? Not at all. In both cases it is the profit which is affected. The man who, for instance, lays out only $1/5$ of his capital in variable capital—provided wages and the rate of surplus-labour are constant—can only produce [a surplus-value of] 4 on 100, if the rate of surplus-value is 20 per cent. On the other hand, another man, who lays out $4/5$ in variable capital would produce a surplus-value of 16 [on 100]. For in the first example the capital laid out in wages is $100/5 = 20$ and $1/5$ of 20 or 20 per cent is 4. And in the second example, the capital laid out in wages equals $4/5 \times 100 = 80$. And $1/5$ of 80 or 20 per cent $= 16$. In the first example the profit would be 4, in the second 16. The average profit for both would be $\frac{16+4}{2}$ or $20/2 = 10$ per cent. This is actually the case to which Ricardo refers. Thus if they both sold at cost-prices—and this Ricardo *assumes*—then they would each sell their commodity at 110. Supposing wages rose, for example, by 20 per cent. Where previously a worker cost £ 1, he now costs £ 1 4s. or 24s. As before, the first [man] still has to lay out £80 in constant capital (since Ricardo leaves raw materials out of account here, we can do the same) and for the 20 workers whom he employs, he has to lay out 80s. that is £ 4 in addition to the £ 20. His capital therefore now amounts to £ 104 and, since the workers are producing a smaller surplus-value instead of a larger one, he is only left with £ 6 profit out of his £ 110. £ 6 on £104 is $5^{10}/13$ per cent. The other man, however, who employs 80 workers, would have to pay out an additional 320s., i.e., £ 16. Thus he would have to lay out £ 116. If he were to sell at £ 110, he would consequently make a loss of £ 6 instead of a gain. This, however,

12*

is only the case because the average profit has already modified
the relation between the labour he has laid out and the surplus-
value which he himself produces.

Instead therefore of investigating the important problem: what
changes have to take place in order that the one who lays out
£80 of his capital of 100 in wages does not make four times as
much profit as the other who only lays out 20 of his £100 in
wages, Ricardo examines the subsidiary question of how it is
that after this great difference has been levelled out, i.e., with a
given rate of profit, any alteration of the rate of profit, due to
rising wages for instance, would affect the man who employs
many workers with his £100 far more than the man who employs
few workers with his £100, and hence—provided the rate of
profit is the same—the commodity prices of the one must rise
and of the other must fall, if the rate of profit—or the *cost-prices*
—is to remain the same.

Ricardo's first illustration has absolutely nothing to do with
"*a rise in the value of labour*" although he originally stated that
the whole of the variation in "the relative values" were to arise
from this cause. This is the example:

"Suppose two men employ one hundred men each for a year in the
construction of two machines, and another man employs the same number
of men in cultivating corn, each of the machines at the end of the year will
be of the same value as the corn, for they will each be produced by the
same quantity of labour. Suppose one of the owners of one of the machines
to employ it, with the assistance of one hundred men, the following year
in making cloth, and the owner of the other machine to employ his also,
with the assistance likewise of one hundred men, in making cotton goods,
while the farmer continues to employ one hundred men as before in the
cultivation of corn. During the second year they will all have employed the
same quantity of labour"

⟨in other words they will have laid out the same capital in
wages, but they will by no means have employed *the same
quantity of labour*⟩

"but the goods and machine together ||532| of the clothier, and also of the·
cotton manufacturer, will be the result of the labour of two hundred men,
employed for a year; or, rather, of the labour of one hundred men for two
years; whereas the corn will be produced by the labour of one hundred men
for one year, consequently if the corn be of the value of £500 the machine
and cloth of the clothier together, ought to be of the value of £1,000 and the
machine and cotton goods of the cotton manufacturer, *ought to be also of
twice the value of the corn. But they will be of more than twice the value of
the corn,* for *the profit of the clothier's and cotton manufacturer's capital
for the first year has been added to their capitals,* while that of the farmer
has been expended and enjoyed. On account then *of the different degrees*

of durability of their capitals, or, which is the same thing, on *account of the time which must elapse* before one set of commodities can be brought to market, they will be valuable, not exactly in *proportion to the quantity of labour bestowed on them,*—they will not be as two to one, but something more, *to compensate for the greater length of time which must elapse before the most valuable can be brought to market.* Suppose that for the labour of each workman £50 per annum were paid, or that £5,000 capital were employed and *profits were 10 per cent,* the value of each of the machines as well as of the corn, at the end of the first year, would be £ 5,500. The second year the manufacturers and farmers will again employ £5,000 each in support of labour, and will therefore again sell their goods for £5,500; but the men using the machines, to *be on a par with the farmer,* must not only obtain £5,500, for the equal capitals of £5,000 employed on labour, but they must obtain a further *sum of £550; for the profit on £5,500, which they have invested in machinery,* and *consequently*" (because actually, *an equal annual rate of profit of 10 per cent is assumed* as a necessity and a law) "their goods must *sell for £6,050*" [l.c., pp. 29-30].

⟨That is, *average prices* or *cost-prices different* from the values of the commodities come into being as a result of the average profit—the *general rate of profit presupposed* by Ricardo.⟩

"Here then are capitalists employing precisely the *same quantity of labour annually* on the production of their commodities, and yet *the goods they produce differ in value on account of the different quantities of fixed capital,* or accumulated labour, employed by each respectively" [l.c., pp. 30-31].

⟨Not on account of that, but on account of both those ragamuffins having the fixed idea that both of them must draw the same spoils from "the support they have given to labour"; or that, whatever the respective *values* of their commodities, those commodities must be sold at *average prices,* giving each of them the same rate of profit.⟩[a]

"The cloth and cotton goods are of the same value, because they are the produce of equal quantities of labour, and equal quantities of fixed capital; but corn is not of the *same value*" ⟨should read cost-price⟩ "as these commodities, *because it is produced, as far as regards fixed capital, under different circumstances*" (l.c., p. 31).

This exceedingly clumsy illustration of an exceedingly simple matter is so complicated in order to avoid saying simply: Since capitals of equal size, whatever the ratio of their organic components or their period of circulation, yield *profits of equal size* —which would be impossible if the commodities were sold at *their values etc.*—there exist *cost-prices* which differ from the values of commodities. And this is indeed implied in the concept of a *general rate of profit.*

---

[a] Marx wrote this paragraph in English.—*Ed.*

Let us examine this complicated example and reduce it to its genuine dimensions, which are hardly "complicated". And for this purpose let us begin from the end and note at the outset, in order to reach a clearer understanding, that Ricardo "presupposes" that the farmer and the cotton manufacturer spend nothing on raw material, that, furthermore, the farmer does not lay out any capital for instruments of labour and, finally, that no part of the fixed capital laid out by the cotton-manufacturer enters into his product as wear and tear. Though all these assumptions are absurd, they do not in themselves affect the illustration.

Having made these assumptions, and starting Ricardo's example from the end, it runs as follows: The farmer lays out £5,000 in wages; the cotton fellow lays out £5,000 in wages and £5,500 in machinery. The first therefore spends £5,000 and the second £10,500; the second ||533| thus spends as much again as the first. If therefore both are to make a profit of 10 per cent, the farmer must sell his commodity at £ 5,500 and the cotton fellow his at £6,050 (since it has been assumed that no part of the £5,500 expended in machinery forms part of the value of the product as wear and tear). One absolutely cannot conceive what Ricardo intended to elucidate in this example, apart from the fact that the cost-prices of commodities—in so far as they are determined by the value of the outlay embodied in the commodities plus the same annual rate of profit—*differ* from the values of the commodities and that this difference arises because the commodities are sold at prices that will yield the *same rate of profit* on the capital advanced; in short, that this difference between *cost-prices* and *values* is identical with a *general rate of profit*. Even the difference between fixed capital and circulating capital which he introduces here is, in this example, sheer humbug. Since if, for instance, the additional £5,500 which the cotton spinner employs, consisted of raw materials, while the farmer did not require any seeds etc., the result would be exactly the same. Neither does the example show, as Ricardo asserts, that

"the goods they" (the cotton-manufacturer and the farmer) "produce differ in value *on account of the different quantities of fixed capital*, or accumulated labour, employed by each respectively" (l.c., p. 31).

For according to his assumption, the cotton-manufacturer employs a fixed capital of £5,500 and the farmer nil; the one employs fixed capital, the other does not. By no means do they, therefore, employ it "in different quantities", any more than one could say that, if one person eats meat and the other eats no meat, they consume meat "in different quantities". On the other hand it is correct (though very wrong to introduce the term surreptitiously with an "or") that they employ "accumulated labour", i.e., materialised labour, "in different quantities", namely, one to the amount of £10,500 and the other only £5,000. However, the fact that they employ "different quantities of accumulated labour" only means that they lay out "different quantities of capital" in their respective trades, that the amount of profit is proportionate to this difference in the size of the capitals they employ, because *the same rate of profit* is assumed, and that, finally, this difference in the amount of profit, proportionate to the size of the capitals, is expressed, represented, in the respective cost-prices of the commodities. But whence the clumsiness in Ricardo's illustration?

"Here then are capitalists employing precisely the *same quantity of labour annually* on the production of their commodities, and yet the goods they produce differ in value" (l.c., pp. 30-31).

This means that they do not employ the same quantity of labour—immediate and accumulated labour taken together—but they do employ the same quantity of variable capital, capital laid out in wages, the same quantity of living labour. And since money exchanges for accumulated labour, i.e., existing commodities, in the form of machines etc., only according to the law of commodities, since *surplus-value* comes into being only as the result of the appropriation without payment of a part of the living labour employed—it is clear (since, according to the assumption, no part of the machinery enters into the commodity as wear and tear) that both can only make the same profit if profit and surplus-value are identical. The cotton-manufacturer would have to sell his commodity for £5,500, like the farmer, although he lays out more than twice as much capital. And even if the whole of his machinery passed into the commodity, he could only sell his commodity for £11,000; he would make a profit of less than 5 per cent, while the farmer makes 10. But with these *unequal* profits, the farmer and the manufacturer would have sold the commodities at their *values,* provided that the 10 per cent made by the farmer represented actual unpaid labour embodied in his commodity. If therefore, they sell their commodities at an equal profit, then this must be due to one of two things: either the manufacturer arbitrarily adds 5 per cent

on to his commodities and then the commodities of the manufacturer and the farmer, taken together, are sold *above* their
value; or the actual surplus-value which the farmer makes is,
for instance, 15 per cent and both add the average of 10 per cent
on to their commodity. In this case, although the cost price of
the respective commodity is either above or below its value, both
commodities *taken together* are *sold at their value* and the equalisation of the profits is itself determined by the total surplus-
values they contain. Here, in Ricardo's above proposition, when
correctly modified, lies the truth, [namely] that capitals of equal
size, containing [different] proportions of variable to constant
capital, must result in commodities of unequal values and thus
yield different profit; the levelling out of these profits must therefore result in *cost-prices* which *differ* from the values of the
commodities.

"Here then are capitalists employing precisely the same quantity of" (immediate, living) "labour annually on the production
of the commodities, and yet the goods they produce differ in
value" (i.e., have cost-prices different from their values) "on
account of the different quantities of ... accumulated labour
employed by each respectively" [l.c., pp. 30-31.]

But the idea foreshadowed in this passage is never clearly
stated by Ricardo. It only explains the meanderings and obvious
fallaciousness of the illustration, which up to this point had
nothing to do with the "different quantities of *fixed capital*
employed".

Let us now go further back in the analysis. In the first year,
the manufacturer builds a machine with a hundred men; the
farmer, meanwhile, produces corn, also with a hundred men. In
the second year the manufacturer uses the machine to manufacture cotton, for which he again employs a hundred men. The
farmer, on the other hand, again employs a hundred men for the
cultivation of corn. Suppose, says Ricardo, the value of corn is
£500 per annum. Let us assume that the unpaid labour contained
therein equals 25 per cent [of the labour paid for], i.e., [of]
400 = 100. Then at the end of the first year, the machine would
also be worth £500, of which £400 would be paid labour and
£100 the value of the unpaid labour. Let us ||534| assume that
by the end of the second year, the whole of the machine has been
used up, has passed into the value of the cotton. In fact Ricardo
assumes this, in that, at the end of the second year, he compares
not only the value of the cotton goods, but "the value of the

cotton goods and the machine" with "the value of the corn" [l.c., p. 29].

Well then. At the end of the second year, the value of the cottons must be equal to £1,000, namely, £500 the value of the machine, and £500 the value of the newly-added labour. The value of the corn, on the other hand, is £500, namely, £400 the value of the wages and £100 unpaid labour. So far, there is nothing in this case which *contradicts the law of value*. The cotton-manufacturer makes a profit of 25 per cent just as the corn-manufacturer does. But the commodities of the former equal £1,000 and those of the latter equal £500, because the former commodity embodies the labour of 200 men and the latter the labour of only 100 in each year. Furthermore, the £100 profit (surplus-value), which the cotton-manufacturer has made on the machine in the first year—by absorbing $1/5$ of the labour of the workers who constructed it, without paying for it—are only realised for him in the second year, since it is only then that he realises in the value of the cotton, simultaneously the value of the machine. But now we come to the point. The cotton-manufacturer sells for more than £1,000, i.e., at a higher value than his commodity has, while the farmer sells his corn at £500, thus, according to our assumption, at its value. If, therefore, there were only these two people to exchange with one another, the manufacturer obtaining corn from the farmer and the farmer cotton from the manufacturer, then it would amount to the same as if the farmer sold his commodity *below* its value, making less than 25 per cent [profit] and the manufacturer sold his cotton *above* its value. Let us do without the two capitalists (the clothman and the cotton-man) whom Ricardo introduces here quite superfluously, and let us modify his example by only referring to the cotton-manufacturer. Ricardo's double calculation is of no value at all to the illustration at this point. Thus:

"But they" (the cottons) "*will be of more than twice the value of the corn*, for the *profit* on the ... *cotton-manufacturer's capital for the first year* has been added to their capitals, while that of the farmer has been expended and enjoyed" [l.c., p. 30].

(This latter bourgeois extenuating phrase is here quite meaningless from a theoretical standpoint. Moral considerations have nothing to do with the matter.)

"*On account then of the different degrees of durability of their capitals, or*, which is the same thing, on *account of the time which must elapse before one set of commodities can be brought to market*, they will be valuable, not exactly in proportion to the quantity of labour bestowed on them,—they will not be as two to one, but something more, to *compensate for the greater length of time which must elapse before the most valuable can be brought to market*" (l.c., p. 30).

If the manufacturer sold the commodity at its value, then he would sell it at £1,000, twice the price of corn, because it embodies twice as much labour, £500 of accumulated labour in the machinery (£100 of which he has not paid for) and £500 labour employed in the production of cotton, 100 of which again he has not paid for. But he calculates like this: the first year I laid out £400 and by exploiting the workers, I produced a machine with this, which is worth £500. I thus made a profit of 25 per cent. The second year I laid out £900, namely, £500 in the said machine and again £400 in labour. If I am again to make 25 per cent, I must sell the cotton at £1,125, i.e., £125 *above* its value. For this £125 does not represent any labour contained in the cotton, neither labour accumulated in the first year nor labour added in the second. The aggregate amount of labour contained in the cotton only amounts to £1,000. On the other hand, suppose the two exchange with one another, or that half the capitalists find themselves in the position of the cotton-manufacturer and the other half in the position of the farmer. How are the first half to be paid £ 125? *From what fund? Obviously only from the second half. But then it is clear* that this second half does not make a profit of 25 per cent. Thus the first half would cheat the second under the pretext of a *general rate of profit*, while, in fact, the rate of profit would be 25 per cent for the manufacturer and below 25 per cent for the farmer. It must, therefore, come about in a different way.

In order to make the illustration clearer and more accurate, let us suppose the farmer uses £900 in the second year. Then, with a profit of 25 per cent, he has made £100 on the £400 laid out in the *first year*, and £225 in the second, altogether £325. As against this, the manufacturer makes 25 per cent on the £400 in the first year, but in the second only £100 on £900, i.e., only $11^1/_9$ per cent (since only the £400 laid out in labour yield surplus-value, whereas the £500 in machinery yield none). Or let us suppose the farmer lays out £400 again, then he has made 25 per cent in the first year as well as in the second; which taken together is 25 per cent or £200 on an outlay of £800 in two years. As against this, the manufacturer will have made 25 per cent in the first year and $11^1/_9$ in the second; i.e., £200 on an outlay of £1,300 in two years which amounts to $15^5/_{13}$ per cent. If this were levelled out, the manufacturer would receive $20^5/_{26}$ per cent and so would the farmer.[71] In other words, this would be the average profit. This would result in [a price of] less than £500 for the farmer's commodity and more than £1,000 for the manufacturer's commodity.

||535| At all events, the manufacturer here lays out £400 in the first year and £900 in the second, while the farmer lays out only £400 on each occasion. If the manufacturer instead of producing cotton had built a house (if he were a builder) then at the end of the first year, the unfinished house would embody £500 and he would have to spend a further £400 on labour in order to complete it. The farmer, however, whose capital turned over within the year, can recapitalise a part, say 50, of his £100 profit and spend it again on labour, which the manufacturer, in the supposed case, cannot do. If the rate of profit is to be *the same* in both cases, then the commodity of one must be sold *above* its value and that of the other *below* its value. Since competition strives to level out values into cost-prices, this is what happens.

But it is incorrect to say, as Ricardo does, that here a variation in the relative values takes place "on account of the different degrees of durability of capitals" (p. 30) or "on account of the time which must elapse before one set of commodities can be brought to market" (p. 30). It is, rather, the adoption of a *general rate of profit,* which despite the different values brought about by the circulation process, gives rise to equal *cost-prices* which are *different* from values, for values are determined only by labour-time.

Ricardo's illustration consists of two examples. The *durability* of capital, or the character of capital as fixed capital, does not enter into the second example at all. It only deals with capitals of different size, but of which the same amount is laid out in wages, as variable capital, and where profits are to be equal, although the surplus-values and values must be different.

Neither does *durability* enter into the first example. It is concerned with the *longer labour-process*—the longer period during which the commodity has to remain within the sphere of production, before it *becomes a finished commodity* and can enter into circulation. In this example of Ricardo the manufacturer also employs more capital in the second year than the farmer although he employs the same amount of variable capital in both years. The farmer, however, could employ a greater variable capital in the second year, because his commodity remains within the labour-process for a shorter period and is converted more quickly into money. Besides, that part of profit which is consumed as revenue, is already available to the farmer at the end of the first year, but to the manufacturer only at the end of the second. The latter must therefore spend an additional amount of capital for his keep which he *advances* to himself. Incidentally, whether in the second case a compensation can take place and profits can be *equalised* depends here entirely on the degree to which the profits of the capitals which are turned over in one year are recapitalised, in other words, on the actual amount of profits produced. Where there is nothing, there is nothing to equalise. Here the capitals again produce values, hence surplus-values, hence profits not in proportion to the size of the capital. If profits are to be proportionate to their size, then there must be *cost-prices* different from the values.

Ricardo gives a third illustration, which, however, is again *exactly* the same as the first example of the first illustration and contains nothing new at all.

> "Suppose I employ twenty men at an expense of £1,000 for a year in the production of a commodity, and at the end of the year I employ twenty men again for another year, at a further expense of £1,000 in finishing or perfecting the same commodity, and that I bring it to market at the end of two years, if profits be 10 per cent, my commodity must sell for £2,310; *for* I have employed £1,000 capital for one year, and £2,100 capital for one year more. Another man employs precisely the same quantity of labour, but he employs it all in the first year; he employs forty men at an expense of £2,000, and at the end of the first year he sells it with 10 per cent *profit*, or for £2,200. Here then are two commodities having precisely the same quantity of labour bestowed on them, one of which sells for £2,310—the other for £2,200. This case *appears* to differ from the last, but is, *in fact*, the same" (l.c., pp. 34-35).

It is not only the same "in fact", but "in appearance" too, except that in the one case the commodity is called "machine" and here simply "commodity". In the first example, the manufacturer laid out £400 in the first year and £900 in the second. This time he lays out £1,000 in the first and £2,100 in the second. The farmer laid out £400 in the first year and £400 in the second. This time, the second man lays out £2,000 in the first year and nothing in the second. That is the whole difference. In both cases, however, the fable turns on the fact that one of the men lays out in the second year the whole of the product of the first (including surplus-value) plus an additional sum.

The clumsiness of these examples shows that Ricardo is wrestling with a difficulty which he does not understand and succeeds even less in overcoming. The clumsiness consists in this: The first example of the first illustration is meant to bring in the *durability* of capital; it does nothing of the sort; Ricardo himself has made this *impossible* because he does not let any part of fixed capital enter into the commodity as wear and tear, thus excluding the very factor through which the *peculiar mode of circulation of fixed capital* becomes evident. He merely demonstrates that as a consequence of the longer duration of the labour-process, a *greater* capital is employed than where the labour-process takes a shorter time. The third example is supposed to illustrate something different, but in reality illustrates the same thing. The *second example* of the first ||536| illustration, however, is intended to show what differences arise as a result of different ratios of fixed capital. Instead it only shows the difference brought about by two capitals of *unequal* size, although the same amount of capital is laid out in wages. And, furthermore, the manufacturer operates without cotton and yarn and the farmer without seeds or implements! The complete inconsistency, even absurdity, of this illustration necessarily arises from this underlying lack of clarity.

[b) Ricardo's Confusion of Cost-Prices with Value and the Contradictions in His Theory of Value Arising Therefrom. His Lack of Understanding of the Process of Equalisation of the Rate of Profit and of the Transformation of Values into Cost-Prices]

Finally he states the practical conclusions to be drawn from all these illustrations:

"The difference in value arises in both cases from the *profits* being accumulated as capital, and is only a *just compensation*" (as though it were a question of justice here) "*for the time that the profits were withheld*" (l.c., p. 35).

What does this mean, other than that in *a definite period of circulation, for instance a year,* a capital must yield 10 per cent whatever its specific period of circulation may be and quite independently of the *various surplus-values* which according to the proportion of their organic component parts *capitals of equal size* must produce in different branches of production, irrespective of the circulation process.

Ricardo should have drawn the following conclusions:

[*Firstly:*] Capitals of equal size produce commodities of un-equal *values* and therefore yield *unequal surplus-values* or *profits*, because value is determined by labour-time, and the amount of labour-time realised by a capital does not depend on its absolute size but on the size of the variable capital, the capital laid out in wages. *Secondly:* Even assuming that capitals of equal size produce *equal values* (although the inequality in the sphere of production usually coincides with that in the sphere of circula-tion), the *period* within which they *appropriate equal quantities of unpaid labour* and *convert* these *into money*, still varies in accordance with their *turnover period*. Thus arises a second dif-ference in the values, surplus-values and profits which capitals of *equal size* must yield in different branches of production in a given *period of time*.

Hence, if *profits* as a percentage of capital are to be equal over a period, say of a year, so that capitals of equal size yield equal profits in the same period of time, then the *prices* of the com-modities must be different from their *values*. The sum total of these *cost-prices* of all the commodities taken together will *be equal to their value*. Similarly the total profit will be equal to the total surplus-value which all these capitals yield, for instance, during one year. If one did not take the definition of value as the basis, the *average profit*, and therefore also the cost-prices, would be purely imaginary and untenable. The equalisation of the surplus-values in different spheres of production does not affect the absolute size of this total surplus-value; but merely alters its *distribution* among the different spheres of production. The *determination of this surplus-value* itself, however, only arises out of the determination of value by labour-time. Without this, the average profit is the average *of nothing*, pure fancy. And it could then equally well be 1,000 per cent or 10 per cent.

All Ricardo's illustrations only serve him as a means to smug-gle in the *presupposition of a general rate of profit*. And this happens in the first chapter "On Value", while wages are sup-posed to be dealt with only in the fifth chapter and profits in the sixth. How from the mere determination of the "*value*" of the commodities their surplus-value, the profit and even a *general rate of profit* are derived remains obscure with Ricardo. In fact the only thing which he proves in the above illustrations is that the *prices* of the commodities, in so far as they are determined by the general rate of profit, are entirely different from their *values.* And he arrives at this difference by postulating the *rate of profit* to be law. One can see that though Ricardo is accused of being too abstract, one would be justified in accusing him of the opposite: lack of the power of abstraction, inability, when dealing with the values of commodities, to forget profits, a factor which confronts him as a result of competition.

Because Ricardo, instead of deriving the difference between cost-prices and values from the determination of value itself, admits that "values" themselves (here it would have been appropriate to define the concept of "absolute" or "real value" or "value" as such) are determined by influences that are independent of labour-time and that the law of value is sporadically invalidated by these influences, this was used by his opponents, such as Malthus, in order to attack his whole ||537| theory of value. Malthus correctly remarks that the differences between the organic component parts of capital and the turnover periods of capitals in different branches of production develop simultaneously with the progress of production, so that one would arrive at Adam Smith's standpoint, that the determination of value by labour-time was no longer applicable to "civilised" times. (See also *Torrens.*) On the other hand his disciples have resorted to the most pitiful scholastic inventions, to make these phenomena consistent with the fundamental principle (see [*James*] *Mill* and the miserable *McCulloch*).[72]

Ricardo *does not dwell on the conclusion which follows from his own illustrations,* namely, that—*quite apart* from the rise or fall of wages—on the assumption of constant wages, the cost-prices of commodities must differ from their values, if cost-prices are determined by the same percentage of profit. But he passes on, in this section, to the influence which the rise or fall of wages exerts on *cost-prices* to which the values have already been levelled out.

The matter is in itself extraordinarily simple.

The farmer lays out £5,000 at 10 per cent; his commodity equals £5,500. If the profit falls by 1 per cent from 10 to 9, because wages have risen and the rise in wages has brought about this reduction, then he continues to sell at £5,500 (since it is assumed that he lays out the whole of his capital in wages). But of these £5,500 only £454$^{14}/_{109}$ belong to him and not £500. The capital of the manufacturer consists of £5,500 for machinery and £5,000 for labour. As before, the latter £5,000 results in a product of £ 5,500, except that now the manufacturer does not lay out

£5,000 but £5,045$^{95}/_{109}$ and on this he makes a profit of only £454$^{14}/_{109}$, like the farmer. On the other hand he can no longer reckon 10 per cent or £550 on his fixed capital of £5,500 but only 9 per cent or £ 495. He will therefore sell his commodity at £5,995 instead of at £6,050. Thus, as a result of the rise in wages, the money price of the farmer's commodity has remained the same, while that of the manufacturer has fallen, the value of the farmer's commodity compared with that of the manufacturer has therefore risen. The whole point of the matter is that if the manufacturer sold his commodity at the same value as before, he would make a higher profit than the average, because only the part of his capital that has been laid out in wages is directly affected by the rise in wages. This illustration in itself already *assumes* cost-prices regulated by an average profit of 10 per cent and *differing from the values of the commodities*. The question is, how are these cost-prices affected by the rise or fall in profit, when the capitals employed contain different proportion of fixed and circulating capital. This illustration (Ricardo, l.c., pp. 31-32) has nothing to do with the essential question of the *transformation of values into cost-prices*. But it is a nice point because Ricardo in fact demonstrates here that, if the composition of the capitals were the same, a rise in wages—contrary to the vulgar view—would only bring about a lowering of profits without affecting the values of the commodities; if the composition of the capitals is unequal, then it will only bring about a *fall* in the price of some commodities instead of—as vulgar opinion maintains—a rise in the *price of all commodities*. Here the fall in the prices of commodities results from a fall in the rate of profit or, which amounts to the same thing, a rise in wages. In the case of the manufacturer a large part of the *cost-price* of the commodity is determined by the average profit which he reckons on his fixed capital. If therefore this rate of profit falls or rises as a result of the rise or fall in wages, then the *price of these* commodities will fall or rise correspondingly—that is in accordance with that part of the price which results from the profit calculated upon the fixed capital. The same applies to "circulating capitals *returnable* at *distant* periods, and vice versa". (J. R. McCulloch [*The Principles of Political Economy,* Edinburgh, 1825, p. 300].) If the capitalists who employ less variable capital were to continue to chalk up their fixed capital at the same rate of profit, and add it to the price of the commodity then their rate of profit would rise and it would rise in the proportion in which they employ more fixed capital than those whose capital consists to a greater extent of variable capital. This would be levelled out by competition.

"Ricardo," says Mac., "was the first who endeavoured to analyse and discover the effects of fluctuations in the rate of wages on the value of commodities, when the capitals employed in their production were not of the same degree of durability." "Ricardo has not only shown that it is impossible for any rise of wages to raise the price of *all* commodities; but ... that in many cases a *rise of wages* necessarily leads to a *fall of prices*, and a *fall of wages* to a *rise of prices*" (l.c., pp. 298-99).

Ricardo proves his point by firstly postulating *cost-prices re-gulated by a general rate of profit.*

Secondly: *"There can be no rise in the value of labour without a fall of profits".* (David Ricardo, *On the Principles of Political Economy, and Taxation,* third edition, London, 1821, p. 31.)

Thus already in Chapter I *"On Value",* those laws are presupposed, which in chapters V and VI "On Wages" and "On Profits" should be deduced from the Chapter *"On Value".* Incidentally, ||538| Ricardo concludes quite wrongly, that because "there can be no rise in the value of labour without a fall of profits", there can be no rise of profits without a fall in the value of labour. The first law refers to surplus-value. But since profit equals the proportion of surplus-value to the total capital advanced, profit can rise though the value of labour remains the same, if the value of constant capital falls. Altogether Ricardo mixes up surplus-value and profit. Hence he arrives at erroneous laws on profit and the rate of profit.

The general conclusion of the last illustration is as follows:

"The degree of alteration in the relative value of goods, on account of a rise or fall of labour" (or, which amounts to the same thing, rise or fall in the rate of profit), "would depend on the proportion which the fixed capital bore to the whole capital employed. All commodities which are produced by very valuable machinery, or in very valuable buildings, or which require a great length of time before they can be brought to market, would fall in relative value, while all those which were chiefly produced by labour, or which would be speedily brought to market would rise in relative value" (l.c., p. 32).

Again Ricardo comes to the one point with which he is really concerned in his investigation. These variations in the cost-prices of commodities resulting from a rise or fall in wages are insignificant compared with those variations in the same cost-prices which are brought about by changes in the values of commodities, that is changes in the quantity of labour employed in their production ⟨Ricardo is far from expressing this truth in these adequate terms⟩. One can therefore, by and large, "abstract" from this and, accordingly, the law of value remains virtually correct. (He should have added that the cost-prices remain unintelligible without values determined by labour-time.) This is the true course of his investigation. In fact it is clear that despite the transformation of the values of commodities into *cost-prices,* the latter having been assumed, a *change* in cost-prices—in so far as it does not arise from a permanent fall or rise, a permanent alteration, in the rate of profit which can only establish itself in the course of many years—can only and solely be caused by a *change* in the values of commodities, in the labour-time necessary for their production. {And these cost-prices must not be confused with *market-prices*: they are the average market-prices of the commodities in the different branches of production. *Market-price* itself already includes an average in so far as *commodities of the same sphere* are determined by the prices of those commodities which are produced *under the mean, average conditions of production of this sphere.* By no means under the *worst conditions,* as Ricardo assumes with rent, because the average demand is related to a certain price, even with corn. A certain amount of the supply is therefore not sold *above* this price. Otherwise the demand would fall. Those whose conditions of production are not average but *below* average, must therefore often sell their commodity not only below its value but below its *cost price.*}

"The reader, however, should remark, that this cause of the variation of commodities" (this should read variations of cost-prices or, as he *calls them,* relative values of commodities) "is comparatively slight in its effects.... Not so with the other great cause of the variation in the value of commodities, namely, the increase or diminution in the quantity of labour necessary to produce them.... An alteration in the permanent rate of profits, to any great amount, is the effect of causes which do not operate but in the course of years; whereas alterations in the quantity of labour necessary to produce commodities, are of daily occurrence. Every improvement in machinery, in tools, in buildings, in raising the raw material, saves labour, and enables us to produce the commodity to which the improvement is applied with more facility, and consequently its *value* alters. In estimating, then, the causes of the variations in the value of commodities, although it would be wrong wholly to omit the consideration of the effect produced by a rise or fall of labour, it would be equally incorrect to attach much importance to it..." (l.c., pp. 32-33).

He therefore takes no further account of this.

The whole of this Section IV of Chapter I *"On Value"* is so extraordinarily confused, that, although Ricardo announces at the start that he intends to *consider the variations* in the values of commodities brought about by the *rise or fall in wages* in conjunction with different composition of capital, he actually does this only occasionally. In fact, he fills the major part of Section IV with illustrations which prove that, *quite indepen-dently* of the *rise or fall* of wages—he himself assumes that wages remain *constant*—the *postulation* ||539| of a *general rate of profit* must result in cost-prices which differ from the values of the commodities and, moreover, that this does not even depend on the difference [in the proportion] of fixed and circulating capital. He forgets this again at the end of the section.

He announces the subject of his inquiry in Section IV with the words:

"This difference in the degree of *durability* of fixed capital, and this *variety in the proportion* in which the two sorts of capital may be combined, introduce *another cause*, besides the greater or less quantity of labour neces-sary to produce commodities, for the variations in their relative value—*this cause is the rise or fall in the value of labour*" (l.c., pp. 25-26).

In fact, he shows by his illustrations, in the first place, that it is only the *general rate of profit* which enables the different com-binations of types of capital (namely, variable and constant etc.) to differentiate the prices of commodities from their values, that therefore the *cause* of those variations is the general rate of profit and not the value of labour, which is assumed to be con-stant. Then—only in the second place—he assumes cost-prices already differentiated from values as a result of the general rate of profit and he examines how variations in the value of labour affect these. Number 1, the main point, he does not investigate; he loses sight of it altogether and he closes the section as he began it:

"... it being shown in this section that without any variation in the quantity of labour, *the rise of its value* merely will occasion a fall in the exchangeable value of those goods, in the production of which *fixed capital* is employed; the larger the amount of fixed capital, the greater will be the fall" (l.c., p. 35).

And in the following Section V (Chapter I) he continues on the same lines, in other words, he only investigates how the *cost-prices* of commodities can be altered by a *variation in the value of labour, or wages,* not when the proportion of fixed and cir-culating capitals is different in two capitals of equal size em-

13*

ployed in two different spheres of production, but when there is *"unequal durability* of the capital"[a] or *"unequal rapidity* with which it is *returned* to its *employer"*[b] [l.c., p. 36]. The correct surmise implied in Section IV, regarding the *difference between cost-prices and values* brought about by the general rate of profit is here no longer noticeable. *Only a secondary question is examined here, namely, the variation in the cost-prices them-selves.* This section, therefore, is in fact of hardly any theoretical interest, apart from the occasional mention of differences in the form of capital arising from the circulation process.

"In proportion as fixed capital is less durable, it approaches to the nature of circulating capital. It will be consumed and its *value reproduced in a shorter time,* in order to preserve the capital of the manufacturer" (l.c., p. 36).

Thus the lesser durability and the difference between fixed and circulating capital in general, are reduced to the difference in the *period of reproduction.* This is certainly a factor of decisive importance. But by no means the only one. Fixed capital enters wholly into the labour-process and only in successive stages and by instalments into the process of creating value. This is another major distinction in their form of circulation. Furthermore: fixed capital enters—*necessarily* enters—only as *exchange-value* into the process of circulation, while its *use-value* is consumed in the labour-process and never goes outside it. This is another important distinction in the *form of circulation.* Both distinctions in the form of circulation also concern the period of circulation; but they are not identical with the degrees [of durability of fixed capital] and the differences [in the period of circulation].

Less durable capital *constantly* requires a greater quantity of *labour,*

"to keep it in its original state of efficiency; but the labour so bestowed may be considered as really expended on the commodity manufactured, which must bear a value in proportion to such labour". (l.c., pp. 36-37.) ". . . if the wear and tear of the machine were great, if the quantity of labour requisite to keep it in an efficient state were that of fifty men annually, I should require an additional price for my goods, equal to that which would be obtained by any other manufacturer who employed fifty men in the production of other goods, and who used no machinery at all. But a rise in the wages of labour would not equally affect commodities produced with machinery quickly consumed, and commodities produced with machinery slowly consumed. In the production of the one, a *great deal of labour would be continually transferred to the commodity* produced. . ." [l.c., p. 37].

---

[a] In the manuscript: "of fixed capital".—*Ed.*

[b] In the manuscript: "unequal rapidity in the return of the capitals to their owners".—*Ed.*

⟨but he is so occupied with his general rate of profit, that he does not see that thereby a relatively great deal of surplus-labour would be continually transferred to the commodity⟩ "in the other very little would be so transferred" [l.c., p. 37].

⟨Hence very little surplus-labour, hence much less [surplus]-value, if the commodities exchanged according to their values.⟩

"Every rise of wages, therefore, or, which is the same thing, ||540| every fall of profits, would lower the relative value of those commodities which were produced with a capital of a durable nature, and would proportionally elevate those which were produced with capital more perishable. A fall of wages would have precisely the contrary effect" (l.c., pp. 37-38).

In other words: The manufacturer who employs fixed capital of less durability employs relatively less fixed capital and more capital expended in wages, than the one who employs capital of greater durability. This case is therefore identical with the previous one, illustrating how a variation in wages affects capitals, one of which consists of relatively, proportionately, more fixed capital than the other. There is nothing new [here].

What Ricardo further says about *machinery* on pp. 38-40 should be held over until we come to Chapter XXXI *"On Machinery"*.[a]

It is curious how Ricardo, at the end, almost expresses the correct idea in a passing *phrase* only to let it go again and after touching upon it in the passages we are about to quote, returns again to his dominating idea of the effect of a change in the value of labour on cost-prices and finally concludes the investigation with this *secondary consideration*.

The passage containing the allusion is the following:

"It will be seen, then, that in the early stages of society, before much machinery or durable capital is used, the commodities produced by *equal capitals* will be nearly of *equal value*, and will rise or fall only relatively to each other on account of more or less labour being required for their production" [l.c., p. 40].

⟨The final clause is badly worded; it refers moreover not to value but to *commodities,* and is meaningless, unless it refers to their *prices*; for to say that *values* fall in proportion to labour-time means that values fall or rise as they fall or rise.⟩

"but after the introduction of these expensive and durable instruments, the *commodities produced by the employment of equal capitals will be of very unequal value*; and although they will still be liable to rise or fall relatively to

---

a See this volume, pp. 550-52.—*Ed.*

each other, as more or less labour becomes necessary to their production, they will be subject to another, though a minor variation, also, from the rise or fall of wages and profits. Since goods which sell for £5,000 may be the produce of a capital equal in amount to that from which are produced other goods which sell for £10,000, the *profits on their manufacture will be the same*; but those *profits would be unequal*, if *the prices of the goods* did not vary with a rise or fall in *the rate of profits*" (l.c., pp. 40-41).

In fact Ricardo says:

Capitals of equal size produce commodities of *equal values,* if the ratio of their organic component parts is *the same;* if equally large portions of them are expended on wages and on means of production. The same quantities of labour, therefore equal values (apart from the difference which might arise through the circulation process) are then embodied in their commodities. On the other hand, capitals *of equal size* produce commodities *of very unequal value,* when their organic composition is different, namely, when the proportion between the part existing as fixed capital and the part laid out in wages differs considerably.

Firstly, only a part of the fixed capital enters into the commodity as a component part of value, consequently the *magnitude of their values* will greatly vary according to whether much or little fixed capital is employed in the production of the commodity. Secondly, the part laid out in wages—calculated as a percentage on capital of equal size—is much smaller, therefore also the total [newly added] labour embodied in the commodity, and consequently the surplus-labour (given a working-day of equal length) which constitutes the surplus-value. If, therefore, these capitals of equal size—whose commodities are of *unequal values* and these unequal values *contain unequal surplus-values,* and therefore *unequal profits*—if these capitals because of their equal size are to yield equal profits, then the *prices of commodities* (as determined by the general rate of profit on a given outlay) must be very different from the *values of the commodities.* Hence it follows, not that the values have altered their nature, but that the *prices* are different from the *values.* It is all the more surprising that Ricardo did not arrive at this conclusion, for he sees that even if one presupposes cost-prices determined by the general rate of profit, a change in the rate of profit (or rate of wages) must change these cost-prices, so that the rate of profit ||541| in the different spheres of production may remain the same. How much more therefore must the establishment of a general rate of profit change unequal values since this *general rate of profit*

is in fact nothing other than the levelling out of the different rates
of surplus-value in different commodities produced by equal
capitals.

Having thus, if not set forth and comprehended, at any rate
virtually demonstrated, the difference between cost and value,
cost-prices and values of commodities, Ricardo ends with the following sentence:

"Mr. Malthus appears to think that it is a part of my doctrine, that *the
cost* and *value* of a thing should be the same;—*it is*, if he means by cost, '*cost
of production' including profits*" (l.c., p. 46, note). (That is, outlay plus
profit as determined by the general rate of profit.)

With this erroneous confusion of cost-prices and values, which
he has himself refuted, he then proceeds to consider rent.

With regard to the influence of the variations in the value of
labour upon the cost-price of gold, Ricardo says the following in
Section VI, Chapter I:

"May not gold be considered as a commodity produced with such proportions of the two kinds of capital as approach nearest to the average quantity
employed in the production of most commodities? May not these proportions
be so nearly equally distant from the two extremes, the one where little fixed
capital is used, the other where little labour is employed, as to form a just
mean between them?" (l.c., p. 44).

This is far more applicable to those commodities into whose
composition the various organic constituents enter in the average
proportion, and whose period of circulation and reproduction is
also of average length. For these, cost-price and value coincide,
because for them, and only for them, average profit coincides
with their actual surplus-value.

As inadequate as sections IV and V of Chapter I appear in
their consideration of the influence of the variations in the value
of labour on "relative values", theoretically a secondary matter compared with the transformation of values into cost-prices
through the average rate of profits, so important is the conclusion which Ricardo draws from this, thereby demolishing one of
the major errors that had persisted since Adam Smith, namely,
that the raising of wages, instead of reducing profits, raises the
prices of commodities. This is indeed already implied in the
very concept of *values* and is in no way altered by the transformation of values into cost-prices, since this, in any case, only
affects the *distribution of the surplus-value made by the total
capital* among the various branches of production or different
capitals in different spheres of production. But it was important

that Ricardo stressed this point and even proved the opposite to be the case. He is therefore justified in saying in Section VI, Chapter I:

"Before I quit this subject, it may be proper to observe, that Adam Smith, and all the writers who have followed him, have, without one exception that I know of, maintained that a rise in the price of labour would be uniformly followed by a rise in the price of all commodities" [l.c., p. 45].

⟨This corresponds to Adam Smith's second explanation of value, according to which it is equal to the quantity of labour a commodity can purchase.⟩

"I hope I have succeeded in showing that there are no grounds for such an opinion and that only those commodities would rise which had less fixed capital employed upon them *than the medium in which price was estimated*," (here relative value is equivalent to the expression of the value in money), "and that all those which had more, would positively fall in price when wages rose. On the contrary, if wages fell, those commodities only would fall, which had a less proportion of fixed capital employed on them, than the medium in which price was estimated; all those which had more, would positively rise in price" (l.c., p. 45).

With regard to *money* prices this seems *wrong*. When gold rises or falls in value, from whatever causes, then it does so to the same extent for all commodities which are reckoned in gold. Since it thus represents a relatively unchangeable medium despite its changeability, it is not at all clear how any relative combination of fixed capital and circulating capital in gold, compared with commodities, can bring about a difference. But this is due to Ricardo's *false assumption* that money, in so far as it serves as a medium of circulation, exchanges as a commodity for commodities. Commodities are assessed in gold before it circulates them. Supposing wheat were the medium instead of gold. If, for example, consequent upon a rise in wages, wheat as a commodity into which enters more than the average variable instead of constant capital, were to rise relatively in its price of production, then all commodities would be assessed in wheat of higher "relative value". The commodities into which more fixed capital entered, would be expressed in less wheat than before, not because their specific price had fallen compared with wheat but because their price had fallen in general. A commodity which contained just as much [living] labour—as against accumulated labour—as wheat, would show its rise [in price] by being expressed in more wheat ||542| than a commodity whose price had fallen as compared with wheat. If the same causes which raised the price of wheat, raised, for example, the price of clothes, then although the clothes would not be expressed in more wheat than previously, those [commodities], whose price had fallen compared with wheat, for instance cotton, would be expressed in less. Wheat would be the medium in which the difference in the price of cotton and clothes would be expressed.

But what Ricardo means is something different. He means that: because of a rise in wages, wheat has risen as against cotton but not as against clothes. Thus clothes would exchange for wheat at the old price, whereas cottons would exchange against wheat at the higher price. In itself, the assumption that variations in the price of wages in England, for instance, would alter the cost-price of gold in California where wages have not risen, is utterly absurd. The levelling out of *values* by labour-time and even less the levelling out of *cost-prices* by a general rate of profit does not take place in this direct form between different countries. But take even wheat, a home product. Say that the quarter of wheat has risen from 40s. to 50s., i.e., by 25 per cent. If the dress has also risen by 25 per cent, then it is worth 1 quarter of wheat as before. If the cotton has fallen by 25 per cent, then the same amount of cotton which was previously worth 1 quarter is now only worth 6 bushels of wheat.[73] And this expression in wheat represents exactly the ratio of the prices of cotton and clothes, because they are being measured in *the same* medium, in 1 quarter wheat.

Moreover, this notion is absurd in another way too. The *price* of the commodity which serves as a measure of value and hence as money, does not exist at all, because otherwise, apart from the commodity which serves as money I would need a second commodity to serve as money—a double measure of values. The relative value of money is expressed in the innumerable prices of all commodities; for in each of these prices in which the exchange-value of the commodity is expressed in money, the exchange-value of money is expressed in the use-value of the commodity. There can therefore be no talk of a rise or fall in *the* price of money. I can say: the price of money in terms of wheat or of clothes has remained the same; its price in terms of cotton has risen, or, which is the same, that the money price of cotton has fallen. But I cannot say that the *price* of money has risen or fallen. But Ricardo actually maintains that, for instance, the price of money in terms of cotton has risen or the price of cotton in terms of money has fallen, because the relative value

of money has risen as against that of cotton while it has retained
the same value as against clothes or wheat. Thus the two are
measured with an *unequal* measure.

This Section VI *"On an Invariable Measure of Value"* [l. c.,
p. 41] deals with the *"measure of value"* but contains nothing
important. The connection between value, its immanent measure
—i.e., labour-time—and the necessity for an *external* measure of the values of commodities is not understood or even raised
as a problem.

The very opening of this section shows the superficial manner
in which it is handled.

> "When commodities varied in relative value, it *would be desirable* to have
> the means of ascertaining which of them fell and which rose in real value,
> and this could be effected only by comparing them one after another with
> some invariable standard measure [...], which should itself be subject to
> none of the fluctuations to which other commodities are exposed." (l.c.,
> pp. 41-42). But "... there is no commodity which is not itself exposed to the
> same variations ... that is, there is none which is not subject to require more
> or less labour for its production" (l.c., p. 42).

Even if there were such a commodity, the influence of the rise
or fall in wages, the different combinations of fixed and circulating capital, the different degrees of durability of the fixed capital employed and the [different] length of time before the commodity can be brought to market, etc., would prevent it from
being:

> "... a perfect measure of value, by which we could accurately ascertain
> the variations in all other things...." "It would be a perfect measure of
> value for all things produced under the same circumstances precisely as itself,
> but for no others" (l.c., p. 43).

That is to say, if the [prices of this latter group of] "things"
varied, we could say (provided the value of money did not rise
or fall) that the variations were caused by the rise or fall "in
their *values*", in the labour-time necessary for their production.
With regard to the other things, we could not know whether the
"variations" in their money prices were due to *other reasons,*
etc. Later we shall have to come back to this matter which is
quite unsatisfactory. (During a subsequent revision of the theory
of money.)

Chapter I, Section VII. Apart from the important doctrine on
"relative" wages, profits and rents, to which we shall return later,[a]

---

[a] See this volume, pp. 419-25.—*Ed.*

this section contains nothing but the theory that a fall or rise in the value of money accompanied by a corresponding rise or fall in wages etc. does not alter the relations but only their monetary expression. If the same commodity is expressed in double the number of pounds sterling, so also is that part of it which resolves into profit, wages or rent. But the ratio of these three to one another and the real values they represent, remain the same. The same applies when the profit is expressed by double the number of pounds, £ 100 is then however represented by £ 200 so that the relation between profit and capital, the rate of profit, remains unaltered. The changes in the monetary expression affect profit and capital simultaneously, ditto profit, wages and rent. This applies to rent as well in so far as it is not calculated on the acre but on the capital advanced in agriculture etc. In short, in this case the variation is not in the commodities etc.

"A rise of wages from this cause will, indeed, be invariably accompanied by a rise in the price of commodities; but in such cases, it will be found that labour and all commodities have not varied in regard to each other, and that the variation has been confined to money" (l.c., p. 47).

[5.] Average or Cost-Prices and Market-Prices

[a) Introductory Remarks: Individual Value and Market-Value; Market-Value and Market-Price]

||543| In developing his theory of differential rent, in Chapter II, "*On Rent*", Ricardo puts forward the following thesis:

"The *exchangeable value of all commodities,* whether they be manufactured, or the produce of the mines, or the produce of land, is always regulated, not by the less quantity of labour that will suffice for their production under circumstances highly favourable, and exclusively enjoyed by those who have peculiar facilities of production; but by the greater quantity of labour necessarily bestowed on their production by those who have no such facilities; by those who *continue* to produce them under the most unfavourable circumstances; meaning—by the most unfavourable circumstances, *the most unfavourable under which the quantity of produce required, renders it necessary to* carry on the production" (l.c., pp. 60-61).

The last sentence is not entirely correct. The "quantity of produce required" [is] not a fixed magnitude. [It would be correct to say:] A certain quantity of produce required within certain limits of price. If the latter rises above these limits then the "quantity required" falls with the demand.

The thesis set out above can be expressed in general terms as follows: The value of the commodity—which is the product of a particular sphere of production—is determined by the labour which is required in order to produce the *whole amount,* the *total sum* of the commodities appertaining to this sphere of production and not by the particular labour-time that each individual capitalist or employer within this sphere of production requires. The general conditions of production and the general productivity of labour in this particular sphere of production, for example in cotton manufacture, are the average conditions of production and the average productivity in this sphere, in cotton-manufacture. The quantity of labour by which, for example, [the value of] a yard of cotton is determined is therefore not the quantity of labour it contains, the quantity the manufacturer expended upon it, but the average quantity with which all the cotton-manufacturers produce one yard of cotton for the market. Now the particular conditions under which the individual capitalists produce, for example, in cotton manufacture, necessarily fall into three categories. Some produce under *medium* conditions, i.e., the individual conditions of production under which they produce coincide with the *general* conditions of production in the sphere. The average conditions are their *actual conditions.* The productivity of their labour is at the average level. The *individual* value of their commodities coincides with the *general* value of these commodities. If, for example, they sell the yard of cotton at 2s.—the average value—then they sell it at the *value* which the yards they produce represent *in natura.* Another category produces under *better* than average conditions. The *individual* value of their commodities is *below* their general value. If they sell their commodities at the general value, they sell them *above* their individual value. Finally, a third category produces under conditions of production that are *below* the average.

Now the "quantity of produce required" from this particular sphere of production is not a fixed magnitude. If the rise of the value of the commodities above the average value exceeds certain limits, the "quantity of produce required" falls, that is, this quantity is only required at a given price—or at least within certain limits of price. Hence it is just as *possible* that the last-mentioned category has to sell *below* the individual value of its commodities as the better placed category always sells its products *above* their individual value. Which of the categories has a decisive effect on the average value, will in particular depend on the numerical ratio or the proportional size of the categories.[74] If numerically the middle category greatly outweighs the others, it will determine [the average value]. If this group is numerically weak and that which works *below the average conditions* is numerically strong and predominant, then the latter determines the general value of the produce of this sphere, although this by no means implies and it is even very unlikely, that the individual capitalist who is the most *unfavourably* placed in the last group, is the determining factor. (See *Corbet*.[75])

But let us leave this aside. The general result is that: the *general* value of the products of this group is *the same* for all, whatever may be its relation to the particular value of each individual commodity. This *common* value is the *market-value* of these commodities, the value at which they appear on the market. Expressed in money, this market-value is the *market-price,* just as in general, value expressed in money is price. The actual market-price is now above, now below this market-value and coincides with it only by chance. Over a certain period, however, the fluctuations equal each other out and it can be said that the average of the actual market-prices is *the market-price* which represents *the market-value.* Whether, at a given moment, the actual market-price corresponds to this market-value   in magnitude, i.e., *quantitatively* or not, at any rate it shares the *qualitative* characteristic with it, that all commodities of the same sphere of production available on the market have *the same* price (assuming of course that they are of the same quality), that is, in practice, they represent the *general* value of the commodities of this sphere.

||544| The above thesis put forward by Ricardo for the purpose of his theory of rent has therefore been interpreted by his disciples to mean that *two different market-prices* cannot exist simultaneously on the same market or: products *of the same* kind found on the market simultaneously, have *the same price* or—since we can leave out of account here the accidental features of this price—*the same market-value.*

Thus competition, partly among the capitalists themselves, partly between them and the buyers of the commodity and partly among the latter themselves, brings it about here that the value of each individual commodity in a particular sphere of production is determined by the *total mass of social labour-time* required by the *total mass of the   commodities of this particular sphere of social production* and not by the *individual values of the separate commodities* or the labour-time the individual commodity has cost its *particular* producer and seller.

It obviously follows from this, however, that, whatever the circumstances, the capitalists belonging to the first group—whose conditions of production are more favourable than the average —make an excess profit, in other words their profit is *above* the general rate of profit of this sphere. Competition, therefore, does not bring about the *market-value* or *market-price* by the *equalisation of profits within* a particular sphere of production. (For the purpose of this investigation, the distinction [between market-value and market-price] is irrelevant since the differences in the conditions of production—hence the different rates of profit for the individual capitalist—in *the same sphere,* remain, whatever may be the relationship of market-price to market-value.) *On the contrary,* competition here equalises the *different individual values* to the same, *equal, undifferentiated market-value,* by permitting *differences between individual profits,* profits of individual capitalists, and their *deviations from the average rate of profit* in the sphere. It even creates differences by establishing *the same market-value* for commodities produced under unequal conditions of production, therefore with unequal productivity of labour, the commodities thus represent individual *unequal quantities of labour-time.* The commodity produced under more favourable conditions, contains less labour-time than that produced under less favourable conditions, but it sells at the same price, and has the same value, as if it contained the same labour-time though this is not the case.

[b) Ricardo Confuses the Process of the Formation of Market-Value and the Formation of Cost-Prices]

For the establishment of his theory of rent, Ricardo needs two propositions which express not only *different* but *contradictory* effects of competition. According to the first, the products of the same sphere sell at *one and the same market-value,* competition therefore enforces different *rates of profit,* i.e., deviations from the general rate of profit. According to the second, the *rate of profit* must be *the same* for each capital investment, that is competition brings about a *general rate of profit.* The first law applies to the various independent capitals invested in *the same sphere of production.* The second applies to capitals in so far as they are invested in *different spheres* of production. By the first action, competition creates the *market*-value, that is, *the same value* for commodities of the same sphere of production, although this *identical value* must result in *different profits*, it thus creates *the same* value *despite of, or rather by means of, different rates of profit*. The second action (which, incidentally, is brought about in a different way; namely, the competition between capitalists of *different* spheres throws the capital from one sphere into another, while the other competition, in so far as it is not competition between buyers, occurs between capitals of *the same* sphere) enables competition to create the *cost-price,* in other words *the same rate of profit* in the various spheres of production, although this *identical rate of profit* is contrary to the inequality of values, and can hence only be enforced by *prices which are different* from values.

Since Ricardo needs both these propositions—*equal value* or *price with unequal rate of profit,* and equal *rate of profit* with *unequal values,*—for his theory of rent, it is most remarkable that he does not sense this twofold determination and that even in the Section where he deals *ex professo* with *market-price,* in *Chapter IV "On Natural Price and Market-Price",* he does not deal with *market-price* or *market-value* at all, although in the above-quoted passage[a] he uses it as a basis to explain *differential rent*, the excess profit crystallised in the form of rent. ||545| But he deals here merely with the reduction of the *prices* in the *different spheres of production* to *cost-prices* or *average prices,* i.e., with the relationship between the market-values of the different spheres of production and not with the establishment of the market-value in each particular sphere, and unless this is established market-values do not exist at all.

The *market-values* of each particular sphere, therefore the *market-prices* of each particular sphere (if the market-price corresponds to the *"natural price",* in other words if it merely represents the value in the form of money) would yield very different rates of profit, for capitals of equal size in *different* spheres—quite apart from the differences arising from their different processes of circulation—employ very unequal proportions of constant and variable capital and therefore yield very unequal surplus-values, hence very unequal profits. The levelling out of the various market-values, so that *the same* rate of profit is produced in the different spheres of production, and capitals of

---

a See this volume, p. 203.—*Ed.*

equal size yield equal average profits, is therefore only possible by the transformation of *market-values* into *cost-prices* which are different from the actual values.*

What competition within *the same* sphere of production brings about, is the determination of the *value of the commodity in a given sphere* by the average labour-time required in it, i.e., the creation of the *market-value*. What competition between the *different* spheres of production brings about is the *creation of the same general rate of profit* in the *different* spheres through the levelling out of the different market-values into market-prices, which are *cost-prices* that are different from the actual market-values. Competition in this second instance by no means tends to assimilate the prices of the commodities to their values, but on the contrary, to reduce their values to cost-prices that differ from these values, to abolish the differences between their values and cost-prices.

It is only this latter process which Ricardo considers in Chapter IV and, oddly enough, he regards it as the reduction of the prices of commodities—through competition—to their values, the reduction of the market-price (a price which is different from value) to the natural price (the value expressed in terms of money). This blunder, however, arises from the error he committed already in Chapter I *"On Value"*, where he identified cost-price and value,[a] this in turn was due to the fact that at a point where as yet he was only concerned with explaining "value", where he, therefore, as yet, only had to deal with "*commodity*", he plunged in with the *general rate of profit* and all the conditions arising from the more developed capitalist relations of production.

Ricardo's whole procedure in Chapter IV is therefore quite superficial. He starts out from the "... accidental and temporary variations of [the] price" (l. c., p. 80) of commodities resulting from the fluctuating relations between demand and supply.

"With the rise or fall of price, *profits* are elevated above, or depressed below *their general level*, and capital is either encouraged to enter into, or is warned to depart from *the particular employment* in which the variation has taken place" (l.c., p. 80).

---

* It is possible that the *rate of surplus-value* is not equalised in the different spheres of production (for instance because of unequal length of working time). This is *not necessary* because the surplus-values themselves are equalised.

a See this volume, p. 199.—*Ed.*

Here the *general level of profit* prevailing between the particular spheres of production, between "the particular employments" is already presupposed. But he should have considered first, how the *general level of price* in the same employment and the *general level of profit* between different employments is brought about. Ricardo would then have seen that the latter operation already presupposes movements of capital in all directions —or a *distribution,* determined by competition, *of the whole social capital between its different spheres of employment.* Once it is assumed that the market-values or average market-prices in the different spheres are reduced to *cost-prices* yielding the same average rate of profit ⟨this is however only the case in spheres where landed property does not interfere; where it interferes, competition—within the same sphere—can convert the price to the value and the value to the market-price, but it cannot reduce the market-price to the cost-price⟩, persistent deviations of the market-price from the cost-price, when it rises above or falls below it in particular spheres, will bring about new migrations and a new distribution of social capital. The first migration occurs in order to establish *cost-prices* which differ from *values.* The second migration occurs in order to equalise the *actual market-prices* with the cost-prices—as soon as they rise above or fall below the latter. The first is a transformation of the values into cost-prices. The second is a rotation of the actual ||546| market-prices of the moment in the various spheres, around the cost-price, which now appears as the *natural price,* although it is different from the value and only the result of social action.

It is this latter, more superficial movement which Ricardo examines and at times unconsciously confuses with the other. Both are of course brought about by "the same principle", namely, the principle that while

"every man" [is] "free to employ his capital where he pleases," [he] "will naturally seek for it that employment which is most advantageous; he will naturally be dissatisfied with a profit of 10 per cent, if by removing his capital he can obtain a profit of 15 per cent. This *restless desire on the part of all the employers of stock, to quit a less profitable for a more advantageous business, has a strong tendency to equalise the rate of profits of all,* or to fix them *in such proportions*, as may, in the estimation of the parties, compensate for any advantage which one may have, or may appear to have over the other" (l.c., p. 81).

This tendency has the effect of distributing the total mass of social labour-time *among the various spheres of production* according to the social need. In this way, the values in the different spheres of production are transformed into cost-prices, and on the other hand, the variations of the actual prices in particular spheres from the cost-prices are levelled out.

All this is contained in Adam Smith's work. Ricardo himself says:

"No writer has more satisfactorily and ably shewn than Dr. Smith, the tendency of capital to move from employments in which the goods produced do not repay by *their price the whole expenses, including the ordinary profits*," (that is to say, the cost-price) "of producing and bringing them to market" (l.c., p. 342, note).

The achievement of Ricardo, whose blunder is on the whole caused by his *lack of criticism* of Adam Smith in this respect, consists in his more precise exposition of this migration of capital from one sphere to the other, or rather of the manner in which this occurs. He was, however, only able to do this because the credit system was more highly developed in his time than in the time of Adam Smith. Ricardo says:

"It is perhaps very difficult to trace *the steps* by which this change is *effected*: it is probably effected, by a manufacturer *not absolutely changing his employment, but only lessening the quantity of capital he has in that employment*. In all rich countries, there is a number of men forming what is called the *monied class**; these men are engaged in *no trade*, but live on the interest of their money, which is employed in discounting bills, or in loans to the more *industrious* part of the community. The bankers too employ a large capital on the same objects. The capital so employed forms a circulating capital of a large amount, and is employed, in larger or smaller proportions, by all the different trades of a country. There is perhaps no manufacturer, however rich, who limits his business to the extent that his own funds alone will allow: he has always some portion of this floating capital, increasing or diminishing according to the activity of the demand for his commodities. When the demand for silks increases, and that for cloth diminishes, the clothier does not remove with his capital to the silk trade, but he dismisses some of his workmen, he discontinues his demand for the loan from bankers and monied men; while the case of the silk manufacturer is the reverse: [...] he *borrows more*, and *thus capital is transferred from one employment to another, without the necessity of a manufacturer discontinuing his usual occupation*. When we look to the markets of a large town, and observe how regularly they are supplied both with home and foreign commodities, in the quantity in which they are required, under all the circumstances of varying demand, arising from the caprice of taste, or a change in the amount of population, without often producing either the effects of a glut from a too abundant supply, or an enormously high price from the

---

* Here Roscher could have seen once again what the Englishman understands by the term "monied class". The "monied class" is here diametrically opposed to the "industrious part of the community".[76]

supply being unequal to the demand, we must confess that *the principle which apportions capital to each trade* in the precise amount that it is required, is more active than is generally supposed" (l.c., pp. 81-82).

Credit therefore is the means by which the capital of the whole capitalist class is placed at the disposal of each sphere of production, not in proportion to the capital belonging to the capitalists in a given sphere but in proportion to their production requirements—whereas in competition the individual capitals appear to be independent of each other. Credit is both the result and the condition of capitalist production and this provides us with a convenient transition from the *competition between capitals* to *capital as credit*.

[c) Ricardo's Two Different Definitions of "Natural Price". Changes in Cost-Price Caused by Changes in the Productivity of Labour]

At the beginning of Chapter IV, Ricardo says that by *natural price* he understands the *value* of the commodities, that is, the *price* as determined by their relative labour-time, and that by *market-price* he understands the accidental and temporary deviations from this natural price or value ||547|. Throughout the further course of the chapter—and he is quite explicit in this— he understands something quite different by *natural price,* namely, *cost-price* which is different from value. Thus, instead of showing how competition transforms values into cost-prices, i.e., creates permanent deviations from values, he shows, following Adam Smith, how competition reduces the market-prices in different trades to cost-prices.

Thus Chapter IV opens like this:

"In making *labour* the *foundation* of the value of commodities, and the *comparative quantity of labour* which is necessary to their production, the rule which determines the respective quantities of goods which shall be given in exchange for each other, we must not be supposed to deny the *accidental and temporary deviations of the actual* or *market price* of commodities from this, *their primary and natural price*" (l.c., p. 80).

Here therefore *natural price* equals *value* and market-price is nothing but the deviation of actual price from value.

As against this:

"Let us suppose that all commodities are at their *natural price*, and consequently that the *profits of capital* in *all employments* are exactly at the *same rate*, or differ only so much as, in the estimation of the parties, is equivalent to any real or fancied advantage which they possess or forego" (l.c., p. 83).

14*

Here therefore, *natural price* equals *cost-price*, that is, the price at which the relation between the profit and the advances embodied in the commodity is the same, although equal *values* of commodities produced by capitals in different spheres of production, contain very *unequal* surplus-values, and thus *unequal profits*. If the price is to yield the same profit, it must therefore be different from the value of the commodity. On the other hand, capitals of equal size produce *commodities of very unequal value*, according to whether a larger or a smaller portion of the fixed capital enters into the commodity. But more about this when dealing with the circulation of capitals.

By equalisation through competition, Ricardo therefore understands only the rotation of the actual prices or actual market-prices around the *cost-prices* or the *natural price* as distinct from the *value*, the levelling out of the market-price in different branches of production to general cost-prices, i.e., precisely to prices which are different from the real values in different trades:

"It is then the desire, which every capitalist has, of diverting his funds from a less to a more profitable employment, that prevents the *market-price* of commodities from continuing for any length of time either much above, or much below their *natural price*. It is this competition which so adjusts the *changeable value* of commodities," (and also the *different real* values) "that after paying the wages for the labour necessary to their production, and all other expenses required to put the capital employed in its original state of efficiency, the *remaining value or overplus* will in *each trade* be in proportion to the *value of the capital* employed" (l.c., p. 84).

This is exactly the case. Competition adjusts the prices in the different trades so that *"the remaining value or overplus"*, the profit, corresponds to the *value of the capital employed,* but not to the real value of the commodity, not to the real overplus which it contains after the deduction of expenses. To bring this adjustment about the price of one commodity must be raised above, and that of the other must be depressed below their respective real values. It is not the value of the commodities but their cost-price, i.e., the expenses they contain plus the general rate of profit, around which competition forces the market-prices in the different trades to rotate.

Ricardo continues:

"In the 7th Chap. of the *Wealth of Nations*, all that concerns this question is most ably treated" (l.c., p. 84).

In fact it is his uncritical belief in the Smithian tradition, which here leads Ricardo astray.

As usual, Ricardo closes the chapter by saying that in the following investigations, he wants to "... leave [...] entirely out of [...] consideration" (l.c., p. 85) the accidental deviations of market-prices from the cost-price; but he overlooks the fact that he has paid no regard at all to the *constant* deviations of market-prices, in so far as they correspond to cost-prices, from the real values of the commodities and that he has substituted cost-price for value.

Chapter XXX "On the Influence of Demand and Supply on Prices". Here Ricardo defends the proposition that the permanent price is determined by the *cost-price*, and not by *supply or demand*: that, therefore, the permanent price is determined by the *value* of the commodities only in so far as this value determines the cost-price. Provided that the prices of the commodities are so adjusted that they all yield a profit of 10 per cent, then every lasting change in these prices will be determined by a change in their values, in the labour-time required for their production. As this value continues to determine the general rate of profit, so the changes in it continue to determine the variations in cost-prices, although of course *the difference between cost-prices and values is thereby not superseded*. What is superseded is only that the difference between value and actual price should not ||548| be greater *than the difference between cost-prices and values, a difference that is brought about by the general rate of profit*. With the changes in the values of commodities, their cost-prices also change. A *"new natural price"* (p. 460) is formed. If, for example, the worker can now produce twenty hats in the same period of time which it previously took him to produce ten hats, and if wages accounted for half the cost of the hat, then the expenses, the costs of production, of the twenty hats, in so far as they consist of wages, have fallen by half. For the same wages are now paid for the production of twenty hats as previously for ten. Thus each hat now contains only half the expenditure for wages. If the hat manufacturer were to sell the hats at the same price he would sell them above the cost-price. If the profit had previously been 10 per cent then it would now be $46^2/_3$ per cent, assuming the outlay for the manufacture of a certain quantity of hats was originally 50 for raw material, etc. and 50 for labour. [The outlay] would now be 50 for raw material etc. and 25 for wages. If the commodity is sold at the old price then the profit is $^{35}/_{75}$ or $46^2/_3$ per cent. As a result of the fall in value, the new natural price will therefore fall to such an extent that the price only yields 10 per cent profit. The fall in the value or in the labour-time necessary for the production of the commodity reveals itself in the fact that less labour-time is used for *the same amount* of commodity, hence also less *paid labour-time*, less *wages* and, consequently, the costs, the wages paid (i.e., the *amount* of wages; this does not presuppose a fall *in the rate of wages*) proportionately decline for the production of *each individual* commodity.

This is the case if the change in value has taken place in the hat making itself. Had it occurred in the production of the raw material or of the tools, then this would have been similarly expressed as a diminution of outlay in wages for the production of a certain given quantity of product in these spheres; but to the hat manufacturer it would denote that his constant capital had cost him less. The *cost-prices* or *"natural prices"* (which have nothing to do with "nature") can fall in two ways as a result of a change—here a fall—*in the value* of the commodities:

[*Firstly*] because the wages laid out in the production of a given quantity of commodities fall, owing to a fall in the aggregate absolute amount of labour, paid labour and unpaid labour, expended on this quantity of commodities.

Secondly: If, as a result of the increased or diminished productivity of labour (both can occur, the one when the proportion of variable capital to constant capital falls, the other when wages rise owing to the means of subsistence becoming dearer), the ratio of surplus-value to the value of the commodity or to the value of the labour contained in it, changes, then the rate of profit rises or falls, and the amount of labour is differently divided up.

In the latter case, the prices of production or cost-prices could change only in so far as they are affected by variations in the value of labour. In the first case, the value of labour remains the same. In the second case, however, it is not the *values* of the commodities which alter, but only the division between [necessary] labour and surplus-labour. A change in the productivity and therefore in the value of the *individual* commodity would nevertheless take place in this case. The same capital will produce more commodities than previously in the one case and less in the other. The aggregate volume of the commodities in which it is materialised would have *the same value*, but the *individual commodity* would have a different value. Although the value of the wage does not determine the value of the commodities, the value of the commodities (which enter into the consumption of the worker) determines the value of the wage.

Once the cost-prices of the commodities in the various branches of production are established, they rise or fall relatively to each other with any change in the values of the commodities. If the productivity of labour rises, the labour-time required for the production of a *particular commodity* decreases and therefore its *value falls*; whether this change in productivity occurs in the labour used in the final process or in the constant capital, the cost-price of this commodity must also fall correspondingly. The *absolute amount of labour employed on it* has been reduced, hence also the amount of paid labour it contains and the amount of wages expended on it, even though the rate of wages has remained the same. If the commodity were sold at its former cost-price, then it would yield a higher profit than the general rate of profit, since formerly, this profit was equal to 10 per cent on the higher outlay. It would therefore be now more than 10 per cent on the diminished outlay. If on the contrary the productivity of labour decreases, the real values of the commodities rise. When the rate of profit is given—or, which is the same thing, the cost-prices are given—the relative rise or fall of the cost-prices is dependent on the rise or fall, the variation, in the real values of the commodities. As a result of this variation, new cost-prices or, as Ricardo says, following Smith, "new natural prices" take the place of the old.

In Chapter XXX, from which we have just been quoting, Ricardo expressly identifies natural price, that is, cost-price, with natural value, i.e., value as determined by labour-time.

"Their price" (of monopolised commodities) "has no necessary connexion with their *natural value*: but the *prices* of commodities, which are subject to competition, ... will ultimately depend ... on [the] ... *cost of their production*" (l.c., p. 465).

Here therefore are cost-prices or natural prices directly ||549| identified with "*natural value*", that is, with "*value*".

This confusion explains how later a whole lot of fellows post Ricardum, like Say himself, could accept "the cost of production" as the ultimate regulator of prices, without having the slightest inkling of the determination of value by labour-time, indeed they directly deny the latter while maintaining the former.

This whole blunder of Ricardo's and the consequent erroneous exposition of rent etc., as well as the erroneous laws about the *rate of profit* etc. spring from his failure to distinguish between *surplus-value* and *profit*; and in general his *treatment of definitions* is crude and uncomprehending, just as that of the other economists. The following will show how he allowed himself to be ensnared by Smith. |549||

* * *

||XII-636| Just to add a further comment to what has already been said: Ricardo knows no other difference between *value* and *natural price* than that the latter is the monetary expression of value, and that it can therefore change because of a change in value of the precious metals, without value itself changing. This change, however, only affects the evaluation or the expression of value in money. Thus, he says, for instance:

"It" (foreign trade) "can only be regulated by altering the *natural price*, not the *natural value*, at which commodities can be produced in those countries, and that is effected by altering the distribution of the precious metals" (l.c., p. 409). |XII-636||.

[B. ADAM SMITH'S THEORY OF COST-PRICE]

[1. Smith's False Assumptions in the Theory of Cost-Prices. Ricardo's Inconsistency Owing to His Retention of the Smithian Identification of Value and Cost-Price]

||XI-549| It must first be noted that according to Adam Smith as well,

"there are always a few commodities of which the price resolves itself into *two* parts only, the wages of labour, and the profits of stock". ([*The Wealth of Nations*, Oxford University Press, London, 1928, Vol. I, p. 56; Garnier,] t. 1, l. 1, ch. VI, p. 103.[a])

This difference between Ricardo's and Smith's views can therefore be ignored here.

---

[a] Marx quotes here from *Recherches sur la nature et les causes de la richesse des nations.* Paris, 1802, Garnier's translation of Adam Smith's work. All passages taken by Marx from the French translation are marked "Garnier" in this edition and are printed in English according to A. Smith, *An Inquiry into the Nature and Causes of the Wealth of Nations*, Oxford University Press, London, 1928 (referred to hereafter as O.U.P.). The French text, as that of all other quotations taken by Marx from French and German sources, can be found in the Appendices.—*Ed.*

Adam Smith first explains that exchange-value resolves itself into a certain quantity of labour and that after deducting raw materials etc., the value contained in exchange-value is resolved into that part of labour for which the labourer is paid and that part for which he is not paid, the latter part consists of profit and rent (the profit in turn may. be resolved into profit and interest). Having shown this, he suddenly turns about and instead of resolving exchange-value into wages, profit and rent, he declares these to be the elements forming exchange-value, he makes them into independent exchange-values that form the exchange-value of the product; he constructs the exchange-value of the commodity from the values of wages, profit and rent, which are determined independently and separately. Instead of having their source in value, they become the source of value.

"*Wages*, *profit*, and *rent*, are *the three original sources* of all revenue, as well as of *all exchangeable value*" ([O.U.P., Vol. I, p. 57; Garnier,] t. 1, l. 1, ch. VI, p. 105).

Having revealed the intrinsic connection, he is suddenly obsessed again with the aspect of the phenomenon, with the *connection, as it appears in competition*, and in competition everything always appears in inverted[a] form, always standing on its head.

Now it is from this latter inverted starting-point that Smith develops the distinction between the "*natural price* of the commodities" and their "*market-price*". Ricardo accepts this from him, but forgets that Adam Smith's "natural price" is, according to Smith's premises, nothing other than the *cost-price* resulting from competition and that for Smith himself, this cost-price is only identical with the "*value*" of the commodity, in so far as he forgets his more profound conception and sticks to the false concept derived from the external *appearance*, namely that the exchange-value of commodities is formed by putting together the independently determined values of wages, profit and rent. While Ricardo contests this concept throughout, he accepts Smith's confusion or identification of *exchange-value* with *cost-price* or *natural price*, which is based on *that very* concept. In the case of Adam Smith this confusion is legitimate, because his whole examination of *natural price starts out* from his second, false conception of *value*. But in Ricardo's case, it is wholly

---

a In the German original: "*verkehrt*" which may mean: upside down, reversed, or: wrong.—*Ed.*

unjustifiable, because he nowhere accepts this wrong conception of Adam Smith's, but contests it *ex professo* as an inconsistency. Adam Smith, however, succeeded in ensnaring him again with his *natural price.*

Having *compounded* the value of the commodity from the separate and independently determined *values of wages, profit* and *rent,* Adam Smith now asks himself how these primary values are determined. And here he starts out from the phenomena as they appear in competition.

[In] Chapter VII, Book I "Of the Natural and Market Price of Commodities" [he says:]

"There is in every society or neighbourhood an *ordinary* or *average rate* of ... wages and profit ... and rent. ... These ordinary or average rates may be called the *natural rates* of wages, profit, and rent, at the time and place in which they commonly prevail" ([O.U.P., Vol. I, p. 60; Garnier,] l.c., t. I, pp. 110-11). "When the *price* of any commodity is neither more nor less than what is sufficient to pay the rent [...] the wages [...] and the profits [...] according to their *natural* rates, the commodity is then sold for [...] its *natural price*" ([O.U.P., Vol. I, p. 61; Garnier,] l.c., p. 111).

This natural price is then the *cost-price* of the commodity and the cost-price coincides with the *value* of the commodity, since it is presupposed that the value of the commodity is compounded of the values of wages, profit and rent.

"The commodity is then ||550| *sold precisely for what it is worth*" (the commodity is sold at its *value*) "or for what *it* really *costs* the person who brings it to market" (at its *v a l u e* or at the *c o s t-p r i c e* for the person who brings it to market) "for though, in common language, what is called the *prime cost* of any commodity does *not comprehend the profit* of the person who is to sell it again, yet, if he sells it at a *price* which *does not allow him* the *ordinary rate of profit* in his neighbourhood, he is evidently a loser by the trade; since *by employing his stock in some other way,* he might have made *that profit*" ([O.U.P., Vol. I, p. 61; Garnier,] l.c., p. 111).

Here we have the whole genesis of natural price and, besides, set out in quite appropriate language and logic, since the value of the commodity is composed of the prices of wages, profit and rent, while the true value of the latter is, in turn, constituted by their *natural rates*; thus it is clear that the value of the *commodity* is identical with its *cost-price* and the latter with the *natural price* of the commodity. The rate of profit, as of wages, is *presupposed*. They are indeed given for the *formation* of the cost-price. They are *antecedent* to the cost-price. To the individual capitalist therefore they also appear as given. The hows, whys and wherefores do not concern him. Adam Smith here adopts the standpoint of the individual capitalist, the agent of capitalist production, who fixes the cost-price of his commodity. So much for wages etc., so much for the general rate of profit. *Ergo*: This is how this capitalist *sees* the operation by which the *cost-price* of the commodity is fixed or, as it further seems to him, the *value* of the commodity, for he also knows that the market-price is now above, now below, this cost-price, which therefore appears to him as the ideal price of the commodity, its absolute price as distinct from its price fluctuations, in short as its *value*, in so far as he has any time at all to reflect on matters of this sort. And since Smith transports himself right into the midst of competition, he immediately reasons and argues with the peculiar logic of the capitalist caught up in this sphere. He interjects: In common language, *costs* do not include the *profit* made by the seller (which necessarily forms a surplus above his expenses). Why then do you include profit in the cost-price? Adam Smith answers like the profound capitalist to whom this question is put:

Profit in general must enter into cost-price, because I would be cheated if *only* a profit of 9 instead of 10 per cent were to enter into cost-price.[77]

The naïve way in which Adam Smith on the one hand expresses the thoughts of the agent of capitalist production and presents things boldly and comprehensively, as they appear to and are thought of by the latter, as they influence him in practice, and as, indeed, they appear on the surface, while, on the other hand, he sporadically reveals their more profound relationships, gives his book its great charm.

One can see here too why Adam Smith—despite his considerable scruples on this point—resolves the entire value of the commodity into rent, profit and wages and omits constant capital, although of course he admits its existence for each "individual" capitalist. For otherwise he would have to say: The value of a commodity consists of wages, profit, rent and that part of the value of the commodity which does not consist of wages, profit, rent. It would therefore be necessary to determine value independently of wages, profit and rent.

If, besides the outlay on average wages etc., the price of the commodity also covers the average profit and—if rent enters into the commodity—the average rent, then the commodity is sold at its *natural* or *cost-price*, and this cost-price is equal to its *value*, for its value is nothing but the sum of the natural values of wages, profit and rent.

||551| Having taken his stand in competition and *assumed* the rate of profit etc. as *given*, Adam Smith for the rest interprets correctly *natural price* or *cost-price*, namely, the cost-price as distinct from the market-price.

"... the *natural price* of the commodity, o r the whole *value* of the rent, labour, and profit, which must be paid in order to bring it" to market ([O.U.P., Vol. I, pp. 61-62; Garnier,] l.c., p. 112).

This cost-price of the commodity is different from the *actual price* or *market-price* of the commodity. ([O.U.P., Vol. I, p. 62; Garnier,] l.c., p. 112.) The latter is dependent on demand and supply.

The [sum of the] *costs of production* or the *cost-price* of the commodity is precisely "the *whole value* of the rent, labour, and profit, *which must be paid in order to bring it*" to market ([O.U.P., Vol. I, p. 62; Garnier,] p. 113). If demand corresponds to supply, then the market-price is equal to the natural price.

"When the quantity brought to market is just sufficient to supply the effectual demand, and no more, the *market-price* naturally comes to be exactly ... the same with the *natural price*" ([O.U.P., Vol. I, p. 63; Garnier,] l.c., p. 114). "The *natural* price, therefore, is, as it were, the central price, to which the prices of all commodities are continually gravitating. Different accidents may sometimes keep them suspended a good deal above it, and sometimes force them down even somewhat below it" ([O.U.P., Vol. I, p. 64; Garnier,] l.c., p. 116).

Hence Adam Smith concludes that in general, the

"whole quantity of industry annually employed in order to bring any commodity to market" will correspond to the needs of society or the "effectual demand" ([O.U.P., Vol. I, p. 64; Garnier,] l.c., p. 117).

What Ricardo conceives as the distribution of total capital among the various branches of production appears here in the as yet more naïve form of the [quantity of] industry needed in order to produce "a *particular* commodity". The levelling out of prices among the sellers of *the same* commodity to the *market*-price and the *levelling out of the market-prices* of the *various* commodities to the cost-price are here as yet jumbled up in complete confusion.

At this point Smith, only quite incidentally, touches upon the influence of the variation in the real values of commodities on the natural prices or cost-prices.

Namely in agriculture
"the same quantity of industry will, in different years, produce very different quantities of commodities; while, in others, it will produce always the same, or very nearly the same. The same number of labourers in husbandry will, in different years, produce very different quantities of corn, wine, oil, hops, etc. But the same number of spinners and weavers will every year produce the same, or very nearly the same, quantity of linen and woollen cloth. ... In the other" (the non-agricultural) "species of industry, the *produce of equal quantities of labour being always the same*, or very nearly the same", (i.e., so long as the conditions of production remain *the same*) "it can be more exactly suited to the effectual demand" ([O.U.P., Vol. I, pp. 64-65; Garnier,] l.c., pp. 117-18).

Adam Smith sees here that a mere change in the productivity of "equal quantities of labour", therefore, in the actual values of commodities, alters cost-prices. But he makes this again more shallow by reducing it to the relation between supply and demand. According to his own arguments, the proposition as he presents it, is wrong. For, while in agriculture, as a result of varying seasons etc., "equal quantities of labour" yield different quantities of products, he himself has demonstrated that as a result of machinery, division of labour etc. "equal quantities of labour" yield very different amounts of product in manufacture etc. It is therefore not *this* difference which distinguishes agriculture from the other branches of industry; but the fact that in industry the degree of productive power applied is determined beforehand, while in the former, it depends on accidents of nature. But the result remains the same: the *value of the commodities* or the quantity of labour which, depending on its productivity, has to be expended on a given commodity, affects cost-prices.

In the following passage Adam Smith has also [shown] how the migration of capitals from one sphere of production to another establishes cost-prices in the various branches of production. But he is not so clear on this as Ricardo. For if the ||552| price of the commodity falls *below* its *natural price* then, according to his argument, this is due to one of the elements of this price falling *below* the natural rate. Thus it is not due to the withdrawal of *capitals alone* or to the migration of capitals, but to the migration of labour, capital or land from one branch to another. In this respect his view is more consistent than Ricardo's, but it is wrong.

"Whatever part of it" (the natural price) "was paid below the *natural* rate, the persons whose interest it affected would immediately feel the loss, and would immediately *withdraw either so much land, or so much labour,*

or so much stock, from being employed about it, that the quantity brought
to market would soon be no more than sufficient to supply the effectual
demand. Its *market-price,* therefore, would soon rise to the *natural price.*
This at least would be the case where there was perfect liberty" ([O.U.P.,
Vol. I, p. 69; Garnier,] l.c., p. 125).

This represents an essential difference between Smith's and
Ricardo's conceptions of the levelling out to the *natural price.*
Smith's [conception] is based on his false assumption, that the
three elements independently determine the value of the commodity, while Ricardo's is based on the correct assumption that
it is the *average rate of profit* (at a given level of wages), which
alone determines the cost-prices.

[2. Adam Smith's Theory of the "Natural Rate" of Wages, Profit and Rent]

"The *natural price* itself varies with the *natural rate* of each of its component parts, of wages, profit, and rent" ([O.U.P., Vol. I, p. 70; Garnier,]
l.c., p. 127).

In chapters VIII, IX, X and XI of Book I, Adam Smith then
seeks to determine the natural rate of these "component parts",
wages, rent and profit, and the fluctuations in these rates.

Chapter VIII: "Of the Wages of Labour"

At the start of the chapter on wages, Smith—forsaking the
illusory standpoint of competition—in the first place shows the
true nature of surplus-value and [regards] profit and rent as
mere forms of surplus-value.

The basis from which he determines the natural rate of wages
is the value of labour-power itself, the *necessary wage.*

"A man must always live by his work, and his wages must at least be sufficient to maintain him. They must even upon most occasions be somewhat
more, otherwise it would be impossible for him to bring up a family, and
the race of such workmen could not last beyond the first generation" ([O.U.P.,
Vol. I, p. 75; Garnier,] l.c., p. 136).

This, however, becomes meaningless again because he never
asks himself how the value of the necessary means of subsistence, i.e., of the *commodity* in general is determined. And here,
since he has moved away from his main conception, Adam Smith
would have to say: The price of wages is determined by the
price of the means of subsistence and the price of the means
of subsistence is determined by the price of wages. Having once

assumed that the *value* of wages is fixed, he gives an exact description of its fluctuations, as they appear in competition, and the circumstances that cause these fluctuations. This belongs to the exoteric part [of his work] and does not concern us here.

⟨In particular [he deals with] the *accumulation* of capital, but he does not tell us what determines it, since this accumulation can only be rapid either if the rate of wages is relatively low and the productivity of labour high (in this case a rise in wages is always the result of a permanently low level of wages during the preceding period) or if the rate of accumulation is low but the productivity of labour is high. From his standpoint, he would have to deduce the rate of wages in the first case from the rate of profit (i.e., from the rate of wages), and in the second case from the gross amount of profit, but this would in turn necessitate his investigating the *value* of the commodity.⟩

He tries to derive the value of the commodity from the value of labour which is one of its constituent parts. And on the other hand he explains the level of wages by saying that

"the wages of labour do not ... fluctuate with the price of provisions" ([O.U.P., Vol. I, p. 82; Garnier,] l.c., p. 149) and that "the wages of labour vary more from place to place than the price of provisions" ([O.U.P., Vol. I, p. 82; Garnier,] l.c., p. 150).

In fact the chapter contains nothing relevant to the question except the definition of the *minimum wage*, alias the value of labour-power. Here Adam Smith instinctively resumes the thread of his more profound argument, only to lose it again, so that even the above-cited definition [signifies] nothing. For how [does he propose to] determine the *value* of the necessary means of subsistence—and therefore of commodities in general? Partly by the natural price of labour. And how is this to be determined? By the value of necessaries, or commodities in general. A vicious circle. As to the rest, the chapter contains not a word on the issue, the *natural price* of labour, ||553| but only investigations into the rise of wages above the level of the natural rate, demonstrating that the rise of wages is proportionate to the rapidity with which capital accumulates, that is, to the progressive accumulation of capital. Then he examines the various conditions of society in which this takes place, and finally he gives a slap in the face to the determination of the value of the commodity by wages and of wages by the value of the necessary means of subsistence, by showing that this does not appear to be the case in England. In between comes a piece of Malthusian population theory—because wages are determined by the means of subsistence necessary, not only to maintain the life of the worker, but [should be sufficient] for the reproduction of the population.

Namely after attempting to prove that wages *rose* during the eighteenth century, especially in England, Adam Smith raises the question whether this is to be regarded "as an advantage, or as an inconveniency, to the society" ([O.U.P., Vol. I, p. 87; Garnier,] l.c., p. 159). In this connection he returns temporarily to his more profound approach, according to which profit and rent are merely parts *of the product* of the worker. The workmen, he says:

"make up the far greater part of every great political society. But what improves the circumstances of the greater part, can never be regarded as any inconveniency to the whole. No society can surely be flourishing and happy, of which the far greater part of the members are poor and miserable. It is but equity, besides, that they who feed, clothe, and lodge the *whole body of the people*, should have *such a share of the produce of their own labour* as to be themselves tolerably well fed, clothed, and lodged" ([O.U.P., Vol. I, p. 87; Garnier,] l.c., pp. 159-60).

In this connection he touches upon the theory of population:

"Poverty, though it no doubt discourages, does not always prevent marriage. It seems even to be favourable to generation.... Barrenness, so frequent among women of fashion, is very rare among those of inferior station.... But poverty, though it does not prevent the generation, is extremely unfavourable to the rearing of children. The tender plant is produced; but in so cold a soil, and so severe a climate, soon withers and dies.... Every species of animals naturally multiplies in proportion to the means of their subsistence, and no species can ever multiply beyond it. But in civilised society, it is only among the inferior ranks of people that the scantiness of subsistence can set limits to the further multiplication of the human species.... *The demand for men*, like that for any other commodity, *necessarily regulates the production of men*, quickens it when it goes on too slowly, and stops it when it advances too fast" ([O.U.P., Vol. I, pp. 87-89; Garnier,] l.c., pp. 160-63 passim).

The connection between the wages minimum and the varying conditions of society is as follows:

"The wages paid to journeymen and servants of every kind must be such as may enable them, one with another, *to continue the race of journeymen and servants*, according as the increasing, diminishing, or stationary demand of the society, may happen to require" ([O.U.P., Vol. I, pp. 89-90; Garnier,] l.c., p. 164). (Of the society! That is to say—of capital.)

He then shows that the slave is "dearer" than the free labourer, because the latter himself *looks after his "wear and tear" whereas that of the former* is [controlled] "by a negligent master or careless overseer" ([O.U.P., Vol. I, p. 90; Garnier,] l.c., p. 164). The "fund" for replacing the "wear and tear" is frugally used by the free labourer whereas for the slave it is wastefully and disorderly administered.

"The fund destined for replacing or repairing, if I may say so, the *wear and tear* of the slave, is commonly managed by a negligent master or careless overseer. That destined for performing the same office with regard to the freeman is managed by the freeman himself. The disorders which generally prevail in the economy of the rich, naturally introduce themselves into the management of the former; the strict frugality and parsimonious attention of the poor as naturally establish themselves in that of the latter" ([O.U.P., Vol. I, p. 90; Garnier,] l.c., p. 164).

It is characteristic in the determination of the minimum wage or the natural price of labour, that it is lower for the free wage-labourer than for the slave. This occurs also to Adam Smith:

"The work done by freemen comes cheaper in the end than that performed by slaves.... The liberal reward of labour, therefore, as it is the effect of increasing wealth, so it is the cause of increasing population. To complain of it, is ||554| to lament over the necessary cause and effect of the greatest public prosperity" ([O.U.P., Vol. I, p. 90; Garnier,] l.c., p. 165).

Adam Smith continues to plead for a high wage.

It not only "encourages the propagation", but also "increases the industry of the common people. The wages of labour are the encouragement of industry, which, like every other human quality, improves in proportion to the encouragement it receives. A plentiful subsistence increases the bodily strength of the labourer, and the comfortable hope of bettering his condition... animates him to exert that strength to the utmost. Where wages are high, accordingly, we shall always find the workmen more active, diligent, and expeditious than where they are low" ([O.U.P., Vol. I, pp. 90-91; Garnier,] l.c., p. 166).

But high wages spur the workmen on to over-exertion and to premature destruction of their labour-power.

"Workmen ... when they are liberally paid by the piece, are very apt to overwork themselves, and to ruin their health and constitution in a few years" ([O.U.P., Vol. I, p. 91; Garnier,] l.c., pp. 166-67). "If masters would always listen to the dictates of reason and humanity, they have frequently occasion rather to moderate, than to animate the application of many of their workmen" ([O.U.P., Vol. I, p. 92; Garnier,] l.c., p. 168).

He goes on to argue against the view that "a little more plenty than ordinary may render some workmen idle" ([O.U.P., Vol. I, p. 92; Garnier,] l.c., p. 169).

Then he examines whether it is true that the workmen are more idle in years of plenty than in years of scarcity and what is the general relation between wages and the price of the means of subsistence. Here again comes the inconsistency.

"*The money price of labour* is necessarily regulated by two circumstances, the demand for labour, and *the price* of the necessaries and conveniencies of life.... The money price of labour is determined by what is requisite for purchasing this quantity" (of the necessaries and conveniencies of life) ([O.U.P., Vol. I, pp. 95-96; Garnier,] l.c., p. 175).

[He then examines] why—because of the demand for labour—wages can rise in years of plenty and fall in years of scarcity. ([O.U.P., Vol. I, p. 96 et seq.; Garnier,] l.c., p. 176 et seq.) The causes [of the rise and fall] in good and bad years counterbalance one another.

"The scarcity of a dear year, by diminishing the demand for labour, tends to lower its price, as the high price of provisions tends to raise it. The plenty of a cheap year, on the contrary, by increasing the demand, tends to raise the price of labour, as the cheapness of provisions tends to lower it. In the ordinary variations of the prices of provisions, those two opposite causes seem to counterbalance one another, which is probably, in part, the reason why the wages of labour are everywhere so much more steady and permanent than the price of provisions" ([O.U.P., Vol. I, p. 96; Garnier,] l.c., p. 177).

As against the concept of wages as the source of the value of commodities, he finally, after all this zigzagging, again advances his original, more profound view, that the value of commodities is determined by the quantity of labour; and if in good years, or with the growth of capital, the worker receives *more* commodities, then he also produces far more commodities, that is to say the individual commodity contains a smaller quantity of labour. He can therefore receive a greater quantity of commodities of less value and thus—this is the implied conclusion—profit can grow, despite rising absolute wages.

"The increase in the wages of labour necessarily increases the price of many commodities, *by increasing that part of it which resolves itself into wages*, and so far tends to diminish their consumption, both at home and abroad. The same cause, however, which raises the wages of labour, the increase of stock, tends to increase its productive powers, and to make a smaller quantity of labour produce a greater quantity of work." [This is due to] the division of labour, the use of machinery, inventions, etc. ... "There are many commodities, therefore, which, in consequence of these improvements, come to be produced *by so much less labour than before*, that *the increase of its price* is more than *compensated* by the *diminution of its quantity*" ([O.U.P., Vol. I, p. 97; Garnier,] l.c., pp. 177-78).

The labour is better paid, but less labour is contained in the individual commodity, hence a smaller amount has to be paid out. He thus allows his false theory, according to which the value of the commodity is determined by the wage as a constituent element of the value, to be annulled, or rather paralysed, counterbalanced by his correct theory, according to which the value [of the commodity] is determined by the quantity of labour it contains.

||555|*Chapter IX: "Of the Profits of Stock".*

Here accordingly the natural rate of the second element that determines and constitutes the natural price *or* value of the commodities is to be ascertained. What Adam Smith says about the cause of the *fall in the rate of profit* ([Garnier,] l.c., pp. 179, 189, 190, 193, 196, 197, etc.) shall be considered at a later stage.[a]

Adam Smith is confronted here by considerable difficulties. He says that even the determination of average wages amounts merely to ascertaining "the most usual wages" ([O.U.P., Vol. I, p. 98; Garnier], l.c., p. 179), the actual given rate of wages.

"But *even this can seldom be done with regard to the profits* of stock" ([O.U.P., Vol. I, p. 98; Garnier,] l.c., p. 179). Apart from the good or bad fortune of the entrepreneur, this profit "is affected by every variation of price in the commodities" ([O.U.P., Vol. I, p. 98; Garnier,] l.c., p. 180)

although it is precisely through the natural rate of profit, as one of the component elements of "value", that we are supposed to determine the natural price of these commodities. This [the determination of the natural rate of profit] is already difficult for a single capitalist in a single trade.

"To ascertain what is the average profit of all the different trades carried on in a great kingdom, must be much more difficult" ([O.U.P., Vol. I, p. 98; Garnier,] l.c., p. 180).

But one may form some notion of the "average profits of stock" "from the *interest of money*".

"It may be laid down as a maxim, that wherever a great deal can be made by the use of money, a great deal will commonly be given for the use of it; and that, wherever little can be made by it, less will commonly be given for it" ([O.U.P., Vol. I, p. 98; Garnier,] l.c., pp. 180-81).

Adam Smith does not say the rate of interest determines profits. He expressly states the reverse. But there are records of the rate of interest for different epochs etc.; such records do not exist for the rate of profit. The rates of interest are therefore indices from which the approximate level of the rate of profit can be judged. But the task set was not to compare the levels of actual rates of profit, but to determine the *natural level*

---

a See this volume, pp. 438 and 467.—*Ed.*

of the rate of profit. Adam Smith seeks refuge in a subsidiary investigation into the level of the rate of interest in different periods, which in no way touches upon the problem he has set himself. He makes a cursory examination of various periods in England and then compares these with Scotland, France and Holland and finds that—with the exception of the American colonies—

"*high wages of labour and high profits of stock* ... *are things, perhaps,*[a] which scarce ever go together, except in the peculiar circumstances of new colonies" ([O.U.P., Vol. I, p. 102; Garnier,] l.c., p. 187).

Here Adam Smith tries, like Ricardo—but to a certain extent with more success—to give some approximate explanation of high profits:

"A new colony must always, for some time, be more under-stocked in proportion to the extent of its territory, and more under-peopled in proportion to the extent of its stock, than the greater part of other countries. They have more land than they have stock to cultivate. What they have, therefore, is applied *to the cultivation only of what is most fertile and most favourably situated*, the land near the sea shore and along the banks of navigable rivers. Such land, too, is frequently purchased at a price below the value even of its natural produce." (In fact, therefore, it costs *nothing*.) "Stock employed in the purchase and improvement of such lands must yield a very large profit, and, consequently, afford to pay a very large interest. Its rapid accumulation in so profitable an employment enables the planter to increase the number of his hands faster than he can find them in a new settlement. Those whom he can find, therefore, are very liberally rewarded. *As the colony increases, the profits of stock gradually diminish. When the most fertile and best situated lands have been all occupied, less profit can be made by the cultivation of what is inferior both in soil and situation,* and less interest can be afforded for the stock which is so employed. In the greater part of our colonies, accordingly, the ... rate of interest has been considerably reduced during the course of the present century" ([O.U.P., Vol. I, pp. 102-03; Garnier,] l.c., pp. 187-89).

This is one of the foundations of the Ricardian explanation of why profits fall, although it is presented in a different way. On the whole, Smith explains everything here by the competition between capitals; as capitals grow, profit falls and as they diminish, profit grows, and accordingly wages rise or fall conversely.

||556| "The diminution of the capital stock of the society, or of the funds destined for the maintenance of industry, however, as it lowers the wages of labour, so it raises the profits of stock, and consequently the interest of money. By the wages of labour being lowered, the owners of what stock

---

[a] In Garnier's translation: "naturellement".—*Ed.*

remains in the society can bring their goods at less expense to market than before, and less stock being employed in supplying the market than before, they can sell them dearer" ([O.U.P., Vol. I, p. 104; Garnier,] l.c., pp. 191-92).

Then he talks about the highest possible and the lowest possible rates [of profit].

The "highest rate" is that which, "in the price of the greater part of commodities, eats up the whole of what should go to the rent of the land, and leaves only what is sufficient to pay the labour of preparing and bringing them to market, according to the lowest rate at which labour can anywhere be paid, the bare subsistence of the labourer" ([O.U.P., Vol. I, p. 108; Garnier,] l.c., pp. 197-98).

"The lowest ordinary rate of profit must always be something more than what is sufficient to compensate the occasional losses to which every employment of stock is exposed. It is this surplus only which is neat or clear profit" ([O.U.P., Vol. I, p. 107; Garnier,] l.c., p. 196).

Adam Smith himself in fact characterises what he says about the "*natural rate of profit*":

"Double interest is in Great Britain reckoned what the merchants call a *good, moderate, reasonable profit*; terms which, I apprehend, mean no more *than a common and usual profit*" ([O.U.P., Vol. I, p. 108; Garnier,] l.c., p. 198).

And indeed, Smith calls this "common and usual profit" neither moderate nor good, but his term for it is "the *natural rate* of profit". However, he does not tell us at all what it is or how it is determined although we are supposed to determine the "natural price" of the commodity by means of this "natural rate of profit".

"In countries which are fast advancing to riches, the low rate of profit may, in the price of many commodities, compensate the high wages of labour, and enable those countries to sell as cheap as their less thriving neighbours, among whom the wages of labour may be lower" ([O.U.P., Vol. I, p. 109; Garnier,] l.c., p. 199).

Low profits and high wages are not reciprocally opposed here, but the same cause—the quick growth or accumulation of capital—produces both. Both enter into the price; they *constitute* it. If therefore one is high while the other is low, the price remains the same, and so on.

Adam Smith here regards profit purely as a surcharge, for at the end of the chapter he says:

"In reality, high profits tend much more to raise *the price* of work than high wages" ([O.U.P., Vol. I, p. 109; Garnier,] l.c., p. 199). If, for example, the wages of all the working people in linen manufacture were to rise by twopence a day, this would only raise the price of the "piece of linen" by the number of twopences equal to the number of people employed, "multiplied by the number of days during which they had been so employed. That part of the price of the commodity which resolved itself into wages would, through all the different stages of the manufacture, rise only in arithmetical proportion to this rise of wages. But if the profits of all the different employers of those working people should be raised five per cent, that part of the price of the commodity which resolved itself into profit would, through all the different stages of manufacture, rise in *geometrical proportion* to this rise of profit.... In raising the price of commodities the rise of wages operates in the same manner as simple interest does in the accumulation of debt. The rise of profit operates like compound interest" ([O.U.P., Vol. I, pp. 109-10; Garnier,] l.c., pp. 200-01).

At the end of this chapter Adam Smith also tells us *the source* of the whole notion, that the price of the commodity, or its value, is made up out of the values of wages and profits—namely, the *amis du commerce*,[a] the faithful practitioners of competition:

"Our merchants and master-manufacturers complain much of the bad effects of high wages in raising the price, and thereby lessening the sale of their goods, both at home and abroad. They say nothing concerning the bad effects of high profits. They are silent ||557| with regard to the pernicious effects of their own gains. They complain only of those of other people" ([O.U.P., Vol. I, p. 110; Garnier,] l.c., p. 201).

Chapter X [is entitled] "Of Wages and Profit in the Different Employments of Labour and Stock." This is only concerned with detail and therefore belongs into the chapter on competition. In its way, it is very good. It is completely exoteric.

{*Productive and unproductive labour*:

"The lottery of the law ... is very far from being a perfectly fair lottery; and that, as well as many other liberal and honourable professions, is, in point of pecuniary gain, evidently under-recompensed" ([O.U.P., Vol. I, p. 118; Garnier,] Book I, Chapter X, pp. 216-17).

Similarly he says of *soldiers*:

"Their pay is less than that of common labourers, and, in actual service, their fatigues are much greater" ([O.U.P., Vol. I, pp. 121-22; Garnier,] l.c., p. 223).

And of *sailors* in the navy:

"Though their skill and dexterity are much superior to that of almost any artificers; and though their whole life is one continual scene of hardship and danger ... their wages are not greater than those of common labourers at the port which regulates the rate of seamen's wages" ([O.U.P., Vol. I, p. 122; Garnier,] l.c., p. 224).

---

[a] Friends of commerce (an expression used by Fourier).—*Ed.*

Ironically:

"It would be indecent, no doubt, to compare either a curate or a chaplain with a journeyman in any common trade. The pay of a curate or chaplain, however, may very properly be considered as of the same nature with the wages of a journeyman" ([O.U.P., Vol. I, p. 148; Garnier,] l.c., p. 271).

He expressly says of *"men of letters"* that they are underpaid because of their too great numbers and he recalls that before the invention of printing, *"a scholar and a beggar"* ([O.U.P., Vol. I, p. 151; Garnier,] l.c., pp. 276-77) were synonymous and seems to apply this, in a certain sense, to men of letters.}
The chapter is full of acute observations and important comments.

"In the same society or neighbourhood, the average and ordinary rates of profit in the different employments of stock should be more nearly upon a level than the pecuniary wages of different sorts of labour" ([O.U.P., Vol. I, p. 124; Garnier,] l.c., p. 228).
"The *extent of the market*, by giving employment to greater stocks, diminishes *apparent* profit; but by requiring supplies from a greater distance, it increases prime cost. This diminution of the one and increase of the other seem, in most cases, nearly to counterbalance one another" (in the case of such articles as bread, meat, etc.) ([O.U.P., Vol. I, p. 126; Garnier,] l.c., p. 232).
"In small towns and country villages, on account of *the narrowness of the market*, trade cannot always be extended as stock extends. In such places, therefore, though the rate of a particular person's profits may be very high, the sum or amount of them can never be very great, nor consequently that of his annual accumulation. In great towns, on the contrary, trade can be extended as stock increases, and the credit of a frugal and thriving man increases much faster than his stock. His trade is extended in proportion to the amount of both" ([O.U.P., Vol. I, p. 127; Garnier,] l.c., p. 233).

Regarding the *false statistical* presentation of wages, for instance in the sixteenth and seventeenth etc. centuries, Adam Smith quite rightly observes that the wages here were only, for example, the wages of cotters, who, when not occupied around their cottages or working for their masters (who gave them a house, "a small garden for pot-herbs, as much grass as will feed a cow, and, perhaps, an acre or two of bad arable land", and, when he employed them, a very poor wage)

"are said to have been willing to give their spare time for a very small recompense to anybody, and to have wrought for less wages than other labourers.... This *daily or weekly recompense*, however, seems to have been considered as *the whole of it*, by many writers who have collected the prices of labour and provisions in ancient times, and who have taken pleasure in representing both as wonderfully low" ([O.U.P., Vol. I, pp. 131-32; Garnier,] l.c., p. 242).

He makes the altogether true observation that:

"this equality in the whole of the advantages and disadvantages of the different employments of labour and stock, can take place only in such as are
the sole or principal employments of those who occupy them" ([O.U.P.,
Vol. I, p. 131; Garnier,] l.c., p. 240).

This point, incidentally, has already been quite well set forth
by Steuart, particularly in relation to agricultural wages—as
soon as time becomes precious.[78]

||558| With regard to the *accumulation of capital in the towns
during the Middle Ages*, Adam Smith very correctly notes in this
chapter, that it was principally due to the exploitation of the
country (by trade as well as by manufacture). (There were in
addition the usurers and even haute finance; in short, the money
merchants.)

"In consequence of such regulations" [i.e., regulations made by the guilds],
"indeed, each class" (*within the town corporate*) "was obliged to buy the
goods they had occasion for from every other within the town, somewhat
dearer than they otherwise might have done. But, in recompense, they were
enabled to sell their own just as much dearer; so that, so far it was as broad
as long, as they say; and in the dealings of the different classes within the
town with one another, none of them were losers by these regulations. *But
in their dealings with the country they were all great gainers*; and in these
latter dealings consists the whole trade which supports and enriches every
town.
"Every town draws its whole subsistence, and all the materials of its
industry, from the country. It pays for these chiefly in two ways. First, by
sending back to the country a part of those materials wrought up and manufactured; in which case, the price is augmented by the *wages of the
workmen, and the profits of their masters or immediate employers*; secondly,
by sending to it a part both of the rude and manufactured produce, either of
other countries, or of distant parts of the same country, imported into the
town; in which case, too, the original price of those goods is augmented by
*the wages of the carriers or sailors, and by the profits of the merchants who
employ them*. In what is gained upon the first of those branches of commerce,
consists *the advantage which the town makes by its manufactures*; in what
is gained *upon the second, the advantage of its inland and foreign trade*. The
wages of the workmen, and the profits of their different employers, make
up the whole of what is gained upon both. Whatever regulations, therefore,
tend *to increase those wages and profits beyond what they otherwise would
be*, tend *to enable the town to purchase, with a smaller quantity of its labour,
the produce of a greater quantity of the labour of the country*" ([O.U.P.,
Vol. I, pp. 140-41; Garnier,] l.c., pp. 258-59).

{Here, therefore,—l.c., t. 1, l. 1, ch. X, p. 259—Adam Smith
returns to the correct determination of value, the determination
of value by the *quantity of labour*. This should be quoted as
an example when dealing with his theory of surplus-value. If

the prices of the commodities which are exchanged between town and country are such that they represent equal quantities of labour, then they are equal to their values. Profit and wages on both sides of the exchange cannot, therefore, determine these values, but the division of these values determines profit and wages. That is why Adam Smith finds that the town, which exchanges a smaller quantity of labour against a greater quantity of labour from the countryside, draws excess profit and excess wages compared with the country. This would not be the case if it did not sell its commodities to the country for *more than* their value. In that case "wages and profits" would not increase "beyond *what they otherwise would be*". If, therefore, wages and profits are at their natural level, then they do not determine the value of the commodity, but are determined by it. Profit and wages can then only arise from the division of the *given value*, which is their precondition, this value however cannot be the result of preconceived profits and wages.}

"They give the traders and artificers in the town an advantage over the landlords, farmers, and labourers in the country, and break down that natural equality which would otherwise take place in the commerce which is carried on between them. The *whole annual produce of the labour of the society is* annually *divided* between those two different sets of people. By means of those" (town) "regulations, *a greater share* of it is given to the inhabitants of the town than would otherwise fall to them; and a less to those of the country.

"The *price* which the town really pays for the provisions and materials annually imported into it, is the quantity of manufactures and other goods annually exported from it. *The dearer the latter are sold*, the cheaper the former are bought. The industry of the town becomes more, and that of the country less advantageous" ([O.U.P., Vol. I, pp. 141-42; Garnier,] l.c., pp. 259-60).

Thus, according to Smith's presentation of the matter, if the commodities of the town and those of the country were sold in proportion to the *quantity of labour* which they each contain, then they would be sold at their *values*, and consequently the profit and wages on both sides of the exchange could not determine *these values*, but would be determined by them. The levelling out of profits—which vary because of the varying organic composition of capitals—does not concern us here, since it does not lead to differences between profits; but equalises them.

||559| "The inhabitants of a town, *being collected into one place*, can easily combine together. The most insignificant trades carried on in towns have, accordingly, in some place or other, been incorporated" ([O.U.P., Vol. I, p. 142; Garnier,] l.c., p. 261). "The inhabitants of the country, dispersed in distant places, cannot easily combine together. They have not only never

been incorporated, but the incorporation spirit never has prevailed among them. No apprenticeship has ever been thought necessary to qualify for husbandry, the great trade of the country" ([O.U.P., Vol. I, p. 143; Garnier,] l.c., p. 262).

In *this connection* Smith comes to speak of the disadvantages of the "division of labour". The farmer practises a trade requiring more intelligence than the manufacturing worker, who is subject to the division of labour.

"The direction of operations, besides, which must be varied with every change of the weather, as well as with many other accidents, requires much more judgement and discretion, than that of those which are always the same, or very nearly the same" ([O.U.P., Vol. I, p. 143; Garnier,] l.c., p. 263).

The division of labour develops the *social* productive power of labour or the productive power of *social* labour, but at the expense of the *general productive ability* of the worker. This increase in *social productive power* confronts the worker therefore as an increased productive power, *not of his* labour, but of *capital*, the force that dominates his labour. If the town labourer is more developed than the country labourer, this is only due to the circumstance that his mode of work causes him to live in *society*, whereas that of the agricultural labourer makes him live directly with nature.

"The superiority which the industry of the towns has everywhere in Europe over that of the country, is not altogether owing to corporations and corporation laws. It is supported by many other regulations. *The high duties* upon foreign manufactures, and upon all goods imported by alien merchants, all tend to the same purpose" ([O.U.P., Vol. I, p. 144; Garnier,] l.c., p. 265). These "regulations secure them" (the towns) against the competition of foreigners.

This is an act, no longer of the town bourgeoisie, but of the bourgeoisie already legislating on a national scale as the *corps de nation* or as the Third Estate of the State Assembly or the Lower House. The specific acts of the town bourgeoisie—directed against the country—are the excise and duties levied at the gates, and, in general, the indirect taxes, which have their origin in the towns (see Hüllmann),[79] while the direct taxes are of country origin. It might appear that the excise, for example, is a tax which the town imposed indirectly upon itself. The countryman must advance it, but reimburses himself in the price of the product. But this was not the case in the Middle Ages. The demand for his products—in so far as he converted these into commodities and money at all—[was, in so far as it came] from the town, mostly compulsorily restricted to the area under the jurisdiction of the town, so that he did not have the power to raise the price of his product by the full amount of the town tax.

"In Great Britain, the superiority of the industry of the towns over that of the country seems to have been greater formerly than in the present times. The wages of country labour approach nearer to those of manufacturing labour, and the profits of stock employed in agriculture to those of trading and manufacturing stock, than they are said to have done in the last century" (the seventeenth) "or in the beginning of the present" (the eighteenth). "This change may be regarded as the necessary, though very late consequence of the extraordinary encouragement given to the industry of the towns. The stocks accumulated in them come in time to be so great, that it can no longer be employed with the ancient profit in that species of industry which is peculiar to them. That industry has its limits like every other; and the *increase of stock*, by *increasing the competition*, necessarily reduces the profit. *The lowering of profit in the town forces out stock to the country*, where, by creating a new demand for country labour, it necessarily raises its wages. *It then spreads itself*, if I may say so, *over the face of the land*, and, by being employed in agriculture, *is in part restored to the country, at the expense of which, in a great measure, it had originally been accumulated in the town*" ([O.U.P., Vol. I, p. 145; Garnier,] l.c., pp. 266-67).

In *Chapter XI of Book I*, Smith then seeks to determine the *natural rate of rent*, the third element which constitutes the value of the commodity. We shall postpone consideration of this and first return again to Ricardo.

This much is clear from the foregoing: When Adam Smith identifies the *natural price* or *cost-price of the commodity* with *its value*, he does so after first abandoning his correct conception of *value*, and substituting for it the view which is evoked by and arises from the phenomena of competition. In competition, the *cost-price* and not the *value* appears as the regulator of the *market-price*—so to speak, as the *immanent price*, the value of the commodity. But in competition this cost-price appears to be represented by the given average rate of wages, profit and rent. Hence Adam Smith tries to establish these separately and independently of the *value* of the commodity— rather as elements of the natural price. Ricardo, whose main concern has been the refutation of this Smithian ||560| aberration, accepts the result that *necessarily* follows from it—namely *the identity of values and cost-prices*—although with Ricardo this result is logically *impossible*.

[CHAPTER XI]

RICARDO'S THEORY OF RENT

[1. Historical Conditions for the Development of the Theory of Rent by Anderson and Ricardo]

The main points were dealt with when discussing Rodbertus. Just a few more gleanings here.

Firstly, some comments on the historical aspect:

Ricardo was first of all concerned with the period 1770-1815, which came approximately within his own experience, and during which wheat prices were constantly rising. Anderson [on the other hand] was concerned with the eighteenth century, at the close of which he was writing. During the first half of that century wheat prices were falling and during the second half they were rising. Hence for Anderson, the law he discovered was in no way connected with a diminishing productivity of agriculture or a normal ⟨for Anderson an unnatural⟩ rise in the price of the product. For Ricardo however such a connection existed. Anderson believed that the abolition of the corn laws (at that time export premiums) caused the rise in prices during the second half of the eighteenth century. Ricardo knew that the introduction of corn laws (1815) was intended to prevent the fall in prices, and to a certain degree was bound to do so. With regard to the latter [it was] therefore necessary to point out that, if left to itself, the law of rent—*within a definite territory*—was bound to result in recourse to less fertile land, thus leading to dearer agricultural products and increased rent at the cost of industry and the mass of the population. And here Ricardo was right, both historically and in practice. Anderson on the other hand [maintained] that corn laws (and he also favours a duty on imports) must further the even development of agriculture within *a definite territory* and that for this even development agriculture needs security. Consequently he [maintained] that this *progressive development in itself*—through the law of rent he discovered—would lead to increased productivity in agriculture and thereby to a fall in the average prices of agricultural produce.

Both of them, however, start out from the viewpoint which, on the continent, seems so strange: 1. That there is no landed property to shackle any desired investment of capital in land. 2. That expansion takes place from better land to worse (this process is absolute for Ricardo, provided one leaves out of account the interruptions caused by the response of science and industry; for Anderson the worse land is in turn transformed into better land and so it is relative). 3. That a sufficient amount of capital is always available for investment in agriculture.

Now so far as 1. and 2. are concerned, it must seem very odd to the continentals, that in the country in which, according to their conception, feudal landed property has maintained itself most stubbornly, the economists, Anderson as well as Ricardo, start out from the conception that *no* landed property exists. The explanation for this is:

firstly: the peculiarity of the English "law of enclosures", which is in no way analogous with the continental portioning out of common land;

secondly: nowhere in the world has capitalist production, since Henry VII, dealt so ruthlessly with the *traditional* relations of agriculture, adapting and subordinating the conditions to its own requirements. In this respect England is the most revolutionary country in the world. Wherever the conditions handed down from history were at variance with, or did not correspond to, the requirements of capitalist production on the land, they were ruthlessly swept away; this applies not only to the position of the village communities but to the village communities themselves, not only to the habitats of the agricultural population but to the agricultural population itself, not only to the original centres of cultivation, but to cultivation itself. The German, for example, meets with economic relations that are determined by traditional circumstances such as land boundaries, the position of the economic centres, given conglomerations of the population. The Englishman meets with historical conditions of agriculture which have been progressively *created* by capital since the end of the 15th century. *"Clearing of estates"*, a technical term [well-known] in the United Kingdom, will not be found in any continental country. But what is the meaning of this "clearing of estates"? It means that without any consideration for the local inhabitants, who are driven away, for existing village communities, which are obliterated, for agricultural buildings, which are torn down, for the type of agriculture, which is transformed in one fell swoop, for instance arable land converted into grazing pasture—[in short] none of the conditions of production are accepted as they have traditionally existed but are historically *transformed* in such a way that under the circumstances, they will provide the most profitable investment for capital. To that extent, therefore, *no landed property* exists; it gives capital—i.e., the farmer—full scope, since it is only concerned with monetary income. A Pomeranian landowner, therefore, with his head full of ancestral land boundaries, centres of economy and lectures on agriculture etc., may well be amazed by Ricardo's "unhistorical" view of the ||561| development of conditions in agriculture. This shows merely that he naïvely confuses Pomeranian conditions with those prevailing in England. But it cannot be said that Ricardo, who in this case starts from the conditions in England, is just as narrow-minded as the Pomeranian landowner, who can think only in terms of Pomeranian conditions. English conditions are the only ones in which *modern landownership,* i.e., landownership which has been *modified* by capitalist production, has been adequately developed. For the modern—the capitalist—mode of production, the English view is here the classical view. The Pomeranian, on the other hand, judges the developed relations from a historically lower and as yet inadequate form.

Indeed, most of Ricardo's continental critics even take as their starting-point conditions in which the capitalist mode of production, adequate or inadequate, does not as yet exist at all. It is as if a guild-master wanted, lock, stock and barrel, to apply Adam Smith's laws—which presuppose free competition—to his guild economy.

The presupposition of the movement from better to worse land—relatively to the particular stage in the development of the productive power of labour as with Anderson, and not absolutely as with Ricardo—could only arise in a country such as England, where within a relatively very small territory capital has farmed so ruthlessly and has for centuries mercilessly sought to adapt to its own needs all traditional relationships of agriculture. Thus it [the presupposition] could only arise where, unlike the continent, capitalist production in agriculture does not date from yesterday and does not have to fight against old traditions.

A second factor influencing the English was the knowledge they gained through their *colonies.* We have seen[a] that Adam Smith's work—with direct reference to the colonies—already contains the basis for the entire Ricardian viewpoint. In these colonies, and especially in those which produced only merchandise such as tobacco, cotton, sugar etc. and not the usual foodstuffs, where, right from the start, the colonists did not seek subsistence but set up a business, fertility was of course decisive, *given the situation* [of the land], and given the fertility, *the situation* of the land was decisive. They did not act like the Germans, who settled in Germany in order to make their home there, but like people who, driven by motives of *bourgeois production*, wanted to produce *commodities*, and their point of view was, from the outset, determined not by the product but by the sale of the product. That *Ricardo* and other English writers transferred this point of view—which emanated from people who were themselves already the product of the capitalist mode of production—from the colonies to the course of world history and that they took the *capitalist mode of production* as a premise for agriculture in general, as it was for *their* colonists, is due to the fact that they saw in these colonies, only in more obvious form, *without the fight against traditional relations,* and therefore *untarnished,* the same domination of capitalist production in agriculture as hits the eye everywhere in their own country. Hence, if a German professor or landowner—belonging to a country which differs from all others in its complete lack of colonies—considers such a view to be "false", then this is quite understandable.

Finally the presupposition of a continuous flow of capital from one sphere of production into another, this *basic assumption of Ricardo's* amounts to nothing more than the assumption that developed capitalist production predominates. Where this domination is not yet established, this presupposition does not exist. For instance, a Pomeranian landowner will find it strange that neither Ricardo nor indeed any English writer ever suspects that agriculture might *lack capital.* The Englishman does, indeed, complain of lack of land in proportion to capital, but *never* of a lack of capital in proportion to the land. *Wakefield, Chalmers,* etc. try to explain the fall in the rate of profit from the former circumstance. The latter does not exist for any English writer;

---

[a] See this volume, p. 228.—*Ed.*

Corbet notes as a self-explanatory fact, that *capital is always redundant in all branches of production*. On the other hand, bearing in mind the situation in Germany, the landowner's difficulties in borrowing money—because mostly it is the land-owner himself who cultivates the land and not a capitalist class which is quite independent of him—it is understandable that Herr Rodbertus, for example, is surprised at "the Ricardian fiction, that the *supply* of capital is regulated by the desire to invest it". (*[Sociale Briefe an v. Kirchmann. Dritter Brief*, Berlin, 1851]* p. 211.) What the Englishman lacks is a "field of action", opportunity for investment of the available stock of capital. But a "desire for capital" to "invest", on the part of the only class which has capital to invest—the capitalist class—this does not exist in England.

||562| This "desire for capital" is Pomeranian.

The objection made by English writers against Ricardo was not that capital was not available in any desired quantity for particular investments, but that the return flow of capital from agriculture encountered specific technical etc. obstacles.

This kind of critical-continental censoriousness of Ricardo, therefore, only shows the lower stage in the conditions of pro-duction from which these "sages" start out.

[2. The Connection Between Ricardo's Theory of Rent and His Explanation of Cost-Prices]

Now to the matter in hand.

In the first place, in order to isolate the problem, we must leave aside entirely *differential rent*, which *alone* exists for Ri-cardo. By *differential rent* I understand the *difference in the magnitude* of rent—the greater or smaller rent which is due to the *different fertility of the various types of land*. (Given equal fertility, differential rent can only arise from differences in the amounts of capital invested. This case does not exist for our problem and does not affect it.) This differential rent merely corresponds to the *excess profits* which, given the *market-price* or, more correctly, the *market-value*, will be made in every branch of industry, for example cotton spinning, by *that* capi-talist whose conditions of production are *better* than the average conditions of this particular trade. For the *value* of the com-modity of a particular sphere of production is determined, not by the *quantity of labour* which the individual commodity costs, but by the quantity which *the* commodity costs that is produced under the *average* conditions of the sphere. Manufacture and agriculture only differ from one another here in that in the one, the excess profits fall into the pocket of the capitalist himself, whereas in the other they are pocketed by the landowner, and furthermore, that in the former they are *f l u i d*, they are not lasting, are made by this capitalist or that, and always disappear again, while in the latter they *become fixed* because of their enduring (at least for a long period) natural basis in the *variations in the land.*

This differential rent must therefore be left out of account, but it should be noted that it may exist not only when a movement from better to inferior land takes place but also from inferior to better land. In both cases the only requirement is that the newly cultivated land is necessary but at the same time only just sufficient to satisfy the additional demand. If the newly cultivated, better land were *more* than sufficient to satisfy the additional demand then, according to the volume of the additional demand, part or all of the inferior land would be thrown *out of cultivation* or, at any rate, out of *cultivation of that product* which forms the basis of the agricultural rent, i.e., in England of wheat and in India of rice. Thus differential rent does not presuppose a *progressive deterioration of agriculture*, but can equally well spring from a *progressive improvement* in it. Even where it is based on the descent to worse types of land, firstly this *descent* may be due to an improvement in the productive forces of agriculture, in that the cultivation of the worse land, at the *price* which is set by demand, is *only* made possible by greater productive power. Secondly, the *worse land* can be improved; the differences will nevertheless remain, although they will become smaller, so that as a result there is only a *relative, comparative* decrease in productivity— whereas *absolute* productivity *increases*. This was in fact the presupposition made by Anderson, the original author of the Ricardian law.

Then, in the second instance, only the *agricultural rent in the strict sense* should be considered here, in other words the rent of the land which supplies the chief vegetable foods. Smith has already explained that the rents of land which supplies the other products, such as stock-raising etc., are determined by *that rent*; that they are themselves *derived*, determined by the law of rent and not determining it. In themselves therefore these rents do not furnish any useful material for the understanding of the law of rent in its original, pure condition: There is nothing primary about them.

This settled, the question is reduced to the following: Does an *absolute rent* exist? That is, a rent which arises from the fact that capital is invested in agriculture rather than manufacture; a rent which is quite independent of *differential rent* or *excess profits* which are yielded by capital invested in better land?

It is clear that Ricardo correctly answers this question in the *negative*, since he starts from *the false* assumption that *values* and *average prices of commodities are identical*. If this were the case, it would be a tautology to say that the price of agricultural products is *above* their *cost-price*—when ||563| the constant price of agricultural products yields, beyond the average profits, also an *extra rent*, a constant surplus over and above the average profit—for this cost-price equals the advances plus the average profit and nothing else. Were the prices of agricultural products to stand *above* their cost-prices, and always to yield an excess profit, they would consequently stand *above* their value. There would be no alternative but to assume that agricultural products are perpetually sold *above* their value, which, however, equally presupposes that all other products are sold *below* their value, or that value in general is something quite different from that which the theory requires it to be. Taking into account all compensations which take place between the different capitals owing to differences arising from the process of circulation, *the same quantity of labour* (immediate and accumulated) would produce a *higher* value in agriculture than in manufacture. The value of the commodity would therefore *not* be determined by the quantity of labour contained in it. The whole foundation of political economy would thus be thrown overboard. Ergo, Ricardo rightly concludes: no absolute rents. Only differential rent is possible; in other words the value of the agricultural product grown on the worst land equals the *cost-price* of the product, as [with] every other commodity, [this is equal to its] value. The capital invested in the worst land differs from capital invested in manufacture only by *the type of investment,* by its being a particular species of investment. Here therefore the universal validity of the law of value becomes apparent. *Differential rent*—and this is the sole rent on better land—is nothing but the excess profit yielded by capitals employed in above-average conditions owing to the [establishment of] *one identical market-value* in *every* sphere of production. This excess profit consolidates itself only in agriculture because of its *natural basis* and, furthermore, the excess profit flows not into the pocket of the capitalist but into that of the landowner since it is the *landowner* who represents this natural basis.

The entire argument collapses together with Ricardo's assumption, that *cost-price* equals *value*. The *theoretical interest* which forces him into a denial of absolute rent disappears. If the value of the commodities differs from their cost-price, then they necessarily fall into three categories. In the first category, cost-price is equal to the value of the commodity, in the second, the value is *below* its cost-price and in the third it is *above* its cost-price. The fact, therefore, that the *price* of the agricultural product yields a rent, only shows that the agricultural product belongs to that group of commodities whose value is *above* their cost-price. The only remaining problem requiring solution would be: why, in contrast to other commodities whose value is also *above* their cost-price, competition between capitals does not reduce the value of agricultural products to their *cost-price*. The question already contains the answer. Because, according to the presupposition, this can only happen in so far as the competition between capitals is able to effect such an equalisation, and this in turn can only occur to the extent that all the conditions of production are either directly created by capital or are equally—elementally—at its disposal as if it had created them. With land this is not the case, because *landed property* exists and capitalist production starts its career on the *presupposition* of *landed property*, which is not its own creation, but which was already there *before* it. The mere existence of landed property thus answers the question. All that capital can do is to subject agriculture to the conditions of capitalist production. But it cannot deprive *landed property* of its hold on that part of the agricultural product which capital could appropriate—not through its own action—but *only* on the assumption of the *non-existence of landed property*. Since landed property exists, capital must however leave the excess of value over cost-price to the landowner. But this difference [between value and cost-price] itself only arises from a difference in the composition of the *organic* component parts of capital. All commodities whose value, in accordance with this organic composition, is *above* the cost-price, thereby show that the labour expended on them is *relatively* less productive than that expended on the commodities whose value is equal to the cost-price and even less productive than that expended on the commodities whose value is *below* the cost-price; for they require a greater quantity of *immediate* labour in proportion to the *past labour* contained in the constant capital; they require more labour in order to set in motion a definite capital. This is a *historical* difference and can therefore disappear. The same chain of reasoning which demonstrates the possibility of the existence of *absolute rent*, shows its reality, its existence, as a purely historical fact, which belongs to a *certain* stage of development of agriculture and which may disappear at a higher stage.

Ricardo explained differential rent from an *absolute decrease in productivity* in agriculture. Differential rent does not presuppose this, nor does Anderson make this assumption. On the other hand Ricardo denies the existence of absolute rent because he ||564| assumes the *organic composition of capital* to be the same in industry and agriculture and so denies the purely historical fact of the *lower development* of the productive power of labour in agriculture as compared with manufacture. Hence he falls into a twofold historical error: On the one hand, he assumes that the productivity of labour in agriculture is *absolutely the same* as in industry, thus denying a purely *historical* difference in their actual stage of development. On the other hand, he assumes an *absolute decrease in the productivity of agriculture* and regards this as its law of development. He does the one in order to make *cost-price* on the worst land equal *value* and he does the other in order to explain the differences between the *cost-prices* [of the products] of the better kinds of land and their *values*. The whole blunder originates in the confusion of *cost-price* with *value*.

Thus the Ricardian theory is disposed of. The rest was dealt with earlier, in the chapter on Rodbertus.

[3. The Inadequacy of the Ricardian Definition of Rent]

I have already indicated[a] that Ricardo opens the chapter by stating that it is necessary to examine "whether the *appropriation* of land, and the consequent creation of rent" ([David

---

a See this volume, p. 168.—*Ed.*

Ricardo, *On the Principles of Political Economy, and Taxation,*
third edition, London, 1821], p. 53) do not interfere with the
determination of value by labour-time. And he says later:

"Adam Smith ... cannot be correct in supposing that the *original rule
which regulated the exchangeable value of commodities,* namely, the comparative quantity of labour by which they were produced, can *be at all
altered by the appropriation of land and the payment of rent*" (l.c., p. 67).

This direct and conscious connection which Ricardo's theory
of rent has with the determination *of value* is its theoretical
merit. Apart from that this *Chapter II "On Rent"* is rather inferior to West's exposition. It contains much that is queer,
petitio principii and unfair dealing with the problem.

Actual agricultural rent, which Ricardo justifiably here treats
as rent proper, is that which is paid for the permission to
invest capital, to produce capitalistically, *in the element land.*
Here land is the *element of production.* This does not apply,
for example, to rent for buildings, waterfalls etc. The powers
of nature which are paid for in these cases enter into production as a *condition,* be it as productive power or as *sine qua
non,* but they are not the *element* in which this particular
branch of production is carried on. Again, in rents for mines,
coal-mines etc., the earth is the reservoir, from whose bowels
the use-values are to be torn. In this case payment is made for
the land, not because it is the *element* in which production is
to take place, as in agriculture, not because it enters *into* production as one of the conditions of production, as in the case
of the waterfall or the building site, but because it is a reservoir
containing the *use-values,* which are to be got hold of through
industry.

Ricardo's explanation that:

"*Rent* is that portion of the produce of the earth, which is paid to the
landlord for *the use* of the *original* and *indestructible powers of the soil*"
(l.c., p. 53)

is poor. Firstly, the soil has no "indestructible powers". (A note
on this is to follow at the end of this chapter.) Secondly, it has
no "original" powers either, since the land is in no way "original", but rather the product of an historical and natural process. But let that pass. By "original" powers of the land we
understand here those, which it possesses independently of the
action of human industry, although, on the other hand, the
powers given to it by human industry, become just as much its

original powers as those given to it by the process of nature. Apart from this, it is correct to say that rent is a payment for the *"use"* of natural things, irrespective of whether it is for the use of the "original powers" of the soil or of the power of the waterfall or of land for building or of the treasures to be found in the water or in the bowels of the earth.

As distinct from the *agricultural rent proper*, Adam Smith (says Ricardo) speaks of the rent paid for wood from virgin forests, rent of coal-mines and stone-quarries. The way in which Ricardo disposes of this is rather strange.

He begins by saying that the rent of land must not be confused with the interest and profit of capital (l.c., p. 53), that is:

"capital [...] employed in ameliorating the quality of the land, and in erecting such buildings as were necessary to secure and preserve the produce" (l.c., p. 54).

From this he immediately [passes on] to the above-mentioned examples from Adam Smith. With regard to virgin forests:

"Is it not, however, evident, that the person who paid what he" (Adam Smith) "calls rent, paid it in consideration of the *valuable commodity* which was then standing on the land, and that he actually *repaid himself with a profit, by the sale of the timber*?" (l.c., p. 54).

Similarly with the stone-quarries and coal-mines.

"...the compensation ||565| [...] for the mine or quarry, is paid for the *value* of the coal or stone which can be removed from them, and has no connection with the original and indestructible powers of the land. This is a distinction of great importance, in an enquiry concerning rent and profits; for it is found, that the laws which regulate the progress of rent, are widely different from those which regulate the progress of profits, and seldom operate in the same direction" (l.c., pp. 54-55).

This is very strange logic. One must distinguish *rent* paid to the owner of the land for the *use* of the *"original and indestructible powers of the soil"* from the *interest and profit* which is paid to him for the capital he has invested in *ameliorating* the land, etc. The *"compensation"* which is paid to the owner of naturally-grown forests for the right to "remove" wood, or to the owner of stone-quarries and coal-mines for the right to remove stones and coal, is not *rent*, because it is not a payment for the "use of the original and indestructible powers of the soil". Very well. But Ricardo argues as though this "compensation" were the same as the profit and interest which are paid for capital invested in ameliorations of the land. But this is wrong. Has the owner of a "virgin forest" invested

"capital" in it so that it may bear "wood" or has the owner
of stone-quarries and coal-mines invested "capital" in these,
so that they may contain "stones" and "coal"? Whence, therefore, his "compensation"? It is by no means—as Ricardo tries
to make out—profit or interest of capital. Therefore it is
"rent" and nothing else, even if it is not *rent* as defined by
Ricardo. But this only shows that his definition of rent excludes
those forms of it where the "compensation" is paid for mere
natural things, in which no human labour is embodied, and
where it is paid to the *owner* of these natural things only because he is the "owner", *the owner of land*, whether this consists of soil, forest, fish pond, waterfall, building land or anything else. But, says Ricardo, the man who *paid* for the right to
fell trees in the forest, paid "in consideration of the *valuable
commodity* which was then *standing on the land* and [...] actually *repaid himself with a profit*, by the sale of the timber"
[p. 54]. Stop! When Ricardo here calls the wood, i.e., the trees
"standing on the land" in the virgin forest a *"valuable* commodity", then this means only that it is potentially a *use-value*.
And this use-value is expressed here in the word "valuable".
But it is not a *"commodity"*. Because for this it would, at the
same time, have to be exchange-value, in other words, to contain a certain quantity of labour expended upon it. It only
becomes a commodity by being separated from the virgin
forest, by being felled, removed and transported—by being transformed from wood into timber. Or does it only become a commodity by the fact it is *sold*? Then arable land too becomes
a commodity by the mere act of *selling*?

Then we would have to say: *Rent is the price paid to the
owner of natural forces or mere products of nature* for the right
of using those forces or appropriating (by labour) those products. This is in fact the form in which all rent *appears* originally. But then the question remains to be solved, how things
which have no *value* can have a *price* and how this is compatible with the general theory *of value*. The question: for *what
purpose* does the man pay "a compensation" for the right to
remove timber from the land upon which it stands, has nothing to do with the real question. The question is: from what
fund does he pay? Well, says Ricardo, *"by the sale of the timber"*. That is, out of the *price* of the timber. And furthermore,
this price was such that, as Ricardo says, the man "actually repaid himself *with a profit*". Now we know where we are. The

price of the timber must at any rate equal the sum of money representing the quantity of labour necessary to fell the timber, to remove it, to transport it, to bring it to market. Now is the profit with which the man "repays" himself, an addition over and above this *value*, this exchange-value just imparted to the wood through the labour expended upon it? If Ricardo said this then he would fall into the crudest conception, far beneath his own doctrine. No. Given that the man was a capitalist, the profit is part of the labour he employed in the production of the "timber", the part for which he did *not pay*; and the man would have made the same profit, if he had set in motion the same amount of labour, shall we say, in cotton spinning. (If the man is not a capitalist, then the profit is equal to that quantity of his labour which he exerts beyond that which is necessary to cover his wages, and which would have constituted the profit of the capitalist, had a capitalist employed him, but which now constitutes his own profit because he is his own wage-labourer and his own capitalist in *one and the same* person.) But here we come to the *ugly word* that this timber man "actually *repaid* himself with a profit". This gives the whole transaction a very ordinary look and corresponds to the crude manner of thinking which this capitalist, who removes timber, may himself have of the source of his profit. First he pays the owner of the virgin forest for the use-value wood, which, however, has no "value" (value in exchange) and which, so long as it "stands upon the land" has not even a use-value. He may pay him £5 per ton. And then he sells the same wood to the public (setting aside his other costs) at £6 and so actually pays back to himself the £5 with a profit of 20 per cent. [He] "actually repaid himself with a profit". If the owner of the forest had only demanded "compensation" of £2 (40s.), then the timber man would have sold the ton at £2 8s. instead of at [£] 6. ||566| Since he always adds the same rate of profit, the price of timber would be high or low here because the rent is high or low. The latter would enter into the price as a constituent part but would in no way be the result of the price. Whether the "rent"—compensation—is paid to the owner of the land for the use of the "power" of the land or for the "use" of the "natural products" of the land, in no way alters the economic relations, in no way alters the fact that money is paid for "a natural thing" (power or produce of the earth) upon which no previous human labour has been spent. And thus on the second page of his chapter *"On Rent"* Ricardo would have overthrown his whole theory in order to avoid a difficulty. It would appear that Adam Smith was a great deal more far-sighted here.

The same case with the stone-quarries and coal-mines.

"The compensation *given* for the mine or quarry, is paid for the *value* of the coal or stone which can be removed from them, and has no connection with the *original* and indestructible *powers* of the land"[a] (l.c., pp. 54-55).

No! But there is a very significant connection with the *"original* and destructible *productions* of the soil". The word *"value"* is just as ugly here as the phrase *"repaid* himself with a profit" was above.

Ricardo never uses the word *value* for utility or usefulness or "value in use". Does he therefore mean to say that the "compensation" is paid to the owner of the quarries and coal-mines for the *"value"* the coal and stone have before they are removed from the quarry and the mine—in their original state? Then he invalidates his entire doctrine of value. Or does *value* mean here, as it must do, the *possible* use-value and hence also the *prospective exchange*-value of coal and stone? Then it means nothing but that their owner is paid *rent* for the permission to use the "original composition of the soil" for the production of coal and stones. And it is absolutely incomprehensible why this should not be called "rent", in the same way as if the permission were given to use the "powers" of the land for the production of wheat. Or we end up again with the annulment of the whole theory of rent, as explained in connection with wood. According to the correct theory, there are no difficulties involved here at all. The labour, or capital, employed in the "production" ⟨not reproduction⟩ of wood, coal or stone (this labour, it is true, does not create these natural products, but separates them from their elementary connection with the earth and so "produces" them as usable wood, coal or stone) evidently belongs to those spheres of production in which the part of capital laid out in wages is greater than that laid out in constant capital, [where consequently the amount of] direct labour is greater than that of "past" labour the result of which serves as a means of production. If, therefore, the commodity is sold at its value here, then this value

---

[a] In the manuscript: "soil".—*Ed.*

will be above its *cost-price,* i.e., the wear and tear of the instruments of labour, the wages, and the average profit. The *excess*
can thus be paid as rent to the owner of forest, quarry or coal-
mine.

But why these clumsy manoeuvres of Ricardo's, such as the
wrong use of value etc.? Why this clinging to the explanation
of rent as a payment for the use of the "original and indestructible powers of the land"? Perhaps the answer will emerge
later. In any case, he wants to distinguish, to mention specifically, the agricultural rent in the strict sense and at the same
time to open the way for differential rent, by saying that payment for this elementary power can only be made in so far
as it develops different degrees of power.

[CHAPTER XII]

TABLES OF DIFFERENTIAL RENT AND COMMENT

[1. Changes in the Amount and Rate of Rent]

A further comment on the above: Supposing more productive or better situated coal-mines and stone-quarries were
discovered, so that, with the same quantity of labour, they yielded a larger product than the older ones, and indeed *so large
a product* that it covered the entire demand. Then the value
and therefore the price of coal, stones, timber, would fall and
as a result the old coal-mines and stone-quarries would have
to be closed. They would yield neither profit, nor wages, nor
rent. Nevertheless, the *new* ones would yield rent just as the
old ones did previously although *less* (at a lower rate). For
every increase in the productivity of labour reduces the amount
of capital laid out [in] wages, in proportion to the constant capital which is in this case laid out in tools. Is this correct? Does
this also apply here, where the change in the productivity of
labour does not arise from a change in the *method of production* itself, but from the natural fertility of the coal-mine
or the stone-quarry, or from their situations? One can only
say here that in this case *the same* quantity of capital yields
more tons of coal or stone and that therefore each individual
ton contains less labour; the total tonnage, however, contains
as much as, or even more [labour], if the new mines or quarries satisfy not only the old demand which was previously
supplied by the old mines and quarries, but also an additional
demand, and, moreover, an additional demand which is greater
than the difference between the productivity of the old and
that of the new mines and quarries. But this would not alter

the *organic composition* of the capital *employed*. It would be true to say that the price of a ton, an individual ton, contained less rent, but only because altogether it contained less labour, hence also less wages and less profit. The *proportion* of the *rate of rent* to profit would, however, not be affected by this. Hence we can ||567| only say the following:

If demand remains the same, if, therefore, *the same* quantity of coal and stone is to be produced as before, then *less capital* is employed now in the new richer mines and quarries than before, in the old ones, in order to produce *the same* mass of commodities. The total value of the latter thus falls, hence also the total amount of rent, profit, wages and constant capital employed. But the proportions of rent and profit change no more than those of profit and wages or of profit and the capital laid out, because there has been no *organic* change in the capital employed. Only the *size* and not the *composition* of the capital employed has changed, hence neither has the method of production.

If there is an *additional demand* to be satisfied, an additional demand moreover that equals the difference in fertility between the new and the old mines and quarries, then *the same amount of capital* will be used now as previously. The value of the individual ton falls. But the total tonnage has the same value as before. As regards the individual ton, the size of the portions of value which resolve into profit and rent decreased together with the value it contained. But since the amount of *capital* has remained the same and with it the total value of its product and no *organic* change has taken place in its composition, the *absolute amount of rent and profit* has remained the same.

If the *additional demand* is so great that with the same capital investment it is not covered by the difference in fertility between the new and the old mines and quarries, then additional capital will have to be employed in the new mines. In this case—provided the growth of the total capital invested is not accompanied by a change in the distribution of labour, the application of machinery, in other words provided there is *no* change in the *organic* composition of the capital—*the amount of rent and profit* grows because the value of the total product grows, the value of the total tonnage, although the value of each individual ton falls and therefore also that part of its value which resolves into rent and profit.

In all these instances, there is *no change* in the rate of rent, because there is no *change* in the *organic composition* of the capital employed (however much its *magnitude* may *alter*). If, on the other hand, the change arose out of such a change—i.e., from a decrease in the amount of capital laid out in wages as compared with that laid out in machinery, etc., so that the method of production itself is altered—then the *rate of rent* would fall, because the difference between the value of the commodity and the cost-price would have decreased. In the three cases considered above, this does not decrease. For though the value falls, the cost-price of the individual commodity falls likewise, in that less labour is expended upon it, less paid and unpaid labour.

Accordingly, therefore, when the greater productivity of labour, or the lower value of a certain measure of commodities produced, arises only from a change in the productivity of the natural elements, from the difference between the natural degree of fertility of soils, mines, quarries etc., then the amount of rent may fall because, under the altered conditions, a lesser quantity of capital is employed; it may remain constant if there is an additional demand; it may grow, if the additional demand is greater than the difference in productivity between the previously employed and the newly employed natural agencies. The rate of rent, however, could only grow with a change in the organic composition of the capital employed.

Thus the *amount of rent* does not necessarily fall if the worse soil, quarry, coal-mine etc. is abandoned. The *rate of rent*, moreover, can never fall if this abandoning is purely the result of *lesser* natural fertility.

Ricardo distorts the correct idea, that in this case, depending on the state of demand, the *amount of rent* may fall, in other words depending upon whether the *amount of capital employed* decreases, remains the same or grows; he confuses it with the fundamentally wrong idea, that the *rate of rent* must fall, which is an *impossibility* on the assumption made, since it has been assumed that *no change* in *the organic composition of capital* has taken place, therefore no change affecting the *relationship between value and cost-price*, the only relationship that determines the *rate of rent*.

[2. Various Combinations of Differential and Absolute Rent. Tables A, B, C, D, E]

But what happens to *differential rents* in this case?

Supposing that three groups of coal-mines were being worked: I, II and III. Of these, I bore the absolute rent, II a rent which was twice that of I, and III a rent which was twice that of II or four times that of I. In this example, I bears the absolute rent R, II 2R and III 4R. Now if No. IV is opened up, and if this is more productive than I, II and III, and if it is so extensive that the capital invested in it can be as great as that in I, [then] in this case—the former *state of demand remaining constant*—the same amount of capital as was previously invested in I would now be invested in IV. I would thereupon be closed and a part of the capital invested in II would have to be withdrawn. IV would suffice to replace I and a part of II, but III and IV would not suffice to supply the whole demand, without part of II continuing to be worked. Let us assume, for the sake of the illustration, that IV—using the same amount of capital as was previously invested in I—is capable of providing the whole of the supply from I and half the supply from II. If, therefore, half the previous capital were invested in II, the old capital in III and the new in IV, then the whole market would be supplied.

||568| What changes had taken place, or how would the changes accomplished affect the general rental, the rents of I, II, III and IV?

The[a] *absolute rent*, derived from IV, would, in amount and rate, be absolutely the same as that formerly derived from I; in fact the *absolute rent*, in amount and rate, would also before have been the same on I, II and III, always supposing that the *same amount of capital* was employed in those different classes. The value of the produce of IV would be exactly identical to that formerly employed on I, because it is the produce of a capital *of the same magnitude* and of a capital of the same *organic composition*. Hence the difference between [the] value [of the product] and its cost-price must be the same; hence [also] the rate of rent. Besides, the amount [of rent] must be the same, because—at a *given rate* of rent—capitals of the same magnitude would have been employed. But, since the [market]-value of the coal is not determined by the [individual]

---

[a] This paragraph is in English in the manuscript.—*Ed.*

value of the coal derived from IV, it would bear an excess rent, or an overplus over its *absolute rent*; a rent derived, not from any difference between value and cost-price, but from the difference between the *market-value* and the *individual value* of the produce No. IV.

When we say that the absolute rent or the difference between value and cost-price on I, II, III, IV, is *the same*, provided the *magnitude* of the capital invested in them, and therefore the amount of rent with a given rate of rent is the same, then this is to be understood in the following way: The (individual) value of the coal from I is higher than that from II and that from II is higher than that from III, because *one* ton from I contains more labour than one ton from II and one ton from II more than one ton from III. But since the *organic composition* of the capital is in all three cases the same, this difference does not affect the *individual absolute rent* yielded by I, II, III. For if the value of a ton from I is greater, so is its cost-price; it is only greater in the proportion that *more capital* of the same organic composition is employed for the production of *one* ton in I than in II and of one ton in II than in III. This difference in their values is, therefore, exactly equal to the difference in their *cost-prices*, in other words to [the difference in] the relative amount of capital expended to produce one ton of coal in I, II and III. The variation in the magnitudes of value in the three groups does not, therefore, affect the *difference between value and cost-price* in the various classes. If the value is greater, then the *cost-price is greater in the same proportion*, for the value is only greater in proportion as more *capital* or labour is expended; hence the relation between value and cost-price remains the same, and hence *absolute rent* is the same.

But now let us go on to see what is the situation regarding *differential rent*.

Firstly, *less* capital is now being employed in the entire production of coal in II, III and IV. For the capital in IV is as great as the capital in I had been. Furthermore, half the capital employed in II is now withdrawn. The amount of rent on II therefore will at all events drop by a half. Only one change has taken place in capital investment, namely in II, because in IV the same amount of capital is invested as was previously invested in I. We have, moreover, assumed that capitals of the same size were invested in I, II and III, for example £ 100 in each, altogether £ 300; now therefore only

£ 250 are invested in II, III and IV, or one-sixth of the capital has been withdrawn from the production of coal.

Moreover, the *market-value* of coal has fallen. We saw that I yielded R, II 2R and III 4R. Let us assume that the product of £ 100 on I was £ 120, of which R equalled £ 10 and £ 10 equalled the profit, then the market-value of II was £ 130 (£ 10 profit and £ 20 rent), and of III £ 150 (£ 10 profit and £ 40 rent). If the product of I was 60 tons (£ 2 per ton), then that of II was 65 tons and that of III was 75 tons and the total production was 60+65+75 tons=200 tons. Now 100 will produce as much in IV as the total product of I and half the product of II, namely, 60+32$^{1}/_{2}$ tons=92$^{1}/_{2}$ tons, which, according to the old market-value, would have cost £ 185 and since the profit was 10 would thus have yielded a rent of £ 75, amounting to 7$^{1}/_{2}$ R, for the absolute rent equalled £ 10.

II, III and IV continue to yield the same number of tons, 200, since 32$^{1}/_{2}$+75+92$^{1}/_{2}$=200 tons.

But what is the position now, with regard to market-value and differential rents?

In order to answer this we must see what is the amount of the *absolute individual rent* of II. We assume that the absolute difference between *value and cost-price* in this sphere of production equals £ 10, i.e. equals the rent yielded by the worst mine, although this is not necessary unless the *market-value* was absolutely determined by the value of I. ||569| If this was, indeed, the case, then the rent on I (if the coal from I were sold at its value) in fact represented the excess of value over its own cost-price and the general cost-price of commodities in this *sphere of production*. II would therefore be selling its products at their value, if it sold its tonnage (the 65 tons) at £ 120, i.e., the individual ton at £ 1$^{11}/_{13}$. That instead it sold them at £ 2 was only due to the excess of the market-value, as determined by I, over its individual value; it was due to the excess, not of its *value*, but of its *market-value over its cost-price*.

Moreover, on the assumption made, II now sells instead of 65, only 32$^{1}/_{2}$ tons, because a capital of only £ 50 instead of a capital of £ 100, is now invested in the mine.

II therefore now sells 32$^{1}/_{2}$ tons at £ 60. £ 10 on £ 50 [the capital advanced] is 20 per cent. Of the £ 60, 5 are profit and 5 rent.

Thus we have for II: Value of the product, £ 1$^{11}/_{13}$ per ton; number of tons is 32$^{1}/_{2}$; total value of the product is £ 60; *rent* is £ 5. The rent has fallen from £ 20 to £ 5. If *the same amount* of capital were still employed, then it would only have fallen to £ 10. The rate has therefore only fallen by half. That is, it has fallen by the total difference that existed between the *market-value* as determined by I and its own value, the difference therefore that existed over and above the difference between its own value and cost-price. Its differential rent was £ 10; its rent is now £ 10, equal to its absolute rent. In II, therefore, with the reduction of the market-value to the *value* (of coal from II) differential rent has disappeared and consequently also the increased rate of rent which was doubled by this differential rent. Thus it has been reduced from £ 20 to £ 10; with this *given rate of rent*, however, the rent has been further reduced from £ 10 to £ 5, because the capital invested in II has fallen by half.

Since the *market-value* is now determined by the value of II, i.e., by £ $1^{11}/_{13}$ per ton, the *market-value* of the 75 tons produced by III is now £ $138^6/_{13}$, of which £ $28^6/_{13}$ are rent. Previously the rent was £ 40. It has, therefore, fallen by £ $11^7/_{13}$. The difference between this rent and the absolute rent used to be [£] 30; now it only amounts to [£] $18^6/_{13}$ (for $18^6/_{13}+10=28^6/_{13}$). Previously it was 4R, now it is only 2R+£ $8^6/_{13}$. As the amount of capital invested in III has remained the same, this fall is entirely due to the fall in the *rate of differential rent*, i.e., the fall in the excess of the market-value of III over its individual value. Previously, the whole amount of the rent in III was equal to the excess of the *higher market-value* over the price of production, now it is only equal to the excess of the *lower* market-value over the cost-price[80]; the difference is thus coming closer to the absolute rent of III. With a capital of £ 100, III produces 75 tons, whose [individual] value is £ 120; one ton is therefore equal to £ $1^3/_5$. But III sold the ton at £ 2, the previous market-price, therefore, at £ $2/_5$ more [than its individual value]. On 75 tons, this amounted to [£] $2/_5 \times 75 = £$ 30, and this was in fact the differential rent of rent III, for the rent was [£] 40 ([£] 10 absolute and [£] 30 differential rent). Now, according to the new market-value, the ton is sold at only £ $1^{11}/_{13}$. How much above its [individual] value is this? [£] $1^3/_5 = $ $= £ 1^{39}/_{65}$ and [£] $1^{11}/_{13} = 1^{55}/_{65}$ $(1^{55}/_{65} - 1^{39}/_{65} = {}^{16}/_{65})$. Thus the price at which the ton is sold is [£] $^{16}/_{65}$ above its [individual] value.[81] On 75 tons this amounts to [£] $18^6/_{13}$, and this is exactly the differential rent, which is thus always equal to the number of tons multiplied by the excess of the market-value of the ton over the [individual] value of the ton. It now remains to work out the fall in rent by £ $11^7/_{13}$. The excess of the market-value over the value of III has fallen from $2/_5$ of a £ per ton (when it was sold at £ 2) to $16/_{65}$ per ton (at £ $1^{11}/_{13}$), i.e., from $2/_5=26/_{65}$ to $16/_{65}$, [which is by] $10/_{65}$. On 75 tons this amounts to $750/_{65}=$ $=150/_{13}=11^7/_{13}$, and this is exactly the amount by which the rent in III has fallen.

||570| The $92^1/_2$ tons from IV, at £ $1^{11}/_{13}$ [per ton], cost £ $170^{10}/_{13}$.The rent here is £ $60^{10}/_{13}$ and the differential rent is £ $50^{10}/_{13}$.

If the $92^1/_2$ tons were sold at their value (£ 120), then 1 ton would cost £ $1^{11}/_{37}$. Instead it is being sold at £ $1^{11}/_{13}$. But £ $1^{11}/_{13}=$£ $1^{407}/_{481}$ and £ $1^{11}/_{37}=$£ $1^{143}/_{481}$. This makes the excess of the market-value of IV over its value equal to $264/_{481}$. On $92^1/_2$ tons this amounts to exactly £ $50^{10}/_{13}$, which is the differential rent of IV.

Now let us put these two cases together, under A and B.

A

Class	Capital	Absolute rent	Number of tons	Market-value per ton	Individual value per ton	Total value	Differential rent
	£	£		£	£	£	£
I	100	10	60	2	2	120	0
II	100	10	65	2	$1^{11}/_{13}$	130	10
III	100	10	75	2	$1^3/_5$	150	30
Total	300	30	200			400	40

The total number of tons = 200. Total absolute rent = £30. Total *differential rent* = £40. Total rent = £70.

B

Class	Capital	Absolute rent	Number of tons	Market-value per ton	Individual value per ton	Total value	Different-ial rent
	£	£		£	£	£	£
II	50	5	$32^1/_2$	$1^{11}/_{13}$	$1^{11}/_{13}$	60	0
III	100	10	75	$1^{11}/_{13}$	$1^3/_5$	$138^6/_{13}$	$18^6/_{13}$
IV	100	10	$92^1/_2$	$1^{11}/_{13}$	$1^{11}/_{37}$	$170^{10}/_{13}$	$50^{10}/_{13}$
Total	250	25	200			$369^3/_{13}$	$69^3/_{13}$

Total capital = £250. Absolute rent = £25. Differential rent = £$69^3/_{13}$. *Total rent* = £$94^3/_{13}$. The total value of the 200 tons has fallen from £400 to £$369^3/_{13}$.

These two tables give rise to some very important considerations.

First of all we see that the amount of *absolute rent* rises or falls proportionately to the capital invested in agriculture,[82] that is, to the total amount of capital invested in I, II, III. The *rate of this absolute rent* is quite independent of the size of the capitals invested for it does not depend on the difference in the various types of land but is derived from the difference between value and cost-price; this latter difference however is itself determined by the *organic composition* of the agricultural capital, by the method of production and not by the land. In II B, the *amount* of the absolute rent falls from £ 10 to £ 5, because the capital has fallen from £ 100 to £ 50; half ||571| the capital has been withdrawn [from the land].

Before making any further observations on the two tables, let us construct some other tables. We saw that in B the market-value fell to £ $1^{11}/_{13}$ per ton. But [let us assume that] at this *value*, there is no necessity either for I A to disappear completely from the market, or for II B to employ only half the previous capital. Since in I, the rent is £ 10 out of the total value of the commodity of £ 120, or $^1/_{12}$ of the total value, [this applies] equally to the value of the individual ton which is worth £ 2. £$^2/_{12}$, however, is £$^1/_6$ or $3^1/_3$s. ($3^1/_3$s.×60=£10). The *cost-price* of a ton from I is thus [£ 2—$3^1/_3$s.=] £ 1 $16^2/_3$s. The [new] market-value is £ $1^{11}/_{13}$, or £ 1 $16^{12}/_{13}$s. £ 1 $16^2/_3$s., however, is £ 1 16s. 8d. or £ 1 $16^{26}/_{39}$s. Against this, £ 1 $16^{12}/_{13}$s. are £1 $16^{36}/_{39}$s. or $^{10}/_{39}$s. more. This would be the rent per ton, at the new market-value and would amount to a total rent of $15^5/_{13}$s. for 60 tons. Therefore I put less than 1 per cent rent on the capital of £ 100. For I A to yield no rent at all, the market-value would have to fall to *its* cost-price, namely, to £ 1 $16^2/_3$s. or to £ $1^5/_6$ (or to £ $1^{10}/_{12}$). In this case the rent on I A would have disappeared. It could, however, continue to be exploited with a profit of 10 per cent. This would only cease if the market-value were to fall further, below [the cost-price of] £ $1^5/_6$.

So far as II B is concerned, it has been assumed in Table *B* that half of the capital is withdrawn. But since the market-value of £ $1^{11}/_{13}$ still yields a rent of 10 per cent, it will do so just as well on £ 100 as on £ 50. If, therefore, it is assumed that half the capital has been withdrawn, then only because under these circumstances, II B still yields an absolute rent of 10 per cent. For if II B had continued to produce 65 tons instead of $32^1/_2$, then the market would be over-supplied and the market-value of IV, which dominates the market, would fall to such an extent, that the capital investment in II B would have to be reduced in order to yield the absolute rent. It is however clear that, if the whole capital [of] £ 100 yields rent at 9 per cent, the sum total is greater than that yielded by [a capital of] £ 50 at 10 per cent. Thus if, according to the state of the market, a capital of only £50 were required in II to satisfy the demand, the rent would have to be forced down to £ 5. It would, in fact, fall even lower, if it is assumed that the $32^1/_2$ tons cannot always be disposed of, i.e., if they were thrown out of the market. The market-value would fall so low, that not only the rent on II B would disappear, but the profit would also be affected. Then capital would be withdrawn in order to diminish supply, until the correct point of £ 50 had been reached and then the market-value would have been re-established at £ $1^{11}/_{13}$, at which II B would again yield the absolute rent, but only on half the capital previously invested in it. In this instance too, the whole process would emanate from IV and III, who dominate the market.

But it does not by any means follow that if the market only absorbs 200 tons at £ $1^{11}/_{13}$ per ton, it will not absorb an additional $32^1/_2$ tons if the market-value falls, i.e., if the market-value of $232^1/_2$ tons is forced down through the pressure of $32^1/_2$ surplus tons on the market. The cost-price in II B is £ $1^9/_{13}$ or £1 $13^{11}/_{13}$s. But the market-value is £$1^{11}/_{13}$ or £1 $16^{12}/_{13}$s. If the market-value fell to such an extent that I A no longer yielded a rent, i.e., [if the market-value fell] to the cost-price of I A, to £1 $16^2/_3$s. or £$1^5/_6$ or £$1^{10}/_{12}$, then for II B to use his whole capital, demand would have to grow considerably; since I A could continue to be exploited, as it yields the normal profit. The market would have to absorb not $32^1/_2$ but $92^1/_2$ additional tons, $292^1/_2$ tons instead of 200, i.e. [almost] half as much again. This is a very significant increase. If a moderate increase is to take place, the market-value would have to fall to such an extent that I A is driven out of the market. That is, the market-price would have to fall below the cost-price of I A, i.e., below £ $1^{10}/_{12}$, say, to £$1^9/_{12}$ or £1 15s. It would then still be well above the cost-price of II B.

We shall therefore add a further three tables to the tables A and B, namely, C and D and E. And we shall assume in C that the demand grows, that all classes of A and B can continue to produce, but at the market-value of B, at which I A still yields a rent. In D we assume that [the demand] is sufficient for I A to continue to yield the normal profit but no longer a rent. And we shall assume in E that the price falls sufficiently to eliminate I A from the market ||572| but that the fall of the price simultaneously leads to the absorption of the $32^{1}/_{2}$ surplus tons from II B.

The case assumed in A and B is possible. It is possible that if the rent is reduced from £10 to barely 16s., I A would withdraw his land from this particular form of exploitation and let it out to another sphere of exploitation, in which it can yield a higher rent. But in this case, II B would be forced through the process described above, to withdraw half his capital, if the market did not expand upon the appearance of the new market-value.

C

Class	Capital	Absolute rent	Number of tons	Market-value per ton	Iudividual value per ton	Total value	Rent	Differential rent
	£	£		£	£	£	£	£
I	100	$^{10}/_{13}$	60	$1^{11}/_{13}$	2	$110^{10}/_{13}$	$^{10}/_{13}$	$-9^{3}/_{13}$
II	100	10	65	$1^{11}/_{13}$	$1^{11}/_{13}$	120		0
III	100	10	75	$1^{11}/_{13}$	$1^{3}/_{5}$	$138^{6}/_{13}$		$+18^{6}/_{13}$
IV	100	10	$92^{1}/_{2}$	$1^{11}/_{13}$	$1^{11}/_{37}$	$170^{10}/_{13}$		$+50^{10}/_{13}$
Total	400	$30^{10}/_{13}$	$292^{1}/_{2}$			540		$69^{3}/_{13}$

D

Class	Capital	Absolute rent	Market-value per ton	Cost-price	Number of tons	Total value	Differential rent
	£	£	£	£		£	£
I	100	0	$1^{5}/_{6}$	$1^{5}/_{6}$	60	110	0 (—)
II	100	$9^{1}/_{6}$	$1^{5}/_{6}$	$[1^{9}/_{13}]$	65	$119^{1}/_{6}$	—(latent)
III	100	10	$1^{5}/_{6}$	$[1^{7}/_{15}]$	75	$137^{1}/_{2}$	$+17^{1}/_{2}$
IV	100	10	$1^{5}/_{6}$	$[1^{7}/_{37}]$	$92^{1}/_{2}$	$169^{7}/_{12}$	$+49^{7}/_{12}$
Total	400	$29^{1}/_{6}$			$292^{1}/_{2}$	$536^{1}/_{4}$	$67^{1}/_{12}$

E

Class	Capital	Absolute rent	Market-value per ton	Cost-price	Number of tons	Total value	Different-ial rent
	£	£	£	£		£	£
II	100	$3^3/_4$	$1^3/_4$	$1^9/_{13}$	65	$113^3/_4$	—(none)
III	100	10	$1^3/_4$	$[1^7/_{15}]$	75	$131^1/_4$	$+11^1/_4$
IV	100	10	$1^3/_4$	$[1^7/_{37}]$	$92^1/_2$	$161^7/_8$	$+41^7/_8$
Total	300	$23^3/_4$			$232^1/_2$	$406^7/_8$	$+53^1/_8$

||573| Now let us compile the tables *A, B, C, D* and E, but in
the manner which should have been adopted from the outset.
*Capital, Total value, Total product, Market-value per ton, In-
dividual value [per ton], Differential Value [per ton],*[83] *Cost-
Price [per ton], Absolute rent, Absolute rent in tons, Differential
rent, Differential rent in tons, Total rent.* And then the totals
of all classes in each table.[84]

||575| *Comment on the Table* (p. 574)[a]

It is assumed that a capital of 100 (constant and variable
capital) is laid out and that the labour it employs provides
surplus-labour (unpaid labour) amounting to one-fifth of the
capital advanced, or a surplus-value of $^{100}/_5$. If, therefore, the
capital advanced equals £ 100, the *value* of the total product
must be £ 120. Supposing furthermore that the average profit
is 10 per cent, then £ 110 is the *cost-price* of total product, in
the above example, of coal. With the given rate of surplus-
value or surplus-labour, the £ 100 capital transforms itself into
a *value* of £ 120, whether poor or rich mines are being exploited;
in a word: The *varying productivity* of labour—whether this
variation be due to varying natural conditions of labour or
varying social conditions of labour or varying technological
conditions—does not alter the fact that the value of the commodities equals the quantity of labour materialised in them.

Thus to say the *value* of the *product* created by the capital
of £ 100 *equals £ 120*, simply means that the *product* contains
the labour-time materialised in the £ 100 capital, plus one-sixth
of labour-time which is unpaid but appropriated by the capitalist. The total value of the product equals £ 120, whether the

---

[a] See the sheet inserted between pages 264 and 265.—*Ed.*

capital of £100 produces 60 tons in one class of mines or 65, 75 or $92\frac{1}{2}$ in another. But clearly, the value of the individual part, be it measured by the quarter or yard etc., varies greatly according to the productivity. But to stick to our table (the same applies to every other mass of commodities brought about by capitalist production) the value of 1 ton equals £2, if the total product of the capital is 60 tons, i.e., 60 tons are worth £120 or represent labour-time equal to that which is materialised in £120. If the total product amounts to 65 tons, then the value of the individual ton is £ $1\frac{11}{13}$ or £ 1 $16\frac{12}{13}$s., if it amounts to 75 tons, then the value of the individual ton is £ $1\frac{9}{15}$ or £ 1 12s.; finally, if it comes to $92\frac{1}{2}$ tons, then the value per ton is £ $1\frac{11}{37}$ or £ 1 $5\frac{35}{37}$s. Because the total mass of commodities or tons produced by the capital of £100 always has the same *value*, equal to £120, since it always represents the same *total quantity of labour* contained in £ *120*, the *value* of the individual ton varies, according to whether *the same* value is represented in 60, 65, 75 or $92\frac{1}{2}$ tons, in other words, it varies with the different productivity of labour. It is this difference in the productivity of labour which causes *the same quantity of labour* to be represented sometimes in a smaller and sometimes in a larger total quantity of commodities, so that the *individual part* of this total contains now more, now less, of the absolute amount of labour expended, and, therefore, accordingly has sometimes a larger and sometimes a smaller value. This value of the individual ton, which varies according to whether the capital of £100 is invested in more fertile or less fertile mines, and therefore according to the different productivity of labour, figures in the table as the *individual value* of the individual ton.

Hence nothing could be further from the truth than the notion that when the value of the individual commodity falls with the rising productivity of labour, the *total value* of a product produced by a particular capital—for instance, £ 100— rises because of the increased mass of commodities in which it is [now] represented. For the value of the individual commodity only falls because the *total value*—the total quantity of labour expended—is represented by a larger quantity of use-values, of products. Hence a relatively smaller part of the total value or of the labour expended falls to the individual product and this only *to the extent* to which a smaller quantity of labour is absorbed in it or a smaller amout of the total value falls to its share.

Originally, we regarded the *individual commodity* as the result and direct product of a particular quantity of labour. Now, that the commodity appears as the *product of capitalist production*, there is a formal change in this respect: The mass of use-values which has been produced represents a *quantity of labour-time*, which is equal to the quantity of labour-time contained in the capital (constant and variable) consumed in its production, plus the unpaid labour-time appropriated by the capitalist. If the labour-time contained in the capital, as expressed in terms of money, amounts to £ 100 and this capital of £ 100 comprises £ 40 laid out in wages, and if the surplus labour-time amounts to 50 per cent on the variable capital, in other words, the rate of surplus-value is 50 per cent, then the value of the total mass of commodities produced by the capital of £ 100 equals £ 120. As we have seen in the first part of this work,[85] if the commodities are to circulate, their exchange-value must first be converted into a *price*, i.e., expressed in terms of money. Thus ||576| before the capitalist throws the commodities on to the market, he must first work out the *price* of the individual commodity, unless the total product is a single indivisible object, such as, for example, a house, in which the total capital is represented, *a single commodity*, whose price according to the assumption would then be £ 120, equal to the total value as expressed in terms of money. *Price* here equals monetary expression of value.

According to the varying productivity of labour the total value of £ 120 will be distributed over more or fewer products. Thus the value of the *individual* product will, accordingly, be proportionally equal to a larger or a smaller part of £ 120. The whole operation is quite simple. For example, if the total product equals 60 tons of coal, 60 tons are equal to £ 120 and 1 ton equals £ $120/60$, i.e., £ 2; if the product is 65 tons, the value of the individual ton equals £ $120/65$, i.e., £ $1^{11}/_{13}$ or £ 1 $16^{12}/_{13}$ s. (£ 1 16 s. $11^{1}/_{13}$ d). If the product equals 75 tons, the value of the individual ton is $120/75$, i.e., £ 1 12 s.; if it equals $92^{1}/_{2}$ tons, then it is £ 1 $^{11}/_{37}$, which is £ 1 $5^{35}/_{37}$ s. The value (price) of the individual commodity is thus equal to the *total value* of the product divided by the total number of products, which are measured according to the standard of measurement—such as tons, quarters, yards etc.—appropriate to them as use-values.

If, therefore, the price of the individual commodity equals the total value of the mass of commodities produced by a capital of £100, divided by the total number of commodities, then the total value equals the price of the individual commodity multiplied by the total number of individual commodities or it equals the price of a definite quantity of individual commodities multiplied by the total amount of commodities, measured by this standard of measurement. Furthermore: The total value consists of the value of the capital advanced to production plus the surplus-value; that is of the labour-time contained in the capital advanced plus the surplus labour-time or unpaid labour-time appropriated by the capital. Thus the surplus-value contained in each individual part of the commodity is proportional to its value. In the same way as the £120 is distributed among 60, 65, 75 or $92\frac{1}{2}$ tons, so the £20 surplus-value is distributed among them. When the number of tons is 60, and therefore the value of the individual ton equals $^{120}/_{60}$, which is £2 or 40s., then one-sixth of this 40s. or £2, that is, $6\frac{2}{3}$s., is the share of the surplus-value which falls to the individual ton; the proportion of surplus-value in the ton which costs £2 is the same as in the 60 which cost £120. The [ratio of] surplus-value to value remains the same in the price of the individual commodity as in the total value of the mass of commodities. In the above example, the total surplus-value in each individual ton is $^{20}/_{60}=^{2}/_{6}=^{1}/_{3}$ of [20], which is equal to $^{1}/_{6}$ of 40 as above. Hence the surplus-value of the single ton multiplied by 60 is equal to the total surplus-value which the capital has produced. If the portion of value which falls to the individual product—the corresponding part of the total value—is smaller because of the larger number of products, i.e., because of the greater productivity of labour, then the portion of surplus-value which falls to it, the corresponding part of the total surplus-value which adheres to it, is also smaller. But this does not affect the ratio of the surplus-value, of the newly-created value, to the value advanced and merely reproduced. Although, as we have seen,[86] the productivity of labour does not affect the total value of the product, it may however increase the surplus-value, if the product enters into the consumption of the worker; then the falling price of the individual commodities or, which is the same, of a given quantity of commodities, may reduce the normal wage or, amounts to the same, the *value of the labour-power*. In so far as the greater productivity of labour creates relative surplus-value, it increases not the total value of the product, but that part of this total value which

• represents surplus-value, i.e., unpaid labour. Although, therefore, with greater productivity of labour, a smaller portion of
value falls to the individual product—because the total mass
of commodities which represents this value has grown—and
thus the price of the individual product falls, that part of this
price which represents *surplus-value*, nevertheless, rises under
the above-mentioned circumstances, and, therefore, the proportion of surplus-value to reproduced value grows (actually here
one should still refer to variable capital, for profit has not yet
been mentioned). But this is only the case because, as a result
of the increased productivity of labour, the surplus-value has
grown within the *total value*. The same factor—the increased
productivity of labour—which enables a larger mass of products
to contain the same quantity of labour thus lowering the value
of a given part of this mass or the *price* of the individual
commodity, reduces the value of the labour-power, therefore
increases the surplus or unpaid labour contained in the *value
of the total product* and hence in the *price* of the individual
commodity. Although thus the *price of the individual commodity*
falls, although the *total quantity of labour contained in it*, and
therefore its value, falls, the proportion of surplus-value, which
is a component part of this value, increases. In other words,
the smaller total quantity ||577| of labour contained in the
individual commodity comprises a *greater quantity of unpaid
labour* than previously, when labour was less productive, when
the price of the individual commodity was therefore higher,
and the total quantity of labour contained in the individual
commodity greater. Although in the present case one ton contains less labour and is therefore cheaper, it contains more
surplus-labour and therefore yields more surplus-value.

Since in competition everything appears in a false form,
upside down, the individual capitalist imagines 1. that he [has]
reduced his profit on the individual commodity by reducing
its price, but that he makes a greater profit *because of the
increased* mass [of commodities] (here a further confusion is
caused by the greater amount of profit which is derived from
the increase in capital employed, even with a lower rate of
profit); 2. that he fixes the price of the individual commodity
and by multiplication determines the total value of the product
whereas the original procedure is division and multiplication
is only correct as a derivative method based on that division.
The vulgar economist in fact does nothing but translate the

queer notions of the capitalists who are caught up in competition into seemingly more theoretical language and seeks to build up a justification of these notions.

Now to return to our table.

The *total value* of the product or of the quantity of commodities created by a capital of £ 100, equals £ 120, however great or small—according to the varying degree of the productivity of labour—the quantity of commodities may be. The *cost-price* of this total product, whatever its size, equals £ 110 if, as has been assumed, the average profit is 10 per cent. The excess in *value* of the total product, whatever its size, equals £ 10, which is one-twelfth of the total value or one-tenth of the capital advanced. This £ 10, the excess of *value* over the *cost-price* of the total product, constitutes the *rent*. It is evidently quite independent of the varying productivity of labour resulting from the different degrees of natural fertility of the mines, types of soil, in short, of the natural element in which the capital of £ 100 has been employed, for those different degrees in the productivity of the labour employed, arising from the different degrees of fertility of the natural agent, do not prevent the total product from having a value of £ 120, a cost-price of £ 110, and therefore an excess of value over cost-price of £ 10. All that the *competition between capitals* can bring about, is that the *cost-price* of the commodities which a capitalist can produce with £ 100 in coal-mining, this particular sphere of production, is equal to £ 110. But competition cannot compel the capitalist to sell the product at £ 110 which is worth £ 120—although such compulsion exists in other industries. Because the landlord steps in and lays his hands on the £ 10. Hence I call this rent the *absolute rent*. Accordingly it always remains *the same* in the table, however the fertility of the coal-mines and hence the productivity of labour may change. But, because of the different degrees of fertility of the mines and thus of the productivity of labour, it is not always expressed in the *same number of tons*. For, according to the varying productivity of labour, the quantity of labour contained in £ 10 represents more or less use-values, more or less tons. Whether with the variation in degrees of fertility, this *absolute rent* is always paid in full or only in part, will be seen in the further analysis of the table.

There is furthermore on the market coal produced in mines of different productivity. Starting with the lowest degree of productivity, I have called these, I, II, III, IV. Thus, for instance, the first class produces 60 tons with a capital of £100, the second class produces 65 tons etc. Capital of the same size— £100, of the same organic composition, within the same sphere of production—does not have the same productivity here, because the degree of productivity of labour varies according to the degree of productivity of the mine, type of soil, in short of the natural agent. But competition establishes *one market-value* for these products, which have varying *individual values*. This market-value itself can *never* be *greater* than the individual value of the product of the *least fertile* class. If it were higher, then this would only show that the *market-price* stood above the *market-value*. But the market-*value* must represent real *value*. As regards products of separate classes, it is quite possible, that their [individual] *value* is above or below the market-value. If it is *above* the market-value, the difference between the market-value and their cost-price is *smaller* than the difference between their individual value and their cost-price. But as the absolute rent equals the difference between their individual ||578| value and their cost-price, the market-value cannot, in this case, yield the *entire absolute rent* for these products. If the market-value sank down to *their* cost-price, it would yield *no rent* for them *at all*. They could pay no rent, since rent is only the difference between value and cost-price, and for them, individually, this difference would have disappeared, because of the [fall in the] market-value. In this case, the difference between the market-value and their individual value is *negative*, that is, the market-value differs from their individual value by a *negative amount*. The difference between market-value and individual value in general I call *differential value*. Commodities belonging to the category described here have a minus sign in front of their differential value.

If, on the other hand, the *individual value* of the products of a class of mines (class of land) is *below* the market-value, then the *market-value* is a b o v e their individual value. The value or market-value prevailing in their sphere of production thus yields an *excess above* their individual value. If, for example, the market-value of a ton is £2, and the individual value of a ton is £1 12s., then its differential value is 8s. And since in the class in which the individual value of a ton is £1 12s. the capital of £100 produces 75 tons, the total differential value of these 75 tons is 8 s.×75=£30. This excess of the market-value for the total product of this class *over* the individual value of its product, which is due to the relatively greater fertility of the soil or the mine, forms the *differential rent*, since the cost-price for the capital remains the same as before. This differential rent is greater or smaller, according to the greater or smaller excess of the *market-value* over the *individual value*. This excess in turn is greater or smaller, according to the *relatively greater or smaller fertility* of the class of mine or land to which this product belongs, compared with the less fertile class whose product determines the market-value.

Finally, the *individual cost-price* of the products is different in the different classes. For instance, for the class in which a capital of £100 yields 75 tons the cost-price of the individual commodity would be £1 9$\frac{1}{3}$s., since the total value is £120 and the *cost-price* £110, and if the market-value were equal to the individual value in this class, i.e., £1 12 s., then the 75 tons sold at £120 would yield a rent of £10, while £110 would represent their cost-price.

But of course, the *individual cost-price* of a single ton varies according to the number of tons in which the capital of £100 is represented, or according to the *individual value* of the individual products of the various classes. If, for example, the capital of £100 produces 60 tons, then the value per ton is £2 and its cost-price £1 16$\frac{2}{3}$s.; 55 tons would be equal to £110 or to the cost-price of the total product. If, however, the £100 capital produces 75 tons, then the value per ton is £1 12s., its cost-price £1 9$\frac{1}{3}$s., and 68$\frac{3}{4}$ tons of the total product would cost £110 or would replace the cost-price. The individual *cost-price*, i.e., the *cost-price of the individual ton*, varies in the different classes in the same proportion as the *individual value*.

It now becomes evident from all the five tables, that *absolute rent* always equals the excess of the value of the commodity over its own cost-price. The *differential rent*, on the other hand, is equal to the excess of the market-value over its individual value. The total rent, if there is a differential rent (apart from the absolute rent), is equal to the excess of the market-value over the individual value plus the excess of the individual value over the cost-price, or the excess of the market-value over the individual cost-price.

Because here the purpose is only to set forth the general law of rent as an illustration of my theory of value and cost-prices—since I do not intend to give a detailed exposition of rent ||579| till dealing with landed property *ex professo*—I have removed all those factors which complicate the matter: namely the *influence of the location* of the mines or types of land; different degree of productivity of different amounts of capital applied to *the same* mine or *the same* type of land; the inter-relationship of rents yielded by different lines of production within the same sphere of production, for example, by different branches of agriculture; the interrelationship of rents yielded by different branches of production which are, however, inter-changeable, such as, for instance, when land is withdrawn from agriculture in order to be used for building houses, etc. All this does not belong here.

[3. Analysis of the Tables]

Now for a consideration of the tables. They show how the general law explains a great multiplicity of combinations, while Ricardo, because he had a false conception of the general law of rent, perceived only one side of differential rent and there-fore wanted to reduce the great multiplicity of phenomena to one single case by means of forcible abstraction. The tables are not intended to show all the combinations but only those which are most important, particularly for our specific purpose.

[a)] Table A [The Relation Between Market-Value and Individual Value in the Various Classes]

In Table *A*, the market-value of a ton of coal is determined by the individual value of a ton in class I, where the mine is least fertile, hence the productivity of labour is the lowest, hence the mass of products yielded by the capital investment of £ 100 is the smallest and, therefore, the price of the individual product (the price as determined by its value) is the highest.

It is assumed that the market absorbs 200 tons, neither more nor less.

The *market-value* cannot be *above* the [individual] value of a ton in I, i.e., of that commodity which is produced under the least favourable conditions of production. II and III sell the ton above its *individual value* because their conditions of production are more favourable than those of other commodities produced within *the same* sphere, this does not, therefore, offend against the law of value. On the other hand, the market-value could only be above the value of a ton in I, if the product of I were sold *above* its value, *quite* regardless of market-value. A difference between market-value and [individual] value arises in general not because products are sold absolutely *above* their value, but only because the value of the individual product may be different from the value of the product of a whole sphere; in other words because the *labour-time necessary* to supply the total product—in this case 200 tons—may differ from the labour-time which produces some of the tons—in this case those from II and III—in short, because the *total product* supplied has been produced by labour of varying degrees of productivity. The difference between the market-value and the individual value of a product can therefore only be due to the fact that the definite quantities of labour with which different parts of the total product are manufactured have different *degrees of productivity*. It can never be due to the value being determined *irrespective* of the quantity of labour altogether employed in this sphere. The market-value could be above £ 2 per ton, only if I, on the whole, quite apart from its relation to II and III, were to sell its product *above* its value. In this case the *market-price* would be above the *market-value* because of the state of the market, because of demand and supply. But the market-value which concerns us here—and which here is assumed to be equal to the market-price—cannot rise *above itself*.

The market-value here *equals* the value of I, which, moreover, supplies three-tenths of the entire product on the market, since II and III only supply sufficient amounts to meet the total demand, i.e., to satisfy the additional demand over and above that which is supplied by I. II and III have no cause, therefore, to sell below £ 2 since the entire product can be sold at £ 2. They cannot ||580| sell *above* £ 2 because I sells at £ 2 per ton.

This law, that the *market-value* cannot be *above* the individual *value* of that product which is produced under the *worst conditions of production* but provides a part of the necessary supply, Ricardo distorts into the assertion that the market-value cannot fall *below* the value of that product and must therefore always be determined by it. We shall see later how wrong this is.

Because the market-value of a ton coincides with the individual value of a ton in I, *the rent* it yields represents the absolute excess of the value over its cost-price, the *absolute rent*, which is £ 10. II yields a differential rent of £ 10 and III of £ 30, because the market-value, which is determined by I, yields an excess of £ 10 for II and of £ 30 for III, over their *individual value* and therefore over the absolute rent of £ 10, which represents the excess of the individual value over the cost-price. Hence II yields a total rent of £ 20 and III of £ 40, because the market-value yields an excess over their cost-price of £ 20 and £ 40 respectively.

We shall assume that the transition is from I, the least fertile mine, to the more fertile II, and from this to the yet more fertile mine III. It is true that II and III are more fertile than I, but they satisfy only seven-tenths of the total demand and, as we have just explained, can therefore sell their product at £ 2, although its value is only £ 1 $16^{12}/_{13}$s. and £ 1 12s. respectively. It is clear that when the particular quantity required to satisfy demand is supplied, and gradation takes place in the productivity of labour which satisfies the various portions of this demand, whether the transition is in one direction or the other, in both cases the market-value of the more fertile classes will rise *above their individual value*; in one case because they *find* that the market-value is *determined* by the unfertile class and the additional supply provided by them is not great enough to occasion any change in the market-value as determined by class I; in the other case, because the market-value originally determined by them—determined by class III or II—is now determined by class I, which provides the additional supply required by the market and can only meet this at a higher value, which now determines the market-value.   .

[b) The Connection Between Ricardo's Theory of Rent and the Conception of Falling Productivity in Agriculture. Changes in the Rate of Absolute Rent and Their Relation to the Changes in the Rate of Profit]

In the case under consideration, for example, Ricardo would say: We start out from class III. The additional supply will, in the first place, come from II. Finally, the last additional supply—demanded by the market—comes from I, and since I can provide the additional supply of 60 tons only at £ 120, that is at £ 2 per ton, and since this supply is needed, the market-value of a ton which was originally £ 1 12 s. and later £ 1 $16^{12}/_{13}$ s., now rises to £ 2. But, on the other hand, it is equally true. that

if we start out from I, which satisfied the demand for 60 tons
at £ 2, then, however, the additional supply is provided by II,
the product of II is sold at the market-value of £ 2 although
the individual value of it is only £ 1 16$^{12}/_{13}$ s., for it is still only
possible to supply the 125 tons required if I provides 60 tons
at a value of £ 2 per ton. The same applies, if a new additional
supply of 75 tons is required, but III provides *only* 75 tons,
only supplies the additional demand, and therefore, as before,
60 tons have to be supplied by I at £ 2. Had I supplied the whole
demand of 200 tons, they would have been sold at £ 400. And
this is what they are [sold] at now, because II and III do not
sell at the price at which they can satisfy the additional demand
for 140 tons, ||XII-581| but at the price at which I, which only
supplies three-tenths of the product, could satisfy it. The entire
product required, 200 tons, is in this case sold at £ 2 per ton, because three-tenths of it can only be supplied at a value of £ 2 per
ton, irrespective of whether the additional portions of the demand
were met by proceeding from III via II to I or from I via II
to III.

Ricardo says: If III and II are the starting-points, their
market-value must rise to the value (cost-price with him) of I,
because the three-tenths supplied by I are required to meet
the demand and the decisive point here is therefore the *re-*
quired volume of the product and not the individual value of
particular portions of it. But it is equally true that the three-
tenths from I are just as essential as before when I is the
starting-point and II and III *only* provide the additional supply.
If, therefore, I determined the market-value in the descending
line, it determines it in the ascending line *for the same reasons*.
Table *A* thus shows us the incorrectness of the Ricardian concept that differential rent *depends* on the diminishing productivity of labour, on the movement from the more productive mine
or land to the less productive. It is just as compatible with the
reverse process and hence with the growing productivity of
labour. Whether the one or the other takes place has nothing
to do with the nature and existence of differential rent but is a
historical question. In reality, the ascending and descending
lines will cut across one another, the additional demand will
sometimes be supplied by going over to more, sometimes to
less fertile types of land, mine or natural agent. [In this it is]
always supposed that the supply provided by the natural agent
of a new, different class—be it more fertile or less fertile—

only equals the additional demand and does not, therefore, bring about a change in the *relation between demand and supply*. Hence it can only bring about *a change in the market-value* itself, if the supply can only be made available at higher cost not however if it can be made available at lower cost.

Table A thus reveals to us from the outset the falseness of this fundamental assumption of Ricardo's, which, as Anderson shows, was not required, even on the basis of a wrong conception of absolute rent.

If production proceeds in a descending line, from III to II and from II to I with recourse to natural agents of a gradually decreasing fertility—then III, in which a capital of 100 has been invested, will at first sell its commodities at their value, at £ 120. This, since it produces 75 tons, will amount to £ 1 12 s. per ton. If an additional supply of 65 is then required, II, which invests a capital of 100, will similarly sell its product at a value of £ 120. This amounts to £ 1 16^{12}/$_{13}$s. per ton. And if, finally, an additional supply of 60 tons were required, which can only be provided by I, then it too will sell its product at its value of £ 120, which amounts to £ 2 per ton. In this process III would yield a differential rent of £ 18^{6}/$_{13}$ as soon as II came on the market, whereas previously it only yielded the absolute rent of £ 10. II would yield a differential rent of £ 10 as soon as I came into the picture and differential rent of III would then rise to £ 30.

Descending from III to I, Ricardo discovers that I does not yield a rent, because in considering III he started out from the assumption that no absolute rent exists.

There is indeed a difference between the ascending and descending line. If the passage is from I to III, so that II and III only provide the additional supply, then the market-value remains equal to the individual value of I which is £ 2. And if, as the supposition is here, the average profit is 10 per cent, then it can be assumed that the price of coal ([or] price of wheat—a quarter of wheat etc. can always be substituted for a ton of coal) will have entered into its calculation, since coal enters into the consumption of the worker as a means of subsistence as well as figuring as an auxiliary material of considerable importance in constant capital. It can therefore also be assumed that the rate of surplus-value would have been higher and therefore the surplus-value itself greater, hence also the *rate of profit* higher than 10 per cent, if I [were] more productive or the value of the ton had been *below* £ 2. This, however, would be the case if III was the starting-point. The [market]-value of the ton of coal was then only £ 1 12 s.; when ||582| II entered, it rose to £1 16¹²/₁₃ s. and finally when I appeared, it rose to £ 2. It can thus be assumed that when only III was being worked—all other circumstances, length of surplus labour-time and other conditions of production etc. being taken as constant and unchanged—the rate of profit was higher (the *rate of surplus-value* was higher because one element of the wage was cheaper; because of the higher rate of surplus-value, the mass of surplus-value, and therefore also the rate of profit, was higher; in addition however—with the surplus-value thus modified—the rate of profit was higher because an element of cost in the constant capital was lower). The rate of profit became lower with the appearance of II and finally sank to 10 per cent, as the lowest level, when I appeared. In this case therefore one would have to assume that (regardless of the data) for instance the rate of profit was 12 per cent when only III was being worked; that it sank to 11 per cent when II came into play and finally to 10 per cent when I entered into it. In this case the absolute rent would have been £ 8 with III because the cost-price would have been £ 112; it would have become £ 9 as soon as II came into play because now the cost-price would have been £ 111 and it would finally have been raised to £ 10 because the cost-price would have fallen to £ 110. Here then a change in the rate of *absolute rent* itself would have taken place and this in inverse ratio to the change in the *rate of profit*. The rate of rent would have progressively grown *because* the rate of profit had progressively fallen. The latter would, however, have fallen because of the decreasing productivity of labour in the mines, in agriculture, etc. and the corresponding increase in the price of the means of subsistence and auxiliary materials.

[c)] Observations on the Influence of the Change in the Value of the Means of Subsistence and of Raw Material (Hence also the Value of Machinery) on the Organic Composition of Capital

In this case the *rate of rent* rose *because* the *rate of profit* fell. Now did it fall because there was a change in the organic composition of the capital? If the average composition of the

18*

capital was £80c+£20v, did this composition remain the same? It is assumed that the normal working-day remains the same. Otherwise the influence of the increased price of the means of subsistence could be neutralised. We must differentiate between two factors here. Firstly, an increase may occur in the price of the means of subsistence, hence reduction in surplus-labour and surplus-value. Secondly, constant capital may become more expensive because, as in the case of coal, the auxiliary material, or in the case of wheat, another element of constant capital, namely seeds, rises in value or also, [because] due to the increased price of wheat, the cost-price of other raw produce (raw material) may rise. Finally, if the product was iron, copper etc., the raw material of certain branches of industry and the raw material of machinery (including containers) of all branches of industry would rise.

On the one hand it is assumed that no change has taken place in the organic composition of capital; in other words that no change has taken place in the manner of production decreasing or increasing the amount of living labour employed in proportion to the amount of constant capital employed. *The same number of workers* as before is required (the limits of the normal working-day remaining the same) in order to work up the same volume of raw material with the same amount of machinery etc., or, where there is no raw material, to set into motion the same amount of machinery, tools, etc. Besides this first aspect of the organic composition of capital, however, a second aspect has to be considered, namely, the change in the *value* of the elements of capital although as use-values they may be· employed in the same portions. Here again we must distinguish:

The[a] *change in value* affects both elements—variable and constant—*equally*. This may *never* occur in practice. A rise in the price of certain agricultural products such as wheat etc., raises the (necessary) wage and the raw material (for instance seeds). A rise in coal prices raises the necessary wage and the auxiliary material of most industries. While in the first case the rise in wages occurs in all branches of industry, that in raw materials occurs only in some. With coal, the proportion in which it enters into wages is lower than that in which it enters into production. As regards *total capital*, the change in the value

---

    [a] In the manuscript: "First. The".—*Ed.*

of coal and wheat is thus hardly likely to affect both elements of capital *equally*. But let us suppose this to be the case.

Let the value of the product of a capital £ 80c+£ 20v be £ 120. *Considering capital as a whole*, the *value* of the product and its *cost-price* coincide, for the difference is equalised out for the aggregate capital [of the country]. The rise in value of an article such as coal which, according to the assumption, enters into both component parts of capital in *equal proportions*, brings about a rise in cost by one-tenth for both elements. Thus £ 80c would now only buy as many commodities as could previously be bought with [approximately] £ 70c and with £ 20v only as many workers could be paid as previously with [approximately] £ 18v. Or, in order to continue production on the old scale, [approximately] £ 90c and £ 22v would now have to be laid out. The value of the product, as previously, is now £ 120, of which, however, the outlay amounts to £ 112 (£ 90 constant and £ 22 variable). Thus the profit is £ 8 and on £ 112 this works out at $1/_{14}$, which is $7^1/_7$ per cent. Hence the value of the product from £ 100 capital advanced is now equal to £ $107^1/_7$.

What is the ratio in which c and v now enter into this new capital? Previously the ratio v:c was as 20:80, as 1:4; now it is as 22:90 [or] as 11:45. $1/_4=^{45}/_{180}$; $^{11}/_{45}=^{44}/_{180}$. That means that variable capital has decreased by $1/_{180}$ ||583| as against constant capital. In keeping with the assumption that the increase in price of coal etc. has *proportionally the same* effect on both parts of the capital, we must put it as £ 88c+£ 22v. For the value of the product is £ 120; from this has to be deducted an outlay of £ 88+£ 22=£ 110. This leaves a profit of £ 10. 22:88=20:80. The *ratio* of c to v would have remained *the same* as in the old capital. As before, the ratio would be v:c as 1:4. But £ 10 profit on £ 110 is $1/_{11}$, which is $9^1/_{11}$ per cent. If production is to be continued on the same scale, £ 110 capital will have to be invested instead of £ 100, and the value of the product [would continue to be] £ 120.[87] The composition of a capital of £ 100 however would be £ 80c+£ 20v, the value of the product being £ $109^1/_{11}$.

If, in the above case, the value £ 80c had remained constant and only v had varied, i.e., £ 22v instead of £ 20v, then the previous ratio having been 20:80 or 10:40, it would now be 22:80 or 11:40. Now if this change had taken place, then [the capital would amount to] £ 80c+£ 22v [and the] value of the product would be £ 120; therefore the outlay [would be] £ 102 and the profit £ 18 i.e., $17^{33}/_{51}$ per cent. [But] 22:18 is as $21^{29}/_{51}$:$17^{33}/_{51}$. If £ $22v$ capital need to be laid out in wages, in order to set in motion a constant capital of £ 80 in value, then £ $21^{29}/_{51}$ are required in order to move a constant capital of £ $78^{22}/_{51}$ in value. According to this ratio, only £ $78^{22}/_{51}$ would be laid out in machinery and raw material from a capital of £ 100; £ $21^{29}/_{51}$ would have to go to wages, whereas previously £ 80 was spent on raw material etc. and only £ 20 on wages. The value of the product is now £ $117^{33}/_{51}$. And the composition of the capital: £ $78^{22}/_{51}c$+£ $21^{29}/_{51}v$. But £ $21^{29}/_{51}$+£ $17^{33}/_{51}$= £ $39^{11}/_{51}$. Under the previous composition [of capital], the total labour put in was equal to 40; now it is $39^{11}/_{51}$ or less by $^{40}/_{51}$, not *because* the constant capital has altered in value, but *because* there is less constant capital to be worked on, hence a capital of £ 100 can set in motion a little less labour than before, although more dearly paid for.

If, therefore, a change in an element of cost, here a rise in price—a rise in value—only alters (the necessary) wage, then the following takes place: Firstly, the rate of surplus-value falls; secondly, with a given capital, less constant capital, less raw material and machinery, can be employed. The absolute amount of this part of the capital decreases in proportion to the variable capital, and provided other conditions *remain the same*, this must always bring about a rise in the rate of profit (if the value of constant capital remains the same). The [physical] *volume* of the constant capital decreases although its *value* remains *the same*. But the *rate of surplus-value* decreases and also the [amount of] *surplus-value* itself, because the falling rate is not accompanied by an increase in the number of workers employed. The rate of surplus-value—of surplus-labour—falls more than the ratio of variable to constant capital. For *the same number of workers* as before, that is the same absolute quantity of labour, needs to be employed in order to set in motion *the same amount of constant capital*. Of this absolute quantity of labour more, however, is necessary labour and less of it is surplus-labour. Thus *the same quantity of labour* must be paid for more dearly. Of *the same* capital—£ 100 for instance—less can thus be laid out in constant capital, since more has to be laid out in variable capital to set in motion a smaller constant capital. The fall in the rate of surplus-value in this case is not connected with an increase in the absolute quantity of labour which a particular capital employs, or with the increase in the number of workers employed by it. The [amount of] surplus-value itself cannot therefore rise here, although the rate of surplus-value falls.

Provided, therefore, that the organic composition of the capital remains the same, in so far as its physical component parts regarded as use-values are concerned; that is, if change in the composition of the capital is not due to a change in the *method of production* within the sphere in which the capital is invested, but only to a rise in the *value of the labour-power* and hence to a rise in the necessary wage, which is equal to a decrease in surplus-labour or the rate of surplus-value, which in this case can be neither partly nor wholly neutralised by an increase in the number of workers employed by a capital of given size—for instance £100—then the fall in the rate of profit is simply due to the fall in surplus-value itself. If the method of production and the ratio between the amounts of immediate and accumulated labour used remain constant, this same cause then gives rise to the change in the organic composition of capital—a change which is only due to the fact that the *value (the proportional value) of the amounts employed* has changed. The same capital employs ||584| less immediate labour proportionately as it employs less constant capital, but it pays more for this smaller amount of labour. It can therefore only employ less constant capital because the smaller amount of labour which sets in motion this smaller amount of constant capital, absorbs a greater part of the total capital. In order, for example, to set in motion £78 of constant capital, it must lay out £22 in variable capital, while previously £20*v* sufficed to set in motion £80*c*.

This therefore happens when an increase in the price of a product subjected to landed property, only affects wages. The converse would result from the product becoming cheaper.

But now let us take the case assumed above. The increased price of the agricultural product is supposed to affect constant and variable capital *proportionately to the same degree*. According to the assumption, therefore, there is no change in the *organic composition of the capital*. Firstly, no *change in the method of production*. The same absolute amount of immediate labour sets in motion the same amount of *accumulated labour* as before. The ratio of the amounts remains the same. Secondly, no *change in the proportion of value* as between accumulated and immediate labour. If the value of one rises or falls, so does that of the other in the same *proportion* to its relative size, which thus remains unchanged. But previously [we had]: £ 80c+£ 20v; *value of the product* £ 120. Now £ 88c+£ 22v, value of the product [likewise] £ 120. This yields £ 10 on £ 110 or $9^1/_{11}$ per cent [profit; for a capital of] £ 80c+£ 20v therefore the value of [the product is] £ $109^1/_{11}$.

Previously we had:

Constant capital	Variable capital	Surplus-value	Rate of profit	Rate of surplus-value
£80	£20	£20	20 per cent	100 per cent

Now we have:

Constant capital	Variable capital	Surplus-value	Rate of profit	Rate of surplus-value
£80	£20	£$9^1/_{11}$	$9^1/_{11}$ per cent	$45^5/_{11}$ per cent

£ 80c represents less raw material etc. here and £ 20v less absolute labour in the same proportion. The raw material etc. has become dearer and [a capital of] £ 80 therefore buys a smaller quantity of raw material etc.; thus, because the *method of production* has remained *the same*, it requires less immediate labour. But the smaller quantity of immediate labour costs as much as the larger quantity of immediate labour did before, and it has become dearer exactly to the same extent as the raw material etc. and has therefore decreased in the same proportion. If, therefore, the surplus-value had remained the same, then the rate of profit would have sunk in the same proportion in which the raw material etc. had become dearer and in which the ratio of the value of the variable to the constant capital had changed. The rate of surplus-value however has not remained the same, but has changed in the same proportion as the value of the variable capital has grown. Let us take [another] example.

The value of a pound of cotton has gone up from 1s. to 2s. Previously, £ 80 (we take machinery etc. here as equal to nil) could buy 1,600 lbs. Now £ 80 will only buy 800 lbs. Previously, in order to spin 1,600 lbs., £ 20 [were] required to pay the wages of, say, 20 workers. In order to spin the 800 lbs. only 10 [workers are needed], since the method of production has remained *the same*. The 10 had previously cost £ 10, now they cost £ 20, just as the 800 lbs. would previously have cost £ 40, and now cost £ 80. Assume now that the profit was previously 20 per cent. This would involve:

	Constant capital	Variable capital	Surplus-value	Rate of surplus-value	Rate of profit	Product	Price per lb. of yarn
I	£80=1,600 lbs. cotton	£20 = 20 workers	£20	100 per cent	20 per cent	1,600 lbs. yarn	1s. 6d.
II	£80=800 lbs. cotton	£20 = 10 workers	£10	50 per cent	10 per cent	800 lbs. yarn	2s. 9d.

For if the surplus-value created by 20 workers is 20, then that created by 10 is 10; in order to produce it, however, £ 20 needs to be paid out, as before, whereas according to the earlier relationship, only 10 was paid. The value of the product, of the ||585| lb. of yarn, must in this case rise at any rate, because it contains more labour, accumulated labour (in the cotton which enters into it) and immediate labour.

If only cotton had risen and wages had remained the same, then the 800 lbs. of cotton would also have been spun by 10 workers. But these 10 workers would only have cost £ 10. That is, the surplus-value of 10 [would] as before have amounted to 100 per cent. In order to spin 800 lbs. of cotton, 10 workers [would be] needed with a capital outlay of 10. Thus total capital outlay would have been £ 90. Now according to the assumption there would always be 1 worker per 80 lbs. of cotton. Hence on 800 lbs. 10 workers and on 1,600 lbs. 20. How many pounds therefore could the total capital of £ 100 spin now? £ 88⁸/₉ could be used to buy cotton and £ 11¹/₉ could be laid out in wages. The relative proportions would be:

	Constant capital	Variable capital	Surplus-value	Rate of surplus-value	Rate of profit	Product	Price per lb. of yarn
III	£88⁸/₉ = 888⁸/₉ lbs.	£11¹/₉ = 11¹/₉ workers	£11¹/₉	100 per cent	11¹/₉ per cent	888⁸/₉ lb. yarn	2 s. 6d.

In this case, where no *change* in the *value* of *variable* capital takes place, and the rate of surplus-value therefore remains the same, [we have the following]:

In I, variable capital is to constant capital as 20:80=1:4. In III, it is as $11^{1}/_{9}$:$88^{8}/_{9}$=1:8; it has thus fallen proportionally by one half, because the *value* of constant capital has doubled. The same number of workers spin up the same amount of cotton, but £100 now only employ $11^{1}/_{9}$ workers, while the remaining £$88^{8}/_{9}$ only buy $888^{8}/_{9}$ lbs. of cotton instead of 1,600 lbs. [as in] I. The *rate of surplus-value* has remained the same. But owing to the change in the value of the constant capital, the same number of workers can no longer be employed by a capital of £100; the ratio between variable and constant capital has changed. Consequently the amount of surplus-value falls and with it the profit, since this surplus-value is calculated on the same amount of capital outlay as before. In the first case, the variable capital (i.e. 20) was $^{1}/_{4}$ of the constant capital (20:80) and $^{1}/_{5}$ of the total capital. Now it is only $^{1}/_{8}$ of the constant capital ($11^{1}/_{9}$:$88^{8}/_{9}$) and $^{1}/_{9}$ of 100, the total capital. But 100 per cent on $^{100}/_{5}$ or 20 is 20 and 100 per cent on $^{100}/_{9}$ or $11^{1}/_{9}$ is only $11^{1}/_{9}$. If the wage remains the same here, or the value of the variable capital remains the same, its absolute amount falls, because the *value of the constant capital* has risen. Therefore the percentage of the variable capital falls and with it surplus-value itself, its absolute amount, and hence the rate of profit.

If the *value of the variable capital remains the same* and *the method of production remains the same*, and therefore the ratio between the amounts of labour, raw material and machinery employed remains the same, a *change in the value of the constant capital* brings about the same variation in the composition of capital as if the *value of constant capital* had remained the same, but a *greater amount* of capital of unchanged value (*thus* also a *greater capital value*) had been employed, in proportion to the capital laid out in labour. The consequence is necessarily a fall in profit. (The opposite takes place if the value of constant capital falls.)

Conversely, a *change in the value of the variable capital*—in this case a rise—increases the proportion of *variable* to *constant capital* and therefore also the percentage of variable capital, or its proportional share in the total capital. Nevertheless, *the rate of profit falls here,* instead of rising, for the *method of production* has remained *the same.* The same amount of living labour as before is employed now, in order to convert the same amount of raw materials, machinery etc. into products. Here, as in the above case, only a smaller total amount of immediate and accumulated labour can be set in motion with the same capital of £ 100 ||586|; but the smaller amount of labour costs more. The necessary wage has risen. A larger share of this smaller amount of labour represents necessary labour and therefore a smaller amount forms surplus-labour. The rate of surplus-value has fallen, while at the same time the number of workers or the total quantity of labour under the command of the same capital has diminished. The variable capital has increased in proportion to constant capital and hence also in proportion to total capital, although the *amount of labour* employed in proportion to the amount of constant capital has decreased. The surplus-value consequently falls and with it the rate of profit. Previously, the *rate of surplus-value remained the same,* while the rate of profit fell, because the variable capital *fell* in proportion to the constant capital and hence in proportion to the total capital, or the surplus-value fell because the number of workers decreased, its multiplier decreased, *while the rate remained the same.* This time the rate of profit falls because the variable capital *rises* in proportion to the constant capital, hence also to the total capital; this rise in variable capital is, however, accompanied by a fall in the amount of labour employed (of labour employed by *the same* capital), in other words, the surplus-value falls, because its *decreasing rate* is bound up with the decreasing amount of labour employed. The *paid* labour has increased in proportion to the constant capital, but the total quantity of labour employed has decreased.

These variations in the value therefore always affect the surplus-value itself, whose absolute amount decreases in both cases because either one or both of its two factors fall. In one case it decreases because the number of workers decreases while the rate of surplus-value remains the same, in the other, because both the rate decreases and the number of workers employed by a capital of £ 100 decreases.

Finally we come to case II, where the change in the value of an agricultural product affects both parts of capital in the *same proportion* and where this *change of value* is therefore not accompanied by a change in the organic composition of capital.

In this case (see p. 584)[a] the pound of yarn rises from 1s. 6d. to 2s. 9d., since it is the product of more labour-time than before. It contains *just as much immediate* (although more paid and less unpaid) labour as before, but more accumulated labour. Due to the change in the value of cotton from 1s. to 2s., 2s. instead of 1s. is incorporated in the value of the lb. of yarn. Example II on page 584 however is incorrect. We had:

	Constant capital	Variable capital	Surplus-value	Rate of surplus-value	Rate of profit	Product	Price per lb. of yarn
I	£80 = 1,600 lbs. cotton	£20 = 20 workers	£20	100 per cent	20 per cent	1,600 lbs. yarn	1s. 6d.

The labour of 20 workers is represented by £ 40. Of this, half is unpaid labour here, hence [£] 20 surplus-value. According to this ratio, 10 workers will produce [a value of] £ 20 and of this [£] 10 [are] wages and [£] 10 surplus-value.

If, therefore, the value of the labour-power rose in the same proportion as that of the raw material, i.e., if it doubled, then it would be £ 20 for 10 workers as compared with £ 20 for 20 workers before. In this case, there would be no surplus-labour left. For the value, in terms of money, which the 10 workers produce is equal to £ 20, if that which the 20 produce is equal to £ 40. This is impossible. If this were the case, the basis of capitalist production would have disappeared.

Since, however, the changes in value of constant and variable capital are supposed to be *the same* (proportionally), we must put this case differently. Therefore say the value of cotton rose by one-third; £ 80 now buy 1,200 lbs. cotton, whereas previously they bought 1,600. Previously £ 1 = 20 lbs. [cotton] or 1 lb. [cotton] = £ $\frac{1}{20}$ = 1s. Now £ 1 = 15 lbs. or 1 lb. = £ $\frac{1}{15}$ = = 1$\frac{1}{3}$s. or 1s. 4d. Previously 1 worker cost £ 1, now £ 1$\frac{1}{3}$ = = £ 1 6$\frac{2}{3}$s. or £ 1 6s. 8d. and for 15 men [that] amounts to £ 20 (£ 15 + £ $\frac{15}{3}$). ||587| Since 20 men produce a value of £ 40, 15 men produce a value of £ 30. Of this value, £ 20 [are] now their wages and £ 10 surplus-value or unpaid labour.

---

[a] See this volume, p. 281.—*Ed.*

Thus we have the following:

	Constant capital	Variable capital	Surplus-value	Rate of surplus-value	Rate of profit	Product	Price per lb. of yarn
IV	£80 = 1,200 lbs. cotton	£20 = 15 men	£10	50 per cent	10 per cent	1,200 lbs. yarn	1s. 10d.

This 1s. 10d. [contains] cotton worth 1s. 4d. and labour worth 6d.

The product becomes dearer because the cotton has become dearer by a third. But the product is not dearer by a third. Previously, in I, it was equal to 18d.; if, therefore, it had become dearer by one-third, it would now be 18d.+6d.=24d., but it is only equal to 22d. Previously 1,600 lbs. yarn contained £40 labour, i.e., 1 lb., £$^1/_{40}$ or $^{20}/_{40}$s. or $^1/_2$s.=6d. labour. Now 1,200 lbs. [yarn] contain £30 labour, 1 lb. therefore contains £$^1/_{40}$=$^1/_2$s. or 6d. labour. Although the labour has become dearer in the same ratio as the raw material, the quantity of immediate labour contained in 1 lb. of yarn has remained *the same,* though more of this quantity is now paid and less unpaid labour. This change in the value of wages does not, therefore, in any way affected the value of the lb. of yarn, of the product. Now as before, labour only accounts for 6d., while cotton now accounts for 1s. 4d., instead of 1s., as previously. Thus, if the commodity is sold *at its value,* the change in the value of wages cannot after all bring about a change in the price of the product. Previously, however, 3d. of the 6d. were wages and 3d. surplus-value; now 4d. are wages and 2d. surplus-value. In fact 3d. on wages per lb. of yarn comes to 3×1,600.=£20 for 1,600 lbs. yarn. And 4d. per pound amounts to 4×1,200= =£20 for 1,200 lbs. And 3d. on 15d. (1s. cotton plus 3d. wages) in the first example comes to $^1/_5$ profit=20 per cent. On the other hand, 2d. on 20d. (16d. cotton and 4d. wages) comes to $^1/_{10}$ or 10 per cent.

If, in the above example, the price of cotton had remained the same [then we would have the following]: 1 man spins 80 lbs., since the method of production has remained *the same* in all the examples, and the pound is again equal to 1s.

Now the capital is made up as follows:

Constant capital	Variable capital	Surplus-value	Rate of surplus-value	Rate of profit	Product	Price per lb. of yarn
£73$^1/_3$= 1,466$^2/_3$ lbs. cotton	£26$^2/_3$ (20 men)	£13$^1/_3$	50 per cent	13$^1/_3$ per cent	1,466$^2/_3$ lbs.	1$^6/_{11}$s.

This calculation is wrong; for if a man spins 80 lbs., 20 [men] spin 1,600 and not 1,466$^2/_3$, since it is assumed that the *method of production* has remained *the same*. This fact can in no way be altered by the difference in the remuneration of the man. The example must therefore be constructed differently.

	Constant capital	Variable capital	Surplus-value	Rate of surplus-value	Rate of profit	Product	Price per lb. of yarn
II	£75 = 1,500 lbs. cotton	£25 (18$^3/_4$ men)	£12$^1/_2$	50 per cent	12$^1/_2$ per cent	1,500 lbs. yarn	1s. 6d.

Of this 6d., 4d. wages and 2d. profit. 2 on 16=$^1/_8$=12$^1/_2$ per cent.

Finally, if the value of the variable capital remained the same as before, [i.e.], 1 man received £1, whereas the value of the constant capital altered, so that 1 lb. cotton cost 1s. 4d. or 16d., instead of 1s. then:

	Constant capital	Variable capital	Surplus-value	Rate of surplus-value	Rate of profit	Product	Price per lb. of yarn
III	£84$^4/_{19}$ = 1,263$^3/_{19}$ lbs. cotton	£15$^{15}/_{19}$ = (15$^{15}/_{19}$ men)	£15$^{15}/_{19}$	100 per cent	15$^{15}/_{19}$ per cent	1,263$^3/_{19}$ lbs. [yarn]	1s. 10d.

||588| The profit [would be] 3d. On 19d. this comes to exactly 15$^{15}/_{19}$ per cent.

Now let us put all these examples together, beginning with I, where no change of value has as yet taken place.

	Constant capital	Variable capital	Surplus-value	Rate of surplus-value	Rate of profit	Product	Price per lb. of yarn	Profit
I	£80 = 1,600 lbs. cotton	£20 = 20 workers	£20	100 per cent	20 per cent	1,600 lbs. yarn	1s. 6d.	3d.
II	£75 = 1,500 lbs. cotton	£25=18$^3/_4$ workers	£12$^1/_2$	50 per cent	12$^1/_2$ per cent	1,500 lbs. yarn	1s. 6d.	2d.
III	£84$^4/_{19}$ = 1,263$^3/_{19}$ lbs. [cotton]	£15$^{15}/_{19}$= 15$^{15}/_{19}$ workers	£15$^{15}/_{19}$	100 per cent	15$^{15}/_{19}$ per cent	1,263$^3/_{19}$ lbs. yarn	1s. 10d.	3d.
IV	£80 = 1,200 lbs. [cotton]	£20= 15 workers	£10	50 per cent	10 per cent	1,200 lbs. yarn	1s. 10d.	2d.

The price of the product has changed in III and IV, because the value of constant capital has changed. On the other hand, a change in the value of variable capital does not bring about a change in price because the absolute quantity of immediate labour remains the same and is only differently apportioned between necessary labour and surplus-labour.

Now what happens in example IV, where the change in value affects constant and variable capital in *equal proportions,* where both rise by one-third?

If only wages had risen (II), then the profit would have fallen from 20 per cent to 12$^1/_2$, i.e., by 7$^1/_2$ per cent. If constant capital alone had risen (III), profit would have fallen from 20 per cent to 15$^{15}/_{19}$ per cent, i.e., by 4$^4/_{19}$ per cent. Since both rise to the same extent, profit falls from 20 per cent to 10 per cent, i.e., by 10 per cent. But why not by 7$^1/_2$+4$^4/_{19}$ per cent or by 11$^{27}/_{38}$, which is the *sum* of the differences of II and III? This 1$^{27}/_{38}$ must be accounted for; in accordance with that, the profit should have fallen (IV) to 8$^{11}/_{38}$, instead of to 10. The amount of profit is determined by the amount of surplus-value and this is determined by the *number* of workers, when the rate of surplus-labour is given. In I there are 20 workers and half their labour-time is unpaid. In II, only a third of the total labour is unpaid, thus the rate of surplus-value falls; moreover, 1$^1/_4$ less workers are employed and therefore the *number* [of workers] or the total labour decreases. In III the rate of surplus-value is again the same as in I, one-half of the working-day is unpaid, but as a result of the rise in value of the constant capital, the number of workers falls from 20 to 15$^{15}/_{19}$ or by

$4^4/_{19}$. In IV (the rate of surplus-value having fallen again to the level of that in II, namely, one-third of the working-day), the number of workers decreases by 5, namely, from 20 to 15. Compared with I, the number of workers in IV decreases by 5, compared with II by $3^3/_4$ and compared with III by $^{15}/_{19}$; but compared with I it does not decrease by $1^1/_4 + 4^4/_{19}$, i.e., by $5^{35}/_{76}$. Otherwise the number of workers employed in IV would be $14^{41}/_{76}$.

Hence it follows that *variations in the value* of commodities which enter into constant or variable capital—when the *method of production*, or the *physical composition of capital*, remains the same, in other words, when the ratio of immediate and accumulated labour remains constant—do *not* bring about a change in the organic composition of the capital if they affect variable and constant capital *in the same proportion*, as in IV (where for instance cotton becomes dearer to the same degree as the wheat which is consumed by the workers). The rate of profit falls here (while the value of constant and variable capital increases), firstly because the rate of surplus-value falls due to the rise in wages, and secondly, because the *number* of workers decreases.

The change in value—if it affects only constant capital or only variable capital—acts like a change in the organic composition of capital and changes the *relative value* of the component parts of capital, although the method of production remains the same. When only the variable capital is affected, it rises in relation to the constant capital ||589| and to the total capital; and not only the rate of surplus-value decreases, but also the number of workers employed. Consequently the amount of constant capital (whose value [remains] unchanged) employed is also smaller (II).

If the change in value only affects the constant capital, then the variable capital falls in proportion to the constant capital and to the total capital. Although the rate of surplus-value remains the same, its amount decreases because the *number of* workers employed falls (III).

Finally, it would be possible for the change in value to affect both constant and variable capital, but in *uneven* proportions. This case only requires to be fitted into the above categories. Suppose, for instance, that constant and variable capital were affected in such a way that the value of the former rose by 10 per cent and the latter by 5. Then in so far as they both rose by 5 per cent, one by 5+5 and the other by 5, we would have case IV. But in so far as the constant capital changed by a further 5 per cent, we would have case III.

In the above, we have only assumed a rise in value. With a fall we have the opposite effect. For example, going from IV to I can be considered as a fall in value which affected both component parts *in equal proportions*. To assess the effect of a fall in only [one component part], II and III would have to be modified. |589||

* * *

||600| I would make the following further observation on the influence of the variation of value upon the organic composition of capital: With capitals in *different branches of production*—with an otherwise equal physical composition—it is possible that the higher *value* of the machinery or of the material used, may bring about a difference. For instance, if the cotton, silk, linen and wool [industries] had exactly the same physical composition, the mere difference in the cost of the material used would create such a variation. |600||

[d) Changes in the Total Rent, Dependent on Changes in the Market-Value]

||589| Returning to Table A it thus follows,[a] that the assumption, that the profit of 10 per cent has come about through a decrease (in that the rate of profit, starting from III was higher, in II it was lower than in III, but still higher than in I, where it was 10 per cent) may be correct, namely, if the development actually proceeded along the descending line; but this assumption by no means necessarily follows from the gradation of rents, the mere existence of differential rents; on the contrary with the ascending line, this [gradation of rents] presupposes that the rate of profit remains the same over a long period.

Table B. As has already been explained above,[b] in this example the competition from III and IV, forces [the cultivator of] II to withdraw half his capital. With a descending line, it

---

a See this volume, pp. 273-75.—*Ed.*
b See this volume, p. 254 et seqq.—*Ed.*

would on the contrary appear that an additional supply of only $32\frac{1}{2}$ tons is required, hence only a capital of £ 50 has to be invested in II.

But the most interesting aspect of the table is this: Previously a capital of £ 300 was invested, now only £ 250, i.e., one-sixth less. The amount of product has however remained the same— 200 tons. The productivity of labour has thus risen and the value of the individual commodity fallen. The *total value* of the commodities has likewise fallen, from £ 400 to £ $369^3/_{13}$. As compared with A, the market-value per ton has fallen from £ 2 to £ 1 $16^{12}/_{13}$s., since the new market-value is determined by the *individual value* of II instead of, as previously, by the higher one of I. Despite all these circumstances—decrease in the capital invested, decrease in the total value of the product with the same volume of production, fall in the market-value, exploitation of more fertile classes—the rent in *B*, as compared with *A*, has risen absolutely, by £ $24^3/_{13}$ (£ $94^3/_{13}$ as against £ 70). If we examine how far the individual classes participate in the increase in total rent, we find that in class II the absolute rent, in so far as its rate is concerned, has remained the same for £ 5 on £ 50 equals 10 per cent; but its *amount* has fallen by half, from £ 10 to £ 5, because the capital investment in II B has fallen by half, from £ 100 to £ 50. Class II B, instead of effecting an increase in the rental, effects a decrease by £ 5. Furthermore, the differential rent for II B has completely disappeared, because the market-value is now equal to the individual value of II; this results in a second loss of £ 10. Altogether then the reduction in rent for class II amounts to £ 15.

In III the amount of absolute rent is the same; but as a result of the fall in market-value, its differential value has also fallen; hence also the differential rent. It amounted to £ 30, now it amounts only to [£] $18^6/_{13}$. This is a reduction by [£] $11^7/_{13}$. The rent for II and III taken together has therefore fallen by [£] $26^7/_{13}$. It remains to account for a rise, not of $24^3/_{13}$, as at first sight it would seem, but of £ $50^{10}/_{13}$. Furthermore, however, for B as compared with A, the absolute rent of I A has disappeared as class I itself has disappeared. This represents a further reduction by £ 10. Thus, all in all, £ $60^{10}/_{13}$ must be accounted for. But this is the rental of the new class IV B. The rise in the rental of B is therefore only to be explained by the rent from IV B. The absolute rent for IV B, like that of all other classes, is £ 10. The differential rent of £ $50^{10}/_{13}$

however, is due to ||590| the fact that the differential value of
IV is $10^{470}/_{481}$s. per ton, and this has to be multiplied by $92^1/_2$
for that is the number of tons. The fertility of II and III has
remained the same. The least fertile class has been removed
entirely and yet the rental rises because, due to its relatively
great fertility, the differential rent of IV alone is greater than
the total differential rent of A had been previously. Differential rent does not depend on the absolute fertility of the classes
that are cultivated for $^1/_2$ II, III, IV [B are] more fertile than
I, II, III [A], and yet the differential rent for $^1/_2$ II, III, IV [B]
is greater than it was for I, II, III [A] because the greatest portion of the product—$92^1/_2$ tons—is supplied by a class whose
differential value is greater than that occurring in I, II, III A.
When the differential value for a class is *given*, the absolute
amount of its differential rent naturally depends on the amount
of its product. But this *amount* itself is already taken into account in the calculation and formation of the differential value.
Because with £ 100, IV produced $92^1/_2$ tons, no more and no
less, its differential value in B where the market-value is £ 1
$16^{12}/_{13}$s. per ton, amounts to 10 $^{470}/_{481}$s. per ton.

The whole rental in A amounts to £ 70 on £ 300 capital, which
is $23^1/_3$ per cent. On the other hand in B, leaving out of account
the $^3/_{13}$, it is £ 94 on £ 250, which is $37^3/_5$ per cent.

Table C. Here it is assumed that class IV having come into
the picture and class II determining the market-value, demand
does not remain the same, as in Table B, but it increases with
the falling price, so that the whole of the $92^1/_2$ tons which have
been newly added by IV is absorbed by the market. At £ 2 per
ton only 200 tons would be absorbed; at £ $1^{11}/_{13}$, the demand
grows to $292^1/_2$. It is wrong to assume that the limits of the
market are necessarily the same at £ $1^{11}/_{13}$ per ton as at £ 2 per
ton. On the contrary, the market expands to a certain extent
with the falling price—even in the case of a general means of
subsistence, such as wheat.

This, *for the time being*, is the only point to which we want
to draw attention in Table C.

Table D. Here it is assumed that the $292^1/_2$ tons are absorbed by the market only if the market-value falls to £ $1^5/_6$,
which is the *cost-price* per ton for class I, which therefore bears
no rent but only yields the normal profit of 10 per cent. This
is the case which Ricardo assumes to be the normal case and
on which we should therefore dwell at somewhat greater length.

19*

As in the preceding tables, the ascending line is here presupposed at the outset; later we shall look at the same process in the descending line.

If II, III and IV only provided an additional supply of 140, that is, an additional supply which the market absorbs at £2 per ton, then I would continue to determine the market-value.

But this is not the case. There is an overplus of $92\frac{1}{2}$ tons on the market, produced by class IV. If this were, in fact, surplus production, which exceeded the absolute requirements of the market, then I would be completely thrown out of the market and II would have to withdraw half its capital as in B. II would then determine the market-value as in B. But it is assumed that if the market-value decreases, the market can absorb the $92\frac{1}{2}$ tons. How does this occur? IV, III and $\frac{1}{2}$II dominate the market absolutely. In other words if the market could only absorb 200 tons, they would throw out I.

But to begin with let us take the actual position. There are now $292\frac{1}{2}$ tons on the market whereas previously there were only 200. II would sell at its individual value, at £$1\frac{11}{13}$, in order to make room for itself and to drive I, whose individual value is £2, out of the market. But since, even at this market-value, there is no room for the $292\frac{1}{2}$ tons, IV and III exert pressure on II, until the market-price falls to £$1\frac{5}{6}$, at which price the classes IV, III, II and I find room for their product on the market, which at *this* ||591| market-price absorbs the *whole* product. Through this fall in price, supply and demand are balanced. As soon as the additional supply surpasses the capacity of the market, as determined by the old market-value, each class naturally seeks to force the whole of its product *on to* the market to the exclusion of the product of the other classes. This can only be brought about through a fall in price, and moreover a fall to the level where the market can absorb *all* products. If this reduction in price is so great that the classes I, II etc. have to sell *below* their costs of production,[88] they naturally have to withdraw [their capital from production]. If, however, the situation is such that the reduction does not have to be so great in order to bring the output into line with the state of the market, then the total capital can continue to work in this sphere of production at this new market-value.

But it is further clear that in these circumstances it is not the worst land, I and II, but the best, III and IV, which determines the market-value, and so also the rent on the *best sorts of land* determines those on the worse, as *Storch*[89] correctly grasped in relation to this case.

IV sells at the price at which it can force its entire product on to the market overcoming all resistance from the other classes. This price is £ $1^5/_6$. If the price were higher, the market would contract and the process of mutual exclusion would begin anew.

That I determines the market-value [is correct] only on the assumption that the additional supply from II etc. is only the additional supply which the market can absorb at the market-value of I. If it is greater, then I is quite passive and by the room it takes up, only compels II, III, IV to react until the price has contracted sufficiently for the market to be large enough for the whole product. Now it happens that at this market-value, which is in fact determined by IV, IV itself pays a differential rent of £ $49^7/_{12}$ in addition to the absolute rent, III pays a differential rent of £ $17^1/_2$ in addition to the absolute rent, II, on the other hand, pays no differential rent and moreover, only pays a part of the absolute rent, £ $9^1/_6$, instead of £ 10, i.e., not the full amount of the absolute rent. Why? Although the new market-value of £ $1^5/_6$ is above its cost-price, it is *below* its individual value. If market-value were *equal* to its individual value, it would pay the absolute rent of £ 10, which is equal to the difference between individual value and cost-price. But since it is below that, it only pays a part of its absolute rent, £ $9^1/_6$ instead of £ 10; the actual rent it pays is equal to the difference between market-value and cost-price, but this difference is smaller than that between its individual value and its cost-price.

⟨The *actual rent* is equal to the difference between market-value and cost-price.⟩

The *absolute rent* is equal to the difference between individual value and cost-price.

The *differential rent* is equal to the difference between market-value and individual value.

The actual or *total rent* is equal to the absolute rent plus the differential rent, in other words, it is equal to the excess of the market-value over the individual value plus the excess of the individual value over the cost-price or [it is] equal to the difference between market-value and cost-price.

If, therefore, the market-value is equal to the individual value, the differential rent is nil and the total rent is equal to the difference between individual value and cost-price.

If the market-value is greater than the individual value, the *differential rent* is equal to the excess of the market-value over the individual value, the total rent, however, is equal to this differential rent plus the absolute rent.

If the market-value is smaller than the individual value, but greater than the cost-price, the differential rent is a negative quantity, hence the total rent is equal to the absolute rent plus this negative differential rent, i.e., the excess of the individual value over the market-value.

If the market-value is equal to the cost-price, then on the whole rent is nil.

In order to put this down in the form of equations, we shall call the absolute rent AR, the differential rent DR, the total rent TR, the market-value MV, the individual value IV and the cost-price CP. We then have the following equations:

||592| 1. AR=IV—CP=+y
2. DR=MV—IV=x
3. TR=AR+DR=MV—IV+IV—CP=y+x=MV—CP

If MV>IV then MV—IV=+x. Hence: DR positive and TR=$=y+x$.

And MV—CP=$y+x$. Or MV—y—x=CP or MV=$y+x$+CP.

If MV<IV then MV—IV=—x. Hence: DR negative and TR=$=y—x$.

And MV—CP=y—x. Or MV+x=IV. Or MV +x—y=CP. Or MV=y—x+CP.

If MV=IV, then DR=0, x=0, because MV—IV=0.

Hence TR=AR+DR=AR+0=MV—IV+IV—CP=0+IV—$—CP=IV—CP=MV—CP=+$y$.

If MV=CP [then] TR or MV—CP=0

In the circumstances assumed, I pays no rent. Why not? Because the absolute rent is equal to the difference between the individual value and the cost-price. The differential rent, however, is equal to the difference between the market-value and the individual value. But the market-value here is equal to the cost-price of I. The individual value of I is £2 per ton, the market-value £$1^5/_6$. The differential rent of I is therefore £$1^5/_6$—£2, which is —£$^1/_6$. The absolute rent of I, however, is £2—£$1^5/_6$, in other words, it is equal to the difference between its individual value and its cost-price, which is +£$^1/_6$.

Since, therefore, the actual rent of I is equal to the absolute rent $(+£^1/_6)$ and the differential rent $(-£^1/_6)$, it is equal to $+£^1/_6-£^1/_6=0$. Thus category I pays neither differential rent nor absolute rent, but only the cost-price. The value of its product is £2; [it is] sold at £$1^5/_6$, that means $^1/_{12}$ *below* its value which is $8^1/_3$ per cent *below* its value. Category I cannot sell at a higher price, because the market is determined not by I but by IV, III, II in opposition to I. Category I can merely provide an additional supply at the price of £$1^5/_6$.

That I pays no rent, is due to the fact that the market-value is equal to its cost-price.

This fact, however, is the result:

Firstly of the relatively low productivity of I. What it has to supply, is 60 additional tons at £$1^5/_6$. Suppose instead of supplying only 60 tons for [£] 100, I supplied 64 tons for [£] 100, i.e., 1 ton less than class II. Then only £$93^3/_4$ capital would have to be invested in I in order to supply 60 tons. The individual value of one ton in I would then be £$1^7/_8$ or £1 $17^1/_2$s.; its cost-price: £1 $14^3/_8$s. And since the market-value is £$1^5/_6=$ $=£1$ $16^2/_3$s., the difference between cost-price and market-value is $2^7/_{24}$s. And on 60 tons this would amount to ||593| a rent of £6 $17^1/_2$s.

If therefore all the circumstances remained the same and I were more productive than it is by $^1/_{15}$ (since $^{60}/_{15}=4$), it would still pay a part of the absolute rent because there would be a difference between the market-value and its cost-price, although a smaller difference than between its individual value and its cost-price. Here the worst land would therefore still bear a rent if it were more fertile than it is. If I were absolutely more fertile than it is, II, III IV would be *relatively less fertile* compared with it. The difference between its [value] and their individual values would be smaller. The fact that I bears *no rent* is therefore just as much due to the circumstance that it is not absolutely more fertile as to the fact that II, III, IV are not *relatively less fertile.*

Secondly, however: Given the productivity of I as 60 tons for £100. If II, III, IV, and especially IV, which enters the market as a new competitor, were less fertile, not only relatively as against I, but *absolutely,* then category I could yield a rent, even though this would only consist of a fraction of the absolute rent. For since the market absorbs $292^1/_2$ tons at £$1^5/_6$, it would absorb a smaller number of tons, for instance

280 tons at a market-value higher than £ 1⁵/₆. Every market-value, however, which is higher than £ 1⁵/₆, i.e., higher than the production costs of I, yields a rent for I, equal to the market-value minus the cost-price of I.

It can thus equally well be said that I yields no rent because of the absolute productivity of IV, for as long as II and III were the only competitors on the market, it yielded a rent and would continue to do so even despite the advent of IV, despite the additional supply—although it would be a lower rent—if for a capital outlay of £ 100 IV produced 80 tons instead of 92¹/₂ tons.

Thirdly: We have assumed that the absolute rent for a capital outlay of £ 100 is £ 10, that is, 10 per cent on the capital or ¹/₁₁ on the cost-price, and that therefore the value [of the product yielded by] a capital of £ 100 in agriculture is £ 120 of which £ 10 are profit.

It would be wrong to assume that if we [say]: £ 100 capital is laid out in agriculture and if one working-day equals £ 1, then 100 working-days are laid out. In general, if a capital of £ 100 equals 100 working-days then, in whatever branch of production this capital may be laid out, [the newly-created value] is never [equal to 100 working-days]. Supposing that one gold sovereign equals one working-day of 12 hours, and that this is the normal working-day, then the first question is, what is the rate of exploitation of labour? That is, how many of these 12 hours does the worker work for himself, for the re-production (of the equivalent) of his wage, and how many does he work for the capitalist *gratis*? [How great], therefore, is the labour-time which the capitalist *sells* without having *paid* for it and which is therefore the source of the surplus-value and serves to augment the capital? If the rate of exploitation is 50 per cent, then the worker works 8 hours for himself and 4 gratis for the capitalist. The product equals 12 hours, which is £ 1 (since according to the assumption, 12 hours labour-time are contained in one gold sovereign). Of these 12 hours, equal to £ 1, 8 recoup the capitalist for the wage and 4 form his surplus-value. Thus on a wage of 13¹/₃s., surplus-value equals 6²/₃s.; or on a capital outlay of £ 1, it is 10s. and on £ 100, £ 50. Then the value of the commodity produced with the £ 100 capital would be £ 150. The profit of the capitalist in fact consists in the sale of the unpaid labour contained in the product. The normal profit is derived from this sale of that which has not been paid for.

||594| But the second question is this: What is the *organic composition* of the capital? That part of the value of the capital which consists of machinery etc. and raw material is *simply reproduced* in the product, it reappears remaining unaltered. This part of the capital the capitalist must pay for at its *value*. It thus enters into the product as a given *predetermined* value. Only the labour used by the capitalist is merely partly paid for by him, although it enters *wholly* into the value of the product [and] is wholly bought by him. Assuming the above to be the rate of exploitation of labour, the amount of surplus-value for capital *of the same* size will, therefore, depend on its organic composition. If the capital A consists of £ 80c+£ 20v, then the value of the product is £ 110 and the profit is £ 10 (although it contains 50 per cent unpaid labour). If the capital B consists of £ 40c+£ 60v, then the value of the product is £ 130, and the profit is £ 30 although it too contains only 50 per cent unpaid labour. If the capital C consists of £ 60c+ +£ 40v, then the value of the product is £ 120 and the profit is £ 20 although, in this case too, it comprises 50 per cent unpaid labour. Thus the three capitals, equal to £ 300, yield a total profit of £ 10+£ 30+£ 20=£ 60, and this makes an average of 20 per cent for £ 100. This average profit is made by each of the capitals if it sells the commodity it produces at £ 120. The capital A: £ 80c+£ 20v, sells at £ 10 *above* its value; capital B: £ 40c+£ 60v, sells at £ 10 *below* its value; capital C: £ 60c+£ 40v sells *at* its value. All the commodities taken together, are sold at their value: £ 120+£ 120+ £ 120=£ 360. In fact the value of A+B+C equals £ 110+£ 130+£ 120=£ 360. But the prices of the individual categories are partly *above*, partly *below* and partly *at* their value so that each yields a profit of 20 per cent. The values of the commodities, thus modified, are their cost-prices, which competition constantly sets as centres of gravitation for market-prices.

Now assume that the £ 100 laid out in agriculture is composed of £ 60c+£ 40v (which, incidentally, is perhaps still too low for v), then the value [of the product] is £ 120. But this would be equal to the *cost-price* in the industry. Suppose therefore in the above case that the average price [of the product produced] by a capital of [£]100 is £110. We now say that if the agricultural product is sold at its value, its value is £ 10 *above* its cost-price. It then yields a rent of 10 per cent and this we assume to be the *normal* thing in capitalist production, that in contrast to other products, the agricultural product is not sold at its *cost-price,* but at its *value,* as a result of *landed property.* The composition of the aggregate capital is £ 80c+£ 20v, if the average profit is 10 per cent. We assume that that of the agricultural capital is £ 60c+£ 40v, that is, in its composition wages— immediate labour—have a larger share than in the total capital invested in the other branches of industry. This indicates a *relatively lower* productivity of labour in this branch. It is true, that in some types of agriculture, for instance in stock-raising, the composition may be £ 90c+£ 10v, i.e., the ratio of v:c may be smaller than in the total industrial capital. Rent is, however, not determined by this branch, but by agriculture proper, and, furthermore, by that part of it which produces the principal *means of subsistence,* such as wheat, etc. The rent in the other branches is not determined by the composition of ||595| the capital invested in these branches themselves, but by the composition of the capital which is used in the production of the principal means of subsistence. The mere existence of capitalist production presupposes that vegetable food, not animal food, is the largest element in the means of subsistence. The interrelationship of the rents in the various branches is a secondary question that does not interest us here and is [therefore] left out of consideration.

In order, therefore, to make the absolute rent equal to 10 per cent, it is assumed that the general average composition of the non-agricultural capital is £ 80c+£ 20v and that of agricultural capital is £ 60c+£ 40v.

The question now is whether it would make any difference to case D, where class I pays no rent, if the agricultural capital were differently constituted, for example £ 50c+£ 50v or £ 70c+£ 30v? In the first case, the value of the product would be £ 125, in the second, £ 115. In the first case, the difference arising from the different composition of the non-agricultural capital would be £ 15, in the second it would be 5. That is, the difference between the value of the agricultural product and cost-price would in the first case be 50 per cent higher than has been assumed above, and in the second 50 per cent lower.

If the former were the case, if the value [of the product] of £ 100 were £ 125, then the value per ton for I [would be] equal to £ $2^1/_{12}$ in Table A. And this would be the market-value for A, for class I determines the market-value here. The cost-price for I A, on the other hand, would be £ $1^5/_6$, as before. Since, according to the assumption, the $292^1/_2$ tons are only saleable at £ $1^5/_6$, this would therefore make no difference, just as it would make no difference if the agricultural capital [were] composed of £ 70c+£ 30v or the difference between the value of the agricultural produce and its cost-price [were] only £ 5, i.e., half the amount [previously] assumed. If the *cost-price,* and therefore the average organic composition of the non-agricultural capital, were assumed to be constant at £ 80c+£ 20v, then it would make no difference to this case ⟨I D⟩ whether it [the organic composition of the agricultural capital] were higher or lower, although it would make a considerable difference to Table A and it would make a difference of 50 per cent in the absolute rent.

But let us now assume the opposite, that the composition of the agricultural capital remains £ 60c+£ 40v, as before and that of the non-agricultural capital varies. Instead of being £ 80c+£ 20v, let it be either £ 70c+£ 30v or £ 90c+£ 10v. In the first case the average profit [would be] [£] 15 or 50 per cent higher than in the supposed case; in the other, £ 5 or 50 per cent lower. In the first case the absolute rent [would be] £ 5. This would again make no difference to I D. In the second case the absolute rent [would be] £ 15. This too would make no difference to the case I D. All this would therefore be of no consequence to I D, however important it may continue to be for tables A, B, C, and E, i.e., for the absolute determination of the absolute and differential rent, whenever the new class— be it in the ascending or the descending line—only supplies the necessary additional demand at the old market-value.

*   *   *

Now the following question arises:

Can this *case D* occur in practice? And even before this, we must ask: is it, as Ricardo assumes, the *normal* case? It can only be the normal case:

Either: if the agricultural capital is equal to £ 80c+£ 20v, that is, to the average composition of the non-agricultural capital, so that the *value* of the agricultural produce would be equal to the *cost-price* of the *non-agricultural produce.* For the time being this is statistically wrong. The assumption of this *rela-*

tively lower productivity of agriculture is at any rate more appropriate than Ricardo's assumption of a *progressive* absolute decrease in its productivity.

||596| In Chapter I *"On Value"* Ricardo assumes that the average composition of capital prevails in gold and silver mines (although he only speaks of fixed and circulating capital here; but we shall "correct" this). According to this assumption, these mines could only yield a differential rent, never an absolute rent. The assumption itself, however, in turn rests on the other assumption, that the additional supply provided by the richer mines is always greater than the additional supply required at the old market-value. But it is absolutely incomprehensible why the opposite cannot equally well take place. The mere existence of differential rent already proves that an additional supply is possible, without altering the *given market-value*. For IV or III or II would yield no differential rents if they did not sell at the market-value of I, however this may have been determined, that is, if they did not sell at a market-value which is determined *independently* of the absolute amount of their supply.

Or: *case D* would always have to be the normal one, if the [conditions] presupposed in it are always the normal ones; in other words, if I is always forced by the competition from IV, III and II, especially from IV, to sell its product *below* its value by the whole amount of the absolute rent, that is, at the *cost-price*. The mere existence of differential rent in IV, III, II proves that they sell at a market-value which is *above* their individual value. If Ricardo assumes that this cannot be the case with I, then it is only because he *presupposes* the impossibility of absolute rent, and the latter, because he presupposes the *identity of value and cost-price*.

Let us take *case C* where the $292^{1}/_{2}$ tons find a sale at a market-value of £1 $16^{12}/_{13}$ s. And, like Ricardo, let us start out from IV. So long as only $92^{1}/_{2}$ tons are required, IV will sell at £1 $5^{35}/_{37}$ s. per ton, i.e., it will sell commodities that have been produced with a capital of £100 at their value of £120, which yields the absolute rent of £10. Why should IV sell its commodity *below* its value, at its *cost-price*? So long as it alone is there, III, II, I cannot compete with it. The mere *cost-price* of III is *above* the value which yields IV a rent of £10, and even more so the cost-price of II and I. Therefore III etc. could not compete, even if they sold these tons at the bare cost-price.

Let us assume that there is only one class—the best or the worst type of land, IV or I or III or II, this makes no difference whatsoever to the theory—let us assume that its supply is *unlimited*, that is, *relatively* unlimited compared to the amount of the given capital and labour which is in general available and can be absorbed in this branch of production, so that land forms no barriers and provides a relatively unlimited field of action for the available amount of labour and capital. Let us assume, therefore, that there is no differential rent because there is no cultivation of land of *varying* natural fertility, hence there is no differential rent (or else only to a negligible extent). Furthermore, let us assume that there is *no landed property*; then clearly there is no absolute rent and, therefore (as, according to our assumption, there is no differential rent), there is *no* rent at all. This is a tautology. For the existence of *absolute rent* not only presupposes landed property, but it is the *posited landed property*, i.e., landed property contingent on and modified by the action of capitalist production. This tautology in *no* way helps to settle the question, since we explain that absolute rent is formed as the result of the *resistance* offered by landed property in agriculture to the capitalist levelling out of the values of commodities to average prices. If we remove this action on the part of landed property—this resistance, the specific resistance which the competition between capitals comes up against in this field of action—we naturally abolish the precondition on which the existence of rent is based. Incidentally (as Mr. Wakefield sees very well in his colonial theory[90]), there is a contradiction in the assumption itself: on the one hand, developed capitalist production, on the other hand, the non-existence of landed property. Where are the wage-labourers to come from in this case?

A somewhat *analogous* development takes place in the colonies, even where, *legally*, landed property exists, in so far as the government gives [land] gratis as happened originally in the colonisation from England; and even where the ||597| government actually institutes landed property by selling the land, though at a negligible price, as in the United States, at 1 dollar or something of the sort per acre.

Two different aspects must be distinguished here.

Firstly: There are the colonies proper, such as in the United States, Australia, etc. Here the mass of the farming colonists, although they bring with them a larger or smaller amount of capital from the motherland, are not *capitalists*, nor do they carry on *capitalist* production. They are more or less peasants who work themselves and whose main object, in the first place, is to produce *their own livelihood*, their means of subsistence. Their main product therefore does not become a *commodity* and is not intended for trade. They sell or exchange the excess of their products over their own consumption for imported manufactured commodities etc. The other, smaller section of the colonists who settle near the sea, navigable rivers etc., form trading towns. There is no question of capitalist production here either. Even if capitalist production gradually comes into being, so that the sale of his products and the profit he makes from this sale become decisive for the farmer who himself works and owns his land; so long as, compared with capital and labour, land still exists in elemental abundance providing a practically unlimited field of action, the first type of colonisation will continue as well and production will therefore *never* be regulated according to the needs of the market—at a given market-value. Everything the colonists of the first type produce *over and above* their immediate consumption, they will throw on the market and sell at any price that will bring in more than their wages. They are, and continue for a long time to be, competitors of the farmers who are already producing more or less capitalistically, and thus keep the market-price of the agricultural product constantly *below* its value. The farmer who therefore cultivates land of the worst kind, will be quite satisfied if he makes the average profit on the sale of his farm, i.e., if he gets back the capital invested, this is not the case in very many instances. Here therefore we have two essentially different conditions competing with one another: capitalist production is not as yet dominant in agriculture; secondly, although landed property exists legally, in practice it only exists as yet sporadically, and strictly speaking there is only possession of land. Or although landed property exists in a legal sense, it is—in view of the *elemental* abundance of land relative to labour and capital—as yet unable to offer resistance to capital, to transform agriculture into a field of action which, in contrast to non-agricultural industry, offers specific resistance to the *investment of capital*.

In the second type of colonies—plantations—where commercial speculations figure from the start and production is intended for the world market, the capitalist mode of production exists, although only in a formal sense, since the slavery of Negroes precludes free wage-labour, which is the basis of capitalist production. But the business in which slaves are used is conducted by *capitalists*. The method of production which they introduce has not arisen out of slavery but is grafted on to it. In this case the same person is capitalist and landowner. And the *elemental* [profusion] existence of the land confronting capital and labour does not offer any resistance to capital investment, hence none to the competition between capitals. Neither does a class of farmers as distinct from landlords develop here. So long as these conditions endure, nothing will stand in the way of cost-price regulating market-value.

All these preconditions have nothing to do with the preconditions in which an *absolute rent* exists: that is, on the one hand, developed capitalist production, and on the other, landed property, not only existing in the legal sense but actually offering resistance and defending the field of action against capital, only making way for it under certain conditions.

In these circumstances an absolute rent will exist, even if only IV or III or II or I are cultivated. Capital can only win new ground in that solely existing class [of land] by paying rent, that is, by selling the agricultural product at its *value*. It is, moreover, only in these circumstances that there can first be talk of a comparison and a difference between the capital invested in agriculture (i.e., in a natural element as such, in primary production) and that invested in non-agricultural industry.

But the next question is this:

If one starts out from I, then clearly II, III, IV, if they only provide the additional supply admissible at the old market-value, will sell at the market-value determined by I, and therefore, apart from the absolute rent, they will yield a differential rent in proportion to their relative fertility. On the other hand, if IV is the starting-point, then it appears that certain objections ||598| could be made.

For we saw that II [in tables B and C] draws the absolute rent if the product is sold at its value of £ $1^{11}/_{13}$ or at £ 1 $16^{12}/_{13}$s.

In Table D the *cost-price* of III, the next class (in the descending line) is higher than the *value* of IV, which yields a rent of £ 10. Thus there cannot be any question of competition or underselling here—even if III sold at cost-price. If IV, however, no longer satisfies the demand, if more than $92^{1}/_{2}$ tons are required, then its price will rise. In the above case, it would have to rise by $3^{43}/_{111}$s. per ton, before III could enter the field as a competitor, even at its *cost-price*. The question is, will it enter into it in these circumstances? Let us put this case in another way. For the price of IV to rise to £1 12s., the individual value of III, the demand would not have to rise by 75 tons. This applies especially to the *dominant agricultural product*, where an insufficiency in supply will bring about a much greater rise in *price* than corresponds to the *arithmetical* deficiency in supply. But if IV had risen to £1 12s., then at this market-value, which is equal to III's individual value, the latter would pay the absolute rent and IV a differential rent. If there is any additional demand at all, III can sell at its individual value, since it would then dominate the market-value and there would be no reason at all for the *landowner* to forgo the rent.

But say the market-price of IV only rose to £1 $9^{1}/_{3}$s., the *cost-price* of III. Or in order to make the example even more striking: suppose the cost-price of III is only £1 5s., i.e., only $1^{8}/_{37}$s. higher than the *cost-price* of IV. It must be higher because its fertility is lower than that of IV. Can III be taken in hand now and thus compete with IV, which sells above III's cost-price, namely, at £1 $5^{35}/_{37}$s.? Either there is an additional demand or not. In the first case the market-price of IV has risen above its value, above £1 $5^{35}/_{37}$s. And then, whatever the circumstances, III would sell *above* its cost-price, even if not to the full amount of its absolute rent.

Or there is *no* additional demand. Here in turn we have two possibilities. Competition from III could only enter into it if the farmer of III were at the same time its *owner*, if to him as a capitalist landed property would not be an obstacle, would offer no resistance, because he has control of it, not as capitalist but as landowner. His competition would force IV to sell below its hitherto prevailing price of £1 $5^{35}/_{37}$s. and even below the price of £1 5s. And in this way III would be driven out of the field. And IV would be capable of driving III out every time. It would only have no reduce the price to the level of its own costs of production, which are lower than those of III. But if the market expanded as a result of the *reduction in price* engendered by III, what then? Either the market expands to such an extent that IV can dispose of its $92^{1}/_{2}$ tons as before, despite the newly-added 75, or it does not expand to this degree, so that a part of the product of IV and III would be surplus.

In this case IV, since it dominates the market, would continue to lower [the price] until the capital in III is reduced to the appropriate size, that is until only that amount of capital is invested in it as is just sufficient for the entire product of IV to be absorbed. But at £1 5 s. the whole product would be saleable and since III sold a part of the product at this price, IV could not sell above that. This however would be the only possible case: temporary over-production not engendered by an additional demand, but leading to an expansion of the market. And this can only be the case if capitalist and landowner are identical in III—i.e., if it is assumed once again that landed property does not exist as a power confronting capital, because the capitalist himself is landowner and sacrifices the landowner to the capitalist. But if landed property as such confronts capital in III, then there is no reason at all why the landowner should hand over his acres for cultivation without drawing a rent from them, why he should hand over his land before the price of IV has risen to a level which is at least *above* the cost-price of III. If this rise is only ||599| small, then, in any country under capitalist production, III will continue to be withheld from capital as a field of action, unless there is no other form in which it can yield a rent. But it will never be put under cultivation before it yields a rent, before the price of IV is *above* the cost-price of III, i.e., before IV yields a differential rent in addition to its old rent. With the further growth of demand, the price of III would rise to its value, since the *cost-price* of II is *above* the individual value of III. II would be cultivated as soon as the price of III had risen above £ $1,13^{11}/_{13}$s., and so yielded some rent for II.

But it has been assumed in D that I yields *no* rent. But this only because I has been assumed to be already cultivated land which is being forced to sell *below* its value, at its *cost-price* because of the change in market-value brought about by the entry of IV. It will only continue to be thus exploited, if the owner is himself the farmer, and therefore in this *individual case* landed property *does not* confront capital, or if the farmer is a small capitalist prepared to accept less than 10 per cent or a worker who only wants to make his wage or a little more and hands over his surplus-labour, which is equal to [£] 10 or £ 9 or less, to the landowner instead of the capitalist. Although in the two latter cases *fermage* is paid, yet economically speaking, no rent, and we are concerned with the latter. In the one case the farmer is a mere labourer, in the other something between labourer and capitalist.

Nothing could be more absurd than the assertion that the landowner cannot *withdraw* his acres from the market just as easily as the capitalist can withdraw his capital from a branch of production. The best proof of this is the large amount of fertile land that is uncultivated in the most developed countries of Europe, such as England, the land which is taken out of agriculture and put to the building of railways or houses or is reserved for this purpose, or is transformed by the landlord into rifle-ranges or hunting-grounds as in the highlands of Scotland etc. The best proof of this is the vain struggle of the English workers to lay their hands on the waste land.

Nota bene: In all cases where the absolute rent, as in II D, falls below its normal amount, because, as here, the market-value is below the individual value of the class or, as in II B, owing to competition from the better land, a part of the capital must be withdrawn from the worse land or where, as in I D, rent is completely absent, it is presupposed:

1. that where rent is entirely absent, the landowner and capitalist [are] *one and the same* person; here therefore the resistance of landed property against capital and the limitation of the field of action of capital by landed property disappear but only in individual cases and as an exception. The presupposition of landed property is abolished as in the colonies, but only in separate cases;

2. that the competition of the better lands—or possibly the competition from the worse lands (in the descending line)—leads to over-production and forcibly expands the market, creates an additional demand by forcing prices down. This however is the very case which Ricardo does not foresee because he always argues on the assumption that the supply is only sufficient to satisfy the additional demand;

3. that II and I in B, C, D either do not pay the full amount of the absolute rent or pay no absolute rent at all, because they are forced by the competition from the better lands to sell their product *below* its value. Ricardo on the other hand presupposes that they sell their product at *its value* and that the *worst land* always determines the market-value, whereas in case I D, which he regards as the normal case, just the opposite takes place. Furthermore his argument is always based on the assumption of a descending line of production.

If the average composition of the non-agricultural capital is
£ 80c+£ 20v, and the rate of surplus-value is 50 per cent, and
if the composition of the agricultural capital is £ 90c+£ 10v, i.e.,
higher than that of industrial capital—which ||600| is histori-
cally incorrect for capitalist production—[then there is] no
absolute rent; if it is £ 80c+£ 20v, which has not so far been the
case, [there is] *no* absolute rent; if it is lower, for instance
£ 60c+£ 40v, [there is an] *absolute rent.*

On the basis of the theory, the following possibilities can
arise, according to the relationship of the different categories
to the market—i.e., depending on the extent to which one or
another category dominates the market:

A. The last class pays absolute rent. It determines the market-
value because all classes *o n l y provide the necessary supply at
this market-value.*

B. The last class determines the market-value; it pays absolute
rent, the full rate of rent, but not the full previous amount
because competition from III and IV has forced it to withdraw
part of the capital from production.

C. The *excess* supply which classes I, II, III, IV provide *at
the old market-value*, forces the latter to fall; this however,
being regulated by the higher classes, leads to the expansion of
the market. I pays only a part of the absolute rent, II pays
only the absolute rent.

D. The same domination of *market-value* by the better classes
or of the inferior classes by oversupply destroys rent in I
altogether and reduces it to below its absolute amount in II;
finally in

E. The better classes oust I from the market by bringing down
the market-value below the cost-price [of I]. II now regulates
the market-value because *at this new market-value* only the
necessary supply [is] forthcoming from all three classes. |600||

||600| Now back to Ricardo.

*   *   *

It goes without saying that when dealing with the composition of the agricultural capital the value or price of the land
does not enter into this. The latter is nothing but the capitalist rent.

20*

[CHAPTER XIII]

RICARDO'S THEORY OF RENT (CONCLUSION)

[1. Ricardo's Assumption of the Non-Existence of Landed Property. Transition to New Land Is Contingent on Its Situation and Fertility]

Back to *Ricardo*, Chapter II *"On Rent"*:
He begins by presenting the "colonial theory", already known from Smith,[a] and here it is sufficient to state briefly the logical sequence of ideas.

"On the *first settling of a country*, in which there is an *abundance* of rich and fertile land, a *very small proportion of which is required to be cultivated for the support of the actual* population, or indeed *can be cultivated with the capital* which the population can command, there will be *no rent*; for no one would *pay* for the *use of land*, when there *was an abundant quantity not yet appropriated*, and, *therefore*," (because *not appropriated*, which Ricardo entirely forgets later on), "at the *disposal of whosoever might choose* to cultivate it." ([David Ricardo, *On the Principles of Political Economy, and Taxation,* third edition, London, 1821], p. 55.)

⟨Here the assumption therefore is: no landed property. Although this description of the process is *approximately* correct for the settlings of modern peoples, it is, firstly, inapplicable to developed capitalist production; and [secondly] equally false if put forward as the *historical* course of events in the old Europe.⟩

"On the common principles of supply and demand, *no rent could be paid for such land*, for the reason stated why nothing is given for the use of air and water, or for any other of the gifts of nature which exist in *boundless quantity* ... no charge is made for the use of these ||601| natural aids, because they are inexhaustible, and at every man's disposal.... If all land had *the same* properties, if it were *unlimited in quantity*, and *uniform in quality*, no charge could be made for its use" (because it could *not* be converted

---

[a] See this volume, pp. 228 and 239.—*Ed.*

into private property at all), "unless where it possessed *peculiar advantages of situation*" (and, he should add, were at the disposal of a proprietor). "It is only, then, because land is *not unlimited in quantity* and uniform in quality, and because in the progress of population, land of an *inferior quality,* or *less advantageously situated,* is called into cultivation, that *rent is ever paid for the use of* it. When in the progress of society, land of the second degree of fertility is taken into cultivation, *rent immediately commences on that of the first quality,* and the amount of that *rent will depend on the difference in the quality of these two portions of land*" (l.c., pp. 56-57).

We shall examine this point more closely. The logical sequence is this:

If land, rich and fertile land exists in elemental abundance in practically unlimited quantity compared to the actual population and capital—and Ricardo *assumes* this on the *"first settling of a country*" (*Smith's* colonial theory)—and if, furthermore, an "abundant quantity" of this land is "*not yet appropriated*" and *therefore,* because it is "*not yet appropriated*", is "*at the disposal of whosoever might choose to cultivate it*", in this case, naturally, nothing is paid for the use of land, [there is] no rent. If land were [available] "in unlimited quantity"—not only relatively to capital and population, but if it were *in fact* an unlimited element (unlimited like air and water)—then indeed its appropriation by one person could not exclude its appropriation by another. No private (also no "public" or state) property in land could exist. In this case—if all land is of *the same* quality—no rent could be paid for it at all. At most, [rent would be paid] to the possessor of land which "possessed peculiar advantages of situation".

Thus, under the circumstances assumed by Ricardo—namely, that land is "*not appropriated*" and uncultivated land is "*therefore* at the disposal of whosoever might choose to cultivate it"— if rent is paid, then this is only possible because "land is not unlimited in quantity and uniform in quality", in other words, because different types of land exist and land of the same type is "limited". We say that, on Ricardo's assumption, only a differential rent can be paid. But instead of confining it to this, he jumps at once to the conclusion that—quite apart from his assumption of the *non-existence of landed property*—absolute rent is never paid for the use of land, only differential rent.

The whole point therefore is: If land confronts capital in *elemental* abundance, then capital operates in agriculture in *the same* way as in every other branch of industry. There is then no *landed property*, no rent. At most, where one piece of land is more fertile than another, there can be excess profits as in industry. In this case these will consolidate themselves as differential rent, because of their natural basis in the different degrees of fertility of the soil.

If, on the other hand, land is 1. limited, 2. appropriated, and capital finds *landed* property as a precondition—and this is the case where capitalist production develops: where capital does not find this precondition, as it does in the old Europe, it creates it itself, as in the United States—thus land is from the outset not an elementary field of action for capital. Hence [there is absolute] rent, in addition to differential rent. But in this case also the transitions from one type of land to another—be it ascending: I, II, III, IV or descending IV, III, II, I—work out differently than they did under *Ricardo's assumption.* For the employment of capital meets with the resistance of landed property both in category I and in II, III, IV; and similarly, in the reverse process, when the transition is from IV to III etc. In the transition from IV to III etc., it is not sufficient for the price of IV to rise high enough to enable the capital to be employed in III with an average profit. The price must rise to such an extent that rent can be paid on III. If the transition is made from I to II etc., then it is self-evident that the price which paid a rent for I, must not only pay this rent for II, but a differential rent besides. By postulating the *non-existence of landed property*, Ricardo has not, of course, eliminated the law that arises *with* the *existence* and *from the existence of landed property.*

Having just shown how, *on his assumption,* a differential rent can come into being, Ricardo continues:

"When land of the third quality is taken into cultivation, rent immediately commences on the second, and it is regulated, as before, by the difference in their productive powers. At the same time, the rent of the first quality will rise, for that must always be above the rent of the second, by the difference between the produce which they yield with a given quantity of capital and labour. With every *step in the progress of population, which shall oblige a country to have recourse to land of a worse quality*" (l.c., p. 57)

(which, however, by no means implies *that every step in the progress of population will oblige a country to have recourse to land of worse quality*),

"to enable it to raise its supply ||602| of food, rent, on all the more fertile land, will rise" (l.c., p. 57).

This is all right.

Ricardo now passes on to [an] example. But, quite apart from other points to be noted later, this example presupposes the *descending line*. This, however, is mere *presupposition*. In order to smuggle it in, he says:

"On the first settling of a country, in which there is *an abundance of rich and fertile* land[a] ... *not yet appropriated*" (l.c., p. 55).

But the case would [be] the same, if, relatively to the colonists, there was "an abundance of poor and sterile land—not yet appropriated". The *non*-payment of *rents* does not depend on the richness or fertility of the land, but on the fact that it is unlimited, unappropriated and of uniform quality, whatever might be *that* quality as regards the degree of its fertility. Hence Ricardo himself goes on to formulate his *assumption* thus:

"If *all land* had *the same* properties, if it were *unlimited in quantity,* and *uniform in quality,* no charge could be made for its use" (l.c., p. 56).

He does not say and cannot say, if it *"were rich and fertile"*, because this condition would have *absolutely nothing* to do with the law. If, instead of being rich and fertile, the land were poor and sterile, then each colonist would have to cultivate a greater proportion of the whole land, and thus, even where the land is unappropriated, they would, with the growth of population, more rapidly approach the point where the practical abundance of land, its actual unlimitedness in proportion to population and capital, would cease to exist.

It is of course quite certain that the colonists will not pick out the least fertile land, but will choose the most fertile, i.e., the land that will produce most, with the means of cultivation at their disposal. But this is not the sole limiting factor in their choice. The first deciding factor for them is the *situation*, the situation near the sea, large rivers etc. The land in West America etc. may be as fertile as any; but the settlers of course established themselves in New England, Pennsylvania, North Carolina, Virginia etc., in short, on the east coast of the Atlantic. If they selected the most fertile land, then they only selected the *most fertile land in this region.* This did not prevent them from cultivating *more fertile* land in the West, at a later stage, as soon as growth of population, formation of capital, development of means of communication, building of towns, made the *more fertile land* in this *more distant* region accessible to them. They do not look for the

---

[a] In the manuscript: "soil."—*Ed.*

most fertile region, but for the *most favourably situated region*, and within this, of course—given *equal* conditions so far as the situation is concerned—they look for the *most fertile* land. But this certainly does not prove that they progress from the more fertile region to the less fertile region, only that within *the same* region—provided the situation is the same—the more fertile land is naturally cultivated before the unfertile.

Ricardo, however, having rightly *amended* "...abundance of rich and fertile land ..." to read land of the "*same properties* [...] unlimited in quantity [...] uniform in quality", comes to his example and from there jumps back into the first false assumption:

"The most *fertile, and* most *favourably situated*, land will be *first culti-vated*" (l.c., p. 60).

He senses the weakness and spuriousness [in this] and there-fore adds the *new* condition to the "most fertile land": "and the most favourably situated", which was missing at the outset. "The most fertile land *within* the most favourable situation" is how it should obviously read, and surely this absurdity can-not be carried so far [as to say] that the region of the country that happens to be the most favourably situated for the new-comers, since it enables them to keep in contact with the mother country and the old folks at home and the outside world, is "the most fertile region" in the whole of the land, which the colonists have not yet explored and are as yet unable to explore.

The assumption of the descending line, the transition from the more fertile to the less fertile region, is thus surreptitiously brought in. All that can be said is this: In the region that is first cultivated, because it is the most favourably situated, *no rent* is paid until, *within* this region, there is a transition from the more fertile to the less fertile land. Now if, however, there is a transition to a second, *more fertile* region than the first, then, according to the assumption, this is *worse situated*. Hence it is possible that the greater fertility of the soil is more than counterbalanced by the greater disadvantage of the situation, and in this case the land of region I will continue to pay rent. But the "situation" is a circumstance which changes histori-cally, according to the economic development, and *must* con-tinually *improve* with the installation of means of communica-tion, the building of towns, etc., and the growth of the population. Hence it is clear that by and by, the product produced in region II will be brought on to the market at a price which will lower the rent in region I again (for the same product), and that in time it will emerge as the more fertile soil in the measure in which the disadvantage of situation disappears.

||603| It is therefore clear,

that where Ricardo himself states the condition for the formation of differential rent correctly and in general form: "...all land had[a] the *same properties* ... *unlimited in quantity* ... *uniform in quality* ...", the circumstance of the transition from more fertile to less fertile land is *not* included,

that this [transition] is also historically incorrect for the settlement in the United States which, in common with Adam Smith, he has in mind; therefore Carey's objections, which were justified on this point,

that Ricardo himself reverses the problem again, by his addendum on "situation": "The most fertile, and *most favourably situated*, land will be first cultivated ...",

that Ricardo *proves* his *arbitrary* presupposition by an *example* in which that which is to be proved, is *postulated*, namely, the transition from the best to increasingly worse land,

that, finally ⟨it is true, already with an eye to the explanation of the tendency of the general rate of profit to fall⟩ he presupposes this, because he could not otherwise account for *differential rent*, although the latter in no way depends on whether there is a transition from I to II, III, IV or from IV to III, II, I.

[2. The Ricardian Assertion that Rent Cannot Possibly Influence the Price of Corn. Absolute Rent Causes the Prices of Agricultural Products to Rise]

In the example, three sorts of land are postulated, Nos. 1, 2, 3, which, with an equal capital investment, yield "a net produce" of 100, 90, 80 quarters of corn. No. 1 is the first to be cultivated

"in a new country, where there is an abundance of fertile land compared with the population, and where therefore it is only necessary to cultivate No. 1" (l.c., p. 57).

---

[a] In the manuscript: ... "of" instead of "had".—*Ed.*

In this case the "whole net produce" belongs to the "culti-vator" and "will be the profits of the stock which he advances" (l. c., p. 57). That this "net produce" is immediately regarded as profit of stock, although *no capitalist production* has been postulated in this case (we are not speaking of plantations) is also unsatisfactory here. But it may be that the colonist, coming from "the old country", looks at it in this way himself. If the population grows only to such an extent that No. 2 has to be cultivated, then No. 1 bears a rent of 10 quarters. It is of course assumed here that No. 2 and No. 3 are *"unappro-priated"* and that their quantity has remained practically "unlimited" in proportion to population and capital. Otherwise there *could* be a different turn to events. Under this assumption, therefore, No. 1 will bear a rent of 10 quarters:

"For either there must *be two rates of profit on agricultural capital,* or ten quarters, or the value of ten quarters, *must be withdrawn* from the prod-uce of No. 1, for some other purpose. Whether the *proprietor of the land,* or any other person, cultivated No. 1, these ten quarters would equally con-stitute rent; for the cultivator of No. 2 would get the same result with his capital, whether he cultivated No. 1, paying ten quarters for rent, or continued to cultivate No. 2, paying no rent" (l.c., p. 58).

In fact, there would be two rates of profit in agricultural capital, that is, No. 1 supplied an *excess profit* of 10 quarters (which, in this case, *can* consolidate itself as rent). But two pages later, Ricardo himself says that not only two but many very different rates of profit on capital of the same description within *the same sphere of production*, hence also on agricultural capital, are not only possible but inevitable:

"The most fertile, and most favorably situated, land will be first cultivated, and the exchangeable value of its produce will be adjusted in the same man-ner as the exchangeable value of all other commodities, by the total quan-tity of labour necessary in various forms, from first to last, to produce it, and bring it to market. When land of an inferior quality is taken into culti-vation, the exchangeable value of raw produce will rise, because more labour is required to produce it.

"The *exchangeable value* of *all* commodities, whether they be manufac-tured, or the produce of the mines, or the produce of land, *is always regulated,* not by *the less quantity of labour that will suffice for their production under circumstances highly favorable,* and *exclusively enjoyed by those who have peculiar facilities of production*; but by the *greater quantity of labour neces-sarily bestowed on their production by those who have no such facilities*; by those who continue to produce them under the most *unfavorable circum-stances*; meaning—by the most unfavorable circumstances, the most unfavo-rable under which the *quantity of produce required,"* (at the old price) "renders it necessary to carry on the production" (l.c., pp. 60-61).

Thus in each *particular* industry [there are] not only two, but *many rates* of profit, that is to say, deviations from the general rate of profit.

At this point it is not necessary to go into the further details of the example (pp. 58-59), which is concerned with the effect of employing different amounts of capital on the same land. Only these two propositions [to be noted]:

1. "Rent is always the difference between the produce obtained by the employment of two ||604| equal quantities of capital and labour" (l.c., p. 59).

In other words, there is only a differential rent (according to the assumption that there is no *landed property*). For:

2. "there cannot be two rates of profit" (l.c., p. 59).

"It is true, that on the best land, the same produce would still be obtained with the same labour as before, but its value would be enhanced in consequence of the diminished returns obtained by those who employed fresh labour and stock on the less fertile land. Notwithstanding, then, that the advantages of fertile over inferior lands are in no case lost, but only *transferred* from the cultivator, or consumer, to the landlord, yet, since more labour is required on the inferior lands, and *since it is from such land o n l y that we are enabled to furnish ourselves* with the *additional supply* of raw produce, the comparative value of that produce will continue *permanently* above its former level, and make it exchange for more hats, cloth, shoes, etc. [...], in the production of which no such additional quantity of labour is required.

"The reason then, *why* raw *produce rises in comparative value,* is because more labour is employed in the production of the last portion obtained, and *not because a rent is paid to the landlord.* The *value of corn is regulated* by the quantity of labour bestowed on its production on that quality of land, or with that portion of capital, which pays no rent. *Corn is not high because a rent is p a i d, but a rent is paid because corn is high*; and it has been *justly* observed, that *no reduction would take place in the price of corn, although landlords should forego the whole of their rent.* Such a measure would only enable some farmers to live like gentlemen, but would not diminish the quantity of labour necessary to raise raw produce on the least productive land in cultivation" (l.c., pp. 62-63).

My earlier explanations render it unnecessary to expand here on the erroneousness of the proposition that "the value of corn is regulated by the quantity of labour bestowed on its production on that quality of land ... which pays no rent" (l. c., p. 63). I have shown that whether the last type of land pays rent, [or] pays no rent, [whether it] pays the whole of the absolute rent, [only a] part of it, or it pays besides the absolute rent a differential rent (if the line is ascending), partly depends on the direction of the line, whether it is ascending or descending, and at all events, it depends on the relative composition of agricultural capital as compared with the composition of non-agricultural capital and, if as a result of the difference in this composition absolute rent is presupposed, the above cases depend on the state of the market. But the Ricardian case in particular can only occur under two circumstances (although even then *fermage* can yet be paid, though no rent); either when landed property does not exist, in law or in fact, or when the best land provides an additional supply which can only find its place within the market if there is a fall in market-value.

But there is more besides which is wrong or one-sided in the above passage. The comparative value—which here means nothing but market-value—of raw produce can rise for reasons other than the above. [Firstly] if, up to now, it was sold below its value, perhaps below its cost-price; this is always the case in a certain state of society, where the production of raw produce is as yet largely directed to the subsistence of the cultivator (also in the Middle Ages, when the product of the town secured a monopoly price); secondly, it can also happen when the raw produce—*in contrast* to the other commodities which are sold at their cost-price—is not yet sold at its value.

Finally, it is correct to say that it makes no difference to the price of corn if the landlord forgoes the differential rent and the farmer pockets it. But this does not apply to absolute rent. It is wrong to say here that landed property does *not* enhance the price of the raw produce. On the contrary the price goes up because the intervention of landed property causes the raw produce to be sold at its *value* which exceeds its *cost-price*. Supposing, as above, that the average non-agricultural capital consists of $80c+20v$ and the surplus-value is 50 per cent, then the rate of profit is 10 [per cent] and the value of the produce is 110. The agricultural ||605| capital on the other hand consists of $60c+40v$, the value [of the produce] is 120. The raw produce is sold at this value. If landed property did not exist legally—or in practice, because of the relative abundance of land as in the colonies—then it would be sold at 115. For the total profit of the first and the second capital (i.e., on the 200) equals 30, hence average profit equals 15. The non-agricultural produce would be sold at 115 instead of 110; the agricultural produce at 115 instead of 120. The relative value of the agricultural produce compared with the non-agricultural produce would thus fall by one-twelfth; the *average profit* for both capitals—or the total capital, agricultural as well as industrial—would, however, rise by 50 per cent, from 10 to 15. |605||

* * *

||636| Of his own conception of rent, Ricardo says:

"I always consider it as the result of a *partial monopoly,* never really regulating price" [l.c., pp. 332-33]

(that is, never acting as a *monopoly,* hence also never the *result* of monopoly. For him the only result of monopoly could be that the rent is pocketed by the owner of the better types of land rather than by the farmer),

"...but rather as the effect of it. If *all rent were relinquished by land-lords,* I am of opinion, that the commodities produced on the land would be no cheaper, because there is always a portion of the same commodities produced on land, for which *no rent* is or can be paid, as the *surplus produce* is only sufficient to pay the profits of stock" (l.c., p. 333).

Here surplus produce is equal to the excess over the product absorbed by the wages. Assuming that certain land never pays rent Ricardo's assertion is only correct if this land, or rather its product, regulates the market-value. If, on the other hand, its product pays no rent because the market-value is regulated by the more fertile land, then this fact proves nothing.

It would, indeed, benefit the farmers if the differential rent were "relinquished by landlords". The relinquishment of absolute rent, on the other hand, would reduce the price of agricultural products and increase that of industrial products to the extent that the average profit grew by this process. |636||

* * *

||605| "The rise of rent is *always* the effect of the increasing wealth of the country, *and of the difficulty of providing food for its augmented population*" (l.c., pp. 65-66).

The latter is wrong.

"Wealth increases most rapidly in those countries where the disposable land is most fertile, where importation is least restricted, and where through agricultural improvements, productions can be multiplied without any increase in the proportional quantity of labour, and where *consequently the progress of rent is slow*" (l.c., pp. 66-67).

The absolute amount of rent can also grow when the *rate of rent* remains the same and only the capital invested in agriculture is growing with the growth of population; it can grow when no rent is paid on I and only a part of the absolute rent on II, but the differential rent has risen considerably as a result of their relative fertility etc. (See the *table*.)[a]

[3. Smith's and Ricardo's Conception of the "Natural Price" of the Agricultural Product]

"If the high price of corn were the effect, and not the cause of rent, price would be proportionally influenced as rents were high or low, and *rent would be a component part of price*. But that corn which is produced by the greatest quantity of labour is the regulator of the price of corn; and rent does not and cannot enter in the least degree as a *component part of its price....* Raw material enters into the composition of most commodities, but the *v a l u e* of that raw material, as well as corn, is regulated by the *productiveness of the portion of capital last employed on the land, and paying no rent*; and *therefore* rent is not *a component part of the p r i c e* of commodities" (l.c., p. 67).

There is much confusion here, resulting from the jumbling up of "natural *price*" (for that is the price under discussion here) and *value*. Ricardo has adopted this confusion from Smith. In the case of the latter it is relatively correct, because, and in so far as, Smith departs from his own correct explanation of value. Neither rent nor profit nor wages form *a component part of the value* of a commodity. On the contrary, *the value of a commodity being given*, the different parts into which that value may be *divided*, belong either to the category of accumulated labour (constant capital) or wages or profit or rent. On the other hand, when referring to the *natural price* or *cost-price*, Smith can speak of its *component parts* as given preconditions. But by confusing natural price with value, he carries this over to the value of the commodity.

Apart from the fact that the raw material and machinery (in short the constant capital) enter into production with a *fixed* price, which to the capitalist in each particular sphere of production appears as determined from outside, there are two things the capitalist must do when calculating the price of his commodity: he has to add the *price of the wages*, and this also appears to him as given (within certain limits). The

---

[a] See the insertion between pages 264 and 265.—*Ed.*

natural price of the commodity is not the *market-price* but the average market-price over a long period, or the central point towards which the market-price gravitates. In this context therefore the *price of wages* is on the whole determined by the value of labour-power. But the *rate of profit*—the natural rate of profit—is determined by the *value* of the aggregate of commodities created by the aggregate of capitals employed in non-agricultural industry. For it is the excess of this value over the value of the constant capital contained in the commodity plus the value of wages. The total surplus-value which the total capital creates, forms the absolute amount of profit. The ratio of this absolute amount to the whole capital advanced determines the general rate of profit. Thus this general rate of profit too, appears—not only to the individual capitalist, but to the capital in each particular sphere of production—to be determined externally. The capitalist must add the general profit, say of 10 per cent, ||606| to the price of the raw material, etc., contained in the product, and the natural price of wages thus—as it must appear to him by way of addition of component parts, or by composition—to form the natural price of a given commodity. Whether the natural price is paid, or more, or less, depends on the level of the market-price prevailing at the time. Only wages and profit enter into *cost-price* as distinguished from *value*; rent enters only in so far as it is already contained in the price of the expended raw material, machinery, etc. That is, it does not enter as rent for the capitalist, to whom, in any case, the price of raw produce, machinery, in short of the constant capital, appears as a *predetermined total.*

Rent does not enter into *cost-price* as a component part. If, in special circumstances, the agricultural product is sold at its cost-price, then *no rent exists. Economically* landed property does not then exist for capital, that is, when the product of the type of land that sells at the cost-price, regulates the market-value of the product of its sphere. (The position in I, Table *D* is different.[a])

Or (absolute) *rent exists.* In this case the agricultural product is sold *above* its *cost-price.* It is sold at its *value,* which is above its *cost-price.* Rent, however, enters into the *market-value* of the product, or, rather, forms a part of the market-value. But to the farmer rent appears as predetermined, in the same way

---

a See this volume, pp. 293 and 295.—*Ed.*

as profit does to the industrialist. It is determined by the excess of the *value* of the agricultural product over its *cost-price*. The farmer, however, calculates just like the capitalist: First the outlay, secondly wages, thirdly the average profit, finally the rent, which likewise appears to him as fixed. This is *for him* the natural price of wheat, for instance. Whether he obtains it, depends, in turn, on the prevailing state of the market.

If the *distinction* between *cost-price* and *value* is properly maintained, then rent can *never* enter into cost-price as a *constituent part*, and one can talk of constituent parts only in relation to the cost-price as distinguished from the value of the commodity. (Like excess profit, differential rent never enters into *cost-price*, because it is nothing but the excess of the market cost-price[91] over individual cost-price, or the excess of the market-value over individual value.)

Accordingly, Ricardo is in substance right when, in opposition to Adam Smith, he declares that rent *never* enters into cost-price. But again he is wrong in that he proves this, not by differentiating between cost-price and value, but by identifying the two, as Adam Smith did, for neither rent nor profit, nor wages form *constituent parts of value,* although value is dissolvable into wages and profits and rent, and, furthermore, the three parts are of equal importance, *if* all three exist. Ricardo reasons thus: Rent forms no constituent part of the natural price of agricultural produce, *because* the price of the product of the worst land, which is equal to the *cost-price* of this product, and to the *value of this product*, determines the market-value of agricultural produce. Thus rent forms no [constituent] part of the value because it forms no [constituent] part of the *natural price* and this latter is equal to *value*. This however is wrong. The price of the product grown on the worst land equals its *cost-price*, either because this product is sold *below* its value—therefore not as Ricardo says, because it is sold *at its value*—or because the agricultural product belongs to that type, to that class, of commodities in which, *by way of exception*, value and cost-price are *identical*. This is the case when the surplus-value which is made in a particular sphere of production on a given capital, of say £ 100, happens to coincide with the surplus-value which on the average falls to *the same* relative portion of the total capital (say £ 100). This then is Ricardo's confusion.

As to *Adam Smith*: in so far as he identifies cost-price with value, he is justified, on the basis of this false assumption, in saying that rent, as well as profit and wages, form "constituent parts of the natural price". On the contrary it is rather inconsistent that later in his further exposition he asserts that rent does not enter into the natural price in the same way as wages and profits. He commits this inconsistency because observation and correct analysis compel him nevertheless to recognise that there is a difference in the determination of the natural price of non-agricultural produce and the market-value of agricultural produce. But more about this when discussing Smith's theory of rent.

[4. Ricardo's Views on Improvements in Agriculture. His Failure to Understand the Economic Consequences of Changes in the Organic Composition of Agricultural Capital]

||607| "We have seen, that with every portion of additional capital which it becomes necessary to employ on the land with a less productive return, rent would rise."

(But not every portion of additional capital yields a less productive return.)

"It follows from the same principles, that any circumstances in the society which should make it unnecessary to employ the same amount of capital on the land, and which should therefore make the portion last employed more productive, would lower rent" (l.c., p. 68).

That is [lower] absolute rent, not necessarily differential rent. (See Table *B*.)

Such circumstances might be the "reduction in the capital of a country" followed by a reduction in the population. But also a higher development of the productive powers of agricultural labour.

"The same effects may however be produced, when the wealth and population of a country are increased, if that increase is accompanied by such marked improvements in agriculture, as shall have the same effect of diminishing the necessity of cultivating the poorer lands, or of expending the same amount of capital on the cultivation of the more fertile portions" (l.c., pp. 68-69).

(Oddly enough, Ricardo forgets here: improvements as shall have the effect of improving the quality of poorer lands and converting these into richer ones, an aspect stressed by Anderson.)

21-244

The following proposition of Ricardo's is entirely wrong:

"With the same population, and no more, there can be no demand for any additional quantity of corn" (l.c., p. 69).

Quite apart from the fact that, with a fall in the price of corn, an additional demand for other raw produce, green vegetables, meat, etc., will spring up and that schnaps, etc., can be made from corn, Ricardo assumes here that the entire population consumes as much corn as it likes. This is wrong.

{"Our enormous increase of consumption in 1848, 49, 50, shows that we were previously *underfed*, and that prices were forced up by the deficiency of supply." (F. W. Newman, *Lectures on Political Economy*, London, 1851, p. 158.)

The same Newman says:

"The Ricardo argument," that rent cannot enhance price, "turns on the assumption that the power of demanding rent can in no case of real life *diminish supply*. But why not? There are very considerable tracts which would immediately have been cultivated if no rent could have been demanded for them, but which were *artificially kept vacant,* either because landlords could let them advantageously as shooting ground, or [...] prefer the [...] romantic wilderness to the[a] petty and nominal rent which alone they could get by allowing them to be cultivated." (l.c., p. 159.) }

Indeed, [it is] in any case wrong to say that if he withdraws the land from the production of corn, he may not get a rent by converting it into pasture or building grounds or, as in some counties in the highlands of Scotland, into artificial woods for hunting purposes.

Ricardo distinguishes two kinds of improvements in agriculture. The *one* type

"[those which] ... increase the *productive powers of the land* ... [are] *such as the more skilful rotation of crops, or the better choice of manure.* These improvements absolutely enable us to obtain the same produce from a smaller quantity of land." (David Ricardo, *On the Principles of Political Economy, and Taxation*, third edition, London, 1821, p. 70.)

In this case, according to Ricardo, the rent *must fall.*

"If, for example, the successive portions of capital yielded 100, 90, 80, 70; whilst I employed these four portions, my rent would be 60, or the difference between

70 and 100 = 30		
70 and 90 = 20	whilst the produce would be	100
70 and 80 = 10	[340]	90
		80
———		70
60		——
		340

a In the manuscript: "a".—*Ed.*

and while I employed these portions, the *rent would remain the same,* although the produce of each should have an *equal* augmentation."

(If it had an *unequal* augmentation, it would be possible for the rent to rise *despite the increased* fertility.)

"If, instead of 100, 90, 80, 70, the produce should be increased to 125, 115, 105, 95, the rent would still be 60, or the difference between

$$
\left.
\begin{array}{l}
\text{||608|}\ \ 95\ \text{and}\ 125 = 30 \\
\phantom{\text{||608|}}\ \ 95\ \text{and}\ 115 = 20 \\
\phantom{\text{||608|}}\ \ 95\ \text{and}\ 105 = 10 \\
\hline
\phantom{\text{||608|}\ \ 95\ \text{and}}\ 60
\end{array}
\right\}
\begin{array}{l}
\text{whilst the produce would be} \\
\text{increased to 440}
\end{array}
\left\{
\begin{array}{r}
125 \\
115 \\
105 \\
95 \\
\hline
440
\end{array}
\right.
$$

"But with such an increase of produce, *without an increase of demand,* there could be no motive for employing so much capital on the land; one portion would be withdrawn, and consequently the last portion of capital would yield 105 instead of 95, and rent would fall to 30, or the difference between

$$
\left.
\begin{array}{l}
105\ \text{and}\ 125 = 20 \\
105\ \text{and}\ 115 = 10 \\
\hline
\phantom{105\ \text{and}}\ 30
\end{array}
\right\}
\begin{array}{l}
\text{whilst the produce will be still adequate to the} \\
\text{wants of the population, for it would be 345} \\
\text{quarters} \ldots
\end{array}
\left\{
\begin{array}{r}
125 \\
115 \\
105 \\
\hline
345"
\end{array}
\right.
$$

(l.c., pp. 71-72).

Apart from demand being able to rise *without a growth* in population when the price falls (Ricardo himself assumes that it has risen by 5 quarters), there is a constant going over to soils of decreasing fertility, because the population grows every year, i.e., the part of the population that consumes corn, eats bread, and this part grows more rapidly than the population [as a whole], because bread is the chief means of subsistence of the majority. It is thus not *necessary* to assume that the demand does not grow with the productivity of capital, and that consequently the rent falls. And the rent can rise, if the difference in the degree of fertility has been unevenly affected by the improvement.

Otherwise it is certain (Tables *B* and *E*), that the increase in fertility—while demand remains constant—can not only throw the worst land out of the market but can even force a part of the capital on better land (Table *B*) to withdraw from the production of corn. In this case the *corn rent falls,* if the augmentation of the produce is *equal* on the different types of land.

Now Ricardo passes on to the second aspect of *agricultural improvements.*

"But there are improvements which may lower the relative value of produce without lowering the *corn rent,* though they will lower the *money*

21*

rent of land. Such improvements do not increase the productive powers of the land; but they enable us to obtain its produce *with less labour.* They are rather directed to the *formation of the capital applied to the land,* than to the *cultivation of the land itself. Improvements in agricultural implements,* such as the plough and the thrashing machine, economy in the use of horses employed in husbandry, and a better knowledge of the veterinary art, are of this nature. *Less capital,* which *is the same thing as less labour,* will be employed on the land; but to *obtain the same produce, less land cannot be cultivated.* Whether improvements of this kind, however, affect *corn rent,* must depend on the question, whether the difference between the produce obtained by the employment of different portions of capital be increased, stationary, or diminished" (l.c., p. 73).

⟨Ricardo should also have adhered to this when dealing with the *natural fertility of the soils.* Whether the transition to these reduces the differential rent, leaves it stationary, or increases it, depends on whether the difference in the produce of the capital employed on these different more fertile soils, be increased, stationary, or diminished.⟩

"If four portions of capital, 50, 60, 70, 80, be employed on the land, giving each *the same results,* and any improvement in the formation of such capital should enable me to withdraw 5 from each, so that they should be 45, 55, 65 and 75, no alteration would take place in the corn rent; but if the improvements were such as to enable me to make the whole saving on that portion of capital, which is least productively employed, corn rent would immediately fall, because the difference between the capital most productive, and the capital least productive, ||609| would be diminished; and *it is this difference which constitutes rent*" (l.c., pp. 73-74).

This is correct for *differential rent,* which alone exists for Ricardo.

On the other hand, Ricardo does not touch upon the real question at all. For the solution of this question it does not matter whether the value of the individual quarter falls or whether the same *quantity of land,* the same types of land as previously, needs to be cultivated, but whether as a result of the *reduction in the price of constant capital*—which, according to the assumption, costs less labour—the quantity of immediate labour employed in agriculture is *reduced, increased* or *unaltered.* In short, whether or not the capital undergoes an organic change.

Let us take our example from Table *A* (page 574, notebook XI)[a] and let us substitute quarters of corn for tons.

It is assumed here that the composition of the non-agricultural capital is £80c+£20v, that of the agricultural capital

---

a See the insertion between pages 264 and 265.—*Ed.*

£$60c+$£$40v$, the rate of surplus-value in both cases being 50 per cent. Hence the rent on the agricultural capital, or the excess of its value over its cost-price, is £10. Thus we have the following:

Class	Capital £	Qrs. of corn	Total value £	Market-value per qr. £	Individual value per qr.
I	100	60	120	2	£2=40s.
II	100	65	130	2	£1$^{11}/_{13}$ = £1 16$^{12}/_{13}$s.
III	100	75	150	2	£1$^3/_5$ = £1 12s.
Total	300	200	400		

	Differential value per qr.	Cost-price per qr.	Absolute rent £	Differential rent £
I	0	£1$^5/_6$ = £1 16$^2/_3$s.	10	0
II	£$^2/_{13}$ = 3$^1/_{13}$s.	£1$^9/_{13}$=£1 13$^{11}/_{13}$s.	10	10
III	£$^2/_5$ = 8s.	£1$^7/_{15}$ = £1 9$^1/_3$s.	10	30
			30	40

	Absolute rent in qrs.	Differential rent in qrs.	Rental £	Rental in qrs.
I	5	0	10	5
II	5	5	20	10
III	5	15	40	20
	15	20	70	35

In order to examine the problem in its pure form, one must assume that the *magnitude of the capital employed in I, II, III* is in all three classes affected *equally* by the reduction in the price of *constant capital* (100). For the *uneven* effect only concerns differential rent, and has nothing to do with the matter in hand. Supposing, therefore, that as a result of *improvements,* the same amount of capital, which previously cost £ 100, now only costs 90, it would thus be reduced by one-tenth, or 10 per cent. The question is then how the improvements affect the composition of agricultural capital.

If the proportion of capital used as wages [to constant capital] remains the same, then if [£] 100 consists of £ 60c+£40v, £ 90 consists of £ 54c+£ 36v, and in this case the value of the 60 quarters on land I is £ 108. But if the *reduction in price* were such that the same constant capital which previously cost £ 60, now only cost £ 54, but that v (or the capital laid out in wages) now only cost £ 32$^2/_5$ instead of 36 (had also fallen by $^1/_{10}$), then £ 86$^2/_5$ would be laid out instead of £ 100. The composition of this capital would be 54c+32$^2/_5v$. And reckoned on £ 100, the composition would be £ 62$^1/_2c$+£ 37$^1/_2v$. Under these circumstances, the value of the 60 quarters on I would be equal to £ 102$^3/_5$. Finally, let us assume that although the value of the constant capital decreases, the capital laid out in wages remains *the same* absolutely, it therefore grows in *proportion* to the constant capital; so that the capital of £ 90 which has been laid out consists of 50c+40v, the composition of [a capital of] 100 would be 55$^5/_9c$+44$^4/_9v$.

Now let us see what happens to corn and money rent in these three cases. In case *B* the proportion of c to v remains the same although the value of both decreases. In *C* the ||610| value of c decreases, but proportionately, that of v decreases even more. In *D*, only the value of c decreases, not that of v.

First let us reproduce the original table contained on the previous page [and then let us compare it with the new tables *B*, *C* and *D*, representing the cases just described illustrating changes in value of the organic component parts of the agricultural capital.][a]

* * *

||611| From the accompanying table it is evident that:

Originally in *A* the ratio is £ 60c+£ 40v; the capital invested in each class is 100. The rent in money amounts to £ 70, in corn to 35 quarters.

---

[a] There follow the tables, which are reproduced on the sheet inserted between pages 328 and 329. Marx did not fill in some columns in tables *C* and *D*. The missing figures, as well as the heading of the last column, have been inserted by the editors.—*Ed.*

In *B* the constant capital becomes cheaper so that only £ 90 [are] invested in each class, the variable capital however becomes cheaper in the same proportion, so that the *ratio* remains the same. Here the *money rent* falls, the corn rent remains the same; [the] *absolute rent*[92] is also *the same*. Money rent decreases because the capital invested decreases. Corn rent remains the same, because less money [produces relatively] more corn the ratio remaining the same.

In *C* cheaper constant capital; but [the value of] *v* decreases even more, so that the constant capital becomes relatively dearer. *Absolute rent* falls. Corn rent falls and money rent falls. Money rent, because capital in general has decreased significantly, and corn rent, because absolute rent has fallen while the differences [between the various categories] have remained the same, therefore all of them fall equally.

In *D*, however, the case is completely the reverse. Only the constant capital falls; the variable capital remains the same. *This was Ricardo's assumption.* In this case, because of the fall in capital, the money rent falls, though the fall is quite insignificant, in absolute figures it is only [£] $1/3$, but in proportion to the capital laid out, it rises considerably. The corn rent, on the other hand, grows absolutely. Why? Because the absolute rent has risen from 10 to $12 2/9$ per cent, because *v* has grown in proportion to *c*. Hence:

Capital	Absolute rent per cent	Absolute rent £	Differential rent £	Absolute rent qrs.	Differential rent qrs.	Rental £	Rental qrs.
A) $60c + 40v$	10	30	40	15	20	70	35
B) $54c + 36v$ $(60c + 40v)$	10	27	36	15	20	63	35
C) $54c + 32 2/5 v$ $(62 1/2 c + 37 1/2 v)$	$8 3/4$	$22 17/25$	$34 1/5$	$13 5/19$	20	$56 22/25$	$33 5/19$
D) $50c + 40v$ $(55 5/9 c + 44 4/9 v)$	$12 2/9$	33	$36 2/3$	18	20	$69 2/3$	38

Ricardo continues:

"Whatever diminishes the *inequality in the produce* obtained from successive portions of capital employed on the same or on new land, tends to lower rent; and [...] whatever *increases that inequality*, necessarily produces an opposite effect, and tends to raise it" (l.c., p. 74).

The inequality can be increased, while capital is withdrawn and while fertility increases, or even while the less fertile land is thrown out of the market.

{Landlord and capitalist. In a leader of 15th July, 1862, the *Morning Star*[93] [examines] whose duty it is (voluntarily or compulsorily) to support the distressed (as a result of the cotton famine and the civil war in America) workmen in the cotton manufacture districts of Lancashire, etc. It says:

"These people have a legal right to maintenance *out of the property they have mostly created by their industry....* It is said that the men who have made fortunes by the cotton industry are those upon whom it is especially incumbent to come forward with a generous relief. No doubt it is so ... the mercantile and manufacturing sections [...] have done so.... But are these the only class which has made money by the cotton manufacture? Assuredly not. The landed proprietors of Lancashire and North Cheshire have enormously participated in the wealth thus produced. And it is the peculiar advantage of these proprietors to have participated in the wealth without lending a hand or a thought to the industry that [...] created it.... The mill-owner has given his capital, his skill, and his unwinking vigilance to the ||612| creation of this great industry, now staggering under so heavy a blow; the mill-hand has given his skill, his time, and his bodily labour; but what have the landed proprietors of Lancashire given? Nothing at all—literally nothing; and yet they have made from it more substantial gains than either of the other classes ... it is certain that the increase of the yearly income of these great landlords, attributable to this single cause, is something enormous, probably not less than threefold."

The capitalist is the direct exploiter of the workers, not only the direct appropriator, but the direct creator of *surplus-labour*. But since (for the industrial capitalist) this can only take place through and in the process of production, he is himself a functionary of this production, its director. The landlord, on the other hand, has a claim—through landed property (to absolute rent) and because of the physical differences of the various types of land (differential rent)—which enables him to pocket a part of this surplus-labour or surplus-value, to whose direction and creation he contributes nothing. Where there is a conflict, therefore, the capitalist regards him as a mere superfetation, a Sybarite excrescence, a parasite on capitalist production, the louse that sits upon him.}

Chapter III "On the Rent of Mines" [David Ricardo, *On the Principles of Political Economy, and Taxation*, third edition, London, 1821, p. 76].

Here again:

"...this rent" (of mines) "as well as the rent of land, is the effect, and never the cause of the *high value* of their produce" (l.c., p. 76).

So far as absolute rent is concerned, it is neither effect nor cause of the *"high value"*, but the effect of the excess of value over cost-price. That this excess is paid for the produce of the mine, or the land, and thus absolute rent is formed, is the effect, not of that *excess*, because it exists for a whole class of trades, where it does not enter into the price of the produce of those particular branches of production, but is the effect of *landed property*.

In regard to *differential rent* it may be said, that it is the effect of *"high value"*; so far as by "high value" is understood the excess of the market-value of the produce over its real or individual value, for the relatively more fertile classes of land or mine.

That Ricardo understands by the "exchangeable value" regulating the produce of the poorest land or mine, nothing but *cost-price*, by cost-price nothing but the advances plus the ordinary profit, and that he falsely identifies this cost-price with real value, will also be seen from the following passage:

"The metal produced from the poorest mine that is worked, must at least have an exchangeable value, not only sufficient to procure all the clothes, food, and other necessaries consumed by those employed in working it, and bringing the produce to market, but *also to afford the common and ordinary profits* to him who advances the stock necessary to carry on the undertaking. The return for capital from the poorest mine paying no rent, would regulate the rent of all the other more productive mines. *This mine is supposed to yield the usual profits of stock. All that the other mines pro- duce more than this,* will necessarily be paid to the owners for rent" (l.c., pp. 76-77).

Here, therefore, [he says] in plain language: rent equals *excess* of *the price (exchangeable value is the same here) of the agricultural produce over its cost-price*, that is over the value of capital advanced plus the usual (average) profits of stock. Hence, if the *value* of the agricultural produce is higher than its cost-price, it can pay rent quite irrespectively of differences in land, the poorest land and the poorest mine can pay the same absolute rent as the richest. If its *value* were no higher than its cost-price, rent could only arise from the excess of the market-value over the real value of the produce derived from relatively more fertile soils, etc.

"If *equal quantities of labour, with equal quantities of fixed capital,* could at all times obtain, from that mine which paid no rent, *equal quantities of gold....* The quantity" (of gold) "indeed would *enlarge with the demand,* but *its value would be invariable"* (l.c., p. 79).

What applies to gold and mines, applies to corn and land. Hence if the same types of land continued to be exploited and continued to yield the same product for the same outlay in labour ||613|, then the *value* of the pound of gold or the quarter of wheat would remain the same, although its quantity would increase with the *demand.* Thus *its rent* (the amount, not the rate of rent) [would] also *grow* without any change in the price of produce. More capital would be employed, although productivity would remain constant. This is one of the major causes of the rise in the absolute amount of rent, quite apart from any rise in the price of produce, and, therefore, without any proportional change in the rents paid by produce of different soils and mines.

[5. Ricardo's Criticism of Adam Smith's and Malthus's Views on Rent]

Chapter XXIV "Doctrine of Adam Smith concerning the Rent of Land."

This chapter is of great importance for the difference between Ricardo and Adam Smith. We shall postpone a fuller discussion of this (in so far as it affects Adam Smith), to when we consider *ex professo* Adam Smith's doctrine after that of Ricardo.

Ricardo begins by quoting a passage from Adam Smith showing that he correctly determined when the price of the agricultural produce yields a rent and when it does not. But on the other hand Smith thought that some parts of the produce of land, such as food, must always yield a rent.

In this context Ricardo says the following, which is significant for *him*:

"I believe that as yet in every country, from the rudest to the most refined, there is land of such a quality that it cannot *yield a produce more than sufficiently valuable* to replace the stock employed upon it, together with the *profits ordinary and usual* in that country. In *America* we all know that is the case, and yet no one maintains that the principles which regulate rent, are different in that country and in Europe" (l.c., pp. 389-90).

Indeed, these principles are substantially "different". Where *no landed property* exists—actual or legal—no absolute rent can exist. It is absolute rent, not differential rent, which is the adequate expression of landed property. To say that *the same* principles regulate rent, where landed property exists and where it does not exist, means that the *economic form of landed property* is independent of whether landed property exists or not.

Besides, what is the meaning of "there is land of such a quality that it cannot yield a produce more than *sufficiently valuable* to replace the stock ... with the ordinary profits..." (l. c., pp. 389-390). If the same quantity of labour produces 4 quarters, the product is no more valuable than if it produces two, although the value of the individual quarter is in one case twice as great as in the other. Whether or not it yields a rent, is therefore in no way independent on the magnitude of this "value" of the produce as such. It can only yield a rent if its value is higher than its cost-price, which depends on the cost-price of all other products or, in other words, on the quota of unpaid labour which is, on an average, appropriated by a capital of £100 in each sphere of production. But whether its value is higher than its cost-price is in no way dependent on its absolute size, but on the composition of the capital employed on it, compared with the average composition of the capital employed in non-agricultural industry.

"But if it were true that England had so far advanced in cultivation, that at this time there were no lands remaining which did not afford a rent, it would be equally true, that there formerly must have been such lands; and that whether there be or not, is of no importance to this question, for it is the same thing if there be any capital employed in Great Britain on land which yields only the return of stock with its ordinary profits, whether it be employed on old or on new land. If a farmer agrees for land on a lease of seven or fourteen years, he may propose to employ on it a capital of £10,000, knowing that at the existing price of grain and raw produce, he can replace that part of his stock which he is obliged to expend, pay his rent, and obtain the general rate of profit. He will not employ £11,000, unless the last £1,000 can be employed so productively as to afford him the usual profits of stock. In *his calculation, whether he shall employ it or not, he considers only whether the price of raw produce is sufficient to replace his expenses and profits, for he knows that he shall have no additional rent to pay.* Even at the expiration of his lease his rent will not be raised; for if his landlord should require rent, because this additional £1,000 was employed, he would withdraw it; since, by employing it, he gets, by the supposition, only the ordinary and usual profits which he may obtain by any other employment of stock; and, therefore, he *cannot afford to pay rent for it,* unless the *price of raw produce should further rise,* or, *which is the same thing,* unless *the usual and general rate of profits should fall*" (l.c., pp. 390-91).

Ricardo admits here that also the worst land *can* bear a rent. How does he explain this? To provide the additional supply which has become necessary in consequence of an additional demand, a second amount of capital is employed on the worst land ||614|. This will only yield the cost-price if the price of grain is rising. Hence the first amount would now yield a surplus—that is rent—over and above this cost-price. In fact therefore *before* the second amount is invested the *first amount* of capital yields a rent *on the worst* land, because the market-value is above the cost-price. Thus the only question is whether, for this to happen, the market-value has to be *above* the value of the worst product, or whether on the contrary its *value* is *above* its *cost-price*, and the rise in price merely enables it to be sold at *its value*.

Furthermore: Why must the *price* be so high that it equals the cost-price, i.e., the capital advanced plus average profit? Because of the competition of capitals in the different branches of production and the transfer of capital from one branch to another. That is, as a result of the action of capital upon capital. But by what action could capital compel landed property to allow the value of the product to fall to the cost-price? Withdrawal of capital from agriculture cannot have this effect, unless it is accompanied by a fall of the demand for agricultural produce. It would achieve the reverse, and cause the market-price of agricultural produce to rise above its value. Transfer of new capital to land cannot have this effect either. For it is precisely the competition of capitals amongst themselves, which enables the landlord to demand from the individual capitalist that he should be satisfied with "an average profit" and pay over to him the overplus of the value over the price affording this profit.

But, it may be asked: If landed property gives the power to sell the product *above* its cost-price, *at* its value, why does it not equally well give the power to sell the product *above* its value, at an arbitrary monopoly price? On a small island, where there is no foreign trade in corn, the corn, food, like every other product, could unquestionably be sold at a monopoly price, that is, at a price only limited by the state of demand, i.e., of *demand backed by ability to pay,* and according to the price level of the product supplied the magnitude and extent of this effective demand can vary greatly.

Leaving out of account exceptions of this kind—which cannot occur in European countries; even in England a large part of the fertile land is *artificially* withdrawn from agriculture and from the market in general, in order to raise the value of the other part—landed property can only affect and paralyse the action of capitals, their competition, in so far as the competition of capitals modifies the determination of the *values of the commodities*. The conversion of values into cost-prices is only the consequence and result of the development of capitalist production. Originally commodities are (on the average) sold at their values. Deviation from this is in agriculture prevented by landed property.

Ricardo says that when a farmer takes land on a lease of seven or fourteen years, he calculates that with a capital investment of, say, £10,000, the *value of the corn* (average market-value) permits him to replace his outlay plus average profit, plus the contracted rent. In so far as he takes a "lease" of a piece of land, therefore, his first consideration is the average market-value, which is equivalent to the value of the product; profit and rent are only parts into which this value is *resolved,* but they do not constitute it. The *existing market-price* is for the capitalist what the presupposed *value* of the product is for the theory and the inner relationships of production. Now to the conclusion which Ricardo draws from this. If the farmer adds another £1,000, he only considers whether, at the *given market-price*, it yields him the usual profit. Ricardo therefore seems to think that the *cost-price* is the determining factor and that *profit* enters into this cost-price as a regulating element, but *rent* does not.

Firstly, profit too does not enter into it as a constituent element. For, according to the assumption, the farmer takes the *market-price* as his starting-point, and weighs up whether, at this given market-price, the £1,000 will yield him the usual profit. This profit is therefore not the cause, but the effect of that price. But—Ricardo continues his train of thought—the investment of the £1,000 itself is determined by the calculation of whether or not the price yields the profit. Thus the profit is the decisive factor for the investment of the £1,000, and for the price of production.

Furthermore: If the capitalist found that the £1,000 did not yield the usual profit, he would not invest it. The production of the additional food would not take place. If it were necessary for the additional demand, then the demand would have to

raise the price, i.e., the market-price, until it yielded the profit.
Thus profit—in contradistinction to rent—enters as a constituent
element, not because it creates the *value* of the product, but
because the product ||615| itself would not be created if its
price did not rise high enough to pay the usual rate of profit
as well as the capital expended. In *this* case, however, it is not
necessary for it to rise so high as to pay rent. Hence, there
exists an essential difference between rent and profit, and in
a certain sense, it can be said that profit is a constituent element
of price, whereas rent is not. (This thought is evidently also
at the back of Adam Smith's mind.)

In this case, it is correct.

But why?

Because in *this* case landed property *cannot* confront capital
as landed property, thus the very combination [of circumstances]
under which rent, absolute rent, is formed, is *not* present—according to the assumption. The additional corn produced with
the second investment of £1,000, provided *the market-value
remains the same*, in other words when an additional demand
arises only *on* the assumption that the *price* remains *the same,*
must be sold *below* its value at the cost-price. This additional
produce of the £1,000 thus occurs under the same circumstances
as when new worse land is cultivated, which *does not* determine the market-value, but can provide the additional supply
only on the condition that it supplies it at the *previously existing* market-value, i.e., at a price *determined independently of
this new production.* Under these circumstances it depends entirely on the relative fertility of the additional soil whether it
yields a rent precisely because it does *not* determine the market-
value. It is just the same with the additional £1,000 on the old
land. And for this very reason, Ricardo concludes *conversely,*
that the additional land or the additional amount of capital *determines the market-value* because, with a given, quite *independently determined market-value,* the price of its product
yields not rent, but only profit, and only covers the cost-price
but not the value of the product. This is a contradiction   in
terms.

Nevertheless, the product is produced *in this case,* although
it yields no rent! Certainly. Landed property as an independent
opposing element does not exist *for the farmer,* i.e., the capitalist, during the period in which the lease in fact makes him the
landowner of the land which he has *rented.* Capital moves un-

impeded in this element, and capital is satisfied with the cost-price of the product. Even when the lease expires, the farmer will naturally make the amount of rent dependent on how far capital investment in the land will supply a product which can be sold at its *value* thus yielding a rent. Capital investment which, with the given *market-value,* yields no excess over the cost-price, no more enters into the calculation than would the payment of rent—or contractual undertaking to pay rent—on land whose relative fertility is so low that the market-price is merely equal to the cost-price [of its product]. ·

In practice matters do not always work out in the Ricardian manner. If the farmer possesses some spare capital or acquires some during the first years of a lease of 14 years, he does not demand the *usual profit,* unless he has borrowed additional capital. For what is he to do with the spare capital? Conclude a new lease for additional land? Agricultural production favours to a much higher degree more intensive capital investment, than a more extensive cultivation of land with a larger capital. More-over, if no land could be leased in the immediate vicinity of the old land, two farms would split up the farmer's work of super-intending them to a much greater extent, than six factories would split up the work of one capitalist in manufacture. Or should he invest the money with the bank, for interest, in government bonds, railway shares, etc.? Then, from the outset, he forgoes at least a half or a third of the usual profit. Hence, if he can invest it as additional capital on the old farm, even below the average rate of profit, say at 10 per cent, if his profit was 12, then, he will still be gaining 100 per cent if the rate of interest is 5 per cent. To invest the additional £1,000 in the old farm is, therefore, still a profitable speculation for him. ||616|

Hence it is quite wrong for Ricardo to identify this invest-ment of additional capital with the application of additional capital to new soils. In the first case, the product does not have to yield the usual profit, even in capitalist production. It must only yield as much above the usual rate of interest as will make worth while the trouble and risk of the farmer to prefer the industrial employment of his spare capital to its employment as money capital.

But the following conclusion which Ricardo draws from this observation is, as has been shown, quite absurd.

"If the comprehensive mind of Adam Smith had been directed to this fact, he would not have maintained that rent forms *one of the component parts of the price of raw produce*; for price is everywhere *regulated* by the return obtained by this last portion of capital, for which no rent whatever is paid" (l.c., p. 391).

His illustration proves just the *reverse*: that the application to land of this last portion of capital has been regulated by a *market-price* which, independent of that application, existed before it took place—and, therefore comprises no rent, but only profit. That profit is the only regulator for capitalist production is quite true. And it is therefore true that no absolute rent would exist if production were regulated *solely* by capital. It arises precisely at the point where the conditions of production enable the landowner to set up barriers against the exclusive regulation of production by capital.

Secondly, Ricardo reproaches Adam Smith (p. 391, et seq.) for developing the correct principles of rent [only] with regard to coal-mines; [he] even says:

"The whole principle of rent is here admirably and perspicuously explained, but every word is as applicable to land as it is to mines; yet he affirms that 'it is otherwise in estates above ground...'" (l.c., p. 392).

Adam Smith senses that, under certain circumstances, the landlord has the power to offer effective resistance to capital, to bring landed property into play, and thus to demand absolute rent, though, under different circumstances, he does not possess this power; that in particular however the production of food establishes the law of rent, whereas in other applications of capital to land, the rent is determined by the agricultural rent.

"The proportion, both of their produce and of their rent, is in proportion" (says Adam Smith) "to their *absolute*, and not to their *relative* fertility" (l.c., p. 392).

In his reply, Ricardo comes closest to the real principle of rent. He says:

"But, suppose that *there were no land which did not afford a rent; then, the amount of rent on the worst land would be in proportion to the excess of the v a l u e o f t h e p r o d u c e above the expenditure of capital and the ordinary profits of stock*: the same principle would govern the rent of land of a somewhat better quality, or more favourably situated, and, therefore, the rent of this land would exceed the rent of that inferior to it, by the superior advantages which it possessed; the same might be said of that of the third quality, and so on to the very best. Is it not, then, as certain, that it is *the relative fertility of the land*, which determines the portion of the produce, which shall be paid for the rent of land, as it is that the *relative fertility of mines*, determines the portion of their produce, which shall be paid for the rent of mines?" (l.c., pp. 392-93.)

Here Ricardo formulates the correct principle of rent. If the worst land pays a rent, if therefore rent is paid independently of the different natural fertility of the land—i.e., absolute rent —then this rent must equal "the excess of the *value* of the produce *above* the expenditure of capital and the ordinary profits of stock" [l. c., pp. 392-93] that is to say, it must equal the excess of the *value* of the produce *above* its cost-price. Ricardo presupposes that such an excess cannot exist, because, in contradiction to his own principles, he wrongly accepts the Smithian doctrine ||617| that value equals cost-price of the produce.

As for the rest, he falls again into error.

Differential rent would of course be determined by the "relative fertility". Absolute rent would have nothing to do with the "natural fertility".

Smith however would indeed be right when he asserts that the *actual* rent paid by the worst land *may* depend on the absolute fertility of the other soils and the relative fertility of the worst soil, or on the absolute fertility of the worst soil and the relative fertility of the other soils.

For the actual amount of rent paid by the worst land depends not, as Ricardo thinks, on the excess of the *value* of its own produce over its cost-price, but on the excess of the *market-value* over its cost-price. But these are very different things If the market-price were determined by the *product of the worst land*, then the market-value would be equal to its real value, hence, the excess of its market-value over its cost-price would be equal to the excess of its own individual value, its real value, over its cost-price. But this is not the case if quite irrespective of this product the market-price is determined by the other types of land. Ricardo assumes a descending line. He assumes that the worst land is cultivated *last* and is only cultivated (in the case postulated), when the additional demand has necessitated an additional supply at the value of the produce derived from the worst and last cultivated soil. In this case the value of the worst land regulates the market-value. In the ascending line (even according to him) this will only occur when the additional supply of the better sorts of land only equals the additional demand at the old market-value. If the additional supply is greater, Ricardo assumes that the old land must be thrown *out of cultivation*, but it only follows from this that it will yield a *lower rent* than before (or no rent at all).

The same happens in the descending line. Whether, and to what extent, the worse land yields rent, if the additional supply can only by provided at the *old market-value*, depends on how much this market-value stands above the cost-price of the product of the new, worse land. In both cases its rent is determined by the *absolute* fertility, not the relative fertility. It depends on the absolute fertility of the new land how far the market-value of the produce of better lands stands *above* its own real, individual value.

Adam Smith makes a correct distinction here between land and mines, because with the latter he presupposes that there is *never* a transition to worse sorts—always to *better* ones—and that they always provide more than the necessary additional supply. The rent of the worst land is then dependent on its absolute fertility.

"After Adam Smith has declared that there are some mines *which can only be worked by the owners*, as they will afford only sufficient to defray the expense of working, together with the ordinary profits of the capital employed, *we should expect that he would admit that it was these particular mines which regulated the price of the produce from a l l mines*. If the old mines are insufficient to supply the quantity of coal required, the *price of coal will rise*, and will continue rising till the owner of a new and inferior mine finds that he can obtain the usual profits of stock by working his[a] mine.... It appears, then, that *it is always the least fertile mine which regulates the price of coal*. Adam Smith, however, is of a different opinion: he observes that 'the most fertile coal-mine, too, regulates the price of coals at all the other mines in its neighbourhood. Both the proprietor and the undertaker of the work find, the one, that he can get a greater rent, the other, that he can get a greater profit, by somewhat underselling all their neighbours. Their neighbours are soon obliged to sell *at the same price*, though they cannot so well afford it, and though it always diminishes, and sometimes takes away altogether, both their rent and their profit. Some works are abandoned altogether; others can afford no rent, *and can be wrought only by the proprietor*'. If the demand for coal should be diminished, ||617a| or if by new processes the quantity should be increased, the *price would fall*, and some mines would be *abandoned*; but in *every case*, the *price must be sufficient* to *pay the expenses and profit of that mine which is worked without being charged with rent*. It is, *therefore*, the least fertile mine which regulates price. Indeed, it is so stated in another place by Adam Smith himself, for he says: '*The lowest price* at which coals can be *sold* for any considerable time is like that of all other commodities, the price which is barely sufficient to replace, together with its ordinary profits, the stock which must be employed in bringing them to market. At a coal-mine for which the landlord can get no rent, but which he must either work himself, or let it alone all together, *the price of coals must generally be nearly about this price*'" (l.c., pp. 393-95).

---

[a] In the manuscript: "of".—*Ed.*

Adam Smith is mistaken when he declares the particular set of circumstances on the market, under which the most fertile mine (or land) dominates the market, to be the *rule*. But provided such a case is assumed his reasoning is correct (on the whole) and Ricardo's wrong. Adam Smith presupposes that as a result of the state of demand and because of its relative superior fertility, the best mine can only force the whole of its product on to the market if it undersells its competitors, if its product is *below* the old market-value. This causes the price to fall for the worse mines too. The market-price falls. This in any case *lowers the rent* on worse mines and can even make it disappear completely. For the rent is equal to the excess of market-value over cost-price of the produce, whether that market-value be like the individual value of the produce of a certain class [of land], or mines, or not. What Smith fails to notice, is that the profit can only be diminished by this if it becomes necessary to withdraw capital and reduce the scale of production. If the market-price—regulated, as it is under the given circumstances, by the produce of the best mines— falls so low as to afford no excess above cost-price for the product of the worst mine, then it can be worked only by its owner. At this market-price, no capitalist will pay him a rent. His ownership of land does not, in this case, give him power over capital, but as far as he is concerned it annuls the resistance which other capitalists meet who wish to apply capital to land. Landed property does *not exist* for him because he himself is the landed proprietor. Hence he can use his land as a mine, or in any other sphere of production, i.e., he can employ it if the market-price, which he *finds* predetermined and does not determine himself—if the market-price of the product yields him the average profit, that is, his *cost-price*.

And from this Ricardo concludes that Smith contradicts himself! Because the old market-price determines how far new mines can be opened up by their owners—in other words they can be worked in circumstances where landed property disappears, since at the old market-price they yield their cultivators the *cost-price*—he concludes that this cost-price determines the market-price! But again he takes refuge in the descending line and allows the less fertile mine to be cultivated only when the market-price of the product rises above the value of the product of the better mines, whereas it is only necessary that it rises *above* the cost-price or even that it equals the cost-price in

22*

the case of the worse mines exploited by their proprietors themselves. Incidentally, his assumption that "... if by new processes the quantity" (of coal) "should be increased, the *price
would fall*, and *some mines would be abandoned*" [l.c., p. 394],
depends only on the degree of the fall in price and the state
of demand. If, with this fall of prices, the market can absorb
the whole product, then the bad mines will still yield a rent
provided the fall of market-price still leaves an excess of market-
value over the cost-price of the poorer mines, and [the mines
will] be worked by their owners, if the market-value only covers, or is equal to, the cost-price. In either case, however, [it is]
absurd to say that the cost-price of the worst mine regulates
the market-price. Although the cost-price of the worst mine
determines the relation of the price of its produce to the ruling
market-price, and *therefore* decides the question whether or
not ||618| the mine can be worked. But the fact that a piece
of land or a mine of a particular degree of fertility can be exploited at a *given market-price*, is obviously not related to or
identical with the determination of the market-price by the
cost-price of the produce of these mines. If an *increased market-
value* would make an *additional supply* necessary or possible
then the worst land would regulate the market-value, but then
it would also yield absolute rent. This is the exact *opposite* of
the case assumed by Adam Smith.

Thirdly, Ricardo reproaches Smith for believing (p. 395, et.
seq.) that cheapness of raw produce, for instance substitution
of potatoes for corn, which would lower the wage and diminish
the cost of production, would cause a larger share as well as
a larger quantity to fall to the landlord. Ricardo on the other
hand [maintains that]:

"No part of that additional proportion would go to rent, but the whole
invariably to profits ... while lands of the same quality were cultivated, and
there was no alteration in their relative fertility or advantages, *rent would
always bear the same proportion to the gross produce*" (l.c., p. 396).

This is positively wrong. The share of rent would fall and,
therefore, its quantity would decrease *relatively*. The introduction of potatoes as the principal means of subsistence, would
reduce the value of labour-power, shorten the necessary labour-
time, increase the surplus labour-time and therefore the *rate* of
surplus-value, hence—other circumstances remaining the same
—the composition of the capital would be altered, the value
of the variable part would diminish in comparison with that of

the constant part, although the *quantity* of living labour employed remained the same. The *rate of profit* would therefore rise. In this case [there would be] a fall in absolute rent and proportionately in differential rent. (See page 610 Table *C*.)[a] This factor would affect equally agricultural and non-agricultural capital. The general rate of profit would rise and the rent would *consequently* fall.

Chapter XXVIII. "On the comparative Value of Gold, Corn, and Labour, in Rich and Poor Countries."

"Dr. Smith's error, throughout his whole work, lies in supposing that the value of corn is constant; that though the value of all other things may, the value of corn never can be raised. Corn, according to him, is always of the same value because it will always feed the same number of people. In the same manner, it might be said, that cloth is always of the same value, because it will always make the same number of coats. What can value have to do with the power of feeding and clothing?" (l.c., pp. 449-50.)

"Dr. Smith ... has so ably supported the doctrine of the natural price of commodities ultimately regulating their market-price ..." (l.c., p. 451).

"Estimated in corn, gold may be of very different value in two countries. I have endeavoured to shew that it will be low in rich countries, and high in poor countries; Adam Smith is of a different opinion: he thinks that the value of gold, estimated in corn, is highest in rich countries" (l.c., p. 454).

Chapter XXXII. "Mr. Malthus's Opinions on Rent."

"Rent is a creation of value ... but not a creation of wealth"[94] (l.c., p. 485).

"In speaking of the high price of corn, Mr. Malthus evidently does not mean the price per quarter or per bushel, but rather the excess of price for which the whole produce will sell, above the cost of its production, including always in the term 'cost of its production', profits as well as wages. One hundred and fifty quarters of corn at £3 10s. per quarter, would yield a larger rent to the landlord than 100 quarters at £4, provided the cost of production were in both cases the same" (l.c., p. 487). "Whatever the nature of the land may be, high rent must depend on the high price of the produce; but, given the high price, rent must be high in proportion to abundance and not to scarcity" (l.c., p. 492).

"As rent is the effect of the high price of corn, the loss of rent is the effect of a low price. Foreign corn never enters into competition with such home corn as affords a rent; the fall of price invariably affects the landlord till the whole of his rent is absorbed;—if it fall still more, the price will not afford even the common profits of stock; capital will then quit the land for some other employment, and the corn, which was before grown upon it, will then, and not till then, be imported. From the loss of rent, there will be a loss of value, of estimated money value, but, there will be a gain of wealth. The amount of the raw produce and other productions together will be increased; from the greater facility with which they are produced, they will, though augmented in quantity, be diminished in value" (l.c., p. 519).

---

[a] See the insertion between pages 328 and 329.—*Ed.*

[C H A P T E R XIV]

ADAM SMITH'S THEORY OF RENT

[1. Contradictions in Smith's Formulation of the Problem of Rent]

||619| At this stage we shall not examine Smith's interesting account of how the rent of the principal vegetable food dominates all other strictly agricultural rents (stock raising, timber, industrial crops), because each of these branches of production can easily be transformed into one of the others. Adam Smith excludes rice from this, wherever it is the principal vegetable food, since rice fields (or bogs) are not convertible into grass land, wheat lands, etc. and vice versa.

[In Chapter XI, Book I] Adam Smith correctly defines *rent* as "the price paid for *the use of land*" ([O.U.P., Vol. I, p. 162; Garnier,] t. I, p. 299), the term land is intended to mean every power of nature as such, therefore also water, etc.

In contrast to Rodbertus's peculiar notion,[95] Smith, from the outset, enumerates the items of agricultural capital:

"The stock from which he furnishes the seed" (the raw material), "pays the labour, and purchases and maintains the cattle and other *instruments* of husbandry" ([O.U.P., Vol. I, p. 163; Garnier,] l.c.).

Now what is this price paid for the use of land?

"Whatever part of the produce or ... of its price, is over and above this share" (which pays for the capital advanced "together with the ordinary profits"), "he" (the *landlord*) "naturally endeavours to reserve to himself as the *rent* of his land" ([O.U.P., Vol. I, p. 163; Garnier,] l.c., p. 300).

This *excess* may "be considered as the *natural rent* of land" ([O.U.P., Vol. I, p. 163; Garnier,] l.c., p. 300).

Smith refuses to confuse rent with the interest on capital invested in the land.

"The landlord demands a rent even for unimproved land" ([O.U.P., Vol. I, p. 163; Garnier,] l.c., pp. 300-01).

and, he adds, even this second form of rent [i.e., the rent on the improved land] is peculiar in that the interest from the capital used on improvement is interest on a capital which has not been laid out by the landlord, but by the farmer.

"He" (the landlord) "sometimes demands rent for what is altogether incapable of human improvements" ([O.U.P., Vol. I, pp. 163-64; Garnier,] l.c., p. 301).

Smith stresses very strongly, that it is *landed property,* the *landlord,* who as *landlord* "demands the rent". [Regarded] as a mere effluence of *landed property,* rent is *monopoly price,* this is perfectly correct, since it is only the intervention of landed property which enables the product to be sold for more than the cost-price, to be sold at its value.

"The rent of land considered as the price paid for the use of the land, is naturally a monopoly price" ([O.U.P., Vol. I, p. 164; Garnier,] l.c., p. 302).

It is in fact a price which is only enforced through the monopoly of landed property, and as a monopoly price, it differs from the price of the industrial product.

From the standpoint of capital—and capital dominates production—the *cost-price* only requires that the product should pay the average profit in addition to the capital advanced. In this case, the product, be it product of the land or any other product, can *"be brought to market".*

"If the ordinary price is more than this, the *surplus* part of it will naturally go to the rent of the land. If it is not more, though the commodity *may* be brought to market, it can afford no rent to the landlord. Whether the price is, or is not more, depends upon the demand" ([O.U.P., Vol. I, p. 164; Garnier,] l.c., p. 303).

Why does rent enter into price differently from wages and profit? That is the question. Originally, Smith had resolved value correctly, into wages, profits and rents (apart from constant capital). But almost at once he takes the opposite course and identifies value with natural price (the average price determined by competition or the cost-price of the commodities) and builds up the latter from wages, profit and rent.

"These three parts seem either immediately or ultimately to make up the whole price" ([O.U.P., Vol. I, p. 55; Garnier,] l. I, ch. VI, p. 101).

"In the most improved societies, however, there are always a few commodities *of which the price resolves itself into two parts only,* the *wages of labour and the profits of stock;* and a still smaller number, in which *it consists altogether in the wages of labour.* In the price of sea-fish, for example, one part pays the labour of the fishermen, and the other the profits of the capital employed in the fishery. *Rent* very seldom makes any part ||620| of it.... In some parts of Scotland, a few poor people make a trade of gathering, along the sea-shore, those little variegated stones commonly known by the name of *Scotch pebbles.* The price which is paid to them by the *stone-cutter,* is altogether the *wages of their labour; neither rent nor profit makes any part of it.*

"But the *whole price of any commodity* must still finally resolve itself *into some one or other or all of those three parts*" ([O.U.P., Vol. I, pp. 56-57; Garnier,] l. I, ch. VI, pp. 103-04).

In these passages, the resolving of value into wages, etc. and the compounding of price from wages, etc., are jumbled together (this applies to Chapter VI in general which deals with *"the Component Parts of the Price of Commodities"). (Natural price and market-price are for the first time discussed in Chapter VII).

Book I, Chapters I, II, III deal with the "division of labour", *Chapter IV* with money. In these, as in the following chapters, *value* is determined in passing. *Chapter V* deals with the *real and nominal price* of commodities, with the transformation of *value into price*; "the Component Parts of the Price of Commodities" are considered in *Chapter VI*; the *natural and market-price* in *Chapter VII*. Then *Chapter VIII* deals with the wages of labour, *Chapter IX* with the profits of stock; *Chapter X* with the *Wages and Profit in the different Employments of Labour and Stock;* finally, *Chapter XI* with the *Rent of Land.*

But in this connection we want first to draw attention to the following: According to the passages cited above, there are commodities whose *price* consists solely of wages, others, whose price consists only of wages and profit, and finally a third group of commodities, whose price consists of wages, profit and rent. Hence:

"The *whole price of any commodity* must still ... resolve itself *into some one or other* or *all of those three parts.*"

According to this, there would be no grounds for saying that rent enters into price in a different manner from profit and wages, but one could say that rent and profit enter into price in a different way from wages, since the latter always enters [into price], the former not always. *Whence, then, the difference?*

Moreover, Smith should have investigated, whether it is possible that the few commodities which only *comprise wages,* are sold at *their value,* or whether the poor people who gather the Scotch pebbles are not in fact the wage-labourers of the *stone-cutters,* who pay them only the usual wages for the commodity, in other words for a *whole working-day, which apparently belongs to them,* these people receive only as much as a worker in other trades, where *part of the working-day* forms profit and belongs not to him but to the capitalist. Smith should have either affirmed this or else asserted that in this case the profit only *seems* to be confounded with wages. He says himself:

"When those three different sorts of revenue belong to different persons, they are readily distinguished; but when they belong to the same, they are sometimes confounded with one another, at least in common language" ([O.U.P., Vol. I, p. 58; Garnier,] l. I, ch. VI, p. 106).

He nevertheless works out this problem in the following manner:

If an independent labourer (like those poor people of Scotland) uses only labour (without recourse to capital), if, altogether, he only employs his labour and the elements, then the price resolves itself solely into wages. If he employs a small capital as well, then the same individual receives wages and profit. If, finally, he employs his labour, his capital and his landed property, then he unites in his person the characters of landowner, farmer and worker.

{The whole absurdity of Smith's approach comes to light in one of the final passages of Chapter VI, Book I:

"As in a civilised country there are but few commodities of which the *exchangeable value* arises *from labour only*" (here labour is identified with *wages*) "*rent* and *profit* contributing largely to that of the far greater part of them, so the *annual produce of its labour*" (here, after all, the commodities are the *produce* of *labour*, although the whole value of this produce does not arise from labour) "will always be sufficient *to purchase* or *command a much greater quantity of labour than what was employed in raising, preparing, and bringing that produce to market*" ([O.U.P., Vol. I, pp. 59-60; Garnier,] l.c., pp. 108-09).

The produce of *labour* [is] not equal to the *value* of this produce. On the contrary (one may gather) this value is *increased* by the addition of profit and rent. The produce of labour can therefore command, purchase, more labour, i.e., pay a greater value in labour, than the labour contained in it. This proposition would be correct if it ran like this:

||621| *Smith says:*	*According to him himself, it should read:*
"As in a civilised country there are but few commodities of which the *exchangeable value* arises *from labour only*, rent and profit *con-*	"As in a civilised country there are but few commodities of which the *exchangeable value* resolves itself into *wages* only and since,

tributing largely to that of the far greater part of them, so the annual produce of its labour will always be sufficient to purchase or command a much greater *quantity of labour* than *what was employed in raising, preparing, and bringing that produce to market.*"

for a far greater part of them, this value largely *resolves* itself into rent and profit, so the annual produce of its labour will always be sufficient to purchase or command a much greater *quantity of labour* than what had to be *paid*" (and therefore employed) "in raising, preparing, and bringing that produce to market."

(Here Smith returns again to his second conception of value, a concept of which he writes the following in the same chapter.

"The real value of all the different component parts of price, it must be observed, is measured by the *quantity of labour which they can, each of them, purchase or command.* Labour" (in this sense) "measures the value, not only of that part of price which *resolves* itself into *labour*" (should read: into wages) "but of that which resolves itself into rent, and of that which *resolves* itself into *profit*" ([O.U.P., Vol. I, p. 55; Garnier,] l. I, ch. VI, p. 100).

(In Chapter VI, the resolution of *value* into wages, profit and rent is still dominant. It is only in Chapter VII, on the natural price and market-price, that the compounding of the price from these constituent elements wins the upper hand.)

Hence: The *exchangeable value of the annual product of labour* consists not only of the wages of the labour employed in order to bring forth this product, but also of profit and rent. This labour however is only *commanded* or *purchased* with that part of the value which resolves into wages. It is thus possible to set into motion a much larger amount of labour, if a part of the profit and rent is used to command or purchase labour, i.e., if it is converted into wages. So it amounts to this: the exchangeable value of the annual product of labour resolves itself into *paid labour* (wages) and *unpaid labour* (profit and rent). If therefore a part of that part of the value which resolves itself into unpaid labour is converted into wages, one can purchase a greater quantity of labour than if one merely assigns that part of the value which consists of wages, to the purchase of new labour.}

Let us go back then:

"An independent manufacturer, who has *stock enough* both to purchase materials, and to maintain himself till he can carry his work to market, should gain both the *wages of a journeyman* who works under a *master*, and the profit which that master makes by the sale of that journeyman's work. His whole gains, however, are commonly called *profit*, and wages are, in this case too, confounded with profit.

"A gardener who cultivates his own garden with his own hands, unites in his own person the *three different characters of landlord, farmer, and labourer*. His produce, therefore, should pay him the rent of the first, the profit of the second, and the wages of the third. The whole, however, is commonly considered as the *earnings of his labour*. Both rent and profit are, in this case, confounded with wages" ([O.U.P., Vol. I, p. 59; Garnier,] 1. I, ch. VI, p. 108).

This is indeed confounded. Is not the *whole* "the earnings of his labour"? And are not, on the contrary, the conditions of capitalist production—in which, with the alienation of labour from its objective conditions, the worker, capitalist and landowner confront one another as different characters too—transferred to this gardener, so that the product of his labour or rather the value of the product is regarded, part of it as wages, in payment of his labour, part of it as profit, on account of the capital employed, and part of it as rent, as the portion due to the land or rather the proprietor of the land? *Within* capitalist production ⟨it is⟩ quite correct, when considering those conditions of labour in which these elements are *not* separated (in actual fact), to assume them to be separated and so to regard this gardener as his own ||622| journeyman and as his own landowner in one person. The vulgar conception however that wages arise from labour, but profit and rent—independently of the labour of the worker—arise out of capital and land as separate sources, not for the appropriation of alien labour, but of wealth itself, evident· ly creeps into Adam Smith's writing already at this stage. In this fantastic fashion, the profoundest concepts intermingle with the craziest notions, such as the common mind forms in an abstract manner from the phenomena of competition.

Having first *resolved* value into wages, profits, rents, he then on the contrary *compounds* value out of wages, profit and rent, whose magnitudes are determined independently of value. Since Adam Smith has thus forgotten the origin of profit and rent correctly explained by himself, he is able to say:

"Wages, profit, and rent, are the *three original sources* of all *revenue, as well as of all exchangeable value*" ([O.U.P., Vol. I, p. 57; Garnier,] 1. I, ch. VI, p. 105).

In accordance with his own explanation, he should have said:

"The *value* of a commodity arises exclusively out of the labour (the amount of labour) which is embodied in this commodity. This value resolves itself into wages, profit and rent. Wages, profit and rent are the original forms in which the worker, the capitalist and the landlord participate in the value created by the labour of the worker. In this sense they are the three original *sources of all revenue*, although none of these so-called sources enters into the formation of the value."

From the passages quoted it can be seen how in Chapter VI, on the *"Component Parts of the Price of Commodities"*, Adam Smith arrives at the resolution of price into wages, where only (immediate) labour enters into the production; into wages and profit, where, instead of the independent workman, a journeyman is employed by a capitalist (i.e., capital); and finally into wages, profit and rent, where "land" enters into the production besides capital and labour. In this latter case, however, it is assumed that the land is appropriated, that consequently alongside the worker and the capitalist, there is also a landowner (although he notes that it is possible for all three or two of these characters to be united in one person).

In *Chapter VII,* on *natural price* and *market-price,* rent (where land enters into the production) is presented as a component part of the natural price in exactly the same way as wages and profit. The following passages will show this:

(Book I, *Chapter VII*)

"When the price of any commodity is neither more nor less than what is sufficient to pay the *r e n t o f t h e l a n d, the wages of the labour,* and *the profits of the stock* employed in raising, preparing, and bringing it to market, according to their *natural* rates, the commodity is then sold for what may be called *its natural price.*

"The commodity is then sold *precisely* for *what it is worth"* ([O.U.P., Vol. I, p. 61; Garnier,] l.c., p. 111). (At the same time, it is stated here that the natural price is identical with the value of the commodity.)

"The *market price* of every particular commodity is regulated by the proportion between the quantity which is actually brought to market, and the demand of those who are willing to pay the *natural price* of the commodity, or the *whole value of the rent,* labour, and profit, *which must be paid in order to bring it thither"* ([O.U.P., Vol. I, pp. 61-62; Garnier,] l.c., p. 112).

"When the quantity of any commodity which is brought to market *falls short of* the effectual demand, all those who are willing to pay the *whole value o f the r e n t, wages, and profit,* which must be paid in order to bring it thither, cannot be supplied with the quantity which they want ... the *market price* will rise more or less *above* the *natural price,* according as either the *greatness of the deficiency,* or *the wealth* and wanton luxury of the competitors, happen to animate more or less the eagerness of the competition" ([O.U.P., Vol. I, p. 62; Garnier,] l.c., p. 113).

"When the quantity brought to market exceeds the effectual demand, it cannot be all sold to those who are willing to pay the whole value of the rent, wages, and profit, which must be paid in order to bring it thither.... The *market price* will sink more or less below the *natural price,* according as the greatness of the excess increases more or less the competition of the sellers, or according as it happens to be more or less important to them to get immediately rid of the commodity" ([O.U.P., Vol. I, pp. 62-63; Garnier,] l.c., p. 114).

"When the quantity brought to market is just sufficient to supply the effectual demand, and no more, the *market price* naturally comes to be ... exactly ... the same with the *natural price*.... The competition of the different dealers obliges them all to accept of this price, but does not oblige them to accept of less" ([O.U.P., Vol. I, p. 63; Garnier,] l.c., pp. 114-15).

||623| If, in consequence of the state of the market, his rent sinks below, or rises above, its natural rate, Adam Smith allows the landowner to *withdraw his land* or transfer it from the production of one commodity (such as wheat) to that of *another* (such as pasture for instance).

"If at any time it" (the quantity brought to market) "exceeds the effectual demand, some of the component parts of its price must be paid below their *natural rate. If it is rent,* the interest of the landlords will immediately prompt them *to withdraw a part of their land*" ([O.U.P., Vol. I, p. 63; Garnier,] l. c., p. 115).

"If, on the contrary, the quantity brought to market should at any time *fall short of the effectual demand*, some of the component parts of its price must rise above their *natural* rate. *If it is rent,* the interest of all other landlords will naturally prompt them to prepare more land for the raising of this commodity" ([O.U.P., Vol. I, p. 63; Garnier,] l.c., p. 116).

"The occasional and temporary fluctuations in the *market price* of any commodity fall chiefly upon those parts of its price which resolve themselves into wages and profit. That part which resolves itself into rent is less affected by them" ([O.U.P., Vol. I, p. 65; Garnier,] l.c., pp. 118-19).

"The *price of monopoly* is upon every occasion the highest which can be got. The *natural price*, or the price of free competition, on the contrary, is the lowest which can be taken, not upon every occasion indeed, but for any considerable time together" ([O.U.P., Vol. I, p. 68; Garnier,] l.c., p. 124).

"The *market price* of any particular commodity, though it may continue long above, can seldom continue long below, its *natural price*. *Whatever part of it was paid below the natural rate*, the persons whose interest it affected would immediately feel the loss, and would *immediately withdraw* either *so much land*, or so much labour, or so much stock, from being employed about it, that the quantity brought to market would soon be no more than sufficient to supply the effectual demand. Its *market price*, therefore, would soon rise to the *natural price*; this at least would be the case where there was perfect liberty" ([O.U.P., Vol. I, pp. 68-69; Garnier,] l.c., p. 125).

After this exposition of the subject in Chapter VII, it is difficult to see how Adam Smith can justify his proposition in Book I, Chapter XI, "*Of the Rent of Land*", that rent does not always enter into price where appropriated land enters into production; how he can differentiate between the manner in which rent enters into price from that in which profit and wages enter into it, since in chapters VI and VII he has turned rent into a *com-*

ponent part of the *natural price*, in just the same way as profit and wages. Now let us return to this Chapter XI (Book I).

We have seen that there rent is defined as the *surplus* which remains from the *price of the product,* after the expenses of the capitalist (farmer) plus the average profit have been paid.

In this Chapter XI, Smith makes a complete turn-about. Rent no longer enters into the *natural price*. Or, rather, Adam Smith takes refuge in an *ordinary price* which is as a rule different from the natural price, although we were told in Chapter VII, that the ordinary price can never, for any length of time, be *below* the natural price and that none of the component parts of the natural price can for any length of time, be paid below its natural rate and even less, not paid at all, as he now asserts in relation to rent. Neither does Adam Smith tell us whether the produce is sold *below its value* when it pays no rent, or whether it is sold *above* its value, when it pays rent.

Previously, the *natural price* of the commodity was

"the *whole value of the rent,* labour, and profit, *which must be paid in order to bring it thither*" [to market] ([O.U.P., Vol. I, pp. 61-62, Garnier,] l.c., p. 112).

Now we are told that:

"Such parts *only* of the produce of land *can commonly be brought to market,* of which the *ordinary price* is sufficient *to replace the stock which must be employed in bringing them thither, together with its ordinary profits*" ([O.U.P., Vol. I, p. 164; Garnier,] l.c., pp. 302-03).

The *ordinary price* is therefore not the *natural price,* and the natural price need not be paid, in order to bring these commodities to market.

||624| Previously we were told that if the *ordinary price* (that time, the *market-price*) were not sufficient to pay the *whole rent* ("the whole value of the rent," etc.), land will be withdrawn until the market-price rises to the level of the natural price and pays the whole rent. Now, on the other hand:

"If the *ordinary price is more than this*" (sufficient to replace the stock together with its ordinary profits), "the *surplus* part of it will naturally go to the rent of the land. If it is not more, though the *commodity may be brought to market,* it can afford no rent to the landlord. Whether the price is, or is not more, depends upon the demand" ([O.U.P., Vol. I, p. 164; Garnier,] l. I, ch. XI, p. 303).

Thus rent, from being a component part of the *natural price,* suddenly turns into a *surplus* over the *sufficient price,*[a] a sur-

---

[a] The term "prix suffisant" (sufficient price) is used in the French translation of the *Wealth of Nations* from which Marx quotes.—*Ed.*

plus whose existence or non-existence depends on the state of demand. But the *sufficient price* is that price which is required for the commodity to appear on the market, and therefore to be produced, thus it is the *price of production* of the commodity. For the price which is required for the supply of the commodity, the price which is required for it to come into existence at all, to appear as a commodity on the market, is of course its *price of production* or *cost-price*. That [is the condition] *sine qua non* of the existence of the commodity. On the other hand the demand for certain products of the land must always be such that their *ordinary price* pays a surplus over and above the price of production, that is, a rent. For others it may or may not be so.

"There are some parts of the produce of land for which the demand must always be such as to afford a greater price than what is sufficient to bring them to market; and there are others for which it either may or may not be such as to *afford* this greater *price*. The former must always afford a rent to the landlord. The latter sometimes may, and sometimes may not, according to different circumstances" ([O.U.P., Vol. I, pp. 164-65; Garnier,] l. I, ch. XI, p. 303).

So instead of the *natural price* we have the *sufficient price* here. The *ordinary price,* in turn, is different from this *sufficient price*. The ordinary price if it *includes* the rent is *above* the sufficient price. If it does not comprise rent it is equal to the sufficient price. It is even characteristic of the *sufficient price that rent is excluded*. The ordinary price is *below* the sufficient price, when it does not pay the average profit, in addition to replacing the capital. Thus the *sufficient price* is in fact the *price of production* or *cost-price* as abstracted by Ricardo from Adam Smith and as it indeed presents itself from the standpoint of capitalist production, in other words the price which, apart from the outlay of the capitalist, pays the ordinary profit; [it is] the average price brought about by the competition of capitalists in the different employments of capital. It is this abstraction based on competition which induces Adam Smith to confront his *natural price* with the *sufficient price*, although in his presentation of the natural price he on the contrary declares that in the long run only the ordinary price which pays rent, profit and wages, the component parts of the natural price, is sufficient. Since the capitalist controls the production of commodities, the sufficient price is [that] which is sufficient for capitalist production from the standpoint of capital and the price which is sufficient for capital does not include rent, but, on the contrary, excludes it.

On the other hand: This *sufficient price* is not sufficient for some products of the land. For them the *ordinary price* must be high enough to yield a surplus over and above the sufficient price, a rent for the landowner. For others it depends on the circumstances. The contradiction that the sufficient price is not sufficient—that the price which suffices to bring the product to market does not suffice to bring it to market—does not worry Adam Smith.

Although he does not turn back, even for one moment, to glance at chapters V, VI and VII, he admits to himself (not as a contradiction, but as a new discovery which he has suddenly hit upon), that with the sufficient price, he has overthrown his whole doctrine of natural price.

"*Rent*, it is to be *observed*, therefore" (in this extraordinarily naive fashion Adam Smith progresses from an assertion to its very opposite), "*e n t e r s i n t o   t h e   c o m p o s i t i o n of the price of commodities i n   a   d i f f e r e n t w a y   f r o m   w a g e s   a n d   p r o f i t. High or low wages and profit are t h e   c a u s e s   of high or law price* ||625|; *h i g h   o r   l o w   r e n t* is **the effect** *of it. It is because high or low wages and profit must be paid, in order to bring a particular commodity to market, that its price is high or low.* But it is because its price is high or low, *a great deal more, or very little more, or no more, than what is sufficient to pay those wages and profit,* that it affords a high rent, or a low rent, or no rent at all" ([O.U.P., Vol. I, p. 165; Garnier,] l.c., pp. 303-04).

Let us take the final proposition first. The *sufficient price,* the cost-price, which only pays wages and profit, *excludes rent.* If the product pays *a great deal more than the sufficient price,* then it pays a high rent. If it pays only a little more, then it pays a low rent. If it pays *only exactly the sufficient price,* then it pays *no* rent. It pays *no* rent if the actual price of the product coincides with the *sufficient price*, which pays profit and wages. Rent is always a *surplus* over and above the sufficient price. By its very nature, the sufficient price excludes rent. *This is Ricardo's theory.* He accepts the concept of the *sufficient price*, the cost-price, from Adam Smith; but avoids Adam Smith's inconsistency of differentiating it from the natural price, and sets it forth consistently. Having committed all these inconsistencies, Smith is sufficiently inconsistent to demand, for certain products of the land, a price which is *higher* than their *sufficient price.* But this inconsistency itself is in turn the result of a *more correct* "observation".

The beginning of the passage is truly amazing in its naiveté. In Chapter VII Smith explained that rent, profit and wages enter equally into the *composition of the natural price*, having first turned the *dissolution of value* into rent, profit and wages upside down and transformed it into the composition of value from the natural price of rent, profit and wages. Now he tells us that rent enters into "the *composition of the price* of commodities" *differently* from profit and wages. And in what way does it enter *differently* into *that composition?* By *not* entering into that composition *at all*. And here we are first given a true explanation of the sufficient price. The *price of the commodities* is dear or cheap, high or low, because wages and profit—their natural rates—are high or low. The commodity will not be brought to market, will not be produced, unless these high or low profits and wages are paid. They form the *price of production* of the commodity, its *cost-price*; and are thus in fact, the *constituent elements of its value* or *price. Rent,* on the other hand, does not enter into the *cost-price,* the *price of production.* It is not a constituent element of the exchangeable value of the commodity. It is *only* paid when the *ordinary price* of the commodity is *above* its *sufficient* price. Profit and wages as *constituent elements* of the price are *causes* of the price; rent, on the other hand, is only its *effect,* its *result.* It does not, therefore, enter into the composition of the price as an element, as do profit and wages. And this is what Smith calls entering into this composition in a *different* way from profit and wages. He does not appear to be in the slightest bit aware of the fact that he has thrown over his doctrine of natural price. For what was the natural price? The central point around which the market-price gravitated: the *sufficient price, below* which in the long run the product could not fall, if it were to be produced and brought to market.

Thus rent is now the *surplus over the natural price,* previously [it was] a *component part of the natural price;* now [it is the] effect, previously [it was] the cause, of price.

There is however no contradiction in Adam Smith's assertion that for certain products of the land, the circumstances of the market are always such that their ordinary price must be above their sufficient price, in other words: that *landed property* has the power to force the price above that level which would be sufficient for the capitalist if he were not confronted by a counteracting influence.

||626| Having thus, in Chapter XI, thrown overboard chapters V, VI and VII, he calmly proceeds by saying that: he will

now make it his business to consider 1. the produce of the land which always affords rent; 2. the produce of the land which sometimes affords rent and sometimes not; finally 3. the variations which take place, in the different periods of development of society, in the relative value, partly of these two sorts of produce compared with one another and partly in their relationship to manufactured commodities.

[2. Adam Smith's Hypothesis Regarding the Special Character of the Demand for Agricultural Produce. Physiocratic Elements in Smith's Theory of Rent]

"Part I. Of the Produce of Land which always affords Rent."
Adam Smith begins with the theory of population. The *means of subsistence* always create a *demand* for themselves. If the means of subsistence increase, then the people, the consumers of the means of subsistence, also increase. The supply of these commodities thus *creates* the demand for them.

"As men, like all other animals, *naturally multiply in proportion to the means of their subsistence, food is always more or less in demand.* It can always purchase or command a greater or smaller quantity of labour, and somebody can always be found who is willing to do something in order to obtain it" ([O.U.P., Vol. I, p. 165; Garnier,] l. I, ch. XI p. 305).

"But ⟨why?⟩ "*land*, in almost any situation, *produces a greater quantity of food* than what is sufficient *to maintain all the labour* necessary for bringing it to market, in the most liberal way in which that labour is ever maintained. The *surplus*, too, is always more than sufficient *to replace the stock which employed that labour, together with its profits.* Something, therefore, always remains for a rent to the landlord" ([O.U.P., Vol. I, p. 166; Garnier,] l.c., pp. 305-06).

This sounds quite *physiocratic* and contains neither proof nor explanation of why the "*price*" of these particular commodities pays a rent, a surplus over and *above* the "sufficient price".

As an example he immediately refers to *pasture* and *uncultivated pasture*. Then follows the proposition on *differential rent:*

"The rent of land not only varies with its fertility, whatever be its produce, but with its situation, whatever be its fertility" ([ibid., p. 166] l.c., p. 133).

On this occasion rent and profit appear as mere *surplus* of the *product,* after that part of it has been deducted *in kind* which *feeds* the *worker.* (This is really the physiocratic view, which is based on the fact that in an agricultural country man lives almost exclusively on the agricultural product, and industry, manufacture, itself appears as a rural side-line which uses the *local product* of nature.)

"A greater quantity of labour, therefore, must be maintained out of it[a]; and the *surplus, from which are drawn both the profit of the farmer* and *the rent of the landlord*, must be diminished" ([O.U.P., Vol. I, p. 166; Garnier,] l.c., p. 307).

The growing of corn must therefore yield a greater profit than *pasture*.

"A *cornfield* of moderate fertility produces a much *greater quantity of food for man* than the best pasture of equal extent."

(Thus it is not a question of price here, but of the absolute quantity of food for man.)

"Though its cultivation requires *much more labour*, yet the *surplus* which remains after replacing the seed and *maintaining all that labour*, is likewise much greater."

(Although corn costs *more labour*, the cornfield yields a larger *surplus* of food, after labour has been paid, than a meadow used for stock raising. And it is *worth more,* not because corn costs more labour, but because the surplus in corn contains more nourishment.)

"If a pound of butcher's meat, therefore, was *never* supposed to be *worth more* than a pound of bread, this *greater surplus*" (because the same area of land yields more pounds of corn than meat) "would everywhere be of *greater value*," (because it is *assumed*, that a pound of bread equals a pound of meat (in value), and that, after the workers have been fed, more pounds of bread than pounds of meat are left over from the same area of land) "and constitute a greater fund both for the profit of the farmer and the *rent* of the landlord" ([O.U.P., Vol. I, pp. 167-68; Garnier,] l.c., pp. 308-09).

Having replaced the natural price by the sufficient price, and declared rent to be the surplus over and above the sufficient price, Smith forgets altogether, that it is a question of *price,* and derives rent from the ratio between the amount of *food* yielded by agriculture and the amount of *food* consumed by the agricultural worker.

In point of fact—apart from this *physiocratic* interpretation— he *postulates* that the *price* of the agricultural product which supplies the principal food pays *rent* in addition to profit. This is the starting-point for his further arguments. With the extension

---

a i.e., out of the product of the land situated at a greater distance from the market.—*Ed.*

of cultivation, the natural pastures become insufficient for stock raising and cannot satisfy the demand for butcher's meat. Cultivated land has to be employed for this purpose. ||627| The price of meat therefore has to rise to the point where it pays not only the *labour* which is employed in stock raising, but also:

"*the rent which the landlord, and the profit which the farmer, could have drawn from such land employed in tillage.* The cattle bred upon the most uncultivated moors, when brought to the same market, are, in proportion to their weight or goodness, sold at the same price as those which are reared upon the most improved land. The proprietors of those moors profit by it, and raise the rent of their land in *proportion to the price of their cattle.*"

(In this passage Adam Smith correctly derives the differential rent from the surplus of the market-value over the individual value. In this case, however, the market-value rises, not because there is a transition from better to worse, but from less fertile to more fertile land.)

"It is thus that, in the progress of improvement, the *rent and profit of unimproved pasture* come to be regulated in some measure by the rent and profit of what is improved, and *these again by the rent and profit of corn*" ([O.U.P., Vol. I, pp. 168-69; Garnier,] pp. 310-11).

"But where there is no local advantage of this kind, the rent and profit of corn, or whatever else is the common vegetable food of the people, must naturally regulate, upon the land which is fit for producing it, the rent and profit of pasture.

"The use of the artificial grasses, of turnips, carrots, cabbages, and *the other expedients* which have been fallen upon to make an *equal quantity of land feed a greater number of cattle than when in natural grass,* should somewhat reduce, it might be expected, the superiority which, in an improved country, the price of butcher's meat naturally has over that of bread. It seems accordingly to have done so" etc. ([O.U.P., Vol. I, p. 171; Garnier,] l.c., p. 315).

Having thus set forth the *relationship between rent yielded by pasture and by tilled land,* Smith continues:

"In all great countries, the greater part of the cultivated lands are employed in producing either food for men or food for cattle. The rent and profit of these regulate the rent and profit of all other cultivated land. If any particular produce afforded less, the land would soon be turned into corn or pasture; and if any afforded more, some part of the lands in corn or pasture would soon be turned to that produce" ([O.U.P., Vol. I, pp. 172-73; Garnier,] l.c., p. 318).

Then he speaks of vineyards, fruit and vegetable gardens, etc

"The rent and profit of those productions, therefore, which require either a greater original expense of improvement in order to fit the land for them, or a greater annual expense of cultivation, though often much superior to those of corn and pasture, yet when they do no more than compensate such extraordinary expense, are in reality regulated by the rent and profit of those common crops" ([O.U.P., Vol. I, p. 176; Garnier,] pp. 323-24).

Then he passes on to sugar cultivation in the colonies [and] tobacco.

"It is in this manner that the rent of the cultivated land, of which the produce is human food, regulates the rent of the greater part of other cultivated land."

"In Europe, corn is the principal produce of land, which serves immediately for human food. Except in particular situations, therefore, the rent of corn-land regulates in Europe that of all other cultivated land" ([O.U.P., Vol. I, p. 180; Garnier,] l.c., pp. 331-32).

Adam Smith then returns to the physiocratic theory, as interpreted by him, namely that food creates consumers for itself. [He asserts that] if corn were replaced by some other crop, which with the same amount of labour yielded a much greater quantity of food on the most common land, then

"*the rent* of the landlord, o r *the surplus quantity of food* which would remain to him, after paying the labour, and replacing the stock of the farmer, together with its ordinary profits, would necessarily be much greater. Whatever was the rate at which labour was commonly maintained in that country, this *greater surplus could always maintain a greater quantity of it*, and, *consequently*, enable the landlord to purchase or command a greater quantity of it" ([O.U.P., Vol. I, p. 181; Garnier,] l.c., p. 332).

Adam Smith cites rice as an *example*.

"In Carolina ... the *planters*, as in other British colonies, *are generally both farmers and landlords*, and *rent, consequently, is confounded with profit*" ([O.U.P., Vol. I, p. 181; Garnier,] l.c., p. 333).

||628| The rice field, however

"is unfit either for corn, or pasture, or vineyard, or, indeed, for any other vegetable produce that is very useful to men; and the lands which are fit for those purposes are not fit for rice. Even in the rice countries, therefore, the rent of rice lands cannot regulate the rent of the other cultivated land which can never be turned to that produce" ([O.U.P., Vol. I, pp. 181-82; Garnier,] l.c., p. 334).

Second example potatoes (Ricardo's criticism of this has been mentioned earlier[a]). If potatoes became the principal food, in place of corn,

"...*the same quantity of cultivated land* would *maintain a much greater number of people*; and the labourers being generally fed with potatoes, a greater *surplus* would remain after replacing all the stock, and maintaining all the labour employed in cultivation. A greater share of this surplus, too,

---

a See this volume, p. 340.—*Ed.*

would belong to the landlord. Population would increase, and rents would rise much beyond what they are at present" ([O.U.P., Vol. I, p. 182; Garnier,] l.c., p. 335).

A few more comments on wheaten bread, bread made of oatmeal, and on potatoes conclude the first section of Chapter XI.

One can therefore sum up this section, which deals with the product of land *which always pays a rent,* as follows: after *postulating* the rent of the principal vegetable food, it sets forth how this rent regulates the rent of cattle-breeding, wine-growing, market gardening, etc. There is *nothing* about the nature of rent itself, except the general thesis that, *provided* rent exists, its amount is determined by fertility and situation. But this only relates to differences in rents, differences in the magnitude of rents. But why does his product always pay a rent? Why is its *ordinary price* always higher than its *sufficient price?* Smith leaves price out of account here and reverts to the physiocratic theory. What runs through it, however, is that the *demand* is always so great because the product itself creates the demand, [since it creates] its own consumers. Even provided that this were so it is incomprehensible why the demand should rise above the supply and thus force the price *above* the sufficient price. But there is here a secret recollection of the image of the *natural price* which includes rent as well as profit and wages and which is paid when supply corresponds with demand.

"When the quantity brought to market is just sufficient to supply the effectual demand, and no more, the *market price* naturally comes to be ... exactly ... the same with the *natural price*" ([O.U.P., Vol. I, p. 63; Garnier,] l.c., p. 114).

It is however characteristic that Adam Smith nowhere in this section states this clearly. In opening Chapter XI, he had just said that rent does not enter into price as a component part. The contradiction was too conspicuous.

[3. Adam Smith's Explanation of How the Relation Between Supply and Demand Affects the Various Types of Products from the Land. Smith's Conclusions Regarding the Theory of Rent]

"Part II: Of the Produce of Land which sometimes does, and sometimes does not, afford Rent."

It is actually only in this section that the general nature of rent is first discussed.

"Human *food* seems to be the only produce of land, which *always* and *necessarily* affords *some rent to the landlord*." (Why "always" and "necessarily", has not been shown.) "Other sorts of produce sometimes may, and sometimes may not, according to different circumstances" ([O.U.P., Vol. I, p. 183; Garnier,] l. c., p. 337).

"*After food, clothing and lodging* are the two great wants of mankind.

"Land, in its original rude state, can afford the materials of clothing and lodging to a *much greater number of people* than it can *feed*." As a result of this "*superabundance* of those materials" in proportion to the number of people the land can feed, i.e., in proportion to the population, these materials "cost" little or nothing. A large part of these "materials" lies around unused and useless "and the price of what is used is *considered as equal only to the labour and expense of fitting it for use*." This price however affords "no rent to the landlord". On the other hand, where the land is in an improved state, the number of people whom "it can feed", i.e., the population, is greater than the quantity of those materials which it supplies, at least "in the way in which they require them, and are willing to pay for them". There is a relative "scarcity" of these materials "which necessarily augments their value" ... "there is *frequently a demand for more than can be had*." More is paid for them than "the expense of bringing them to market. Their price, therefore, can always *afford some rent* to the landlord" ([O.U.P., Vol. I, p. 184; Garnier,] l. c., pp. 338 to 339).

||629| Here therefore an explanation of rent [is] derived, from the *excess of demand* over the *supply* which can be provided at the *sufficient price*.

The original materials of clothing were the furs and skins "of the larger animals". Among nations of hunters and shepherds, whose food consists chiefly of the flesh of animals, "every man, *by providing himself with food, provides himself with the materials of more clothing than he can wear*". Without foreign trade, the greater part of them would be thrown away as useless. Through the additional demand provided by foreign trade, the price of this surplus of materials is raised "*above what it costs to send them*" to be sold. This price "affords, *therefore*, some rent to the landlord". Through its market in Flanders, English wool thus added "something to the rent of the land which produced it" ([O.U.P., Vol. I, pp. 184-85; Garnier,] l.c., pp. 339-40).

Foreign trade here raises the *price* of an agricultural by-product to such an extent, that the land which produces it can yield some rent.

"The *materials of lodging* cannot always be transported to so great a distance as those of clothing, and do not so readily become an object of foreign commerce. When they are *superabundant* in the country which produces them, it frequently happens, even in the present commercial state of the world, that they are *of no value to the landlord*." Thus a stone quarry in the neighbourhood of London may yield a rent, whereas in many parts of Scotland and Wales, it may not. Similarly with timber. "In a populous and well-cultivated country" it will provide a rent, but "in many parts of North America" it will rot on the ground. The landowner would be glad to get rid of it. "When the materials of lodging are so superabundant, the part made use of is worth only the labour and expense of fitting it for that use. It affords no rent to the landlord, who generally grants the use of it to whoever takes the trouble of asking it. The *demand* of wealthier nations, however, sometimes enables him to get a rent for it" ([O.U.P., Vol. I, pp. 185-86; Garnier,] l.c., pp. 340-41).

Countries are populated, not in proportion to the "number of people whom their produce *can clothe and lodge*, but in proportion to that *of those whom it can feed*. When food is provided, it is easy to find the necessary clothing and lodging. But though these are at hand, it may often be difficult to find food. In some parts of the British Dominions, what is called a house may be built by one day's labour of one man." Among savage and barbarous nations, a hundredth of the labour of a whole year will be sufficient to provide them with what they require in clothing and lodging. The other 99 hundredths [are] often necessary to provide them with the food they need. "But when, by the improvement and cultivation of land, the *labour of one family can provide food for two*, the labour of half the society becomes sufficient to provide food for the whole." The other half can then satisfy the other wants and fancies of mankind. The principal objects of those wants and fancies are *clothing, lodging, household furniture*, and what is called *luxury*. The desire for food is limited. Those other desires are unlimited. Those who possess a surplus of food "are always willing to exchange the surplus". "The poor, in order *to obtain food*", exert themselves to satisfy those "fancies" of the rich, and, moreover, compete with one another in their endeavours. The number of workmen increases with the quantity of food, i.e., in proportion to the progress of agriculture. [The nature of] their "business admits of the utmost subdivisions of labour"; the quantity of materials which they work up therefore increases even more rapidly than their numbers. "Hence arises a demand for every sort of material which human invention can employ, either usefully or ornamentally, in building, dress, equipage, or household furniture; for the fossils and minerals contained in the bowels of the earth, the precious metals, and the precious stones.

"*Food* is, *in this manner*, not only the original source of *rent*, but every other part of the produce of land which afterwards affords rent, derives *that part of its value from the improvement of the powers of labour in producing food*, by means of the improvement and cultivation of land" ([O.U.P., Vol. I, pp. 186-88; Garnier,] l.c., pp. 342-45).

What Smith says here, is the true physical basis of Physiocracy, namely, that the creation of surplus-value (including rent) always has its basis in the relative productivity of agriculture. The first real form of surplus-value is surplus of agricultural produce (food), and the first real form of surplus labour arises when one person is able to produce the food for two. Otherwise this has nothing to do with the development of rent, this specific form of surplus-value, which presupposes capitalist production. Adam Smith continues:

The other parts of the produce of the land (apart from food), which later afford rent, do not afford it always. The *demand* for them, even in the most cultivated countries, is not always *great enough*, "to afford a greater *price*

*than what is sufficient to pay the labour, and replace, together with its ordi-
nary profits, the stock which must be employed in bringing them to market.
||630| Whether it is or is not such, depends upon different circumstances"*
([O.U.P., Vol. I, p. 188; Garnier,] l. c., p. 345).

Here therefore again: Rent arises from the *demand* being greater than the supply at the *sufficient price* which *only includes
wages and profits, but no rent.* What else does this mean, but
that the *supply* at the sufficient price is so great that *landed property* cannot offer any resistance to the equalisation of capitals
or labour? That therefore, even though landed property exists
legally, it does not exist in practice, or cannot be effective as such
in practice? Adam Smith's mistake is that he fails to recognise
that if landed property sells [products] *above* the sufficient price,
it sells [them] at their *value.* His positive point, compared with
Ricardo, is that he realises it depends on the circumstances,
whether or not landed property can assert itself economically. It
is therefore essential to follow this part of his argument step by
step. He begins with the coal mine, then goes over to timber and
then returns to the coal mine, etc. Accordingly we shall let him
start with *timber.*

The *price of wood* varies with the state of agriculture, for the same reasons as does the price of cattle. When agriculture was in its infancy, forests
were dominant and a sheer nuisance to the landowner, who would gladly
give it to anyone for the cutting. As agriculture advances, there is clearance
of forests, partly through the expansion of tillage, partly through the increase
in herds of cattle, which eat up, gnaw at, roots and young trees. "These"
[cattle] though they do not increase in the same proportion as corn, *which is
altogether the acquisition of human industry,* yet multiply under the care
and protection of men." The scarcity of wood, thus created, raises its *price.*
Hence it can afford so high a rent that tilled land (or land that could be
used for tillage) is converted into woodland. This is the case in Great Britain.
The rent of wood can never, for any length of time, rise above that of corn
or pasture, but it may reach that level ([O.U.P., Vol. I, pp. 189-90; Garnier,]
l.c., pp. 347-49).

Thus in fact, the rent of woodland is by nature identical with
that of pasture. It belongs therefore in this category, although
wood does not serve for food. The economic category does not
depend on the *use-value* of the product, but on whether or not
it is convertible into arable land and vice versa.

Coal mines. Smith observes correctly, that the fertility or infertility of mines in general depends on whether the same quantity of labour can extract a larger or a smaller amount of mineral
from the mine. *Infertility* can offset the *favourable* situation, so

that such mines cannot be exploited at all. On the other hand, an *unfavourable* situation can offset the *fertility,* so that despite its natural fertility, such a mine cannot be exploited. This is in particular the case where there are neither good roads, nor shipping ([O.U.P., Vol. I, pp. 188-89; Garnier,] l.c., pp. 346-47).

There are mines whose produce just reaches the *sufficient price.* Hence they pay profit for the entrepreneur but no rent. They can therefore be worked only by the landowner himself. In this way he gets "the ordinary profit of the capital which he employs". There are many mines of this type in Scotland. These could not be exploited in any other way.

"*The landlord will allow nobody else to work them without paying some rent, and nobody can afford to pay any*" ([O.U.P., Vol. I, p. 188; Garnier,] l.c., p. 346).

Here Adam Smith has correctly defined under what circumstances land which has been *appropriated* pays no rent, namely where landowner and entrepreneur are *one* person. He has already told us earlier that this is so in the colonies.

A farmer cannot cultivate the land there because he cannot pay any rent. But the owner can cultivate it with profit, although it does not pay him a rent. This is the case, for example, in the colonies in Western America, because new land can always be appropriated. The land as such is not an element that offers resistance, and the competition of landowners who cultivate the land themselves is here in fact competition between workers or capitalists. The position of coal mines, or mines in general, is different in the supposed circumstances. The market-value, as determined by the mines which supply their product at this value, yields a smaller rent, or no rent at all but just covers the cost-price in the case of mines that are less fertile or less favourably situated. These mines can only be worked by persons for whom the resistance of landed property and the consequent exclusion of others from the land, does not exist, because they are landowners and capitalists in one person; [this] only happens where in fact *landed property* disappears as an independent element opposed to capital. The position differs from that of the colonies in that: in the latter, the landowner cannot prohibit the exploitation of *new* land by anyone. In the former he can do so. He only gives himself the permission to exploit the mine. This does not enable him to draw a rent, but it does enable him to exclude others and to invest his capital in the mine, with profit.

What Adam Smith writes about the regulation of rent by the most fertile mine, I have already commented on, when discussing Ricardo and his polemic.[a] Here only one proposition needs to be stressed:

"The *lowest price*" (previously sufficient price) "at which coals can be sold for any considerable time, is, like that of all other commodities, the *price which is barely sufficient to replace, together with its ordinary profits, the stock which must be employed in bringing them to market*" ([O.U.P., Vol. I, p. 191; Garnier,] l. c., p. 350).

It is evident that the *sufficient price* has taken the place of the *natural price*. Ricardo regards them as identical, and rightly so. ||631| Smith maintains,

that the rent of coal mines is much smaller than that of agricultural products: while with the latter the rent commonly amount to one third [of the gross produce], in coal mines a fifth is a very great rent, and a tenth the common rent. *Metal mines* are not so dependent on their situation, since [their products] are more easily transported and the world market is therefore open to them. Their value, therefore, is more dependent on their fertility than their situation, while with coal mines, the opposite is the case. The products of the most distant metal mines compete with one another. "The price, therefore, of the coarse, and still more that of the precious metals, *at the most fertile mines* in the world, must necessarily more or less affect their price at every other in it" ([O.U.P., Vol. I, pp. 191-92; Garnier,] l.c., pp. 351-52).

"The price of every metal, at every mine, therefore, being regulated in some measure by its price at the most fertile mine in the world that is actually wrought, *it* can, at the greater part of mines, do *very little more than pay the expense of working*, and can *seldom* afford a very high rent to the landlord. Rent accordingly, seems at the greater part of mines to have but a small share in the price of the coarse, and a still smaller in that of the precious metals. Labour and profit make up the greater part of both" ([O.U.P., Vol. I, p. 192; Garnier,] l.c., pp. 353-54).

Adam Smith correctly sets forth here the case presented in *Table C*.[b]

When speaking of *rent* in connection with precious metals, Adam Smith again gives his interpretation of the sufficient price, which he puts in the place of the natural price. Where he speaks of non-agricultural industry, he has no need for this, since the sufficient and the natural price coincide here, according to his original explanation namely that it is the price which repays the capital outlay plus the average profit.

"The lowest price at which the precious metals can be sold ... during any considerable time, is regulated by the same principles which fix the lowest ordinary price of all other goods. The stock which must commonly be

---

a See this volume, pp. 338-40.—*Ed.*

b See the insertion between pages 264 and 265.—*Ed.*

employed, the food, clothes, and lodging, which must commonly be consumed in bringing them from the mine to the market, determine it. It must at least be sufficient to replace that stock, with the ordinary profits" ([O.U.P., Vol. I, p. 195; Garnier,] l.c., p. 359).

With regard to *precious stones,* he observes that:

"The *demand for the precious stones* arises altogether from their beauty. They are of no use but as ornaments; and the merit of their beauty is *greatly enhanced by their scarcity, or by the difficulty and expense of getting them from the mine.* Wages and profit accordingly make up, upon most occasions, almost the whole of the high price. Rent comes in but for a very small share, frequently no share; and the most fertile mines only afford any considerable rent" ([O.U.P., Vol. I, p. 197; Garnier,] l.c., p. 361).

There can only be a differential rent here.

"As the price, both of the precious metals and of the precious stones, is regulated all over the world by their price at the most fertile mine in it, the rent which a mine of either can afford to its proprietor is in proportion, not to its *absolute,* but to what may be called its *relative* fertility, or to its superiority over other mines of the same kind. If new mines were discovered as much superior to those of Potosi as they were superior to those of Europe, the value of silver might be so much degraded as to render even the mines of Potosi not worth the working" ([O.U.P., Vol. I, p. 197; Garnier,] l.c., p. 362).

The products of the less fertile precious metal and precious stone mines carry no rent, because it is *always* the most fertile mine which determines market-value and ever more fertile new mines are being opened up—the line is always in the ascending direction. Hence they are sold *below* their value, merely at their cost-price.

"A produce, of which the value is principally derived from its scarcity, is necessarily degraded by its abundance" ([O.U.P., Vol. I, p. 198; Garnier,] l. c., p. 363).

Then Adam Smith's argument again goes somewhat wrong.

"It is otherwise in estates above ground. The value, both of their produce and of their rent, is in proportion to their *absolute,* and not to their *relative* fertility. The land which produces a certain quantity of food, clothes, and lodging, can always feed, clothe, and lodge a certain number of people; and *whatever may be the proportion of the landlord"* (the very question is whether he takes any share of the produce, and in what proportion) ||632| "it will always give him a proportionable command of the labour of those people, and of the commodities with which that labour can supply him" ([O.U.P., Vol. I, p. 198; Garnier,] l.c., pp. 363-64).

"The value of the most barren lands is not diminished by the neighbourhood of the most fertile. On the contrary, it is generally increased by it. The great number of people maintained by the fertile lands *afford a market to many parts of the produce of the barren,* which they could never have found among those whom their own produce could maintain."

(But only if it does *not* produce *the same product* as the fertile lands in its neighbourhood; only if this product of the barren lands *does not compete* with that of the more fertile. In this case Adam Smith is right and indeed, this is of importance to the way in which the total amount of rent from different kinds of natural products may increase in consequence of the fertility of the land which yields food.)

"Whatever increases the fertility of land in producing food, increases not only the value of the lands upon which the improvement is bestowed" (it may reduce this value and even destroy it), "but contributes likewise to increase that of many other lands, by creating a new demand for their produce" or, *rather* by creating a demand for *new* products." ([O.U.P., Vol. I, p. 198; Garnier,] l. c., p. 364.)

But in all this, Adam Smith does not offer any explanation for absolute rent, which he presupposes to exist for land that produces food. He is correct when he observes that it does not necessarily exist for other lands, mines, for instance, because they are always available in such *relatively* unlimited quantities (in comparison with demand), that landed property cannot offer any resistance to capital [so that] even if it exists in a legal sense, it does not exist in the economic sense.

(See *p. 641* on *house rent*.)[96] |632||

*   *   *

||641| See p. 632. On *house rent Adam Smith* says:

"Whatever part of the whole rent of a house is *over and above what is sufficient* for affording this reasonable *profit*" (to the builder) "naturally goes to the ground-rent; and where the owner of the ground, and the owner of the building, are two different persons, it is in most cases, completely paid to the former. In country houses, at a distance from any great town, where there is a plentiful choice of ground, the ground-rent is scarcely any thing, or no more than what the space upon which the house stands, would pay employed in agriculture." (Book V, Chapter II.)[97]

In the case of the ground-rent of houses, *situation* constitutes just as decisive a factor for the differential rent, as fertility (and situation) in the case of agricultural rent.

Adam Smith shares with the Physiocrats, not only the partiality for agriculture and the landlord, but also the view that they are particularly suitable objects of taxation. He says:

"Both ground-rents, and the ordinary rent of land, are a species of revenue, which the owner in many cases enjoys, without any care or attention of his own. Though a part of this revenue should be taken from him, in order to defray the expenses of the State, no discouragement will thereby be given to any sort of industry. The annual produce of the land and labour of the society, the real wealth and revenue of the great body of the people, might be the same after such a tax as before. Ground-rents, and the ordinary rent of land are, therefore, perhaps, the species of revenue, which can best bear to have a peculiar tax imposed upon them" (Book V, Ch. II).

The considerations which Ricardo (p. 230)[98] advances against Adam Smith's views on the subject, are very philistine. |641||

[4. Adam Smith's Analysis of the Variations in the Prices of Products of the Land]

||632| *"Part III. Of the variations in the Proportion between the respective Values of that sort of Produce which always af-fords Rent, and of that which sometimes does, and sometimes does not, afford Rent."* ([Garnier,] Book I, Vol. II, Ch. XI.)

"In a country naturally fertile, but of which the far greater part is altogether uncultivated, cattle, poultry, game of all kinds, etc., *as they can be acquired with a very small quantity of labour, so they will purchase or command but a very small quantity."* ([O.U.P.,] Vol. I, p. 212; Garnier,] Vol. II, p. 25.)

The *peculiar* manner in which Adam Smith mixes up the measuring of value by the quantity of labour, with the price of labour or the quantity of labour which a commodity can command, is evident from the above quotation, and especially from the following passage, which also shows how it has come about that at times he elevates corn to the measure of value.

"In every state of society, in every stage of improvement, *corn is the production of human industry.* But the average produce of every sort of industry is always suited, more or less exactly, to the average consumption; the average supply to the average demand. *In every different stage of improvement,* besides, *the raising* of equal quantities of corn in the same soil and climate, will, at an average, *require* nearly *equal quantities of labour; o r,* what comes to the same thing, *the price of nearly equal quantities;* the continual increase of the productive powers of labour, in an improved state of cultivation, being more or less counterbalanced by the *continual* increasing *price of cattle,* the *principal instruments* of agriculture. Upon all these accounts, therefore, we may rest assured, that *equal quantities of corn* will, *in every state of society,* in every state of improvement, more nearly *represent, o r be equivalent to, equal quantities of labour,* than equal quantities of any other part of the rude produce of land. Corn, accordingly ... is, in all the different stages of wealth and improvement, a more accurate measure of value than any other commodity or set of commodities. ... *Corn,* besides, or whatever else is the common and favourite vegetable food of the people, constitutes, in every civilised country, the *principal part of the subsistence of the labourer....* The money price of labour, therefore, depends much more upon the average money price of corn, the subsistence of the labour, than upon that of butcher's meat, or of any other part of the rude produce of land. The real value of gold and silver, therefore, the real quantity of labour which they can purchase or command, depends much more upon the quantity of corn which they can purchase or command, than upon that of butcher's meat, or any other part of the rude produce of land" ([O.U.P., Vol. I, pp. 213-14; Garnier,] l.c., pp. 26-28).

When comparing the value of gold and silver, Adam Smith once more sets forth his views on the sufficient price and notes ||633| expressly that *it excludes rent:*

"A commodity may be said to be *dear* or *cheap* not only according to the absolute greatness or smallness of its usual price, but according as that price is more or less above the lowest for which it is possible to bring it to market for any considerable time together. *This lowest price is that which barely replaces, with a moderate profit, the stock which must be employed in bringing the commodity thither. It is the price which affords nothing to the landlord, of which rent makes not any component part, but which resolves itself altogether into wages and profit*" ([O.U.P., Vol. I, p. 243; Garnier,] Vol. II, p. 81).
"The price of diamonds and other precious stones may, perhaps, be still nearer to the lowest price at which it is possible to bring them to market, than even the price of gold" ([O.U.P., Vol. I, p. 244; Garnier,] Vol. II, p. 83).

There are three sorts of raw products ([O.U.P., Vol. I, p. 248; Garnier,] Vol. II, p. 89). The *first,* whose increase is almost, or entirely, independent of human industry; the *second,* which can be increased in proportion to the demand; the *third,* upon whose increase human industry only exercises a "limited or uncertain" influence.

First sort: Fishes, rare birds, different sorts of game, almost all wild-fowl, in particular the birds of passage, etc. The demand for these increases greatly with wealth and luxury.

"The quantity of such commodities, therefore, remaining the same, or nearly the same, while the competition to purchase them is continually increasing, their price may rise to any degree of extravagance" ([O.U.P., Vol. I, pp. 248-49; Garnier,] Vol. II, p. 91).
Second sort: "It consists in those useful plants and animals, which, in uncultivated countries, nature produces with such profuse abundance, that they are of little or no value, and which, as cultivation advances, are therefore forced to give place to some more profitable produce. During a long period in the progress of improvement, the quantity of these is continually diminishing, while, at the same time, the demand for them is continually increasing. Their real value, therefore, the real quantity of labour which they will purchase or command, gradually rises, till at last it gets so high as to render them as profitable a produce as any thing else which human industry can raise upon the most fertile and best cultivated land. When it has got so high, it cannot

well go higher. If it did, more land and more industry would soon be employed to increase their quantity" ([O.U.P., Vol. I, pp. 250-51; Garnier,] Vol. II, pp. 94-95). So, for instance, with cattle.

"Of all the different substances, however, which compose this second sort of rude produce, cattle is, perhaps, that of which the price, in the progress of improvement, rises first to this height" ([O.U.P., Vol. I, p. 252; Garnier,] Vol. II, pp. 96-97). "As cattle are among the first, so perhaps *venison* is among the last parts of this sort of rude produce which bring this price" (i.e., that price which makes it worth while cultivating the soil in order to feed them). "The price of venison in Great Britain, how extravagant soever it may appear, is not near sufficient to compensate the expense of a deer park, as is well known to all those who have had any experience in the feeding of deer" ([O.U.P., Vol. I, p. 256; Garnier,] Vol. II, p. 104).

"Thus, in every farm, the offals of the barn and stable will maintain a certain number of *poultry*. These, as they are fed with what would otherwise be lost, are a mere save-all; and as they cost the farmer scarce any thing, so he can afford to sell them for very little." While this supply is sufficient, poultry [is] as cheap as butcher's meat. With the growth of wealth, the demand grows, and consequently the price of poultry [rises] *above* that of butcher's meat, until "it becomes profitable to cultivate land for the sake of feeding them" ([O.U.P., Vol. I, p. 257; Garnier,] Vol. II, pp. 105-06). Thus in *France*, etc.

The *hog*, like poultry, is "originally kept as a save-all." It lives on refuse. In the end the price rises until land must be cultivated specifically for its food ([O.U.P., Vol. I, pp. 258-59; Garnier,] Vol. II, pp. 108-09).

Milk, dairy farming ([O.U.P., Vol. I, p. 259, et. seq.; Garnier,] Vol. II, p. 110, et. seq.). (Butter, cheese ibid.)

According to Adam Smith, the gradual rise in the *price* of these raw products only proves that, little by little, they are becoming *products of human industry*, while previously, they were practically only *products of nature*. Their transformation from products of nature into products of industry is itself the result of the advance of cultivation, which is increasingly limiting the scope of the spontaneous productions of nature. On the other hand, under less developed conditions of production, a large part of these products was sold *below its value*. The commodities are sold *at* their value (hence the rise in prices), as soon as they cease to be a by-product and become an independent product of some branch of agriculture.

"The lands of no country, it is evident, can ever be completely cultivated and improved, till once the *price* of every produce, which human industry is obliged to raise upon them, has got so high as *to pay for the expense of complete improvement and cultivation*. In order to do this, the price of each particular produce must be sufficient, first, to pay the rent of good corn land, as it is that which regulates the rent of the greater part of other cultivated land; and, secondly, to pay the labour and expense of the farmer as well as they are commonly paid upon good corn land; or, in other words, *to replace with the ordinary profits the stock which he employs about it*. This *rise in the price* of each particular produce must evidently ||634| *be previous to* the improvement and cultivation of the land which is destined for raising it". "... those different sorts of rude produce ... *have become worth*, not only a greater quantity of silver, but a greater quantity of labour and subsistence than before. As it *costs a greater quantity of labour and subsistence to bring them to market*, so, when they are *brought thither*, they *represent or are equivalent to a greater quantity*" ([O.U.P., Vol I, pp. 261-62; Garnier,] Vol. II, pp. 113-15).

Here it is once more evident, how Smith is only able to use value as determined by the quantity of labour it [value] can buy, in so far as he confuses it with value as determined by the quantity of labour required for the production of the commodities.

Third sort: This is the raw product,

"in which the efficacy of human industry, in augmenting the quantity, is either limited or uncertain" ([O.U.P., Vol. I, p. 262; Garnier,] Vol. II, p. 115).

Wool and *raw hides* are limited by the number of large and small cattle that are kept. But the first *by-products* already have a *large market,* while the animal itself does not yet have this. The market for butcher's meat is almost always confined to the inland market. Wool and raw hides, even in the rude beginnings [of cultivation], are in most cases already sold in foreign markets. They are easily transported and furnish the raw material of many manufactured goods. They may thus find a market in countries which are more developed industrially when the industry in the country where they are produced does not yet require them.

"In countries ill cultivated, and therefore but thinly inhabited, the price of the wool and the hide bears always a much greater proportion to that of the whole beast, than in countries where, improvement and population being further advanced, there is more demand for butcher's meat." The same applies to "tallow". In the progress of industry and population, the rise in price of cattle affects the *carcase* more than the *wool* or *hide*. For with the increase in industry and population of a country, the market for meat expands, whereas that for the by-products already previously extended beyond the boundaries of the country. But with the development of industry in the country itself, the price for wool, etc., will nevertheless also rise somewhat. ([O.U.P., Vol. I, pp. 263-64; Garnier,] Vol. II, pp. 115-19).

Fish. ([Garnier,] Vol. II, pp. 129-30.) If the demand for fish rises, then its supply requires more labour. "The fish must generally be sought for at a greater distance, larger vessels must be employed, and more expensive machinery of every kind made use of." "... it will generally be impossible to supply the ... extended market, without employing a quantity of labour greater than in proportion to what had been requisite for supplying the narrow and confined one." "The *real price* of this commodity, therefore, naturally rises in the progress of improvement" ([O.U.P., Vol. I, p. 270; Garnier,] Vol. II, p. 130).

Here Adam Smith therefore determines the *real price* by the quantity of labour necessary for the production of the commodity.

According to Adam Smith, the *real price* of *vegetable food* (corn, etc.) must *fall* in the course of civilisation.

"The extension of improvement and cultivation, as it *necessarily raises* more or less, in proportion to the price of corn, *that of every sort of animal food*, so it as necessarily *lowers* that of, I believe, every sort of *vegetable food*. It raises the price of animal food; because a great part of the land which produces it, being rendered fit for producing corn, must afford to the landlord and farmer the rent and profit of corn land. It *lowers the price of vegetable food*; because, *by increasing the fertility of the land*, it increases its abundance. The improvements of agriculture, too, introduce many sorts of vegetable food, which requiring less land, and not more labour than corn, come much cheaper to market. Such are potatoes and maize.... Many sorts of vegetable food, besides, which in the rude state of agriculture are confined to the kitchen garden, and raised only by the spade, come, in its improved state, to be introduced into common fields, and to be raised by the plough; such as turnips, carrots, cabbages, etc." ([O.U.P., Vol. I, pp. 278-79; Garnier,] Vol. II, pp. 145-46).

Adam Smith sees that the *price of manufactured commodities* in general has fallen wherever

"the real price of the *rude materials* either does not rise at all, or does not rise very much" ([O.U.P., Vol. I, p. 280; Garnier,] p. 149).

On the other hand, he asserts that the real price of labour, i.e., wages, has risen with the progress in production. Hence also, according to him, the prices of commodities do not necessarily rise because of a rise in wages, or the price of labour, although wages [form] "a component part of the natural price" and even of the "sufficient price" or the "lowest price at which commodities can be brought to market". So how does Adam Smith explain this? By a fall in profits? No. (Although he assumes that the general rate of profit falls in the course of civilisation.) Or of rent? No again. He says:

"In consequence of better machinery, ||635| of greater dexterity, and of a more proper division and distribution of work, all of which are the natural effects of improvement, *a much smaller quantity of labour becomes requisite* for executing *any particular piece of work*; and though, in consequence of the *flourishing circumstances* of society, the *real price of labour should rise* very considerably, yet *the great diminution of the quantity*," requisite *for each particular article*,[a] "will generally much more than compensate the

---

[a] "requisite for each particular article" inserted by Garnier in the French version.—*Ed.*

greatest rise which can happen in the price." ([O.U.P., Vol. I, p. 280; Garnier,] Vol. II, p. 148.)

Thus the *value* of the commodities falls, because a smaller quantity of labour is required to produce them; the value moreover falls although the *real price* of labour rises. If here the *real price* of labour means the *value* [of labour], then the profit must fall, if the price of the commodity falls as a result of the fall in its value. If, on the other hand, it means the quantity of the means of subsistence received by the worker, then the Smithian thesis is correct even where profit is rising.

The extent to which Adam Smith uses the correct definition of value, wherever he actually analyses [facts] can be seen at the end of the chapter where he examines why *woollen cloths* were dearer in the 16th century, etc.

"It *cost a greater quantity of labour to bring the goods to market*. When they were brought thither, therefore, they must have purchased, or exchanged for the *price* of, a greater quantity" ([O.U.P., Vol. I, p. 284; Garnier,] Vol. II, p. 156).

The mistake here consists only in the use of the word *price*.

[5. Adam Smith's Views on the Movements of Rent and His Estimation of the Interests of the Various Social Classes]

Conclusion of the Chapter. Adam Smith concludes his chapter on rent with the observation that

"every improvement in the circumstances of the society tends, either directly or indirectly, to raise the real rent of land."

"The extension of improvement and cultivation tends to raise it directly. The landlord's share of the produce necessarily increases with the increase of the produce." The "rise in the real price of those parts of the rude produce of land, which is first the effect of the extended improvement and cultivation, and afterwards the cause of their being still further extended" for instance the rise in the price of cattle, raises, firstly, the real value of the landlord's share, but also the proportion of that share, because: "That produce, after the rise in its real price, *requires no more labour to collect it than before.* A *smaller proportion of it will*, therefore, *be sufficient to replace, with the ordinary profit, the stock which employs that labour.* A greater proportion of it must consequently belong to the landlord" ([O.U.P., Vol. I, pp. 285-86; Garnier,] Vol. II, pp. 158-59).

In exactly the same way Ricardo explains the increase in the proportion of rent, as the price of corn rises on the more fertile land. Only this rise in price is not the result of improvement, and

24*

therefore leads Ricardo to the opposite conclusion from Adam
Smith.

Adam Smith says that the landlord moreover benefits from
every development of the productive power of labour in manufacture.

"Whatever reduces the real price of the latter" [i.e., manufactured goods]
"raises that of the former" [i.e., of agricultural produce]. Furthermore, with
every increase of the real wealth of the society, the population increases;
with the population increases the demand for agricultural produce and
consequently the capital employed in agriculture; "and the rent increases
with the produce". On the other hand all circumstances which hinder the
growth of general wealth, will have the opposite effect and lead to a fall
in rent and hence a decrease in the real wealth of the landowners ([O.U.P.,
Vol. I, pp. 286-87; Garnier,] Vol. II, pp. 159-60).

From this Adam Smith concludes that the interests of the landlord are always in harmony with the "general interest of society".
This also applies to the *labourers* ([O.U.P., Vol. I, pp. 287-88;
Garnier,] Vol. II, pp. 161-62). But Adam Smith is honest enough
to make the following distinction:

"The order of proprietors may perhaps gain more by the prosperity of
the society than that of labourers; but there is no order that suffers so cruelly
from its" [society's] "decline" [as do the labourers] ([O.U.P., Vol. p. 288;
Garnier,] Vol. II, p. 162).

The interests of the capitalists (manufacturers and merchants),
on the other hand, are not identical with the

"general interest of the society...." "The interest of the dealers, however, in
any particular branch of trade or manufactures, is *always* in some respects
different from, and even *opposite* to, that of the public." [The dealers are]
"... an order of men, whose interest ||636| is never exactly the same with that
of the public, who have generally an interest to deceive and even to oppress
the public, and who accordingly have, upon many occasions, both deceived
and oppressed it" ([O.U.P., Vol. I, pp. 289-90; Garnier,] Vol. II, pp.
163-65).[99] |636||.

[CHAPTER XV]

RICARDO'S THEORY OF SURPLUS-VALUE

[A. THE CONNECTION BETWEEN RICARDO'S CONCEPTION OF SURPLUS-VALUE AND HIS VIEWS ON PROFIT AND RENT]

[1. Ricardo's Confusion of the Laws of Surplus-Value with the Laws of Profit]

||636| Nowhere does Ricardo consider *surplus-value* separately and independently from its particular forms—profit (interest) and rent. His observations on the organic composition of capital, which is of such decisive importance, are therefore confined to those differences in the organic composition which he took over from Adam Smith (actually from the Physiocrats), namely, those arising from the process of circulation (fixed and circulating capital). Nowhere does he touch on or perceive the differences in the organic composition within the actual process of production. Hence his confusion of *value* with *cost-price*, his wrong theory of rent, his erroneous laws relating to the causes of the rise and fall in the rate of profit, etc.

Profit and surplus-value are only identical when the capital advanced is identical with the capital laid out directly in wages. (Rent is not taken into account here since the surplus-value is, in the first place, entirely appropriated by the capitalist, [irrespective of] what portion he has subsequently to hand over to his co-partners. Furthermore, Ricardo himself presents rent as an item which is separated, detached from profit.) In his observations on profit and wages, Ricardo also abstracts from the constant part of capital, which is not laid out in wages. He treats the matter as though the entire capital were laid out directly in wages. *To this extent*, therefore, he considers *surplus-value* and *not profit*, hence it is possible to speak of his theory of surplus-value. On the other hand, however, he thinks that he is dealing with profit as such, and in fact views which are based on the assumption of profit and not of surplus-value, constantly creep in. Where he correctly sets forth the laws of surplus-value, he distorts them by immediately expressing them as laws of profit. On the other hand, he seeks to present the laws of profit directly, without the intermediate links, as laws of surplus-value.

When we speak of his theory of surplus-value, we are, therefore, speaking of his theory of profit, in so far as he confuses the latter with surplus-value, i.e., in so far as he only considers profit in relation to variable capital, the part of capital laid out in wages. We shall later deal with what he says of profit as distinct from surplus-value.

It is so much in the nature of the subject-matter that surplus-value can only be considered in relation to the variable capital, i.e., capital laid out directly in wages—and without an understanding of surplus-value no theory of profit is possible—that Ricardo treats the entire capital as variable capital and *abstracts* from constant capital, although he occasionally mentions it in the form of advances.

||637| In Chapter XXVI *"On Gross and Net Revenue"* Ricardo speaks of:

"trades where *profits* are in *proportion to the capital*, and not in proportion to the *quantity of labour* employed" ([David Ricardo, *On the Principles of Political Economy, and Taxation*, third edition,] p. 418).

What does his whole doctrine of average profit (on which his theory of rent depends) mean, but that profits are "in proportion to the *capital*, and *not* in proportion to the *quantity of labour* employed"? If they were "in proportion to the quantity of labour employed", then equal capitals would yield very *unequal* profits, since their profit would be equal to the surplus-value created in their own sphere of production; the surplus-value however depends not on the size of the capital as a whole, but on the size of the variable capital, which is equivalent to the quantity of labour employed. What then is the meaning of attributing to a specific use of capital, to *specific trades*, by way of exception, that in them profits are proportionate to the amount of capital and not to the quantity of labour employed? With a given rate of surplus-value, the amount of surplus-value for a particular capital must always depend, not on the absolute size of the capital, but on the quantity of labour employed. On the other hand, if the average rate of profit is given, the amount of profit must always depend on the size of the capital employed and not on the quantity of labour employed. Ricardo expressly mentions the

"carrying trade, the distant foreign trade, and trades where expensive machinery is required" (l.c., p. 418).

That is to say, he speaks of trades which employ relatively large amounts of constant, and little variable capital. At the same time, they are trades in which, compared with others, the *total amount* of the capital advanced is large, or which can only be carried on with *large capitals*. If the rate of profit is given, the amount of profit depends entirely on the *size* of the capitals advanced. This, however, by no means distinguishes the trades in which large capitals and much constant capital are employed (the two always go together) from those in which small capitals are employed, but is merely an application of the theory that equal capitals yield equal profits, a larger capital therefore yields more profit than a smaller capital. This has nothing to do with the "quantity of labour employed". But whether the rate of profit in general is great or small, depends indeed on the total quantity of labour employed by the capital of the whole class of capitalists and on the proportion of *unpaid* labour; and, lastly, on the ratio of the capital spent on labour and the capital that is merely reproduced as a condition of production.

Ricardo himself argues against Adam Smith's view,

"... that the great profits which are sometimes made by particular merchants in foreign trade, will elevate the general rate of profits in the country..." (l.c., Chapter VII "*On Foreign Trade*", p. 132).

He says:

"... They contend, that the equality of profits will be brought about by the general rise of profits; and I am of opinion, that the profits of the favoured trade will speedily subside to the general level" (l.c., pp. 132-33).

We shall see later, how far his view is correct that exceptional profits (when they are not caused by the rise in market-price above the value) do not raise the general rate of profit *in spite of the equalisation* of profits, and also how far his view is correct that foreign trade and the expansion of the market can*not* raise the rate of profit.[a] But granted that he is right, and, on the whole granted "the equality of profits", how can he distinguish between trades "where profits are in *proportion to the capital*"

---

[a] See this volume, pp. 436-37 and 468-69.—*Ed.*

and others where they are "in proportion to the quantity of labour employed"?

In Chapter XXVI, "*On Gross and Net Revenue*", quoted above, Ricardo says:

"I admit, that from the nature of rent, a given capital employed in agriculture, on any but the land last cultivated, puts in motion a greater quantity of labour than an equal capital employed in manufactures and trade" (l.c., p. 419).

The whole statement is nonsense. In the first place, according to Ricardo, a greater quantity of labour is employed on the land last cultivated than on all the other land. That is why, according to him, rent arises on the other land. How, therefore, is a given capital to set in motion a greater quantity of labour than in manufactures and trade, on all other land *except* the land last cultivated? That the product of the better land has a *market-value* that is *higher* than the *individual* value, which is determined by the quantity of labour employed by the capital that cultivates it, is surely not the same thing as that this capital "puts in motion a greater quantity of labour than an equal capital employed in manufactures and trade"? But it would have been correct, had Ricardo said that, apart from differences in the fertility of the land, altogether rent arises because agricultural capital sets in motion a greater quantity of labour in proportion to the constant part of the capital, than does the average non-agricultural capital.

||638| Ricardo overlooks the fact that, *with a given surplus-value,* various factors may raise or lower and in general influence the rate of profit. Because he identifies surplus-value with profit, he quite consistently seeks to demonstrate that the rise and fall in the rate of profit is caused only by circumstances that make the rate of surplus-value rise or fall. Apart from the circumstances which, when the amount of surplus-value is given, influence the *rate of profit*, although not the *amount of profit*, he furthermore overlooks the fact that the rate of profit depends on the *a m o u n t   o f   s u r p l u s-v a l u e*, and by no means on the *rate of surplus-value*. When the rate of surplus-value, i.e., of surplus-labour, is given, the amount of surplus-value depends on the organic composition of the capital, that is to say, on the number of workers which a capital of given value, for instance £ 100, employs. It depends on the rate of surplus-value if the organic composition of the capital is given. It is thus determined by two factors: the number of workers simultaneously employed

and the rate of surplus-labour. If the capital increases, then the amount of surplus-value also increases whatever its organic composition, provided it remains unchanged. But this in no way alters the fact that for a capital of given value, for example 100, it [the amount of surplus-value] remains the same. If in this case it is 10, then it is 100 for £ 1,000, but this does not alter the proportion.

⟨Ricardo:

"There cannot be *two rates of profit in the same employment*, and therefore when the value of produce is in different proportions to capital, it is the rent which will differ, and not the profit" (l.c., Chapter XII *"Land-Tax,"* pp. 212-13).

This only applies to the normal rate of profit "in the same employment". Otherwise it is in direct contradiction to the statements quoted earlier on[a]:

"The exchangeable value of all commodities, whether they be manufactured, or the produce of the mines, or the produce of land, is always regulated, not by the less quantity of labour that will suffice for their production under circumstances highly favourable, and exclusively enjoyed by those who have peculiar facilities of production; but by the greater quantity of labour necessarily bestowed on their production by those who have no such facilities; by those who continue to produce them under the most unfavourable circumstances; meaning—*by the most unfavourable circumstances, the most unfavourable under which the quantity of produce required, renders it necessary to carry on the production"* (l.c., Chapter II *"On Rent"*, pp. 60-61).⟩

In Chapter XII *"Land-Tax"*, Ricardo incidentally makes the following remark directed against Say; it shows that the Englishman is always very conscious of the economic distinctions whereas the Continental constantly forgets them:

"M. Say supposes, 'A landlord by his *assiduity, economy and skill*, to increase his annual revenue by 5,000 francs;' but a landlord has no means of employing his assiduity, economy and skill on his land, unless he farms it himself; and then it is in quality of capitalist and farmer that he makes the improvement, and not in quality of landlord. It is not conceivable that he could so augment the produce of his farm by any *peculiar* skill" ⟨the "skill" therefore is more or less empty talk⟩ "on his part, without first increasing the quantity of capital employed upon it" (l.c., p. 209).

In *Chapter XIII "Taxes on Gold"* (important for Ricardo's theory of money), Ricardo makes some additional reflections or further definitions relating to *market-price* and *natural price*. They amount to this, how long the equalisation of the two prices takes depends on whether the particular sphere of production

---

[a] See this volume, pp. 203 and 314.—*Ed.*

permits a rapid or slow increase or reduction of supply, which in turn is equivalent to a *rapid or slow transfer* or *withdrawal* of capital to or from the sphere in question. Ricardo has been criticised by many writers (Sismondi, etc.) because, in his observations on rent, he disregards the difficulties that the *withdrawal of capital* presents for the farmer who employs a great deal of fixed capital, etc. (The history of England from 1815 to 1830 provides *strong* proof for this.) Although this objection is quite correct, it does *not in any way* affect the theory, it leaves it *quite untouched,* because in this case it is invariably only a question of the more or less rapid or slow operation of the economic law. But as regards the *reverse* objection, which refers to the application of new capital to new land, the situation is quite different. Ricardo assumes that this can take place *without the intervention* of the landlord, that in this case capital is operating in a field of action ||639|, in which it does not meet with any resistance. But this is *fundamentally wrong.* In order to prove this assumption, that this is indeed so, where capitalist production and landed property are developed, Ricardo always presupposes cases in which landed property does *not* exist, either in fact or in law, and where capitalist production too is *not yet* developed, at least not on the land.

The statements just referred to are the following:

"The rise in the price of commodities, in consequence of taxation or of difficulty of production, will in all cases ultimately ensue; but the *duration of the interval*, before the market-price will conform to the natural price, *must depend on the nature of the commodity*, and *on the facility with which it can be reduced in quantity.* If the quantity of the commodity taxed could not be diminished, if the capital of the farmer or of the hatter for instance, could not be withdrawn to other employments, it would be of no consequence that their profits were reduced below the general level by means of a tax; unless the demand for their commodities should increase, they would never be able to elevate the market-price of corn and of hats up to their increased natural price. Their threats to leave their employments, and remove their capitals to more favoured trades, would be treated as an idle menace which could not be carried into effect; and consequently the price would not be raised by diminished production. *Commodities*, however, of all descriptions *can be reduced in quantity*, and *capital can be removed from trades which are less profitable to those which are more so, but with different degrees of rapidity.* In proportion as the supply of a particular commodity can be more easily reduced, without inconvenience to the producer, the price of it will more quickly rise after the difficulty of its production has been increased by taxation, or by any other means" (l.c., pp. 214-15).

"The agreement of the market and natural price of all commodities, depends at all times on the facility with which the supply can be increased or diminished. In the case of gold, houses, and labour, as well as many other things, this effect cannot, under some circumstances, be speedily produced. But it is different with those commodities which are consumed and reproduced from year to year, such as hats, shoes, corn, and cloth; they may be reduced, if necessary, and the interval cannot be long before the supply is contracted in proportion to the increased charge of producing them" (l.c., pp. 220-21).

[2. Changes in the Rate of Profit Caused by Various Factors]

In the same Chapter XIII *"Taxes on Gold"*, Ricardo speaks of

"rent being not a creation, but merely a transfer of wealth" (l.c., p. 221).

Is profit *a creation* of wealth, or is it not rather a *transfer* of the surplus-labour, from the workman to the capitalist? In fact *wages* too, are not a *creation* of wealth. But they are not a transfer. They are the appropriation of part of the produce of labour by those who produced it.

In the same chapter Ricardo says:

"A *tax on raw produce* from the surface of the earth, will ... fall on the consumer, and will in no way affect rent; unless, by diminishing the funds for the maintenance of labour, it lowers wages, reduces the population, and diminishes the demand for corn" (l.c., p. 221).

Whether Ricardo is right when he says that "a tax on *raw produce* from the surface of the earth" falls neither on the landlord nor on the farmer but on the *consumer,* does not concern us here. I maintain, however, that, if he is right, such a tax may *raise the rent,* whereas he thinks that it does not affect it, unless, by increasing the price of the means of subsistence, etc., it diminishes capital, population and the demand for corn, etc. For Ricardo imagines that an increase in the price of raw produce only affects the *rate of profit* in so far as it raises the price of the *means of subsistence* of the worker. And it is true that an increase in the price of *raw produce* can only in this way affect the *rate of surplus-value* and consequently *surplus-value* itself, *thereby* affecting the rate of profit. But assuming a given *surplus-value,* an increase in the price of the "raw produce from the surface of the earth" would *raise* the value of constant capital in proportion to the variable, would increase the ratio of constant capital to variable and *therefore* reduce the *rate of profit,* thus raising the *rent.* Ricardo starts out from the view point ||640| that in so far as the rise or fall in the price of the *raw produce* does not affect wages, it does not affect profit; for, he argues

⟨except in one passage to which we shall return at a later stage⟩[a] that the rate of profit remains the same, whether the value of the capital advanced falls or rises. If the value of the capital advanced grows, then the value of the product grows and also the part of the product which forms the surplus-product, i.e., profit. The reverse happens when the value of the capital advanced falls. This [Ricardo's assertion] is only correct, if the values of variable and constant capital change in the *same proportion,* whether the change is caused by a rise in the price of raw materials or by taxes, etc. In this case the rate remains unaffected, because no change has occurred in the organic composition of the capital. And even then it must be *assumed*—as is the case with temporary changes—that wages remain the same, whether the price of raw produce rises or falls (in other words wages remain the same, that is, their value remains unchanged irrespective of any rise or fall in the use-value of the wages).

The following possibilities exist:

First the two major differences:

A. A *change in the method of production* brings about a change in the *proportion* between the amounts of constant and variable capital employed. In this case the rate of surplus-value remains the same provided wages remain constant (in terms of value) ⟨i.e., in terms of the labour-time they represent⟩. But the surplus-value itself is affected if a different number of workers is employed by the same capital, i.e., if there is an alteration in the variable capital. If the change in the method of production results in a relative fall in constant capital, the surplus-value grows and thus the rate of profit. The reverse case produces the opposite result.

It is here assumed throughout that the value *pro tanto,* per £ *100* for example, of constant and variable capital remains *the same.*

In this case the change in the method of production cannot affect constant and variable capital equally; that is, for instance, constant and variable capital—without a change in value—cannot increase or diminish to the same extent, for the fall or rise is here always the result of a change in the productivity of labour. A change in the method of production has not the same but a *different* effect [on constant and variable capital]; and this has nothing to do with whether a large or small amount of capital has to be employed with a given *organic composition of capital.*

---

[a] See this volume, pp. 431-32.—*Ed.*

B. *The method of production remains the same.* There is a *change in the ratio of constant to variable capital,* while their relative volume [in physical units] remains the same (so that each of them forms the same proportion of the total capital as before). This change in their ratio is caused by a *change in the value* of the commodities which enter into constant or variable capital.

The following possibilities exist here:

[1.] The value of the constant capital remains the same while that of the variable capital rises or falls. This would always affect the surplus-value, and thereby the rate of profit.

[2.] The value of the variable capital remains the same while that of the constant rises or falls. Then the rate of profit would fall in the first case and rise in the second.

[3.] If both fall simultaneously, but in different proportions, then the one has always risen or fallen as compared with the other.

[4.] The value of the constant and of the variable capital is *equally* affected, whether both rise or both fall. If both rise, then the rate of profit falls, not because the constant capital rises but because the variable capital *rises* and accordingly the surplus-value falls (for only the value [of the variable capital] rises, although it sets in motion the same number of workers as before, or perhaps even a smaller number). If both fall, then the rate of profit rises, not because constant capital falls, but because the variable falls (in terms of value) and therefore the surplus-value increases.

C. *Change in the method of production and change in the value of the elements that form constant or variable capital.* Here one change may neutralise the other, for example, when the amount of constant capital grows while its value falls or remains the same (i.e., it falls *pro tanto,* per £ 100) or when its amount falls but its value rises in the same proportion or remains the same (i.e., it rises *pro tanto*). In this case there would be no change at all in the organic composition. The rate of profit would remain unchanged. But it can never happen—except in the case of agricultural capital—that the amount of the constant capital falls as compared with the variable capital, while its value *rises.*

This type of nullification cannot possibly apply to variable capital (while the real wage remains unchanged).

Except for this one case, it is therefore only possible for the value and amount of the constant capital to   fall   or   rise simultaneously in relation to the variable capital, its value therefore rises or falls absolutely as compared with the variable capital. This case has already been considered. Or they may fall or rise simultaneously ||641| but in unequal proportion. On the assumption made, this possibility always reduces itself to the case in which the value of the constant capital rises or falls relatively to the variable.

This also includes the other case. For if the amount of the constant capital rises, then the amount of the variable capital falls relatively, and vice versa. Similarly with the value. |641||

[3. The Value of Constant Capital Decreases While That of Variable Capital Increases and Vice Versa, and the Effect of These Changes on the Rate of Profit]

||642| *In regard to case* C, [*page*], *640*, it should also be noted:

It would be possible for the wages to rise but for constant capital to fall *in terms of value*, not in physical *terms*. If the rise and fall were proportional on both sides, the rate of profit could remain unchanged. For instance, if the constant capital were £ 60, wages [£] 40 and the rate of surplus-value 50 per cent, then the product would be [£] 120. The rate of profit would be 20 per cent. If the constant capital fell to [£] 40, although its volume [in physical terms] remained unchanged, and wages rose to £ 60, while the surplus-value fell from 50 per cent to $33^1/_3$ per cent, then the product would be £ 120 and the rate of profit 20 per cent. This is wrong.

According to the assumption, the total value of the quantity of labour employed is £ 60. Hence, if the wage rose to £ 60, surplus-value and therefore the rate of profit would be nil. But if it did not rise to such an extent, then any rise in the wage would bring about a fall in the surplus-value. If wages rose to £ 50, then the surplus-value would be £ 10, if [they rose] to £ 45, then [the surplus-value would be] £ 15, etc. Under all circumstances, therefore, the surplus-value and the rate of profit would fall to the same degree. For we are measuring the unchanged total capital here. While the magnitude of the capital (the total capital) remains the same the rate of profit must always rise and fall, not with the rate of surplus-value but with the absolute amount of surplus-value. But if, in the above example, the flax fell so low that the amount which the same number of workers were spinning could be bought for £ 40, then we would have the following:

Constant capital	Variable capital	Surplus-value	Value of the product	Capital advanced	Rate of profit
40	50	10	100	90	$11^1/_9$ per cent

The rate of profit would have fallen below 20 per cent.

But supposing:

Constant capital	Variable capital	Surplus-value	Value of the product	Capital advanced	Rate of profit
30	50	10	90	80	$12^1/_2$ per cent

Supposing:

Constant capital	Variable capital	Surplus-value	Value of the product	Capital advanced	Rate of profit
20	50	10	80	70	$14^2/_7$ per cent

According to the assumption, the fall in the value of the constant capital never completely counterbalances the rise in the value of the variable capital. On the assumption made, it can never entirely cancel it out, since for the rate of profit to be 20, [£] 10 would have to be a fifth of the total capital advanced. But in the case in which the variable capital amounts to [£] 50, this would only be possible when the constant capital is nil. Assume, on the other hand, that variable capital rose only to [£] 45; in this case the surplus-value would be [£] 15. And, say, the constant capital fell

Constant capital	Variable capital	Surplus-value	Value of the product	Capital advanced	Rate of profit
30	45	15	90	75	20 per cent

In this case the two movements cancel each other out entirely.

||643| Assume further:

Constant capital	Variable capital	Surplus-value	Value of the product	Capital advanced	Rate of profit
20	45	15	80	65	$23^1/_{13}$ per cent

Even with the fall in the surplus-value, therefore, the rate of profit could *rise* in this case, because of the proportionately greater fall in the value of the constant capital. More workers could be employed with the same capital of 100, despite the rise in wages and the fall in the rate of surplus-value. Despite the fall in the rate of surplus-value, the amount of surplus-value, and hence the profit, would increase, because the number of workers had increased. For the above ratio of $20c + 45v$ gives us the following proportions with a capital outlay of 100:

Constant capital	Variable capital	Surplus-value	Value of the product	Capital advanced	Rate of profit
$30^{10}/_{13}$	$69^3/_{13}$	$23^1/_{13}$	$123^1/_{13}$	100	$23^1/_{13}$ per cent

The relation between the rate of surplus-value and the number of workers becomes very important here. Ricardo never considers it. |643||

* * *

||641| It is clear that what has been regarded here as a *variation* within the *organic composition* of one capital, can apply equally to the difference in the *organic composition* between *different capitals*, capitals in different spheres of production.

Firstly: Instead of a variation in the organic composition of *one* capital—a difference in the *organic composition of different* capitals.

Secondly: Alteration in the organic composition through a *change in value* in the two parts of one capital, similarly a difference in the *value* of the *raw materials* and *machinery employed* by different capitals. This does not apply to variable capital, since equal wages in the different branches of production are assumed. The difference in the *value* of different days of labour in different *spheres* has nothing to do with it. If the labour of a goldsmith is dearer than that of a labourer, then the surplus-time of the goldsmith is proportionately dearer than that of the labourer.[100] |641||

[4. Confusion of Cost-Prices with Value in the Ricardian Theory of Profit]

||641| *In Chapter XV "Taxes on Profits"* Ricardo says:

"Taxes on those commodities, which are generally denominated luxuries, fall on those only who make use of them.... But taxes on necessaries do not affect the consumers of necessaries, in proportion to the quantity that may be consumed by them, but often in a much higher proportion." "For example, a tax on corn.... it alters the rate of profits of stock.... Whatever raises the wages of labour, lowers the profits of stock; therefore every tax on any commodity consumed by the labourer, has a tendency to lower the rate of profits" (l.c. p. 231).

Taxes on consumers are at the same time taxes on producers, in so far as the object taxed enters not only into individual consumption but also into industrial consumption, or only into the latter. This does not, however, apply only to the necessaries consumed by workmen. It applies to all materials industrially consumed by the capitalist. Every tax of this kind reduces the rate of profit, because it raises the value of the constant capital in relation to the variable. For example, a tax imposed on flax or wool. ||642| The flax rises in price. The flax spinner can therefore no longer purchase the same quantity of flax with a capital of £ 100. Since the method of production has remained the same, he needs the same number of workers to spin the same quantity of flax. But the flax has a greater value than before, in relation to the capital laid out in wages. The rate of profit therefore falls. It does not help him at all that the price of linen-yarn rises. The absolute level of this price is in fact immaterial to him, What matters is only the excess of this price over the price of the capital advanced. If he wanted to raise [the price of] the total product, not only by [the amount necessary to cover the increase in] the price of the flax, but to such an extent that the same quantity of yarn would yield him the same profit as before, then the demand —which is already falling as a result of the rising price of the raw material of the yarn—would fall still further because of the artificial rise due to the higher profit. Although the average rate of profit is given, it is not possible in such cases to raise the price in this way.[101] |642||

||643| [In] *Chapter XV "Taxes on Profits"* Ricardo says:

"In a former part of this work, we discussed the effects of the division of capital into *fixed and circulating*, or rather into *durable and perishable capital*, on the prices of commodities. We shewed that two manufacturers might employ precisely the same amount of capital, and might derive from it precisely the same amount of profits, but that they would sell their commodities for very different sums of money, according as the capitals they employed were rapidly, or slowly, consumed and reproduced. The one might sell his goods for £ 4,000, the other for £ 10,000, and they might both employ £ 10,000 of capital, and obtain 20 per cent profit, or £ 2,000. The capital of one might consist, for example,[a] of £ 2,000 circulating capital, to be reproduced, and £ 8,000 fixed, in buildings and machinery; the capital of the other, on the contrary, might consist of £ 8,000 of circulating, and of only £ 2,000 fixed capital in machinery and buildings. Now, if each of these persons were to be taxed ten per cent on his income, or £ 200, the one, to make his business yield him the *general rate of profit*, must raise his goods from £ 10,000 to £ 10,200; the other would also be obliged to raise the price of his goods from

---

[a] In the manuscript: "f.i."—*Ed.*

£ 4,000 to £ 4,200. Before the tax, the goods sold by one of these manufacturers were 2¹/₂ times more valuable than the goods of the other; after the tax they will be 2.42 times more valuable: the one kind will have risen two per cent; the other five per cent: consequently a tax upon income, whilst money continued unaltered in value, would alter the relative prices *and* value of commodities" (l.c., pp. 234-35).

The error lies in this final "and"—"prices *and* value". This change of prices would only show—just as in the case of capital containing different proportions of fixed and circulating capital —that the establishment of the *general rate of profit* requires that the prices or cost-prices which are determined and regulated by that general rate of profit [are] very different from the *values* of the commodities. And this most important aspect of the question does not exist for Ricardo at all.

In the same chapter he says:

"If a country were not taxed, and money should fall in value, its abundance in every market" ⟨here [he expresses] the absurd notion that a fall in the value of money ought to be accompanied by its abundance in every market⟩ ||644| "would produce similar effects in each. If meat rose 20 per cent, bread, beer, shoes, labour, and *every commodity*, would also rise 20 per cent; it is necessary they should do so, to secure to each trade the same rate of profits. But this is no longer true when any of these commodities is taxed; if, in that case, they should all rise in proportion to the fall in the value of money, *profits would be rendered unequal*; in the case of the commodities taxed, *profits would be raised above the general level*, and capital *would be removed from one employment to another, till an equilibrium of profits was restored*, which could only be, after *the relative prices were altered*" (l.c., pp. 236-37).

And so this equilibrium of profits is after all brought about by the relative *values,* the *"real values"* of the commodities being altered, and so adjusted that they correspond, not to their real value, but to the average profit which they must yield.

[5. The General Rate of Profit and the Rate of Absolute Rent in Their Relation to Each Other. The Influence on Cost-Prices of a Reduction in Wages]

In Chapter XVII: *"Taxes on other Commodities than Raw Produce"*, Ricardo says:

"Mr. Buchanan considers corn and raw produce as at a monopoly price, because they yield a rent: all commodities which yield a rent, he supposes must be at a monopoly price; and thence he infers, that all taxes on raw produce would fall on the landlord, and not on the consumer. 'The *price of corn*,' he says, 'which always affords a rent, *being in no respect influenced by the expenses of its production*, those *expenses must be paid out of the rent*; and when they rise or fall, therefore, the consequence is not a higher or lower price, but a higher or [...] lower rent. In this view, all taxes on farm servants, horses, or the implements of agriculture, are in reality land-taxes; the burden falling on the farmer during the currency of his lease, and on the landlord, when the lease comes to be renewed. In like manner all those improved implements of husbandry which save expense to the farmer, such as machines for threshing and reaping, whatever gives him easier access to the market, such as good roads, canals and bridges, though they lessen the original cost of corn, *do not lessen its market price*. Whatever is saved by those improvements, therefore, belongs to the landlord as part of his rent.'

"It is evident" (says Ricardo) "that if we yield to Mr. Buchanan the basis on which his argument is built, namely, that the price of corn always yields a rent, all the consequences which he contends for would follow of course" (l.c., pp. 292-93).

This is by no means evident. What Buchanan bases his argument on is not that all corn yields a rent, but that all corn which yields a rent is sold at a *monopoly price*, and that monopoly price—in the sense in which Adam Smith explains it and it has the same meaning with Ricardo—is "the very highest price at which the consumers are willing to purchase it".[a][102]

But this is wrong. Corn which yields a rent (apart from differential rent) is not sold at a monopoly price in Buchanan's sense. It is sold at a monopoly price, only in so far as it is sold above its *cost-price and at its value*. Its price is determined by the quantity of labour embodied in it, not by the cost of pro-ducing it, and the rent is the excess of the value over the cost-price, it is therefore determined by the latter. The smaller is the cost-price relatively to the value, the greater will be the rent, and the greater the cost-price in relation to the value, the smaller the rent. All improvements lower the value of the corn because [they reduce] the quantity of labour required for its production. Wheth-er they reduce the rent, depends on various circumstances. If the corn becomes cheaper, and if wages are thereby reduced, then the rate of surplus-value rises. Furthermore, the farmer's expenses in seeds, fodder, etc., would fall. And therewith the rate of profit in all other, non-agricultural, branches of production would rise, hence *also* in agriculture. The relative amounts of immediate and accumulated labour would remain unchanged in the non-agricultural spheres of production; the number of workers (in relation to constant capital) would remain the same, but the value of the variable capital [would] fall, the surplus-

---

a In the manuscript: "the commodity".—*Ed.*

value ||645| would therefore rise, and also the rate of profit. *Consequently* [they would] also rise in agriculture. Rent falls here because the rate of profit rises. *Corn becomes cheaper, but its cost-price rises. Hence the difference between its value and its cost-price falls.*

According to our assumption the ratio for the average non-agricultural capital was £ 80c+£ 20v, the rate of surplus-value 50 per cent, hence surplus-value £ 10 and the rate of profit 10 per cent. The value of the product of the average capital of £ 100 was therefore £ 110.

If one assumes, that as a result of the lowering of the price of grain, wages fell by one-quarter, then *the same number of workers* employed on a constant capital of £ 80, that is on the same amount of raw material and machinery, would now cost only £ 15. And the same amount of commodities would be worth £ 80c+£ 15v+£ 15s, since, according to the assumption, the quantity of labour which they perform equals £ 30. Thus the value of the same amount of commodities is £ 110, as before. But the capital advanced would now amount only to £ 95 and [the rate of profit], £ 15 on £ 95, would be $15^{15}/_{19}$ per cent. If, however, the same amount of capital were laid out, that is £ 100, then the ratio would be: £ $84^4/_{19}$c+£ $15^{15}/_{19}$v. The profit, however, would be £ $15^{15}/_{19}$. And the value of the product would amount to £ $115^{15}/_{19}$. According to the assumption, however, the agricultural capital was £ 60c+£ 40v and the value of its product was £ 120. Rent was £ 10, while the cost-price was £ 110. Now the rent would only be £ $4^4/_{19}$. For £ $115^{15}/_{19}$+£ $4^4/_{19}$=£ 120.

We see here that the average capital of £ 100 produces commodities at a cost-price of £ $115^{15}/_{19}$ instead of the previous £ 110. Has this caused the average price of the commodity to rise?

Its value has remained the same, since the same amount of labour is required to transform the same amount of raw material and machinery into product. But the same capital of £ 100 sets in motion more labour, and while previously it transformed £ 80, now it transforms £ $84^4/_{19}$ constant capital into product. A greater proportion of this labour is, however, now unpaid. Hence there is an increase in profit and in the *total value* of the commodities produced by [a capital of] £ 100. The value of the individual commodity has remained the same, but more commodities *at the same value* are being produced with a capital of £ 100. What is however the position of the cost-price in the individual branches of production?

Let us assume that the non-agricultural capital consisted of the following capitals:

		[the price of the] product [must be:]	Difference between value and cost-price
I. $80c + 20v$	In order to sell at the same cost-prices	110 (value = 110)	0
II. $60c + 40v$		110 (value = 120)	—10
III. $85c + 15v$		110 (value = $107^1/_2$)	$+2^1/_2$
IV. $95c + 5v$		110 (value = $102^1/_2$)	$+7^1/_2$
Thus the average capital = $80c + 20v$			

For II the difference is —10, for III and IV [taken together] +10. For the whole capital of £ 400, it is 0—10+10=0. If the product of the capital of £ 400 is sold at £ 440, then the commodities produced by it are sold at *their value*. This yields [a profit of] 10 per cent. But in case II, the commodities are sold at £ 10 below their value, in case III at [£] $2^1/_4$ above their value and in case IV at [£] $7^1/_2$ above their value. Only in case I are they sold at their value if they are sold at their cost-price, i.e., £ 100 capital + £ 10 profit.

||646| But what would be the situation as a result of the fall in wages by one-quarter?

For capital I: Instead of £ 80 c+£ 20v, [the outlay is] now $84^4/_{19}c+15^{15}/_{19}v$, *profit* £ $15^{15}/_{19}$, *value of the product* £ $115^{15}/_{19}$.

For capital II: Now only £ 30 laid out in wages, since $^1/_4$ of 40=10 and 40—10=30. The product is £ 60c+£ 30v and the surplus-value £ 30. (For the *value of the labour applied is* £ 60.) [30 surplus-value] on a capital of £ 90 equals $33^1/_3$ per cent. For a [capital of] £ 100 the ratio is: £ $66^2/_3c$+£ $33^1/_3v$ *and the value [of the product] is* £ $133^1/_3$. The rate of profit is $33^1/_3$.

For capital III: Now only $11^1/_4$ [laid out] in wages, for $^1/_4$ of 15=$3^3/_4$ and 15—$3^3/_4$=$11^1/_4$. The product would be £ 85c+£ $11^1/_4v$ and surplus-value £ $11^1/_4$. (Value of labour applied is £ $22^1/_2$.) [$11^1/_4$] on a capital of £ $96^1/_4$. This amounts to $11^{53}/_{77}$ per cent. For £ 100 the ratio is $88^{24}/_{77}c+11^{53}/_{77}v$. The rate of profit is £ $11^{53}/_{77}$ and [the value of the] product £ $111^{53}/_{77}$.

For capital IV: Now only $3^3/_4$ laid out in wages, for $^1/_4$ of 5=$1^1/_4$ and 5—$1^1/_4$=$3^3/_4$. The product is £ 95c+£ $3^3/_4v$ and the surplus-value £ $3^3/_4$ (for the value of the total labour is $7^1/_2$). [$3^3/_4$] on a capital of $98^3/_4$. This amounts to $3^{63}/_{79}$ per cent. For 100 the ratio is: $96^{16}/_{79}c + 3^{63}/_{79}v$. The rate of profit is $3^{63}/_{79}$. The value [of the product] is $103^{63}/_{79}$.

We would therefore have the following:

	Rate of profit		[The price of the] product [must be:]	Difference between cost-price and value
I. $84^4/_{19}c + 15^{15}/_{19}v$	$15^{15}/_{19}$	In order to sell at the same cost-prices	116(value=$115^{15}/_{19}$)	$+ \ ^4/_{19}$
II. $66^2/_3c + 33^1/_3v$	$33^1/_3$		116(value=$133^1/_3$)	$-17^1/_3$
III. $88^{24}/_{77}c + 11^{53}/_{77}v$	$11^{53}/_{77}$		116(value=$111^{53}/_{77}$)	$+4^{24}/_{77}$
IV. $96^{16}/_{79}c + 3^{63}/_{79}v$	$3^{63}/_{79}$		116(value=$103^{63}/_{79}$)	$+12^{16}/_{79}$
Total 400		64 (to the nearest whole number)		

This makes 16 per cent. More exactly, a little more than $16^1/_7$ per cent. The calculation is not quite correct because we have disregarded, not taken into account a fraction of the average profit; this makes the negative difference in II appear a little too large and [the positive] in I, III, IV a little too small. But it can be seen that otherwise the positive and negative differences would cancel out; further, it can be seen that on the one hand the sale of II *below* its value and of III and particularly of IV *above* their value would increase considerably. True, the addition to or reduction of the price would not be so great for the individual product as might appear here, since in all four categories more labour is employed and hence more constant capital (raw materials and machinery) is transformed into product. The increase or reduction in price would thus be spread over a larger volume of commodities. Nevertheless it would still be considerable.

It is thus evident that a fall in wages would cause a rise in the cost-prices of I, III, IV, in fact a very considerable rise in the cost-price of IV. It is the same law as that developed by Ricardo in relation to the difference between circulating and fixed capital,[103] but he did not by any means prove, nor could he have proved, that this is reconcilable with the law of value and that the value of the products remains the same for the total capital.

||647| The calculation and the adjustment becomes much more complicated if we take into account those differences in the or-

ganic composition of the capital which arise from the circulation process. For in our calculation, above, we assumed that the whole of the *constant capital* which has been advanced, enters into the product, i.e., that it contains only the *wear and tear* of the fixed capital, for one year, for example (since we have to calculate the profit for the year). The values of the total product would otherwise be very different, whereas here they only change with the variable capital. Secondly, with a constant rate of surplus-value but varying periods of circulation, there would be greater differences in the *amount of surplus-value created,* relatively to the capital advanced. Leaving out of account any differences in variable capital, the amounts of the surplus-values would be proportionate to the amounts of the values created by the same capitals. The rate of profit would be even lower where a relatively large part of the constant capital consisted of fixed capital and considerably higher, where a relatively large part of the capital consisted of circulating capital. It would be highest where the variable capital was relatively large as compared with the constant capital and where the fixed portion of the latter was at the same time relatively small. If the ratio of circulating to fixed capital in the constant capital were *the same* in the different capitals, then the only determining factor would be the difference between variable and constant capital. If the ratio of variable to constant capital were the same, then it would be the difference between fixed and circulating capital, that is, only the difference within the constant capital itself.

As we have seen above, the farmer's rate of profit would rise, in any case, if, as a result of the lower price of corn, the general rate of profit of the non-agricultural capital increased. The question is whether his rate of profit would rise directly, and this appears to depend on the nature of the improvements. If the improvements were of such a kind that the capital laid out in wages decreased considerably compared with that laid out in machinery, etc., then his rate of profit need not necessarily rise directly. If, for example, it was such that he required one-quarter less workers, then instead of his original outlay of £ 40 in wages, he would now pay only £ 30. Thus his capital would be £ $60c+$£ $30v$, or on £ 100 it would be £ $66^2/_3c+$£ $33^1/_3v$. And since the labour costing £ 40 [provides a surplus-value of] £ 20, the labour costing £ 30 provides £ 15. And £ $16^2/_3$ [surplus-value is derived] from the labour. costing £ $33^1/_3$. Thus the organic composition would approach that of the non-agricultural capital. And in the above case,

with a simultaneous decrease in wages by one-quarter, it would
fall even *below* that of the non-agricultural capital.[104] In this
case, rent (absolute rent) would disappear.

Following upon the above-quoted passage on Buchanan, Ricardo says:

> "I hope I have made it sufficiently clear, that until a country is cultivated
> in every part, and up to the highest degree, there is always *a portion of
> capital employed on the land* which yields no rent, *and*" (!) "that it is this
> portion of capital, the result of which, as in manufactures, is divided between
> profits and wages that *regulates the price of corn*. The price of corn, then,
> which does not afford a rent, being influenced by the expenses of its produc-
> tion, those expenses cannot be paid out of rent. The consequence therefore
> of those expenses increasing, is a higher price, and not a lower rent" (l.c.,
> p. 293).

Since absolute rent is equal to the excess of the value of the
agricultural product over its price of production, it is clear that
all factors which reduce the *total quantity* of labour required in
the production of corn, etc., reduce the rent, because they reduce
the value, hence the excess of the value over the price of production. In so far as the price of production consists of expenses,
its fall is identical and goes hand in hand with the fall in
value. But in so far as the price of production (or the expenses)
is equal to the capital advanced plus the average profit, the
very reverse is the case. The market-value of the product falls,
but that part of it, which is equal to the price of production,
rises, if the general rate of profit rises as a result of the fall in
the market-value of corn. The rent, therefore, falls, because the
expenses in this sense rise—and this is how Ricardo takes expenses elsewhere, when he speaks of cost of production. Improvements in agriculture, which bring about an increase in constant capital as compared with variable, would reduce rent considerably, even if the total quantity of labour employed fell only
slightly, or so slightly that it did not influence wages (surplus-
value, directly) at all. Suppose, as a result of such improvements,
the composition of the capital altered from £ 60c+£ 40v to
£ 66$^2/_3$$c$+£ 33$^1/_3$$v$ (this might occur, for example, as a result of
rising wages, caused by emigration, war, discovery of new markets, prosperity in the non-agricultural industry [or it could occur as a result of the] competition of foreign corn, the
farmer might feel impelled to find means of employing more
constant capital and less variable; the same circumstances could
continue to operate after the introduction of the improvement
and wages therefore might not fall despite the improvement).

||648| Then the value of the agricultural product would be reduced from £ 120 to £ 116²/₃, that is, by £ 3¹/₃. The rate of profit would continue to be 10 per cent. The rent would fall from £ 10 to £ 6²/₃ and, moreover, this reduction would have taken place without any reduction whatsoever in wages.

The absolute rent may rise because the general rate of profit falls, owing to new advances in industry. The rate of profit may fall due to a rise in rent, because of an increase in the value of agricultural produce which is accompanied by an increase in the difference between its value and its cost-price. (At the same time, the rate of profit falls because wages rise.)

The absolute rent can fall, because the value of agricultural produce falls and the general rate of profit rises. It can fall, because the value of the agricultural produce falls as a result of a fundamental change in the organic composition of capital, without the rate of profit rising. It can disappear completely, as soon as the *value of the agricultural produce* becomes equal to the *cost-price,* in other words when the agricultural capital has the same composition as the non-agricultural, average capital.

Ricardo's proposition would only be correct if expressed like this: When the value of agricultural produce equals its cost-price, then there is no absolute rent. But he is wrong because he says: There is no absolute rent *because* value and cost-price are altogether identical, both in industry and in agriculture.* On the contrary, agriculture would belong to an exceptional class of industry, if its value and cost-price were identical.

Even when admitting that there may be no portion of land which does not pay a rent, Ricardo believes that by referring to the fact that at least some portion of the capital employed on the land pays no rent he substantially improves his case. The one fact is as irrelevant to the theory as the other. The real question is this: Do the products of these lands or of this capital regulate the market-value? Or must they not rather sell their products *below* their value, because their additional supply is only saleable *at,* not *above,* this market-value which is regulated without them. So far as the portion of capital is concerned, the

* ||663| (The following passage shows that Ricardo consciously identifies *value* with *cost of production:* "Mr. Malthus appears to think that it is a part of my doctrine, that the *cost* and *value* of a thing should be the same; —it is, if he means by cost, '*cost of production*' *including profits*" (l.c., p. 46, note).) |663||

matter is simple, because for the farmer who invests an *additional amount of capital landed property does not exist* and as a capitalist he is only concerned with the cost-price; if he possesses the additional capital, it is more advantageous for him to invest it on his farm, even *below* the average profit, than to *lend it out* and to receive only interest and no profit. So far as the land is concerned, those portions of land which do not pay a rent form component parts of estates that pay rent and are not separable from the estates with which they are let; they cannot however be let in isolation from the rest to a capitalist farmer (but perhaps to a cottager or to a small capitalist). In relation to these bits of land, the farmer is again not confronted by "landed property". Alternatively, the owner of the land must cultivate it himself. The farmer cannot pay a rent for it and the landlord does not let it *for nothing,* unless he wants to have his land made arable in this fashion without incurring any expense.

The situation would be different in a country in which the composition of the agricultural capital was equal to the average composition of the non-agricultural capital, which presupposes a high level of development in agriculture or a low level of development in industry. In this case the value of the agricultural produce would be equal to its cost-price. Only differential rent could be paid then. The land which yields no differential rent but *only* an agricultural rent, could then pay no rent. For if the farmer sells the agricultural produce at its value, it only covers its cost-price. *He* therefore pays no rent. The landowner must then cultivate the land himself, or the so-called rent collected by him is a part of his tenant's profit or even of his wages. That this might be the case in one country does not mean that the opposite might not happen in another country. Where, however, industry—and therefore capitalist production—is at a low level of development, there are no capitalist farmers, whose existence would presuppose capitalist production on the land. Thus, quite different circumstances have to be considered here, from those involved in the economic organisation in which landed property as an economic category exists only in the form of rent.

In the same Chapter XVII, Ricardo says:

"Raw produce is not at a monopoly price, because the market price of barley and wheat is as much regulated by their *cost of production*, as the market price of cloth and linen. The only difference is this, that *one portion of the capital* employed in agriculture regulates the price of corn, namely, that portion which pays no rent; whereas, in the *production of manufactured commodities, every portion of capital is employed with the same results*; and as *no portion pays rent, every portion is equally a regulator of price*" (l.c., pp. 290-91).

This assertion, that every portion of capital is employed with the same results and that none pays rent (which is, however, called excess profit here) is not only wrong, but has been refuted by Ricardo himself ||650|[105] as we have seen previously.[a]

We now come to the presentation of Ricardo's theory of surplus-value.

[B. RICARDO ON THE PROBLEM OF SURPLUS-VALUE]

1. Quantity of Labour and Value of Labour. [As Presented by Ricardo the Problem of the Exchange of Labour for Capital Cannot Be Solved]

Ricardo opens *Chapter I, "On Value"*, with the following heading of *Section I:*

"The value of a commodity, or the quantity of any other commodity for which it will exchange, depends on the relative *quantity of labour* which is necessary for its production, and not on the greater or less compensation which is paid for *that labour*" (l.c., p. 1).

In the style which runs through the whole of his enquiry, Ricardo begins his book here by stating that the determination of the value of commodities by labour-time is *not* incompatible with *wages*, in other words with the varying compensation paid for that labour-time or that quantity of labour. From the very outset, he turns against Adam Smith's confusion between the determination of the value of commodities by the relative *quantity of labour* required for their production and the *value of labour* (or the compensation paid for labour).

It is clear that the proportional quantity of labour contained in two commodities A and B, is absolutely unaffected by whether the workers who produce A and B receive much or little of the product of their labour. The value of A and B is determined by the *quantity of labour* which their production costs, and not by the *costs of labour* to the owners of A and B. Quantity of labour and value of labour are two different things. The quantity of labour which is contained in A and B respectively, has nothing to do with how much of the *labour* contained in A and B the owners of A and B, have *paid* or even *performed themselves*. A and B are

---

[a] See this volume, pp. 203, 314 and 347.—*Ed.*

exchanged not in proportion to the *paid* labour contained in them, but in proportion to the total quantity of labour they contain, paid and unpaid.

"Adam Smith, who so accurately defined the original source of exchangeable value, and who was bound in consistency to maintain, that all things became more or less valuable in proportion as more or less labour was bestowed on their production, has himself erected another standard measure of value, and speaks of things being more or less valuable, in proportion as they will *exchange for more or less of this standard measure* ... as if *these were two equivalent expressions*, and as if because a man's labour had become doubly efficient, and he could therefore produce twice the quantity of a commodity, he would necessarily receive twice the former quantity in exchange for it" (that is for his labour).

"If this indeed were true, *if the reward of the labourer were always in proportion to what he produced, the quantity of labour bestowed on a commodity, and the quantity of labour which that commodity would purchase, would be equal*, and either might accurately measure the variations of other things: *but they are not equal*" (l.c., p. 5).

Adam Smith nowhere asserts that "these were two equivalent expressions". On the contrary, he says: Because in capitalist production, the wage of the worker is *no* longer equal to his product, therefore, the quantity of labour which a commodity costs and the quantity of commodities that the worker can purchase with this labour are two different things—*for this very reason* the relative quantity of labour contained in commodities ceases to determine their value, which is now determined rather by the *value of labour,* by the quantity of labour that I can purchase, or command with a given amount of commodities. Thus the *value of labour,* instead of the *relative quantity* of labour becomes the measure of value. Ricardo's reply to Adam Smith is correct—that the *relative quantity of labour* which is contained in two commodities is in no way affected by how much of this quantity of labour falls to the workers themselves and by the way this labour is remunerated; if the *relative quantity of labour* was the measure of value of commodities *before* the supervention of wages (wages that differ from the value of the products themselves), there is therefore no reason at all, why it should not continue to be so *after* wages have come into being. He argues correctly, that Adam Smith could use both expressions so long as they were equivalent, but that this is no reason for using the wrong expression instead of the right one when they have ceased to be equivalent.

But Ricardo has by no means thereby solved the problem which is the real cause of Adam Smith's contradiction. *Value of labour* and *quantity of labour* remain "equivalent expressions", so long as it is a question of *materialised labour.* ||651| They cease to be equivalents as soon as *materialised labour* is exchanged for *living labour.*

Two *commodities* exchange in proportion to the *labour materialised in them.* Equal quantities of materialised labour are exchanged for one another. Labour-time is their standard measure, but precisely for this reason they are "more or less valuable, in proportion as they will exchange for more or less of this standard measure" [l.c., p. 5]. If the commodity A contains one working-day, then it will exchange against any quantity of commodities which likewise contains one working-day and it is "more or less valuable" in proportion as it exchanges for more or less materialised labour in other commodities, since this exchange relationship expresses, is identical with, the relative quantity of labour which it itself contains.

Now wage-labour, however, is a *commodity.* It is even the basis on which the production of *products* as *commodities* takes place. The *law of values* is not applicable to it. Capitalist production therefore is not governed at all by this law. Therein lies a contradiction. This is the first of Adam Smith's problems. The second—which we shall find further amplified by Malthus—lies in the fact that the *utilisation* of a commodity (as capital) is proportional not to the amount of labour it contains, but to the extent to which it commands the *labour of others,* gives power over *more* labour of others than it itself contains. This is in fact a second latent reason for asserting that since the beginning of capitalist production, the value of commodities is determined not by the labour they contain but by the living labour which they command, in other words, by the *value of labour.*

Ricardo simply answers that this is how matters are in capitalist production. Not only does he fail to solve the problem; he does not even realise its existence in Adam Smith's work. In conformity with the whole arrangement of his investigation. Ricardo is satisfied with demonstrating that the changing value of labour —in short, wages—*does not invalidate* the determination of the value of the *commodities,* which are distinct from labour itself, by the relative quantity of labour contained in them. "*They are not equal*", that is "the quantity of labour bestowed on a commodity, and the quantity of labour which that commodity would purchase" [l.c., p. 5]. He contents himself with stating this fact. But how does the commodity labour differ from other commodities? One is *living labour* and the other *materialised* labour. They are, therefore, only two different forms of labour. Since the difference is only a matter of form, why should a law apply to one and not to the other? Ricardo does not answer—he does not even raise this question.

Nor does it help when he says:

"Is not the value of labour ... variable; being not only affected, as all other things" (should read commodities) "are, by the proportion between the supply and demand, which uniformly varies with every change in the condition of the community, but also by the varying price of food and other necessaries, on which the *wages of labour are expended?*" (l.c., p. 7).

That the price of labour, like that of other commodities, changes with supply and demand proves nothing in regard to the *value* of labour, according to Ricardo, just as this change of price with supply and demand proves nothing in regard to the value of other commodities. But that the "wages of labour" —which is only another expression for the value of labour—are affected by "the varying price of food and other necessaries, on which the wages of labour are expended", shows just as little why the value of labour is (or appears to be) determined differently from the value of other commodities. For these too are affected by the varying price of other commodities which enter into their production and against which they are *exchanged.* That the wages of labour are *spent* upon food and necessaries, means after all only that the value of labour is *exchanged* against food and necessaries. The question is just why *labour* and the *commodities against which it is exchanged,* do not exchange according to the law of value, i.e., according to the relative quantities of labour.

Posed in this way, *presupposing* the *law of value,* the question is intrinsically insoluble, because *labour* as such is counterposed to *commodity*, a definite quantity of immediate labour as such is counterposed to a definite quantity of materialised labour.

This weakness in Ricardo's discourse, as we shall see later, has contributed to the disintegration of his school, and led to the proposition of absurd hypotheses.

||652| *Wakefield* is right when he says:

"Treating *labour* as a *commodity,* and *capital,* the produce of labour, as another, then, if the *value of these two commodities were regulated by equal quantities of labour,* a given amount of labour would, under all circumstances, exchange for that quantity of capital which had been produced by the same amount of labour, *antecedent labour* [...] *would always exchange for the same amount of present labour* [....] It follows, that[a] the value of labour in relation to other commodities, in so far, at least, as wages depend upon share, is determined, *not by equal quantities of labour*, but by the proportion between supply and demand." (E. G. Wakefield, Note on p. 230 of Vol. I of his edition of Adam Smith's *Wealth of Nations*, London, 1835.)

This is also one of *Bailey's* hobby-horses; to be looked up later. Also *Say*, who is very pleased to find that here, all of a sudden, supply and demand are said to be the decisive factors.[106] |652||

* * *

||652| *Re 1.* Another point to be noted here: Chapter I, *Section 3*, bears the following superscription:

"Not only *the labour applied immediately* to commodities affects their value, but the *labour also* which is *bestowed* on the implements, tools, and buildings, with which such labour is assisted" (David Ricardo, *On the Principles of Political Economy, and Taxation*, London, 1821, p. 16).

Thus the value of a commodity is equally determined by the quantity of *materialised* (*past*) labour and by the quantity of *living* (*immediate*) labour required for its production. In other words: the quantities of labour are in no way affected by the *formal difference* of whether the labour is materialised or living, past or present (immediate). If this difference is of no significance in the determination of the value of commodities, why does it assume such decisive importance when past labour (capital) is exchanged against living labour? Why should it, in this case, invalidate the law of value, since the difference *in itself,* as shown in the case of commodities, has no effect on the determination of value? Ricardo does not answer this question, he does not even raise it. |652||

2. Value of Labour-Power. Value of Labour.
[Ricardo's Confusion of Labour with Labour-Power.
Concept of the "Natural Price of Labour"]

||652| In order to determine surplus-value, Ricardo, like the Physiocrats, Adam Smith, etc., must first determine the *value of labour-power* or, as he puts it—following Adam Smith and his predecessors—the *value of labour.* |652||

||652| How then is the *value* or *natural price* of labour determined? According to *Ricardo,* the *natural price* is in fact nothing but the *monetary* expression of *value.*

---

[a] In the manuscript "but" instead of "It follows, that".—*Ed.*

"*Labour*, like all other things which are purchased and sold, and which may be increased or diminished in quantity" (that is like all other commodities) "has its natural and its market price. *The natural price of labour* is that price which is necessary to enable the labourers, one with another, to subsist and to perpetuate their race, without either increase or diminution." (Should read: with that rate of increase, required by the average progress of production.)

"The power of the labourer to support himself, and the family which may be necessary to keep up the number of labourers ... depends on *the price of the food, necessaries, and conveniences required for the support of the labourer and his family*. With a rise in the price of food and necessaries, the natural price of labour will rise; with the fall in their price, the natural price of labour will fall" (l.c., p. 86).

"It is not to be understood that the natural price of labour, estimated even in food and necessaries, is absolutely fixed and constant. It varies at different times in the same country, and very materially differs in different countries. It essentially depends on the habits and customs of the people" (l.c., p. 91).

The *value of labour* is therefore determined by the *means of subsistence* which, in a given society, are traditionally *necessary* for the maintenance and reproduction of the labourers.

But why? By what law is the *value of labour* determined in this way?

Ricardo has in fact no answer, other than that the law of supply and demand reduces the average price of labour to the means of subsistence that are necessary (physically or socially necessary in a given society) for the maintenance of the labourer. ||653| He determines *value* here, in one of the basic propositions of the whole system, by *demand and supply*—as Say notes with malicious pleasure (see Constancio's translation).[107]

Instead of *labour,* Ricardo should have discussed labour-*power*. But had he done so, *capital* would also have been revealed as the material conditions of labour, confronting the labourer as power that had acquired an independent existence and capital would at once have been revealed as a *definite social relationship.* Ricardo thus only distinguishes capital as "accumulated labour" from "immediate labour". And it is something purely physical, only an element in the *labour-process,* from which the relation between labour and capital, wages and profits, could never be developed.

"*Capital* is that part of the wealth of a country which is employed in production, and consists of food, clothing, tools, raw materials, machinery, etc., necessary to give effect to labour" (l.c., p. 89). "*Less capital*, which is the *same* thing as *less labour* ..." (l.c., p. 73). "Labour and *capital* (that is *accumulated labour*)a" (l.c., p. 499).

---

a The brackets are omitted in the manuscript.—*Ed.*

The jump which Ricardo makes here is correctly sensed by *Bailey:* •

"Mr. Ricardo, ingeniously enough, avoids a difficulty, which, on a first view, threatens to encumber his doctrine, that value depends on the quantity of labour employed in production. If this principle is rigidly adhered to, it follows, that the *value of labour* depends *on the quantity of labour employed in producing it*—which is evidently absurd. By a dexterous turn, therefore, Mr. Ricardo makes the value of labour depend on the quantity of labour required to produce wages, or, to give him the benefit of his own language, he maintains, that the *value of labour is to be estimated* by the quantity of labour required to produce wages, by which he means, the quantity of labour required to produce the money or commodities given to the labourer. This is similar to saying, that the value of cloth is to be estimated, not by the quantity of labour bestowed on[a] its production, but by the quantity of labour bestowed on the production of the silver, for which the cloth is exchanged." (Samuel Bailey, *A Critical Dissertation on the Nature, Measures, and Causes of Value, etc.,* London, 1825, pp. 50-51.)

Literally the objection raised here is correct. Ricardo distinguishes between *nominal* and *real wages.* Nominal wages are wages expressed in money, money wages.

Nominal wages are "the number of pounds that may be annually paid to the labourer" but *real wages* are "the *number of day's work,* necessary to obtain those pounds" (David Ricardo, l.c., p. 152).

As wages are equal to the necessary means of subsistence of the labourer, and the value of these wages (the real wages) is equal to the value of these means of subsistence, it is obvious that the value of these necessary means of subsistence is also equal to the real wages, that is, to the labour which they can command. If the value of the means of subsistence changes, then the value of the real wages changes. Assume that the means of subsistence of the labourer consist only of corn, and that the quantity of means of subsistence which he requires is 1 quarter of corn per month. Then the value of his wages [for one month] equals the value of 1 quarter of corn; if the value of the quarter of corn rises or falls, then the value of the month's labour rises or falls. But however much the value of the quarter of corn rises or falls (however much or little labour the quarter of corn contains), it is always equal to the value of one month's labour.

And here we have the *hidden reason* for Adam Smith's assertion, that as soon as capital, and consequently wage-labour, intervenes, the value of the product is not regulated by the quantity of labour bestowed upon it, but by the quantity of labour it

---

[a] In the manuscript: "upon".—*Ed.*

can command. The value of corn (and of other means of subsistence) determined by labour-time, changes; but, so long as the natural price of labour is paid, the quantity of labour that the quarter of corn can command remains the same. Labour has therefore, a *permanent relative value as compared with corn*. That is why for Smith too, the value of labour and the value of corn ([representing] *food* [in general]. See *Deacon Hume*)[108] are standard measures of value, because so long as the natural price of labour is paid, a given quantity of corn always commands [the same] quantity of labour, whatever the quantity of labour bestowed upon one quarter of corn may be. The same quantity of labour always commands the same *use-value*, or rather the same use-value always commands *the same quantity of labour*.

Even Ricardo determines the value of labour, its natural price, in this way. Ricardo says: The quarter of corn may have very different values, although it always commands—or is commanded by—the same ||654| quantity of labour. Yes, says Adam Smith: However much the value of the quarter of corn, determined by labour-time, may change, the worker must always pay (sacrifice) the same quantity of labour in order to buy it. The value of corn therefore alters, but the value of labour does not, since one month's labour equals one quarter of corn. The value of the corn too changes only in so far as we are considering the labour required for its production. If, on the other hand, we examine the quantity of labour against which it exchanges, which it sets into motion, its value does not change. And that is precisely why the quantity of labour, against which a quarter of corn is exchanged, is the *standard measure of value*. But the values of the other commodities have the same relation to labour as they have to corn. A given quantity of corn commands a given quantity of labour. A given quantity of every other commodity commands a certain quantity of corn. Hence every other commodity—or rather the value of every other commodity—is expressed by the quantity of labour it commands, since it is expressed by the quantity of corn it commands, and the latter is expressed by the quantity of labour it commands.

But how is the value of other commodities in relation to corn (means of subsistence) determined? By the quantity of labour they command. And how is the quantity of labour they command determined? By the quantity of corn that labour commands. Here Adam Smith is inevitably caught up in a vicious circle. (Incidentally, he *never* uses this measure of value when making an actual analysis.) Moreover here he confuses—as Ricardo also often does—labour, the *intrinsic* measure of value, with *money,* the *external measure,* which presupposes that value is already determined; although he and Ricardo have declared that labour is "the *foundation of the value* of commodities" while "the comparative quantity of labour which is necessary to their production" is "the rule which determines the respective quantities of goods which shall be given in exchange for each other" (Ricardo, l. c., p. 80).

Adam Smith errs when he concludes from the fact that a definite quantity of labour is exchangeable for a definite quantity of use-value, that this *definite quantity of labour* is the measure of value and that it always has *the same value,* whereas the same quantity of use-value can represent very different exchange-values. But Ricardo errs twice over; firstly because he does not understand the problem which causes Adam Smith's errors; secondly because disregarding the law of value of commodities and taking refuge in the law of supply and demand, he himself determines the *value of labour,* not by the quantity of labour expended in the production of *labour-power,* but by the quantity of labour expended in the production of the wages which the labourer receives. Thus in fact he says: The value of labour is determined by the value of the money which is paid for it! And what determines this? What determines the amount of money that is paid for it? The quantity of use-value that a given amount of labour commands or the quantity of labour that a definite quantity of use-value commands. And thereby he falls *literally* into the very inconsistency which he himself condemned in Smith.

This, as we have seen, also prevents him from grasping the specific distinction between *commodity* and *capital,* between the exchange of commodity for commodity and the exchange of capital for commodity—in accordance with the law of exchange of commodities.

The above example was this: 1 quarter of corn equals 1 month's labour, say 30 working-days. (A working-day of 12 hours.) In this case the value of 1 quarter corn is less than 30 working-days. If 1 quarter corn were the product of 30 working-days, the value of the labour would be equal to its product. There would be no surplus-value, and therefore no profit. No capital. In actual fact, therefore, if 1 quarter corn represents the wages for 30 working-days, the value of 1 quarter corn is always less than 30 working-days. The surplus-value depends on how much less it is. For example, 1 quarter corn may be equal to 25 working-days. Then the surplus-value equals 5 working-days, which is $^1/_6$ of the total labour-time. If 1 quarter (8 bushels) equals 25 working-days, then 30 working-days are equal to 1 quarter $1^3/_5$ bushels. The *value* of the 30 working-days (i.e., the wage) is therefore always smaller than the value of the product which contains the labour of 30 days. The value of the corn is thus determined not by the ||655| labour which it commands, for which it exchanges, but by the labour which is contained in it. On the other hand, the *value of the 30 days' labour* is always determined by 1 quarter corn, whatever this may be.

3. Surplus-Value. [An Analysis of the Source of Surplus-Value Is Lacking in Ricardo's Work. His Concept of Working-Day as a Fixed Magnitude]

Apart from the confusion between labour and labour-power, Ricardo defines the average wages or the value of labour correctly. For he says that it [the value of labour] is determined neither by the money nor by the means of subsistence which the labourer receives, but by the *labour-time which it costs to produce it*; that is, by the *quantity of labour materialised* in the means of subsistence of the labourer. This he calls the *real* wages. (See later.)

This definition [of the value of labour], moreover, necessarily follows from his theory. Since the value of labour is determined by the *value of the necessary means of subsistence* on which this value is to be expended, and the *value of the means of subsistence*, like that of all other commodities, is determined by the *quantity of labour they contain,* it naturally follows that the value of labour equals the value of the means of subsistence, which equals *the quantity of labour expended upon them.*

However correct this formula is (apart from the direct opposition of labour and capital), it is, nevertheless, inadequate. Although in replacement of his wages the individual labourer does not directly *produce—or reproduce,* taking into account the continuity of this process—products on which he lives (he may produce products which do not enter into his consumption at all, and even if he produces necessary means of subsistence, he may, due to the division of labour, only produce a single part of the necessary means of subsistence, for instance corn—and even that only in one form (for example in that of corn, not bread)),

but he *produces* commodities to the *value* of his means of subsistence, that is, he produces the *value* of his means of subsistence.
This means, therefore, if we consider his daily average consumption, that the labour-time which is contained in his daily means
of subsistence, forms one part of *h i s working-day*. He works one
part of the day in order to reproduce the *value* of his means of
subsistence; the commodities which he produces in this part of
the working-day have the same value, or represent a *quantity* of
labour-time equal to that contained in his daily means of subsistence. *It depends on the value of these means of subsistence*—in
other words on the social productivity of labour and not on the
productivity of the individual branch of production in which he
works—*how great a part of his working-day* is devoted to the
reproduction or production of the *value,* i.e., the equivalent, of
his means of subsistence.

Ricardo of course assumes that the labour-time contained in
the daily means of subsistence is equal to the labour-time which
the labourer must work daily in order to reproduce the value of
these means of subsistence. But by not *directly* showing that one
part of the labourer's *working-day* is assigned to the reproduction of the value of his own labour-power, he introduces a difficulty and obscures the clear understanding of the relationship.
A twofold confusion arises from this. The *origin of surplus-value*
does not become clear and consequently Ricardo is reproached by
his successors for having failed to grasp and expound the nature
of surplus-value. That is part of the reason for their scholastic
attempts at explaining it. But because thus the origin and nature
of surplus-value is not clearly comprehended, the surplus-labour
plus the necessary labour, in short, the *total working-day,* is regarded as a fixed magnitude, the differences in the amount of
surplus-value are overlooked, and the productivity of capital, the
compulsion to perform surplus-labour—on the one hand [to per-
form] absolute surplus-labour, and on the other its innate urge to
shorten the necessary labour-time—are not recognised, and therefore the *historical* justification for capital is not set forth. Adam
Smith, however, had already stated the correct formula. Important as it was, to resolve value into labour, it was equally important to resolve surplus-value into surplus-labour, and to do
so in explicit terms.

Ricardo starts out from the actual fact of capitalist production.
The value of labour is smaller than the value of the product
which it creates. The value of the product is therefore greater

than the value of the labour which produces it, or the value of the wages. The excess of the value of the product *over* the value of the wages is the surplus-value. (Ricardo wrongly uses the word *profit,* but, as we noted earlier, he identifies profit with surplus-value here and is really speaking of the latter.) For him it is a fact, that the value of the product is greater than the value of the wages. How this fact arises, remains unclear. The total working-day *is greater* than that part of the working-day which is required for the production of the wages. Why? That does not emerge. The *magnitude of the total working-day* is therefore wrongly assumed to be *fixed,* and directly entails wrong conclusions. The increase or decrease in surplus-value can therefore be explained *only* from the growing or diminishing productivity of social labour which produces the means of subsistence. That is to say, only relative surplus-value is understood.

||656| It is obvious that if the labourer needed his whole day to produce his own means of subsistence (i.e., commodities equal to the value of his own means of subsistence), there could be no surplus-value, and therefore no capitalist production and no wage-labour. This can only exist when the productivity of social labour is sufficiently developed to make possible some sort of excess of the total working-day over the labour-time required for the reproduction of the wage—i.e., *surplus-labour,* whatever its magnitude. But it is equally obvious, that with a given labour-time (a given length of the working-day) the productivity of labour [may be very different], on the other hand, with a given productivity of labour, the labour-time, the length of the working-day, may be very different. Furthermore, it is clear that though the existence of *surplus-labour* presupposes that the productivity of labour has reached a certain level, the mere *possibility* of this surplus-labour (i.e., the existence of that necessary minimum productivity of labour), does not in itself make it a *reality.* For this to occur, the labourer must first be *compelled* to work in excess of the [necessary] time, and this compulsion is exerted by capital. This is missing in Ricardo's work, and therefore also the whole struggle over the regulation of the normal working-day.

At a low stage of development of the social productivity of labour, that is to say, where the surplus-labour is relatively small, the class of those who live on the labour of others will generally be small in relation to the number of labourers. It can considerably grow (proportionately) in the measure in which productivity and therefore relative surplus-value develop.

It is moreover understood that the *value of labour* varies greatly in the same country at different periods and in different countries during the same period. The temperate zones are however the home of capitalist production. The *social* productive power of labour may be very undeveloped; yet this may be compensated precisely in the production of the means of subsistence, on the one hand, by the fertility of the natural agents, such as the land; on the other hand, by the limited requirements of the population, due to climate, etc.—this is, for instance, the case in India. Where conditions are primitive, the minimum wage may be very small (quantitatively in use-values) because the social needs are not yet developed though it may cost much labour. But even if an average amount of labour were required to produce this minimum wage, the surplus-value created, although it would be high in proportion to the wage (to the necessary labour-time), would, even with a high rate of surplus-value, be just as meagre (proportionately) —when expressed in terms of use-values—as the wage itself.

Let the necessary labour-time be 10 hours, the surplus-labour 2 hours, and the total working-day 12 hours. If the necessary labour-time were 12 hours, the surplus-labour $2^2/_5$ hours and the total working-day $14^2/_5$ hours, then the values produced would be very different. In the first case they would amount to 12 hours, in the second to $14^2/_5$ hours. Similarly, the absolute magnitude of the surplus-value: In the former case it would be 2 hours, in the latter $2^2/_5$. And yet the *rate of surplus-value* or of *surplus-labour* would be the same, because $2:10=2^2/_5:12$. If, in the second case, the variable capital which is laid out were greater, then so also would be the surplus-value or surplus-labour appropriated by it. If in the latter case, the surplus-labour were to rise by $5/_5$ hours instead of by $2/_5$ hours, so that it would amount to 3 hours and the total working-day to 15 hours, then, although the *necessary labour-time* or the minimum wage had increased, the *rate of surplus-value* would have risen, for $2:10=^1/_5$; but $3:12=^1/_4$. Both could occur if, as a result of the corn, etc., becoming dearer, the minimum wage had increased from 10 to 12 hours. Even in this case, therefore, not only might the rate of surplus-value remain the same, but the amount and rate of surplus-value might grow.

But let us suppose that the necessary wage amounted to 10 hours, as previously, the surplus-labour to 2 hours and all other conditions remained the same (that is, leaving out of account here any lowering in the production costs of constant capital). Now let the labourer work $2^2/_5$ hours longer, and appropriate 2 hours, while the $^2/_5$ forms surplus-labour. In this case wages and surplus-value would increase in equal proportion, the former, however, representing more than the necessary wage or the necessary labour-time.

If one takes a *given* magnitude and divides it into two parts, it is clear that one part can only increase in so far as the other decreases, and vice versa. But this is by no means the case with expanding (elastic) magnitudes. And the working-day represents such an elastic magnitude, as long as no normal working-day has been won. With such magnitudes, both parts can grow, either to an equal or unequal extent. An increase in one is not brought about by a decrease in the other and vice versa. This is moreover the only case in which wages and surplus-value, in terms of *exchange-value*, can both *increase* and possibly even in *equal proportions*. That they can increase in terms of use-value is self-evident; this can increase ||657| even if, for example, the value of labour decreases. From 1797 to 1815, when the price of corn and [also] the nominal wage rose considerably in England, the daily hours of labour increased greatly in the principal industries, which were then in a phase of ruthless expansion; and I believe that this arrested the fall in the rate of profit, because it arrested the fall in the rate of surplus-value. In this case, however, whatever the circumstances, the normal working-day is lengthened and the normal span of life of the labourer, hence the normal duration of his labour-power, is correspondingly shortened. This applies where a permanent lengthening of the working-day occurs. If it is only temporary, in order to compensate for a temporary rise in wages, it may (except in the case of children and women) have no other result than to prevent a fall in the rate of profit in those enterprises where the nature of the work makes a prolongation of labour-time possible. (This is least possible in agriculture.)

Ricardo did not consider this at all since he investigated neither the origin of surplus-value nor absolute surplus-value and therefore regarded the working-day as a given magnitude. For this case, therefore, *his law*—that surplus-value and wages (he erroneously says profit and wages) in terms of exchange-value can rise or fall only in *inverse* proportion—*is incorrect*.

Firstly let us assume that the necessary labour-time and the surplus-labour remain constant. That is 10 hours + 2 hours; the working-day equals 12 hours, surplus-value equals 2 hours; the rate of surplus-value is $^1/_5$.

[In the second example] the necessary labour-time remains the same; surplus-labour increases from 2 to 4 hours. Hence 10+4=a working-day of 14 hours; surplus-value equals 4 hours; rate of surplus-value is $4:10=^4/_{10}=^2/_5$.

In both cases the necessary labour-time is the same; but the surplus-value in the one case is twice as great as in the other and the working-day in the second case is one-sixth longer than in the first. Furthermore, although the wage is the same, the values produced, corresponding to the quantities of labour, would be very different; in the first case it would be equal to 12 hours, in the second to $12+^{12}/_6=14$ hours. It is therefore wrong to say that, provided the *wage is the same* (in terms of value, of necessary labour-time), the surplus-value contained in two commodities is proportionate to the quantities of labour contained in them. This is only correct where the *normal working-day* is the same.

Let us further assume that as a result of the rise in the productive power of labour, the necessary wage (although it remains constant in terms of use-values) falls from 10 to 9 hours and similarly that the surplus labour-time falls from 2 to $1^4/_5$ hours ($^9/_5$). In this case $10:9=2:1^4/_5$. Thus the surplus labour-time would fall in the same proportion as the necessary labour-time. The rate of surplus-value would be the same in both cases, for $2=^{10}/_5$ and $1^4/_5=^9/_5$. $1^4/_5:9=2:10$. The quantity of use-values that could be bought with the surplus-value, would—according to the assumption—also remain the same. (But this would apply only to those use-values which are necessary means of subsistence.) The working-day would decrease from 12 to $10^4/_5$ [hours]. The amount of value produced in the second case would be smaller than that produced in the first. And despite these unequal quantities of labour, the rate of surplus-value would be the same in both cases.

In discussing surplus-value we have distinguished between surplus-value and the rate of surplus-value. Considered in relation to one working-day, the surplus-value is equal to the absolute number of hours which it represents, 2, 3, etc. The rate is equal to the proportion of this number of hours to the number of hours which makes up the necessary labour-time. This distinction is very important, because it indicates the varying length of the working-day. If the surplus-value equals 2 hours, then [the rate] is $1/5$, if the necessary labour-time is 10 hours; and $1/6$, if the necessary labour-time is 12 hours. In the first case the working-day consists of 12 hours and in the second of 14. In the first case the rate of surplus-value is greater, while at the same time the labourer works a smaller number of hours per day. In the second case the rate of surplus-value is smaller, the value of the labour-power is greater, while at the same time the labourer works a greater number of hours per day. This shows that, with a constant surplus-value, but a working-day of unequal length, the rate of surplus-value may be different. The earlier case, 10:2 and $9:1^4/5$, shows how with a constant rate of surplus-value, but a working-day of unequal length, the surplus-value itself may be different, in one case 2 hours and in the other $1^4/5$ hours.

I have shown previously (Chapter II), that if the length of the working-day and the necessary labour-time, and therefore the rate of surplus-value are given, the amount of surplus-value depends on the *number* of workers simultaneously employed by the same capital.[109] This was a tautological statement. For if 1 working-day gives me 2 surplus hours, then 12 working-days give me 24 surplus hours or 2 surplus days. The statement, however, becomes very important in connection with the determination of profit, which is equal to the proportion of surplus-value to the capital advanced, thus depending on the absolute amount of surplus-value. It becomes important because capitals of equal size but different organic composition employ unequal numbers of labourers; they must thus produce unequal amounts of surplus-value, and therefore unequal profits. With a falling rate of surplus-value, the profit may rise and with a rising rate of surplus-value, the profit may fall; or the profit may remain unchanged, if a rise or fall in the rate of surplus-value is compensated by a counter movement affecting the number of workers employed. Here we see immediately, how extremely wrong it is ||658| to identify the laws relating to the rise and fall of surplus-value with the laws relating to the rise and fall of profit. If one merely considers the simple law of surplus-value, then it seems a tautology to say that with a given rate of surplus-value (and a given length of the working-day), the absolute amount of surplus-value depends on the amount of capital employed. For an increase in this amount of capital and an increase in the number of labourers simultaneously employed are, on the assumption made, identical, or merely [different] expressions of the same fact. But when one turns to an examination of profit, where the amount of the total capital employed and the number of workers employed vary greatly for capitals of equal size, then the importance of the law becomes clear.

Ricardo starts by considering *commodities* of a given value, that is to say, commodities which represent a *given* quantity of labour. And from this starting-point, absolute and relative surplus-value appear to be always identical. (This at any rate explains the one-sidedness of his mode of procedure and corresponds with his whole method of investigation: to start with the *value* of the commodities as determined by the definite labour-time they contain, and then to examine to what extent this is affected by wages, profits, etc.) This appearance is nevertheless false, since it is not a question of commodities here, but of capitalist production, of commodities as products of capital.

Assume that a capital employs a certain number of workers, for example 20, and that wages amount to £ 20. To simplify matters let us assume that the fixed capital is nil, i.e., we leave it out of account. Further, assume that these 20 workers spin £ 80 of cotton into yarn, if they work 12 hours per day. If 1 lb. of cotton costs 1s. then 20lbs. cost £ 1 and £ 80 represents, 1,600 lbs. If 20 workers spin 1,600 lbs. in 12 hours, then they spin $^{1,600}/_{12}$ lbs., which is $133^{1}/_{3}$ lbs. in one hour. Thus, if the necessary labour-time is 10 hours, then the surplus labour-time is 2 hours and this equals $266^{2}/_{3}$ lbs. yarn. The value of the 1,600 lbs. would be £ 104. For if 10 hours of work equal £ 20, then 1 hour of work equals £ 2 and 2 hours of work £ 4, hence 12 [hours of work] are equal to £ 24. ([Raw material] £ 80+£ 24 [the newly-created value] are equal to £ 104.)

But if each of the workers worked 4 hours of surplus-labour, then their product would be equal to £ 8 (I mean the surplus-value which he creates—his product is in fact equal to £ 28.[110]) The total product would be £ $121^{1}/_{3}$[111]. And this £ $121^{1}/_{3}$ would be the equivalent of 1,866$^{2}/_{3}$ lbs. of yarn. As before, since the conditions of production remained the same, 1 lb. of yarn would have the same value; it would contain the same amount of labour-time. Moreover, according to the assumption, the necessary wages—their value, the labour-time they contained—would have remained unchanged.

Whether these 1,866$^{2}/_{3}$ lbs. of yarn were being produced under the first set of conditions or under the second, i.e., with 2 or with 4 hours surplus-labour, they would have the same value in both cases. The value therefore of the additional 266$^{2}/_{3}$ lbs. of cotton that are spun, is £ 13$^1/_3$. This, added to the £ 80 for the 1,600 lbs., amounts to £ 93$^1/_3$ and in both cases 4 working-hours more for 20 men amount to £ 8. Altogether £ 28 for the labour, that is £ 121$^1/_3$. The wages are, in both cases, the same. The pound of yarn costs in both cases 1$^3/_{10}$ s. Since the value of the pound of cotton is 1s., what remained for the newly-added labour in 1 lb. of yarn would in both cases amount to $^3/_{10}$ s., equal to 3$^3/_5$ d (or $^{18}/_5$ d.).

Nevertheless, under the conditions assumed, the relation between value and surplus-value in each pound of yarn would be very different. In the first case, since the necessary labour was equal to £ 20 and the surplus-labour to £ 4, or since the former amounted to 10 hours and the latter to 2 hours, the ratio of surplus-labour to necessary labour would be 2:10=$^2/_{10}$=$^1/_5$. (Similarly £ 4:£ 20=$^4/_{20}$=$^1/_5$.) The 3$^3/_5$ d. [newly-added labour] in a pound of yarn would in this case contain $^1/_5$ unpaid labour, that is $^{18}/_{25}$ d. or $^{72}/_{25}$ farthings equal to 2$^{22}/_{25}$ farthings. In the second case, on the other hand, the necessary labour would be £ 20 (10 working-hours), the surplus-labour £ 8 (4 working-hours). The ratio of surplus-labour to necessary labour would be 8:20=$^8/_{20}$=$^4/_{10}$=$^2/_5$. Thus the 3 $^3/_5$ d. [of newly-added labour] in a pound of yarn would contain $^2/_5$ unpaid labour, i.e., 5$^{19}/_{25}$ farthings or 1 d. 1$^{19}/_{25}$ farthings. ||659| Although the yarn has the same value in both cases and although the same wages are paid in both cases, the surplus-value in a pound of yarn is in one case twice as large as in the other. The ratio of value of labour to surplus-value is of course the same in the individual commodity, that is, in a portion of the product, as in the whole product.

In the one case, the capital advanced is £ 93$^1/_3$ for cotton, and how much for wages? The wages for 1,600 lbs. amount to £ 20 here, hence for the additional 266$^2/_3$ lbs. a further £ 3$^1/_3$. This makes £ 23$^1/_3$. And the total capital outlay is £ 93$^1/_3$+£ 23$^1/_3$=£ 116$^2/_3$. The product comes to £ 121$^1/_3$. (The additional outlay in [variable] capital, of £ 3$^1/_3$, only yields 13$^1/_3$ s. [£ $^2/_3$] surplus-value. £ 20:£ 4=£ 3$^1/_3$+£ $^2/_3$).

In the other case, however, the capital outlay would amount to only £ 93$^1/_9$+£ 20=£ 113$^1/_3$ and £ 4 would have to be added to the £ 4 surplus-value. The same number of pounds of yarn are produced in both cases and both have the same value, that is to say, they represent equal total quantities of labour, but these equal total quatities of labour are set in motion by capitals of unequal size, although the wages are the same; but the working-days are of unequal length and, *therefore,* unequal quantities of unpaid labour are produced. Taking the individual pound of yarn, the wages paid for it, or the amounts of *paid* labour a pound contains, are different. The same wages are spread over a larger volume of commodities here, not because labour is more productive in the one case than in the other, but because the total amount of unpaid labour which is set into motion in one case is greater than in the other. With *the same* quantity of *paid* labour, therefore, more pounds of yarn are produced in the one case than in the other, although in both cases the same quantities of yarn are produced, representing the same quantity of total labour (paid and unpaid). If, on the other hand, the productivity of labour had increased in the second case, then the value of the pound of yarn would at all events have fallen, whatever the ratio of surplus-value to variable capital.

In such a case, therefore, it would be wrong to say that—because the *value* of the pound of yarn is fixed at 1s. $3^3/_5$d., the value of the labour which is added is also fixed and amounts to $3^3/_5$ d., and the wages, i.e., the *necessary labour-time,* remain, according to the assumption, unchanged—the surplus-value [must] be the same and the two capitals under otherwise equal conditions would have produced the yarn with equal profits. This would be correct if we were concerned with one pound of yarn, but we are in fact concerned here with a capital which has produced 1,866$^2/_3$ lbs. yarn. And in order to know the amount of profit (actually of surplus-value) on one pound, we must know the length of the working-day, or the quantity of unpaid labour (when the productivity is given) that the capital sets in motion. But this information cannot be gathered by looking at the individual commodity.

Thus Ricardo deals only with what I have called the *relative surplus-value.* From the outset he assumes, as Adam Smith and his predecessors seem to have done as well, that the *length of the working-day is given.* (At most, Adam Smith mentions differences in the length of the working-day in *different* branches of labour, which are levelled out or compensated by the relatively greater intensity of labour, difficulty, unpleasantness, etc.) On the basis of this postulate Ricardo, on the whole, explains relative surplus-value correctly. Before we give the principal points of his theory, we shall cite a few more passages to illustrate Ricardo's point of view.

"The labour of a million of men in manufactures, will always produce the *same value*, but will not always produce the same riches" (l.c., p. 320).

This means that the product of their daily labour will always be the product of a million working-days containing *the same* labour-time; this is wrong, or is only true where *the same* normal working-day—taking into account the various difficulties etc. in different branches of labour—has been generally established.

Even then, however, the statement is wrong in the general form in which it is expressed here. If the normal working-day is 12 hours, and the annual product of one man is, in terms of money, £ 50 and the value of money remains unchanged, then, in this case, the product of 1 million men would always amount to £ 50 million per year. If the necessary labour is 6 hours, then the capital laid out for these million men would be £ 25,000,000 per annum. The surplus-value would also be £ 25 million. The product would always be 50 million, whether the workers received 25 or 30 or 40 million. But in the first case the surplus-value would be 25 million, in the second it would be 20 million and in the third 10 million. If the capital advanced consisted only of *variable* capital, i.e., only of the capital which is laid out in the *wages* of these 1 million men, then Ricardo would be right. He is, therefore, only right in the *one* case, where the total capital equals the variable capital; a presupposition which pervades all his, and Adam Smith's, ||660| observations regarding the capital of society as a whole, but in capitalist production this precondition does not exist in a single branch of industry, much less in the production of society as a whole.

That *part of the constant capital* which enters into the labour-process without entering into the process of the creation of value, does not enter into the product, into the *value of the product*, and, therefore, important as it is in the determination of the general rate of profit, it does not concern us here, where we are considering the *value* of the *annual product*. But matters are quite different with that part of constant capital which enters into the annual product. We have seen that a portion of this part of constant capital, or what appears as constant capital in one sphere of production, appears as a direct product of labour within another sphere of production, during *the same* production period of one year; a large part of the capital laid out annually, which *appears* to be constant capital from the standpoint of the individual capitalist or the particular sphere of production, therefore, resolves itself into *variable* capital from the standpoint of society or of the capitalist class. This part is thus included in the 50 million, in that part of the 50 million which forms variable capital or is laid out in wages.

But the position is different with that *part of constant capital* which is used up in order to replace the constant capital consumed in industry and agriculture—with the consumed part of the constant capital employed in those branches of production which produce constant capital, raw material in its primary form, fixed capital and auxiliary materials. The value of this part reappears, it is reproduced in the product. In what proportion it enters into the value of the whole product depends entirely on its actual magnitude—provided the productivity of labour does not change; but however the productivity may change, this part of the constant capital will always have a *definite* magnitude. (On the average, apart from certain exceptions in agriculture, the amount of the product, i.e., the *riches*—which Ricardo distinguishes from the *value*—produced by one million men will, indeed, also depend on the magnitude of this constant capital which is antecedent to production.) This part of the value of the product would not exist without the new labour of the million men during the year. On the other hand, the labour of the million men would not yield the same amount of product without this constant capital which exists independently of their year's labour. It enters into the labour-process as a condition of production but not a single additional hour is worked in order to reproduce the value of this part. As value it is, therefore, not the result of the year's labour, although its value would not have been reproduced *without* this year's labour.

If the part of the constant capital which enters into the product were 25 million, then the value of the product of the one million men would be 75 million; if this part of the constant capital were 10 million, then the value of the product would only be 60 million, etc. And since the ratio of constant capital to variable capital increases in the course of capitalist development, the value of the annual product of a million men will tend to rise continuously, in proportion to the growth of the past labour which plays a part in their annual production. This alone shows that Ricardo was unable to understand either the essence of accumulation or the nature of profit.

With the growth in the proportion of constant to variable capital, grows also the productivity of labour, the productive forces brought into being, with which social labour operates. As a result of this increasing productivity of labour, however, a part of the existing constant capital is continuously depreciated in value, for its value depends not on the labour-time that it cost originally, but on the labour-time with which it can be reproduced, and this is continuously diminishing as the productivity of labour grows. Although, therefore, the value of the constant capital does not increase in proportion to its amount, it increases nevertheless, because its amount increases even more rapidly than its value falls. But we shall return later to Ricardo's views on accumulation.

It is evident, however, that if the length of the working-day is given, the value of the annual product of the labour of one million men will differ greatly according to the different amount of constant capital that enters into the product; and that, despite the growing productivity of labour, the value of this product will be greater where the constant capital forms a large part of the total capital, than under social conditions where it forms a relatively small part of the total capital. With the advance in the productivity of social labour, accompanied as it is by the growth of constant capital, a relatively ever increasing part of the annual product of labour will, therefore, fall to the share of capital as such, and thus property in the form of capital (apart from revenue) will be constantly increasing and proportionately that part of value which the individual worker and even the working class creates, will be steadily decreasing, ||661| compared with the product of their past labour that confronts them as capital. The alienation and the antagonism between labour-power and the objective conditions of labour which have become independent in the form of capital, thereby grow continuously. (Not taking into account the variable capital, i.e., that part of the product of the annual labour which is required for the reproduction of the working class; even these means of subsistence, however, confront them as capital.)

Ricardo's view, that the working-day is *given, limited, a fixed magnitude,* is also expressed by him in other forms, for instance:

"They" (the wages of labour and profit of stock) are "*together* always *of the same value*" (l.c., p. 499, [in] Chapter XXXII "Mr. Malthus's Opinions on Rent"),

in other words this only means that the (daily) labour-time whose product is *divided* between the wages of labour and the profits of stock, is always *the same,* is *constant.*

"Wages and profits together will be of *the same value*" (l.c., p. 491, note).

I hardly need to repeat here that in these passages one should always read "surplus-value" instead of "profit".

"Wages and profits taken together will continue *always* of the same value" (l.c., pp. 490-91).

"Wages are to be estimated by their *real value*, viz., by the *quantity of labour and capital employed in producing* them, and not by their *nominal value* either in coats, hats, money, or corn" (l.c., Chapter I, "*On Value*" p. 50).

The value of the means of subsistence which the worker obtains (buys with his wages), corn, clothes, etc., is determined by the total labour-time required for their production, the quantity of immediate labour as well as the quantity of materialised labour necessary for their production. But Ricardo confuses the issue because he does not state it plainly, he does not say: "their *real value*, viz., that quantity of the working-day required to reproduce the value of their [the workers] own necessaries, the equivalent of the necessaries paid to them, or exchanged for their labour". Real wages have to be determined by the average time which the worker must work each day in order to produce or reproduce his own wages.

"The labourer is only paid a really high price for his labour, when his wages will purchase the produce of a great deal of labour" (l.c., p. 322, [note]).

4. Relative Surplus-Value.
[The Analysis of Relative Wages Is One of Ricardo's Scientific Achievements]

This is in fact the only form of surplus-value which Ricardo analyses under the name of *profit*. [According to him:]

The quantity of labour required for the production of a commodity, and contained in it, determines its value, which is thus a *given* factor, a *definite amount*. This amount is divided between wage-labourer and capitalist. (Ricardo, like Adam Smith, does not take constant capital into account here.) It is obvious that the share of one can only rise or fall in proportion to the fall or rise of the share of the other. Since the value of the commodities is due to the labour of the workers, labour is under all circumstances the precondition of value, but there can be no labour unless the worker lives and maintains himself, i.e., receives the necessary wages (the minimum wages—wages is synonymous

with the value of his labour-power). Wages and surplus-value—
these two categories into which the value of the commodity or the
product itself is divided—are therefore not only in inverse proportion to each other, but the primary, the determinant factor is
the movement of wages. Their rise or fall causes the opposite
movement on the part of profit (surplus-value). Wages do not rise
or fall because profit (surplus-value) falls or rises, but on the
contrary surplus-value (profit) falls or rises because wages rise
or fall. The *surplus-product* (one should really say *surplus-value*)
which remains after the working class has received its share of
its own annual production forms the substance on which the
capitalist class lives.

Since the value of the commodities is determined by the quantity of labour contained in them, and since wages and surplus-
value (profit) are only *shares,* proportions in which two classes
of producers divide the value of the commodity between themselves, it is clear that a rise or fall in wages, although it determines the rate of surplus-value (profit), does not affect the value
of the commodity or the price (as the monetary expression of the
value of a commodity). The proportion in which a whole is divided between two shareholders makes the whole neither larger
nor smaller. It is, therefore, an erroneous preconception to assume that a *rise in wages raises the prices of commodities;* it
only makes profit (surplus-value) fall. Even the exceptions cited
by Ricardo, where a rise in wages is supposed to make the exchange-values of some commodities fall and those of others rise,
are wrong so far as *value* is concerned and only correct for *cost-
prices.*

||662| Since the rate of surplus-value (profit) is determined
by the relative height of wages, how is the latter determined?
Apart from competition, by the price of the necessary means of
subsistence. This, in turn, depends on the productivity of labour,
which increases with the fertility of the land (Ricardo assumes
capitalist production here). Every "improvement" reduces the
prices of commodities, of the means of subsistence. Wages or the
value of labour, thus rise and fall in inverse proportion to the
development of the productive power of labour, in so far as the
latter produces necessary means of subsistence which enter into
the average consumption of the working class. The rate of surplus-value (profit) falls or rises, therefore, in direct proportion
to the development of the productive power of labour, because
this development reduces or raises wages.

The rate of profit (surplus-value) cannot fall unless wages rise, and cannot rise unless wages fall.

The value of wages has to be reckoned not according to the quantity of the means of subsistence received by the worker, but according to the quantity of labour which these means of subsistence cost (in fact the proportion of the working-day which he appropriates for himself), that is according to the *relative share* of the total product, or rather of the total value of this product, which the worker receives. It is possible that, reckoned in terms of use-values (quantity of commodities or money), his wages rise as productivity increases and yet the value of the wages may fall and vice versa. It is one of Ricardo's great merits that he examined relative or proportionate wages, and established them as a definite category. Up to this time, wages had always been regarded as something simple and consequently the worker was considered an animal. But here he is considered in his social relationships. The position of the classes to one another depends more on relative wages than on the absolute amount of wages.

Now these propositions have to be substantiated by quotations from Ricardo.

"The *value* of the deer, the produce of the hunter's *day's labour*, would be exactly equal to the value of the fish, the produce of the fisherman's *day's labour*. The comparative value of the fish and the game, would be entirely regulated by the quantity of labour realised in each, *whatever might be the quantity of production*, or however *high or low general wages or profits might be*. If ... the fisherman ... employed ten men, whose annual labour cost £100 and who *in one day* obtained *by their* labour twenty salmon: If ... the hunter [...] also employed ten men, whose *annual labour* cost £100 and who in *one day* procured him ten deer; then the natural price of a deer would be two salmon, whether *the proportion of the whole produce bestowed on the men who obtained* [it,] were large or small. The *proportion* which might be paid for *wages*, is of the utmost importance in the question of *profits*; for it must at once be seen, that profits would be high or low, exactly in proportion as wages were low or high; but it could not in the least affect the relative value of fish and game, as wages would be high or low at the same time in both occupations" (l.c., Chapter I "*On Value*", pp. 20-21).

It can be seen that Ricardo derives the whole value of the commodity from the *labour* of the men employed. It is their own labour or the product of that labour or the value of this product, which is divided between them and capital.

"No alteration in the wages of labour could produce any alteration in the relative value of these commodities; for suppose them to rise, no *greater quantity of labour* would be required in any of these occupations, but it would be *paid* for at a *higher price*.... Wages might rise twenty per cent and profits consequently fall in a greater or less proportion, without occasioning the least alteration in the relative value of these commodities" (l.c., p. 23).

"There can be no rise in the *value of labour* without a fall of profits. If the corn is to be *divided* between the farmer and the labourer, *the larger the proportion* that is given to the latter, the less will remain for the former. So if cloth or cotton goods be *divided* between the workman and his employer, the *larger the proportion* given to the former, the less remains for the latter" (l.c., p. 31).

||663| "Adam Smith, and all the writers who have followed him, have, without one exception that I know of, maintained that *a rise in the price of labour* would be uniformly followed by *a rise in the price of all commodities.* I hope I have succeeded in showing, that there are no grounds for such an opinion" (l.c., p. 45).

"A rise of[a] wages, from the circumstance of the labourer being more liberally rewarded, or from a difficulty of procuring the necessaries on which wages are expended, does not, except in some instances, produce the effect of raising price, but has a great effect in lowering profits."

The position is different, however, when the rise of wages is due to "... an alteration in the value of money.... "In the one case" ⟨namely, in the last-mentioned case⟩ "no *greater proportion of the annual labour of the country* is devoted to the *support of* [the] *labourers*; in the other case, a larger portion is so devoted" (l.c., p. 48). |663||.

||663| "With a rise in the price of food and necessaries, the natural price of labour will rise; with the[b] fall in their price, the natural price of labour will fall" (l.c., p. 86).

"The *surplus produce* remaining, after satisfying the wants of the existing population, must necessarily be in proportion to the *facility of production,* viz., to the *smaller number of persons* employed in production" (l.c., p. 93).

"Neither the farmer who cultivates that quantity of land, which regulates price, nor the manufacturer, who manufactures goods, sacrifice any portion of the produce for rent. The *whole value of their commodities is divided* into *two portions* only: one constitutes the profits of stock, the other the wages of labour" (l.c., p. 107).

"Suppose the price of silks, velvets, furniture, and any other commodities, not required by the labourer, to rise in consequence of more labour being expended on them, would not that affect profits? Certainly not: for nothing can affect profits but a rise in wages; silks and velvets are not consumed by the labourer, and therefore cannot raise wages" (l.c., p. 118).

"If the labour of ten men will, on land of a certain quality, obtain 180 quarters of wheat, and its value be £ 4 per quarter, or £ 720" (l.c., p. 110), "... in all cases, the same sum of £ 720 must be divided between wages and profits.... Whether wages or profits rise or fall, it is this sum of £ 720 from which they must both be provided. On the one hand, profits can never rise so high as to absorb so much of this £ 720 that enough will not be left to furnish the labourers with absolute necessaries; on the other hand, wages can never rise so high as to leave no portion of this sum for profits" (l.c., p. 113).

"Profits *depend on high or low wages,* wages on the price of necessaries, and the price of necessaries chiefly on the price of food, because all other

---

  a In the manuscript: "in".—*Ed.*
  b In the manuscript: "a".—*Ed.*

requisites may be increased almost without limit" (l.c., p. 119).

"Although a greater value is produced" (with a deterioration of the land) "a *greater proportion of what remains of that value*, after paying rent, is consumed by the producers," (he identifies labourers with producers here) "and it is this, *and this alone*, which regulates profits" (l.c., p. 127).

"It is the essential quality of an *improvement to diminish the quantity of labour* before required to produce a commodity; and this diminution cannot take place without a *fall of its price or relative value*" (l.c., p. 70).

"Diminish the cost of production of hats, and their price will ultimately fall to their new natural price, although the demand should be doubled, trebled, or quadrupled. Diminish the cost of subsistence of men, by diminishing the natural price of the food and clothing, by which life is sustained, and wages will ultimately fall, notwithstanding that the demand for labourers ||664| may very greatly increase" (l.c., p. 460).

"In proportion as less is appropriated for wages, more will be appropriated for profits, and vice versa" (l.c., p. 500).

"It has been one of the objects of this work to shew, that with every fall in the real value of necessaries, the wages of labour would fall, and that the profits of stock would rise—in other words, that of any given *annual value a less portion would be paid to the labouring class*, and a larger portion to those *whose funds employed this class*."

⟨It is only in this statement, which has now become a commonplace, that Ricardo expresses the nature of capital, though he may not be aware of it. It is not accumulated labour which is employed by the labouring class, by the labourers themselves, but the "funds", "accumulated labour", which "employ this class", employ present, immediate labour.⟩

"Suppose the *value* of the commodities produced in a particular manufacture to be £ 1,000, and to be *divided* between *the master* and *his* labourers" ⟨here again he expresses the nature of capital; the capitalist is the *master*, the workers are *his* labourers⟩ "in the proportion of £ 800 to labourers, and £ 200 to the master; if the value of these commodities should fall to £ 900, and £ 100 be saved from the wages of labour, in consequence of the fall of necessaries, the net income of the masters would be in no degree impaired" (l.c., pp. 511-12).

"If the shoes and clothing of the labourer, could, by improvements in machinery, be produced by one-fourth of the labour now necessary to their production, they would probably fall 75 per cent; but so far is it from being true, that the labourer would thereby be enabled permanently to consume four coats, or four pair of shoes, instead of one, that it is probable his *wages would in no long time be adjusted* by the effects of competition, and the stimulus to population, to the *new value of the necessaries* on which they were expended. If these improvements extended to all the objects of the labourer's consumption, we should find him probably at the end of a very few years, in possession of only a small, if any, addition to his enjoyments, although the exchangeable value of those commodities, compared with any other commodity [...] had sustained a very considerable reduction; and though they were the produce of a very considerably diminished quantity of labour" (l.c., p. 8).

"When wages rise, it is always at the expense of profits, and when they fall, profits always rise" (l.c., p. 491, note).

"It has been my endeavour to shew throughout this work, that the rate of profits can never be increased but by a fall in wages, and that there can be no permanent fall of wages but in consequence of a fall of the necessaries on which wages are expended. If, therefore, by the *extension of foreign* trade, or by *improvements in machinery*, the food and necessaries of the labourer can be brought to market, at a reduced price, profits will rise. If, instead of growing our own corn, or manufacturing the clothing and other necessaries of the labourer, we discover a new market from which we can supply ourselves with these commodities at a cheaper price, wages will fall and profits rise; but if the commodities obtained at a cheaper rate[a], by the extension of foreign commerce, or by the improvement of machinery, be exclusively the commodities consumed by the rich, no alteration will take place in the rate of profits. The rate of wages would not be affected, although wine, velvets, silks, and other expensive commodities should fall 50 per cent, and consequently profits would continue unaltered.

"Foreign trade, then, though highly beneficial to a country, as it increases the amount and variety of the objects on which revenue may be expended, and affords, by the abundance and cheapness of commodities, incentives to saving" (and why not incentives to spending?), "and to the *accumulation of capital*, has no tendency to raise the profits of stock, *unless the commodities imported be of that description on which the wages of labour are expended.*

"The remarks which have been made respecting foreign trade, apply equally to home trade. The rate of profits is *never increased*"

⟨he has just said the very opposite; evidently he means never, unless the value of labour is diminished by the improvements mentioned⟩

"by a *better distribution of labour*, by the *invention of machinery*, by the *establishment of roads and canals*, or by *any means of abridging labour* [...] *in the manufacture or in the conveyance of goods*. These are causes which operate on price, and never fail to be highly beneficial to consumers; since they enable them, with the same labour [...] to obtain in exchange a greater quantity of the commodity to *which the improvement* is applied; but they have no effect whatever on profit. On the other hand, |665| every diminution in the wages of labour raises profits, but produces no effect on the price of commodities. One is advantageous to all classes, for all classes are consumers"

⟨but how is it advantageous to the labouring class? For Ricardo presupposes that if these commodities enter into the consumption of the wage-earner they reduce wages, and if these commodities become cheaper without reducing wages they are not commodities on which wages are expended⟩;

"the other is beneficial only to producers; they gain more, but every thing remains at its former price."

---

a In the manuscript: "price".—*Ed.*

⟨Again, how is this possible, since Ricardo presupposes that the reduction of wages which raises profits takes place precisely because the price of the necessaries has fallen and therefore by no means does "every thing remain at its former price".⟩

"In the first case they get the same as before; but *every thing*" ⟨wrong again; should read every thing, with the exception of the necessaries⟩ "on which their gains are expended, is diminished in exchangeable value" (l.c., pp. 137-38).

It is evident that this passage is rather loosely worded. But apart from this formal aspect, the statements are only true if one reads "rate of surplus-value" for rate of profit, and this applies to the whole of this investigation into relative surplus-value. Even in the case of luxury articles, such improvements can raise the general rate of profit, since the rate of profit in these spheres of production, as in all others, bears a share in the levelling out of all particular rates of profit into the average rate of profit. If in such cases, as a result of the above-mentioned influences, the value of the constant capital falls proportionately to the variable, or the period of turnover is reduced (i.e., a change takes place in the circulation process), then the rate of profit rises. Furthermore, the influence of foreign trade is expounded in an entirely one-sided way. The development of the product into a commodity is fundamental to capitalist production and this is intrinsically bound up with the expansion of the market, the creation of the world market, and therefore foreign trade.

Apart from this, Ricardo is right when he states that all improvements, be they brought about through the division of labour, improvements in machinery, the perfection of means of communication, foreign trade—in short all measures that reduce the necessary labour-time involved in the manufacture or transport of commodities increase the surplus-value (hence profit) and thus enrich the capitalist class because, and in so far as, these "improvements" reduce the value of labour.

Finally, in this section, we must quote a few passages in which Ricardo analyses the nature of *relative* wages.

"If I have to hire a labourer for a week, and instead of ten shillings I pay him eight, no variation having taken place in the value of money, the labourer can probably obtain more food and necessaries, with his eight shillings, than he before obtained for ten: but this is owing, not to a rise in the *real value of his wages*, as stated by Adam Smith, and more recently by Mr. Malthus, but to a fall in the value of the things on which his wages are expended, things perfectly distinct; and yet *for calling this a fall in the real value of wages*, I am told that I adopt new and unusual language, not reconcilable with the true principles of the science" (l.c., pp. 11-12).

"It is not by the *absolute quantity of produce* obtained by either class, that we can correctly judge of the rate of profit, rent, and wages, but by the quantity of labour required to obtain that produce. By improvements in machinery and agriculture, the whole produce may be doubled; but if wages, rent, and profit be also doubled, these three will bear *the same proportions to one another as before*, and neither could be said to have *relatively varied*. But if wages partook not of the whole of this increase; if they, instead of being doubled, were only increased one-half ... it would, I apprehend, be correct for me to say that ... wages had fallen while profits had risen; for if we had an invariable standard by which to measure the *value* of this produce, we should find that a less value had fallen to the class of labourers ..., and a greater to the class of capitalists, than had been given before" (l.c., p. 49).

"It will not the less be a real fall, because they" (the wages) "might furnish him with a greater quantity of cheap commodities than his former wages" (l.c., p. 51).

* * *

De Quincey points out the contrast between some of the propositions developed by Ricardo and those of the other economists.

"When it was asked" [by the economists before Ricardo] "what determined the value of all commodities: it was answered that this value was chiefly determined by wages. When again it was asked—what determined wages?—it was recollected that wages must [...] be adjusted to the value of the commodities upon which they were spent; and the answer was in effect that wages were determined by the value of commodities." ([Thomas de Quincey], *Dialogues of Three Templars on Political Economy, Chiefly in Relation to the Principles of Mr. Ricardo* in *The London Magazine*, Vol. IX, 1824, p. 560.)

||666| The same *Dialogues* contains the following passage about the law governing the measurement of value by the *quantity of labour* and *by the value of labour:*

"So far are the two formulae from presenting merely two different expressions of the same law, that the very best way of expressing negatively Mr. Ricardo's law (viz. A is to B in value as the *quantities* of the producing labour) would be to say—A is *not* to B in value as the *values* of the producing labour" [l.c., p. 348].

(If the organic composition of the capital in A and B were the same, then it could in fact be said that their *relation* to one another is proportionate to the *values* of the producing labour. For the accumulated labour in each would be in the same proportion as the immediate labour in each. The quantities of paid labour in each, however, would be proportionate to the total quantities of immediate labour in each. Assume the composition to be

$80c+20v$ and the rate of surplus-value equal to 50 per cent. If one capital were equal to £ 500 and the other to £ 300, then the product in the first case would be £ 550 and in the second £ 330. The products would then be as $5 \times 20 = 100$ (wages) to $3 \times 20 = 60$; that is as 100:60, as 10:6, as 5:3. [And] $550:330 = 55:33$ or as $^{55}/_{11} : ^{33}/_{11}$ ($5 \times 11 = 55$ and $3 \times 11 = 33$); i.e., as 5:3. But even then one would only know their relation to one another and not their true values, since many different values correspond to the ratio 5:3.)

"If the price is ten shillings, then [...] wages and profits, taken as a whole, cannot exceed ten shillings. [...] But do not the wages and profits as a whole, themselves, on the contrary, predetermine the price? No; that is the old superannuated doctrine." (Thomas de Quincey, *The Logic of Political Economy*, Edinburgh and London, 1844, p. 204.)

"The new economy has shown that all price is governed by proportional quantity of the producing labour, and by that only. Being itself once settled, then, *ipso facto*, price settles the *fund* out of which both *wages and profits must draw their separate dividends*" (l.c., p. 204). "Any change that can disturb the existing relations between wages and profits, *must originate in wages*" (l. c., p. 205).

Ricardo's doctrine is new in so far as he poses the question whether in fact it sets aside the law of actual value (l. c., p. 158).[a]

---

[a] Marx summarises very briefly here—in his own words—the idea developed by de Quincey.—*Ed.*

[CHAPTER XVI]

RICARDO'S THEORY OF PROFIT

[1. Individual Instances in Which Ricardo Distinguishes Between Surplus-Value and Profit]

It has already been shown in some detail, that the laws of surplus-value—or rather of the rate of surplus-value—(assuming the working-day as given) do not so directly and simply coincide with, nor are they applicable to, the laws of profit, as Ricardo supposes. It has been shown that he wrongly identifies surplus-value with profit and that these are only identical in so far as the total capital consists of variable capital or is laid out directly in wages; and that therefore what Ricardo deals with under the name of "profit" is in fact surplus-value. Only in this case can the total product simply be resolved into wages and surplus-value. Ricardo evidently shares Smith's view, that the *total value* of the annual product resolves itself into revenues. Hence also his confusion of value with cost-price.

It is not necessary to repeat here that the rate of profit is not directly governed by the same laws as the rate of surplus-value.

Firstly: We have seen that the rate of profit can rise or fall as a result of a fall or rise in rent, independently of any change in the value of labour.

Secondly: The absolute amount of profit is equal to the absolute amount of surplus-value. The latter, however, is determined not only by the rate of surplus-value but just as much by the number of workers employed. The same amount of profit is therefore possible, with a falling rate of surplus-value and a rising number of workers and vice versa, etc.

Thirdly: With *a given rate of surplus-value,* the rate of profit depends on the organic composition of capital.

Fourthly: With a *given surplus-value* (the *organic composition of capital* per £100 is also assumed to be given) the rate of profit depends on the *relative value* of the different parts of the capital, which may be differently affected, partly by economy of power etc. in the use of the means of production, partly by variations in value which may affect one part of capital while they leave the rest untouched.

Finally, one has to take into account the differences in the composition of capital arising from the process of circulation.

||667| Some of the observations that occur in Ricardo's writing should have led him to the distinction between surplus-value and profit. Because he fails to make this distinction, he appears in some passages to descend to the vulgar view—as has already been indicated in the analysis of Chapter I *"On Value"*—the view that profit is a mere addition over and above the value of the commodity; for instance when he speaks of the determination of profit on capital in which the fixed capital predominates, etc.[a] This was the source of much nonsense among his successors. This vulgar view is bound to arise, if the proposition (which in practice is correct) that on the average, *capitals of equal size yield equal profits* or that profit depends on the size of the capital employed, is not connected by a series of intermediary links with the general laws of value etc.: in short, if profit and surplus-value are treated as identical, which is only correct for the aggregate capital. Accordingly Ricardo has no means for determining a *general rate of profit.*

Ricardo realises that the *rate of profit* is *not* modified by those variations of the value of commodities which affect all parts of capital *equally* as, for example, variations in the value of money. He should therefore have concluded that *it is affected* by such variations in the value of commodities which do *not* affect all parts of capital *equally;* that therefore variations in the rate of profit may occur while the value of labour remains unchanged, and that even the rate of profit may move in the opposite direction to variations in the value of labour. Above all, however, he should have kept in mind that here the *surplus-product,* or what is for him the same thing, *surplus-value,* or again the same thing, *surplus-labour,* when he is considering it *sub specie* profit, is not calculated in proportion to the variable capital alone, but in proportion to the *total capital advanced.*

With reference to a change in the value of money, he says:

---

a See this volume, pp. 181-82.—*Ed.*

"The variation in the value of money, however great, makes no difference in the *rate of profits*; for suppose the goods of the manufacturer to rise from £ 1,000 to £ 2,000, or 100 per cent, if *his capital*, on which the variations of money have as much effect as on the value of produce, if his machinery, buildings, and stock in trade rise also 100 per cent, his *rate of profits* will be the same....

"If, with a capital of a given value, he can, by economy in labour, double the quantity of produce, and it fall to half its former price, it *will bear the same proportion to the capital that produced it* which it did before, and *consequently* profits will still be at the same rate.

"If, at the same time that he doubles the quantity of produce by the employment of the same capital, the value of money is by any accident lowered one half, the produce will sell for twice the money value that it did before; but the capital employed to produce it will also be of twice its former money value; and therefore in this case too, *the value of the produce will bear the same proportion to the value of the capital as it did before*." (David Ricardo, *On the Principles of Political Economy, and Taxation*, third edition, London, 1821, pp. 51-52.)

If Ricardo means *surplus produce* when he writes *produce* in the last passage then this is correct. For the rate of profit is equal to the *surplus produce (value)* divided by the capital employed. Thus if the surplus produce is 10 and the capital 100, the rate of profit is $^{10}/_{100}$, which equals $^{1}/_{10}$, which equals 10 per cent. If however he means the total product, then the way he puts it is not accurate. In that case by proportion of the value of the produce to the value of capital, he evidently means nothing but the excess of the value of the commodity over the value of the capital advanced. In any case, it is obvious that *here* he does not identify profit with surplus-value or the rate of profit with the rate of surplus-value, [the latter is] equal to the *surplus-value* divided by the value of labour or the variable capital.

Ricardo says (Chapter XXXII):

"The *raw produce* of which commodities are made, is supposed to have fallen in price, and, therefore, commodities will fall on that account. True, they will fall, but their fall will not be attended with any diminution in the money income of the producer. If he sell his commodity for less money, it is only because *one of the materials from which it is made has fallen in value*. If the clothier sell his cloth for £ 900 instead of £ 1,000, his income will not be less, if the wool from which it is made, has declined £ 100 in value" (l. c., p. 518).

(The particular point with which Ricardo is actually dealing, the effect in a practical case, does not concern us here. But a sudden fall in the value of wool would of course affect (adversely) the money income of those clothiers who had on their hands a large stock of finished cloth manufactured at a time when wool was dearer and which has to be sold after the price ||668| of wool has dropped.)

If, as Ricardo assumes here, the clothiers set in motion the same amount of labour as before ⟨they could set in motion a much greater amount of labour because a part of the capital which was previously expended *only* on raw material is now at their disposal and can be expended on raw material plus labour⟩, it is clear that their "money income" taken in absolute terms, "will not be less" but their *rate of profit* will be *greater* than previously; for—say it was 10 per cent, i.e., £ 100—the same amount as before would now have to be reckoned on £ 900 instead of £ 1,000. In the first case the rate of profit was 10 per cent. In the second it is $1/9$ or $11^1/9$ per cent. Since Ricardo moreover presupposes that the raw produce of which commodities are made has fallen generally, the general rate of profit would rise and not only the rate of profit in one branch of production. It is all the more strange that Ricardo does not realise this, because he understands it when the opposite takes place.

For in Chapter VI "*On Profits*" Ricardo deals with the case where, as a result of an increase in the price of necessaries owing to the cultivation of worse land and the consequent rise in differential rent, firstly wages rise and secondly all raw produce from the surface of the earth. (This assumption is by no means necessary; cotton may very well fall in price, so can silk and even wool and linen, although the price of corn may be rising.)

In the first place he says that the *surplus-value* (he calls it profit) of the farmer will fall because the value of the product of the ten men whom he employs, continues to be £ 720 and from this fund of £ 720 he has to hand over more in wages. And he continues:

"But the *rate of profits* will fall still more, because the *capital* of the farmer ... consists in a great measure of raw produce, such as his corn and hay-ricks, his unthreshed wheat and barley, his horses and cows, which would all rise in price in consequence of the *rise of produce*. His *absolute profits* would fall from £ 480 to £ 445 15s.; but if from the cause which I have just stated, his capital should rise from £ 3,000 to £ 3,200, the *rate of his profits* would, when corn was at £ 5 2s. 10d., be under 14 per cent.

"If a manufacturer had also employed £ 3,000 in his business, he would be obliged in consequence of the rise of wages, to increase his capital, in order to be enabled to carry on the same business. If his commodities sold before for £ 720 they would continue to sell at the same price; but the wages of labour, which were before £ 240, would rise when corn was at £ 5 2s. 10d., to £ 274 5s. In the first case he would have a balance of £ 480 as profit on £ 3,000, in the second he would have a profit only of £ 445 15s., on an increased capital, and therefore his profits would conform to the altered rate of those of the farmer" (l.c., pp. 116-17).

In this passage, therefore, Ricardo distinguishes between *absolute profit* (equal to *surplus-value*) and *rate of profit* and also shows that the rate of profit falls more as a result of the change in the value of the capital advanced, than the absolute profit (surplus-value) falls as a result of the rise in the value of labour. The rate of profit would have also fallen, if the value of labour [had] remained *the same*, because *the same* absolute profit would have to be calculated on a greater capital. The reverse result, i.e., a rise in the rate of profit (as distinct from a rise in surplus-value or absolute profit), would take place in the first instance cited from him, where the value of the raw produce falls. It is evident, therefore, that rises and falls in the rate of profit may also be brought about by circumstances other than the rise and fall in the absolute profit and the rise and fall in its rate, reckoned on the capital laid out in wages.

In connection with the last quoted passage Ricardo writes:

"Articles of jewellery, of iron, of plate, and of copper, would not *rise*, because none of the raw produce from the surface of the earth enters into their composition" (l. c., p. 117).

The prices of these commodities would not rise, but the rate of profit in these branches of production would rise above that in the others. For in the latter, a smaller surplus-value (because of the rise in wages) would correspond to a capital outlay that had grown in value for two reasons: firstly, because the outlay in wages had increased; secondly, because the outlay in raw materials had increased. In the second case [i.e. jewellery etc.] ||669| there is a smaller surplus-value on a capital outlay in which only the variable part has grown because of the rise in wages.

In these passages, Ricardo himself throws overboard his whole theory of profit, which is based on the false identification of the rate of surplus-value with the rate of profit.

"In every case, agricultural, as well as manufacturing profits are lowered by a rise in the *price of raw produce*, if it be accompanied by a rise of wages" (l. c., pp. 113-14).

It follows from what Ricardo himself has said, that, even if [the rise in the price of raw produce] is not accompanied by a rise of wages, the *rate of profit* would be lowered by an increase of that part of the advanced capital which consists of raw produce.

"Suppose the price of silks, velvets, furniture, and any other commodities, not required by the labourer, to rise in consequence of more labour being *expended on them, would not that affect profits?* Certainly not: for *nothing can affect profits but a rise in wages*; silks and velvets are not consumed by the labourer, and therefore cannot raise wages" (l. c., p. 118).

The *rate of profit* in these particular spheres of production would certainly fall, although the value of labour—wages—remained the same. The raw material used by the silk manufacturers, piano manufacturers, furniture manufacturers, etc. would have become dearer, and therefore the proportion borne by the same surplus-value to the capital laid out would have fallen and hence the rate of profit. And the *general rate of profit* consists of the average of the particular rates of profit in all branches of business. Or, in order to make the same average profit as before, these manufacturers would raise the price of their commodities. Such a nominal rise in prices does not directly affect the rate of profit, but the distribution of profit.

Ricardo returns once more to the case considered above, where the surplus-value (absolute profit) falls, because the price of the necessaries (and along with these, also rent) rises.

"I must again observe that the *rate of profits* would fall much more rapidly than I have estimated in my calculation: for the *value of the produce* being what I have stated it under the circumstances supposed, the value of *the farmer's stock* would be *greatly increased from its necessarily consisting of many of the commodities which had risen in value.* Before corn could rise from £ 4 to £ 12, *his capital* would probably be doubled in exchangeable value, and be worth £ 6,000 instead of £ 3,000. If then his profit were £ 180, or 6 per cent on his *original capital*, profits would not at that time be really at a *higher rate* than 3 per cent; for £ 6,000 at 3 per cent gives £ 180; and on *those terms only could a new farmer with £6,000 money in his pocket enter into the farming business.*

"Many trades would derive some advantage, more or less, from the same source. The brewer, the distiller, the clothier, the linen manufacturer, would be *partly compensated for the diminution of their profits, by the rise in the value of their stock of raw and finished materials*; but a manufacturer of hardware, of jewellery, and of many other commodities, as well as those whose capitals uniformly consisted of money, would be subject to the *whole fall in the rate of profits*, without any compensation whatever" (l. c., pp. 123-24).

What is important here is only something of which Ricardo is not aware, namely, that he throws overboard his identification of profit with surplus-value and [admits] that the rate of profit can be affected by a variation in the value of the constant capital independently of the value of labour. Moreover, his illustration is only partially correct. The advantage which the farmer, clothier etc. would derive from the rise in price of the stock of commodities they have on hand and on the market, would of course cease as soon as they had sold these commodities. The increased value of their capital would similarly no longer represent a gain for them, when this capital was used up and had to be replaced. They would then all find themselves in the position of the new farmer cited by Ricardo himself, who would have to advance a capital of £ 6,000 in order to make a profit of 3 per cent. On the other hand, ||XIII-670| the jeweller, manufacturer of hardware, money-dealer etc.—although at first they would not [receive] any compensation for their losses—would realise a rate of profit of more than 3 per cent, for only the capital laid out in wages would have risen in value whereas their constant capital remained unchanged.

One further point of importance in connection with this compensation of the falling profit by the rise in value of the capital, mentioned by Ricardo, is that for the capitalist—and generally, as far as the division of the product of annual labour is concerned—it is a question not only of the distribution of the product among the various shareholders in the revenue, but also of the division of this product into capital and revenue.

[2.] Formation of the General Rate of Profit.
(Average Profit or "Usual Profit")

[a] The Starting-Point of the Ricardian Theory
of Profit Is the Antecedent Predetermined Average Rate of Profit]

Ricardo is by no means theoretically clear here.

"I have already remarked, that the *market price* of a commodity may *exceed* its *natural or necessary price*, as it may be produced in less abundance than the new demand for it requires. This, however, is but a *temporary* effect. The high profits on capital employed in producing that commodity, will naturally attract capital to that trade; and as soon as the requisite funds are supplied, and the quantity of the commodity is duly increased, *its price will fall*, and the *profits of the trade will conform to the general level*. A *fall in the general rate of profits* is by no means incompatible with *a partial rise of profits in particular employments. I t   i s   t h r o u g h   t h e   i n e q u a l-
i t y   o f   p r o f i t s , t h a t   c a p i t a l   i s   m o v e d   f r o m   o n e   e m p l o y-
m e n t   t o   a n o t h e r*. Whilst then general profits are falling, and gradually settling at a lower level in consequence of the rise of wages, and the increasing difficulty of supplying the increasing population with necessaries, the profits of the farmer may, for an interval of some little duration, be above the former level. An extraordinary stimulus may be also given for a certain time, to a particular branch of foreign and colonial trade..." (l.c., pp. 118-19).

"It should be recollected that prices always vary in the market, and in the first instance, through the comparative state of   demand   and   supply. Although cloth could be furnished at 40s. per yard, and give the *usual profits of stock,* it may rise to 60 or 80s. from a general change of fashion... The makers of cloth will for a time have unusual profits, but capital will naturally flow to that manufacture, till the supply and demand are again at their fair level, when the price of cloth will again sink to 40s., its natural or necessary price. In the same manner, with every increased demand for corn, it may rise so high as to afford more than the general profits to the farmer. If there be plenty of fertile land, the price of corn will again fall to its former standard, after the requisite quantity of capital has been employed in producing it, and profits will be as before; but if there be not plenty of fertile land, if, to produce this additional quantity, more than the usual quantity of capital and labour be required, corn will not fall to its former level. Its natural price will be raised, and the farmer, instead of obtaining permanently larger profits, will find himself obliged to be satisfied with the diminished rate which is the inevitable consequence of the rise of wages, produced by the rise of necessaries" (l.c., pp. 119-20).

If the *working-day* is given (or if only such differences occur in the working-day in different trades as are compensated by the particular characteristics of the different kinds of labour) then the *general rate of surplus-value,* i.e., of *surplus-labour,* is given since wages are on the average the same. Ricardo is preoccupied with this idea, and he confuses the *general rate of surplus-value* with the *general rate of profit.* I have shown that with the same *general rate of surplus-value,* the *rates of profit* in different branches of production must be very different, if the commodities are to be sold at their respective *values.*

The *general rate of profit* is formed through the total surplus-value produced being calculated on the total capital of society (of the class of capitalists). Each capital, therefore, in each particular branch, represents a *portion* of a total capital of the same ||671| *organic composition,* both as regards constant and variable capital, and circulating and fixed capital. As such a portion, it draws its dividends from the surplus-value created by the aggregate capital, in accordance with its size. The surplus-value thus distributed, the amount of surplus-value which falls to the share of a block of capital of given size, for example £100, during a given period of time, for example one year, constitutes the *average profit* or the *general rate of profit,* and as such it enters into the costs of production of every sphere of production. If this share [per 100] is 15, then the usual profit equals 15 per cent and the cost-price is £115. It can be less if, for instance, only a part of the capital advanced enters as wear and tear into the process of the creation of value. But it is always equal to the capital consumed +15 [per cent], the average profit on the capital advanced. If in one case £100 entered into the product and in another only

£ 50, then in the first case the cost-price would be 100+15=115 and in the second case it would be 50+15=65; thus both capitals would have sold their commodities at *the same cost-price,* i.e., at a price which yielded the same rate of profit to both. It is evident, that the emergence, realisation, creation of the *general rate of profit* necessitates the *transformation of values* into *cost-prices* that are *different* from these values. Ricardo on the contrary assumes the identity of values and cost-prices, because he confuses the rate of profit with the rate of surplus-value. Hence he has not the faintest notion of the general change which takes place in the *prices* of commodities, in the course of the establishment of a general rate of profit, before there can be any talk of a general rate of profit. He accepts this rate of profit as something pre-existent which, therefore, even plays a part in his determination of *value.* (See Chapter I *"On Value".*) *Having postulated the general rate of profit,* he only concerns himself with the exceptional modifications in prices which are necessary for the *maintenance,* for the continued existence of this *general rate of profit.* He does not realise at all that in order to *create* the general rate of profit values must first be transformed into cost-prices and that therefore, when he presupposes a general rate of profit, he is no longer dealing directly with the *values* of commodities.

Moreover, the passage under consideration, *only* [expresses] the Smithian concept and even this in a one-sided way, because Ricardo is preoccupied with his notion of a *general rate of surplus-value.* According to him, the rate of profit rises above the [average] *level* only in particular branches of production, because there the market-price rises above the natural price owing to the relation between supply and demand, under-production or over-production. Competition, influx of new capital into one branch of production or withdrawal of old capital from another, will then equalise market-price and natural price and *reduce* the profit of the particular branch to the general level. Here the real level of profit is assumed as *constant* and predetermined, and it is only a question of *reducing* the profit to this level in particular spheres of production in which it has risen above or fallen below it, as a result of the action of supply and demand. Ricardo, moreover, always assumes that the commodities whose prices yield more than the average profit stand *above* their value and that those which yield less than the average profit stand *below* their value. If competition makes their *market-value* conform to their *value,* then the level is established.

According to Ricardo, the *level* itself can only rise or fall if wages fall or rise (for a relatively long period), that is to say, if the *rate of relative surplus-value* falls or rises; and this occurs without any change in prices. (Yet Ricardo himself admits here that there can be very significant variations in prices in different spheres of production, according to the ratio of circulating and fixed capital.)

But even when a *general rate of profit* is established and therefore *cost-prices,* the *rate of profit* in particular branches may rise, because the *hours of work,* in them are *longer* and consequently the *rate of absolute surplus-value* rises. That competition between the workers cannot level this out, is proved by the *intervention of the state.* The rate of profit will rise in these particular spheres without the market-price rising above the natural price. Competition between capitals, however, can and in the long run will prevent that this excess profit accrues entirely to the capitalists in these particular fields. They will have to reduce the prices of their commodities below their "natural prices", or the other spheres will raise *their prices* a little (or if they do not actually raise them, because a fall in *value* of these commodities may supervene, then ||672| at any rate they will not lower them as much as the development of the productive power of labour in their own branches of production required). The general level will rise and the cost-prices will change.

Furthermore: if a new branch of production comes into being in which a disproportionate amount of living labour is employed in relation to accumulated labour, in which therefore the composition of capital is far below the average composition which determines the average profit, the relations of supply and demand in this new trade may make it possible to sell its output above its *cost-price,* at a price approximating more closely to its *actual value.* Competition can level this out, only through the raising of the *general level* [of profit], because capital on the whole realises, sets in motion, a greater quantity of *unpaid surplus-labour.* The relations of supply and demand do not, in the first instance as Ricardo maintains, cause the commodity to be sold *above its value,* but merely cause it to be sold above its cost-price, at a price approximating *to its value.* The equalisation can therefore bring about not its reduction to the old level, but the establishment of a *new level.*

28*

[b) Ricardo's Mistakes Regarding the Influence
of Colonial Trade, and Foreign Trade in General,
on the Rate of Profit]

The same applies, for example, to *colonial trade,* where as a result of slavery and the bounty of nature, the value of labour is lower than in the old country, or perhaps because, in fact or in law, landed property has not developed there. If capitals from the mother country can be freely transferred to this new trade, then they will reduce the specific excess profit in this trade, but will raise the general level of profit (as Adam Smith observes quite correctly).

On this point, Ricardo always helps himself out with the phrase: But in the old trades the quantity of labour employed has nevertheless remained the same, and so have wages. The general rate of profit is, however, determined by the ratio of unpaid labour to paid labour and to the capital advanced not in this or that sphere of the economy, but in all spheres to which the capital may be freely transferred. The ratio may stay the same in nine-tenths; but if it alters in one-tenth, then the general rate of profit in the ten-tenths must change. Whenever there is an increase in the quantity of unpaid labour set in motion by a capital of a given size, the effect of competition can only be that capitals of equal size draw equal dividends, equal shares in this increased surplus-labour; but not that the dividend of each individual capital remains the same or is reduced to its former share in surplus-labour, despite the increase of surplus-labour in proportion to the total capital advanced. If Ricardo makes this assumption he has no grounds whatsoever for contesting Adam Smith's view that the rate of profit is reduced merely by the growing competition between capitals due to their accumulation. For he himself assumes here that the rate of profit is reduced simply by competition, although the rate of surplus-value is increasing. This is indeed connected with his second false assumption, that (leaving out of account the lowering or raising of wages) the rate of profit can never rise or fall, except as a result of temporary deviations of the market-price from the natural price. And what is natural price? That price which is equal to the capital outlay plus the average profit. Thus one arrives again at the assumption that average profit can only fall or rise in the same way as the relative surplus-value.

Ricardo is therefore wrong when, contradicting Adam Smith, he says:

"Any change from one foreign trade to another, or from home to foreign trade, cannot, in my opinion, affect the rate of profits" (l.c., p. 413).

He is equally wrong in supposing that the rate of profit does not affect cost-prices because it does not affect values.

Ricardo is wrong in thinking that if, in consequence of particularly favourable circumstances, profits in a branch of foreign trade [rise above the general level,] the general level [of profits] must always be re-established by reducing [these profits] to the former level and not by raising the general level of profits.

"They contend, that the equality of profits will be brought about by the general rise of profits; and I am of opinion, that the profits of the favoured trade will speedily subside to the general level" (l.c., pp. 132-33).

Because of his completely wrong conception of the rate of profit, Ricardo misunderstands entirely the influence of foreign trade, when it does not directly lower the price of the labourers' food. He does not see how enormously important it is for England, for example, to secure ||673| cheaper raw materials for industry, and that in this case, as I have shown previously,[112] the *rate of profit* rises *although prices fall,* whereas in the reverse case, with *rising prices*, the rate of profit can fall, even if wages remain the same in both cases.

"It is *not*, therefore, in consequence of the extension of the market that the rate of profit is raised" (l. c., p. 136).

The rate of profit does not depend on the price of the individual commodity but on the amount of surplus-labour which can be realised with a given capital. Elsewhere Ricardo also fails to recognise the importance of the *market* because he does not understand the nature of money.

* * *

||673| (In connection with the above it must be noted that Ricardo commits all these blunders, because he attempts to carry through his identification of the rate of surplus-value with the rate of profit by means of forced abstractions. The vulgar mob has therefore concluded that theoretical truths are abstractions which are at variance with reality, instead of seeing, on the contrary, that Ricardo does not carry true abstract thinking far enough and is therefore driven into false abstraction.[113] |673||

[3.] Law of the Diminishing Rate of Profit
[a) Wrong Presuppositions in the Ricardian Conception of the Diminishing Rate of Profit]

This is one of the most important points in the Ricardian system.

The rate of profit has a tendency to fall. Why? Adam Smith says: As a result of the growing accumulation and the growing competition between capitals which accompanies it. Ricardo retorts: Competition can level out profits in the different spheres of production (we have seen above that he is not consistent in this); but it cannot lower the general rate of profit. This would only be possible if, as a result of the accumulation of capital, the capital grew so much more rapidly than the population, that the demand for labour were *constantly* greater than its supply, and therefore wages—both nominal and real wages and in terms of use-value—were constantly rising in value and in use-value. This is not the case. Ricardo is not an optimist who believes such fairy-tales.

But because for Ricardo the *rate of profit* and the *rate of surplus-value*—that is, the relative surplus-value, since he assumes the length of the working-day to be constant—are identical terms, a permanent fall in profit or the tendency of profit to fall can only be explained as the result of *the same causes* that bring about a permanent fall or tendency to fall in the *rate of surplus-value,* i.e., in that part of the day during which the worker does not work for himself but for the capitalist. What are these causes? If the length of the working-day is assumed to remain constant, then the part of it during which the worker works for nothing for the capitalist can only fall, diminish, if the part during which he works for himself grows. And this is only possible (assuming that labour is paid at its *value*), if the *value* of the necessaries—the means of subsistence on which the worker spends his wages—increases. But as a result of the development of the productivity of labour, the value of industrial commodities is constantly decreasing. The diminishing rate of profit can therefore only be explained by the fact that the value of food, the principal component part of the means of subsistence, is constantly rising. This happens because agriculture is becoming less productive. This is the same presupposition which, according to Ricardo's interpretation, explains the existence and growth of rent. The continuous fall in profits is thus bound up with the continuous rise in the

rate of rent. I have already shown that Ricardo's view of rent
is wrong. This then cuts out one of the grounds for his explanation of the fall in the rate of profits. But secondly, it rests on the
false assumption that the *rate of surplus-value* and the *rate of
profit* are identical, that therefore a fall in the rate of profit is
identical with a fall in the rate of surplus-value, which in fact
could only be explained in Ricardo's way. And this puts an end
to his theory. The rate of profit falls, although the rate of surplus-value remains the same or rises, because the proportion of
variable capital to constant capital decreases with the development of the productive power of labour. The rate of profit thus
falls, not because labour becomes less productive, but because it
becomes more productive. Not because the worker is less exploited, but because he is more exploited, whether the absolute surplus-time grows or, when the state prevents this, the relative surplus-time grows, for capitalist production is inseparable from
falling relative value of labour.

Thus Ricardo's theory rests on two false presuppositions:

1. The false supposition that the existence and growth of rent
is determined by the diminishing productivity of agriculture;

2. The false assumption that the rate of profit is equal to the
rate of relative surplus-value and can only rise or fall in inverse
proportion to a fall or rise in wages.

||674| I shall now place together the statements in which Ri-
cardo expounds the view that has just been described.

[b) Analysis of Ricardo's Thesis that the Increasing
Rent Gradually Absorbs the Profit]

First, however, some comments on the way in which, given his
concept of rent, Ricardo thinks that rent gradually swallows up
the rate of profit.

We shall use the tables on page 574[a], but with the necessary
modifications.

In these tables it is assumed that the capital employed consists
of £ 60c+£ 40v, the surplus-value is 50 per cent, the *value* of the
product is therefore £ 120, whatever the productivity of labour.
Of this £ 10 was profit and £ 10 absolute rent. Say, the £ 40 represents wages for 20 men (for a week's labour for example or

---

[a] See the insertion between pages 264 and 265.—*Ed.*

rather, because of the rate of profit, say, a year's labour; but this does not matter here at all). According to Table *A*, where land I determines the market-value, the number of tons is 60, therefore 60 tons=£ 120, 1 ton=$^{120}/_{60}$=£ 2. The wages, £ 40, are thus equal to 20 tons or quarters of grain. This then is the necessary wage for the number of workers employed by the capital of £ 100. Now if it were necessary to descend to an inferior type of soil, where a capital of £ 110 (£ 60 constant capital and the 20 workers which this sets in motion, that is, £ 60 constant capital and £ 50 variable capital) was required, in order to produce 48 tons. In this case the surplus-value would be £ 10, and the price per ton would be £ 2$^1/_2$. If we descended to an even worse type of land where £ 120 would be equal to 40 tons, the price per ton would be $^{120}/_{40}$=£ 3. In this case there would be no surplus-value on the worse type of land. What the 20 men produce is always equal to the value of £ 60 (£ 3 equals a working-day of a given length). Thus if wages grow from £ 40 to £ 60, the surplus-value disappears altogether. It is assumed throughout that one quarter is the necessary wage for one man.

Assume that in both these cases a capital of only £ 100 is to be laid out. Or, which is the same thing, whatever capital may be laid out, what is the proportion for 100? For instead of calculating that, if the same number of workers and the same constant capital is employed as before, the capital outlay will amount to 110 or 120, we shall calculate on the basis of the same organic composition (not measured in value but in amount of labour employed and amount of constant capital) how much constant capital and wages a capital of £ 100 contains (in order to keep to the comparison of 100 with the other classes). The proportion 110:60=100:54$^6/_{11}$ and 110:50=100:45$^5/_{11}$. 20 men set in motion £ 60 constant capital; so how many [men] set in motion 54$^6/_{11}$?

The situation is as follows: The value obtained from employing a number of workers (say 20) is £ 60. In this case 20 quarters or tons, equal to £ 40, will fall to the share of the workers employed, if the value of the ton or quarter is £ 2. If the value of a ton rises to £ 3, the surplus-value disappears. If it rises to 2$^1/_2$, then that half of the surplus-value disappears, which constituted the absolute rent.

In the first case, where a capital of £ 120 (60c+60v) is laid out the product amounts to £ 120, that is 40 tons (40×3). In the second case, where a capital of £ 110 (60c and 50v) is laid out the product amounts to £ 120, which is 48 tons (48×2$^1/_2$).

In the first case, if the capital laid out were £ 100 (50c and 50v) the product would come to £ 100, i.e., $33^1/_3$ tons ($3 \times 33^1/_3 = 100$). Moreover, since only the land has deteriorated while the capital has undergone no change, the proportionate number [of workers] who set in motion the constant capital of £ 50 will be the same as that previously setting in motion the capital of £ 60. Thus if the latter was set in motion by 20 men (who received £ 40 while the value of 1 ton was £ 2) it will now be set in motion by $16^2/_3$ men, who receive £ 50 since the value of a ton has risen to £ 3. As before, 1 man receives 1 ton or 1 quarter equal to £ 3, for $16^2/_3 \times 3 = 50$. If the value created by $16^2/_3$ men is £ 50, then that created by 20 men is £ 60. Thus the assumption that a day's labour of 20 men is equal to £ 60 remains unchanged.

Now let us take the second case. With a capital outlay of £ 100, the product is £ $109^1/_{11}$, equal to $43^7/_{11}$ tons ($2^1/_2 \times 43^7/_{11} = 109^1/_{11}$). The constant capital is £ $54^6/_{11}$ and the variable £ $45^5/_{11}$. How many men does the £ $45^5/_{11}$ represent? $18^2/_{11}$ *men*, ||675| for if the value of a day's labour of 20 men equals £ 60, then that of $18^2/_{11}$ men equals £ $54^6/_{11}$ hence the value of the product is £ $109^1/_{11}$.

It can be seen that in both cases the same capital sets in motion fewer men who, however, cost more. They work for the same length of time, but the surplus-labour [time] decreases or disappears altogether, because they produce a smaller amount of product in the same time (and this product consists of their *necessaries*), therefore they use more labour-time for the production of 1 ton or 1 quarter although they work *the same* length of time as before.

In his calculations, Ricardo always presupposes that the capital must set in motion *more labour* and that therefore a *greater* capital, i.e., £ 120 or £ 110, must be laid out instead of the previous £ 100. This is only correct if *the same quantity* is to be produced, i.e., 60 tons in the cases cited above, instead of 40 tons being produced in case I, with an outlay of £ 120, and 48 in case II with an outlay of £ 110. With an outlay of £ 100, therefore, $33^1/_3$ tons are produced in case I and $43^7/_{11}$ tons in case II. Ricardo thus departs from the correct view point, which is not that more workers must be employed in order to create the same product, but that a given number of workers create a smaller product, a greater share of which is in turn taken up by wages.

We shall now compile two tables, firstly Table A from page 574[a] and the new table which follows from the data given above.

[Class]	Capital £	[Number of] tons	TV [Total value] £	MV [Market-value per ton] £	IV [Individual value] per ton £	DV [Differential value] per ton £	CP [Cost-price] per ton £	AR [Absolute rent] £	DR [Differential rent] £	AR [Absolute rent] tons
I	100	60	120	2	2	0	$1^5/_8$	10	0	5
II	100	65	130	2	$1^{11}/_{13}$	$^2/_{13}$	$1^9/_{13}$	10	10	5
III	100	75	150	2	$1^3/_5$	$^2/_5$	$1^7/_{15}$	10	30	5
	300	200	400					30	40	15

[Class]	DR [Differential rent] tons	Rental £	Rental tons	Composition of capital	Rate of surplus-value per cent	Number of workers	Wages £	Wages tons	Rate of profit per cent
I	0	10	5	$60c + 40v$	50	20	40	20	10
II	5	20	10	$60c + 40v$	50	20	40	20	10
III	15	40	20	$60c + 40v$	50	20	40	20	10
	20	70	35						

If this table were constructed in the reverse direction, according to Ricardo's descending line: that is beginning from III and if at the same time one assumed that the more fertile land which is cultivated first, pays no rent, then we would, in the first place, have a capital of £ 100 in III, [which] produces a value of £ 120, consisting of £ 60 constant capital and £ 60 newly-added labour. According to Ricardo, one would further have to assume, that the rate of profit stood at a higher level than entered in Table A, since, when the ton of coal (quarter of wheat) was £ 2, the 20 men received 20 tons, equal to £ 40; now that, as a result of the fall

---

a See the insertion between pages 264 and 265.—*Ed.*

in the value, the ton is equal to £ $1\frac{9}{15}$, or £ 1 12s., the 20 men receive only £ 32 (equal to 20 tons). The capital advanced to employ the same number of workers would amount to £ 60c and £ 32v=£ 92 and the produced value would be £ 120, since the value of the work carried out by the 20 men equals £ 60 as before. Accordingly, a capital of £ 100 would produce a value of £ $130\frac{10}{23}$, for $92:120=100:130\frac{10}{23}$ (or $23:30=100:130\frac{10}{23}$). Moreover this capital of £ 100 would be composed as follows: £ $65\frac{5}{23}c$ and £ $34\frac{18}{23}v$. Thus the capital would be £ $65\frac{5}{23}c$+£ $34\frac{18}{23}v$; the value of the product would amount to £ $130\frac{10}{23}$. The *number of workers* would be $21\frac{17}{23}$ and the rate of surplus-value $87\frac{1}{2}$ per cent.

1. So we would have:

[Class]	Capital £	Number of tons	TV [Total value] £	MV [Market] value per ton £	IV [Individual value] per ton £	DV [Differential value] per ton £
III	100	$81\frac{12}{23}$	$130\frac{10}{23}$	$1\frac{3}{5}$	$1\frac{3}{5}$	0

Rent £	Profit £	Rate of profit per cent	Composition of capital	Rate of surplus-value per cent	Number of workers
0	$30\frac{10}{23}$	$30\frac{10}{23}$	$65\frac{5}{23}c$ $+34^{18}/23v$	$87\frac{1}{2}$	$21\frac{17}{23}$

Expressed in tons, wages would be equal to $21\frac{17}{23}$ tons and profit to $19\frac{1}{46}$ tons.

||676| Continuing on the Ricardian assumption, let us now suppose that as a result of the increasing population, the market-price rises so high that class II must be cultivated, where the value per ton is £ $1\frac{11}{13}$.

In this case it is impossible to assume as Ricardo wants that the $21\frac{17}{23}$ workers produce always the same value, i.e., £ $65\frac{5}{23}$ (wages added to surplus-value). For the *number of workers* whom III can employ, and therefore exploit, decreases—according to his own assumption—hence also the total amount of surplus-value.

At the same time, the composition of the agricultural capital always remains the same. Whatever their wages may be, 20 workers are always required (with a given length of the working-day) in order to set in motion £ 60c.

Since these 20 workers receive 20 tons and the ton is equal to $£ 1^{11}/_{13}$, 20 workers cost $£ 20 (1+^{11}/_{13})=£ 20+£ 16^{12}/_{13}=£ 36^{12}/_{13}$.

The value which these 20 workers produce, whatever the productivity of their labour, equals [$£$] 60; thus the capital advanced amounts to $£ 96^{12}/_{13}$, the value [of the product] is $£ 120$, and profit $£ 23^{1}/_{13}$. The profit on a capital of $£ 100$ will therefore be [$£$] $23^{17}/_{21}$ and the composition: $£ 61^{19}/_{21}c+£ 38^{2}/_{21}v$. $20^{40}/_{63}$ workers [are] employed.

Since the total value is $£ 123^{17}/_{21}$, and the individual value per ton in class III is $£ 1^{3}/_{5}$, of how many tons does the product consist? $77^{8}/_{21}$ tons. The *rate of surplus-value* is $62^{1}/_{2}$ per cent.

But III sells the ton at $£ 1^{11}/_{13}$. This results in a differential value of $4^{12}/_{13}$ s. or $£ ^{16}/_{65}$ per ton, and on $77^{8}/_{21}$ tons it amounts to $77^{8}/_{21}×^{16}/_{65}=£ 19^{1}/_{21}$.

Instead of selling its product at $£ 123^{17}/_{21}$, III sells at $£ 123^{17}/_{21}+£ 19^{1}/_{21}=£ 142^{6}/_{7}$. The $£ 19^{1}/_{21}$ constitutes the rent.

Thus we would have the following for III:

[Class]	Capital £	[Number of] tons	[ATV] Actual total value £	[TMV] Total market-value £	MV [Market-value per ton] £	IV [Individual value per ton] £
III	100	$77^{8}/_{21}$	$123^{17}/_{21}$	$142^{6}/_{7}$	$1^{11}/_{13}$	$1^{3}/_{5}$

DV Differential value [per ton]	Rent £	Rent in tons	Rate of profit per cent	Composition of capital	Rate of surplus-value per cent	Number of workers
[$+£^{16}/_{65}=$] $+4^{12}/_{13}s.$	$19^{1}/_{21}$	$10^{20}/_{63}$	$23^{17}/_{21}$	$61^{19}/_{21}c+38^{2}/_{21}v$	$62^{1}/_{2}$	$20^{40}/_{63}$

The wages measured in tons are $20^{40}/_{63}$ tons. And the profit is $12^{113}/_{126}$ tons.

We now pass on to class II; there is no rent here. Market-value and individual value are equal. The number of tons produced by II is $67^{4}/_{63}$.

Thus we have the following for II:

[Class]	Capital £	[Number of] tons	TV [Total value] £	MV [Market-value per ton] £	IV [Individual value per ton]
II	100	$67^4/_{63}$	$123^{17}/_{21}$	$1^{11}/_{13}$	$1^{11}/_{23}$

DV [Differential value per ton] £	Rent £	Rate of profit per cent	Composition of capital	Rate of surplus-value per cent	Number of workers
0	0	$23^{17}/_{21}$	$61^{19}/_{21}c+38^2/_{21}v$	$62^1/_2$	$20^{40}/_{63}$

Wages measured in tons are $20^{40}/_{63}$ and profit is $12^{113}/_{126}$ tons.
||677| 2. For the second case, in which class II is introduced and rent comes into existence, we have the following:

[Class]	Capital £	[Number of] tons]	ATV [Actual total value] £	TMV [Total market-value per ton] £	MV [Market-value] per ton £	IV [Individual value per ton] £	DV [Differential value per ton] £
III	100	$77^8/_{21}$	$123^{17}/_{21}$	$142^6/_7$	$1^{11}/_{13}$	$1^3/_5$	$[+£^{16}/_{65}=] + +4^{12}/_{13}\,s.$
II	100	$67^4/_{63}$	$123^{17}/_{21}$	$123^{17}/_{21}$	$1^{11}/_{13}$	$1^{11}/_{13}$	0

Composition of capital	Number of workers	Rate of surplus-value per cent	Rate of profit per cent	Wages in tons	Profit in tons	Rent £	Rent in tons
$61^{19}/_{21}c+38^2/_{21}v$	$20^{40}/_{63}$	$62^1/_2$	$23^{17}/_{21}$	$20^{40}/_{63}$	$12^{113}/_{126}$	$19^1/_{21}$	$10^{20}/_{63}$
$61^{19}/_{21}c+38^2/_{21}v$	$20^{40}/_{63}$	$62^1/_2$	$23^{17}/_{21}$	$20^{40}/_{63}$	$12^{113}/_{126}$	0	0

Let us now pass on to the third case and, like Ricardo, let us assume that mine I, a poorer mine, must and can be worked, because the *market-value* has risen to £2. Since twenty workers are required for a constant capital of £60 and their wages are now £40, we have the same composition of capital as in Table *A* page 574,[a] i.e., £ 60c+£ 40v, and as the value produced by the 20 workers is always equal to £ 60, the total value of the product produced by a capital of £ 100 is £ 120, whatever its productivity. The rate of profit in this case is 20 per cent and the surplus-value 50 per cent. Measured in tons, the profit is 10 tons. We must now see what changes occur in III and II as a result of this change in the market-value and the introduction of I, which determines the rate of profit.

Although III works the most fertile land he can with £ 100 only employ 20 workers, costing him £ 40, for a constant capital of £ 60 requires 20 workers. The number of workers employed with a capital of £ 100 therefore falls to 20. And the actual total value of the product is now £ 120. But how many tons have been produced by III when the individual value of one ton is equal to £ $1^9/_{15}$? 75 tons, since 120 divided by $^{24}/_{15}$ (£ $1^9/_{15}$)=75. The number of tons produced by III decreases because he can employ *less* labour with the same capital, not *more* (as Ricardo wrongly declares, because he always considers merely how much labour is required in order to create *the same* output; and not *how much living labour* can be employed with the new composition of capital though this is the only important point). But he sells these 75 tons at £ 150 (instead of at £ 120, which is their value) and so the rent rises to £ 30 in III.

So far as II is concerned, the value of the product here is also £ 120 etc. But, as the individual value per ton is £ $1^{11}/_{13}$, 65 tons are produced (for 120 divided by $^{24}/_{13}$ ($1^{11}/_{13}$)=65). In short, we arrive here at Table *A* from page 574. But since for our purpose we need new headings here, now that I is introduced and the market-value has risen to £ 2 we set out the table anew.

3. [Third Case:]

[Class]	Capital £	[Number of] tons	ATV [Actual total value] £	TMV [Total market-value] £	MV [Market-value per ton] £	IV [Individual value per ton] £	DV [Differential value per ton] £
III	100	75	120	150	2	$1^3/_5$	[£$^2/_5$=]8s.
II	100	65	120	130	2	$1^{11}/_{13}$	[£$^2/_{13}$=]3$^1/_{13}$s.
I	100	60	120	120	2	2	0

---

[a] See the insertion between pages 264 and 265.—*Ed.*

Composition of capital	Number of workers	Rate of surplus value per cent	Rate of profit per cent	Wages in tons	Profit in tons	Rent £	Rent in tons
$60c + 40v$	20	50	20	20	10	30	15
$60c + 40v$	20	50	20	20	10	10	5
$60c + 40v$	20	50	20	20	10	0	0
						40	20

||678| In short, this case III corresponds to Table A page 574 (apart from absolute rent which appears as a part of profit here) only the order is reversed.

Let us now go on to the newly assumed cases.[a]

First of all the class which still yields a profit. Let it be called Ib. With a capital of £ 100 it only yields $43^7/_{11}$ tons.

The value of a ton has risen to £ $2^1/_2$. The composition of the capital is [£] $54^6/_{11}c + $[£] $45^5/_{11}v$. The value of the product is £ $109^1/_{11}$. £ $45^5/_{11}$ is enough to pay $18/_{11}^2$ men. And since the value of a day's labour of 20 men is £ 60, that of $18^2/_{11}$ men is [£] $54^6/_{11}$. The value of the product is therefore [£] $109^1/_{11}$. The *rate of profit* is £ $9^1/_{11}$, that is, $3^7/_{11}$ tons. The *rate of surplus-value* is 20 per cent.

Since the organic composition of the capitals in III, II, I is the same as in Ib and they must pay the same wages, they too can employ only $18^2/_{11}$ men with £ 100, these men produce a total value of [£] $54^6/_{11}$, and therefore a surplus-value of 20 per cent and a rate of profit of $9^1/_{11}$ per cent as in Ib. The total value of the product here, as in Ib, is £ $109^1/_{11}$.

But since the individual value of a ton in III is £ $1^3/_5$, III produces (or its product is equal to) £ $109^1/_{11}$ divided by $1^3/_5$ or $24/_{15} = 68^2/_{11}$ tons. Moreover, the difference between the market-value of a ton and the individual value amounts to £ $2^1/_2$—£ $1^3/_5$. That is £ 2 10s.—£ 1 12s.=18s. And on $68^2/_{11}$ tons this amounts to $18(68 + 2/_{11})$s.=1,227$^3/_{11}$s.=£ $617^3/_{11}$s. Instead of selling at £ $109^1/_{11}$, III sells at £ 170 $9^5/_{11}$s. And this excess equals the rent of III. This rent, expressed in tons, is $24^6/_{11}$ tons.

Since the individual value of a ton in II is £ $1^{11}/_{13}$, II produces [£] $109^1/_{11}$ divided by $1^{11}/_{13}$ and this is $59^1/_{11}$ tons. The difference

---

a See this volume, pp. 440-42.—*Ed.*

between the market-value of one ton in II and its individual value is £ $2^1/_2$—£ $1^{11}/_{13}$ which is £ $^{17}/_{26}$. And on $59^1/_{11}$ tons, this amounts to £$38^7/_{11}$. And this is the rent. The total market-value [of the product] amounts to £ $147^8/_{11}$. The rent expressed in tons is $15^5/_{11}$ tons.

Finally, since the individual value of a ton in I is £ 2, £ $109^1/_{11}$ is equal to $54^6/_{11}$ tons. The difference between the market-value and the individual-value is £ $2^1/_2$—£ 2=10s. And on $54^6/_{11}$ tons, this amounts to $(59+^6/_{11})$ 10s.=590s.$+^{60}/_{11}$s.=£27$+5^5/_{11}$s. The total market-value [of the product] is therefore £ 136 $7^3/_{11}$s. And the value of the rent expressed in tons is $10^{10}/_{11}$ tons.

Bringing together all the data for case 4, one gets the following:

||679| 4. [Fourth Case:]

[Class]	Capital £	[Number of] tons	ATV [Actual total value] £	TMV [Total market-value] £	MV [Market-value per ton] £	IV [Individual value per ton] £	DV [Differential value per ton]
III	100	$68^2/_{11}$	$109^1/_{11}$	[£$170^5/_{11}$=] £170 $9^1/_{11}$s.	$2^1/_2$	$1^3/_5$	[£$^9/_{10}$]=18s.
II	100	$59^1/_{11}$	$109^1/_{11}$	£$147^8/_{11}$[= £147 $14^6/_{11}$s.]	$2^1/_2$	$1^{11}/_{13}$	[£$^{17}/_{26}$=] $13^1/_{13}$s.
I	100	$54^6/_{11}$	$109^1/_{11}$	[£$136^4/_{11}$=] £136 $7^3/_{11}$s.	$2^1/_2$	2	[£$^1/_2$=]10s.
Ib	100	$43^7/_{11}$	$109^1/_{11}$	£$109^1/_{11}$[= £109 $1^9/_{11}$s.]	$2^1/_2$	$2^1/_2$	0

Composition of capital	Number of workers	[Rate of] surplus-value per cent	Rate of profit per cent	Wages [in] tons	Profit [in] tons	Rent £	Rent [in] tons
$54^6/_{11}c + 45^5/_{11}v$	$18^2/_{11}$	20	$9^1/_{11}$	$18^2/_{11}$	$3^7/_{11}$	[£$61^4/_{11}$=] £61 $7^3/_{11}$s.	$24^6/_{11}$
$54^6/_{11}c + 45^5/_{11}v$	$18^2/_{11}$	20	$9^1/_{11}$	$18^2/_{11}$	$3^7/_{11}$	[£$38^7/_{11}$=] £38 $12^8/_{11}$s.	$15^5/_{11}$
$54^6/_{11}c + 45^5/_{11}v$	$18^2/_{11}$	20	$9^1/_{11}$	$18^2/_{11}$	$3^7/_{11}$	[£$27^3/_{11}$=] £27 $5^5/_{11}$s.	$10^{10}/_{11}$
$54^6/_{11}c + 45^5/_{11}v$	$18^2/_{11}$	20	$9^1/_{11}$	$18^2/_{11}$	$3^7/_{11}$	0	0

Finally let us look at the last case in which, according to Ricardo, the *entire profit* disappears and there is no surplus-value. In this case the value of the product rises to £ 3, so that if 20 men are employed, their wage is £ 60 which is equal to the value produced by them. The composition of the capital is £ 50c+£ 50v. Now $16^2/_3$ *men* are employed. If the value produced by 20 men is £ 60, then that produced by $16^2/_3$ men is £ 50. The wages, therefore, swallow up the whole value. Now, as before, a man receives 1 ton. The value of the product is £ 100 and therefore the number of tons produced is $33^1/_3$ tons, of which one-half merely replaces the value of the constant capital and the other half the value of the variable capital.

Since in III, the individual value of the ton is £ $1^3/_5$ or £ $^{24}/_{15}$, how many tons does III produce? 100 divided by $^{24}/_{15}$, i.e., $62^1/_2$ tons, whose value is £ 100. The difference, however, between market-value and individual value is £ 3—£ $1^3/_5$=£ $1^6/_{15}$ or £ $1^2/_5$. On $62^1/_2$ tons this amounts to £ $87^1/_2$. Hence the total market-value of the product is £ $187^1/_2$. And the rent in tons is $29^1/_6$ tons.

In II the individual value of a ton is £ $1^{11}/_{13}$. Hence the differential value is £ 3—£ $1^{11}/_{13}$=£ $1^2/_{13}$. Since the individual value of a ton is here £ $1^{11}/_{13}$ or £ $^{24}/_{13}$, the capital of £ 100 produces (100 divided by $^{24}/_{13}$) $54^1/_6$ tons. On this number of tons, that difference amounts to £ 62 10s. And the [total] market-value of the product is £ 162 10s. Expressed in tons, the rent is $20^5/_6$ tons.

In I the individual value of a ton is £ 2. The differential value therefore equals £ 3—£ 2=£ 1. Since the individual value of a ton is £ 2 here, a capital of £ 100 produces 50 tons. This makes a difference of £ 50. The [total] market-value of the product is £ 150 and the rent in tons is $16^2/_3$ tons.

We now come to Ib, which until now has not carried a rent. Here the individual value is £ $2^1/_2$. Hence differential value equals 3—$2^1/_2$=£ $^1/_2$ or 10s. And since the individual value of a ton is here equal to £ $2^1/_2$ or £ $^5/_2$, £ 100 produces 40 tons. The differential value on these is £ 20, so that the total market-value [of the product] amounts to £ 120. And the rent expressed in tons is $6^2/_3$ tons.

Let us now construct *case 5* in which, according to Ricardo, profit disappears.

||680| 5. [Fifth Case:]

29–244

[Class]	Capital £	[Number of] tons	ATV [Actual total value] £	TMV [Total market-value] £	MV [Market-value per ton] £	IV [Individual value per ton] £	DV [Differential value per ton] £
III	100	$62^1/_2$	100	$187^1/_2$	3	$1^3/_5$	$1^2/_5$
II	100	$54^1/_6$	100	$162^1/_2$	3	$1^{11}/_{13}$	$1^2/_{13}$
I	100	50	100	150	3	2	1
Ib	100	40	100	120	3	$2^1/_2$	$^1/_2$
Ia	100	$33^1/_3$	100	100	3	3	0

Composition of capital	Number of workers	Rate of surplus-value per cent	Rate of profit per cent	Wages in tons	Rent £	Rent in tons
$50c + 50v$	$16^2/_3$	0	0	$16^2/_3$	$87^1/_2$	$29^1/_6$
$50c + 50v$	$16^2/_3$	0	0	$16^2/_3$	$62^1/_2$	$20^5/_6$
$50c + 50v$	$16^2/_3$	0	0	$16^2/_3$	50	$16^2/_3$
$50c + 50v$	$16^2/_3$	0	0	$16^2/_3$	20	$6^2/_3$
$50c + 50v$	$16^2/_3$	0	0	$16^2/_3$	0	0

On the following page I shall now put all five cases in tabular form.[a] |680||

[c) Transformation of a Part of Profit and a Part of Capital into Rent. The Magnitude of Rent Varies in Accordance with the Amount of Labour Employed in Agriculture]

||683| If in the first place we examine *Table E* on the previous page, we see that the position in the last class, Ia, is very clear. In this case wages swallow up the whole product and the whole value of the [newly-added] labour. Surplus-value is non-existent, hence there is neither profit nor rent. The value of the product is equal to the value of the capital advanced, so that the workers —who are here in possession of their own capital—can invariably reproduce their wages and the conditions of their labour, but no more. In this last class it cannot be said that the rent

---

[a] See the insertion between pages 452 and 453.—*Ed.*

swallows up the profit. There is no rent and no profit because there is no surplus-value. Wages swallow up the surplus-value and therefore the profit.

In the four other classes the position is *prima facie* by no means clear. If there is no surplus-value, how can rent exist? Moreover, the productivity of labour on the types of land Ib, I, II and III has not altered at all. The *non-existence* of surplus-value must therefore be sheer illusion.

Furthermore, another phenomenon becomes apparent and this, *prima facie,* is equally inexplicable. The rent in tons for III amounts to $29^1/_6$ tons or quarters, whereas in Table *A,* where only land III was cultivated, where there was no rent and where, moreover, $21^{17}/_{23}$ men were employed whereas now only $16^2/_3$ men are employed, the profit (which absorbed the entire surplus-value) only amounted to $19^1/_{46}$ tons.

The same contradiction is apparent in II, where the rent in *Table E* amounts to $20^5/_6$ tons or quarters while in Table *B* the profit, which absorbed the entire surplus-value ($20^{40}/_{63}$ men being employed instead of $16^2/_3$ men now), amounted to only $12^{113}/_{126}$ tons or quarters.

Similarly in I, where the rent in *Table E* is $16^2/_3$ tons or quarters, while in Table *C* the profit of I, which absorbs the entire surplus-value, is only 10 tons (20 men being employed, instead of the present $16^2/_3$).

Finally in Ib, where the rent in *Table E* is $6^2/_3$ tons or quarters, while the profit of Ib in Table *D,* where the profit absorbed the entire surplus-value, was only $3^7/_{11}$ tons or quarters (while $18^2/_{11}$ men were employed instead of the $16^2/_3$ now being employed).

It is, however, clear, that whereas the rise in market-value above the individual value of the products of III, II, I, Ib can alter the distribution of the product, shifting it from one class of shareholders to the other, it can by no means increase the product which represents the surplus-value over and above the wages. Since the productivity of the various types of land has remained the same, as has the productivity of capital, how can III to Ib become more productive in tons or quarters through the entry into the market of the less productive type of land or mine Ia?

The riddle is solved in the following manner:

If a day's labour of 20 men produces £60, then that of $16^2/_3$ men produces £50. And since in land of class III, the labour-time contained in $£1^3/_5$ or $£^8/_5$ is represented in 1 ton or 1 quarter,

29*

£ 50 will be represented in $31^1/_4$ tons or quarters. $16^2/_3$ tons or quarters have to be deducted from this for wages, thus leaving $14^7/_{12}$ as *surplus-value*.

Furthermore, because the market-value of a ton has risen from £ $1^3/_5$ or £ $^8/_5$ to £ 3, $16^2/_3$ tons or quarters out of the product of $62^1/_2$ tons or quarters, will suffice to replace the value of the constant capital. On the other hand, so long as the ton or quarter produced on III itself determined the market-value, and the latter was therefore equal to its individual value, $31^1/_4$ tons or quarters were required in order to replace a constant capital of £ 50. Instead of the $31^1/_4$ tons or quarters—the part of the product which was necessary to replace the capital when the value of a ton was £ $1^3/_5$—only $16^2/_3$ are now required. Thus $31^1/_4$—$16^2/_3$ tons or quarters, ||684| i.e., $14^7/_{12}$ tons or quarters, become available and fall to the share of rent.

If one now adds the surplus-value produced by $16^2/_3$ workers with a constant capital of £ 50 on III, which amounts to $14^7/_{12}$ tons or quarters, to $14^7/_{12}$ tons or quarters, the part of the product which instead of replacing the constant capital now takes on the form of surplus-produce, then the total surplus-produce amounts to $28^{14}/_{12}$ tons or quarters $=29^2/_{12}=29^1/_6$ quarters or tons. And this is exactly the ton or corn rent of III in *Table E*. The apparent contradiction in the amount of ton or corn rent in classes II, I, Ib in *Table E* is solved in exactly the same way.

Thus it becomes evident that the *differential rent*—which arises on the better types of land owing to the difference between market-value and individual value of the products raised on them— in its *material form* as *rent in kind, surplus-product, rent in tons* or *corn* in the above example, is made up of *two elements* and due to two *transformations*. [Firstly:] The surplus-product which represents the surplus-labour of the workers or the surplus-value, is changed from the form of profit to the form of rent, and therefore falls to the landlord instead of the capitalist. Secondly: a part of the product which previously—when the product of the better type of land or mine was being sold at its own value—was needed to *replace the value of the constant capital,* is now, when each portion of the product possesses a higher market-value, free and appears in the form of surplus-product, thus falling to the landlord instead of the capitalist.

The *rent in kind* in so far as it is differential rent comes into being as the result of two processes: the transformation of the surplus-produce into rent, and not into profit, and the transformation of a *portion* of the product which was previously allotted for the replacement of the value of the constant capital into surplus-product, and thus into rent. The latter circumstance, that a part of the product is converted into rent instead of capital, has been overlooked by Ricardo and all his followers. They only see the transformation of surplus-product into rent, but not the transformation of a part of the product which previously fell to the share of capital (not of profit) into surplus-product.

The *nominal value* of the *surplus-product* or *differential rent* thus constituted, is determined (according to the presupposition made) by the value of the product produced on the worst land or in the worst mine. But this market-value only instigates the different distribution of this product, it does not bring it about.

These same two elements [are present] in all excess profit, for instance, if as a result of new machinery etc., a cheaply produced product is sold at a higher market-value than its own value. A part of the surplus-labour of the workers appears as surplus-product (excess profit) instead of as profit. And a part of the product which—if the product were sold at its own lower value—would have to replace the value of the capitalist's constant capital, now becomes free, has not got to replace anything, becomes surplus-product and therefore swells the profit. |684||

* * *

||688| {Incidentally, when speaking of the law of the *falling rate of profit* in the course of the development of capitalist production, we mean by profit, the total sum of surplus-value which is seized in the first place by industrial capitalist, [irrespective of] how he may have to share this later with the money-lending capitalist (in the form of interest) and the landlord (in the form of rent). Thus here the rate of profit is equal to surplus-value divided by the capital outlay. The rate of profit in this sense may fall, although, for instance, the industrial profit rises proportionately to interest or vice versa, or although rent rises proportionately to industrial profit or vice versa. If P is the profit, P' the industrial profit, I interest and R rent, then $P=P'+I+R$. And it is clear, that whatever the absolute magnitude of $P-P'$, I, R can increase or decrease as compared with one another, independently of the magnitude of P or the rise and fall of P. The reciprocal rise of P', I and R only represents an altered distribution of P among different persons. A further examination of the circumstances on which this distribution of P depends but which does

not coincide with a rise or fall of P itself, does not belong here, but into a consideration of the competition between capitals. That, however, R can rise to a level higher even than that of P, if it were only divided into P' and I, is therefore—as has already been explained—due to an *illusion* which arises from the fact that a part of the product whose value is rising, becomes free and is converted into rent instead of being reconverted into constant capital.} |688||

* * *

||684| It was assumed throughout this discussion, that the product whose price (according to market-value) had risen did not enter in kind into the composition of the constant capital, but only into wages, only into the variable capital. If the former were the case, Ricardo says that this would cause the rate of profit to fall even more and the rent to rise. This has to be examined.

We have assumed until now, that the *value* of the product has to replace the value of the constant capital, i.e., the £ 50 in the case cited above. Thus if 1 ton or quarter costs £ 3, it is obvious that not so many tons or quarters are required for the replacement of this value than would be needed if the ton or quarter cost only £ $1^9/_{15}$. But supposing that the coal or the corn or whatever other product of the earth, the product produced by agricultural capital, itself enters *in kind* into the formation of the constant capital. Let us assume for instance that it makes up half of the constant capital. In this case it is clear that whatever the price of the coal or the corn ||685| a constant capital of definite size, in other words, one which is set in motion by a definite number of workers, always requires a definite portion of the total product *in kind* for its replacement—since the composition of agricultural capital has, according to the assumption, remained *unchanged* in its proportionate amounts of accumulated and living labour.

If for example, half the constant capital consists of coal or corn and half of other commodities, then the constant capital of £ 50 will consist of £ 25 of other commodities and £ 25 (or $15^5/_8$ quarters or tons) [coal or corn], when the value of a ton is £ $^8/_5$ or £ $1^3/_5$. And however the market-value of a ton or a quarter may change, $16^2/_3$ men require a constant capital of £ 25 plus $15^5/_8$ quarters or tons, for the nature of the constant capital remains the same, and so does the proportionate number of workers required to set it in motion.

Now if, as in *Table E,* the value of a ton or quarter rises to £ 3, then the constant capital required for the $16^2/_3$ men would be £ 25+£ 3 $(15+^5/_8)$=£ 25+£ 45+£ $^{15}/_8$=£71$^7/_8$. And since the $16^2/_3$ men cost £ 50, they would require a total capital outlay of £ 71$^7/_8$+£ 50=£ 121$^7/_8$.

The *correlation of values* within the agricultural capital would have changed while organic composition remained the same.

It would be £71$^7/_8$c+£ 50v (for 16$^2/_3$ workers). For [£] 100 the composition would be £ 58$^{38}/_{39}$c+£ 41$^1/_{39}$v. Slightly more than 13$^2/_3$ workers (that is, leaving out of account the fraction $^1/_{117}$). Since 16$^2/_3$ workers set in motion 15$^5/_8$ tons or quarters constant capital, 13$^{79}/_{117}$ workers set in motion 12$^{32}/_{39}$ tons or quarters, equal to £ 38$^6/_{13}$. The remainder of the constant capital, equal to £ 20$^{20}/_{39}$, would consist of other commodities. Whatever the circumstances, 12$^{32}/_{39}$ tons or quarters would always have to be deducted from the product in order to replace that part of constant capital into which they enter in kind. Since the value produced by 20 workers equals £ 60, that produced by 13$^{79}/_{117}$ equals £ 41$^1/_{39}$. Wages in *Table E,* however, also amount to £ 41$^1/_{39}$. Therefore no surplus-value.

The total number of tons would be [51$^{11}/_{13}$,[114] of which] 12$^{32}/_{39}$ tons are needed to replace [part of the constant capital in kind]; a further 13$^{79}/_{117}$ are for the workers; 6$^{98}/_{117}$ tons, at £ 3 a ton, are used to replace the remainder of the constant capital. That is altogether 33$^1/_3$ tons. This would leave 17$^{37}/_{39}$ tons for the rent.

To shorten the matter, let us take the most extreme case, the one most favourable to Ricardo, i.e., that the constant capital, just as the variable, consists purely of agricultural produce whose value rises to £ 3 per quarter or ton, when class Ia governs the market.

The technological composition of the capital remains the same; that is, the *ratio* between living labour or number of workers (since the normal working-day has been assumed to be constant) represented by the variable capital and the *quantity of the instruments of labour* required, which now, according to our assumption, consist of tons of coal or quarters of corn, remains constant for a given number of workers.

Since with the original composition of the capital, of £ 60c+ £ 40v, and the price per ton of £ 2, £ 40v represented 20 workers or 20 quarters, or tons, £ 60c represented 30 tons; and since these 20 workers produced 75 tons on III, 13$^1/_3$ workers (and £ 40v is equal to $13\frac{1}{3}$ tons or workers if the ton costs £ 3) produce *50 tons* and set in motion a constant capital of $^{60}/_{3}$ ||686| equal to 20 tons or quarters.

Moreover, since 20 workers produce a value of £ 60, $13\frac{1}{3}$ [workers] produce £ 40.

Since the capitalist must pay £ 60 for the 20 tons and £ 40 for the $13\frac{1}{3}$ workers, but the latter only produce a value of £ 40, the value of the product is £ 100; the outlay is £ 100. Surplus-value and profit are nil.

But because the productivity of III has remained the same, as has already been said, $13\frac{1}{3}$ men produce 50 tons or quarters. The outlay in kind of tons, or quarters, however, only amounts to 20 tons for constant capital and $13\frac{1}{3}$ tons for wages, i.e., $33\frac{1}{3}$ tons. The 50 tons thus leave a surplus-product of $16\frac{2}{3}$ and this forms the rent.

But what do the $16\frac{2}{3}$ represent?

Since the *value* of the product is [£] 100 and the product itself equals 50 tons, the value of the ton produced here would in fact be £ 2, which is $^{100}/_{50}$. And so long as the product in kind is greater than what is required for the replacement of the capital in kind, the individual value of a ton must remain smaller than its market-value according to this criterion.

The farmer must pay £ 60 in order to replace the 20 tons [constant capital], and he reckons the 20 tons at £ 3, since this is the market-value per ton and a ton is sold at this price. Similarly he must pay £ 40 for the $13\frac{1}{3}$ workers, or for the tons or quarters which he pays to the workers. Thus the workers only receive $13\frac{1}{3}$ tons in the transaction.

In actual fact, however, so far as class III is concerned, the 20 tons cost £ 40 and the $13\frac{1}{3}$ cost only £ $26\frac{2}{3}$. But the $13\frac{1}{3}$ workers produce a value of £ 40, and therefore a surplus-value of £ $13\frac{1}{3}$. At £ 2 per ton, this amounts to $6\frac{4}{6}$ or $6\frac{2}{3}$ tons.

And since the 20 tons [constant capital] cost only £ 40 on III, this leaves an excess of £ 20 equal to 10 tons.

The $16\frac{2}{3}$ tons rent are thus equal to $6\frac{2}{3}$ tons surplus-value which is converted into rent and 10 tons capital which is converted into rent. But because the market-value per ton has risen to £ 3, the 20 tons cost the farmer £ 60 and the $13\frac{1}{3}$ cost him £ 40, while the $16\frac{2}{3}$ tons, that is the excess of the market-value over the [individual] value of his product, appear as rent, and [cost] £ 50.

How many tons are produced by $13\frac{1}{3}$ men in class II? 20 men produce 65 here, $13^{1}/_{3}$ [men] therefore $43^{1}/_{3}$ tons. The value of the product is £100, as above. Of the $43^{1}/_{3}$ tons, however, $33^{1}/_{3}$ are required for the replacement of the capital. This leaves $43^{1}/_{3}-33^{1}/_{3}=10$ tons as surplus-product or rent.

But this rent of 10 tons can be explained as follows: the value of the product of II is £100, the product amounts to $43^{1}/_{3}$ [tons], thus the value of a ton is $\frac{100}{43^{1}/_{3}}=£2^{4}/_{13}$. The $13^{1}/_{3}$ workers therefore cost £$30^{10}/_{13}$, and this leaves a surplus-value of £$9^{3}/_{13}$. Moreover, the 20 tons constant capital cost [£] $46^{2}/_{13}$ and of the [£] 60 that are paid for this, there remain [£] $13^{11}/_{13}$. Together with the surplus-value this comes to £$23^{1}/_{13}$, which is correct to the last farthing.

Only in class Ia, where in fact $33^{1}/_{3}$ tons or quarters, that is the total product, is required in kind to replace constant capital and wages, there is neither surplus-value, nor surplus-product, nor profit, nor rent. So long as this is not the case, so long as the product is greater than is necessary to replace the capital in kind, there will be conversion of profit (surplus-value) and capital into rent. Conversion of capital into rent takes place when a part of the product is freed, which, with a lower value, would have had to replace the capital, or [when] a part of the product which would have been converted into capital and surplus-value falls to rent.

At the same time it is evident that if constant capital becomes dearer as a result of dearer agricultural produce, the rent is very much reduced, for example, the rent of III and II^{a} [is reduced] from 50 tons, equal to £150 with a market-value of £3, to $26^{2}/_{3}$ tons, i.e., almost to half. Such a reduction is inevitable ||687| since the number of workers employed with the same capital of £100 is reduced for two reasons, firstly, because wages rise, i.e., the value of the variable capital rises, secondly, because the value of the means of production, the constant capital, rises. In itself, the rise in wages necessitates that out of the £100 less can be laid out in labour, hence relatively less (if the value of the commodities that enter into the constant capital remains the same) can be laid out in constant capital; thus £100 represents less accumulated and less living labour. In addition, however, the

---

a Marx has in view the fifth case (see the table between pages 452 and 453 taken together the rent of class III—$29^{1}/_{6}$ tons—and class II—$20^{5}/_{6}$ tons—comes to 50 tons.—*Ed.*

rise in the value of the commodities which enter into the constant capital, reduces the amount of accumulated labour and for this reason of living labour, which can be employed for the same sum of money, as the technological ratio between accumulated and living labour remains the same. But since, with the same productivity of the land and a given technological composition of the capital, the total product depends on the quantity of labour employed, as the latter decreases, so the rent must also decrease.

This only becomes evident when *profit* disappears. So long as there is a profit, the rent can increase despite the absolute decrease in the product in *all* classes, as shown in the table on page 681.[a] It is after all obvious that as soon as rent alone exists, the decrease in the product, hence in the surplus-product, must hit rent itself. This would occur more rapidly at the outset, if the value of the constant capital increased with that of variable capital.

But this apart, the table on page 681 shows that with declining fertility in agriculture, the growth of differential rent is always accompanied, *even on the better classes of land,* by a diminishing volume of total product in proportion to a capital outlay of a definite size, say £ 100. Ricardo has no inkling of this. The rate of profit decreases, because the same capital, say £ 100, sets in motion *less* labour and pays more for this labour, thus yielding an ever smaller surplus. The actual product, however, like the surplus-value, depends on the number of workers employed by the capital, when the productivity is given. This is overlooked by Ricardo. He also ignores the manner in which the rent is formed: not only by transforming surplus-value into rent, but also capital into surplus-value. Of course this is only an apparent transformation of capital into surplus-value. Each particle of surplus-produce would represent surplus-value or surplus-labour, if the market-value were determined by the value of the product of III etc. Ricardo, moreover, only considers that in order to produce the same volume of product, more labour has to be employed, but disregards the fact that with the same capital, an ever diminishing quantity of living labour is employed, of which an ever greater part is necessary labour and an ever smaller part surplus-labour, and this is the decisive factor for the determination of both the rate of profit and the quantity of product produced.

---

a See the insertion between pages 452 and 453.—*Ed.*

All this considered, it must be said that even if rent is taken to
be purely differential rent, Ricardo has not made the slightest
advance over his predecessors. His important achievement in this
field is, as De Quincey pointed out, the *scientific* formulation of
the question. In solving it Ricardo accepts the traditional views.
Namely:

"The innovation that Ricardo introduced into the theory of rent, is that
he resolves it into the question whether it really invalidates the law of
value."[a] (Thomas de Quincey, *The Logic of Political Economy*, Edinburgh
and London, 1844, p. 158.)

On page 163 of the same work, De Quincey says further:

"Rent is [...] that portion of the produce from the soil (or *from any agency
of production*) which is paid to the landlord for the *use of its differential
powers*, as measured by comparison with those of similar agencies operating
on the same market."

Furthermore on page 176:

The objections against Ricardo are that the owners of No. 1 will not give
it away for nothing. But in the *period* ⟨this mythical period⟩, when only
No. 1 is being cultivated "*no separate class of occupants and tenants* distinct
from the *class of owners* ||688| can have been formed".

So according to De Quincey this law of landownership [is valid]
so long as there is *no* landownership in the modern sense of the
word.

Now to the relevant quotations from Ricardo.

**[d] Historical Illustration of the Rise in the Rate
of Profit with a Simultaneous Rise in the Prices
of Agricultural Products. The Possibility of an Increasing
Productivity of Labour in Agriculture]**

(First the following note on *differential rent:* In reality, the
ascending and descending lines alternate, run across one another
and intertwine.

But it cannot by any means be said that if for individual short
periods (such as 1797-1813) the descending line clearly predominates, that *because of this*, the rate of profit must fall (in so
far, that is, as the latter is determined by the rate of surplus-
value). Rather I believe that during that period, the rate of profit
in England rose by way of exception, despite the greatly increased prices of wheat and agricultural produce generally. I do
not know of any English statistician who does not share this

---

[a] Marx gives here, in his own words, a brief summary of the idea developed by De Quincey.—*Ed.*

view on the rise in the rate of profit during that period. Individual economists, such as Chalmers, Blake, etc. have advanced special theories based on this fact. Moreover I must add that it is foolish to attempt to explain the rise in the price of wheat during that period by the depreciation of money. No one who has studied the history of the prices of commodities during that period, can agree with this. Besides, the rise in prices begins much earlier and reaches a high level before any kind of depreciation of money occurs. As soon as it appears it must simply be allowed for. If one asks why the rate of profit rose despite the rising corn prices, this is to be explained from the following circumstances: Prolongation of the working-day, the direct consequence of the newly introduced machinery; depreciation of the manufactured goods and colonial commodities which enter into the consumption of the workers; reduction of wages (although the nominal wage rose) *below* their traditional average level ⟨this fact is acknowledged for that period; J. P. Stirling in *The Philosophy of Trade* etc., Edinburgh, 1846, who, on the whole, accepts Ricardo's theory of rent, seeks, however, to prove that the *immediate* consequence of a permanent (that is, not accidental, dependent on the seasons) rise in the price of corn, is always reduction in the average wage[115]⟩; finally, the rise in the rate of profit was due to rising *nominal* prices of commodities, because loans and government expenditure increased the demand for capital even more rapidly than its supply, and this enabled the manufacturers to retrieve part of the product paid to the landowning rentiers and other persons who have a fixed income in the form of rent etc. This transaction is of no concern to us here, where we are considering the basic relationships, and therefore are concerned only with three classes: landlords, capitalists and workmen. On the other hand it plays a significant part in practice, under appropriate circumstances as *Blake* has shown.[116]) |688||

* * *

||689| {Mr. Hallett from Brighton exhibited "pedigree nursery wheat" at the 1862 exhibition.[117] "Mr. Hallett insists that ears of corn, like race-horses, must be carefully reared, instead of, as is done ordinarily, grown in higgledy-piggledy fashion, with no regard to the theory of natural selection. In illustration of what good education may do, even with wheat, some remarkable examples are given. In 1857, Mr. Hallett, planted [the grains of] an ear of the first quality of the red wheat, exactly 4 $\frac{3}{8}$ inches long, and containing 47 grains. From the product of the small crops ensuing, he again selected, in 1858, the finest ear, $6\frac{1}{2}$ inches long, and with 79 grains; and this was repeated, in 1859, again with the best offspring, this time $7\frac{3}{4}$ inches

long, and containing 91 grains. The next year, 1860, was a bad season for agricultural education, and the wheat refused to grow any bigger and better; but the year after, 1861, the best ear came to be $8^3/_4$ inches long, with no less than 123 grains on the single stalk. Thus the wheat had increased, in five years, to very nearly double its size, and to a threefold amount of productiveness in number of grains. These results were obtained by what Mr. Hallett calls the 'natural system' of cultivating wheat; that is, the planting of single grains at such a distance—about 9 inches from each other—every way—as to afford each sufficient space for full development.... He asserts that the corn produce of England may be doubled by adopting 'pedigree wheat' and the 'natural system' of cultivation. He states that from single grains, planted at the proper time, one only on each square foot of ground, he obtained plants consisting of 23 ears on the average, with about 36 grains in each ear. The produce of an acre at this rate was, accurately counted, 1,001,880 ears of wheat; while, when sown in the ordinary fashion, with an expenditure of more than 20 times the amount of seed, the crop amounted to only 934,120 ears of corn, or 67,760 ears less..."a}

[e) Ricardo's Explanation for the Fall in the Rate of Profit and Its Connection with His Theory of Rent]

[Ricardo establishes the fall in the rate of profit as follows:]

"With the progress of society the *natural price of labour* has always a *tendency to rise, because one of the principal commodities by which its natural price is regulated, has a tendency to become dearer, from the greater difficulty of producing it.* As, however, the improvements in agriculture, the discovery of new markets, whence provisions may be imported, may for a time counteract the tendency to a rise in the price of necessaries, and may even occasion their natural price to fall, so will the same causes produce the correspondent effects on the natural price of labour.

"The natural price of all commodities, excepting raw produce and labour, has a tendency to fall, in the progress of wealth and population; for though, on one hand, they are enhanced in real value, from the rise in the natural price of the raw material of which they are made, this is more than counterbalanced by the improvements in machinery, by the better division and distribution of labour, and by the *increasing skill,* both *in science and art,* of the *producers.*" ([David Ricardo, *On the Principles of Political Economy, and Taxation,* third edition, London, 1821,] pp. 86-87.)

"As population increases, these necessaries will be constantly rising in price, because more labour will be necessary to produce them.... Instead, therefore, of the money wages of labour falling, they would rise; but they would not rise sufficiently to enable the labourer to purchase as many comforts and necessaries as he did before the rise in price of those commodities....

"Notwithstanding, then, that the labourer would be really worse paid, *yet this increase in his wages would necessarily diminish the profits of the manufacturer*; for his goods would sell at no higher price and yet the expense of producing them would be increased....

---

a The source of this quotation has not been established.—*Ed.*

"It appears, then, that *the same cause which raises rent* [...] *the increasing difficulty of providing an additional quantity of food with the same proportional quantity of labour, will also raise wages*; and therefore if money be of an unvarying value, both rent and wages will have a tendency to rise with the progress of wealth and population.

"But there is this essential difference between the rise of rent and the rise of wages. The rise in the money value of rent is accompanied ||6:!0| by an increased share of the produce; not only is the landlord's money rent greater, but his corn rent also.... The fate of the labourer will be less happy; he will receive more money wages, it is true, but his corn wages will be reduced; and not only his command of corn, but his general condition will be deteriorated, by his finding it more difficult to maintain the market rate of wages above their natural rate" (l. c., pp. 96-98).

Supposing[a] corn and manufactured goods always to sell at the same price, profits would be high or low in proportion as wages were low or high. But suppose corn to rise in price because more labour is necessary to produce it; that cause will not raise the price of manufactured goods in the production of which no additional quantity of labour is required.... if, as is absolutely certain, wages should rise with the rise of corn, then their profits[b] would necessarily fall" (l.c., p. 108).

But it may be asked, "...whether the *farmer at least* would not have the same rate of profits, although he should pay an additional sum for wages? Certainly not: for he will not only have to pay, in common with the manufacturer, an increase of wages to each labourer he employs, but he will be *obliged either to pay rent, or to employ an additional number of labourers to obtain the same produce*; and the rise in the price of raw produce[c] will be proportioned only to that rent, or that additional number, and will not compensate him for the rise of wages" (l. c., p. 108).

"We have shewn that in *early stages of society*, both the landlord's and the labourer's share of the *value* of the produce of the earth, would be but small; and that it would increase in proportion to the progress of wealth, and the difficulty of procuring food" (l. c., p. 109).

These "early stages of society" are a peculiar bourgeois fantasy. In these early stages, the labourer is either slave or self-supporting peasant, etc. In the first case he belongs to the landlord, together with the land; in the second case he is his own landlord. In neither case does *any capitalist* stand between the landlord and the labourer. The subjugation of agriculture to capitalist production, and *hence* the transformation of slaves or peasants into wage-labourers and the intervention of the capitalist between landlord and labourer—which is only the final result of capitalist production—is regarded by Ricardo as a phenomenon belonging to the "early stages of society".

"The natural tendency of profits then is to fall; for, in the progress of society and wealth, the additional quantity of food required is obtained by

---

[a] In the manuscript: "Suppose".—*Ed.*

[b] i.e., the profits of manufacturers.—*Ed.*

[c] In the manuscript: "of the raw produce".—*Ed.*

the sacrifice of more and more labour. This tendency, this gravitation as it were of profits, is happily checked at repeated intervals by the improvements in[a] machinery, connected with the production of necessaries, as well as by discoveries in the science of agriculture which enable us to relinquish a portion of labour before required, and therefore to lower the price of the prime necessary of the labourer" (l.c., pp. 120-21).

In the following sentence, Ricardo says in plain terms that by *rate of profit* he understands the *rate of surplus-value*:

"Although a greater *value* is produced, a *greater proportion of what remains of that value*, after paying rent, is consumed by the producers, and *it is this, and this alone, which regulates profits*" (l. c., p. 127).

In other words, apart from rent, the rate of profit is equal to the excess of the value of the commodity over the value of the labour which is paid during its production, or that part of its value which is consumed by the *producers*. [In this context] Ricardo calls only the workers producers.[118] He assumes that the *produced value* is produced by them. He thus defines surplus-value here, as that part of the value created by the workers which the capitalist retains.*

But if Ricardo identifies rate of surplus-value with rate of profit—and at the same time assumes, as he does, that the working-day is of given length—then the tendency of the rate of profit to fall can only be explained by the same factors which make the rate of surplus-value fall. But, with a given working-day, the rate of surplus-value can only fall if the rate of wages is rising permanently. This is only possible if the value of necessaries is rising permanently. And this only if agriculture is constantly deteriorating, in other words, if Ricardo's theory of rent is accepted. Since Ricardo identifies rate of surplus-value with rate of profit, ||691| and since the rate of surplus-value can only be reckoned in relation to variable capital, capital laid out in wages, Ricardo, like Adam Smith, assumes that the *value of the whole product*—after deduction of rent—is divided between

---

[a]) In the manuscript: "of".—*Ed.*

* ||691| Regarding the *origin of surplus-value* [Ricardo says]:

"In the form of money ... capital is productive of no profit; in the form of materials, machinery, and food, for which it might be exchanged, it *would be productive of revenue...*" (l.c., p. 267). "The capital of the stockholder ||692| can never be made productive—*it is, in fact, no capital.* If he were to sell his stock, and employ the capital he obtained for it, productively, he could only do so by detaching the capital of the buyer of his stock from a productive employment" (l.c., p. 289, note). |692||

workmen and capitalists, into wages and profit. This means that he makes the false presupposition that the whole of the capital advanced consists only of variable capital. Thus, for example, after the passage quoted above, he goes on:

"When poor lands are taken into cultivation, or when more capital and labour are expended on the old land, with a less return of produce, the effect must be permanent. A greater proportion of that part of the produce which remains to be divided, after paying rent, between the owners of stock and the labourers, will be apportioned to the latter" (l. c., pp. 127-28).

The passage continues:

"Each man may, and probably will, have a less absolute quantity; but as more labourers are employed in proportion to the whole produce retained by the farmer, the value of a greater proportion of the whole produce will be absorbed by wages, and consequently the value of a smaller proportion will be devoted to profits" (l.c., p. 128).

And shortly before:

"The remaining quantity of the produce of the land, after the landlord and labourer are paid, necessarily belongs to the farmer, and *constitutes the profits of his stock*" (l. c., p. 110).

At the end of the section (Chapter VI) *"On Profits"*, Ricardo says that his thesis on the fall of profits remains true, even if— which is wrong—it were assumed, that the *prices of commodities* rose with a rise in the money wages of the labourers.

"In the Chapter on Wages, we have endeavoured to shew that *the money price of commodities would not be raised by a rise of wages...* But if it were otherwise, if the prices of commodities were permanently raised by high wages, the proposition would not be less true, which asserts that high wages invariably affect the employers of labour, by depriving them of a portion of their real profits. Supposing the hatter, the hosier, and the shoemaker each paid £ 10 more wages in the manufacture of a particular quantity of their commodities, and that the price of hats, stockings, and shoes, rose by a sum sufficient to repay the manufacturer the £ 10; *their situation would be no better than if no such rise took place*. If the hosier sold his stockings for £ 110 instead of £ 100, his profits would be precisely the same money amount as before; but as he would obtain in exchange for this equal sum, one-tenth less of hats, shoes and every other commodity, and as he could *with his former amount of savings*" (that is with the same capital) *"employ fewer labourers at the increased wages*, and purchase fewer raw materials at the increased prices, he would be in no better situation than if his money profits had been really diminished in amount, and every thing had remained at its former price" (l. c., p. 129).

Whereas elsewhere in his argument Ricardo always only stressed that in order to produce *the same quantity of product* on worse land, *more labourers* have to be paid, here at last he stresses what is decisive for the rate of profit, namely, that with the same amount of capital *fewer labourers are employed at increased wages*. Apart from this, he is not quite right in what he says. It makes no difference to the capitalist, if the price of hats etc. rises by 10 per cent, but the landlord would have to give up more of his rent. His rent may have risen for example, from £ 10 to £ 20. But he gets proportionately fewer hats etc. for his £ 20 than for the £ 10.

Ricardo says quite rightly:

"In an improving state of society, the net produce of land is always diminishing in proportion to its gross produce" (l. c., p. 198).

By this he means that the rent diminishes in an improving state of society. The real reason is that in an improving state of society, the variable capital decreases in proportion to the constant capital. |691||

||692| That with the progress of production, the constant capital grows in proportion to the variable, Ricardo himself admits, but only in the form that the fixed capital grows in proportion to the circulating.

"In rich and powerful countries, where large capitals are invested in machinery, more distress will be experienced from a revulsion in trade, than in poorer countries *where there is proportionally a much smaller amount of fixed, and a much larger amount of circulating capital*, and where consequently *more work is done by the labour of men*. It is not so difficult to withdraw a circulating as a fixed capital, from any employment in which it may be engaged. It is often impossible to divert the machinery which may have been erected for one manufacture, to the purposes of another; but the clothing, the food, and the lodging of the labourer in one employment may be devoted to the support of the labourer in another;"

(here, therefore, circulating capital comprises only variable capital, capital laid out in wages)

"or the same labourer may receive the same food, clothing and lodging, whilst his employment is changed. This, however, is an evil to which a rich nation must submit; and it would not be more reasonable to complain of it, than it would be in a rich merchant to lament that his ship was exposed to the dangers of the sea, whilst his poor neighbour's cottage was safe from all such hazard" (l. c., p. 311).

Ricardo himself mentions one reason for the rise in rent, which is quite independent of the rise in the price of agricultural produce:

"Whatever capital becomes fixed on the land, must necessarily be the *landlord's*, and not the tenant's, at the expiration of the lease. Whatever compensation the landlord may receive for this capital, on re-letting his land, *will appear in the form of rent*; but no rent will be paid, if, with a given capital, more corn can be obtained from abroad, than can be grown on this land at home" (l. c., p. 315, note).

On the same subject Ricardo says:

"In a former part of this work, I have noticed the difference between rent, properly so called, and the remuneration paid to the landlord under that name, for the advantages which the expenditure of his capital has procured to his tenant; but I did not perhaps sufficiently distinguish the difference which would arise from the different modes in which this capital might be applied. As a part of this capital, when once expended in the improvement of a farm, is inseparably amalgamated with the land, and tends to increase its productive powers, the *remuneration paid to the landlord for its use is strictly of the nature of rent*, and is subject to all the laws of rent. Whether the improvement be made at the expense of the landlord or the tenant, it will not be undertaken in the first instance, unless there is a strong probability that the return will at least be equal to the *profit* that can be made by the disposition of any other equal capital; but when once made, the return obtained will *ever after be wholly of the nature of rent*, and will be subject to all the variations of rent. Some of these expenses, however, only give advantages to the land for a limited period, and do not add permanently to its productive powers: being bestowed on buildings, and other perishable improvements, they require to be constantly renewed, and therefore do not obtain for the landlord any permanent addition to his real rent" (l.c., p. 306, note).

Ricardo says:

"In all countries, and all times, *profits depend* on the quantity of labour requisite to provide necessaries for the labourers, on that land or with that capital which yields no rent" (l. c., p. 128).

According to this, the profit of the farmer on that land—the worst land, which according to Ricardo pays no rent—regulates the general rate of profit. The reasoning is this: the product of the worst land is sold at its *value* and pays no rent. We see here exactly, therefore, how much surplus-value remains for the capitalist after deduction of the value of that part of the product which is merely an equivalent for the worker. And this surplus-value is the profit. This is based on the assumption that *cost-price* and *value* are identical, that this product, because it is sold at its cost-price, is sold at its value.

This is incorrect, historically and theoretically. I have shown that, where there is capitalist production and where landed property exists, the land or mine of the worst type cannot pay a rent, because the corn is sold *below its* [individual] *value* if it is sold at the market-value, which is not regulated by it. For the market-value only covers its *cost-price*. But what regulates this cost-price? The rate of profit of the *non-agricultural capital*, into whose determination the price of corn naturally enters as well, however far removed the latter may be from being its sole determinant. Ricardo's assertion would only be correct if values and cost-prices were ||693| identical. Historically too, as the capitalist mode of production appears later in agriculture than in industry, agricultural profit is determined by industrial profit, and not the other way about. The only correct point is that on the land which pays a profit but no rent, which sells its product at the cost-price, the average rate of profits becomes *apparent*, is tangibly presented, but this does not mean at all that the average profit is thereby *regulated*; that would be a very different matter.

The *rate of profit* can fall, without any rise in the *rate of interest* and *rate of rent*.

"From the account which has been given of the profits of stock, it will appear, that *no accumulation of capital will permanently lower profits,** *unless there be some permanent cause for the rise of wages....* If the necessaries of the workman could be constantly increased with the same facility, there could be no *permanent alteration in the rate of profit or wages*," (this should read: in the rate of surplus-value and the value of labour) "to whatever amount capital might be accumulated. *Adam Smith,* however, uniformly *ascribes the fall of profits to the accumulation of capital, and to the competition which will result from it,* without ever adverting to the increasing difficulty of providing food for the additional number of labourers which the additional capital will employ" (l. c., pp. 338-39).

The whole thing would only be right if profit were equal to surplus-value.

Thus Adam Smith says that the rate of profit falls with the accumulation of capital, because of the growing competition between the capitalists; Ricardo says that it does so because of the growing deterioration of agriculture (increased price of necessaries). We have refuted his view, which would only be correct if rate of surplus-value and rate of profit were identical, and therefore the rate of profit could not fall unless the rate of wages rose, provided the working-day remained unchanged. Adam Smith's view rests on his compounding value out of wages, profits and rents (in accordance with his false view, which he himself refuted). According to him, the accumulation of capitals forces the reduction in *arbitrary* profits—for which there is no

---

* By *profits* Ricardo means here that part of surplus-value which the capitalist appropriates, but by no means the [entire] surplus-value; and wrong as it is to say that accumulation can cause the surplus-value to fall, so it is right that accumulation can cause a fall in profit.

inherent measure—through the reduction in the prices of commodities; profits, according to this conception, being merely a
nominal addition to the prices of commodities.

Ricardo is of course theoretically right when he maintains, in
opposition to Adam Smith, that the accumulation of capitals
does not alter the determination of the value of commodities; but
Ricardo is quite wrong when he seeks to refute Adam Smith by
asserting that *over-production* in one country is impossible.
Ricardo denies the plethora of capital, which later became an
established axiom in English political economy.

Firstly he overlooks that in reality, where not only the
capitalist confronts the workman, but capitalist, workman,
landlord, moneyed interest, [people receiving] fixed incomes from
the state etc., confront one another, the fall in the prices of commodities which hits both the industrial capitalist and the
workman, benefits the other classes.

Secondly he overlooks that the output level is by no means
arbitrarily chosen, but the more capitalist production develops,
the more it is forced to produce on a scale which has nothing to
do with the immediate demand but depends on a constant expansion of the world market. He has recourse to Say's trite assumption, that the capitalist produces not for the sake of profit,
surplus-value, but produces use-value directly for consumption—
for his own consumption. He overlooks the fact that the commodity has to be converted into money. The demand of the
workers does not suffice, since profit arises precisely from the
fact that the demand of the workers is smaller than the value of
their product, and that it [profit] is all the greater the smaller,
relatively, is this demand. The demand of the capitalists among
themselves is equally insufficient. Over-production does not call
forth a *constant* fall in profit, but *periodic* over-production
recurs constantly. It is followed by periods of under-production
etc. Over-production arises precisely from the fact that the mass
of the people can never consume more than the average quantity
of necessaries, that their consumption therefore does not grow
correspondingly with the productivity of labour. But the whole of
this section belongs to the *competition of capitals*. All that
Ricardo says on this isn't worth a rap. (This is contained in
Chapter XXI, "*Effects of Accumulation on Profits and Interest*".)

"There is only one case, and that will be *temporary*, in which the accumulation of capital with a low price of food may be attended with a fall of
profits; and that is, when the funds for the maintenance of labour increase

much more rapidly than population;—wages will then be high, and profits low" (l. c., p. 343).

[In the same chapter] Ricardo directs against *Say* the following ironical remarks on the relation between profits and interest:

"M. Say allows, that the rate of interest depends on the rate of profits; but it does not therefore follow, that the rate of profits depends on the rate of interest. One is the cause, the other the effect, and it is impossible for any circumstances to make them change places" (l. c., p. 353, note).

However, the same causes which bring down profits can make interest rise, and vice versa.[119]

[In the Chapter "On Colonial Trade" Ricardo writes:]

"M. Say acknowledges that the *cost of production* is the foundation of price, and yet in various parts of his book he maintains that price is regulated by the proportion which demand bears to supply" (l. c., p. 411).

Ricardo should have seen from this that ||694| the *cost of production* is something very different from the quantity of labour employed for the production of a commodity.

Instead he continues:

"The real and ultimate regulator of the relative value of any two commodities, is the cost of their production" (l. c., p. 411).

"And does not Adam Smith agree in this opinion" (that prices are regulated neither by wages nor profits) "when he says, that 'the *prices* of commodities, or the *value* of gold and silver as compared with commodities, depends upon the proportion between the *quantity of labour* which is necessary in order to bring a certain quantity of gold and silver to market, and that which is necessary to bring thither a certain quantity of any other sort of goods?' That quantity will not be affected, whether profits be high or low, or wages low or high. *How then can prices be raised by high profits?*" (l. c., pp. 413-14).

In the passage quoted, Adam Smith means by *prices* nothing other than the monetary expression of the *values* of commodities. That these and the gold and silver against which they exchange, are determined by the relative quantities of labour required for producing those two sorts of commodities (commodities on the one side, gold and silver on the other), in no way contradicts the fact that the *actual* prices of commodities, i.e., their cost-prices "... can [...] be raised by high profits" [l.c., p. 414]. Although not all prices simultaneously, as Smith thinks. But as a result of high profits, some commodities will rise higher above their value, than if the average profits were low, while another group of commodities will sink to a smaller extent below their value.[120]

[CHAPTER XVII]

RICARDO'S THEORY OF ACCUMULATION AND A CRITIQUE OF IT.
(THE VERY NATURE OF CAPITAL LEADS TO CRISES)

[1. Adam Smith's and Ricardo's Error in Failing to Take into Consideration Constant Capital. Reproduction of the Different Parts of Constant Capital]

First we shall compare Ricardo's propositions, which are widely scattered over the whole of his work.

"All the productions of a country are consumed; but it makes the greatest difference imaginable whether they are consumed by *those who reproduce, or by those who do not reproduce another value.* When we say that *revenue is saved,* and *added to capital,* what we mean is, that the *portion of revenue, so said to be added to capital,* is *consumed by productive instead of unproductive labourers.*" (This is the same distinction as Adam Smith makes.) "There can be no greater error than in supposing that *capital is increased by non-consumption.* If the price of labour should rise so high, that notwithstanding the increase of capital, no more could be employed, I should say that such *increase of capital would be still unproductively consumed*" (l. c., p. 163, note).

Here, therefore—as with Adam Smith and others—[it is] only [a question] of whether [the products] are consumed by workers or not. But it is at the same time also a question of the *industrial consumption* of the commodities which form constant capital, and are consumed as instruments of labour or materials of labour, or are consumed in such a way that through this consumption they are transformed into instruments of labour or materials, of labour. The conception that accumulation of capital is identical with conversion of revenue into wages, in other words, that it is synonymous with accumulation of variable capital—is one-sided, that is, incorrect. This leads to a wrong approach to the whole question of accumulation.

Above all it is necessary to have a clear understanding of the *reproduction of constant capital.* We ·are considering the *annual* reproduction here, taking the year as the time measure of the process of reproduction.

A large part of the constant capital—the *fixed capital*—enters into the annual process of labour without entering into the annual process of the creation of value. It is not consumed and, therefore, does not need to be reproduced. Because it enters into the production process and remains in contact with living labour it is *kept in existence*—and along with its use-value, also its exchange-value. The greater this part of capital is in a particular country in one year, the greater, relatively, will be its purely formal reproduction (preservation) in the following year, providing that the production process is renewed, continued and kept flowing, even if only on the same scale. Repairs and so on, which are necessary to maintain the fixed capital, are reckoned as part of its original labour costs. This has nothing in common with preservation in the sense used above.

A second part of the constant capital is consumed annually in the production of commodities and must therefore also be reproduced. This includes the whole of that part of fixed capital which enters annually into the process of creating value, as well as the whole of that part of constant capital which consists of circulating capital, raw materials and auxiliary materials.

As regards this second part of constant capital, the following distinctions must be made:

||695| A large part of what *appears* as constant capital—instruments and materials of labour—in one sphere of production, is *simultaneously* the product of another, parallel sphere of production. For example, yarn which forms part of the constant capital of the weaver, is the product of the spinner, and may still have been in the process of becoming yarn on the previous day. When we use the term *simultaneous* here, we mean produced during *the same* year. The same commodities in different phases pass through various spheres of production in the course of the same year. They emerge as products from one sphere and enter another as commodities constituting constant capital. And as constant capital they are all consumed during the year; whether only their value enters into the commodity, as in the case of fixed capital, or their use-value too, as with circulating capital. While the commodity produced in one sphere of production enters into another, to be consumed there as constant capital—in addition to the same commodity entering a *succession* of spheres of production—the various elements or the various phases of this commod-

ity are being produced *simultaneously*, side by side. In the course of the same year, it is continuously consumed as constant capital in one sphere and in another parallel sphere it is produced as a commodity. The same commodities which are thus consumed as constant capital in the course of the year are also, in the same way continuously being produced during the same year. A machine is wearing out in sphere A. It is simultaneously being produced in sphere B. The constant capital that is consumed during a year in those spheres of production which produce the means of subsistence, is *simultaneously* being produced in other spheres of production, so that *during the course* of the year or *by the end of the year* it is renewed in kind. Both of them, the means of subsistence as well as this part of the constant capital, are the products of new labour employed during the year.

In the spheres producing the means of subsistence, as I have shown earlier,[121] that *portion of the value* of the product which replaces the constant capital in these spheres, forms the revenue of the *producers* of this constant capital.

But there is also a further portion of the constant capital which is *consumed annually,* without entering as a component part into the spheres of production which produce the means of subsistence (consumption goods). Therefore, it cannot be replaced [by products] from these spheres. We mean instruments of labour, raw materials and auxiliary materials, i.e., that portion of constant capital which is itself consumed industrially in the creation or production, of constant capital, that is to say, machinery, raw materials and auxiliary materials. This part, as we have seen,[122] is replaced in kind either directly out of the product of these spheres of production themselves—as in the case of seeds, livestock and to a certain extent coal—or through the exchange of a portion of the products of the various spheres of production manufacturing constant capital. In this case capital is exchanged for capital.

The existence and consumption of this portion of constant capital increases not only the mass of products, but also the *value* of the annual product. The *portion of the value* of the *annual* product which equals the value of this section of the consumed constant capital, buys back in kind or withdraws from the annual product that part of it, which must replace in kind the constant capital that is consumed. For example, the value of the seed sown determines the portion of the value of the harvest (and thus the quantity of corn) which must be returned to the land, to production, as constant capital. This portion would not be reproduced without the labour newly added during the course of the year; but it is in fact *produced* by the labour of the year before, or past labour and—in so far as the productivity of labour remains unchanged—the *value* which it adds to the annual product is not the result of this year's labour, but of that of the previous year. The greater, *proportionately*, is the constant capital employed in a country, the greater will also be the part of the constant capital which is consumed in the production of the constant capital, and which not only expresses itself in a greater quantity of products, but also raises the value of this quantity of products. This *value*, therefore, is the result not only of the current year's labour, but equally the result of the labour of the previous year, of past labour, although *without* the immediate labour of the current year it would not reappear, any more than would the product of which it forms a part. If this portion [of constant capital] grows, not only does the annual mass of products grow, but also their *value,* even if the annual labour remains the same. This growth is one form of the *accumulation of capital,* which it is essential to understand. And nothing could be further removed from such an understanding than Ricardo's proposition:

"The labour of a million of men in manufactures, will always produce the same value, but will not always produce the same riches" (l. c., p. 320).

These million men—with a given working-day—will not only produce very different quantities of commodities depending on the productivity of labour, but the value of these quantities of commodities will be very different, according to whether they are produced with much or little constant capital, that is, whether much or little value originating in the *past* labour of *previous years* is added to them.

[2. Value of the Constant Capital and Value of the Product]

For the sake of simplicity, when we speak of the reproduction of constant capital we shall in the first place assume that the productivity of labour, and consequently the method of production, remain the same. At a given level of production, the constant capital which has to be replaced is a definite quantity in kind. If productivity remains the same, then the value ||696| of this quantity also remains constant. If there are changes in the productivity of labour which make it possible to reproduce the same quantity, at greater or less cost, with more or less labour, then similarly changes will occur in the value of the constant capital, which will affect the surplus-product after deduction of the constant capital.

For example, supposing 20 quarters [of wheat] at £ 3, totalling £ 60, were required for sowing. If a third less labour is used to reproduce a quarter it would now cost only £ 2. 20 quarters have to be deducted from the product, for the sowing, as before; but their share in the value of the whole product only amounts to £ 40. The replacement of the same constant capital thus requires a smaller portion of value, a smaller share in kind out of the total product, although, as previously, 20 quarters have to be returned to the land as seed.[123]

If the constant capital consumed annually by one nation were £ 10 million and that consumed by another were only 1 million and the annual labour of 1 million men amounted to £ 100 million, then the value of the product of the first nation would be 110 and of the second only 101 million. It would be, moreover, not only possible, but certain, that the individual commodity of nation I would be cheaper than of nation II, because the latter would produce a much smaller quantity of commodities with the same amount of labour, much smaller than the difference between 10 and 1. It is true that a greater portion of the value of the product goes to the replacement of capital in nation I as compared with nation II, and therefore also a greater portion of the total product. But the total product is also much greater.

In the case of factory-made commodities, it is known that a million [workers] in England produce not only a much greater product but also a product of much greater value than in Russia for example, although the individual commodity is much cheaper. In the case of agriculture, however, the same relation between capitalistically developed and relatively undeveloped nations does not appear to exist. The product of the more backward nation is cheaper than that of the capitalistically developed nation, in terms of its *money price*. And yet the product of the developed nation appears to be produced by much less (annual) labour than that of the backward one. In England, for example, less than one-third [of the workers] are employed in agriculture, while in Russia it is four-fifths; in the former $5/15$, in the latter $12/15$. These figures are not to be taken literally. In England, for instance, a large number of people in *non-agricultural occupations*—in

engineering, trade, transport etc.—are engaged in the production
and distribution of elements of agricultural production, but this
is not the case in Russia. The proportion of persons engaged in
agriculture cannot therefore be directly determined by the number of individuals immediately employed in agriculture. In countries with a capitalist mode of production, many people participate *indirectly* in agricultural production, who in less developed
countries are directly included in it. The difference therefore
appears to be greater than it is. For the civilisation of the country
as a whole, however, this difference is very important, even in
so far as it only means that a large section of the workers involved in agriculture do not participate in it directly; they are
thus saved from the narrow parochialism of country life and belong to the industrial population.

But let us leave aside this point for the moment and also the
fact that most agricultural peoples are forced, to sell their product
below its value whereas in countries with advanced capitalist production the agricultural product rises to its value. At any rate,
a portion of the value of the constant capital enters into the
value of the product of the English farmer, which does not enter
into the product of the Russian farmer. Let us assume that this
portion of value is equal to a day's labour of 10 men, and that
one English worker sets this constant capital in motion. I am
speaking of that part of the constant capital of the agricultural
product, which is not replaced by new labour, such as is the case,
for example, with agricultural implements. If five Russian
workers were required in order to produce the same product
which one Englishman produces with the help of the constant
capital, and if the constant capital used by the Russian were
equal to one [day's labour], then the English product would be
equal to $10+1=11$ working-days, and that of the Russian would
be $5+1=6$. If the Russian soil were so much more fertile than
the English, that without the application of any constant capital
or with a constant capital that was one-tenth the size, it could
produce as much corn as the Englishmen with a constant capital
ten times as great, then the *values* of the same quantities of
English and Russian corn would compare as 11:6. If the quarter
of Russian corn were sold at £ 2, then the English would be sold
at £ $3^2/_3$, for $2:3^2/_3=6:11$. The money price and the value of the
English corn would thus be much higher than that of the Russian,
but nevertheless, the English corn would be produced with less
labour, since the *past* labour, which reappears in the quantity as

well as in the value of product, costs no additional new labour. This would always be the case, if the Englishman uses less immediate labour than the Russian, but the greater constant capital which he uses—and which costs him *nothing*, although it has cost something and must be paid for—does not raise the productivity of labour to such an extent that it compensates for the natural fertility of the Russian soil. The money prices of agricultural products can, therefore, be higher in countries of capitalist production than in ||697| less developed countries, although in fact they cost less labour. They contain more immediate and past labour, but this past labour costs nothing. The product would be cheaper if the difference in natural fertility did not intervene. This would also explain the higher money price of the labourer's wage.

Up to now we have only spoken of the reproduction of the capital involved. The labourer replaces his wage with a surplus-product or surplus-value, which forms the profit (including rent) of the capitalist. He replaces that part of the annual product which serves him anew as wages. The capitalist has consumed his profit during the course of the year, but the labourer has created a portion of the product which can again be consumed as profit. That part of the constant capital which is consumed in the production of the means of subsistence, is replaced by constant capital which has been produced by new labour, during the course of the year. The producers of this new portion of constant capital realise their revenue (profit and wages) in that part of the means of subsistence which is equal to the value of the constant capital consumed in their production. Finally, the constant capital which is consumed in the production of constant capital, in the production of machinery, raw materials and auxiliary materials, is replaced in kind or through the exchange of capital, out of the total product of the various spheres of production which produce constant capital.

[3. Necessary Conditions for the Accumulation of Capital. Amortisation of Fixed Capital and Its Role in the Process of Accumulation]

What then is the position with regard to the *increase* of capital, its *accumulation* as distinct from reproduction, the *transformation of revenue* into capital?

In order to simplify the question, it is assumed that the productivity of labour remains the same, that no changes occur in the method of production, that therefore the same quantity of labour is required to produce the same quantity of commodities, and consequently that the *increase* in capital costs the same amount of labour as the production of capital of the same size cost the previous year.

A portion of the surplus-value must be transformed into capital, instead of being consumed as revenue. It must be converted partly into constant and partly into variable capital. And the proportion in which it is divided into these two different parts of capital, depends on the given organic composition of the capital, since the method of production remains unaltered and also the proportional value of both parts. The higher the development of production, the greater will be that part of surplus-value which is transformed into constant capital, compared with that part of the surplus-value which is transformed into variable capital.

To begin with, a portion of the surplus-value (and the corresponding surplus-product in the form of means of subsistence) has to be transformed into variable capital, that is to say, new labour has to be bought with it. This is only possible if the number of labourers grows or if the labour-time during which they work, is prolonged. The latter takes place, for instance, when a part of the labouring population was only employed for half or two-thirds [of the normal time], or also, when for longer or shorter periods, the working-day is absolutely prolonged, this however, must be paid for. But that cannot be regarded as a method of accumulation which can be continuously used. The labouring population can increase, when previously unproductive labourers are turned into productive ones, or sections of the population who did not work previously, such as women and children, or paupers, are drawn into the production process. We leave this latter point out of account here. Finally, together with the growth of the population in general, the labouring population can grow absolutely. If accumulation is to be a steady, continuous process, then this absolute growth in population—although it may be decreasing in relation to the capital employed—is a necessary condition. An *increasing population* appears to be the basis of accumulation as a continuous process. But this presupposes an average wage which permits not only reproduction of the labouring population but also its constant growth. Capitalist production provides for unexpected contingencies by overworking one section of the labouring population and keeping the other as a ready reserve army consisting of partially or entirely pauperised people.

What then is the position with regard to the other portion of the surplus-value which has to be converted into constant capital? In order to simplify this question, we shall leave out of account foreign trade and consider a self-sufficing nation. Let us take an example. Let us assume that the surplus-value produced by a linen weaver amounts to £10,000, and that he wants to convert into capital one half of it, i.e., £5,000. Let one-fifth of this be laid out in wages in accordance with the organic composition [of capital] in mechanised weaving. In this case we are disregarding the turnover of capital, which may perhaps enable him to carry on with an amount sufficient for five weeks, after which he would sell [his product] and so receive back from circulation the capital for the payment of wages. We are assuming that in the course of the year he will gradually lay out in wages (for 20 men) £1,000 which he must hold in reserve with his banker. Then £4,000 are to be converted into constant capital. Firstly he must purchase as much yarn as 20 men can weave during the year. (The turnover of the circulating part of capital is disregarded throughout.) Further, he must increase the number of looms in his factory, and perhaps install an additional steam-engine or enlarge the existing one, etc. But in order to purchase all these things, he must find yarn, looms etc. available on the market. He must convert his £4,000 into yarn, looms, coal etc., ||698| i.e., he must buy them. In order to buy them, they must be available. Since we have assumed that the reproduction of the old capital has taken place under the old conditions, the spinner of yarn has spent the whole of his capital in order to supply the amount of yarn required by the weavers during the previous year. How then is he to satisfy the additional demand by an additional supply of yarn?

The position of the manufacturer of machines, who supplies looms etc. is just the same. He has produced only sufficient new looms in order to cover the average consumption in weaving. But the weaver who is keen on accumulation, orders yarn for £3,000 and for £1,000 looms, coal (since the position of the coal producer is the same), etc. Or in fact, he gives £3,000 to the spinner, and £1,000 to the machinery manufacturer and the coal merchant, etc., so that they will transform this money into yarn, looms and coal for him. He would thus have to wait until this process is completed before he could begin with his accumulation—his production of new linen. This would be interruption number I.

But now the owner of the spinning-mill finds himself in the same position with the £ 3,000 as the weaver with the 4,000, only he deducts his profit right away. He can find an additional number of spinners, but he needs flax, spindles, coal, etc. Similarly the coal producer [needs] new machinery or implements apart from the additional workers. And the owner of the engineering works who is supposed to supply the new looms, spindles, etc. [needs] iron and so forth, apart from additional labourers. But the position of the flax-grower is the worst of all, since he can supply the additional quantity of flax only in the following year.

So that accumulation can be a continuous process and the weaver able to transform a portion of his profit into constant capital every year, without long-winded complications and interruptions, he must find an additional quantity of yarn, looms, etc. available on the market. He [the weaver], the spinner, the producer of coal, etc. require additional workers, only if they are able to obtain flax, spindles and machines on the market.

A part of the constant capital which is calculated to be used up annually and enters as wear and tear into the value of the product, is in fact *not* used up. Take, for example, a machine which lasts twelve years and costs £ 12,000; its average wear and tear, which has to be charged each year, amounts to £ 1,000. Thus, since £ 1,000 is incorporated into the product each year, the value of £ 12,000 will have been reproduced at the end of the twelve years and a new machine of the same kind can be bought for this price. The repairs and patching up which are required during the twelve years are reckoned as part of the production costs of the machine and have nothing to do with the question under discussion. In fact, however, reality differs from this calculation of averages. The machine may perhaps run more smoothly in the second year than in the first. And yet after twelve years it is no longer usable. It is the same as with an animal whose average life is ten years, but this does not mean that it dies by one-tenth each year, although at the end of ten years it must be replaced by a new individual. Naturally, during the course of *a particular year*, a certain quantity of machinery etc. always reaches the stage when it must actually be replaced by new machines. Each year, therefore, a certain quantity of old machinery etc. has in fact to be replaced in kind by new machines etc. And the average annual production of machinery etc. corresponds with this. The value with which they are to be paid for, lies ready; it is derived from the [proceeds of the] commodities, according to the reproduction period of the machines. But the fact remains, that although a large part of the value of the annual product, of the value which is paid for it each year, is needed to replace, for example, the old machines after twelve years, it is by no means actually required to replace one-twelfth in kind each year, and in fact this would not be feasible. This fund may be used partly for wages or for the purchase of raw material, before the commodity, which is constantly thrown into circulation but does not immediately return from circulation, is sold and paid for. This cannot, however, be the case throughout the whole year, since the commodities which complete their turnover during the year realise their whole value, and must therefore replace the wages, raw material and used up machinery contained in them, as well as pay surplus-value.

Hence where much constant capital, and therefore also much fixed capital, is employed, that part of the value of the product which replaces the wear and tear of the fixed capital, provides an *accumulation fund,* which can be invested by the person controlling it, as new fixed capital (or also circulating capital), without any deduction whatsoever having to be made from the surplus-value for this part of the accumulation (see McCulloch).[124] This accumulation fund does not exist at levels of production and in nations where there is not much fixed capital. This is an important point. It is a fund for the continuous introduction of improvements, expansions etc.

[4. The Connection Between Different Branches of Production in the Process of Accumulation. The Direct Transformation of a Part of Surplus-Value into Constant Capital—a Characteristic Peculiar to Accumulation in Agriculture and the Machine-building Industry]

But the point we want to make here is the following: Even if the total capital employed in machine-building were only large enough to replace the annual wear and tear of machinery, it would produce much more machinery each year than required, since in part the wear and tear merely exists nominally, and in reality it only has to be replaced in kind after a certain number of years. The capital thus employed, therefore yields annually a mass of machinery which is available for new capital investments and anticipates these new capital investments. For example, the factory of the machine-builder begins production, say, this year. He supplies £ 12,000 worth of machinery during the year. If he were merely to replace the machinery produced by him, he would only have to produce machinery worth £ 1,000 in each of the eleven following years and even this annual production would not be annually consumed. An even smaller part of his production would be used, if he invested the whole of his capital. A continuous expansion of production in the branches of industry which use these machines is required in order to keep his capital employed and merely to reproduce it annually ||699|. (An even greater expansion is required if he himself accumulates.)

Thus *even the mere reproduction of the capital invested in this sphere* requires continuous accumulation in the remaining spheres of production. But because of this, one of the elements of continuous accumulation is always available on the market. Here, in one sphere of production—even if only the existing capital is reproduced in this sphere—exists a continuous supply of commodities for accumulation, for new, additional industrial consumption in other spheres.

As regards the £ 5,000 profit or surplus-value which is to be transformed into capital, for instance by the weaver, there are two possibilities—always assuming that he *finds available* on the market *the labour* which he must buy with part of the £ 5,000, i.e., £ 1,000 in order to transform the £ 5,000 into capital according to the conditions prevailing in his sphere of production. This part [of the capitalised surplus-value] is transformed into variable capital and is laid out in wages. But in order to employ this labour, he requires yarn, additional auxiliary materials and additional machinery ⟨unless the working-day is prolonged. In that case the machinery is merely used up faster, its reproduction period is curtailed, but at the same time more surplus-value is produced; and though the value of the machine has to be distributed over the commodities produced during a shorter period far more commodities are being produced, so that despite this more rapid depreciation of the machine, a smaller portion of machine value enters into the value or price of the individual commodity. In this case, no *new* capital has to be laid out directly in machinery. It is only necessary to replace the value of the machinery a little more rapidly. *But* additional capital must be laid out for auxiliary materials.⟩ Either the weaver

31–244

finds these, his conditions of production, on the market: then the purchase of these commodities only differs from that of other commodities by the fact that he buys commodities for *industrial consumption* instead of for *individual* consumption. Or he does not find these conditions of production on the market: then he must order them (as for instance machines of a new design), just as he has to order articles for his private consumption which are not readily available on the market. If the raw material (flax) were only produced to order (as, for instance, indigo, jute etc. are produced by the Indian Ryots to orders and with advances from English merchants), then the linen weaver could not accumulate in his own business during that year. On the other hand, assuming, that the spinner converts the £ 5,000 into capital and that the weaver does not accumulate, then the spun yarn— although all the conditions for its production were in supply on the market—will be unsaleable and the £ 5,000 have in fact been transformed into yarn but not into capital.

(*Credit*, which does not concern us further here, is the means whereby accumulated capital is not just used in that sphere in which it is created, but wherever it has the best chance of being turned to good account. Every capitalist will however prefer to invest his accumulation as far as possible in his own sphere of production. If he invests it in another, then he becomes a moneyed capitalist and instead of profit he draws only interest— unless he goes in for speculative transactions. We are, however, concerned with average accumulation here and only [assume] for the sake of illustration that it is invested in a particular sphere.)

If, on the other hand, the flax-grower had expanded his production, that is to say, had accumulated, and the spinner and weaver and machine-builder, etc. had not done so, then he would have superfluous flax in store and would probably produce less in the following year.

⟨At present we are leaving individual consumption completely out of account and are only considering the mutual relations between producers. If these relations exist, then in the first place the producers constitute a market for the capitals which they must replace for one another. The newly employed, or more fully employed workers constitute a market for some of the means of subsistence; and since the surplus-value increases in the following year, the capitalists can consume an increasing part of their revenue, to a certain extent therefore they also constitute a market for one another. Even so, a large part of the annual product may still remain unsaleable.⟩

The question has now to be formulated thus: *assuming general accumulation*, in other words, assuming that capital is accumulated to some extent in all branches of production—this is in fact a condition of capitalist production and is just as much the urge of the capitalist as a capitalist, as the urge of the hoarder is the piling up of money (it is also a necessity if capitalist production is to go ahead)—what are the *conditions* of this general accumulation, what does it amount to? Or, since the linen weaver may be taken to represent the capitalist in general, what are the *conditions* in which he can uninterruptedly reconvert the £ 5,000 surplus-value into capital and steadily continue the process of accumulation year in, year out? The accumulation of the £ 5,000 means nothing but the transformation of this money, this amount of value, into capital. *The conditions for the accumulation of capital are thus the very same as those for its original production or for reproduction in general.*

These conditions, however, were: that labour was bought with one part of the money, and with the other, commodities—raw material, machinery, etc.—which could be *consumed industrially* by this labour. ⟨Some commodities can only be consumed industrially, such as machinery, raw material, semi-finished goods; others, such as houses, horses, wheat (from which brandy or starch etc. is made), can be consumed industrially or individually.⟩ These commodities can only be purchased, if they are available on the ||700| *market* as commodities—in the intermediate stage when production is completed and consumption has not as yet begun, in the hands of the seller, in the stage of circulation—or if they can be made to order (produced to order, as is the case with the construction of new factories etc.). Commodities were available—this was presupposed in the production and reproduction of capital—as a result of the division of labour carried out in capitalist production on a social scale (distribution of labour and capital between the different spheres of production); as a result of *parallel* production and reproduction which takes place *simultaneously* over the whole field. This was the condition of the *market*, of the production and the reproduction of capital. The greater the capital, the more developed the productivity of labour and the scale of capitalist production in general, *the greater is also the volume of commodities found on the market, in circulation, in transition between production and*

consumption (individual and industrial), and the greater
the certainty that each particular capital will find its conditions for reproduction readily available on the market. This
is all the more the case, since it is in the nature of capitalist
production that: 1. each particular capital operates on a scale
which is not determined by individual demand (orders etc.,
private needs), but by the endeavour to realise as much labour
and therefore as much surplus-labour as possible and to produce
the largest possible quantity of commodities with a given capital;
2. each individual capital strives to capture the largest possible
share of the market and to supplant its competitors and exclude
them from the market—*competition of capitals.*

⟨The greater the development of the means of communication, the more can the stocks on the market be reduced.

"There will, indeed, where production and consumption are comparatively great, naturally be, at any given moment, a *comparatively great surplus*
in the intermediate state, in the market, on its way from having been produced to the hands of the consumer; unless indeed the quickness with which
things are sold off should have increased so as to counteract what would else
have been the consequence of the increased production." (*An Inquiry into
those Principles, respecting the Nature of Demand and the Necessity of Consumption, lately advocated by Mr. Malthus,* London, 1821, pp. 6-7.)⟩

The accumulation of new capital can therefore proceed only
under the same conditions as the reproduction of already existing capital.
⟨We disregard here the case in which more capital is accumulated than can be invested in production, and for example
lies fallow in the form of money at the bank. This results in
loans abroad, etc., in short speculative investments. Nor do we
consider the case in which it is impossible to sell the mass of
commodities produced, crises etc. This belongs into the section
on competition. Here we examine only the forms of capital in
the various phases of its process, assuming throughout, that the
commodities are sold at their value.⟩
The weaver can reconvert the £ 5,000 surplus-value into
capital, if besides labour for £ 1,000 he finds yarn etc. ready on
the market or is able to obtain it to order; this presupposes the
production of a *surplus-product* consisting of commodities which
enter into his constant capital, particularly of those which require
a longer period of production and whose volume cannot be increased rapidly, or cannot be increased at all during the course
of the year, such as raw material, for example flax.

⟨What comes into play here is the merchants' capital, which keeps warehouses stocked with goods to meet growing individual and industrial consumption; but this is only a *form of intermediary agency,* hence does not belong here, but into the consideration of the competition of capitals.⟩

Just as the production and reproduction of existing capital in one *sphere* presupposes *parallel* production and reproduction in other spheres, so accumulation or the formation of additional capital in one branch of production presupposes *simultaneous or parallel* creation of additional products in other branches of production. Thus the scale of production in all spheres which supply constant capital must grow simultaneously (in accordance with the average participation—determined by the demand—of each particular sphere in the general growth of production) and all spheres which do not produce finished products for individual consumption, supply constant capital. Of the greatest importance, is the increase in machinery (tools), *raw material,* and auxiliary material, for, if these preconditions are present, all other industries into which they enter, whether they produce semi-finished or finished goods, only need to set in motion more labour.

It seems therefore, that for accumulation to take place, continuous *surplus production* in all spheres is necessary.

This will have to be more closely defined.

Then there is the second essential question:

The [part of] the *surplus-value* [or] in this case the part of *profit* (including rent; if the landlord wants to accumulate, to transform rent into capital, it is always the *industrial capitalist* who gets hold of the surplus-value; this applies even when the worker transforms a portion of his revenue into capital), which is reconverted into capital, consists only of *labour newly added* during ||701| the past year. The question is, whether this new capital is entirely expended on wages, i.e., exchanged only against new labour.

The following speakes for this: All value is originally derived from labour. All constant capital is originally just as much the product of labour as is variable capital. And here we seem to encounter again the direct genesis of capital from labour.

An argument against it is: Can one suppose that the formation of additional capital takes place under worse conditions of production than the reproduction of the old capital? Does a reversion to a lower level of production occur? This would have to be the case if the new value [were] spent only on immediate labour, which, *without fixed capital* etc., would thus also first have to produce this fixed capital, just as originally, labour had first to create its constant capital. This is sheer nonsense. But this is the *assumption made by Ricardo, etc.* This needs to be examined more closely.

The first question is this:

Can the capitalist transform a part of the surplus-value into capital by employing it *directly* as capital instead of *selling* the surplus-value, or rather the surplus-product in which it is expressed? An affirmative answer to this question would already imply that the whole of the surplus-value to be transformed into capital is *not* transformed into variable capital, or is not laid out in wages.

With that part of the agricultural produce which consists of corn or livestock, this is clear from the outset. Some of the corn which belongs to that part of the harvest representing the surplus-product or the surplus-value of the farmer (similarly some of the livestock), instead of being sold, can at once serve again as means of production, as seed or draught animals. The same applies to that part of the manure produced on the land itself, which at the same time exists as commodity on the market, that is to say, can be sold. This part of the surplus-product which falls to the share of the farmer as surplus-value, as profit, can be at once transformed by him into means of production within his own branch of production, it is thus *directly* converted into capital. This part is not expended on wages; it is not transformed into variable capital. It is withdrawn from individual consumption without being consumed *productively* in the sense used by Smith and Ricardo. It is consumed *industrially*, but as raw material, not as means of subsistence either of productive or of unproductive workers. Corn, however, serves not only as means of subsistence for productive worker etc., but also as auxiliary material for livestock, as raw material for spirits, starch etc. Livestock (for fattening or draught animals) in turn serves not only as means of subsistence, but its fur, hide, fat, bones, horns etc. supply raw materials for a large number of industries, and it also provides motive power, partly for agriculture itself and partly for the transport industry.

In all industries, in which the *period of reproduction* extends over more than a year, as is the case with a major part of livestock, timber etc., but whose products at the same time have to be continuously reproduced, thus requiring the application of a certain amount of labour, accumulation and reproduction coincide in so far as the *newly-added* labour, which includes not only paid but also unpaid labour, must be accumulated in kind, until the product is ready for sale. (We are not speaking here of the accumulation of the profit which according to the general rate of profit is added [to the capital] each year—this is not *real* accumulation, but only a method of accounting. We are concerned here with the accumulation of the total labour which is repeated in the course of several years, during which not only paid, but also unpaid labour is accumulated in kind and at once reconverted into capital. The accumulation of profit is in such cases however independent of the quantity of newly-added labour.)

The position is the same with *commercial crops* (whether they provide raw materials or auxiliary materials). Their seeds and that part of them which can be used again as manure etc., represent a portion of the total product. Even if this were *unsaleable*, it would not alter the fact that as soon as it becomes a means of production again, it forms a part of the total value and as ||702| such constitutes constant capital for new production.

This settles one major point—the question of raw materials and means of subsistence (food), in so far as they are actually agricultural products. Here therefore, accumulation coincides *directly* with reproduction on a larger scale, so that a part of the surplus-product serves again as a means of production in its own sphere, *without being exchanged for wages or other commodities*.

The second important question relates to *machinery*. Not the machines which produce commodities, but the machines which produce machines, the *constant capital* of the machine producing industry. Given this machinery, the extractive industries require nothing but labour in order to provide the raw material, iron etc. for the production of containers and machines. And with the latter are produced the machines for working up the raw materials themselves. The difficulty here is not to get entangled in a vicious circle of presuppositions. For, in order to produce more machinery, more material is required (iron etc., coal etc.) and in order to produce this, more machinery is required. Whether we assume that industrialists who build machine-building machines and industrialists who manufacture machines (with the machine-building machines) are in one and the same category, does not alter the situation. This much is clear: One part of the surplus-product is embodied in machine-building machines (at least it is up to the manufacturers of machines to see that this happens). These need not be sold but can re-enter the new production in kind, as constant capital. This is therefore a second category of surplus-product which enters directly (or through exchange within the same sphere of production) as constant capital into the new production (accumulation), without having gone through the process of first being transformed into variable capital.

The question whether a part of the *surplus-value* can be directly transformed into constant capital, resolves, in the first place, into the question whether a part of the *surplus-product*, in which the surplus-value is expressed, can directly re-enter its own sphere of production as a means of production, without first having been alienated.

The general law is as follows:

Where a part of the product, and therefore also of the *surplus-product* (i.e., the use-value in which the surplus-value is expressed) can re-enter as a means of production—as instrument of labour or material of labour—into the sphere of production from which it came, directly, without an intermediary phase, accumulation within this sphere of production can and must take place in such a way that a part of the surplus-product, instead of being sold, is as a means of production re-incorporated into the reproduction process directly (or through exchange with other specialists in the same sphere of production who are similarly accumulating), so that accumulation and reproduction on a larger scale coincide here *directly*. They must coincide everywhere, but not in this direct manner.

This also applies to a part of the auxiliary materials. For example to the coal produced in a year. A part of the surplus-product can itself be used to produce more coal and can therefore be used up again directly by its producer, without any intermediary phase, as constant capital for production on a larger scale.

In industrial areas there are machine-builders who build whole factories for the manufacturers. Let us assume one-tenth is surplus-product or unpaid labour. Whether this tenth, the surplus-product, consists of factory buildings which are built for a third party and are sold to them, or of factory buildings which the producer builds for himself—sells to himself—clearly makes no difference. The only thing that matters here is whether the *kind of use-value* in which the surplus-labour is expressed, can re-enter as means of production into the sphere of production ||703| of the capitalist to whom the surplus-product belongs. This is yet another example of how important is the analysis of *use-value for the determination of economic phenomena.*

Here, therefore, we already have a considerable portion of the surplus-product, and therefore of the surplus-value, which can and must be transformed directly into constant capital, in order to be *accumulated* as *capital* and without which no accumulation of capital can take place at all.

Secondly, we have seen that where capitalist production is developed, that is, where the productivity of labour, the constant capital and particularly that part of constant capital which consists of fixed capital are developed, the *mere reproduction of fixed capital in all spheres* and the parallel reproduction of the existing capital which produces fixed capital, forms an accumulation fund, that is to say, provides machinery, i.e., constant capital, for production on an extended scale.

Thirdly: There remains the question: Can a part of the *surplus-product* be re-transformed into capital (that is constant capital) through an (intermediary) exchange between the producer, for example of machinery, implements of labour etc. and the producer of raw material, iron, coal, metals, timber etc., that is, through the exchange of various components of constant capital? If, for example, the manufacturer of iron, coal, timber, etc., buys machinery or tools from the machine-builder and the machine-builder buys metal, timber, coal etc. from the primary producer, then they replace or form new constant capital through this exchange of the reciprocal component parts of their constant capital. The question here is: to what extent is the *surplus-product* converted in this way?

[5. The Transformation of Capitalised Surplus-Value into Constant and Variable Capital]

We saw earlier,[125] that in the simple reproduction of the *advanced* capital, the portion of the constant capital which is used up in the reproduction of *constant capital* is replaced either directly in kind or through exchange between the producers of constant capital—an exchange of capital against capital and not of revenue against revenue or revenue against capital. Moreover, the constant capital which is used up or consumed industrially in the production of consumable goods—commodities which enter into individual consumption—is replaced by new products of the same kind, which are the result of *newly-added* labour, and therefore resolve into revenue (wages and profit). Accordingly, therefore, in the spheres which produce consumable goods, the portion of the total product, which is equal to the portion of their value which replaces their constant capital, represents the revenue of the producers of constant capital; while, on the other hand, in the spheres which produce constant capital, the part of the total product which represents newly-added labour and therefore forms the revenue of the producers of this constant capital, represents the constant capital (replacement capital) of the producers of the means of subsistence. This presupposes, therefore, that the producers of constant capital exchange their surplus-product (which means here, the excess of their product over that part of it which is equal to *their* constant capital) against means of subsistence, and consume its value individually. This surplus-product, however, consists of:

1. wages (or the reproduced fund for wages), and this portion must continue to be allocated (by the capitalist) for paying out wages, that is, for individual consumption (and assuming a minimum wage, the worker too can only convert the wages he receives, into means of subsistence);

2. the profit of the capitalist (including rent). If this portion is large enough, it can be consumed partly individually and partly industrially. And in this latter case, an exchange of products takes place between the producers of constant capital; this is, however, no longer an exchange of the portion of their products representing their constant capital which has to be mutually replaced between them, but is an exchange of a part of their surplus-product, revenue (*newly-added* labour) which is directly transformed into constant capital, thus increasing the amount of constant capital and expanding the scale of reproduction.

In this case, too, therefore a part of the existing surplus-product, that is, of the labour which has been newly added during the year, is transformed directly into constant capital, without first having been converted into variable capital. This demonstrates again that the industrial consumption of the surplus-product—or accumulation—is by no means identical with the conversion of the entire surplus-product into wages paid to productive workers.

It is quite possible that the manufacturer of machines sells (part of) his commodity to the producer, say, of cloth. The latter pays him in money. With this money he purchases iron, coal etc. instead of means of subsistence. But when one considers the process as a whole, it is evident that the producers of means of subsistence cannot purchase any replacement machinery or replacement raw materials, unless the producers of the replacements of constant capital buy their means of subsistence from them, in other words, unless this circulation is fundamentally an exchange between means of subsistence and constant capital. The separation of the acts of buying and selling can of course cause considerable disturbances and complications in this compensatory process.

||704| If a country cannot itself produce the amount of machinery required for the accumulation of capital, then it buys it from abroad. The same happens if it cannot itself produce a sufficient quantity of means of subsistence (for wages) and the raw material. As soon as international trade intervenes, it becomes quite obvious that a part of the surplus-product of a country—in so far as it is intended for accumulation—is not transformed into wages, but directly into constant capital. But then there may remain the notion that over there, in the foreign country, the money thus laid out is spent entirely on wages. We have seen that, even leaving foreign trade out of account, this is not so and cannot be so.

The proportion in which the surplus-product is divided between variable and constant capital, depends on the average composition of capital, and the more developed capitalist production is, the smaller, *relatively*, will be the part which is directly laid out in wages. The idea that, because the surplus-product is solely the product of the labour newly added during the year, it can therefore only be converted into variable capital, i.e., only be laid out in wages, corresponds altogether to the false conception that because the product is only the result, or the materialisation, of labour, its value is resolved only into revenue—wages, profit, and rent—the false conception of Smith and Ricardo.

A large part of constant capital, namely, the fixed capital, may enter directly into the process of the production of means of subsistence, raw materials etc., or it may serve either to shorten the circulation process, like railways, roads, navigation, telegraphs etc. or to store and accumulate stocks of commodities like docks, warehouses etc., alternatively it may increase the yield only after a long period of reproduction, as for instance levelling operations, drainage etc. The direct consequences for the reproduction of the means of subsistence etc. will be very different according to whether a greater or smaller part of the surplus-product is converted into one of these types of fixed capital.

[6. Crises (Introductory Remarks)]

If *expanded production* of constant capital is assumed—that is greater production than is required for the replacement of the former capital and therefore also for the production of the former quantity of means of subsistence—expanded production or accumulation in the spheres using the machinery, raw materials etc. encounters no further difficulties. If sufficient additional labour is available, they [the manufacturers] will find on the market all the means for the formation of new capital, for the transformation of their additional money into new capital.

But the whole process of accumulation in the first place resolves itself into *production on an expanding scale*, which on the one hand corresponds to the natural growth of the population, and on the other hand, forms an inherent basis for the phenomena which appear during *crises*. The criterion of this expansion of production is *capital* itself, the existing level of the conditions of production and the unlimited desire of the capitalists to enrich themselves and to enlarge their capital, but by no means *consumption*, which from the outset is inhibited, since the majority of the population, the working people, can only expand their consumption within very narrow limits, whereas the demand for labour, although it grows *absolutely*, decreases *relatively*, to the same extent as capitalism develops. Moreover, all equalisations are *accidental* and although the proportion of capital employed in individual spheres is equalised by a continuous process, the continuity of this process itself equally presupposes the constant disproportion which it has continuously, often violently, to even out.

Here we need only consider the forms which capital passes through in the various stages of its development. The real conditions within which the actual process of production takes place are therefore not analysed. It is assumed throughout, that the commodity is sold at its value. We do not examine the competition of capitals, nor the credit system, nor the actual composition of society, which by no means consists only of two classes, workers and industrial capitalists, and where therefore consumers and producers are not identical categories. The first category, that of the consumers (whose revenues are in part not primary, but secondary, derived from profit and wages), is much broader than the second category [producers], and therefore the way in which they spend their revenue, and the very size of the revenue give rise to very considerable modifications in the economy and particularly in the circulation and reproduction process of capital. Nevertheless, just as the examination of money[126]— both in so far as it represents a form altogether different from the natural form of commodities, and also in its form as means of payment—has shown that it contained the possibility of crises; the examination of the general nature of capital, even without going further into the actual relations which all constitute prerequisites for the real process of production, reveals this still more clearly.

||705| The conception (which really belongs to [James] Mill), adopted by Ricardo from the tedious Say (and to which we shall return when we discuss that miserable individual), that *over-production* is not possible or at least that no *general glut of the market* is possible, is based on the proposition that *products* are exchanged *against products*,[127] or as Mill put it, on the "metaphysical equilibrium of sellers and buyers",[128] and this led to [the conclusion] that demand is determined only by production, or also that demand and supply are identical. The same proposition exists also in the form, which Ricardo liked particularly, that any amount of capital can be employed productively in any country.

"M. Say," writes Ricardo in Chapter XXI ("*Effects* of Accumulation on Profits and Interest"), "has... most satisfactorily shewn, that there is no amount of capital which may not be employed in a country, because *demand is only limited by production*. No man *produces, but with a view to consume or sell, and he never sells, but* with an *intention to purchase some other commodity*, which may be immediately useful to him, or which may contribute to future production. By producing, then, he necessarily becomes either the consumer of his own goods, or the purchaser and consumer of the goods of some other person. It is not to be supposed that he should, for any length of time, be ill-informed of the commodities which he can most advantageously produce, to attain the object which he has in view, namely, the *possession of other goods*; and, therefore, it is not probable that he will *continually*" (the point in question here is not eternal life) "produce a commodity for which there is no demand." ([David Ricardo, *On the Principles of Political Economy, and Taxation*, London, 1821,] pp. 339-40.)

Ricardo, who always strives to be consistent, discovers that his authority, Say, is playing a trick on him here. He makes the following comment in a footnote to this passage:

"Is the following quite consistent with M. Say's principle? 'The more disposable capitals are abundant in proportion to the extent of employment for them, the more will the rate of interest on loans of capital fall.' (Say, Vol. II, p. 108.) If capital to any extent can be employed by a country, how can it be said to be abundant, compared with the extent of employment for it?" ([Ricardo], l.c., p. 340, note.)

Since Ricardo cites Say, we shall criticise Say's theories later, when we deal with this humbug himself.

Meanwhile we just note here: In reproduction, just as in the accumulation of capital, it is not only a question of replacing *the same* quantity of use-values of which capital consists, on the former scale or on an enlarged scale (in the case of accumulation), but of replacing the *value* of the capital advanced along with the usual rate of profit (surplus-value). If, therefore, through any circumstance or combination of circumstances, the market-prices of the commodities (of all or most of them, it makes no difference) fall far below their cost-prices, then reproduction of capital is curtailed as far as possible. Accumulation, however, stagnates even more. Surplus-value amassed in the form of money (gold or notes) could only be transformed into capital at a loss. It therefore lies idle as a hoard in the banks or in the form of credit money, which in essence makes no difference at all. The same hold up could occur for the opposite reasons, if the *real prerequisites* of reproduction were missing (for instance if grain became more expensive or because not enough constant capital had been accumulated in kind). There occurs a stoppage in reproduction, and thus in the flow of circulation. Purchase and sale get bogged down and unemployed capital appears in the form of idle money. The same phenomenon (and this usually precedes crises) can appear when additional capital is produced at a very rapid rate and its reconversion into productive capital increases the demand for all the elements of the latter to such an extent, that actual production cannot keep pace with it; this brings about a rise in the prices of all commodities, which enter into the formation of capital. In this case the rate of interest falls sharply, however much the profit may rise and this fall in the rate of interest then leads to the most risky speculative ventures. The interruption of the reproduction process leads to the decrease in variable capital, to a fall in wages and in the quantity of labour employed. This in turn reacts anew on prices and leads to their further fall.

It must never be forgotten, that in capitalist production what matters is not the immediate use-value but the exchange-value and, in particular, the expansion of surplus-value. This is the driving motive of capitalist production, and it is a pretty conception that—in order to reason away the contradictions of capitalist production—abstracts from its very basis and depicts it as a production aiming at the direct satisfaction of the consumption of the producers.

Further: since the circulation process of capital is not completed in one day but extends over a fairly long period until the capital returns to its original form, since this period coincides with the period within which market-prices ||706| equalise with cost-prices, and great upheavals and changes take place in the *market* in the course of this period, since great changes take place in the productivity of labour and therefore also in the *real value* of commodities, it is quite clear, that between the starting-point, the prerequisite capital, and the time of its return at the end of one of these periods, great catastrophes must occur and elements of crisis must have gathered and develop, and these cannot in any way be dismissed by the pitiful proposition that products exchange for products. The *comparison* of value in one period with the value of the same commodities in a later period is no scholastic illusion, as Mr. Bailey maintains,[129] but rather forms the fundamental principle of the circulation process of capital.

When speaking of the *destruction of capital* through crises, one must distinguish between two factors.

In so far as the reproduction process is checked and the labour-process is restricted or in some instances is completely stopped, *real* capital is destroyed. Machinery which is not used is not capital. Labour which is not exploited is equivalent to lost production. Raw material which lies unused is no capital. Buildings (also newly built machinery) which are either unused or remain unfinished, commodities which rot in warehouses— all this is destruction of capital. All this means that the process of reproduction is checked and that the *existing* means of production are not really used as means of production, are not put into operation. Thus their use-value and their exchange-value go to the devil.

Secondly, however, the *destruction of capital* through crises means the depreciation of *values* which prevents them from later renewing their reproduction process as capital on the same scale. This is the ruinous effect of the fall in the prices of commodities. It does not cause the destruction of any use-values. What one loses, the other gains. Values used as capital are prevented from acting again as *capital* in the hands of the same person. The old capitalists go bankrupt. If the value of the commodities from whose sale a capitalist reproduces his capital was equal to £ 12,000, of which say £ 2,000 were profit, and their price falls to £ 6,000, then the capitalist can neither meet his contracted obligations nor, even if he had none, could he, with the £ 6,000 restart his business on the former scale, for the commodity prices have risen once more to the level of their cost-prices. In this way, £ 6,000 has been destroyed, although the buyer of these commodities, because he has acquired them at half their cost-price, can go ahead very well once business livens up again, and may even have made a profit. A large part of the nominal capital of the society, i.e., of the *exchange-value* of the existing capital, is once for all destroyed, although this very destruction, since it does not affect the use-value, may very much expedite the new reproduction. This is also the period during which moneyed interest enriches itself at the cost of industrial interest. As regards the fall in the purely nominal capital, State bonds, shares etc.—in so far as it does not lead to the bankruptcy of the state or of the share company, or to the complete stoppage of reproduction through undermining the credit of the industrial capitalists who hold such securities—it amounts only to the transfer of wealth from one hand to another and will, on the whole, act favourably upon reproduction, since the parvenus into whose hands these stocks or shares fall cheaply, are mostly more enterprising than their former owners.

[7. Absurd Denial of the Over-production of Commodities, Accompanied by a Recognition of the Over-abundance of Capital]

To the best of his knowledge, Ricardo is always consistent. For him, therefore, the statement that no *over-production* (of commodities) is possible, is synonymous with the statement that no plethora or over-abundance of capital is possible.*

"There cannot, then, be accumulated in a country any amount of capital which cannot be employed productively, until wages rise so high in consequence of the rise of necessaries, and so little consequently remains for the profits of stock, that the motive for accumulation ceases" ([Ricardo], l. c., p. 340). "It follows then ... that there is no limit to demand—no limit to the employment of capital while it yields any profit, and that *however abundant capital may become*, there is no other adequate reason for a *fall of profit* but a rise of wages, and further it may be added, that the only adequate and permanent cause for the rise of wages is the increasing difficulty of providing food and necessaries ||707| for the increasing number of workmen" (l. c., pp. 347-48).

What then would Ricardo have said to the stupidity of his successors, who deny over-production in one form (as a general glut of commodities in the market) and who, not only admit its existence in another form, as over-production of capital, plethora of capital, over-abundance of capital, but actually turn it into an essential point in their doctrine?

Not a single responsible economist of the post-Ricardian period denies the plethora of capital. On the contrary, all of them regard it as the cause of crises (in so far as they do not explain the latter by factors relating to credit). Therefore, they all admit over-production in one form but deny its existence in another. The only remaining question thus is: what is the relation between these two forms of over-production, i.e., between the form in which it is denied and the form in which it is asserted?

Ricardo himself did not actually know anything of crises, of general crises of the world market, arising out of the production process itself. He could explain that the crises which occurred between 1800 and 1815, were caused by the rise in the price of corn due to poor harvests, by the devaluation of paper currency, the depreciation of colonial products etc., because, in consequence of the continental blockade, the market was forcibly contracted for political and not economic reasons. He was also able to explain the crises after 1815, partly by a bad year and a shortage of corn, and partly by the fall in corn prices, because those causes which, according to his own theory, had forced up the price of

---

* A distinction must be made here. When Adam Smith explains the fall in the rate of profit from an over-abundance of capital, an accumulation of capital, he is speaking of a *permanent* effect and this is wrong. As against this, the transitory over-abundance of capital, over-production and crises are something different. Permanent crises do not exist.

corn during the war when England was cut off from the continent, had ceased to operate; partly by the transition from war to peace which brought about "sudden changes in the channels of trade" [l.c., p. 307]. (See Chapter XIX—"On Sudden Changes in the Channels of Trade"—of his *Principles*.)

Later historical phenomena, especially the almost regular periodicity of crises on the world market, no longer permitted Ricardo's successors to deny the facts or to interpret them as accidental. Instead—apart from those who explain everything by credit, but then have to admit that they themselves are forced to presuppose the over-abundance of capital—they invented the nice distinction between *over-abundance of capital* and *over-production*. Against the latter, they arm themselves with the phrases and good reasons used by Ricardo and Adam Smith, while by means of the over-abundance of capital they attempt to explain phenomena that they are otherwise unable to explain. Wilson, for example, explains certain crises by the over-abundance of fixed capital, while he explains others by the over-abundance of circulating capital. The over-abundance of capital itself is affirmed by the best economists (such as Fullarton), and has already become a matter of course to such an extent, that it can even be found in the learned Roscher's compendium[130] as a self-evident fact.

The question is, therefore, what is the over-abundance of capital and how does it differ from over-production?

(In all fairness however, it must be said, that other economists, such as Ure, Corbet etc., declare over-production to be the *usual condition in large-scale industry*, so far as the home country is concerned and that it thus only leads to crises under certain circumstances, in which the foreign market also contracts.)

According to the same economists, capital is equivalent to money or commodities. Over-production of capital is thus over-production of money or of commodities. And yet these two phenomena are supposed to have nothing in common with each other. Even the over-production of money [is of] no [avail], since money for them is a commodity, so that the entire phenomenon resolves into one of over-production of commodities which they admit under one name and deny under another. Moreover, the statement that there is over-production of fixed capital or of circulating capital, is based on the fact that commodities are here no longer considered in this simple form, but in their designation as capital. This, however, is an admission that in capitalist ||708| production and its phenomena—e.g., over-production—it is a question not only of the simple relationship in which the product appears, is designated, as *commodity*, but of its designation within the social framework, it thereby becomes something *more* than, and also different from, a commodity.

Altogether, the phrase *over-abundance of capital* instead of *over-production of commodities* in so far as it is not merely a prevaricating expression, or unscrupulous thoughtlessness, which admits the existence and necessity of a particular phenomenon when it is called A, but denies it as soon as it is called B, in fact therefore showing scruples and doubts only about the *name* of the phenomenon and not the phenomenon itself; or in so far as it is not merely an attempt to avoid the difficulty of explaining the phenomenon, by denying it in one form (under one name) in which it contradicts existing prejudices and admitting it in a form only in which it becomes meaningless—apart from these aspects, the transition from the phrase *"over-production of commodities"* to the phrase *"over-abundance of capital"* is indeed an *advance*. In what does this consist? In [expressing the fact], that the producers confront one another not purely as owners of commodities, but as capitalists.

[8. Ricardo's Denial of General Over-production. Possibility of a Crisis Inherent in the Inner Contradictions of Commodity and Money]

A few more passages from Ricardo:

"One would be led to think ... that Adam Smith concluded we were *under some necessity*" (this is indeed the case) "of *producing a surplus* of corn, woollen goods, and hardware, and that the capital which produced them could not be otherwise employed. It is, however, always a matter of choice in what way a capital shall be employed, and therefore there can never, *for any length of time*, be a surplus of any commodity; for if there were, it would fall below its natural price, and capital would be removed to some more profitable employment" (l. c., pp. 341-42, note).

"Productions are always bought by productions, or by services; money is only the medium by which the exchange is effected."

(That is to say, money is merely a means of circulation, and exchange-value itself is merely a fleeting aspect of the exchange of product against product—which is wrong.)

"Too much of a particular commodity may be produced, of which there may be such a glut in the market, as not to repay the capital expended on it; *but this cannot be the case with [...] all commodities*" (l. c., pp. 341-42).

32*

"Whether *these increased productions, and consequent demand which they occasion,* shall or shall not lower profits, depends solely on the rise of wages; and the rise of wages, excepting for a limited period, on the facility of producing the food and necessaries of the labourer" (l. c., p. 343).

"When merchants engage their capitals in foreign trade, or in the carrying trade, it is always from choice, and never from necessity: it is because in that trade their profits will be somewhat greater than in the home trade" (l. c., p. 344).

So far as crises are concerned, all those writers who describe the real movement of prices, or all experts, who write in the actual situation of a crisis, have been right in ignoring the allegedly theoretical twaddle and in contenting themselves with the idea that what may be true in abstract theory—namely, that no gluts of the market and so forth are possible—is, nevertheless, wrong in practice. The constant recurrence of crises has in fact reduced the rigmarole of Say and others to a phraseology which is now only used in times of prosperity but is cast aside in times of crises.

||709| In the crises of the world market, the contradictions and antagonisms of bourgeois production are strikingly revealed. Instead of investigating the nature of the conflicting elements which errupt in the catastrophe, the apologists content themselves with denying the catastrophe itself and insisting, in the face of their regular and periodic recurrence, that if production were carried on according to the textbooks, crises would never occur. Thus the apologetics consist in the falsification of the simplest economic relations, and particularly in clinging to the concept of unity in the face of contradiction.

If, for example, purchase and sale—or the metamorphosis of commodities—represent the unity of two processes, or rather the movement of one process through two opposite phases, and thus essentially the unity of the two phases, the movement is essentially just as much the separation of these two phases and their becoming independent of each other. Since, however, they belong together, the independence of the two correlated aspects can only *show itself* forcibly, as a destructive process. It is just the *crisis* in which they assert their unity, the unity of the different aspects. The independence which these two linked and complimentary phases assume in relation to each other is forcibly destroyed. Thus the crisis manifests the unity of the two phases that have become independent of each other. There would be no crisis without this inner unity of factors that are apparently indifferent to each other. But no, says the apologetic economist.

Because there is this unity, there can be *no* crises. Which in turn means nothing but that the unity of contradictory factors excludes contradiction.

In order to prove that capitalist production cannot lead to general crises, all its conditions and distinct forms, all its principles and specific features—in short *capitalist production* itself—are denied. In fact it is demonstrated that if the capitalist mode of production had not developed in a specific way and become a unique form of social production, but were a mode of production dating back to the most rudimentary stages, then its peculiar contradictions and conflicts and hence also their eruption in crises would not exist.

Following Say, Ricardo writes: "Productions are always bought by productions, or by services; money is only the medium by which the exchange is effected" (l. c., p. 341).

Here, therefore, firstly *commodity*, in which the contradiction between exchange-value and use-value exists, becomes mere product (use-value) and therefore the exchange of commodities is transformed into mere barter of products, of simple use-values. This is a return not only to the time before capitalist production, but even to the time before there was simple commodity production; and the most complicated phenomenon of capitalist production—the world market crisis—is flatly denied, by denying the first condition of capitalist production, namely, that the product must be a commodity and therefore express itself as money and undergo the process of metamorphosis. Instead of speaking of wage-labour, the term "services" is used. This word again omits the specific characteristic of wage-labour and of its use—namely, that it increases the value of the commodities against which it is exchanged, that it creates surplus-value—and in doing so, it disregards the specific relationship through which money and commodities are transformed into capital. "*Service*" is labour seen only as *use-value* (which is a side issue in capitalist production) just as the term "productions" fails to express the essence of *commodity* and its inherent contradiction. It is quite consistent that *money* is then regarded merely as an intermediary in the exchange of products, and not as an essential and necessary form of existence of the commodity which must manifest itself as exchange-value, as general social labour. Since the transformation of the commodity into mere use-value (product) obliterates the essence of ||710| exchange-value, it is just as easy to deny, or rather it is necessary to deny, that *money* is an essential aspect of the commodity and that in the process of metamorphosis it is *independent* of the original form of the commodity.

Crises are thus reasoned out of existence here by forgetting or denying the first elements of capitalist production: the existence of the product as a commodity, the duplication of the commodity in commodity and money, the consequent separation which takes place in the exchange of commodities and finally the relation of money or commodities to wage-labour.

Incidentally, those economists are no better, who (like John Stuart Mill) want to explain the crises by these simple *possibilities* of crisis contained in the metamorphosis of commodities—such as the separation between purchase and sale. These factors which explain the possibility of crises, by no means explain their actual occurrence. They do not explain *why* the phases of the process come into such conflict that their inner unity can only assert itself through a crisis, through a violent process. This *separation* appears in the crisis; it is the elementary form of the crisis. To *explain* the crisis on the basis of this, its elementary form, is to explain the existence of the crisis by describing its most abstract form, that is to say, to explain the crisis by the crisis.

Ricardo says: "No man produces, but with a view to consume *or sell*, and he never sells, but with an intention to *purchase* some other commodity, which may be immediately useful to him, or which may contribute to *future production*. By producing, then, he necessarily becomes either the consumer of his own goods, or the purchaser and consumer of the goods of some person. It is not to be supposed that he should, *for any length of time*, be ill-informed of the commodities which he can most advantageously produce, to attain the object which he has in view, namely, the *possession of other goods*; and, *therefore*, it is not probable that he will *continually* produce a commodity for which there is no demand" [l. c., pp. 339-40].

This is the childish babble of a Say, but it is not worthy of Ricardo. In the first place, no capitalist produces in order to consume his product. And when speaking of capitalist production, it is right to say that: "no man produces with a view to consume his own product", even if he uses portions of his product for industrial consumption. But here the point in question is private consumption. Previously it was forgotten that the product is a commodity. Now even the social division of labour is forgotten. In a situation where men produce for themselves, there are indeed no crises, but neither is there capitalist production. Nor have we ever heard that the ancients, with their slave production ever knew crises, although individual producers among the ancients too, did go bankrupt. The first part of the alternative is nonsense. The second as well. A man who has produced, does not have the choice of selling or not selling. He must *sell*. In the crisis there arises the very situation in which he cannot sell or can only sell below the cost-price or must even sell at a positive loss. What difference does it make, therefore, to him or to us that he has produced in order to sell? The very question we want to solve is what has thwarted this good intention of his?

Further:

he "never *sells*, but with an intention to *purchase* some other commodity, which may be immediately useful to him, or which may contribute to future production" (l. c., p. 339).

What a cosy description of bourgeois conditions! Ricardo even forgets that a person may *sell* in order to *pay*, and that these forced sales play a very significant role in the crises. The capitalist's immediate object in selling, is to turn his commodity, or rather his commodity capital, back into *money capital*, and thereby to *realise* his profit. Consumption—revenue—is by no means the guiding motive in this process, although it is for the person who only sells *commodities* in order to transform them into means of subsistence. But this is not capitalist production, in which revenue appears as the result and not as the determining purpose. Everyone *sells* first of all in order to sell, that is to say, in order to transform commodities into money.

||711| During the crisis, a man may be very pleased, if he has *sold* his commodities without immediately thinking of a purchase. On the other hand, if the value that has been realised is again to be used as capital, it must go through the process of reproduction, that is, it must be exchanged for labour and commodities. But the crisis is precisely the phase of disturbance and interruption of the process of reproduction. And this disturbance cannot be explained by the fact that it does not occur in those times when there is no crisis. There is no doubt that no one "will continually produce a commodity for which there is no demand" (l.c., p. 340), but no one is talking about such an absurd hypothesis. Nor has it anything to do with the problem. The immediate purpose of capitalist production is not "the possession of other goods", but the appropriation of value, of money, of abstract wealth.

Ricardo's statements here are also based on James Mills's proposition on the "metaphysical equilibrium of purchases and sales", which I examined previously—an equilibrium which sees *only* the unity, but not the separation in the processes of purchase and sale. Hence also Ricardo's assertion (following James Mill):

"Too much of a *particular* commodity may be produced, of which there may be such a glut in the market, as not to repay the capital expended on it; but this cannot be the case with respect to *all* commodities" (l. c., pp. 341-42).

Money is not only "the medium by which the exchange is effected" (l.c., p. 341), but at the same time the medium by which the exchange of product with product is divided into two acts, which are independent of each other, and separate in time and space. With Ricardo, however, this false conception of money is due to the fact that he concentrates exclusively on the *quantitative determination* of exchange-value, namely, that it is equal to a definite quantity of labour-time, forgetting on the other hand the *qualitative* characteristic, that individual labour must present itself as *abstract, general social* labour only through its alienation.*

That only *particular* commodities, and not *all* kinds of commodities, can form "a glut in the market" and that therefore over-production can always only be partial, is a poor way out. In the first place, if we consider only the nature of the commodity, there is nothing to prevent *all commodities* from being superabundant on the market, and therefore all falling below their price.[131] We are here only concerned with the factor of crisis. That is all commodities, apart from *money* [may be superabundant]. [The proposition] *the* commodity must be converted into money, only means that: *all* commodities must do so. And just as the difficulty of undergoing this metamorphosis exists for an individual commodity, so it can exist for all commodities. The general nature of the metamorphosis of commodities—which includes the separation of purchase and sale just as it does their unity—instead of excluding the *possibility* of a general glut, on the contrary, contains the possibility of a general glut.

Ricardo's and similar types of reasoning are moreover based not only on the relation of *purchase and sale*, but also on that of *demand and supply*, which we have to examine only when considering the competition of capitals. As Mill says purchase is sale

---

* ||718| (That Ricardo, [regards] money merely as *means of circulation* is synonymous with his regarding *exchange-value* as a merely transient form, and altogether as something purely formal in bourgeois or capitalist production, which is consequently for him not a specific definite mode of production, but simply *the* mode of production.) |718||

etc., therefore demand is supply and supply demand. But they also fall apart and can become independent of each other. At a given moment, the supply of all commodities can be greater than the demand for all commodities, since the demand for the *general commodity*, money, exchange-value, is greater than the demand for all particular commodities, in other words the motive to turn the commodity into money, to realise its exchange-value, prevails over the motive to transform the commodity again into use-value.

If the relation of demand and supply is taken in a wider and more concrete sense, then it comprises the relation of *production* and *consumption* as well. Here again, the *unity* of these two phases, which does exist and which forcibly asserts itself during the crisis, must be seen as opposed to the *separation* and *antagonism* of these two phases, separation and antagonism which exist just as much, and are moreover typical of bourgeois production.

With regard to the contradiction between partial and universal over-production, in so far as the existence of the former is affirmed in order to evade the latter, the following observation may be made:

Firstly: Crises are usually preceded by a general inflation in prices of all articles of capitalist production. All of them therefore participate in the subsequent crash and at their former prices they cause a glut in the market. The market can absorb a larger volume of commodities at falling prices, at prices which have fallen below their cost-prices, than it could absorb at their former prices. The excess of commodities is always relative; in other words it is an excess at particular prices. The prices at which the commodities are then absorbed are ruinous for the producer or merchant.

||712| *Secondly*:

For a crisis (and therefore also for over-production) to be general, it suffices for it to affect the principal commercial goods.

[9. Ricardo's Wrong Conception of the Relation Between Production and Consumption under the Conditions of Capitalism]

Let us take a closer look at how Ricardo seeks to deny the possibility of a general glut in the market:

"Too much of a particular commodity may be produced, of which there may be such a glut in the market, as not to repay the capital expended on it; but this cannot be the case with respect to all commodities; the demand for corn is limited by the mouths which are to eat it, for shoes and coats by the persons who are to wear them; but though a community, or a part of a community, may have as much corn, and as many hats and shoes, as it is able or may wish to consume, *the same cannot be said of every commodity produced by nature or by art.* Some would consume more wine, if they had the ability to procure it. Others having enough of wine, would wish to increase the quantity or improve the quality of their furniture. Others might wish to ornament their grounds, or to enlarge their houses. The wish to do all or some of these is implanted in every man's breast; *nothing is required but the means, and nothing can afford the means, but an increase of production"* (l. c., pp. 341-42).

Could there be a more childish argument? It runs like this: more of a particular commodity may be produced than can be consumed of it; but this cannot apply to *all* commodities at the same time. Because the needs, which the commodities satisfy, have no limits and all these needs are not satisfied at the same time. On the contrary. The fulfilment of one need makes another, so to speak, latent. Thus nothing is required, but the means to satisfy these wants, and these means can only be provided through an increase in production. Hence no general over-production is possible.

What is the purpose of all this? In periods of over-production, a large part of the nation (especially the working class) is less well provided than ever with corn, shoes etc., not to speak of wine and furniture. If over-production could only occur when all the members of a nation had satisfied even their most urgent needs, there could never, in the history of bourgeois society up to now, have been a state of general over-production or even of partial over-production. When, for instance, the market is glutted by shoes or calicoes or wines or colonial products, does this perhaps mean that four-sixths of the nation have more than satisfied their needs in shoes, calicoes etc.? What after all has over-production to do with absolute needs? It is only concerned with demand that is backed by ability to pay. It is not a question of absolute over-production—over-production as such in relation to the absolute need or the desire to possess commodities. In this sense there is neither partial nor general over-production; and the one is not opposed to the other.

But—Ricardo will say—when there are a lot of people who want shoes and calicoes, why do they not obtain the means to acquire them, by producing something which will enable them to buy shoes and calicoes? Would it not be even simpler to say: Why do they not produce shoes and calicoes for themselves? An even stranger aspect of over-production is that the workers, the actual producers of the very commodities which glut the market, are in need of these commodities. It cannot be said here that they should produce things in order to obtain them, for they have produced them and yet they have not got them. Nor can it be said that a particular commodity gluts the market, because no one is in want of it. If, therefore, it is even impossible to explain that *partial* over-production arises because the demand for the commodities that glut the market has been more than satisfied, it is quite impossible to explain away *universal* over-production by declaring that needs, unsatisfied needs, exist for many of the commodities which are on the market.

Let us keep to the example of the weaver of calico.[132] So long as reproduction continued uninterruptedly—and therefore also the phase of this reproduction in which the product existing as a saleable commodity, the calico, was reconverted into money, at its value—so long, shall we say, the workers who produced the calico, also consumed a part of it, and with the expansion of reproduction, that is to say, with accumulation, they were consuming more of it, or also more workers were employed in the production of calico, who also consumed part of it.

[10. Crisis, Which Was a Contingency, Becomes a Certainty. The Crisis as the Manifestation of All the Contradictions of Bourgeois Economy]

Now before we proceed further, the following must be said:

The *possibility* of crisis, which became apparent in the *simple metamorphosis* of the commodity, is once more demonstrated, and further developed, by the disjunction between the (direct) process of production and the process of circulation. As soon as these processes do not merge smoothly into one another ||713| but become independent of one another, the crisis is there.

The possibility of crisis is indicated in the metamorphosis of the commodity like this:

Firstly, the commodity which actually exists as use-value, and nominally, in its price, as exchange-value, must be transformed into money. C — M. If this difficulty, the sale, is solved then the purchase, M — C, presents no difficulty, since money is directly exchangeable for everything else. The use-value of the commodity, the usefulness of the labour contained in it, must be assumed from the start, otherwise it is no commodity at all. It is further assumed that the individual value of the commodity is equal to its social value, that is to say, that the labour-time materialised in it is equal to the socially *necessary* labour-time for the production of this commodity. The possibility of a crisis, in so far as it shows itself in the simple form of metamorphosis, thus only arises from the fact that the differences in form—the phases—which it passes through in the course of its progress, are in the first place necessarily complimentary and secondly, despite this intrinsic and necessary correlation, they are distinct parts and forms of the process, independent of each other, diverging in time and space, separable and separated from each other. The possibility of crisis therefore lies solely in the separation of sale from purchase. It is thus only in the form of commodity that the commodity has to pass through this difficulty here. As soon as it assumes the form of money it has got over this difficulty. Subsequently however this too resolves into the separation of sale and purchase. If the commodity could not be withdrawn from circulation in the form of money or its re-transformation into commodity could not be postponed—as with direct barter—if purchase and sale coincided, then the *possibility* of crisis would, under the assumptions made, disappear. For it is assumed that the commodity represents *use-value* for other owners of commodities. In the form of direct barter, the commodity is not exchangeable only if it has no use-value or when there are no other use-values on the other side which can be exchanged for it; therefore, only under these two conditions: either if one side has produced *useless* things or if the other side has nothing *useful* to exchange as an equivalent for the first use-value. In both cases, however, no exchange whatsoever would take place. *But in so far as exchange did take place*, its phases would not be separated. The buyer would be seller and the seller buyer. The *critical* stage, which arises from the form of the exchange—in so far as it is circulation—would therefore cease to exist, and if we say that the simple form of metamorphosis comprises the possibility of crisis, we only say that in this form itself lies the possibility of the rupture and separation of essentially complimentary phases.

But this applies also to the content. In direct barter, the bulk of production is intended by the producer to satisfy his own needs, or, where the division of labour is more developed, to satisfy the needs of his fellow producers, needs that are known to him. What is exchanged as a commodity is the surplus and it is unimportant whether this surplus is exchanged or not. In *commodity production* the conversion of the product into money, the sale, is a *conditio sine qua non*. Direct production for personal needs does not take place. Crisis results from the impossibility to sell. The difficulty of transforming the *commodity*—the particular product of individual labour—into its opposite, money, i.e., abstract general social labour, lies in the fact that *money* is not the particular product of individual labour, and that the person who has effected a sale, who therefore has commodities in the form of money, is not compelled to buy again at once, to transform the money again into a particular product of individual labour. In barter this contradiction does not exist: no one can be a seller without being a buyer or a buyer without being a seller. The difficulty of the seller—on the assumption that his commodity has use-value—only stems from the ease with which the buyer can defer the retransformation of money into commodity. The difficulty of converting the commodity into money, of selling it, only arises from the fact that the commodity must be turned into money but the money need not be immediately turned into commodity, and therefore *sale* and *purchase* can be separated. We have said that this *form* contains the *possibility of crisis*, that is to say, the possibility that elements which are correlated, which are inseparable, are separated and consequently are forcibly reunited, their coherence is violently asserted against their mutual independence. ||714| *Crisis* is nothing but the forcible assertion of the unity of phases of the production process which have become independent of each other.

The general, abstract possibility of crisis denotes no more than the *most abstract form* of crisis, without content, without a compelling motivating factor. Sale and purchase may fall apart. They thus represent potential *crisis* and their coincidence always remains a critical factor for the commodity. The transition from one to the other may, however, proceed smoothly. The *most abstract form of crisis* (and therefore the formal possibility of crisis) is thus the *metamorphosis of the commodity* itself; the contradiction of exchange-value and use-value, and furthermore of money and commodity, comprised within the unity of the commodity, exists in metamorphosis only as an involved movement. The factors which turn this possibility of crisis into [an actual] crisis are not contained in this form itself; it only implies that *the framework* for a crisis exists.

And in a consideration of the bourgeois economy, that is the important thing. The world trade crises must be regarded as the real concentration and forcible adjustment of all the contradictions of bourgeois economy. The individual factors, which are condensed in these crises, must therefore emerge and must be described in each sphere of the bourgeois economy and the further we advance in our examination of the latter, the more aspects of this conflict must be traced on the one hand, and on the other hand it must be shown that its more abstract forms are recurring and are contained in the more concrete forms.

It can therefore be said that the crisis in its first form is the metamorphosis of the commodity itself, the falling asunder of purchase and sale.

The crisis in its second form is the function of money as a means of payment, in which money has two different functions and figures in two different phases, divided from each other in time. Both these forms are as yet quite abstract, although the second is more concrete than the first.

To begin with therefore, in considering the *reproduction process* of capital (which coincides with its circulation) it is necessary to prove that the above forms are simply repeated, or rather, that only here they receive a content, a basis on which to manifest themselves.

Let us look at the movement of capital from the moment in which it leaves the production process as a commodity in order once again to emerge from it as a commodity. If we abstract here from all the other factors determining its content, then the total commodity capital and each individual commodity of which it is made up, must go through the process C—M—C, the metamorphosis of the commodity. The general possibility of crisis, which is contained in this form—the falling apart of purchase and sale —is thus contained in the movement of capital, in so far as the latter is *also* commodity and nothing but commodity. From the interconnection of the metamorphoses of commodities it follows, moreover, that one commodity is transformed into money because another is retransformed from the form of money into commodity. Furthermore, the separation of purchase and sale appears here in such a way that the transformation of one capital from the form commodity into the form money, must correspond to the retransformation of the other capital from the form money into the form commodity. The first metamorphosis of one capital must correspond to the second metamorphosis of the other; one capital leaves the production process as the other capital returns into the production process. This intertwining and coalescence of the processes of reproduction or circulation of different capitals is on the one hand necessitated by the division of labour, on the other hand it is accidental; and thus the definition of the content of crisis is already fuller.

Secondly, however, with regard to the possibility of crisis arising from the form of money as *means of payment*, it appears that capital may provide a much more concrete basis for turning this possibility into reality. For example, the weaver must pay for the whole of the constant capital whose elements have been produced by the spinner, the flax-grower, the machine-builder, the iron and timber manufacturer, the producer of coal etc. In so far as these latter produce constant capital that only enters into the production of constant capital, without entering into the cloth, the final commodity, they replace each other's means of production through the exchange of capital. Supposing the ||715| weaver now sells the cloth for £ 1,000 to the *merchant* but in return for a bill of exchange so that money figures as *means of payment*. The weaver for his part hands over the bill of exchange to the *banker*, to whom he may thus be repaying a debt or, on the other hand, the banker may negotiate the bill for him. The flax-grower has sold to the spinner in return for a bill of exchange, the spinner to the weaver, ditto the machine manufacturer to the weaver, ditto the iron and timber manufacturer to the machine manufacturer, ditto the coal producer to the spinner, weaver, machine manufacturer, iron and timber supplier. Besides, the iron, coal, timber and flax producers have paid one another with bills of exchange. Now if the merchant does not pay, then the weaver cannot pay his bill of exchange to the banker.

The flax-grower has drawn on the spinner, the machine manufacturer on the weaver and the spinner. The spinner cannot pay because the weaver cannot pay, neither of them pay the machine manufacturer, and the latter does not pay the iron, timber or coal supplier. And all of these in turn, as they cannot realise the value of their commodities, cannot replace that portion of value which is to replace their constant capital. Thus the general crisis comes into being. This is nothing other than the *possibility of crisis* described when dealing with money as a means of payment; but here—in capitalist production—we can already see the connection between the mutual claims and obligations, the sales and purchases, through which the possibility can develop into actuality.

In any case: If purchase and sale do not get bogged down, and therefore do not require forcible adjustment—and, on the other hand, money as means of payment functions in such a way that claims are mutually settled, and thus the contradiction inherent in money as a means of payment is not realised—if therefore neither of these two abstract forms of crisis become real, no crisis exists. No crisis can exist unless sale and purchase are separated from one another and come into conflict, or the contradictions contained in money as a means of payment actually come into play; crisis, therefore, cannot exist without manifesting itself at the same time in its simple form, as the contradiction between sale and purchase and the contradiction of money as a means of payment. But these are merely *forms*, general possibilities of crisis, and hence also forms, abstract forms, of actual crisis. In them, the nature of crisis appears in its simplest forms, and, in so far as this form is itself the simplest content of crisis, in its simplest content. But the content is not yet *substantiated*. Simple circulation of money and even the circulation of money as a means of payment—and both come into being long *before* capitalist production, while there are no crises—are possible and actually take place without crises. These forms alone, therefore, do not explain why their crucial aspect becomes prominent and why the potential contradiction contained in them becomes a real contradiction.

This shows how insipid the economists are who, when they are no longer able to explain away the phenomenon of overproduction and crises, are content to say that these forms contain the possibility of *crises*, that it is therefore *accidental* whether or not crises occur and consequently their occurrence is itself merely a *matter of chance*.

The contradictions inherent in the circulation of commodities, which are further developed in the circulation of money—and thus, also, the possibilities of crisis—reproduce themselves, automatically, in capital, since developed circulation of commodities and of money, in fact, only takes place on the basis of capital.

But now the further development of the potential crisis has to be traced—the real crisis can only be educed from the real movement of capitalist production, competition and credit—in so far as crisis arises out of the special aspects of capital which are *peculiar* to it as capital, and not merely comprised in its existence as commodity and money.

||716| The mere (direct) *production process* of capital in itself, cannot add anything new in this context. In order to exist at all, its conditions are presupposed. The first section dealing with capital—the *direct* process of production—does not contribute any new element of crisis. Although it *does* contain such an element, because the production process implies appropriation and hence production of surplus-value. But this cannot be shown when dealing with the production process itself, for the latter is not concerned with the *realisation* either of the reproduced value or of the surplus-value.

This can only emerge in the *circulation process* which is in itself also a *process of reproduction*.

Furthermore it is necessary to describe the circulation or reproduction process *before* dealing with the already existing capital—*capital and profit*—since we have to explain, not only how capital produces, but also how capital is produced. But the actual movement starts from the existing capital—i.e., the actual movement denotes developed capitalist production, which starts from and presupposes its own basis. The process of reproduction and the predisposition to crisis which is further developed in it, are therefore only partially described under this heading and require further elaboration in the chapter on *"Capital and Profit"*.[133]

The circulation process as a whole or the reproduction process of capital as a whole is the unity of its production phase and its circulation phase, so that it comprises both these processes or phases. Therein lies a further developed possibility or abstract form of crisis. The economists who deny crises consequently assert only the unity of these two phases. If they were only separate, without being a unity, then their unity could not be established by force and there could be no crisis. If they were only a unity without being separate, then no violent separation would be possible implying a crisis. Crisis is the forcible establishment of unity between elements that have become independent and the enforced separation from one another of elements which are essentially one. |716||

[11. On the Forms of Crisis]

||770a| Supplement to page 716.
Therefore:
1. The general *possibility* of crisis is given in the process of

metamorphosis of capital itself, and in two ways: in so far as money functions as *means of circulation*, [the possibility of crisis lies in] the separation *of purchase and sale;* and in so far as money functions as *means of payment*, it has two different aspects, it acts as *measure of value* and *as realisation of value.* These two aspects [may] become separated. If *in the interval* between them the value has changed, if the commodity at the moment of its sale is not *worth* what it was *worth* at the moment when money was acting as a measure of value and therefore as a measure of the reciprocal obligations, then the obligation cannot be met from the *proceeds of the sale of the commodity,* and therefore the whole series of transactions which retrogressively depend on this one transaction, cannot be settled. If even for only *a limited period of time* the commodity cannot be sold then, although its value has not altered, *money* cannot function as *means of payment*, since it must function as such in a *definite given period of time.* But as the same sum of money acts for a whole series of reciprocal transactions and obligations here, *inability to pay* occurs not only at one, but at many points, hence a *crisis* arises.

These are the *formal possibilities* of crisis. The form mentioned first is possible without the latter—that is to say, crises are possible without credit, without money functioning as a means of payment. But the second form is not possible *without the first*— that is to say, without the separation between purchase and sale. But in the latter case, the crisis occurs not only because the commodity is unsaleable, but because it is not saleable within a *particular period of time*, and the crisis arises and derives its character not only from the *unsaleability* of the commodity, but from the *non-fulfilment of a whole series of payments* which depend on the sale of this particular commodity within this particular period of time. This is the *characteristic form of money crises.*

If the *crisis* appears, therefore, because purchase and sale become separated, it becomes a *money crisis*, as soon as money has developed as *means of payment*, and this *second form* of crisis follows as a matter of course, when the *first occurs.* In investigating why the general *possibility of crisis* turns into a *real* crisis, in investigating the *conditions* of crisis, it is therefore quite superfluous to concern oneself with the *forms* of crisis which arise out of the development of money as *means of payment.* This is precisely why economists like to suggest that this *obvious* form is the *cause* of crises. (In so far as the development of money as means of payment is linked with the development of credit and of *excess credit* the causes of the latter have to be examined, but this is not yet the place to do it.)

2. In so far as crises arise from *changes in prices and revolutions in prices*, which do not coincide with *changes in the values* of commodities, they naturally cannot be investigated during the examination of capital in general, in which the prices of commodities are assumed to be *identical* with the *values* of commodities.

3. The *general possibility* of crisis is the formal *metamorphosis* of capital itself, the separation, in time and space, of purchase and sale. But this is never the *cause* of the crisis. For it is nothing but the *most general form of crisis*, i.e., the crisis itself in *its most generalised expression*. But it cannot be said that the *abstract form of crisis* is the *cause of crisis*. If one asks what its cause is, one wants to know why *its abstract form*, the form of its possibility, turns from possibility into *actuality*.

4. The *general conditions* of crises, in so far as they are independent of *price fluctuations* (whether these are linked with the credit system or not) as distinct from fluctuations in value, must be explicable from the general conditions of capitalist production. |770a||

||716| (A *crisis* can arise: 1. in the course of the *reconversion* [of money] *into productive capital*; 2. through *changes in the value* of the elements of productive capital, particularly of *raw material*, for example when there is a decrease in the quantity of cotton harvested. Its *value* will thus rise. We are not as yet concerned with prices here but with *values*.) |716||

||770a| *First Phase.* The *reconversion of money into capital.* A definite level of *production or reproduction* is assumed. Fixed capital can be regarded here as given, as remaining unchanged and not entering into the *process of the creation of value*. Since the reproduction of raw material is not dependent solely on the labour employed on it, but on the productivity of this labour which is bound up with *natural conditions*, it is possible for the volume, ||XIV-771a| the *amount* of the product of *the same* quantity of labour, to fall (as a result of bad *harvests*). The *value of the raw material therefore rises*; its *volume* decreases, in other words the *proportions* in which the money has to be reconverted into the *various component parts of capital* in order to continue production on the former scale, are upset. More must be expended on *raw material*, less remains for *labour*, and it is not possible

to absorb the same quantity of labour as before. Firstly this is
physically impossible, because of the deficiency in raw material.
Secondly, it is impossible because a greater *portion of the value
of the product* has to be converted into raw material, thus leaving less for conversion into *variable capital*. Reproduction cannot
be *repeated* on the same scale. A part of *fixed capital* stands idle
and a part of the workers is thrown out on the streets. The *rate
of profit* falls because the value of constant capital has risen as
against that of variable capital and less variable capital is
employed. The fixed charges—interest, rent—which were based
on the anticipation of a *constant* rate of profit and exploitation
of labour, remain the same and in part *cannot be paid*. Hence
crisis. Crisis of labour and crisis of capital. This is therefore a
disturbance in the reproduction process due to the increase in
the value of that part of constant capital which has to be replaced
out of the value of the product. Moreover, although the *rate of
profit* is decreasing, there is a *rise in the price of the product*.
If this product enters into other spheres of production as a means
of production, the rise in its price will result in the same disturbance in *reproduction* in these spheres. If it enters into general
consumption as a means of subsistence, it either enters also into
the consumption of the workers or *not*. If it does so, then its
effects will be the same as those of a disturbance in *variable
capital*, of which we shall speak later. But in so far as it enters
into *general consumption* it may result (if its consumption is
not reduced) in a diminished *demand* for other products and
consequently *prevent their reconversion* into money at their
value, thus disturbing the *other aspect* of their reproduction—
not the *reconversion of money* into productive capital but the
reconversion of commodities into money. In any case, the *volume
of profits* and the *volume of wages* is reduced in this branch of
production thereby reducing a *part of the necessary returns* from
the sale of commodities from other branches of production.
    Such a *shortage* of *raw material* may, however, occur not only
because of the *influence of harvests* or of the *natural productivity*
of the labour which supplies the raw material. For if an *excessive portion of the surplus-value, of the additional capital*, is laid
out in machinery etc. in a particular branch of production, then,
although the raw material would have been sufficient for the
old level of production, it will be insufficient for the *new*. This
therefore arises from the *disproportionate* conversion of additional capital into its various elements. It is a case of *over-pro-*

duction of fixed capital and gives rise to exactly the same phenomena as occur in the first case. (See the previous page.) |XIV-771a||

||XIV-861a| [. . .]ᵃ

Or they [the crises] are due to an *over-production of fixed capital* and therefore a relative under-production of circulating capital.

Since fixed capital, like circulating, consists of commodities, it is quite ridiculous that the same economists who admit the *over-production of fixed capital*, deny the *over-production of commodities*.

5. *Crises* arising *from disturbances in the first phase of reproduction:* that is to say, interrupted conversion of commodities into money or *interruption of sale*. In the case of crises of the first sort [which result from the rise in the price of raw materials] the crisis arises from interruptions in the *flowing back* of the elements of productive capital. |XIV-861a||

[12. Contradictions Between Production and Consumption under Conditions of Capitalism. Over-production of the Principal Consumer Goods Becomes General Over-production]

||XIII-716| Before embarking on an investigation of the new forms of crisis, [134] we shall resume our consideration of Ricardo and the above example. |716||

ᵃ In the manuscript, the upper left-hand corner of this page has been torn away. Consequently, out of the first nine lines of the text, only the right ends of six lines have been preserved. This does not make it possible to reproduce the complete text here, but it does permit us to surmise that Marx speaks here of crises which arise "out of [the] *revolution in the value* of the variable capital". The "increased price of the *necessary means of subsistence*" caused, for example, by a poor harvest, leads to a rise in costs for those workers who "are set in motion by variable capital". "At the same time, this rise" causes a fall in the demand for "*all other commodities*" that do not enter into the consumption" of the workers. It is therefore impossible "to sell the commodities at their value; the first *phase* in their reproduction", the transformation of the commodity into money is interrupted. The increased price of the means of subsistence thus leads to "crisis in other branches" of production.

The two last lines of the damaged part of the page seem to summarise this train of thought, by saying that crises can arise as a result of increased prices of raw materials, "whether these raw materials enter as raw materials into constant capital or as means of subsistence" into the consumption of the workers.—*Ed.*

||716| So long as the owner of the weaving-mill reproduces and accumulates, his workers, too, purchase a part of his product, they spend a part of their wages on calico. Because he produces, they have the means to purchase a part of his product and thus to some extent give him the means to sell it. The worker can only buy—he can represent a demand only for—commodities which enter into individual consumption, for he does not himself turn his labour to account nor does he himself possess the means to do so—the instruments of labour and materials of labour. This already, therefore, excludes the majority of producers, the workers themselves, as consumers, buyers [of many commodities], where capitalist production prevails. They buy no raw material and no instruments of labour; they buy only means of subsistence, commodities which enter directly into individual consumption. Hence nothing is more ridiculous than to speak of the identity of producers and consumers, since for an extraordinarily large number of branches of production—all those that do not supply articles for direct consumption—the mass of those who participate in production are entirely excluded from the *purchase* of their own products. They are never *direct* consumers or buyers of this large part of their own products, although they pay a portion of the value of these products in the articles of consumption that they buy. This also shows the ambiguity of the word consumer and how wrong it is to identify it with the word buyer. As regards industrial consumption, it is precisely the workers who consume machinery and raw material, using them up in the labour-process. But they do not use them up for themselves and they are therefore not *buyers* of them. Machinery and raw material are for them neither use-values nor commodities, but objective conditions of a process of which they themselves are the subjective conditions.

||717| It may, however, be said that their employer represents them in the purchase of means of production and raw materials. But he represents them under different conditions from those in which they would represent themselves on the market. He must sell a quantity of commodities which represents surplus-value, unpaid labour. They [the workers] would only have to sell the quantity of commodities which would reproduce the value advanced in production—the value of the means of production, the raw materials and the wages. He therefore requires a wider market than they would require. It depends, moreover, on him

and not on them, whether he considers the conditions of the market sufficiently favourable to begin reproduction.

They are therefore producers without being consumers—even when no interruption of the reproduction process takes place—in relation to all articles which have to be consumed not individually but industrially.

Thus nothing is more absurd as a means of denying crises, than the assertion that the consumers (buyers) and producers (sellers) are identical in capitalist production. They are entirely distinct categories. In so far as the reproduction process takes place, this identity can be asserted only for one out of 3,000 producers, namely, the capitalist. On the other hand, it is equally wrong to say that the consumers are producers. The landlord does not produce (rent), and yet he consumes. The same applies to all monied interests.

The apologetic phrases used to deny crises are important in so far as they always prove the opposite of what they are meant to prove. In order to deny crises, they assert unity where there is conflict and contradiction. They are therefore important in so far as one can say they prove that there would be no crises if the contradictions which they have erased in their imagination, did not exist in fact. But in reality crises exist because these contradictions exist. Every reason which they put forward against crisis is an exorcised contradiction, and, therefore, a real contradiction, which can cause crises. The desire to convince oneself of the non-existence of contradictions, is at the same time the expression of a pious wish that the contradictions, which are really present, *should not* exist.

What the workers in fact produce, is surplus-value. So long as they produce it, they are able to consume. As soon as they cease [to produce it], their consumption ceases, because their production ceases. But that they are able to consume is by no means due to their having produced an equivalent for their consumption. On the contrary, as soon as they produce merely such an equivalent, their consumption ceases, they have no equivalent to consume. Their work is either stopped or curtailed, or at all events their wages are reduced. In the latter case—if the level of production remains the same—they do not consume an equivalent of what they produce. But they lack these means not because they do not produce enough, but because they receive too little of their product for themselves.

By reducing these relations simply to those of consumer and producer, one leaves out of account that the wage-labourer who produces and the capitalist who produces are two producers of a completely different kind, quite apart from the fact that some consumers do not produce at all. Once again, a *contradiction* is denied, by abstracting from a contradiction which really exists in production. The mere relationship of wage-labourer and capitalist implies:

1. that the majority of the producers (the workers) are non-consumers (non-buyers) of a very large part of their product, namely, of the means of production and the raw material;

2. that the majority of the producers, the workers, can consume an equivalent for their product only so long as they produce more than this equivalent, that is, so long as they produce surplus-value or surplus-product. They must always be *overproducers*, produce over and above their needs, in order to be able to be consumers or buyers within the ||718| limits of their needs.[135]

As regards this class of producers, the unity between production and consumption is, at any rate *prima facie*, false.

When Ricardo says that the only limit to *demand* is production itself, and that this is limited by capital,[136] then this means, in fact, when stripped of false assumptions, nothing more than that capitalist production finds its measure only in capital; in this context, however, the term capital also includes the labour-power which is incorporated in (bought by) capital as one of its conditions of production. The question is whether capital as such is also the limit for consumption. At any rate, it is so in a negative sense, that is, more cannot be consumed than is produced. But the question is, whether this applies in a positive sense too, whether—on the basis of capitalist production—as much can and must be consumed as is produced. Ricardo's proposition, when correctly analysed, says the very opposite of what it is meant to say—namely, that production takes place without regard to the existing limits to consumption, but is limited only by capital itself. And this is indeed characteristic of this mode of production.

Thus according to the assumption, the market is glutted, for instance with cotton cloth, so that part of it remains unsold or all of it, or it can only be sold well below its price. (For the time being, we shall call it *value*, because while we are considering circulation or the reproduction process, we are still concerned with value and not yet with cost-price, even less with market-price.)

It goes without saying that, in the whole of this observation. it is not denied that too much may be produced in individual spheres and *therefore* too little in others; partial crises can thus arise from *disproportionate production* (proportionate production is, however, always only the result of disproportionate production on the basis of competition) and a general form of this disproportionate production may be over-production of fixed capital, or on the other hand, over-production of circulating capital.* Just as it is a condition for the sale of commodities at their value, that they contain only the socially necessary labour-time, so it is for an entire sphere of production of capital, that only the necessary part of the total labour-time of society is used in the particular sphere, only the labour-time which is required for the satisfaction of social need (demand). If more is used, then, even if each individual commodity only contains the necessary labour-time, the total contains more than the socially necessary labour-time; in the same way, although the individual commodity has use-value, the total sum of commodities loses some of its use-value under the conditions assumed.

However, we are not speaking of crisis here in so far as it arises from disproportionate production, that is to say, the disproportion in the distribution of social labour between the individual spheres of production. This can only be dealt with in connection with the competition of capitals. In that context it has already been stated[a] that the rise or fall of market-value which is caused by this disproportion, results in the withdrawal of capital from one branch of production and its transfer to another, the migration of capital from one branch of production to another. This equalisation itself however already implies as a precondition the opposite of equalisation and may therefore comprise *crisis*; the crisis itself may be a form of equalisation. Ricardo etc. admit this form of crisis.

When considering the production process[137] we saw that the whole aim of capitalist production is appropriation of the greatest possible amount of surplus-labour, in other words, the realisation of the greatest possible amount of immediate labour-time with

---

* ||720| (When spinning-machines were invented, there was over-production of yarn in relation to weaving. This disproportion disappeared when mechanical looms were introduced into weaving.) |720||

a See this volume, pp. 206-11.—*Ed.*

the given capital, be it through the prolongation of the labour-day or the reduction of the necessary labour-time, through the development of the productive power of labour by means of co-operation, division of labour, machinery etc., in short, large-scale production, i.e., mass production. It is thus in the nature of capitalist production, to produce without regard to the limits of the market.

During the examination of reproduction, it is, in the first place, assumed that the method of production remains the same and it remains the same, moreover, for a period while production expands. The volume of commodities produced is increased in this case, because more capital is employed and not because capital is employed more productively. But the mere quantitative increase in ||719| capital at the same time implies that its productive power grows. If its quantitative increase is the result of the development of productive power, then the latter in turn develops on the assumption of a broader, extended capitalist basis. Reciprocal interaction takes place in this case. Reproduction on an extended basis, accumulation, even if originally it appears only as a quantitative expansion of production—the use of more capital under the same conditions of production—at a certain point, therefore, always represents also a qualitative expansion in the form of greater productivity of the conditions under which reproduction is carried out. Consequently the volume of products increases not only in simple proportion to the growth of capital in expanded reproduction—accumulation.

Now let us return to our example of calico.

The stagnation in the market, which is glutted with cotton cloth, hampers the reproduction process of the weaver. This disturbance first affects his workers. Thus they are now to a smaller extent, or not at all, consumers of his commodity—cotton cloth—and of other commodities which entered into their consumption. It is true, that they need cotton cloth, but they cannot buy it because they have not the means, and they have not the means because they cannot continue to produce and they cannot continue to produce because too much has been produced, too much cotton cloth is already on the market. Neither Ricardo's advice "to increase their production", nor his alternative "to produce something else" can help them.[138] They now form a part of the temporary surplus population, of the surplus production of workers, in this case of cotton producers, because there is a surplus production of cotton fabrics on the market.

But apart from the workers who are directly employed by the capital invested in cotton weaving, a large number of other producers are hit by this interruption in the reproduction process of cotton: spinners, cotton-growers, engineers (producers of spindles, looms etc.), iron and coal producers and so on. Reproduction in all these spheres would also be impeded because the reproduction of cotton cloth is a condition for their own reproduction. This would happen even if they had not *over-produced* in their own spheres, that is to say, had not produced beyond the limit set and justified by the cotton industry when it was working smoothly. All these industries have this in common, that their revenue (wages and profit, in so far as the latter is consumed as revenue and not accumulated) is not consumed by them in their own product but in the product of other spheres, which produce articles of consumption, calico among others. Thus the consumption of and the demand for calico fall just because there is too much of it on the market. But this also applies to all other commodities on which, as articles of consumption, the revenue of these *indirect* producers of cotton is spent. Their means for buying calico and other articles of consumption shrink, contract, because there is too much calico on the market. This also affects other commodities (articles of consumption). They are now, all of a sudden, *relatively* over-produced, because the means with which to buy them and therefore the demand for them, have contracted. Even if there has been no over-production in these spheres, now they are over-producing.

If over-production has taken place not only in cotton, but also in linen, silk and w,oollen fabrics, then it can be understood how over-production in these few, but leading articles, calls forth a more or less general (*relative*) over-production on the whole market. On the one hand there is a superabundance of all the means of reproduction and a superabundance of all kinds of unsold commodities on the market. On the other hand bankrupt capitalists and destitute, starving workers.

This however is a two-edged argument. If it is easily understood how over-production of some leading articles of consumption must bring in its wake the phenomenon of a more or less general over-production, it is by no means clear how over-production of these articles can arise. For the phenomenon of general over-production is derived from the interdependence not only of the workers directly employed in these industries, but of all branches of industries which produce the elements of their products, the various stages of their constant capital. In the latter branches of industry, over-production is an effect. But whence does it come in the former? For the latter [branches of industry] continue to produce so long as the former go on producing, and along with this continued production, a general growth in revenue, and therefore in their own consumption, seems assured.[139] |719||

[13. The Expansion of the Market Does Not Keep in Step with the Expansion of Production. The Ricardian Conception That an Unlimited Expansion of Consumption and of the Internal Market Is Possible]

||720| If one were to answer the question by pointing out that the constantly expanding production (it expands annually for two reasons; firstly because the capital invested in production is continually growing; secondly because the capital is constantly used more productively; in the course of reproduction and accumulation, small improvements are continuously building up, which eventually alter the whole level of production. There is a piling up of improvements, a cumulative development of productive powers.) requires a constantly expanding market and that production expands more rapidly than the market, then one would merely have used different terms to express the phenomenon which has to be explained—concrete terms instead of abstract terms. The market expands more slowly than production; or in the cycle through which capital passes during its reproduction—a cycle in which it is not simply reproduced but reproduced on an extended scale, in which it describes not a circle but a spiral —there comes a moment at which the market manifests itself as too narrow for production. This occurs at the end of the cycle. But it merely means: the market is glutted. Over-production is manifest. If the expansion of the market had kept pace with the expansion of production there would be no glut of the market, no over-production.

However, the mere admission that the market must expand with production, is, on the other hand, again an admission of the possibility of over-production, for the market is limited externally in the geographical sense, the internal market is limited as compared with a market that is both internal and external, the latter in turn is limited as compared with the world market, which however is, in turn, limited at each moment of time, [though] in itself capable of expansion. The admission that the market must expand if there is to be no over-production, is therefore also an admission that there can be over-production. For it is then possible—since market and production are two independent factors—that the expansion of one does *not* correspond with the expansion of the other; that the limits of the market are not extended rapidly enough for production, or that new markets— new extensions of the market—may be rapidly outpaced by production, so that the expanded market becomes just as much a barrier as the narrower market was formerly.

Ricardo is therefore consistent in denying the necessity of *an expansion of the market* simultaneously with the expansion of production and growth of capital. All the available capital in a country can also be advantageously employed in that country. Hence he polemises against Adam Smith, who on the one hand put forward *his* (Ricardo's) view and, with his usual rational instinct, contradicted it as well. Adam Smith did not yet know the phenomenon of over-production, and crises resulting from over-production. What he knew were only credit and money crises, which automatically appear, along with the credit and banking system. In fact he sees in the accumulation of capital an unqualified increase in the general wealth and well-being of the nation. On the other hand, he regards the mere fact that the internal market develops into an external, colonial and world market, as proof of a so-to-speak relative (potential) over-production in the internal market. It is worth quoting Ricardo's polemic against him at this point:

"When merchants engage their capitals in foreign trade, or in the carrying trade, it is always from choice, and never from necessity: it is because in that trade their profits will be somewhat greater than in the home trade.

"Adam Smith has justly observed 'that the desire of food is limited in every man by the narrow capacity of the human stomach',"

⟨Adam Smith is very much mistaken here, for he excludes the luxury products of agriculture⟩

" 'but the desire of the conveniences and ornaments of building, dress, equipage, and household furniture, seems to have no limit or certain boundary."

"*Nature*" (Ricardo continues) "then has necessarily *limited the amount of capital which can* at any [...] *time be profitably engaged in agriculture*,"

⟨Is that why there are nations which export agricultural products? As if it were impossible, despite nature, to sink all possible capital into agriculture in order to produce, in England for example, melons, figs, grapes etc., flowers etc., and birds and game etc. (See, for example, the capital that the Romans put into artificial fish culture alone.) And as if the raw materials of industry were not produced by means of agricultural capital.⟩

"but she has placed no limits" (as if nature had anything to do with the matter) *"to the amount of capital* that may be employed in procuring 'the conveniences and ornaments' of life. To procure these gratifications in *the greatest abundance* is *the object in view,* and it is only because foreign trade, or the carrying trade, will accomplish it better, that men engage in them in preference to manufacturing the commodities required, or a substitute for them, at home. If, however, from peculiar circumstances, we were precluded from engaging capital in foreign trade, or in the carrying trade, we should, though with less advantage, employ it at home; and *while there is no limit* to the desire of 'conveniences, ornaments of building, dress, equipage, ||721| and household furniture,' *there can be no limit to the capital that may be employed in procuring them,* except that which bounds our power to *maintain the workmen who are to produce them.*

"Adam Smith, however, speaks of the carrying trade as one, not of choice, but of necessity; as if the capital engaged in it would be inert if not so employed, as *if the capital in the home trade could overflow,* if not confined to a limited amount. He says, 'when the capital stock of any country is increased to such a degree, *that it cannot be all employed in supplying the consumption,* and *supporting the productive labour of that particular country',"* (this passage is printed in italics by Ricardo himself) " 'the *surplus part'* of it naturally disgorges itself into the carrying trade, and is employed in performing the same offices to other countries'.

"But could not this portion of the productive labour of Great Britain be employed in preparing some other sort of goods, with which something more in demand at home might be purchased? And if it could not, might we not employ this productive labour, though with less advantage, in making those goods in demand at home, or at least some substitute for them? If we wanted velvets, might we not attempt to make velvets; and if we could not succeed, might we not make more cloth, or some other object desirable to us?

"We manufacture commodities, and with them buy goods abroad, because we can obtain a *greater quantity"* (the qualitative difference does not exist!) "than we could make at home. Deprive us of this trade, and we immediately manufacture again for ourselves. But this opinion of Adam Smith is at variance with all his general doctrines on this subject." (Ricardo now cites Smith:⟩ "If a foreign country can supply us with a commodity cheaper than we ourselves can make it, better buy it of them with some part of the produce of our own industry, employed in a way in which we have some advantage. *The general industry of the country being always in proportion to the capital which employs it',"* (in very different proportion) (this sentence too is emphasised by Ricardo) " 'will not thereby be diminished, but only left to find out the way in which it can be employed with the greatest advantage.'

"Again. 'Those, therefore, who have the command of more food than they themselves can consume, are always willing to *exchange the surplus,* or, what is the same thing, the price of it, for gratifications of another kind. What is over and above satisfying the limited desire, is given for the amusement of *those desires which cannot be satisfied, but seem to be altogether endless*. The poor, in order to obtain food, exert themselves to gratify those fancies of the rich; and to obtain it more certainly, they vie with one another in the cheapness and perfection of their work. The number of workmen increases with the increasing quantity of food, or with the growing improvement and cultivation of the lands; and as the nature of their business admits of the utmost subdivisions of labours, the quantity of materials which they can work up increases in a much greater proportion than their numbers. Hence arises a demand for every sort of material which human invention can employ, either usefully or ornamentally, in building, dress, equipage, or household furniture; for the fossils and minerals contained in the bowels of the earth, the precious metals, and the precious stones.'

"It follows then from these admissions, that *there is no limit to demand— no limit to the employment of capital while it yields any profit*, and that *however abundant capital may become*, there is no other adequate reason for a fall of profit but a rise of wages, and further it may be added, that the only adequate and permanent cause for the rise of wages is the increasing difficulty of providing food and necessaries for the increasing number of workmen" (l.c., pp. 344-48).

[14. The Contradiction Between the Impetuous Development of the Productive Powers and the Limitations of Consumption Leads to Over-production. The Theory of the Impossibility of General Over-production Is Essentially Apologetic in Tendency]

The word *over-production* in itself leads to error. So long as the most urgent needs of a large part of society are not satisfied, or *only* the most immediate needs are satisfied, there can of course be absolutely no talk of an *over-production of products*— in the sense that the amount of products is excessive in relation to the need for them. On the contrary, it must be said that on the basis of capitalist production, there is constant *under-production* in this sense. The limits to production are set by the profit of the capitalist and in no way by the needs of the producers. But over-production of products and over-production of *commodities* are two entirely different things. If Ricardo thinks that the *commodity* form makes no difference to the product, and furthermore, that *commodity circulation* differs only formally from barter, that in this context the exchange-value is only a fleeting form of the exchange of things, and that money is therefore merely a formal means of circulation—then this in fact is in line with his presupposition that the bourgeois mode of production is the absolute mode of production, hence it is a mode of production without any definite specific characteristics, its distinctive traits are merely formal. He cannot therefore admit that the bourgeois mode of production contains within itself a barrier to the free development of the productive forces, a barrier which comes to the surface in crises and, in particular, in *over-production*—the basic phenomenon in crises.

||722| Ricardo saw from the passages of Adam Smith, which he quotes, approves, and therefore also repeats, that the limitless "desire" for all kinds of use-values is always satisfied on the basis of a state of affairs in which the mass of producers remains more or less restricted to necessities—"food" and other "necessaries"—that consequently this great majority of producers remains more or less excluded from the consumption of wealth—in so far as wealth goes beyond the bounds of the necessary means of subsistence.

This was indeed also the case, and to an even higher degree, in the ancient mode of production which depended on slavery. But the ancients never thought of transforming the surplus-product into capital. Or at least only to a very limited extent. (The fact that the hoarding of treasure in the narrow sense was widespread among them shows how much surplus-product lay completely idle.) They used a large part of the surplus-product for unproductive expenditure on art, religious works and public works. Still less was their production directed to the release and development of the material productive forces—division of labour, machinery, the application of the powers of nature and science to private production. In fact, by and large, they never went beyond handicraft labour. The wealth which they produced for private consumption was therefore relatively small and only appears great because it was amassed in the hands of a few persons, who, incidentally, did not know what to do with it. Although, therefore, there was no *over-production* among the ancients, there was *over-consumption* by the rich, which in the final periods of Rome and Greece turned into mad extravagance. The few trading peoples among them lived partly at the expense of all these essentially poor nations. It is the unconditional development of the productive forces and therefore mass production on the basis of a mass of producers who are confined within the bounds of the necessary means of subsistence on the one hand and, on the other, the barrier set up by the capitalists' profit, which [forms] the basis of modern over-production.

All the objections which Ricardo and others raise against over-production etc. rest on the fact that they regard bourgeois production either as a mode of production in which no distinction exists between purchase and sale—direct barter—or as *social* production, implying that society, as if according to a plan, dis-tributes its means of production and productive forces in the degree and measure which is required for the fulfilment of the various social needs, so that each sphere of production receives the *quota* of social capital required to satisfy the corresponding need. This fiction arises entirely from the inability to grasp the specific form of bourgeois production and this inability in turn arises from the obsession that bourgeois production is production as such, just like a man who believes in a particular religion and sees it as *the* religion, and everything outside of it only as *false* religions.

On the contrary, the question that has to be answered is: since, on the basis of capitalist production, everyone works for himself and a particular labour must at the same time appear as its opposite, as abstract general labour and in this form as social labour—how is it possible to achieve the necessary balance and interdependence of the various spheres of production, their di-mensions and the proportions between them, except through the constant neutralisation of a constant disharmony? This is admit-ted by those who speak of adjustments through competition, for these adjustments always presuppose that there is something to adjust, and therefore that harmony is always only a result of the movement which neutralises the existing disharmony.

That is why Ricardo admits that a glut of certain commodities is possible. What is supposed to be *impossible* is only a simul-taneous general glut of the market. The possibility of over-production in any particular sphere of production is therefore not denied. It is the *simultaneity* of this phenomenon for *all* spheres of production which is said to be impossible and there-fore makes impossible [general] over-production and thus a gen-eral glut of the market. (This expression must always be taken *cum grano salis*, since in times of general over-production, the over-production in some spheres is always only the *result*, the *consequence*, of over-production in the leading articles of com-merce; [it is] always only *relative*, i.e., over-production because over-production exists in other spheres.)

Apologetics turns this into its very opposite. [There is only] over-production in the leading articles of commerce, in which alone, active over-production shows itself—these are on the whole articles which can only be produced on a mass scale and by factory methods (also in agriculture), because over-production exists in those articles in which relative or passive over-production manifests itself. According to this, over-production only exists because over-production is not universal. The *relativity* of over-production—that actual over-production in a few spheres calls forth over-production in others—is expressed in this way: There is no *universal* over-production, because if over-production were universal, all spheres of production would retain the same relation to one another; therefore *universal* over-production is proportional production which excludes over-production. And this is supposed to be an argument against universal over-production. ||723| For, since *universal over-production* in the absolute sense would not be over-production but only a greater than usual development of the productive forces in all spheres of production, it is alleged that *actual over-production*, which is precisely not this non-existent, self-abrogating over-production, does *not* exist—although it only exists because it is not this.

If this miserable sophistry is more closely examined, it amounts to this: Suppose, that there is over-production in iron, cotton goods, linen, silk, woollen cloth etc.; then it cannot be said, for example, that too little coal has been produced and that this is the reason for the above over-production. For that over-production of iron etc. involves an exactly similar over-production of coal, as, say, the over-production of woven cloth does of yarn. ⟨Over-production of yarn as compared with cloth, iron as compared with machinery, etc. could occur. This would always be a relative over-production of constant capital.⟩ There cannot, therefore, be any question of the under-production of those articles whose over-production is implied because they enter as an element, raw material, auxiliary material or means of production, into those articles (the "particular commodity of which too much may be produced,[a] of which there may be such a glut in the market, as not to repay the capital expended on it" [l.c., pp. 341-42], whose positive over-production is precisely the fact to be explained. Rather, it is a question of other articles which belong directly to [other] spheres of production and [can] neither [be] subsumed under the leading articles of commerce which, according to the assumption, have been over-produced, nor be

---

[a] In the original: "Too much of a particular commodity may be produced..." See also pp. 499, 504 and 505 of this volume where this quotation from Ricardo is given in full.—*Ed.*

attributed to spheres in which, because they supply the *inter-mediate product* for the leading articles of commerce, production must have reached at least the same level as in the final phases of the product—although there is nothing to prevent production in those spheres from having gone even further ahead thus caus-ing an over-production within the over-production. For example, although sufficient coal must have been produced in order to keep going all those industries into which coal enters as necessary condition of production, and therefore the *over-production* of coal is implied in the *over-production* of iron, yarn etc. (even if coal was produced only in proportion to the production of iron and yarn [etc.]), it is *also* possible that more coal was produced than was required even for the over-production of iron, yarn etc. This is not only possible, but very probable. For *the production of coal and yarn* and of all other spheres of production which produce only the conditions or earlier phases of a product to be completed in another sphere, is governed not by the immediate demand, by the immediate production or reproduction, but by the *degree, measure, proportion* in which these are expanding. And it is self-evident that in this calculation, the target may well be overshot. Thus not enough has been produced of other articles such as, for example, pianos, precious stones etc., they have been *under-produced*. ⟨There are, however, also cases where the over-production of non-leading articles is not the result of over-production, but where, on the contrary, *under-production* is the cause of over-production, as for instance when there has been a failure in the grain crop or the cotton crop.⟩

The absurdity of this statement becomes particularly marked if it is applied to the international scene, as it has been by Say[140] and others after him. For instance, that England has not *over-produced* but Italy has *under-produced*. There would have been no over-production, if in the first place Italy had enough capital to replace the English capital exported to Italy in the form of commodities; and secondly if Italy had invested this capital in such a way that it produced those particular articles which are required by English capital—partly in order to replace itself and partly in order to replace the revenue yielded by it. Thus the fact of the actually existing *over-production in England*—in relation to the *actual* production in Italy—would not have existed, but only the fact of *imaginary under-production* in *Italy*; imaginary because it ||724| presupposes a capital in Italy and a development of the productive forces that do not exist there, and secondly

34*

because it makes the equally utopian assumption, that this capital which does *not* exist in Italy, has been employed in exactly the way required to make English supply and Italian demand, English and Italian production, complementary to each other. In other words, this means nothing but: there would be no over-production, if demand and supply corresponded to each other, if the capital were distributed in such proportions in all spheres of production, that the production of one article involved the consumption of the other, and thus its own consumption. There would be no over-production, if there were no over-production. Since, however, capitalist production can allow itself free rein only in certain spheres, under certain conditions, there could be no capitalist production at all if it had to develop *simultaneously* and *evenly* in all spheres. Because absolute over-production takes place in certain spheres, relative over-production occurs also in the spheres where there has been no over-production.

This explanation of over-production in one field by under-production in another field therefore means merely that if production were proportionate, there would be no over-production. The same could be said if demand and supply corresponded to each other, or if all spheres provided equal opportunities for capitalist production and its expansion—division of labour, machinery, export to distant markets etc., mass production, i.e., if all countries which traded with one another possessed the same capacity for production (and indeed for different and complementary production). Thus over-production takes place because all these pious wishes are not fulfilled. Or, in even more abstract form: There would be no over-production in one place, if over-production took place to the same extent everywhere. But there is not enough capital to over-produce so universally, and therefore there is partial over-production.

Let us examine this fantasy more closely:

It is admitted that there can be over-production in *each particular* industry. The only circumstance which could prevent over production in *all* industries simultaneously is, according to the assertions made, the fact that commodity exchanges against commodity—i.e., recourse is taken to the supposed conditions of barter. But this loop-hole is blocked by the very fact that trade [under capitalist conditions] is not barter, and that therefore the seller of a commodity is not necessarily at the same time the buyer of another. This whole subterfuge then rests on abstracting from *money* and from the fact that we are not concerned with the exchange of products, but with the circulation of commodities, an essential part of which is the separation of purchase and sale.

⟨The circulation of capital contains within itself the *possibilities* of interruptions. In the reconversion of money into its conditions of production, for example, it is not only a question of transforming money into the same use-values (in kind), but for the repetition of the reproduction process [it is] essential that these use-values can again be obtained at their old value (at a lower value would of course be even better). A very significant part of these elements of reproduction, which consists of raw materials, can however rise in price for two reasons. *Firstly,* if the instruments of production increase more rapidly than the amount of raw materials that can be provided at the given time. *Secondly,* as a result of the variable character of the harvests. That is why weather conditions, as Tooke rightly observes,[141] play such an important part in modern industry. (The same applies to the means of subsistence in relation to wages.) The reconversion of money into commodity can thus come up against difficulties and can create the possibilities of crisis, just as well as can the conversion of commodity into money. When one examines simple circulation—not the circulation of capital—these difficulties do not arise.⟩ (There are, besides, a large number of other factors, conditions, possibilities of crises, which can only be examined when considering the concrete conditions, particularly the competition of capitals and credit.)

||725| *The over-production of commodities* is denied but the *over-production of capital* is admitted. Capital itself however consists of commodities or, in so far as it consists of money, it must be reconverted into commodities of one kind or another, in order to be able to function as capital. What then does *over-production of capital* mean? Over-production of value destined to produce surplus-value or, if one considers the material content, over-production of commodities destined for reproduction —that is, *reproduction on too large a scale*, which is the same as over-production pure and simple.

Defined more closely, this means nothing more than that too much has been produced for the purpose of *enrichment*, or that too great a part of the product is intended not for consumption as revenue, but *for making more money* (for accumulation): not to satisfy the personal needs of its owner, but to give him money, abstract social riches and capital, more power over the labour of others, i.e., to increase this power. This is what one side says. (Ricardo denies it.[a]) And the other side, how does it explain the over-production of commodities? By saying that production is not sufficiently diversified, that certain articles of consumption have not been produced in sufficiently large quantities. That it is not a matter of industrial consumption is obvious, for the manufacturer who over-produces linen, thereby necessarily increases his demand for yarn, machinery, labour etc. It is therefore a question of personal consumption. Too much linen has been produced, but perhaps too few oranges. Previously the existence of money was denied, in order to show [that there was no] separation between sale and purchase. Here the existence of capital is denied, in order to transform the capitalists into people who carry out the simple operation C—M—C and who produce for individual consumption and not *as* capitalists with the aim of enrichment, i.e., the reconversion of part of the surplus-value into capital. But the statement that there is *too much capital,* after all means merely that too little is consumed as *revenue,* and that more cannot be consumed in the given conditions. (*Sismondi.*)[142] Why does the producer of linen demand from the producer of corn, that he should consume more linen, or the latter demand that the linen manufacturer should consume more corn? Why does the man who produces linen not himself convert a larger part of his revenue (surplus-value) into linen and the farmer into corn? So far as each individual is concerned, it will be admitted that his desire for capitalisation (apart from the limits of his needs) prevents him from doing this. But for all of them collectively, this is not admitted.

(We are entirely leaving out of account here that element of crises which arises from the fact that commodities are reproduced more cheaply than they were produced. Hence the depreciation of the commodities on the market.)

In world market crises, all the contradictions of bourgeois production erupt collectively; in particular crises (*particular* in their content and in extent) the eruptions are only sporadical, isolated and one-sided.

Over-production is specifically conditioned by the general law of the production of capital: to produce to the limit set by the

---

[a] See this volume, p. 497.—*Ed.*

productive forces, that is to say, to exploit the maximum amount of labour with the given amount of capital, without any consideration for the actual limits of the market or the needs backed by the ability to pay; and this is carried out through continuous expansion of reproduction and accumulation, and therefore constant reconversion of revenue into capital, while ||726| on the other hand, the mass of the producers remain tied to the average level of needs, and must remain tied to it according to the nature of capitalist production.

[15. Ricardo's Views on the Different Types of Accumulation of Capital and on the Economic Consequences of Accumulation]

In Chapter VIII, "*On Taxes*", Ricardo says:

"When the annual productions of a country more than replace its annual consumption, it is said to increase its capital; when its annual consumption is not at least replaced by its annual production, it is said to diminish its capital. Capital may therefore be increased by an increased production, or by a diminished unproductive consumption" (l. c., pp. 162-63).

By "unproductive consumption" Ricardo means here, as he says in the note on p. 163, consumption by unproductive workers, "... by those who do not reproduce another value". By increase in the annual production, therefore, is meant increase in the annual industrial consumption. This can be increased by the direct expansion of it, while non-industrial consumption remains constant or even grows, or by reducing non-industrial consumption.

"When we say," writes Ricardo in the same note, "that revenue is saved, and added to capital, what we mean is, that the portion of revenue, so said to be added to capital, is consumed by productive instead of unproductive labourers" [l.c., p. 163, note].

I have shown[a] that the conversion of revenue into capital is by no means synonymous with the conversion of revenue into variable capital or with its expenditure on wages. Ricardo however thinks so. In the same note he says:

"If the price of labour should rise so high, that notwithstanding the increase of capital, no more could be employed, I should say that such increase of capital would be still unproductively consumed" [l. c., p. 163, note].

---

[a] See this volume, pp. 470-92.—*Ed.*

It is therefore not the consumption of revenue by productive workers, which makes this consumption "productive", but its consumption by workers who produce surplus-value. According to this, capital increases only when it commands *more labour*.

Chapter VII "On Foreign Trade".

"There are two ways in which capital may be accumulated: it may be saved either *in consequence of increased revenue*, or *of diminished consumption*. If my *profits are raised* from £1,000 to £1,200 *while my expenditure continues the same*, I accumulate annually £200 more than I did before. If *I save £200 out of my expenditure, while my profits continue the same*, the same effect will be produced; £200 per annum will be added to my capital" (l. c., p. 135).

"If, by the introduction of machinery, the *generality of the commodities on which revenue was expended* fell 20 per cent in value, I should be enabled to save as effectually as if my revenue had been raised 20 per cent; but in one case the *rate of profits* is stationary, in the other it is raised 20 per cent. —If, by the introduction of cheap foreign goods, I can save 20 per cent from my expenditure, the effect will be precisely the same as if machinery had lowered the expense of their production, but profits would not be raised" (l. c., p. 136).

(That is to say, they would not be raised if the cheaper goods entered neither into the variable nor the constant capital.)

Thus with the *same expenditure of revenue* accumulation is the result of the rise in the rate of profit ⟨but accumulation depends not only on the rate of profit but on the amount of profit⟩; with a *constant rate of profit* accumulation is the result of decreasing expenditure, which is however assumed by Ricardo to occur because of the reduced price ⟨whether this is brought about by machinery or foreign trade⟩ of "commodities on which revenue was expended".

Chapter XX "Value and Riches, their Distinctive Properties".

"The wealth" (Ricardo takes this to mean use-values) "of a country may be increased in two ways: it may be increased by *employing a greater portion of revenue* in *the maintenance of productive labour*,—which will not only add to the *quantity*, but to the *value* of the mass of commodities; or it may be increased, *without employing any additional quantity of labour*, by *making the same quantity more productive*,—which will add to the abundance, but not to the value of commodities.

"In the first case, a country would not only become rich, but the value of its riches would increase. It *would become rich by parsimony*; by diminishing its expenditure on objects of luxury and enjoyment; and *employing those savings in reproduction.*

||727| "In the second case, there will not necessarily be either *any diminished expenditure on luxuries and enjoyments*, or any *increased quantity of productive labour employed*, but *with the same labour more would be produced*; wealth would increase, but not value. Of these two modes of increasing wealth, the last must be preferred, since it produces the same

effect without the privation and diminution of enjoyments, which can never fail to accompany the first mode. *Capital is that part of the wealth of a country which is employed with a view to future production, and may be increased in the same manner as wealth.* An *additional capital* will be equally efficacious in the production of future wealth, whether it *be obtained from improvements in skill and machinery*, or from *using more revenue reproductively*; for wealth always depends on the quantity of commodities produced, without any regard to the facility with which the instruments employed in production may have been procured. A certain quantity of clothes and provisions will maintain and employ the same number of men, and will therefore procure the same quantity of work to be done, whether they be produced by the labour of 100 or 200 men; but they will be of twice the value if 200 have been employed on their production" (l.c., pp. 327-28).

Ricardo's first proposition was:

Accumulation grows, if the rate of profit rises, while expenditure remains the same

or when the rate of profit remains the same, if expenditure (in terms of value) decreases, because the commodities on which the revenue is expended become cheaper.

Now he puts forward another antithetical proposition.

Accumulation grows, capital is accumulated in amount and value, if a larger part of the revenue is withdrawn from individual consumption and directed to industrial consumption, if more productive labour is set in motion with the portion of revenue thus saved. In this case accumulation is brought about by *parsimony*.

Or expenditure remains the same, and no additional productive labour is employed; but the same labour produces more, its productive power is raised. The elements which make up the productive capital, raw materials, machinery etc. (previously it was the commodities upon which revenue is expended; now it is the commodities employed as means of production) are produced with the same labour in greater quantities, better and therefore cheaper. In this case, accumulation depends neither on a rising rate of profit, nor on a greater portion of revenue being converted into capital as a result of parsimony, nor on a smaller portion of the revenue being spent unproductively as a result of a reduction in the price of those commodities on which revenue is expended. It depends here on labour becoming more productive in the spheres of production which produce the elements of capital itself, thus lowering the price of the commodities which enter into the production process as raw materials, instruments etc.

  If the productive power of labour has been increased through greater production of fixed capital in proportion to variable capital, then not only the amount, but also the *value* of reproduction will rise, since a part of the value of the fixed capital enters into the annual reproduction. This can occur simultaneously with the growth of the population and with an increase in the number of workers employed, although the number of workers steadily declines *relatively*, in proportion to the constant capital which they set in motion. There is therefore a growth, not only of wealth, but of value, and a larger quantity of living labour is set in motion, although the labour has become more productive and the quantity of labour in proportion to the quantity of commodities produced, has decreased. Finally, variable and constant capital can grow in equal degree with the natural, annual increase in population while the productivity of labour remains the same. In this case, too, capital will accumulate in volume and in value. These last points are all disregarded by Ricardo.

  In the same chapter Ricardo says:

"The labour of a million men in manufactures, will always produce the same value, but will not always produce the same riches".

(This is quite wrong. The value of the product of a million men does not depend solely on their labour but also on the value of the capital with which they work; it will thus vary considerably, according to the amount of the already produced productive forces with which they work.)

"By the invention of machinery, by improvements in skill, by a better division of labour, or by the discovery of new markets, where more advantageous exchanges may be made, a million of men may produce double, or treble the amount of riches, of 'necessaries, conveniences, and amusements,' in one state of society, that they could produce in another, but they will not on that account add any thing to value"

(they certainly will, since their past ||728| labour enters into the new reproduction to a much greater extent),

"for every thing rises or falls in value, in proportion to the facility or difficulty of producing it, or, in other words, in proportion to the quantity of labour employed on its production."

(Each individual commodity may become cheaper but the value of the increased total mass of commodities [will] rise.)

"Suppose with a given capital the labour of a certain number of men produced 1,000 pair of stockings, and that by inventions in machinery, the same number of men can produce 2,000 pair, or that they can continue to produce 1,000 pair, and can produce besides[a] 500 hats; then the value of the 2,000 pair of stockings or of the 1,000 pair of stockings, and 500 hats, will be neither more nor less than that of the 1,000 pair of stockings before the introduction of machinery; for they will be the produce of the same quantity of labour."

(N.B. provided the newly introduced machinery costs *nothing.*)

"But the *value of the general mass of commodities will nevertheless be diminished*; for, although the value of the increased quantity produced, in consequence of the improvement, will be the same exactly as the value would have been of the less quantity that would have been produced, had no improvement taken place, *an effect is also produced on the portion of goods still unconsumed, which were manufactured previously to the improvement*; the value of those goods will be reduced, inasmuch as they must fall to the level, quantity for quantity, of the goods produced under all the advantages of the improvement: and the society will, notwithstanding the increased quantity of commodities, notwithstanding its augmented riches, and its augmented means of enjoyment, *have a less amount of value.* By *constantly increasing the facility of production, we constantly diminish the value of some of the commodities before produced*, though by the same means we not only add to the national riches, but also to the power of future production" (l.c., pp. 320-22).

Ricardo says here that the continuous development of the productive forces diminishes the value of the commodities produced under less favourable conditions, whether they are still on the market, or functioning as capital in the production process. But, although the value of one part of the commodities will be reduced, it does not by any means follow from this that "the value of the general mass of commodities will [...] be diminished". This would be the only effect if, firstly, the value of the machinery and commodities that have been newly added as a result of the improvements, is smaller than the loss in value suffered by previously existing goods of the same kind; secondly, if one leaves out of account the fact that with the development of the productive forces, the number of spheres of production is also steadily increasing, thus creating possibilities for capital investment which previously did not exist at all. Production not only becomes cheaper in the course of the development, but it is also *diversified.*

Chapter IX, "Taxes on Raw Produce".

"With respect to the third objection against taxes on raw produce, namely, that the raising wages, and lowering profits, is a discouragement to accumulation, and acts in the same way as a natural poverty of soil; I have

---

[a] In the manuscript: "besides produce".—*Ed.*

endeavoured to shew in another part of this work that *savings may be as effectually made from expenditure as from production; from a reduction in the value of commodities, as from a rise in the rate of profits.* By increasing my profits from £ 1,000 to £ 1,200, whilst *prices* continue the same, my power of increasing my capital by savings is increased, but it is not increased so much as it would be if *my profits continued as before*, whilst commodities were so lowered in price, that £ 800 would procure[a] me as much as £ 1,000 purchased before" (l.c., pp. 183-84).

The total value of the product (or rather that part of the product which is divided between capitalist and worker) can decrease, without causing a fall in the net income, in terms of the mass of value it represents. (It may even rise proportionally.) This is dealt with in

Chapter XXXII, "Mr. Malthus's Opinions on Rent".

"The whole argument however of Mr. Malthus, is built on an infirm basis: it supposes, because the *gross income* of the country is diminished, that, therefore, the net income must also be diminished, in the same proportion. It has been one of the objects of his work to shew, that with every fall in the real value of necessaries, the wages of labour would fall, and that the profits of stock would rise—in other words, that of any given annual value a less portion would be paid to the labouring class, and a larger portion to those whose funds employed this class. Suppose the value of the commodities produced in a particular manufacture to be £ 1,000, and to be divided between the master and his labourers, in the proportion of £ 800 to labourers, and £ 200 to the master; ||729| if the value of these commodities should fall to £ 900, and £100 be saved from the wages of labour, in consequence of the fall of necessaries, the net income of the masters would be in no degree impaired, and, therefore, he could with just as much facility pay the same amount of taxes, after, as before the reduction of price" (l.c., pp. 511-12).

Chapter V, "On Wages".

"Notwithstanding the tendency of wages to conform to their natural rate, their market rate may, in an improving society, for an indefinite period, be constantly above it; for no sooner may the impulse, which an increased capital gives to a new demand for labour be obeyed, than another increase of capital may produce the same effect; and thus, if the increase of capital be gradual and constant, the demand for labour may give a continued stimulus to an increase of people" (l.c., p. 88).

From the capitalist standpoint, everything is seen upside down. The number of the labouring population and the degree of the productivity of labour determine both the reproduction of capital and the reproduction of the population. Here, on the contrary, it appears that *capital* determines [the size] of the population.

---

[a] In the manuscript: "produce".—*Ed.*

Chapter IX, "Taxes on Raw Produce".

"An accumulation of capital naturally produces an increased competition among the employers of labour, and a consequent rise in its price" (l.c., p. 178).

This depends on the proportion in which the various component parts of capital grow as a result of accumulation. Capital can be accumulated and the demand for labour can decrease absolutely or relatively.

According to Ricardo's theory of rent, the rate of profit has a tendency to fall, as a result of the accumulation of capital and the growth of the population, because the necessary means of subsistence rise in value, or agriculture becomes less productive. Consequently accumulation has the tendency to check accumulation, and the *law of the falling rate of profit*—since agriculture becomes relatively less productive as industry develops—hangs ominously over bourgeois production. On the other hand, Adam Smith regarded the falling rate of profit with satisfaction. Holland is his model. It compels most capitalists, except the largest ones, to employ their capital in industry, instead of living on interest and is thus a spur to production. The dread of this pernicious tendency assumes tragi-comic forms among Ricardo's disciples.

Let us here compare the passages in which Ricardo refers to this subject:

Chapter V, "On Wages".

"In different stages of society, the accumulation of capital, or of the means of employing labour, is more or less rapid, and *must in all cases depend on the productive powers of labour.* The productive powers of labour are generally greatest when there is an abundance of fertile land: at such periods accumulation is often so rapid, that labourers cannot be supplied with the same rapidity as capital" (l.c., p. 92).

"It has been calculated, that under favourable circumstances population may be doubled in twenty-five years; but under the same favourable circumstances, the whole capital of a country might possibly be doubled in a shorter period. In that case, wages during the whole period would have a tendency to rise, because the demand for labour would increase still faster than the supply.

"In new settlements, where the arts and knowledge of countries far advanced in refinement are introduced, it is probable that capital has a tendency to increase faster than mankind: and if the deficiency of labourers were not supplied by more populous countries, this tendency would very much raise the price of labour. In proportion as these countries become populous, and land of a worse quality is taken into cultivation, the tendency to an increase of capital diminishes; *for the surplus produce remaining, after satisfying the wants of the existing population, must necessarily be in proportion to the facility of production, viz. to the smaller number of persons employed in production.* Although, then, it is probable, that under the most favourable circumstances, the power of production is still greater than that of population, it will not long continue so; for the land being limited in quantity, and differing in quality, with every increased portion of capital employed on it, there will be a decreased rate of production, whilst *the power of population continues always the same*" (l.c., pp. 92-93).

(The latter statement is a parson's fabrication. The power of population decreases with the power of production.)

First it should be noted here that Ricardo admits that "the accumulation of capital ... must in all cases depend on the productive powers of labour", labour therefore is primary and not capital.

Further, according to Ricardo, it would appear that in countries which have been settled for a long time and are industrially developed, more people are engaged in agriculture than are in the colonies—while in fact it is the other way about. In proportion to the output ||730|, England, for example, uses fewer agricultural labourers than any other country, new or old, although a larger section of the non-agricultural population participates indirectly in agricultural production. But even this is by no means equal to the proportion of the population directly engaged in agriculture in the less developed countries. Supposing even that in England grain is dearer, and the costs of production are higher. More capital is employed. More past labour, even though less living labour is used in agricultural production. But the reproduction of this capital, although its value is reproduced in the product, costs less labour because of the already existing technical basis of production.

Chapter VI, "On Profits".

First, however, a few observations. [The amount of] surplus-value, as we saw, depends not only on the rate of surplus-value but on the number of workers simultaneously employed, that is to say, on the size of the variable capital.

Accumulation for its part is not directly determined by the rate of *surplus-value*, but by the ratio of surplus-value to the total capital outlay, that is, by the rate of profit, and even more by the *total amount of profit*. This, as we have seen, is for the total capital of society identical with the aggregate amount of surplus-value, but for individual capitals employed in the different branches of production, it may differ considerably from the amount of surplus-value produced by them. If we consider the accumulation of capital as a whole, then profit equals surplus-value and the rate of profit equals surplus-value divided by capital or rather surplus-value reckoned on a capital of £100.

If the rate of profit (per cent) is given, then the total amount of profit depends on the size of the capital advanced, and therefore accumulation too in so far as it is determined by profit.

If the total sum of capital is given then the total amount of profit depends on the rate of profit.

A small capital with a higher rate of profit may therefore yield more profit than a larger capital with a lower rate of profit.

Let us suppose:

1

Capital £	Rate of profit per cent	Total profit £
100	10	10
$100 \times 2 = 200$	$^{10}/_2$ or 5	10
$100 \times 3 = 300$	$^{10}/_2$ or 5	15
$100 \times 1^1/_2 = 150$	5	$7^1/_2$

2

100	10	10
$2 \times 100 = 200$	$\dfrac{10}{2^1/_2} = 4$	8
$2^1/_2 \times 100 = 250$	4	10
$3 \times 100 = 300$	4	12

3

500	10	50
5,000	1	50
3,000	1	30
10,000	1	100

If the multiplier of the capital and the divisor of the rate of profit are the same, that is to say, if the size of the capital increases in the same proportion as the rate of profit falls, then the total profit remains unchanged. 100 at 10 per cent amounts to 10, and 2×100 at $^{10}/_2$ or 5 per cent also amounts to 10. In other words, the amount of profit remains unchanged if the rate of profit falls in the same proportion in which capital accumulates (grows).

If the rate of profit falls more rapidly than the capital grows, then the amount of profit decreases. 500 at 10 per cent yields a total profit of 50. But six times as much, 6×500 or 3,000 at $^{10}/_{10}$ per cent or 1 per cent yields only 30.

Finally, if capital grows faster than the rate of profit falls, the amount of profit increases in spite of the falling rate of profit. Thus 100 at 10 per cent profit yields a profit of 10. But 300 (3×100) at 4 per cent (i.e., where the rate of profit has fallen by 60 per cent) yields a total profit of 12.

Now to the passages from Ricardo:

Chapter VI, "On Profits".

"The *natural tendency of profits then is to fall*; for, in the progress of society and wealth, the additional quantity of food required is obtained by the sacrifice of more and more labour. This tendency, this *gravitation as it were of profits*, is *happily checked* at repeated intervals by the improvements in machinery, connected with the production of necessaries, as well as by discoveries in the science of agriculture which enable us to relinquish a portion of labour before required, and ||731| therefore to lower the price of the prime necessary of the labourer. The rise in the price of necessaries and in the wages of labour is however limited; for as soon as wages should be equal ... to £ 720, the whole receipts of the farmer, there *must be an end of accumulation; for no capital can then yield any profit whatever*, and no *additional labour can be demanded,* and consequently *population will have reached its highest point.* Long indeed before this period the *very low rate of profits will have arrested all accumulation*, and almost the whole produce of the country, after paying the labourers, will be the property of the owners of land and the receivers of tithes and taxes" (l.c., pp. 120-21).

This, as Ricardo sees it, is the bourgeois "Twilight of the Gods"—the Day of Judgement.

"Long before this state of prices was become permanent, *there would be no motive for accumulation; for no one accumulates but with a view to make his accumulation productive*, and [...] consequently such a state of prices never could take place. The *farmer and manufacturer can no more live without profit, than the labourer without wages. Their motive* for accumulation will *diminish with every diminution of profit*, and will *cease altogether when their profits are so low* as not to afford them *an adequate compensation* for their trouble, and the *risk which they must necessarily encounter in employing their capital productively*" (l.c., p. 123).

"I must again observe, that the rate of profits would fall much more rapidly ... for the value of the produce being what I have stated it under the circumstances supposed, the value of the farmer's stock would be greatly increased from its necessarily consisting of many of the commodities which had risen in value. Before corn could rise from £ 4 to £ 12, *his capital would probably be doubled in exchangeable value*, and be worth £ 6,000 instead of £ 3,000. If then his profit were £ 180, or 6 per cent on his original capital, profits would not at that time be really at a higher *rate* than 3 per cent; for £ 6,000 at 3 per cent gives £ 180; and on *those terms* only could *a new farmer with £ 6 000 money* in his pocket *enter into the farming business*" (l.c., p. 124).

"We should also expect that, however *the rate of the profits of stock* might diminish *in consequence of the accumulation of capital on the land.*

and the rise of wages, yet that *the aggregate amount of profits would increase*.

Thus supposing that, with repeated accumulations of £ 100,000, the rate of profit should fall from 20 to 19, to 18, to 17 per cent, a constantly diminishing rate, we should expect that the whole amount of profits received by those successive owners of capital would be always progressive; that it would be greater when the capital was £ 200,000, than when £ 100,000, still greater when £ 300,000; and so on, *increasing, though at a diminishing rate, with every increase of capital*. This *progression however is only true for a certain time*: thus 19 per cent on £ 200,000 is more than 20 on £ 100,000; again 18 per cent on £ 300,000 is more than 19 per cent on £ 200,000; but after capital has accumulated to a large amount, and profits have fallen, the *further accumulation diminishes the aggregate of profits*. Thus suppose the accumulation should be £ 1,000,000, and the profits 7 per cent the whole amount of profits will be £ 70,000; now if an addition of £ 100,000 capital be made to the million, and profits should fall to 6 per cent, £ 66,000 or a diminution of £ 4,000 will be received by the owners of stock, although the whole amount of stock will be increased from £ 1,000,000 to £ 1,100,000.

"*There can, however, be no accumulation of capital, so long as stock yields any profit at all, without its yielding not only an increase of produce, but an increase of value*. By employing £ 100,000 additional capital, no part of the former capital will be rendered less productive. The produce of the land and labour of the country must increase, and its value will be raised, not only by the value of the addition which is made to the former quantity of productions but by the new value which is given to the whole produce of the land, by the increased difficulty of producing the last portion of it. When the accumulation of capital, however, becomes very great, notwithstanding this increased value, it will be so distributed that a less value than before will be appropriated to profits, while that which is devoted to rent and wages will be increased" (l.c., pp. 124-26).

"Although a greater value is produced, a greater proportion of what remains of that value, after paying rent, is consumed by the producers, and it is this, and this alone, which regulates profits. Whilst the land yields abundantly, wages may temporarily rise, and the producers may consume more than their accustomed proportion; but the stimulus which will thus be given to population, will *speedily reduce the labourers to their usual consumption*. But when poor lands are taken into cultivation, or when more capital and labour are expended on the old land, with a less return of produce, the effect must be permanent" (l.c., p. 127).

||732| "The effects then of accumulation will be different in different countries, and will depend chiefly on the fertility of the land. However extensive a country may be where the land is of a poor quality, and where the importation of food is· prohibited, the most moderate accumulations of capital will be attended with great reductions in the rate of profit, and a rapid rise in rent; and on the contrary a small but fertile country, particularly if it freely permits the importation of food, may accumulate a large stock of capital without any great diminution in the rate of profits, or any great increase in the rent of land" (l.c., pp. 128-29).

[It can] also [happen] as a result of *taxation* that "*sufficient surplus produce* may not be left to stimulate the exertions of those who usually augment by their savings the capital of the State" (Chapter XII on "*Land-Tax*", p. 206).

⟨Chapter XXI, *"Effects of Accumulation on Profits and Interest"*,⟩ "There is only one case, and that will be temporary, in which the accumulation of capital with a low price of food may be attended with a fall of profits; and that is, when the *funds for the maintenance of labour increase much more rapidly than population;*—wages will then be high, and profits low. If every man were to forego the use of luxuries, and be intent only on accumulation, a quantity of necessaries might be produced, for which there could not be any immediate consumption. *Of commodities so limited in number, there might undoubtedly be a universal glut*, and consequently there might neither be demand for an additional quantity of such commodities, nor profits on the employment of more capital. If men ceased to consume, they would cease to produce" (l.c., p. 343).

Thus Ricardo on accumulation and the law of the falling rate of profit.

[CHAPTER XVIII]

RICARDO'S MISCELLANEA. JOHN BARTON

[A.] GROSS AND NET INCOME

Net income, as opposed to gross income (which is equal to
the total product or the value of the total product), is the form
in which the Physiocrats originally conceived surplus-value.
They consider rent to be its sole form, since they think of industrial profit as merely a kind of wage; later economists who
blur the concept of profit by calling it wages for the superintendence of labour, ought to agree with them.

Net revenue is therefore in fact the excess of the product (or
the excess of its value) over that part of it which replaces the
capital outlay, comprising both constant and variable capital.
It thus consists simply of profit and rent, the latter, in turn,
is only a separate portion of the profit, a portion accruing to a
class other than the capitalist class.

The direct purpose of capitalist production is not the production of commodities, but of surplus-value or profit (in its
developed form), the aim is not the product, but the surplus-
product. Labour itself, from this standpoint, is only productive
in so far as it creates profit or surplus-product for capital. If the
worker does not create profit, his labour is unproductive. The
mass of productive labour employed is only of interest to capital in so far as through it—or in proportion to it—the mass
of surplus-labour grows. Only to this extent is what we called
necessary labour-time, necessary. In so far as it does not have
this result, it is superfluous and to be supressed.

It is the constant aim of capitalist production to produce a
maximum of surplus-value or surplus-product with the minimum

35*

capital outlay; and to the extent that this result is not achieved by overworking the workers, it is a tendency of capital to seek to produce a given product with the least possible expenditure— economy of power and expense. It is therefore the economic tendency of capital which teaches humanity to husband its strength and to achieve its productive aim with the least possible expenditure of means.

In this conception, the workers themselves appear as that which they are in capitalist production—mere means of production, not an end in themselves and not the aim of production.

Net income is not determined by the value of the total product, but by the excess of the value of the total product over the value of the capital outlay, or by the size of the surplus-product in relation to the total product. Provided this surplus grows the aim of capitalist production has been achieved even if the value decreases ||733| or, if along with the value, the total quantity of the product also decreases.

Ricardo expressed these tendencies consistently and ruthlessly. Hence much howling against him on the part of the philanthropic philistines.

In considering net income, Ricardo again commits the error of resolving the total product into revenue, wages, profits and rent, and disregarding the constant capital which has to be replaced. But we will leave this out of account here.

Chapter XXXII "Mr. Malthus's Opinions on Rent".

"It is of importance to distinguish clearly between gross revenue and net revenue, for it is from the net revenue of a society that all taxes must be paid. Suppose that all the commodities in the country, all the corn, raw produce, manufactured goods, etc. which could be brought to market in the course of the year, were of the value of 20 millions, and that in order to obtain this value, the labour of a certain number of men was necessary, and that the absolute necessaries of these labourers required an expenditure of 10 millions. I should say that the gross revenue of such society was 20 millions, and its net revenue 10 millions. It does not follow from this supposition, that the labourers should receive only 10 millions for their labour; they might receive 12, 14, or 15 millions, and in that case they would have 2, 4, or 5 millions of the net income. The rest would be divided between landlords and capitalists; but the whole net income would not exceed 10 millions. Suppose such a society paid 2 millions in taxes, its net income would be reduced to 8 millions" (l.c., pp. 512-13.)

[And in Chapter XXVI Ricardo says:]

"What would be the advantage resulting to a country from [...] a great quantity of productive labour, if, whether it employed that quantity or a smaller, its net rent and profits together would be the same. The *whole*

*produce of the land and labour of every country is divided into three por-
tions: of these, one portion is devoted to wages, another to profits, and the
other to rent."*

⟨This is wrong because the portion devoted to replacing the
capital (wages excluded) employed in production has been forgotten.⟩

"It is from the two last portions only, that any deductions can be made
for taxes, or for saving; *the former, if moderate, constituting always the
necessary expenses of production*" [l.c., p. 416].

⟨Ricardo himself makes the following comment on this passage in a note on page 416:

"Perhaps this is expressed too strongly, as more is generally allotted to
the labourer under the name of wages, than the absolutely necessary
expenses of production. In that case a part of the net produce of the country
is received by the labourer, and may be saved or expended by him; or it
may enable him to contribute to the defence of the country" [l.c., p. 416].⟩

"To an individual with a capital of £ 20,000, whose profits were £ 2,000
per annum, it would be a matter quite indifferent whether his capital would
employ a hundred or a thousand men, whether the commodity produced,
sold for £10,000, or for £ 20,000, provided, in all cases, his profits were not
diminished below £ 2,000. *Is not the real interest of the nation similar?
Provided its net real income, its rent and profits be the same, it is of no
importance whether the nation consists of ten or of twelve millions of
inhabitants.* Its power of supporting fleets and armies, and all species of
unproductive labour, must be in proportion to its net, and not in proportion
to its gross income. If five millions of men could produce as much food and
clothing as was necessary for ten millions, food and clothing for five millions
would be the net revenue. Would it be of any advantage to the country, that
to produce this same net revenue, seven millions of men should be required,
that is to say, that seven millions should be employed to produce food and
clothing sufficient for twelve millions? The food and clothing of five millions
would be still the net revenue. The employing a greater number of men
would enable us neither to add a man to our army and navy, nor to contribute one guinea more in taxes" (l.c., pp. 416-17).

To gain a better understanding of Ricardo's views, the following passages must also be considered.

"There is this advantage always resulting from a relatively low price of
corn,—that the division of the actual production is more likely to increase
the *fund for the maintenance of labour*, inasmuch as more will be allotted,
under the name of profit, to the productive class, a[a] less under the name rent,
to the *unproductive class*" (l.c., p. 317).

Productive class here refers only to the industrial capitalists.

"Rent is a creation of value ... but not a creation of wealth. If the price
of corn, from the difficulty of producing any portion of it, should rise from

---

a In the manuscript: "and".—*Ed.*

£ 4 to £ 5 per quarter, a million of quarters will be of the value of £ 5,000,000 instead of £ 4,000,000, ... the society altogether will be possessed of greater value, and in that sense rent is a creation of value. But this value is so far nominal, that it adds nothing to the wealth, that is to say, the necessaries, conveniences, and enjoyments of the society. We should have precisely the same quantity, and no more of commodities, and the same million quarters of corn as before; but the effect of its being rated at £ 5 per quarter, instead of £ 4, *would be to transfer a portion of the value of the corn and commodities from their* former possessors to the landlords. Rent then is a creation of value, but not a creation of wealth; *it adds nothing to the resources of a country*" (l.c., pp. 485-86).

||734| Supposing that through the import of foreign corn the price of corn falls so that rent is decreased by 1 million. Ricardo says that as a result the money incomes of the capitalists will increase, and then continues:

"But it may be said, that the capitalist's income will not be increased; that the million deducted from the landlord's rent, will be paid in additional wages to labourers! Be it so; ... the situation of the society will be improved, and they can[a] bear the same money burthens with greater facility than before; it will only prove what is still more desirable, that the situation of another class, *and by far the most important class in society*, is the one which is chiefly benefited by the new distribution. All that they receive more than 9 millions, *forms part of the net income of the country*, and it cannot be expended without adding to its revenue, its happiness, or its power. Distribute then the net income as you please. Give a little more to one class, and a little less to another, yet you do not thereby diminish it; a greater amount of commodities will be still produced with the same labour, although the amount of the gross money value of such commodities will be diminished; but the net money income of the country, that fund from which taxes are paid and enjoyments procured, would be much more adequate, than before, to maintain the actual population, to afford it enjoyments and luxuries, and to support any given amount of taxation" (l.c., pp. 515-16).

[B.] MACHINERY [RICARDO AND BARTON ON THE INFLUENCE OF MACHINES ON THE CONDITIONS OF THE WORKING CLASS]

[1. Ricardo's Views]

[a) Ricardo's Original Surmise Regarding the Displacement of Sections of the Workers by Machines]

Chapter I (Section V) "On Value".

"Suppose ... a machine which could in any particular trade be employed to do the work of one hundred men for a year, and that it would last only for one year. Suppose too, the machine to cost £ 5,000, and the wages

---

a In the manuscript: "they will be able" instead of "they can".—*Ed.*

annually paid to one hundred men to be £ 5,000, it is evident that it would be a matter of indifference to the manufacturer whether he bought the machine or employed the men. But suppose labour to rise, and consequently the wages of one hundred men for a year to amount to £ 5,500, it is obvious that the manufacturer would now no longer hesitate, it would be for his interest to buy the machine and get his work done for £ 5,000. But will not the machine rise in price, will not that also be worth £ 5,500 in consequence of the rise of labour? It would rise in price if *there were no stock employed on its construction, and no profits to be paid to the maker of it.* If for example, the machine were the produce of the labour of one hundred men, working one year upon it with wages of £ 50 each, and its price were consequently £ 5,000; should those wages rise to £ 55, its price would be £ 5,500, but this cannot be the case; less than one hundred men are employed or it could not be sold for £5,000, for out of the £ 5,000 must be paid the profits of stock which employed the men. Suppose then that only eighty-five men were employed at an expense of £ 50 each, or £ 4,250 per annum, and that the £ 750 which the sale of the machine would produce over and above the wages advanced to the men, constituted the profits of the engineer's stock. When wages rose 10 per cent he would be obliged to employ an *additional capital* of £ 425 and would therefore employ £ 4,675 instead of £ 4,250, on which capital he would only get a profit of £ 325 if he continued to sell his machine for £ 5,000; but this is precisely the case of all manufacturers and capitalists; the rise of wages affects them all. If therefore the maker of the machine should raise the price of it in consequence of a rise of wages, an unusual quantity of capital would be employed in the construction of such machines, till their price afforded only the common rate of profits. We see then that machines would not rise in price, in consequence of a rise of wages.

"The manufacturer, however, who in a general rise of wages, can have recourse to a machine which shall not increase the charge of production on his commodity, would enjoy peculiar advantages if he could continue to charge the same price for his goods; but he, as we have already seen, would be obliged to lower the price of his commodities, or capital would flow to his trade till his profits had sunk to the general level. Thus *then is the public benefited by machinery: these mute agents are always the produce of much less labour than that which they displace, even when they are of the same money value*" (l.c., pp. 38-40).

This point is quite right. At the same time it provides the answer to those who believe that the workers displaced by machines find employment in machine manufacture itself. This view, incidentally, belongs to an epoch in which the engineering workshop was still based entirely on the division of labour, and machines were not as yet employed on the production of machines.

Suppose the annual wage of one man to be £50, then that of 100 is £5,000. If these 100 men are replaced by a machine which costs, similarly, £5,000, then this machine must be the product of the labour of less than 100 men. For besides paid labour it contains unpaid labour which forms the profit of the machine manufacturer. If it were the product of 100 men, then it would contain only paid labour. If the rate of profit were 10 per cent then approximately £4,545 of the £5,000 would represent the capital advanced and approximately £ 455 the profit. At [a wage of] £ 50, £ 4,545 would only represent $90^9/_{10}$ men.

||735| But the capital of £ 4, 545 by no means represents only variable capital (capital laid out directly in wages). It represents also raw materials and the wear and tear of the fixed capital employed by the machine manufacturer. The machine costing £5,000, which replaces 100 men whose wages come to £5,000, thus represents the product of far fewer than 90 men. Moreover, the machine can only be employed profitably, if it ⟨at least that portion of it which enters annually with interest into the product, i.e., into its value⟩ is the (annual) product of far fewer men than it replaces.

Every rise in wages increases the variable capital that has to be laid out, although the *value of the product*—since this is equal to the variable capital plus the surplus-labour—remains the same, for the number of workers which the variable capital sets in motion remains *the same*.

[b) Ricardo on the Influence of Improvements in Production on the Value of Commodities. False Theory of the Availability of the Wages Fund for the Workers Who Have Been Dismissed]

Chapter XX "Value and Riches, their Distinctive[a] *Properties".* Natural agents add nothing to the value of *commodities,* on the contrary, [they reduce it]. But by doing so they add to the *surplus-value,* which alone interests the capitalists.

"In contradiction to the opinion of Adam Smith, M. Say, in the fourth chapter, speaks of the value which is given to commodities by *natural agents,* such as the sun, the air, the pressure of the atmosphere, etc., which are sometimes substituted for the labour of man, and sometimes concur with him in producing. But these natural agents, though they add greatly to *value in use,* never add exchangeable value, of which M. Say is speaking, to a *commodity:* as soon as by the *aid of machinery,* o r *by the knowledge of natural philosophy,* you oblige natural agents to do the work which was before done by man, the exchangeable value of such work falls accordingly" (l.c., pp. 335-36).

---

[a] In the manuscript: "different."—*Ed.*

The machine costs [labour]. Natural agents as such cost nothing. They cannot, therefore, add any value to the product; rather they diminish its value in so far as they replace capital or labour, immediate or accumulated labour. In as much as natural philosophy teaches how to replace human labour by natural agents, without the aid of machinery or only with the same machinery as before (perhaps even more cheaply, as with the steam boiler, many chemical processes etc.), it costs the capitalist, and society as well, nothing and cheapens commodities absolutely.

Ricardo continues the above-quoted passage thus:

> "If ten men turned a corn mill, and it be discovered that by the assistance of wind, or of water, the labour of these ten men may be spared, the flour which is the produce partly of the work performed by the mill, would immediately fall in value, in proportion to the quantity of labour saved; and *the society would be richer by the commodities which the labour of the ten men could produce, the funds destined for their maintenance being in no degree impaired*" (l.c., p. 336).

Society would in the first place be richer by the diminished price of flour. It would either consume more flour or spend the money formerly *destined for flour* upon some other commodity, either existing, or called into life, because a new fund for consumption had become available.

Of this part of the revenue, formerly spent on flour and now, consequent upon the diminished price of flour, set free for some other application, it may be said that it was *"destined"*—by virtue of the whole economy of the society—for a certain thing, and that it is now freed from that "destiny". It is the same as if new capital had been accumulated. And in this way, the application of machinery and natural agents frees capital and enables previously "latent needs" to be satisfied.

On the other hand, it is wrong to speak of "the funds *destined* for the maintenance" of the ten men thrown out of employment by the new discovery. For the first fund which is saved or created through the discovery is that part of the revenue which society previously paid for flour and which it now saves as a result of the diminished price of flour. The second fund which is saved, however, is that which the miller previously paid for the ten men now displaced. This "fund" indeed, as Ricardo notes, is in no degree impaired by the discovery and the displacement of the ten men. But the fund has no natural connection with the ten men. They may become paupers, starve etc.

One thing only is certain, that ten men of the new generation
who should take the place of these ten men in order to turn
the mill, must now be absorbed in other employment; and so
the relative population has increased (independently of the
average increase of population) in that the mill is now driven
[by a natural agent] and the ten men who would otherwise
have had to turn it are employed in producing some other
commodity. The invention of machinery and the employment
of natural agents thus set free capital and men (workers) and
create together with freed capital freed hands (free hands, as
Steuart calls them[143]), whether ||736| [for] newly created
spheres of production or [for] the old ones which are expanded
and operated on a larger scale.

The miller with his freed capital will build new mills or will
lend out his capital if he cannot use it himself as a capitalist.

On no account, however, is there a fund *"destined"* for the ten
men displaced. We shall return to this absurd assumption: namely that, if the introduction of machines (or natural agents)
does not (as is partly the case in agriculture, when horses take
the place of men or stock-raising takes the place of corn growing) reduce the quantity of means of subsistence which can be
laid out in wages, the fund which has thus been set free must
necessarily be laid out as variable capital (as if there was no
possibility of exporting means of subsistence, or spending them
on unproductive workers, or [as if] wages in certain spheres
could not rise etc.) and must even be paid out to the displaced
labourers. Machinery always creates a relative surplus population, a reserve army of workers, which greatly increases the
power of capital.

In the note on page 335, Ricardo also makes the following
observation directed against Say:

"Though Adam Smith, who defined riches to consist in the abundance of
necessaries, convenience and enjoyments of human life, would have allowed
that *machines and natural agents* might very greatly add to the riches of a
country, he would not have allowed that they *add any thing to the value
of those riches*" [l.c., p. 335, note].

Natural agents, indeed, add nothing to *value*, so long as there
are no circumstances in which they give occasion for the creation of *rent*. But machines invariably add *their own value* to
the already existing value and firstly, in so far as their existence
facilitates the further transformation of circulating into fixed
capital, and makes it possible to carry on this transformation

on an ever growing scale, they increase not only wealth but also the *value* which is added by past labour to the product of the annual labour; secondly, since machines make possible the absolute growth of population. and with it the growth of the mass of the annual labour, they increase the value of the annual product in this second way. |736||

[c) Ricardo's Scientific Honesty, Which Led Him to Revise His Views on the Question of Machinery. Certain False Assumptions Are Retained in Ricardo's New Formulation of the Question]

||736| *Chapter XXXI "On Machinery"*.

This section, which Ricardo added to his third edition, bears witness to his *honesty* which so essentially distinguishes him from the vulgar economists.

"It is more incumbent on me to declare my opinions on this question" ⟨viz. "the influence of machinery on the interests of the different classes of society"⟩, "because they have, on further reflection, undergone a considerable change; and although I am not aware that I have ever published any thing respecting machinery which it is necessary for me to retract, yet I have in other ways" ⟨as a Member of Parliament⟩[144] "given my support to doctrines which I now think erroneous; it, therefore, becomes a duty in me to submit my present views to examination, with my reasons for entertaining them" (l.c., p. 466).

"Ever since I first turned my attention to questions of political economy, I have been of opinion, that such an application of machinery to any branch of production, as should have the effect of saving labour, was a general good, accompanied only with that portion of inconvenience which in most cases attends the removal of capital and labour from one employment to another."

⟨This inconvenience is great enough for the worker, if, as in modern production, it is perpetual.⟩

"It appeared to me, that provided the landlords had the same money rents, they would be benefited by the reduction in the prices of some of the commodities on which those rents were expended, and which reduction of price could not fail to be the consequence of the employment of machinery. The capitalist, I thought, was eventually benefited precisely in the same manner. He, indeed, who made the discovery of the machine, or who first usefully applied it, would enjoy an additional advantage, by making great profits for a time; but, in proportion as the machine came into general use, the price of the commodity produced, would, from the effects of competition, sink to its cost of production, when the capitalist would get the same money profits as before, and he would only participate in the general advantage, ||737| as a consumer, by being enabled, with the same money revenue, to command an additional quantity of comforts and enjoyments. *The class of labourers also*, I thought, *was equally benefited by the use of machinery*, as they would have the means of buying more commodities with the same money wages, and I thought that *no reduction of wages would take place, because the capitalist would have the power of demanding and employing the same quantity of labour as before*, although he might be under the necessity of employing it in the production of a new, or at any rate of a different commodity. If, by improved machinery, with the employment of the same quantity of labour, the quantity of stockings could be quadrupled, and the demand for stockings were only doubled, some labourers would necessarily be discharged from the stocking trade; but *as the capital which employed them was still in being, and as it was the interest of those who had it to employ it productively*, it appeared to me that it would be employed on the production of some other commodity, useful to the society, for which there could not fail to be a demand.... As, then, it appeared to me that *there would be the same demand for labour as before*, and that wages would be no lower, I thought that the labouring class would, equally with the other classes, participate in the advantage, from the general cheapness of commodities arising from the use of machinery.

"These were my opinions, and they continue unaltered, as far as regards the landlord and the capitalist; but I am convinced, that *the substitution of machinery for human labour, is often very injurious to ... the class of labourers*" (l.c., pp. 466-68).

In the first place, Ricardo starts from the false assumption that machinery is always introduced into spheres of production in which the capitalist mode of production already exists. But the mechanised loom originally replaced the hand-loom weaver, the spinning jenny the hand spinner, the mowing, threshing and sowing machines often the small peasant who himself cultivated his plot of land, etc. In this case, not only is the labourer displaced, but his instrument of production too ceases to be capital (in the Ricardian sense). This entire or complete devaluation of the old capital also takes place when machinery revolutionises manufacture previously based on the simple division of labour. It is ridiculous to say in this case that the "old capital" continues to make the same demand for labour as before.

The "capital" which was employed by the hand-loom weaver, hand spinner etc. has ceased to exist.

But suppose, for the sake of simplicity, that the machinery is introduced ⟨there is, of course, no question here of the employment of machinery in *new* branches of industry⟩ only into spheres where capitalist production (manufacture) is already [dominant] or it may be introduced into the workshop already based on machinery, thus increasing the mechanisation of the labour processes or bringing into use improved machinery, which makes it possible either to dismiss a section of the workers previously employed or to produce a greater product while employing *the same* number of workers as before. The latter is of course the most favourable case.

In order to reduce confusion, we must distinguish here between 1. the funds of the capitalist who employs machinery
and dismisses workers; 2. the funds of society, that is, of the
consumers of the commodities produced by this capitalist.

ad 1. So far as the capitalist who introduces the machinery is
concerned, it is wrong and absurd to say that he can lay out
the same amount of capital in wages as before. (Even if he
borrows, it is still equally wrong, not for him, but for society.)
One part of his capital he will convert into machinery and
other forms of fixed capital, another part into auxiliary materials which he did not need before, and a larger part into raw
materials, if we assume that he produces more commodities
with fewer workers, thus requiring more raw material. The proportion of variable capital—that is to say, of capital laid out in
wages—to constant capital has decreased in his branch of business. And this reduction in the *proportion will be permanent*
(indeed, the decrease in variable capital relatively to constant
will even continue at a *faster* rate as a result of the productive
power of labour developing along with accumulation), even if
his business on the new scale of production expands to such
an extent that he can re-employ the total number of dismissed
workers, and employ even more workers than before. (The
demand for labour in his business will grow with the accumulation of his capital, but to a much smaller degree than his
capital accumulates, and his capital will in absolute terms never
again require the same amount of labour as before. The immediate result, however, will be that a section of the workers
is thrown on to the street.)

But it may be said that indirectly the demand for workers
will remain the same, for more workers will be required for the
construction of machines. But Ricardo himself has already shown
that machinery never costs as much labour as the labour which
it displaces. It is possible for the hours of labour in the ma-
chine workshops to be lengthened for some time ||738| and that,
in the first instance, not a man more may be employed in them.
Raw material—cotton for example—can come from America
and China and it makes no difference whatsoever to the Englishmen who have been thrown out of work, whether the demand
for Negroes or coolies grows. But even assuming that the raw
materials are supplied within the country, more women and
children will be employed in agriculture, more horses etc., and
perhaps more of one product and less of another will be pro-

duced. But there will be no demand for the dismissed workers, for in agriculture, too, the same process which creates a constant relative surplus population is taking place.

Prima facie it is not likely that the introduction of machinery will set free any of the capital of the manufacturer when he makes his first investment. It merely provides a new type of investment for his capital, its immediate result, according to the assumption, is the dismissal of workers and the conversion of part of the variable capital into constant capital.

ad 2. So far as the general public is concerned, in the first place, *revenue* is set free as a result of the lowering in price of the commodity produced by means of the machine; *capital*—directly—only in so far as the manufactured article enters into constant capital as an element of production. ⟨If it entered into the average consumption of the worker, it would, according to Ricardo, bring in its wake a reduction in *real wages*[145] also in the other branches of industry.⟩ A part of the revenue thus set free, will be consumed in the same article, either because the reduction in price makes it accessible to new classes of consumers (in this case, incidentally, it is not displaced revenue that is expended on the article), or because the old consumers consume more of the cheaper article, for instance four pairs of cotton stockings instead of one pair. Another part of the revenue thus set free may serve to expand the industry into which the machinery has been introduced, or it may be used in the formation of a new industry producing a different commodity, or it may serve to expand a sphere of production which already existed before. For whatever purpose the revenue thus set free and reconverted into capital is used, it will in the first place hardly be sufficient to absorb that part of the increased population which each year streams into each branch of production, and which is now debarred from entering the old industry. It is, however, also possible for a portion of the freed revenue to be exchanged against foreign products or to be consumed by unproductive workers. But *by no means* does a *necessary connection exist between the revenue that has been set free and the workers that have been set free of revenue.*

The absurd fundamental notion, however, which underlies Ricardo's view, is the following:

The capital of the manufacturer who introduces machinery is not set free. It is merely utilised in a *different* manner, namely, in such a manner that it is not, as before, transformed into

wages for the workers who are discharged. A part of the variable capital is converted into constant capital. Even if some of
it were set free, it would be absorbed by spheres in which the
discharged labourers could not *work* and where, at the most,
those who replace them could find refuge.

By expanding old spheres of production or opening up new
ones the revenue set free—in so far as it is not offset by greater
consumption of the cheaper article or is not exchanged against
foreign means of subsistence—only gives the necessary opening (if it does so!) for that part of the annual population increase that is for the time being debarred from the old trade
into which the machinery has been introduced.

But the absurdity which lies concealed at the root of Ricardo's notions, is this:

The means of subsistence which were previously consumed
by the workers now discharged, remain after all in existence
and are still on the market. The workers, on the other hand,
are also available on the market. Thus there are, on the one
hand, means of subsistence (and therefore means of payment)
for workers, i.e., potential variable capital, and on the other,
unemployed workers. Hence the fund is there to set them in
motion. Consequently they will find employment.

Is it possible that even such an economist as Ricardo can
babble such hair-raising nonsense?

According to this, no human being who is capable of work
and willing, could ever starve in bourgeois society, when there
are means of subsistence on the market, at the disposal of the
society, to pay him for any work whatever. These means of
subsistence, in the first place, do not by any means confront
those workers as capital.

Assume that 100,000 workers have suddenly been thrown
out on the streets by machinery. Then in the first place there
is no doubt whatsoever ||739| that the agricultural products on
the market, which on the average suffice for the whole year
and which were previously consumed by these workers, are
still on the market as before. If there were no demand for
them—and if, at the same time, they were not exportable—
what would happen? As the supply relative to the demand
would have grown, they would fall in price, and as a result
of this fall in price, their consumption would rise, even if the
100,000 workers were starving to death. The price need not

even fall. Perhaps less of these means of subsistence is imported or more of them exported.

Ricardo imagines quixotically that the entire bourgeois social mechanism is arranged so nicely that if, for instance, ten men are discharged from their work, the means of subsistence of these workers—now set free—must definitely be consumed in one way or another by the identical ten men and that otherwise they could not be sold; as if a mass of semi-employed or completely unemployed were not for ever crawling around at the bottom of this society—and as if the capital existing in the form of means of subsistence were a fixed amount.

If the market-price of corn fell due to the decreasing demand, then the capital available in the shape of corn would be *diminished* (in terms of money) and would exchange for a smaller portion of the society's money revenue, in so far as it is not exportable. And this applies even more to manufactures. During the many years in which the hand-loom weavers were slowly dying of hunger, the production and export of English cotton cloth increased enormously. At the same time (1838-1841) the prices of provisions rose. And the weavers had only rags in which to clothe themselves and not enough food to keep body and soul together. The constant artificial production of a surplus population, which disappears only in times of feverish prosperity, is one of the necessary conditions of production of modern industry. There is nothing to prevent a part of the money capital lying idle and without employment and the prices of the means of subsistence falling because of relative surplus production while at the same time workers who have been displaced by machinery, are starving.

It is true that in the long run the labour that has been released together with the portion of revenue or capital that has been released, will find an opening in a new sphere of production or in the expansion of the old one, but this is of more benefit to *those who succeed the displaced men* than to the displaced men themselves. New ramifications of more or less unproductive branches of labour are continually being formed and in these revenue is directly expended. Then there is the formation of fixed capital (railways etc.) and the labour connected with superintendence which this opens up; the manufacture of luxuries etc., foreign trade, which increasingly diversifies the articles on which revenue is spent.

From his absurd standpoint, Ricardo therefore assumes that

the introduction of machinery harms the workers only when it diminishes the gross product (and therefore gross revenue), a case which may occur, it is true, in large-scale agriculture, with the introduction of horses which consume corn in place of the workers, with the transition from corn-growing to sheep-raising etc.; but it is quite preposterous [to extend this case] to industry proper, whose ability to sell its gross product is by no means restricted by the internal market. (Incidentally, while one section of the workers starves, another section may be better fed and clothed, as may also the unproductive workers and the middle strata between worker and capitalist.)

It is wrong, in itself, to say that the increase (or the quantity) of articles entering into revenue as such, forms a fund for the workers or forms capital for them. A portion of these articles is consumed by unproductive workers or non-workers, another portion may be transformed by means of foreign trade, from its coarse form, the form in which it serves as wages, into a form in which it enters into the revenue of the wealthy, or in which it serves as an element of production of constant capital. Finally, a portion will be consumed by the discharged workers themselves in the workhouse, or in prison, or as alms, or as stolen goods, or as payment for the prostitution of their daughters.

In the following pages I shall briefly compare the passages in which Ricardo develops this nonsense. As he says himself, he received the impetus for it from *Barton's* work, which must therefore be examined, after citing those passages.

||740| It is self-evident, that in order to employ a certain number of workers each year, a certain quantity of food and other necessary means of subsistence must be produced annually. In large-scale agriculture, stock-raising etc. it is possible for the net income (profit and rent) to be increased while the gross income is reduced, that is to say, while the quantity of necessaries intended for the maintenance of the workers is reduced. But that is not the question here. The quantity of articles entering into consumption or, to use Ricardo's expression, the quantity of articles of which the gross revenue consists, can be increased, without a consequent increase in that portion of this quantity which is transformed into variable capital. This may even decrease. In this case more is consumed as revenue by capitalists, landlords and their retainers, the unproductive classes, the state, the middle strata (merchants) etc.

36–244

What lies behind the view taken by Ricardo (and Barton) is that he originally set out from the assumption that every accumulation of capital is equivalent to an increase in variable capital, that the demand for labour therefore increases directly, in the same proportion, as capital is accumulated. But this is wrong, since with the accumulation of capital a change takes place in its organic composition and the constant part of the capital grows at a faster rate than the variable. This does not, however, prevent revenue from constantly growing, in value and in quantity. But it does not result in a proportionately larger part of the total product being laid out in wages. Those classes and sub-classes who do not live directly from their labour become more numerous and live better than before, and the number of unproductive workers increases as well.

Since, in the first place, it has nothing to do with the question, we will not concern ourselves with the *revenue* of the capitalist who transforms a part of his variable capital into machinery (and who therefore also puts more into raw material relatively to the amount of labour employed in all those spheres of production where raw material is an element of the process of creating value). His revenue and that part of his capital which has actually gone into the production process exist, at first, in the form of *products* or rather *commodities* which he produces himself, for example yarn if he is a spinner. After the introduction of machinery he transforms one part of these commodities—or the money for which he sells them—into machinery, auxiliary materials and raw materials whereas, previously, he paid it out as wages to the workers, thus transforming it indirectly into means of subsistence for the workers. With some exceptions in agriculture, he will produce more of these commodities than before, although his *discharged* workers have ceased to consume, and therefore to buy his own articles, though they did so before. More of these commodities will now be present on the market, although for the workers thrown on the street, they have ceased to exist [as objects of consumption] or have ceased to exist in their previous quantity. Thus, so far as his own product is concerned, in the first place, even if it enters into the consumption of the workers, its increased production in no way contradicts the fact that a part of it has ceased to exist as capital for the workers. A larger part of it (of the total product) on the other hand must now replace that portion of the constant capital which resolves into machinery, auxiliary materials and raw materials, that is to say, it must be exchanged against more of these ingredients of reproduction than formerly. If the increase in commodities through machinery and the decrease in a previously existing demand (*namely in the demand of the workers that have been discharged*) for the commodities produced by this machinery were contradictory, then in most cases, no machinery could in fact be introduced. The mass of commodities produced and the portion of these commodities which is reconverted into wages, therefore, have no definite relationship or necessary connection, when we consider the capital of which a part is transformed into machinery instead of into wage labour.

So far as society in general is concerned, the replacement of its revenue or rather the extension of the limits of its revenue takes place first of all on account of the articles whose price has been lowered by the introduction of machinery. This revenue may continue to be spent as revenue, and if a considerable part of it is transformed into capital, the increased population— apart from the artificially created surplus population—is already there to absorb that part of the revenue which is transformed into variable capital.

Prima facie, therefore, what this comes to is only: the production of all other articles, particularly in the spheres which produce articles entering into the consumption of the workers —despite the discharging of the hundred men etc.—continues on the same scale as before; quite certainly at the moment when the workers are discharged. In so far, therefore, as the dismissed workers represented a demand for these articles, the demand has decreased, although the supply has remained the same. If the reduced demand is not made good, the price will fall (or instead of a fall in price a larger stock may remain on the market for the following year). If the article is not produced for export, too, and if the decrease in demand were to persist, then reproduction would decrease, but it does not follow that the capital employed in this sphere ||741| must necessarily decrease. Perhaps more meat or commercial crops or luxury foods are produced [and] less wheat or more oats for horses etc. or fewer fustian jackets and more bourgeois frock-coats. But none of these consequences need necessarily materialise, if, for instance, as a result of the cheapening of cotton goods, the employed workers are able to spend more on food etc. The same quantity of commodities and even more of them—includ-

36*

ing those consumed by the workers—can be produced, although less capital, a smaller portion of the total product, is transformed into variable capital, that is laid out in wages.

Neither is it the case that part of the capital of the producers of these articles has been set free. At worst the demand for their commodities would have decreased, and the reproduction of their capital impeded by the reduced price of their commodities. Hence their own revenue would immediately decrease, as it would with any fall in the prices of commodities. But it cannot be said that any particular part of their commodities had previously confronted the discharged workers as capital and was now "set free" along with the workers. What confronted the workers as capital, was a part of the commodity now being produced with machinery; this part came to them in the form of money and was exchanged by them for other commodities (means of subsistence), which did not face them as capital, but confronted their money as commodities. This is therefore an entirely different relationship. The farmer and any other producer whose commodity they bought with their wages, did not confront them as capitalist and did not employ them as workers. They *have only ceased to be buyers for him*, which may possibly —if not counterbalanced by other circumstances—bring about a temporary depreciation in his capital, but does not set free any capital for the discharged workers. The capital that employed them "is still in being", but no longer in a form in which it resolves into wages, or only indirectly and to a smaller extent.

Otherwise anyone who through some bad luck ceased to have money, would inevitably set free sufficient capital for his own employment.

[d) Ricardo's Correct Determination of Some of the Consequences of the Introduction of Machines for the Working Class. Apologetic Notions in the Ricardian Explanation of the Problem]

By *gross revenue* Ricardo means that part of the product which replaces wages and surplus-value (profits and rent); by net revenue he means the surplus-product, [which] equals the surplus-value. He forgets here, as throughout his work, that a portion of the gross product must replace the value of the machinery and raw material, in short, the value of the constant capital.

* * *

Ricardo's subsequent treatment is of interest, partly because of some of the observations he makes in passing, partly because, *mutatis mutandis*, it is of practical importance for large-scale agriculture, particularly sheep-rearing, and shows the limitations of capitalist production. Not only is its determining purpose not production *for* the producers (workmen), but its exclusive aim is *net revenue* (profit and rent), even if this is achieved at the cost of the volume of production—at the cost of the volume of commodities produced.

"My mistake arose from the supposition, that whenever the *net income* of a society increased, its *gross income* would also increase; I now, however, see reason to be satisfied that *the one fund, from which landlords and capitalists derive their revenue, may increase*, while the other, *that upon which the labouring class mainly depend, may diminish*, and therefore it follows, if I am right, that the *same cause* which may increase the net revenue of the country, may at the same time *render the population redundant*, and deteriorate the condition of the labourer" (l.c., p. 469).

First it is noteworthy that Ricardo here admits that causes which further the wealth of the capitalists and landlords "may... *render the population redundant* ..." so that redundant population or over-population is presented here as the result of the process of enrichment itself, and of the development of productive forces which conditions this process.

So far as the fund is concerned, out of which the capitalists and landlords draw their revenue and on the other hand the fund from which the workers draw theirs, to begin with, it is the total product which forms this common fund. A large part of the products which enter into the consumption of the capitalists and landlords, does not enter into the consumption of the workers. On the other hand, almost all, in fact more or less all, products which enter into the consumption of the workers also enter into that of the landlords and capitalists, their retainers and hangers-on, including dogs and cats. One cannot suppose that there are two essentially distinct fixed funds in existence. The important point is, what relative portion each of these groups draws from the common fund. The aim of capitalist production is to obtain as large an amount of surplus-product or surplus-value as possible with a given amount of wealth. This aim is achieved by constant capital growing more rapidly in proportion to variable capital or by setting in motion the greatest possible ||742| constant capital with the least possible variable capital. In much more general terms than Ricardo conceives here, the same cause effects an increase in the fund out of which capitalists and landlords draw their revenue, by a decrease in the fund out of which the workers draw theirs.

It does not follow from this that the fund from which the workers draw their revenue is diminished *absolutely*; only that it is diminished *relatively*, in proportion to their total output. And that is the only important factor in the determination of the portion which they appropriate out of the wealth they themselves created.

"A capitalist we will suppose employs a capital of the value of £ 20,000 and that he carries on the joint business of a farmer, and a manufacturer of necessaries. We will further suppose, that £ 7,000 of this capital is invested in fixed capital, viz. in buildings, implements, etc., etc., and that the remaining £ 13,000 is employed as circulating capital in the support of labour. Let us suppose, too, that profits are 10 per cent, and consequently that the capitalist's capital is every year put into its original state of efficiency, and yields a profit of £ 2,000.

"Each year the capitalist begins his operations, by having food and necessaries in his possession of the value of £ 13,000, all of which he sells in the course of the year to his own workmen for that sum of money, and, during the same period, he pays them the like amount of money for wages: *at the end of the year* they replace in his possession food and necessaries of the value of £ 15,000, £ 2,000 of which he consumes himself, or disposes of as may best suit his pleasure and gratification."

⟨The *nature of surplus-value* is very palpably expressed here. The passage is on pp. 469-70.⟩

"As far as these products are concerned, the *gross produce* for that year is £ 15,000, and the net produce £ 2,000. Suppose now, that the following year the capitalist employs half his men in constructing a machine, and the other half in producing food and necessaries as usual. During that year he would pay the sum of £ 13,000 in wages as usual, and would sell food and necessaries to the same amount to his workmen; but what would be the case the following year?

"While the machine was being made, only one-half of the usual quantity of food and necessaries would be obtained, and they would be only one-half the value of the quantity which was produced before. The machine would be worth £ 7,500, and the food and necessaries £ 7,500, and, therefore, the capital of the capitalist would be as great as before; for he would have besides these two values, his fixed capital worth £ 7,000, making in the whole £ 20,000 capital, and £ 2,000 profit. After deducting this latter sum for his own expenses, he would have a no greater circulating capital than £ 5,500 with which to carry on his subsequent operations; and, therefore, his means of employing labour, would be reduced in the proportion of £13,000 to £5,500, and, consequently, *all the labour which was before employed by £7,500, would become redundant*" [l.c., pp. 469-71].

{This would, however, also be the case if by means of the machine which costs £7,500, exactly the same quantity of products were produced as previously with a variable capital of £13,000. Suppose the wear and tear of the machine were equal to one-tenth in one year, that is to £750, then the value of the product—previously £15,000—would now be £8,250. (Apart from the wear and tear of the original fixed capital of £7,000, whose replacement Ricardo does not mention at all.) Of these £8,250, £2,000 would be profit, as previously out of the £15,000. The lower price would be advantageous to the farmer in so far as he himself consumes food and necessaries as revenue. It would also be advantageous to him in so far as it enables him to reduce the wages of the workers he employs thus releasing a portion of his variable capital. It is this portion, which to a certain degree could employ new labour, but only because the *real wage* of the workers who have been retained had fallen. A small number of those who have been discharged could thus—at the cost of those who had been retained—be re-employed. The fact however that the product would be just as great as before, would not help the dismissed workers. If the wage remained the same, no part of the variable capital would be released. The fact that the product of £8,250 represents the same amount of necessaries and food as previously £15,000 does not cause its value to rise. The farmer would have to sell it for £8,250, partly in order to replace the wear and tear of his machinery and partly in order to replace his variable capital. In so far as this lowering of the price of food and necessaries did not bring about a fall in wages in general, or a fall in the ingredients entering into the reproduction of the constant capital, the revenue of society would have expanded only in so far as it is expended on food and necessaries. A section of the unproductive and productive workers etc. would live better. That is all. (They could also save, but that is always action in the future). The discharged workers would remain on the street, although the *physical* possibility of their maintenance existed just as much as before. Moreover, the same capital would be employed in the reproduction process as

before. But a *part of the product* (whose value had fallen),
which previously existed as *capital* has now become *revenue*.⟩

"The reduced quantity of labour which the capitalist can employ, must,
indeed, with the assistance of the machine, and after deductions for its
repairs, produce a value equal to £ 7,500, it must replace the circulating
capital with a profit of £ 2,000 on the whole capital; but if this be done,
||743| if the net income be not diminished, of what importance is it to the
capitalist, whether the gross income be of the value of £ 3,000, of £ 10,000,
or of £ 15,000?"

⟨This is perfectly correct. The gross income is of absolutely
no importance to the capitalist. The only thing which is of
interest to him is the net income.⟩

"In this case, then, although the net produce will not be diminished in
value, although its power of purchasing commodities may be greatly increased,
the gross produce will have fallen from a value of £ 15,000 to a value of
£ 7,500, and as *the power of supporting a population, and employing labour,
depends always on the gross produce of a nation, and not on its net produce*"
[l.c., p. 471]

⟨Hence Adam Smith's partiality for gross produce, a partiality to which Ricardo objects. See *Chapter XXVI "On Gross
and Net Revenue"*, which Ricardo opens with the words:

"Adam Smith constantly magnifies the advantages which a country derives
from a large gross, rather than a large net income" (l.c., p. 415)⟩
". . . there will *necessarily be a diminution in the demand for labour,
population will become redundant*, and the situation of the labouring classes
will be that of distress and poverty" [l.c., p. 471].

⟨Labour therefore *becomes redundant*, because the demand
for labour diminishes, and that demand diminishes in consequence of the development in the productive powers of
labour.⟩

"As, however, *the power of saving from revenue to add to capital, must
depend on the efficiency of the net revenue*, to satisfy the wants of the
capitalist, it *could not fail to follow from the reduction in the price of commodities consequent on the introduction of machinery*, that with the *same*
wants" ⟨but his wants grow larger⟩ "he would *have increased means of
saving,—increased facility of transferring revenue into capital*" (l.c., pp. 471-
72).

⟨According to this, first one part of capital is transformed
into revenue, transferred to revenue—not in terms of value,
but as regards the use-value, the material elements of which
the capital consists—in order later, to transfer a part of the
revenue back into capital. For example, when £13,000 was laid
out in variable capital a part of the product amounting to

£7,500, entered into the consumption of the workers whom the farmer employed, and this part of the product formed part of his capital. Following upon the introduction of machinery, for example, according to our supposition, the same amount of product is produced as previously, but its value does not amount to £15,000, as previously, but only to £8,250; and a larger part of this cheaper product enters into the revenue of the farmer or the revenue of the buyers of food and necessaries. They now consume a part of the product as revenue which was previously consumed industrially, as capital, by the farmer, although his labourers (since dismissed) consumed it as revenue as well. As a result of this growth in revenue—which has come about because a part of the product which was previously consumed as capital is now consumed as revenue—new capital is formed and revenue is reconverted into capital.⟩

"But with every increase of capital he would employ more labourers;"

⟨this *in any case* not in proportion to the increased capital, not to the whole extent of that increase. Perhaps he would buy more horses, or guano, or new implements⟩

"and, therefore, a *portion of the people thrown out of work in the first instance, would be subsequently employed; and if the increased production, in consequence of the employment of the machine, was so great as to afford, in the shape of net produce, as great a quantity of food and necessaries as existed before in the form of gross produce,* there would be *the same ability to employ the whole population,* and, therefore, there would not *necessarily*" ⟨but possibly and probably!⟩ "*be any redundancy of people*" (l.c., pp. 469-72).

In the last lines, Ricardo thus says what I observed above. In order that revenue is transformed in this way into capital, capital is first transformed into revenue. Or, as Ricardo puts it: First the net produce is increased at the expense of the gross produce in order then to reconvert a part of the net produce into gross produce. Produce is produce. Net or gross makes no difference (although this antithesis may also mean that the *excess over and above the outlay* increases, that therefore the net produce grows although the total product, i.e., the gross produce, diminishes). The produce only becomes net or gross, according to the determinate form which it assumes in the process of production.

"All I wish to prove, is, that the discovery and use of machinery may be attended with a diminution of gross produce; and whenever that is the case, it will be injurious to the labouring class. as some of their number will be thrown out of employment, and *population will become redundant, compared with the funds which are to employ it*" (l.c., p. 472).

But the same may, and in most instances ||744| will, be the case, even if the gross produce remains the same or increases; but that part of it which was formerly used as variable capital, is now consumed as revenue.

It is superfluous for us to go into Ricardo's absurd example of the clothier who reduces his production because of the introduction of machinery (pp. 472-74).

"If these views be correct, it follows,

"*1st*. That the discovery, and useful application of machinery, *always leads to the increase* of the *net produce of the country*, although it may not, and will not, after an inconsiderable interval, increase the *value of that net produce*" (l.c., p. 474).

It will always increase that value whenever it diminishes the value of labour.

"*2dly*. That an increase of the net produce of a country is compatible with a diminution of the gross produce, and that the motives for employing machinery are always sufficient to insure its employment, if it will increase the net produce, although it may, and frequently must, diminish both the quantity of the gross produce, and its value.

"*3dly*. That the opinion entertained by the labouring class, that the employment of machinery is frequently detrimental to their interests, is not founded on prejudice and error, but is conformable to the correct principles of political economy.

"*4thly*. That if the improved means of production, in consequence of the use of machinery, should increase the net produce of a country in a degree so great as not to diminish the gross produce, (I mean always quantity of commodities and not value,) then the situation of all classes will be improved. The landlord and capitalist will benefit, not by an increase of rent and profit, but by the advantages resulting from the expenditure of the same rent, and profit, on commodities, very considerably reduced in value"

⟨this sentence contradicts the whole of Ricardo's doctrine, according to which the lowering in the price of necessaries, and therefore of wages, raises profits, whereas machinery, which permits more to be extracted from the same land with less labour, must lower rent⟩,

"while the situation of the labouring classes will also be considerably improved; 1st, *from the increased demand for menial servants;*"

⟨this is indeed a fine result of machinery, that a considerable section of the female and male labouring class is turned into servants;⟩

"2dly, from the stimulus to savings from revenue, which such an abundant net produce will afford; and 3dly, from the low price of all articles of consumption on which their wages will be expended" (and in consequence of this low price their wages will be reduced) (l.c., pp. 474-75).

The entire apologetic bourgeois presentation of machinery does not deny,

1. That machinery—sometimes here, sometimes there, but continually—makes a part of the population redundant, throws a section of the labouring population on the street. It creates a surplus population, thus leading to lower wages in certain spheres of production, here or there, not because the population grows more rapidly than the means of subsistence, but because the rapid growth in the means of subsistence, due to machinery, enables more machinery to be introduced and *therefore* reduces the *immediate demand for labour*. This comes about not because the social fund diminishes, but because of the growth of this fund, the part of it which is spent in wages falls relatively.

2. Even less do these apologetics deny the subjugation of the workers who operate the machines and the wretchedness of the manual workers or craftsmen who are displaced by machinery and perish.

What they assert—and partly rightly—is [*firstly*] that due to machinery and the development of the productivity of labour in general the net revenue (profit and rent) grows to such an extent, that the bourgeois needs more *menial servants* than before; whereas previously he had to lay out more of his product in productive labour, he can now lay out more in unproductive labour, [so that] servants and other workers living on the unproductive class increase in number. This progressive transformation of a section of the workers into servants is a fine prospect. For the worker it is equally consoling that because of the growth in the net product, more spheres are opened up for unproductive workers, who live on his product and whose interest in his exploitation coincides more or less with that of the directly exploiting classes.

Secondly, that because of the spur given to accumulation, on the new basis requiring less living labour in proportion to past labour, the workers who were dismissed and pauperised, or at least that part of the population increase ||745| which replaces them, are either absorbed in the expanding engineering-works themselves, or in branches of production which machinery has made necessary and brought into being, or in new fields of employment opened by the new capital, and satisfying new wants. This then is another wonderful prospect: the labouring class has to bear all the "temporary inconveniences"—unemployment, displacement of labour and capital—*but wage-labour is nevertheless not to be abolished, on the contrary it will be reproduced on an ever growing scale, growing absolutely, even though decreasing relatively to the growing total capital which employs it.*

Thirdly: that consumption becomes more *refined* due to machinery. The reduced price of the immediate necessities of life allows the scope of luxury production to be extended. Thus the third fine prospect opens before the workers: in order to win their means of subsistence, the same amount of them as before, the same number of labourers will enable the higher classes to extend, refine, and diversify the circle of their enjoyments, and thus to widen the economic, social, and political gulf separating them from their betters. Fine prospects, these, for the labourer, and very desirable results of the development of the productive powers of his labour.

Furthermore, Ricardo then shows that it [is in] the interest of the labouring classes,

"that as much of the revenue as possible should be diverted from expenditure on luxuries, to be expended in the support of[a] menial servants" (l.c., p. 476). For whether I [purchase] furniture or keep menial servants, I thereby present a demand for a definite amount of commodities and set in motion approximately the same amount of productive labour in one case as in the other; but in the latter case, I add [a new demand] "to the former demand for labourers, and this addition would take place only because I chose this mode of expending my revenue" (l.c., p. 476).

The same applies to the maintenance of large fleets and armies.

"Whether it" (the revenue) "was expended in the one way or in the other, there would be *the same quantity of labour employed in production*; for the food and clothing of the soldier and sailor would require the same amount of industry to produce it as the more luxurious commodities; but in the case of the war, there would be the additional demand for men as soldiers and sailors; and, consequently, a war which is supported out of the revenue, and not from the capital of a country, is favourable to the increase of population" (l.c., p. 477).

"There is one other case that should be noticed of the possibility of an *increase in the amount of the net revenue of a country*, and *even of its gross revenue*, with a diminution of demand for labour, and that is, when the labour of horses is substituted for that of man. If I employed one hundred men on my farm, and if I found that the food bestowed on fifty of those

---

[a] In the manuscript: "on", instead of: "in the support of".—*Ed.*

men, could be diverted to the support of horses, and afford me a greater
return of raw produce, after allowing for the interest of the capital which
the purchase of the horses would absorb, it would be advantageous to me to
substitute the horses for the men, and I should accordingly do so; but this
would not be for the interest of the men, and unless the income I obtained,
was so much increased as to enable me to employ the men as well as the
horses, *it is evident that the population would become redundant*, and the
labourer's condition would sink in the general scale. It is evident he could
not, under any circumstances, be employed in agriculture;" (why not? if
the field of agriculture were enlarged?) "but if the produce of the land were
increased by the substitution of horses for men, he might be employed in
manufactures, or as a menial servant" (l.c., pp. 477-78).

There are two tendencies which constantly cut across one
another; [firstly,] to employ as little labour as possible, in order
to produce the same or a greater quantity of commodities, in
order to produce the same or a greater net produce, surplus-
value, net revenue; secondly, to employ the largest possible
number of workers (although as few as possible in proportion
to the quantity of commodities produced by them), because—
at a given level of productivity—the mass of surplus-value and
of surplus-product grows with the amount of labour employed.
The one tendency throws the labourers on to the streets and
makes a part of the population redundant, the other absorbs
them again and extends wage-slavery absolutely, so that the
lot of the worker is always fluctuating but he never escapes
from it. The worker, therefore, justifiably regards the development of the productive power of his own labour as
hostile to himself; the capitalist, on the other hand, always
treats him as an element to be eliminated from production.
These are the contradictions with which Ricardo struggles in
this chapter. What he forgets to emphasise ||746| is the con-
stantly growing number of the middle classes, those who stand
between the workman on the one hand and the capitalist and
landlord on the other. The middle classes maintain themselves
to an ever increasing extent directly out of revenue, they are a
burden weighing heavily on the working base and increase the
social security and power of the upper ten thousand.

According to the bourgeoisie the perpetuation of wage-slavery
through the application of machinery is a "vindication" of the
latter.

"I have before observed, too, that *the increase of net incomes, estimated
in commodities, which is always the consequence of improved machinery,*
will lead to new savings and accumulations. *These savings,* it must be
remembered, are *annual,* and must soon create a *fund, much greater than*

the gross· revenue, originally lost by the discovery of the machine, when the demand for labour will be as great as before, and the situation of the people will be still further improved by the increased savings which the increased net revenue will still enable them to make" (l.c., p. 480).

First gross revenue declines and net revenue increases. Then a portion of the increased net revenue is transformed into capital again and hence into gross revenue. Thus the workman must constantly enlarge the power of capital, and then, after very serious disturbances, obtain permission to repeat the process on a larger scale.

"With every increase of capital and population, food will generally rise, on account of its being more difficult to produce" (l.c., pp. 478-79).

It then goes straight on:

"The consequence of a rise of food will be a rise of wages, and every rise of wages will have a tendency to determine *the saved capital in a greater proportion than before to the employment of machinery. Machinery and labour are in constant competition, and the former can frequently not be employed until labour* rises*" (l.c., p. 479).

The machine is thus a means to prevent a rise of labour.

"To elucidate the principle, I have been supposing, that improved machinery is *suddenly* discovered, and extensively used; but the truth is, that these discoveries are gradual, and rather operate in *determining the employment of the capital which is saved and accumulated, than in diverting capital from its actual employment*" (l.c., p. 478).

The truth is, that it is not so much the displaced labour as, rather, the new supply of labour—the part of the growing population which was to replace it—for which, as a result of new accumulation, new fields of employment are opened.

"In America and many other countries, where the food of man is easily provided, there is not nearly such great temptation to employ machinery" ⟨nowhere is it used on such a massive scale and also, so to speak, for domestic needs as in America⟩ "as in England, where food is high, and costs much labour for its production" [l.c., p. 479].

{How little the employment of machinery is dependent on the price of food is shown precisely by America, which employs relatively much more machinery than England, where there is always a redundant population. The use of machinery *may*, however, depend on the relative scarcity of labour as, for instance, in America, where a comparatively small population is spread over immense tracts of land. Thus we read in the

---

* He means "wages".

Standard[146] of September 19, 1862, in an article on the Exhibition[147]:

"'Man is a machine-making animal' ... if we consider the American as a representative man, the definition is ... perfect. It is one of the cardinal points of an American's system to do nothing with his hands that he can do by a machine. From rocking a cradle to making a coffin, from milking a cow to clearing a forest, from sewing on a button to voting for President, almost, he had a machine for everything. He has invented a machine for saving the trouble of masticating food.... The *exceeding scarcity of labour* and its consequent high value" ⟨despite the low value of food⟩, "as well as a certain innate 'cuteness' have stimulated this inventive spirit.... The machines produced in America are, generally speaking, inferior in value to those made in England ... they are rather, as a whole, *makeshifts to save labour* than inventions to accomplish former impossibilities". ⟨And the steam ships?⟩ ... [at the Exhibition] "in the United States department [...] is *Emery's cotton gin.* For many a year after the introduction of cotton to America the crop was very small; because not only was the demand rather limited, but the difficulty of cleaning the crop by manual labour rendered it anything but remunerative. When Eli Whitney, however, invented the saw cotton-gin ||747| there *was an immediate increase in the breadth planted,* and that increase has up to the present time gone on almost in an arithmetical[a] progression. In fact, it is not too much to say that Whitney made the cotton trade. With modifications more or less important and useful his gin has remained in use ever since; and until the invention of the present improvement and addition Whitney's original gin was quite as good as the most of its would-be supplanters. By the present machine, which bears the name of Messrs. Emery of [...] Albany, N.Y., we have no doubt that Whitney's gin, on which it is based, will be almost entirely supplanted. It is simple and more efficacious; it delivers the cotton not only cleaner, but in sheets like wadding, and thus the layers as they leave the machine are at once fit for the cotton press and the bale ... In [the] American Court proper there is little else than machinery [....] *The cow-milker* ... a *belt-shifter* ... *a hemp carding and spinning machine,* which at one operation reels the cliver direct from the bale ... *machines*[b] [...] *for the manufacture of paper-bags,* which it cuts from the sheet, pastes, folds, and perfects at the rate of 300 a minute ... Hawes's clothes-wringer, which by two indiarubber rollers presses from clothes the water, leaving them almost dry, [...] saves time, but does not injure the texture ... *bookbinder's machinery ... machines for making shoes.* It is well known that the uppers have been for a long time made up by machinery in this country, but here are machines for putting on the sole, others for cutting the sole to shape, and others again for trimming the heels.... A *stone-breaking machine* is very powerful and ingenious, and no doubt will come extensively into use for ballasting roads and crushing ores.... A *system of marine signals* by Mr. W. H. Ward of Auburn, New York.... *Reaping and mowing machines* are an American invention coming into very general favour in England. [...] McCormick's" [machine is] "the best ... Hansbrow's California Prize Medal *Force Pump,* is in simplicity and efficiency the best [...] in the Exhibition ... it will throw

---

[a] In the manuscript: "geometrical".—*Ed.*
[b] In the manuscript: "A machine".—*Ed.*

more water with the same power than any pump in the world.... *Sewing machines..."*}

"The same cause that raises labour, does not raise the value of machines, and, therefore, *with every augmentation of capital, a greater proportion of it is employed on machinery. The demand for labour will continue to increase with an increase of capital, but not in proportion to its increase; the ratio will necessarily be a diminishing ratio*" ([David Ricardo, *On the Principles of Political Economy, and Taxation*, third edition, London, 1821,] p. 479).

In the last sentence Ricardo expresses the correct law of growth of capital, although his reasoning is very one-sided. He adds a note to this, from which it is evident that he follows *Barton* here, whose work we will therefore examine briefly.

But first one more comment. When Ricardo discussed revenue expended either on menial servants or luxuries, he wrote:

"In both cases the net revenue would be the same, and so would be the gross revenue, but the *former would be realised in different commodities*" (l.c., p. 476).

Similarly the gross produce, in terms of value, may be the same, but it may "be realised"—and this would strongly affect the workmen—*"in different commodities"* according to whether it had to replace more variable or constant capital.

[2. Barton's Views]

[a) Barton's Thesis that Accumulation of Capital Causes a Relative Decrease in the Demand for Labour. Barton's and Ricardo's Lack of Understanding of the Inner Connection Between This Phenomenon and the Domination of Capital over Labour]

Barton's work is called:

John Barton. *Observations on the Circumstances which Influence the Condition of the Labouring Classes of Society*, London, 1817.

Let us first gather together the small number of theoretical propositions to be found in Barton's work.

"The demand for labour depends on *the increasing of circulating, and not of fixed capital.* Were it true *that the proportion between these two sorts of capital is the same at all times, and in all countries,* then, indeed, it follows that the *number of labourers employed is in proportion to the wealth of the State.* But such a position has not the semblance of probability. As arts are cultivated, and civilization is extended, *fixed capital bears a larger and larger proportion to circulating capital.* The amount of fixed capital employed in the production of a piece of British muslin is at least a hundred, probably a thousand times greater than that employed in the production of a similar piece of Indian muslin. And the ||748| proportion of circulating capital employed is a hundred or a thousand times less. It is easy to conceive that, under certain circumstances, the whole of the annual savings of an industrious people might be added to fixed capital, in which case they would have no effect in increasing the demand for labour" (l.c., pp. 16-17).

⟨Ricardo comments on this passage in a note on page 480 of his work:

"It is not easy, I think, to conceive that under any circumstances, an increase of capital should not be followed by an increased demand for labour; the most that can be said is, that the *demand will be in a diminishing ratio*. Mr. Barton, in the above publication, has, I think, taken *a correct view* of some of the effects of an increasing amount of fixed capital on the condition of the labouring classes. His Essay contains much valuable information."⟩

To Barton's above proposition we must add the following one:

"Fixed capital [...] when once formed, ceases to affect the demand for labour," (incorrect, since it necessitates reproduction, even if only at intervals and gradually) "but during its formation it gives employment to just as many hands as an equal amount would employ, either of circulating capital, or of revenue" (l.c., p. 56).

And:

"The demand for labour [...] depends absolutely on the joint amount of revenue and circulating capital" (l.c., pp. 34-35).

Indisputably, Barton has very great merit.

Adam Smith believes that the demand for labour grows in direct proportion to capital accumulation. Malthus derives surplus population from capital not being accumulated (that is, reproduced on a growing scale) as rapidly as the population. Barton was the first to point out that the different organic component parts of capital do not grow evenly with accumulation and development of the productive forces, that on the contrary in the process of this growth, that part of capital which resolves into wages decreases in proportion to that part (he calls it fixed capital) which in relation to its size, alters the demand for labour only to a very small degree. He is therefore the first to put forward the important proposition "that the number of labourers employed is" *not* "in proportion to the wealth of the state", that relatively more workers are employed in an industrially undeveloped country than in one which is industrially developed.

In the third edition of his *Principles*, Chapter XXXI *"On Machinery"*, Ricardo—having followed exactly in Smith's footsteps in his earlier editions—now takes up Barton's correction on this point, and moreover, in the same *one-sided* formulation in which Barton gives it. The only point in which he makes an advance—and this is important—is that, unlike Barton, he not only says that the demand for labour does *not* grow *proportionally* with the development of machinery, but that the machines themselves *"render the population redundant"* [l.c., p. 469], i.e., create surplus population. But he wrongly limits this effect to the case in which the net produce is increased at the cost of the gross produce. This only occurs in agriculture, but he also transfers it into industry. Essentially, however, the whole of the absurd theory of population was thus overthrown, in particular also the claptrap of the vulgar economists, that the workers must strive to keep their multiplication below the standard of the accumulation of capital. The opposite follows from Barton's and Ricardo's presentation, namely that to keep down the labouring population, thus diminishing the supply of labour, and, consequently, raising its price, would only *accelerate* the application of machinery, the conversion of circulating into fixed capital, and, hence, make the population artificially "redundant"; redundancy exists, generally, not in regard to the quantity of the means of subsistence, but the means of employment, the actual demand for labour.

||749| Barton's error or deficiency lies in his conceiving the organic differentiation or composition of capital only in the form in which it appears in the *circulation process*—as fixed and circulating capital—a difference which the Physiocrats had already discovered, which Adam Smith had developed further and which became a prepossession among the economists who succeeded him; a prepossession in so far as they see *only* this difference—which was handed down to them—in the organic composition of capital. This difference, which arises out of the process of circulation, has a considerable effect on the reproduction of wealth in general, and therefore also on that part of it which forms the wages fund. But that is not decisive here. The difference between fixed capital such as machinery, buildings, breeding cattle etc. and circulating capital, does not *directly* lie in their relation to wages, but in their mode of circulation and reproduction.

The *direct relation* of the different component parts of capital to living labour is not connected with the phenomena of the circulation process. It does not arise from the latter, but from the *immediate process of production*, and its [expression] is the relation of *constant* to *variable capital*, whose difference is based *only* on their relationship to living labour.

Thus Barton says for example: The demand for labour does not depend on *fixed capital*, but only on circulating capital. But a part of circulating capital, *raw material* and *auxiliary materials*, is not exchanged against living labour, any more than is machinery. In all branches of industry in which raw material enters as an element into the process of the creation of value— in so far as we consider only that portion of the fixed capital which enters into the commodity—it forms the *most important* part of that portion of capital which is not laid out in wages. Another part of the circulating capital, namely of the commodity capital, consists of articles of consumption which enter into the revenue of the non-productive class (i.e., [not of] the working class). The growth of these two parts of *circulating* capital therefore does not influence the demand for labour any more than does that of fixed capital. Furthermore, the part of the circulating capital which resolves into raw materials and auxiliary materials increases in the same or even greater proportion as that part of capital which is fixed in machinery etc.

On the basis of the distinction made by Barton, *Ramsay* goes further. He improves on Barton but retains his method of approach. Indeed he reduces the distinction to constant and variable capital, but continues to call constant capital *fixed* capital, although he includes raw materials etc., and [calls] variable capital circulating capital, although he excludes from it all circulating capital which is not directly laid out in wages. More on this later, when we come to Ramsay. It does, however, show the intrinsic necessity of the progress.

Once the distinction between constant capital and variable capital has been grasped, a distinction which arises simply out of the immediate process of production, out of the relationship of the different component parts of capital to living labour, it also becomes evident that in itself it has nothing to do with the absolute amount of the consumption goods produced, although plenty with the way in which these are realised. The way, however, of realising the gross revenue in different commodities is not, as Ricardo has it, and Barton intimates it, *the cause*, but the *effect* of the immanent laws of capitalistic production, leading to a diminishing proportion, compared with the total amount of produce, of that part of it which forms the fund for the reproduction of the labouring class. If a large part of the capital consists of machinery, raw materials, auxiliary materials etc., then a smaller portion of the working class as a whole will be employed in the reproduction of the means of subsistence ||750| which enter into the consumption of the workers. This relative diminution in the reproduction of variable capital, however, is not the reason for the relative decrease in the demand for labour, but on the contrary, its effect. Similarly: A larger section of the workers employed in the production of articles of consumption which enter into revenue in general, will produce articles of consumption that are consumed by— are exchanged against the revenue of—capitalists, landlords and their retainers (state, church etc.), [and a smaller] section [will produce] articles destined for the revenue of the workers. But this again is effect, not cause. A change in the social relation of workers and capitalists, a revolution in the conditions governing capitalist production, would change this at once. The revenue would be "realised in different commodities", to use an expression of Ricardo's.

There is nothing in the, so-to-speak, physical conditions of production which forces the above to take place. The workmen, if they were dominant, if they were allowed to produce for themselves, would very soon, and without great exertion, bring the capital (to use a phrase of the vulgar economists) up to the standard of their needs. The very great difference is whether the available means of production confront the workers as capital and can therefore be employed by them *only* in so far as it is necessary for the increased production of surplus-value and surplus-produce for their employers, in other words whether the means of production employ *the workers*, or whether the workers, as subjects, employ the means of production—in the accusative case—in order to produce wealth for themselves. It is of course assumed here that capitalist production has already developed the productive forces of labour in general to a sufficiently high level for this revolution to take place.

⟨Take for example 1862 (the present autumn). The plight of the Lancashire unemployed labourers; on the other hand, "the difficulty of finding employment for money" on the

London money market, this has almost made necessary the formation of fraudulent companies, since it [is] difficult to obtain two per cent for money. According to Ricardo's theory "some new field of employment ought to have been opened up," for on the one hand there is capital in London, and on the other, unemployed workers in Manchester.⟩

[b) Barton's Views on the Movement of Wages and the Growth of Population]

Barton explains further, that the accumulation of capital increases the demand for labour only very slowly, unless the population has grown to such an extent *previously*, that the rate of wages is low.

"The *proportion which the wages of labour at any particular*[a] *time bear to the whole produce of* [...] *labour* [...] determine the appropriation" of capital "in one way" (as fixed capital) "or the other" (circulating capital) ([John Barton, *Observations on the Circumstances Which Influence the Condition of the Labouring Class of Society*, London, 1817], p. 17).

"For if [...] the rate of wages should decline, while the price of goods remained the same, or if goods should rise, while wages remained the same, the profit of the employer would increase, and he would be induced to hire more hands. If on the other hand, wages should rise in proportion to commodities" [the] "master[b] [...] would [...] keep as few hands as possible.— He would aim at performing every thing by machinery" (l.c., pp. 17-18).

"We have good evidence that population advanced much more slowly under a gradual rise of wages during the earlier part of the last century, than during the latter part of the same century while the real price of labour fell rapidly" (l. c., p. 25).

"A rise of wages, of itself, then, never increases the labouring population;—a fall of wages may sometimes increase it very rapidly. Suppose that" the Englishman's demands should sink to the level of the Irishman's. Then the manufacturer would engage more [workers][c] "in proportion to the diminished expense of maintenance" (l.c., p. 26).

"It is *the difficulty of finding employment*, much more *than the insufficiency of the rate of wages*, which discourages marriage" (l.c., p. 27).

"It is admitted that every increase of wealth has a tendency to create a fresh demand for labour; but as labour, of all commodities, requires the greatest length of time for its production"

⟨for the same reason, the rate of wages can remain below the average for long periods, because of all commodities,

---

[a] In the manuscript: "given".—*Ed.*

[b] In the manuscript: "manufacturers".—*Ed.*

[c] Marx gives this part of the quotation in his own words, summarising the idea expressed by Barton.—*Ed.*

labour is the most difficult to withdraw from the market and thus to bring down to the level of the actual demand⟩

"so, of all commodities ||751| it is the most raised [...] by a given increase of demand; and as every rise of wages produces a tenfold reduction of profits; it is evident that the accumulation of capital can operate *only in an inconsiderable degree in adding to the effectual demand* for labour, *unless preceded by such an increase of population as shall have the effect of keeping down the rate of wages*" (l. c., p. 28).

Barton puts forward various propositions here:

First: It is not the rise of wages in itself which increases the labouring population, but a fall in wages may very easily and rapidly make it rise. Proof: First half of the eighteenth century, gradual rise in wages, slow movement in population; in the second half of the eighteenth century, on the other hand, sharp fall in real wages, rapid increase in the labouring population. Reason: It is not the insufficient rate of wages which prevents marriages, but the difficulty of finding employment.

Secondly: The facility of finding employment stands, however, in inverse ratio to the rate of wages. For capital is transformed into circulating or fixed capital, that is to say, capital which employs labour or capital which does not employ it, in inverse proportion to the high or low level of wages. If wages are low, then the demand for labour is great because it is then profitable for the employer to use much labour, and he can employ *more* with the same circulating capital. If wages are high, then the manufacturer employs as few workers as possible and seeks to do everything with the aid of machines.

Thirdly: The accumulation of capital by itself raises the demand for labour only slowly, because each increase in this demand, if [labour is] scarce, causes [the wages] of labour to rise rapidly and brings about a fall of profit which is ten times greater than the rise in wages. Accumulation can have a rapid effect on the demand for labour only if *accumulation was preceded by a large increase in the labouring population*, and wages are therefore very low so that even a rise of wages still leaves them low because the demand mainly absorbs unemployed workers rather than competing for those fully employed.

This is all, *cum grano salis*, correct so far as fully developed capitalist production is concerned. But it does not explain this development itself.

And even Barton's historical proof therefore contradicts that which it is supposed to prove.

During the first half of the eighteenth century, wages rose gradually, the population grew slowly and [there was] no machinery; moreover, compared with the following half of the century, little other fixed capital [was employed].

During the second half of the eighteenth century, however, wages fell continuously, population grew amazingly—and [so did] machinery. But it was precisely the machinery which on the one hand made the existing population superfluous, thus reducing wages, and on the other hand, as a result of the rapid development of the world market, absorbed the population again, made it redundant once more and then absorbed it again; while at the same time, it speeded up the accumulation of capital to an extraordinary extent, and increased the *amount* of variable capital, although variable capital fell relatively, both compared with the total value of the product and also compared with the number of workers it employed. In the first half of the eighteenth century, however, large-scale industry did not as yet exist, but only *manufacture based on the division of labour*. The principal component part of capital was still variable capital laid out in wages. The productivity of labour developed slowly, compared with the second half of the century. The demand for labour, and therefore also wages, rose almost proportionately to the accumulation of capital. England was as yet essentially an agricultural nation and a very extensive cottage industry—spinning and weaving—which was carried on by the agricultural population, continued to exist, and even to expand. A numerous proletariat could not as yet come into being, any more than there could exist industrial millionaires at the time. In the first half of the eighteenth century, variable capital was relatively dominant; in the second, fixed capital; but the latter requires a large mass of human material. Its introduction on a large scale must be preceded by an increase of population. The whole course of things, however, contradicts Barton's presentation, in as much as it is evident that a general change in the method of production took place. The laws which correspond to large-scale industry are not identical with those corresponding to manufacture ||752|. The latter constitutes merely a phase of development leading to the former.

But in this context some of Barton's historical data—comparing the development in England during the first half and the second half of the eighteenth century—are of interest,

partly because they show the movement of wages, and partly
because they show the movement in corn prices.

"...wages [...] increased from the middle of the seventeenth, till near
the middle of the eighteenth century, for the price of corn declined within
that space of time not less than 35 per cent" [l.c., p. 25]. "The following
statement will shew what proportion the *wages of husbandry* [...] have
borne[a] to the price of corn [...] during the last seventy years.

Periods	Weekly pay	Wheat per quarter	Wages in pints of wheat
1742 to 1752	6s. 0d.	30s. 0d.	102
1761 to 1770	7s. 6d.	42s. 6d.	90
1780 to 1790	8s. 0d.	51s. 2d.	80
1795 to 1799	9s. 0d.	70s. 8d.	65
1800 to 1808	11s. 0d.	86s. 8d.	60

(l.c., pp. 25-26)
"From a table of the number of Bills for the inclosing of land passed
in each session since the revolution, given in the Lord's Report on the Poor
Laws" (1816?), "it appears that in sixty-six years from 1688 to 1754, that
number was 123; in the sixty-nine[b] years from 1754 to 1813 it was 3,315.—
The progress of cultivation was then about twenty-five times more rapid
during the last period than the former. But during the first sixty-six years
more and more corn was grown continually for exportation; whereas, during
the greater part of the last sixty-nine years, we not only consumed all that
we had formerly sent abroad, but likewise imported an increasing, and at
last a very large quantity, for our own consumption ... the increase of population in the former period, as compared with the latter, was still slower
than the progress of cultivation might appear to indicate" (l. c., pp. 11-12).
"In the year 1688, the population of England and Wales was computed
by Gregory King, from the number of houses, at five millions and a half."
The population in "1780 is put down by Mr. Malthus at 7,700,000. In ninety-
two years then it had increased 2,200,000—in the succeeding thirty years it
increased something more than 2,700,000. But of the first increase [...] there
is every probability, that the far greater part took place from 1750 to 1780"
(l. c., p. 13).

Barton calculates from good sources that

"the number of inhabitants in 1750" [was] "5,946,000, making an increase
since the revolution of 446,000, or 7,200 per annum" (l.c., p. 14).

_____

[a] In the manuscript: "been".—*Ed.*

[b] Although Barton says 69 years in fact the period from 1754 to 1813
comprises only 59 years.—*Ed.*

"At the lowest estimate then [...] the progress of population of late years has been ten times more rapid than a century ago. Yet it is impossible to believe, that the accumulation of capital has been ten times greater" (l. c., p. 14).

It is not a question of how great a quantity of means of subsistence is produced annually, but how large a portion of living labour enters into the annual production of fixed and circulating capital. This determines the size of the variable capital in relation to constant.

Barton explains the remarkable increase in population which took place almost all over Europe during the last 50 to 60 years, from the increased productivity of the American mines, since this abundance of precious metals raised commodity prices more than wages, thus in fact, lowering the latter and causing the rate of profit to rise (l.c., pp. 29-35). |XIII-752||

ADDENDA[148]

[1. Early Formulation of the Thesis That the Supply of Agricultural Products Always Corresponds to Demand. Rodbertus and the Practicians among the Economists of the Eighteenth Century]

||XII-580b| The proposition that corn produces its own demand etc.[a] "casually" advanced by Adam Smith, later repeated by *Malthus* with considerable pomposity in his theory of rent and partly used as the basis of his theory of population, is very *concisely* expressed in the following passage:

"Corn [...] is scarce or not scarce in proportion to the consumption of it. If there are *more m o u t h s*, there will be *more corn*, because there will be *more hands* to till the earth; and if there is *more corn*, there will be more mouths, because *plenty* will bring *people...*" ([John Arbuthnot], *An Inquiry into the Connection Between the Present Price of Provisions, and the Size of Farms*, etc. *By a Farmer*, London, 1773, p. 125).

Hence

"the culture of the earth cannot be over-done" (l. c., p. 62).

Rodbertus's fantasy that *seeds* etc. do not enter as an item of capital [into the farmer's calculations],[b] is refuted by the hundreds of treatises, some written by farmers themselves, that appeared in the eighteenth century (particularly since the 60s of that century). But on the contrary, it would be correct to say that *rent* is an item of expenditure for the farmer. He[c] reckons rent among the *costs of production* (and it does belong to his costs of production).

"If ... the *price of corn* is nearly what it ought to be, which can only be determined by the proportion that the *value of land* bears to the *value of money*" (l.c., p. 132).

---

a See this volume, p. 354 et seqq.—*Ed.*
b See this volume, pp. 45-55.—*Ed.*
c Arbuthnot, the author of the anonymous pamphlet.—*Ed.*

As soon as capital takes possession of agriculture, the farming-capitalist himself regards rent only as a deduction from profit and the whole of surplus-value is for him essentially profit:

"The *old* method of calculating the *profits* of the farmer [was] by the *three rents*" (the métayage system). "*In the infancy of agriculture*, it was a conscientious and equal partition of property; such as is now practised in the less enlightened parts of the world ... the one finds land and capital, the other knowledge and labour: but on a well-cultivated and good soil, the rent is now the least object: it is the *sum which a man can sink in stock*, and *in the annual expense of his labour*, on which he is to reckon the interest of his money, or income" (l. c., p. 34). |XII-580b||

[2. Nathaniel Forster on the Hostility Between Landowners and Traders]

||XIII-670a| "The *landed* and *trading interests* are eternally jarring, and jealous of each other's advantages" ([Nathaniel Forster], *An Enquiry into the Causes of the Present High Price of Provisions,* London, 1767, p. 22, note). |XIII-670a||

[3. Hopkins's Views on the Relationship Between Rent and Profit]

||XIII-669b| Hopkins (passage to be looked up)[a] naïvely [describes] *rent of land* as the original form of surplus-value, and profit as derived from this.

He writes:

"When the ... producers were both agriculturists and manufacturers, the landowner received, as *rent of land*, a value of £10. Suppose this rent to have been paid one half in raw produce, and the other half in manufactures;—on the *division* of the producers into the two classes of agriculturists and manufacturers" this could be continued. "In practice, however, it would be found more convenient for the cultivators of the land, *to pay the rent*, and to charge it on their produce, when exchanging it against the produce of the labour of the manufacturers; so as to divide the payment into equitable proportions between the two classes, and to leave wages and profits equal in each department" (Thomas Hopkins, *Economical Enquiries relative to the Laws which Regulate Rent, Profit, etc.* London, 1822, p. 26). |XIII-669b||

---

[a] See this volume, p. 55 and Note 20.—*Ed.*

[4. Carey, Malthus and James Deacon Hume on Improvements in Agriculture]

||XI-490a| "It will be observed that we consider the owner and farmer always as *one and the same person*.... Such it is in the United States." (H. C. Carey, *The Past, the Present, and the Future*, Philadelphia, 1848, p. 97, note).

"Man [...] is always going from a poor soil to better, and then returning on his footsteps to the original poor one, and turning up the marl or the lime; and so on, in continuous succession ... and [...] at each step in this course, he is making a better machine[a]..." (l.c., pp. 128-29). "Capital may be invested in agriculture with *more* advantage than in *engines*, because the last are *only of equal*, whereas the other is of *superior*, power" (l.c., p. 129). "The gain from a steam-engine[b]" (which transforms the wool into cloth, etc.) "is the wages of [...] labour, *minus* the loss by deterioration of the machine. Labour applied to fashioning the earth produces wages, plus the gain by improvement of the machine" (l. c., p. 129). Hence "a piece of land that yields £ 100 per annum will sell" dearer than a steam-engine which produces just as much per annum (l. c., p. 130). "The buyer of the first knows that it will pay his wages and interest, plus the increase of its value by use. The buyer of the other knows it will give him wages and interest, minus the diminution in its value by use [....] The one buys a machine that improves by use. The other, one that deteriorates with use [....] The one is a machine upon which new capital and labour may be expended with constantly increasing return; while upon the other no such expenditure can be made" (l.c., p. 131).

* * *

Even those improvements in agriculture which bring about reduced costs of production and eventually a fall in prices, but which first—so long as prices have not yet fallen—[call forth] a temporary rise of agricultural *profit*, almost never fail,

---

[a] The reference is to the land which has been worked and improved.—*Ed.*
[b] Carey wrote: "from its use".—*Ed.*

"...*to increase rent ultimately. The increased capital*, which is emloyed in consequence of the opportunity of making great temporary profits, *can seldom or ever be entirely removed from the land, at the expiration of the current leases;* and, *on the renewal of these leases*, the landlord feels the benefit of it in *the increase of his rents*" (Thomas Robert Malthus, *An Inquiry into the Nature and Progress of Rent*, London, 1815, p. 26).

* * *

"If until the prevalence of the late high prices, arable land in general bore but *little rent*, chiefly by reason of the *acknowledged necessity of frequent fallows*; the rents must be again reduced, to admit of a return to the same system" (James Deacon Hume, *Thoughts on the Corn-Laws*, London, 1815, p. 72). |XI-490a||

[5. Hodgskin and Anderson on the Growth of Productivity in Agricultural Labour]

||XIII-670a| "A diminishing surface suffices to supply man with food as population multiplies" ([Thomas] Hodgskin (anonymously), *The Natural and Artificial Right of Property Contrasted...*, London, 1832, p. 69).

Similar ideas were expressed by *Anderson* even earlier.[a] |XIII-670a||

---

[a] See this volume, pp. 144-45.—*Ed.*

38*

[6. Decrease in the Rate of Profit]

||XIII-670a| Calculated on the total capital the [rate of] profit of the larger capital, which employs more constant capital (machinery, raw material) and relatively less living labour, will be lower than that of the smaller [amount of] profit yielded by the smaller capital employing more living labour in proportion to the total capital. The [relative] decrease in variable capital and the relative increase in constant capital, although both parts are growing, is only another *expression for the increased productivity of labour.* |XIII-670a||

APPENDICES

QUOTATIONS IN FRENCH AND GERMAN[a]

24. « Le propriétaire fournit le domaine, les bâtiments, et ordinairement tout ou partie du bétail et des instrumens nécessaires à l'exploitation; le colon, de son côté, apporte son travail [...], et rien ou presque rien de plus; les produits de la terre se partagent par moitié.» (Mathieu de Dombasle, *Annales agricoles de Roville...*, Quatrième livraison. Paris, 1828, p. 301.)

24. «...les colons partiaires sont généralement des hommes plongés dans la misère... » (ibidem, p. 302.)

24. «... s'il[b] a o b t e n u[c] un accroissement de produit brut de 1500 fr., au moyen d'une avance de 1000 fr., i l f a u t q u ' i l p a r t a g e p a r m o i t i é [...] a v e c l e p r o p r i é t a i r e, en sorte qu'il ne retire que 750 fr., ou, en d'autres termes, qu'il perd un quart des ses avances... » (ibidem, p. 304.)

24 « Dans l'ancien système de culture, la dépense ou les frais de production sont pris presque entièrement sur les produits eux-mêmes en nature, par la consommation des bestiaux, du cultivateur et de sa famille ; il ne se fait presque aucune dépense en écus. C'est s e u l e m e n t c e t t e c i r c o n s t a n c e q u i a pu donner lieu de croire que le propriétaire et le colon pouvaient partager entre eux tout le produit des récoltes qui n'est pas consommé dans l'exploitation; m a i s i l f a u t q u e l ' o n s a c h e b i e n q u e c e t t e m a n i è r e d u p r o c é d e r n'est applicable qu'à ce genre d'agriculture, c ' e s t - à - d i r e à l'*agriculture misérable ;* c a r, aussitôt que l'on veut a p p o r t e r à l a c u l t u r e q u e l q u e a m é l i o r a t i o n, on s'aperçoit qu'on ne peut le f a i r e q u ' a u m o y e n de quelques avances dont il faut réserver le montant sur le produit brut, pour l'appliquer

---

[a] See Publishers' Note.—*Ed.*
[b] In the manuscript: "If the métayer".—*Ed.*
[c] Words and passages translated by Marx into German are set in spaced type.—*Ed.*

à la production de l'année suivante, en sorte que tout partage du produit brut, entre le propriétaire et le colon, forme un obstacle insurmon-
table à toute amélioration. »[a] (ibidem, p. 307.)

56. „Kapitalgewinnsatz". . . „das Verhältnis des Gewinns zum Kapital aus-
zudrücken", „ein Richtmass zur Gleichstellung der Kapitalgewinne abge-
geben." (Rodbertus, *Sociale Briefe an von Kirchmann. Dritter Brief,*
Berlin, 1851, S. 94.)

56. „der *Vermögensertrag* auf nichts anderes als Kapital berechnet werden
kann." (ibidem, S. 95.)

56. „grössre Teil des Nationalkapitals angewandt wird." (ibidem. S. 95.)

56. „bei der Fabrikation noch der *Wert sämtlichen Produkts der Land-*
wirtschaft als Material mit im Kapital, während dies in der Rohproduktion
nicht vorkommen kann." (ibidem, S. 95.)

56. „dass sich das Rohprodukt wie das Fabrikationsprodukt nach der Kostenarbeit vertauschen, dass der Wert des Rohprodukts nur äqual seiner
Kostenarbeit ist." (ibidem, S. 96.)

57. „Ich habe *angenommen,* dass sich die Rente im *Verhältnis des Werts*
des Rohprodukts und des Fabrikationsprodukts verteilt, und dass dieser
Wert durch die *Kostenarbeit* bestimmt wird." (ibidem, S. 96-97.)

58. „. . . sich die *Rente* im Verhältnis des *Werts* des Rohprodukts und des
Fabrikationsprodukts verteilt" . . . „dieser Wert durch die *Kostenarbeit*
bestimmt wird." (ibidem, S. 96-97.)

58. „Damit ist natürlich auch gesagt, dass die Grösse dieser Rententeile
nicht durch die *Grösse des Kapitals, auf das der Gewinn berechnet wird,*
sondern durch die *unmittelbare Arbeit,* sie sei landwirtschaftliche oder
Fabrikationsarbeit+derjenigen Arbeit, die wegen der vernutzten Werk-
zeuge und Maschinen mit aufzurechnen ist, bestimmt wird." (ibidem,
S. 97.)

58. „derjenige Kapitalteil, der in dem Materialwert besteht", Einfluß auf
die Größe der Rententeile haben, da „zum Beispiel die Kostenarbeit des
besonderen Produkts, das Gespinst oder Gewebe ist, nicht durch die
Kostenarbeit mitbestimmt werden kann, die der Wolle als Rohprodukt
zu berechnen ist". (ibidem, S. 97.)

59. „Dagegen figuriert doch der Wert des Rohprodukts oder der Materialwert als *Kapitalauslage* mit in dem Kapitalvermögen, auf das der
Besitzer den auf das Fabrikationsprodukt fallenden Rentenanteil als
Gewinn zu berechnen hat. In dem *landwirtschaftlichen Kapital* fehlt
aber dieser Kapitalteil. Die Landwirtschaft bedarf nicht Produkt einer
ihr vorangehenden Produktion zu Material, sondern beginnt überhaupt
erst die Produktion, und der dem Material analoge Vermögensteil in
der Landwirtschaft würde der Boden selbst sein, der aber kostenlos
vorausgesetzt wird." (ibidem, S. 97-98.)

59. „Die Landwirtschaft hat also mit der Fabrikation zwar die beiden
Kapitalteile gemein, die auf die Bestimmung der *Grösse* der Rententeile von Einfluss sind, aber nicht denjenigen, der hierzu nicht beiträgt,
auf den aber der durch jene Kapitalteile bestimmte Rententeil mit als

---

[a] Marx summarises part of this passage.—*Ed.*

Gewinn berechnet wird; dieser findet sich in dem Fabrikationskapital allein. Wenn also, auch nach der Annahme, dass sich der Wert des Rohprodukts wie des Fabrikationsprodukts nach der Kostenarbeit richtet, und da die Rente sich im Verhältnis dieses Werts an die Besitzer des Rohprodukts und Fabrikationsprodukts verteilt, *wenn* deshalb auch *die in der Rohproduktion und* |*Fabrikation abfallenden Rententeile im Verhältnis zu den Arbeitsquantitäten stehen, welche das respektive Produkt gekostet hat, so stehen doch die in der Landwirtschaft und Fabrikation angewandten Kapitalien, auf welche die Rententeile als Gewinn repartiert werden* — und zwar in der Fabrikation ganz, in der Landwirtschaft nach dem *dort* resultierenden Gewinnsatz—, nicht in demselben Verhältnis wie jene Arbeitsquantitäten und die durch diese bestimmten Rententeile. Vielmehr ist bei *gleicher Grösse der auf das Rohprodukt und das Fabrikationsprodukt fallenden Rententeile,* das Fabrikationskapital um den ganzen darin enthaltenen Materialwert grösser als das landwirtschaftliche Kapital und da dieser Materialwert zwar das *Fabrikationskapital, auf der abfallende Rententeil als Gewinn berechnet wird, aber nicht auch diesen Gewinn selbst vergrösert,* und also auch zugleich noch dazu dient, *den Kapitalgewinnsatz,* der auch in der *Landwirtschaft* normiert, zu *erniedrigen,* so muss notwendig auch von dem in der Landwirtschaft abfallenden Rententeil ein Teil übrigbleiben, der nicht von der *Gewinnberechnung nach diesem Gewinnsatz* absorbiert wird." (ibidem, S. 98-99.)

65. „Nur wenn der Wert des Rohprodukts *unter* die Kostenarbeit fällt, ist es möglich dass auch in der Landwirtschaft der ganze auf *das Rohprodukt fallende Rententeil von der Kapitalgewinnberechnung absorbiert wird,* denn dann ist es möglich, dass dieser Rententeil so verringert wird, dass dadurch zwischen ihm und dem landwirtschaftlichen Kapital, obwohl darin ein Materialwert fehlt, doch ein gleiches Verhältnis erzeugt wird, wie es zwischen dem auf das Fabrikationsprodukt fallenden Rententeil und dem Fabrikationskapital besteht, obwohl in diesem letztren ein Materialwert enthalten ist; nur dann ist es also möglich, dass auch in der Landwirtschaft keine Rente ausser Kapitalgewinn übrigbleibt. Insofern aber im wirklichen Verkehr wenigstens die Gravitation nach jenem Gesetz, dass der Wert der Kostenarbeit äqual ist, die Regel bildet, bildet auch die Grundrente die Regel, und es ist nicht, wie Ricardo meint, der ursprüngliche Zustand, sondern nur eine Abnormität, wenn keine Grundrente, sondern nur Kapitalgewinn abfällt." (ibidem, S. 100.)

69. „Die *Pacht* ist ihrer Natur nach immer *Grudrente.*" (ibidem, S. 113.)

71. „*Höhe des Kapitalgewinnes und Zinsen.*" (ibidem, S. 113.)

71. „...ergibt sich aus deren Proportion zum Kapital.... Bei allen zivilisierten Nationen ist die Kapitalsumme von 100 als die Einheit angenommen, die den Maßstab für die zu berechnende Höhe abgibt. Je grösser also die Verhältniszahl ist, die der auf das Kapital fallende Gewinn- oder Zinsenbetrag zu 100 gibt, mit anderen Worten, je ‚mehr Prozente' ein Kapital abwirft, desto *höher* stehen Gewinn und Zins." (ibidem, S. 113-14.)

71. „Die Höhe *der Grundrente und der Pacht* argibt sich aus deren Proportion zu einem bestimmten Grundstück." (ibidem, S. 114.)

71. „Die *Höhe des Bodenwerts* ergibt sich aus der Kapitalisation der Grundrente eines bestimmten Grundstücks. Je grösser die Kapitalsumme ist, welche die Kapitalisation der Grundrente eines Grundstücks von einem bestimmten Flächenmass gibt, desto *höher* steht der Bodenwert." (ibidem, S. 114.)

72. „Was *entscheidet nun über die Höhe des Kapitalgewinnes und der Grundrente?"* (ibidem, S. 115.)

72. „I.) Bei einem gegebenen Produktwert oder dem Produkt einer gegebenen Quantität Arbeit oder, was wieder dasselbe ist, bei einem gegebenen Nationalprodukt steht die Höhe der Rente überhaupt in umgekehrtem Verhältnis zu der Höhe des Arbeitslohnes und in gradem Verhältnis zu der Höhe der Produktivität der Arbeit überhaupt. Je niedriger der Arbeitslohn, desto höher die Rente; je höher die Produktivität der Arbeit überhaupt, desto niedriger der Arbeitslohn und desto höher die Rente." (ibidem, S. 115-16.)

72. „...*Grösse* dieses zur Rente übrigbleibenden Teils". (ibidem, S. 117.)

72. „...von *dem* Teile des Produktwerts, der zum Kapital*ersatz* dient ... ausser acht gelassen werden kann". (ibidem, S. 117.)

72. „wenn der Arbeitslohn fällt, das heisst fortan eine kleinere Quote des ganzen Produktwerts ausmacht, das *gesamte* Kapital, auf welches der *andere Teil der Rente* als Gewinn zu berechnen ist, kleiner wird. Nun konstituiert aber allein der Verhältnissatz zwischen dem Wert, der Kapitalgewinn oder Grundrente wird, zu dem Kapital respektive der Grundfläche, auf die er als solche zu *berechnen* ist, die *Höhe* derselben. Lässt also der Arbeitslohn einen grössren Wert zu Rente übrig, so ist auf das selbst *verringerte Kapital* und die gleich grosse Grundfläche ein grösser Wert als Gewinn und Grundrente zu berechnen, die daraus sich ergebende Proportionszahl beider wird grösser, und es sind also beide zusammengenommen oder die Rente überhaupt höher geworden ... es ist vorausgesetzt, dass der Produktwert überhaupt sich gleichbleibt.... Deshalb, *weil der Lohn, welchen die Arbeit kostet, geringer wird,* wird noch *nicht die Arbeit, die das Produkt kostet, geringer."* (ibidem, S. 117-18.)

73. „dem *Betrage des notwendigen Unterhalts,* das heisst einem für ein bestimmtes Land und einen bestimmten Zeitraum *ziemlich gleichen, bestimmten realen Produktquantum."* (ibidem, S. 118.)

73. „...wenn der Arbeitslohn, als notwendiger Unterhalt, ein bestimmtes reales Produktquantum ist, so muss derselbe, wenn der Produktwert hoch ist, einen grossen Wert, wenn er niedrig ist, einen geringen Wert ausmachen, also auch, da ein gleicher Produktwert als zur Teilung kommend angenommen ist, wenn der Produktwert hoch ist, einen grossen Teil, wenn er niedrig ist, einen geringen Teil davon absorbieren, und endlich also auch eine grosse respektive eine kleine Quote des Produktwerts zu Rente übriglassen. Wenn aber die Regel gilt, dass der Wert des Produkts äqual der Quantität Arbeit ist, die dasselbe gekostet hat, so entscheidet wieder über die *Höhe des Produktwerts lediglich die Produktivität der Arbeit* oder das Verhältnis der Menge des Produkts zu der Quantität der Arbeit, die zu seiner Produktion verwandt ist ... wenn dieselbe Quantität Arbeit mehr Produkt hervorbringt, mit

anderen Worten, wenn die Produktivität steigt, so haftet auf demselben
Quantum Produkt weniger Arbeit; und umgekehrt, wenn dieselbe Quantität Arbeit weniger Produkt hervorbringt, mit andren Worten, wenn
die Produktivität sinkt, so haftet auf demselben Quantum Produkt mehr
Arbeit. Nun bestimmt aber *die Quantität Arbeit den Wert des Produkts,* und der *verhältnismässige Wert eines bestimmten Quantums von
Produkt die Höhe des Produktwerts....* die Rente überhaupt ... *desto
höher sein, je höher die Produktivität der Arbeit überhaupt steht.*"
(ibidem, S. 119-20.)

74. „II.) Ist bei einem gegebenen Produktwert die Höhe der Rente überhaupt gegeben, so steht die Höhe der Grundrente respektive des Kapitalgewinnes in umgekehrtem Verhältnis sowohl zueinander als auch
zu der Produktivität respektive der Rohproduktionsarbeit und der Fabrikationsarbeit. Je höher oder niedriger die Grundrente, desto niedriger oder höher der Kapitalgewinn und umgekehrt; je höher oder
niedriger die Produktivität der Rohproduktionsarbeit oder der Fabrikationsarbeit, desto niedriger oder höher die Grundrente oder der
Kapitalgewinn, und wechselweise also auch desto höher oder niedriger
der Kapitalgewinn oder die Grundrente." (ibidem, S. 116.)

75. „... der als Rente überhaupt zur Teilung kommende *Wert des Arbeitsprodukts* ... aus dem Wert des Rohprodukts+dem Wert des Fabrikationsprodukts besteht." (ibidem, S. 120.)

75. „Der Rententeil, welcher auf das Fabrikationsprodukt fällt und den
Kapitalgewinnsatz bestimmt, wird nicht bloss auf das zur Herstellung
dieses Produkts wirklich verwandte Kapital, sondern auch auf den
ganzen Rohproduktwert, der als *Materialwert* im Unternehmungsfonds
des Fabrikanten mitfiguriert, als Gewinn repartiert; bei dem Rententeil hingegen, welcher auf das Rohprodukt fällt und von *dem der
Gewinn für das in der Rohproduktion verwandte Kapital nach dem
in der Fabrikation gegebnen Gewinnsatz* berechnet wird, der Rest aber
zu Grundrente übrigbleibt, fehlt ein solcher Materialwert." (ibidem,
S. 121.)

75. „Die Höhe der Rente überhaupt ist von einem gegebenen Produktwert
gleichfalls gegeben." (ibidem, S. 121.)

79. „... weil der Flächenraum oder die Morgenzahl, auf welche er berechnet
wird, dieselbe geblieben ist, und also auf den einzelnen Morgen eine
grössere Wertsumme kommt." (ibidem, S. 122.)

81. „Zum Beispiel die *Kostenarbeit* des besondren Produkts, das W e i z e n
oder B a u m w o l l e ist, kann nicht durch die Kostenarbeit mitbestimmt
werden, die d e m P f l u g o d e r d e m g i n a l s M a s c h i n e zu
berechnen ist. Dagegen figuriert doch der Wert der M a s c h i n e oder
der M a s c h i n e n w e r t mit in dem Kapitalvermögen, auf das der
Besitzer den auf das R o h p r o d u k t fallenden Rentenanteil als Gewinn zu berechnen hat." (cf. ibidem, S. 97.)

85. „Es ist aber wieder nur die Produktivität der Rohproduktionsarbeit
respektive der Fabrikationsarbeit, welche die verhältnismässige Höhe
des Rohproduktwerts respektive des Fabrikationsproduktwerts oder die
Anteile, die beide vom ganzen Produktwert einnehmen, bestimmen.
Der Rohproduktwert wird desto höher sein, je niedriger die Produk-

tivität der Rohproduktionsarbeit steht, und umgekehrt. Ebenso wird der Fabrikationsproduktwert desto höher sein, je niedriger die Produktivität der Fabrikation steht, und umgekehrt. Es muss also auch bei einer gegebenen Höhe der Rente überhaupt, da hoher Rohproduktwert hohe Grundrente und niedrigen Kapitalgewinn, hoher Fabrikationswert hohen Kapitalgewinn und niedrige Grundrente bewirkt, die Höhe der Grundrente und die des Kapitalgewinns nicht bloss im umgekehrten Verhältnis zueinander, sondern auch zu der Produktivität ihrer respektiven Arbeiten, der Rohproduktions- und der Fabrikationsarbeit stehen." (ibidem, S. 123.)

86. „Die *Höhe des Kapitalgewinnes* wird lediglich durch die *Höhe des Produktwerts* überhaupt und des Rohproduktwerts und Fabrikationsproduktwerts insbesondre oder durch das Produktivitätsverhältnis der Arbeit überhaupt und der Rohproduktions- und Fabrikationsarbeit insbesondre bestimmt; die *Höhe* der Grundrente hängt ausserdem auch von der *Grösse des Produktwerts* oder der *Quantität Arbeit oder Produktivkraft* ab, die bei *einem gegebenen Produktivitätsverhältnis* zur Produktion verwandt wird." (ibidem, S. 116-17.)

87. „In demselben Verhältnis, in welchem sich infolge der *Vermehrung des Produktwerts* die Summe des Kapitalgewinnes vermehrt, vermehrt sich also auch die Summe des Kapitalwerts, auf die der Gewinn zu berechnen ist, und der bisherige Verhältnissatz zwischen Gewinn und Kapital wird durch jene Vermehrung des Kapitalgewinns gar nicht alteriert." (ibidem, S. 125.)

87. „Die Grundrente kann daher aus einem in der nationalökonomischen Entwicklung der Gesellschaft überall eintretenden Grunde, der Vermehrung der zur Produktion verwandten Arbeit, mit anderen Worten, der *zunehmenden Bevölkerung* steigen, ohne dass dabei eine *Steigerung* des Rohproduktwerts zu erfolgen brauchte, da schon der Bezug von Grundrente von *mehr* Rohprodukt solche Wirkung haben muss." (ibidem, S. 127.)

88. „*dass der Kapitalgewinn jemals 100 Prozent betragen könnte,* er muss, so hoch er sein mag, stets bedeutend weniger betragen". (ibidem, S. 128.)

88. „Denn er resultiert lediglich aus dem Teilungsverhältnis des Produktwerts. Er kann daher immer nur einen *Bruchteil* dieser Einheit betragen." (ibidem, S. 127-28.)

89. „auf die gleichgebliebne Morgenzahl des Grundstücks". (ibidem, S. 132.)

89. „...bei den europäischen Nationen ist die Produktivität der Arbeit überhaupt—der Rohproduktions- und der Fabrikationsarbeiten — gestiegen ... infolge davon sich die Quote des Nationalprodukts, die auf Arbeitslohn verwandt wird, verringert, diejenige, die zu Rente übrigbleibt, vergrössert, ... also *ist die Rente überhaupt gestiegen.*" (ibidem, S. 138-39.)

89. „... die Produktivität der Fabrikation hat in *grössrem Verhältnis* zugenommen als die der Rohproduktion ... deshalb ist heute von einem gleichen Quantum Nationalproduktwert die Rentenquote, die auf Rohprodukt fällt, grösser als die, welche auf das Fabrikationsprodukt fällt, deshalb ist also ungeachtet der Steigerung der Rente überhaupt,

doch nur die *Grundrente gestiegen, der Kapitalgewinn hingegen gefallen".* (ibidem, S. 139.)

91. „...infolge der gestiegenen Bevölkerung hat sich auch die Summe des Nationalproduktwerts ausserordentlich vermehrt ... deshalb wird heute *mehr* Lohn, *mehr* Gewinn, *mehr* Grundrente in der Nation bezogen ... auch noch dieser *mehrere* Bezug von Grundrente hat dieselbe erhöht, während eine solche Wirkung des *mehreren* Bezugs beim Lohn und Gewinn nicht hat eintreten können". (ibidem, S. 139.)

106. „Die aus einer *Vermehrung* des nationalen Produktwerts herrührende *Vermehrung* von respektivem Arbeitslohn, Kapitalgewinn und Grundrente können weder den Arbeitslohn noch den Kapitalgewinn der Nation *erhöhen,* da der mehrere Arbeitslohn sich nun auch unter mehrere Arbeiter verteilt, und der mehrere Kapitalgewinn auf ein in demselben Verhältnis vermehrtes Kapital fällt, dagegen die Grundrente allerdings *erhöhen* muss, da diese immer auf die *gleich gross gebliebenen* Grundstücke fällt. So vermag sie die grosse *Steigerung des Bodenwerts,* der nichts als die nach dem üblichen Zinsfuss kapitalisierte Grundrente ist, zu Genüge zu erklären, ohne ihre Zuflucht zu einer steigenden Unproduktivität der landwirtschaftlichen Arbeit zu nehmen, die der Idee der Perfektibilität der menschlichen Gesellschaft wie allen landwirtschaftlichen und statistischen Tatsachen schnurstracks widerspricht." (ibidem, S. 160-61.)

122. „Merkwürdig, wie eine Lehre, die 1777 *fast* unbeachtet blieb, 1815 ff. gleich mit dem grössten Interesse verteidigt und bekämpft wurde, weil sie den inzwischen so schroff ausgebildeten Gegensatz des monied and landed interest berührte." (Wilhelm Roscher, *Die Grundlagen der Nationalökonomie. Ein Hand- und Lesebuch für Geschäftsmänner und Studierende,* Dritte Auflage, Stuttgart und Augsburg, 1858, S. 297-98.)

145. „...la terre, qué, par la labourage et les engrais elle change de nature et devient *toujours* meilleure..." Camillo Tarello da Lonato, *Ricordo d'Agricoltura,* quoted by James Anderson, in *A Calm Investigation of the Circumstances that have led to the Present Scarcity of Grain in Britain,* London, 1801, p. 38., note. (See this volume, Note 56.)

149. „Sie erklärt ... aus *einer Teilung des Arbeitsprodukts,* die mit Notwendigkeit eintritt, wenn zwei Vorbedingungen, hinlängliche Produktivität der Arbeit und Grund- und Kapitaleigentum, gegeben sind, alle Erscheinungen des Arbeitslohns und der Rente, etc. Sie erklärt, dass allein die hinlängliche Produktivität der Arbeit die *wirtschaftliche Möglichkeit einer solchen Teilung* konstituiert, indem diese Produktivität dem Produktwert soviel realen Inhalt gibt, dass noch andre Personen, die nicht arbeiten, davon mitleben können, und sie erklärt, dass allein das Grundeigentum und Kapitaleigentum die *rechtliche Wirklichkeit* einer *solchen Teilung* konstituiert, indem es die Arbeiter zwingt, sich *ihr Produkt* mit den nicht arbeitenden Grund- und Kapitalbesitzern sogar in dem Verhältnis zu *teilen,* dass grade sie, die Arbeiter, nur soviel davon bekommen, dass sie leben können." (Rodbertus, *Sociale Briefe an von Kirchmann. Dritter Brief,* Berlin, 1851, S. 156-57.)

150. „Sie wissen, dass *alle Nationalökonomen* schon seit Adam Smith den *Wert des Produkts in Arbeitslohn, Grundrente und Kapitalgewinn* zer-

fallen lassen und dass also die Idee, das Einkommen der verschiedenen Klassen und namentlich auch die Rententeile *auf eine Teilung des Produkts* zu gründen, nicht neu ist. Allein sofort geraten die Nationalökonomen auf Abwege. Alle—selbst nicht mit Ausnahme der Ricardoschen Schule—begehen *zuvörderst* den Fehler, nicht das *ganze* Produkt, das *vollendete* Gut, das *ganze Nationalprodukt* als die Einheit aufzufassen, an der Arbeiter, Grundbesitzer und Kapitalisten partizipieren, sondern die *Teilung des Rohprodukts* als eine *besondre Teilung,* an der *drei Teilnehmer,* und die Teilung des Fabrikationsprodukts wieder als eine besondre Teilung aufzufassen, an der *nur zwei* Teilnehmer partizipieren. So sehen diese Systeme schon das blosse Rohprodukt und das blosse Fabrikationsprodukt jedes für sich als ein besondres Einkommensgut an." (ibidem, S. 162.)

153. „Auch er teilt nicht das *fertige* Produkt unter die Beteiligten, sondern nimmt ebenso wie die übrigen Nationalökonomen das landwirtschaftliche Produkt wie das Fabrikationsprodukt, jedes als ein besondres der Teilung unterliegendes Produkt an." (ibidem, S. 167.)

153. „Das Kapitaleigentum ist ihm gegeben und *zwar nach früher* als das Grundeigentum. . . . So beginnt er nicht mit den Gründen, sondern mit der *Tatsache* der Teilung des Produkts, und seine ganze Theorie beschränkt sich auf die Ursachen, welche das *Teilungsverhältnis* desselben bestimmen und modifizieren. . . . Die Teilung des Produkts nur in *Lohn* und *Kapitalgewinn* ist ihm die *ursprüngliche* und ursprünglich auch die einzige." (ibidem, S. 167.)

154. „Sie könnten behaupten wollen, dass wie *ursprünglich* das Gesetz der Gleichheit des Kapitalgewinns die Rohproduktpreise so hätte drücken müssen, dass die Grundrente hätte verschwinden müssen, um dann nur wieder infolge einer Preissteigerung aus der Ertragsdifferenz des fruchtbareren und unfruchtbareren Bodens zu entstehn, dass so auch *heute* die Vorteile eines Grundrentenbezugs neben dem üblichen Kapitalgewinn Kapitalisten veranlassen würden, so lange Kapital auf neue Urbarmachungen und Meliorationen zu verwenden, bis durch die dadurch bewirkte Überfüllung des Marktes die Preise hinlänglich erniedrigt wären, um bei den unvorteilhaftesten Kapitalanlagen den Grundrentenbezug verschwinden zu lassen. *Mit andren Worten wäre das die Behauptung, dass das Gesetz der Gleichheit der Kapitalgewinne das andre Gesetz, dass der Wert der Produkte sich nach der Kostenarbeit richtet, für das Rohprodukt aufhöbe,* während gerade *Ricardo* im ersten Kapitel seines Werks jenes benutzt, um dieses darzutun." (ibidem, S. 174.)

155. „Kann es wahr sein, dass, *ehe* überhaupt zum Ackerbau geschritten wird, schon Kapitalisten existieren, die Gewinn beziehen und nach dem Gesetz der Gleichheit desselben ihre Kapitalien anlegen?. . . Ich gestehe zu, dass, wenn heute von zivilisierten Ländern aus nach einem neuen unbebauten Lande eine Expedition unternommen wird, bei welcher die reicheren Teilnehmer mit den Vorräten und Werkzeugen einer schon alten Kultur—mit Kapital—versehen sind und die ärmeren in der Aussicht mitgehen, im Dienst der ersteren einen hohen Lohn zu gewinnen, dass dann die Kapitalisten das, was ihnen über den Lohn der Arbeiter hinaus verbleibt, als ihren Gewinn betrachten werden, denn sie führen längst vor-

handene Dinge und Begriffe aus dem Mutterlande mit sich." (ibidem, S. 174-75.)

155. „*vor* Anbau des Bodens." (ibidem, S. 176.)

155. „Erst wenn ... in der Gesellschaft Kapital entstanden ist und Kapitalgewinn gekannt und bezahlt wird, soll nach... Ricardoscher Auffassung die Kultur des Bodens beginnen." (ibidem, S. 178.)

156. „In jedem Lande ist der grösste Teil des Bodens schon viel früher im Eigentum gewesen, als er angebaut worden ist; namentlich schon längst, wenn in den Gewerben ein Kapitalgewinnsatz gegeben ist." (ibidem, S. 179.)

156. „parzellenweise erst an die Anbauer, freilich auch für einen geringen Preis, der aber doch *jedenfalls* schon eine Grundrente repräsentieren muss." (ibidem, S. 179-80.)

156. „Die sub b enthaltene Ursache der Steigerung, behaupte ich aber, hat die Grundrente vor dem Kapitalgewinn voraus. Dieser kann *niemals* deshalb steigen, weil infolge der Vermehrung des Nationalproduktwerts bei *gleicher Produktivität*, aber vermehrter Produktivkraft (gestiegner Bevölkerung), *mehr* Kapitalgewinn in der Nation abfällt, denn dieser *mehrere* Kapitalgewinn fällt immer auf ein in demselben *Verhältnis vermehrtes Kapital*, der Gewinnsatz bleibt also gleich hoch." (ibidem, S. 184-85.)

157. „Möglich, dass im Lauf dieser dreissig Jahre durch Parzellierungen oder *selbst durch Urbarmachung mehrere* Besitztümer entstanden waren und die vermehrte Grundrente sich also auch unter *mehrere* Besitzer teilte, aber sie *verteilte sich 1830 nicht auf mehr Morgen als 1800*; jene neuen abgezweigten oder neu kultivierten Grundstücke waren mit ihrer ganzen Morgenzahl früher in *den älteren Grundstücken mitbegriffen gewesen*, und die geringere Grundrente von 1800 war also damals so gut auf sie *mitrepartiert* worden und hatte damals die Höhe der englischen Grundrente überhaupt bestimmen helfen, als 1830 die grössere." (ibidem, S. 186.)

157. „Ricardo beschränkt die Bodenrente auf dasjenige, was dem Grundbesitzer für die Benutzung der *unrsprünglichen, natürlichen und unzerstörbaren Bodenkräfte* bezahlt wird. Er will damit alles, was bei schon kultivierten Grundstücken dem Kapital zugut geschrieben werden müsste, von der Grundrente abgezogen wissen. Allein es ist klar, dass er aus dem Ertrage eines Grundstücks niemals mehr als die *vollen landesüblichen Zinsen* dem Kapital anrechnen darf. Denn er würde sonst in der nationalökonomischen Entwicklung eines Landes zwei verschiedne Gewinnsätze annehmen müssen, einen landwirtschaftlichen, der grösseren Gewinn als den in der Fabrikation herrschenden abwürfe, und diesen letzteren— eine Annahme indessen, die gerade sein System, das auf Gleichheit des Gewinnsatzes basiert ist, umstossen würde." (ibidem, S. 215-16.)

158. « La rente, dans le sens de Ricardo, est la propriété foncière à l'état bourgeois : « c'est-à-dire la propriété féodale qui a subi les conditions de la production bourgeoise. » (Karl Marx, *Misère de la Philosophie. Réponse à la Philosophie de la misère de M. Proudhon*, Paris et Bruxelles, **1847**, p. 156.)

158. « Ricardo, après avoir supposé la production bourgeoise comme nécessaire pour déterminer la rente, l'applique néanmoins à la propriété foncière de toutes les époques et de tous les pays. Ce sont là les errements
de tous les économistes, qui représentent les rapports de la production
bourgeoise comme des catégories éternelles. » (ibidem, p. 160.)

158. « Les terres capitaux peuvent être *augmentées* tout aussi bien que tous
les autres instruments de production. On n'y ajoute rien à la matière, pour
parler le langage de M. Proudhon, mais on *multiplie les terres qui servent
d'instrument de production.* Rien qu'à appliquer à des terres déjà trans-
formées en moyen de production de secondes mises de capital, on augmente la terre capital sans rien ajouter à la terre matière, c'est-à-dire à
l'étendue de la terre. » (ibidem, p. 165.)

159. « En premier lieu, on ne peut pas, comme dans l'industrie manufac-
turière, *multiplier à volonté les instruments de production du même
degré de productivité*, c'est-à-dire les terrains du même degré de fécondité. Puis, à mesure que la population s'accroît, on en vient à exploiter
des terrains d'une qualité inférieure, ou à faire sur le même terrain de
nouvelles mises de capital proportionellement moins productives que les
premières. » (ibidem, p. 157.)

159. „Aber ich muss noch auf einen anderen Umstand aufmerksam machen,
der freilich weit allmählicher, aber auch noch weit allgemeiner aus
schlechtern landwirtschaftlichen Maschinen bessre macht. Es ist dies
die *fortgesetzte Bewirtschaftung* eines Grundstücks selbst, lediglich nach
einem vernünftigen System, ohne dass die geringste aussergewöhnliche
Kapitalanlage hinzuträte." (Karl Rodbertus, *Sociale Briefe an von
Kirchmann. Dritter Brief*, Berlin, 1851, S. 222.)

159. „Sie müssten beweisen, dass die mit Ackerbau beschäftigte Arbeiterbe-
völkerung im Laufe der Zeit in grösserem Verhältnisse zugenommen
hätte als die Produktion von Lebensmitteln oder auch nur als der
übrige Teil der Bevölkerung eines Landes. Daraus allein könnte un-
widerleglich hervorgehen, dass mit der Zunahme der landwirtschaftlichen Produktion auch zunehmend mehr Arbeit darauf verwandt werden müsste. Aber gerade darin widerspricht ihnen die Statistik."
(ibidem, S. 274.)

159. „Ja, Sie finden sogar [ziemlich] allgemein die Regel vorherrschend, dass
je dichter die Bevölkerung eines Landes ist, in desto geringerem Verhältnis sich Menschen mit dem Ackerbau beschäftigen.... Dieselbe
Erscheinung zeigt sich bei der Zunahme der Bevölkerung desselben
Landes: der Teil, der sich *nicht* mit Ackerbau beschäftigt, wird fast
überall in stärkerem Verhältnis zunehmen." (ibidem, S. 275.)

159. „...heute der Landwirt das in seiner eignen Wirtschaft gebaute Futter
des Zugviehs nicht als Kapital an".... (ibidem, S. 78.)

159. „Kapital an sich oder im nationalwirtschaftlichen Sinn ist Produkt,
das weiter zur Produktion benutzt wird.... Aber in bezug auf einen
besondren Gewinn, den es abwerfen soll, oder im Sinn der *heutigen
Unternehmer,* muss es als *,Auslage'* auftreten, um Kapital zu sein."
(ibidem, S. 77.)

160. „Der *Wert* der besondren Resultate dieser verschiednen Arbeiten ist noch nicht das ihrem Besitzer zufallende Einkommen selbst, sondern nur erst der Liquidationsmaßstab dafür. Dies respektive Einkommen selbst ist Teil des gesellschaftlichen Einkommens, das lediglich durch die zusammenwirkende Arbeit der Landwirtschaft und Fabrikation hergestellt wird, und dessen *Teile* also auch nur durch diese Zusammenwirkung hergestellt werden." (ibidem, S. 36.)

166. «...sous[a] prétexte de l'étendre, ils l'ont[b] poussée dans le vide.» (Jean-Baptiste Say, *Traité d'économie politique...*, t. I, Paris, 1826, in *Discours préliminaire*, p. LXXXIII à LXXXIV.)

216. «...il y a toujours quelque marchandises ... dont le prix se résout en *deux* parties seulement ; les salaires du travail et les profits des fonds...» (Adam Smith, *Recherches sur la nature et les causes de la richesse des nations*. Traduction nouvelle...par Germain Garnier, t. I, Paris, 1802, p. 103.)

217. «*Salaire, profit* et *rente* sont *les trois sources primitives* de tout revenu, aussi bien que de *toute valeur échangeable.*» (ibidem, p. 105.)

218. «*Du prix naturel des marchandises, et de leur prix de marché.*» (ibidem, p. 110.)

218. «Dans chaque société ou canton, *il y* a un taux *moyen ordinaire* [...] pour les salaires [...] les profits [...] les rentes...» (ibidem, p. 110.)

218. «On peut appeler ce taux moyen [...] le *taux naturel* du salaire, du profit et de la rente, pour le tems et le lieu dans lesquels ce taux domine communément.» (ibidem, pp. 110-11.)

218. «Lorsque *le prix* d'une marchandise n'est ni plus ni moins que ce qu'il faut pour payer suivant leurs taux *naturels,* et la rente de la terre et les salaires de travail, et les profits du capital [...] alors cette marchandise est vendue ce [...] son *prix naturel.*» (ibidem, p. 111.)

218. « La marchandise est alors *vendue précisement ce qu'elle vaut* ou ce qu'*elle coûte* réellement à la personne qui la porte au marché ; car quoique, dans le langage ordinaire, quand on parle de ce qu'une marchandise *coûte en première main,* on *n'y comprenne pas le profit* de la personne qui fait métier de la vendre, cependant si celle-ci la vendait à un *prix qui ne lui rendît pas son profit au taux ordinaire* du canton, il est évident qu'elle perdrait à ce métier, puisqu'elle aurait pu faire *ce profit en employant son capital d'une autre manière.*» (ibidem, p. 111.)

220. «...le *prix naturel o u la valeur* entière des rente, profit et salaire qu'il faut payer pour qu'elle vienne au marché.» (ibidem, p. 112.)

220. «...*valeur entière* des rente, salaires et profits *qu'il en coûte pour amener cette marchandise au marché...*» (ibidem, p. 113.)

---

[a] In the manuscript: "que sous".—*Ed.*
[b] In the manuscript: "on la".—*Ed.*

220. « Quand la quantité amenée au marché suffit tout juste pour remplir la demande effective, et rien de plus, le *prix de marché* se trouve naturellement être précisément ... le même que le *prix naturel.* » (ibidem, p. 114.)

220. « Le prix *naturel* est donc pour ainsi dire le point central vers lequel gravitent continuellement les prix de toutes les marchandises. Différentes circonstances accidentelles peuvent quelquefois les tenir un certain tems élevés au dessus, et quelquefois les forcer à descendre un peu au dessous de ce prix. » (ibidem, p. 116.)

220. « ...somme totale d'industrie employée annuellement à l'effet de faire venir au marché une marchandise ... demande effective. » (ibidem, p. 117.)

221. « ...la même quantité d'industrie produira, en différentes années, des quantités fort différentes de marchandises, pendant que, dans d'autres emplois, elle produira la même ou très-approchant la même quantité. Le même nombre d'ouvriers employés à la culture produira, en différentes années, des quantités fort différentes de blé, de vin, d'huile, de houblon, etc. Mais le même nombre de fileurs et de tisserands produira chaque année la même ou très-approchant la même quantité de toile ou de drap. ...Dans l'autre espèce d'industrie, le *produit de quantités égales de travail étant toujours le même* ou très-approchant le même, il peut s'assortir plus exactement à la demande effective. » (ibidem, p. 117-118.)

221. « ...quantités égales de travail... » (ibidem, p. 118.)

221. « ...quantités[a] égales de travail... » (ibidem, p. 118.)

221. « ...quantités[a] égales de travail... » (ibidem, p. 118.)

221. « Quelle que soit la partie de ce prix qui soit payée au-dessous du taux *naturel*, les personnes qui y ont intérêt sentiront bientôt le dommage qu'elles éprouvent, et aussitôt *elles retireront, ou tant de terre, ou tant de travail, ou tant de capitaux de ce genre d'emploi*, que la quantité de cette marchandise qui sera amenée au marché ne sera bientôt plus que suffisante pour répondre à la demande effective, ainsi son *prix de marché* remontera bientôt au *prix naturel*, au moins sera-ce le cas où règne une entière liberté. » (ibidem, p. 125.)

222. « Le *prix naturel* varie lui-même avec le *taux naturel* de chacune de ses parties constituantes, le salaire, le profit et la rente... » (ibidem, p. 127.)

222. « *Des salaires du travail.* » (ibidem, p. 129.)

222. « Il faut de toute nécessité qu'un homme vive de son travail, et que son salaire suffise au moins à sa subsistance ; il faut même quelque chose de plus dans la plupart des circonstances, autrement il lui serait impossible d'élever une famille, et alors la race de ces ouvriers ne pourrait pas durer au-delà de la première génération. » (ibidem, p. 136.)

223. « ...les salaires du travail ... ne suivent pas les fluctuations du prix des denrées. » (ibidem, p. 149.)

---

[a] In the manuscript: "des quantités".—*Ed.*

223. « ... les salaires varient plus que le prix des denrées d'un lieu à un autre[a]. » (ibidem, p. 150.)

224. « ... comme un avantage ou comme un inconvénient pour la société ? » (ibidem, p. 159.)

224. « ... composent la très-majeure partie de toute grande société politique. Or, peut-on jamais regarder comme un désavantage pour le tout, ce qui améliore le sort de la plus grande partie? Une société ne peut sûrement pas être réputée dans le bonheur et la prospérité, quand la très-majeure partie de ses membres sont pauvres et misérables. La seule équité d'ailleurs exige que ceux qui nourrissent, habillent et logent *tout* le *corps de la nation*, aient *dans le produit de leur propre travail,* une *part suffisante* pour être eux-mêmes passablement nourris, vêtus et logés. » (ibidem, pp. 159-60.)

224. « Quoique, sans aucun doute, la pauvreté décourage le mariage, cependent elle ne l'empêche pas toujours ; elle paraît même être favorable à la génération... La stérilité, qui est si fréquente chez les femmes du grand monde, est extrêmement rare parmi celles d'une condition inférieure... Mais si la pauvreté n'empêche pas d'engendrer des enfants, elle est un très-grand obstacle à ce qu'on puisse les élever. Le tendre rejeton est produit, mais c'est dans un sol si froid, et dans un climat si rigoureux que bientôt il se dessèche et périt.... Naturellement toutes les espèces animales multiplient à proportion de leurs moyens de subsistance, et aucune espèce ne peut jamais multiplier au-delà. Mais dans les sociétés civilisée, ce n'est que parmi les classes inférieures du peuple que la disette de subsistance peut mettre des bornes à la propagation, ultérieure de l'espèce humaine... C'est... *la demande d'hommes règle nécessairement la production des hommes,* comme fait la demande à l'égard de toute autre marchandise ; elle hâte la production quand celle-ci marche trop lentement, et l'arrête quand elle va trop vîte. » (ibidem, pp. 160-63 passim.)

224. « Les salaires qu'on paie à des gens de journée et domestiques de toute espèce, doivent être tels que ceux-ci puissent, l'un dans l'autre, *continuer* à *maintenir leur population,* suivant que peut le requérir l'état croissant ou décroissant, ou bien stationnaire de la demande qu'en fait la société. » (ibidem, p. 164.)

224. « ... sous l'administration d'un maître peu attentif ou d'un inspecteur négligent. » (ibidem, p. 164.)

225. « Le fonds destiné à remplacer et à réparer, pour ainsi dire, le *déchet* résultant du tems et du service dans la personne de l'esclave, est ordinairement sous l'administration d'un maître peu attentif ou d'un inspecteur négligent. Celui qui est destiné au même emploi, à l'égard du serviteur libre, est économisé par les mains mêmes du serviteur libre.

---

[a] In the manuscript: "l'autre."—*Ed.*

Dans l'administration du premier s'introduisent naturellement les dé-
sordres qui règnent en général dans les affaires du riche ; la frugalité
sévère et l'attention parcimonieuse du pauvre s'établissent aussi naturellement dans l'administration du second. » (ibidem, p. 164.)

225. « ... l'ouvrage fait par des mains libres, revient à la fin à meilleur
compte que celui qui est fait par des esclaves. » (ibidem, p. 165.)

225. « Ainsi, si la récompense libérale du travail est l'effet de l'accroissement de la richesse nationale, elle devient aussi la cause de l'accroissement de la population. Se plaindre de la libéralité de cette récompense, c'est se plaindre de ce qui est à la fois l'effet et la cause de la
plus grande prospérité publique. » (ibidem, p. 165.)

225. « ... encourage la population[a]... » (ibidem, p. 166.)

225. « ... augmente l'industrie du commun du peuple. Ce sont les salaires
du travail qui sont l'encouragement de l'industrie, et celle-ci, comme
toute autre qualité de l'homme, se perfectionne à proportion de l'encouragement qu'elle reçoit. Une subsistance abondante augmente la
force corporelle de l'ouvrier ; et la douce espérance d'améliorer sa condition... l'excite à tirer de ses forces tout le parti possible. Aussi
verrons-nous toujours les ouvriers plus actifs, plus diligens, plus expé-
ditifs là où les salaires sont hauts, que là où il sont bas. » (ibidem,
p. 166.)

225. « ... les ouvriers qui sont largement payés à la pièce, sont très-sujets
à se forcer d'ouvrage, et à ruiner leur santé et leur tempérament en
peu d'années. » (ibidem, pp. 166-67.)

225. « Si les maîtres écoutaient toujours ce que leur dictent à la fois la
raison et l'humanité, ils auraient lieu bien souvent de modérer plutôt
que d'exciter l'application au travail, dans une grande partie de leurs
ouvriers. » (ibidem, p. 168.)

225. « ... plus d'aisance [...] puisse rendre certains[b] ouvriers paresseux... »
(ibidem, p. 169.)

226. « *Le prix pécuniaire du travail* est nécessairement réglé par deux circonstances, la demande de travail et *le prix* des choses propres aux
besoins et aisance de la vie ... c'est ce qu'il faut d'argent pour acheter
cette quantité déterminée de choses, qui régle le prix pécuniaire du
travail. » (ibidem, p. 175.)

226. « La disète d'une année de cherté, en diminuant la demande de travail,
tend à en faire baisser le prix, comme la cherté des vivres tend à le
hausser. Au contraire, l'abondance d'un année de bon marché, en
augmentant cette demande, tend à élever le prix du travail, comme
le bon marché des vivres tend à le faire baisser. Dans les variations
ordinaires du prix des vivres, ces deux causes opposées semblent se
contrebalancer l'une l'autre ; ce qui probablement est en partie la
raison pourquoi les salaires du travail sont partout beaucoup **plus**
fixes et plus constants que le prix des vivres. » (ibidem, p. 177.)

---

a In the manuscript: "encourage non seulement la population."—*Ed.*
b In the manuscript: "le".—*Ed.*

226. « L'augmentation qui survient dans les salaires du travail, augmente nécessairement le prix de beaucoup de marchandises *en haussant cette partie du prix qui se résout en salaires,* et elle tend d'autant à diminuer la consommation tant intérieure qu'extérieure de ces marchandises. Cependant la même cause qui fait hausser les salaires du travail, l'accroissement des capitaux, tend à augmenter ses facultés productives, et tend à mettre une plus petite quantité de travail en état de produire une plus grande quantité d'ouvrage. » (ibidem, p. 177.)

226. « Il y a donc une infinité de marchandises qui, en conséquence de tous ces moyens de perfectionner l'industrie, viennent à être produites *avec un travail tellement inférieur à celui* qu'elles *coûtaient auparavant,* que *l'augmentation dans le prix de ce travail* se *trouve plus que compensée* par *la diminution dans la quantité* de *travail.* » (ibidem, p. 178.)

227. « *Des profits des capitaux.* » (ibidem, p. 179.)

227. « ... taux [...] habituel des salaires... » (ibidem, p. 179.)

227. « ... mais *ceci même ne peut guère s'obtenir* à *l'égard des profits* de capitaux. » (ibidem, p. 179.)

227. « Ce profit se ressent ... de chaque variation qui survient dans le prix des marchandises... » (ibidem, p. 180.)

227. « Il serait encore plus difficile de déterminer le profit moyen de tous les différens commerces établis dans un grand royaume... » (ibidem, p. 180.)

227. « ... profits moyens des capitaux... » (ibidem, p. 180.)

227. « ...quelque idée d'après *l'intérêt de l'argent.* On peut établir pour maxime que partout où on pourra faire beaucoup de profits par le moyen de l'argent, on donnera communément beaucoup pour avoir la faculté de s'en servir, et qu'on donnera en général moins quand il n'y aura que peu de profits à faire par son moyen. » (ibidem, pp. 180-81.)

228. ...*de forts salaires et de hauts profits sont naturellement des choses qui vont rarement ensemble,* si ce n'est dans le cas particulier d'une colonie nouvelle. » (ibidem, p. 187.)

228. « Une colonie nouvelle doit nécessairement, pendant quelque tems, plus que la majeure partie des autres pays, avoir la masse de ses capitaux au dessous de la proportion que peut comporter l'étendue de son territoire, et avoir sa population au dessous de la proportion que peut comporter l'étendue de son capital. Les colons ont plus de terres qu'ils n'ont de capitaux à consacrer à la culture ; ainsi, ce qu'ils ont de capitaux, ils l'appliquent *seulement à la culture* des *terres les plus fertiles et les plus favorablement situées,* celles qui sont près des côtes de la mer ou le long des rivières navigables. Ces terres aussi s'achètent très-souvent au dessous même de la valeur de leur produit naturel. Le capital employé à l'achat et à l'amélioration de ces terres doit rendre un très-gros profit, et par conséquent fournir de quoi payer un très-gros intérêt. Son accumulation rapide dans un emploi aussi profitable met le planteur dans le cas d'augmenter le nombre des bras qu'il occupe, beaucoup plus vite qu'un établissement récent ne lui permet d'en

trouver ; aussi ceux qu'il peut se procurer sont-ils très-libéralement payés. *A mesure que la colonie augmente, les profits des capitaux baissent. Quand les terres les plus fertiles et les mieux situées se trouvent toutes occupées, la culture de celles qui sont inférieures, tant pour le sol que pour la situation, offre de moindres profits à faire,* et par conséquent un intérêt plus faible pour le capital qu'on y aura employé. C'est pour cela que le taux de l'intérêt... a considérablement baissé dans la plupart de nos colonie, pendant le cours de ce siècle. » (ibidem, pp. 187-89.)

228. « ... une diminution survenue dans la masse des capitaux d'une société, ou dans le fonds destiné à alimenter l'industrie, en amenant la baisse des salaires, amène pareillement une hausse dans les profits, et par conséquent dans le taux de l'intérêt. Les salaires du travail étant baissés, les propriétaires de ce qui reste de capitaux dans la société, peuvent établir leurs marchandises à meilleur compte qu'auparavant ; et comme il y a moins de capitaux employés à fournir le marché qu'il n'y en avait auparavant, ils peuvent vendre plus cher. » (ibidem, pp. 191-92.)

229. « ... qui, dans la plus grande partie des marchandises, emporte la totalité de ce qui devrait aller à la rente de la terre, et laisse seulement ce qui est nécessaire pour salarier le travail de préparer la marchandise et de la conduire au marché, au taux le plus bas auquel le travail puisse jamais être payé, c'est-à-dire, la simple subsistance de l'ouvrier. » (ibidem, pp. 197-98.)

229. « Le taux le plus bas des profits ordinaires des capitaux doit toujours être quelque chose au-delà de ce qu'il faut pour compenser les pertes accidentelles auxquelles est exposé chaque emploi de capital. Il n'y a que ce surplus qui constitue vraiment le profit ou le bénéfice net. » (ibidem, p. 196.)

229. « Dans la Grande-Bretagne, on porte au double de l'intérêt ce que les commerçans appellent un *profit honnête, modéré, raisonnable;* toutes expressions qui, à mon avis, ne signifient autre chose qu'un *profit commun et d'usage.* » (ibidem, p. 198.)

229. « Dans les pays qui vont en s'enrichissant avec rapidité, le faible taux des profits peut compenser le haut prix des salaires du travail dans le prix de beaucoup de marchandises, et mettre ces pays à portée de vendre à aussi bon marché que leurs voisins, qui s'enrichiront moins vîte, et chez lesquels les salaires seront plus bas. » (ibidem, p. 199.)

229. « Dans le fait, de hauts profits tendent, beaucoup plus que de hauts salaires, à faire monter *le prix* de l'ouvrage. » (ibidem, p. 199.)

229. « ... pièce de toile... » (ibidem, p. 200.)

230. « ...en multipliant [...] par le nombre des journées pendant lesquelles ils auraient été ainsi employés. Dans chacun des différens degrés de main-d'oeuvre que subirait la marchandise, cette partie de son prix, qui se résout en salaires, hausserait seulement dans la proportion arithmétique de cette hausse des salaires. Mais si les profits de tous les différens maîtres qui mettent ces ouvriers à l'ouvrage venaient à

monter de 5 pour 100,[a] cette partie du prix de la marchandise qui se résout en profits, s'éleverait dans chacun des différens degrés de la main-d'oeuvre, en *raison progressive* de cette hausse du taux des profits... La hausse des salaires opère en haussant le prix d'une marchandise, comme opère l'intérêt simple dans l'accumulation d'une dette. La hausse des profits opère comme l'intérêt composé. » (ibidem, pp. 200-01.)

230. « Nos marchands et nos maîtres manufacturiers se plaignent beaucoup des mauvais effets des hauts salaires, en ce que ces hauts salaires renchérissent leurs marchandises, et par-là en diminuent le débit, tant dans l'intérieur que chez l'étranger: ils ne parlent pas des mauvais effets des hauts profits; ils gardent le silence sur les conséquences fâcheuses de leurs propres gains ; ils ne se plaignent que de celles du gain des autres. » (ibidem, p. 201.)

230. « *Des salaires et des profits dans les divers emplois du travail et des capitaux.* » (ibidem, p. 201.)

230. « La loterie du droit est donc bien loin d'être une loterie parfaitement égale, et cet état, comme la plupart des autres professions libérales et honorables est évidemment très mal récompensé, sous le rapport du gain pécuniaire. » (ibidem, pp. 216-17.)

230. « Leur paye est au dessous du salaire des simples manoeuvres, et quand ils sont en activité de service leurs fatigues sont beaucoup plus grandes que celles de ces derniers. » (ibidem, p. 223.)

230. « Quoiqu'il exige[b] bien plus de savoir et de dextérité que presque tout autre métier d'artisan, et quoique toute la vie d'un matelot soit une scène continuelle de travaux et de dangers... Leurs salaires ne sont pas plus forts que ceux que gagne un simple manoeuvre dans le port qui règle le taux de ces salaires. » (ibidem, p. 224.)

231. « Sans doute il ne serait pas convenable de comparer un curé ou un chapelain, à un artisan à la journée. On peut bien pourtant, sans choquer la décence, considérer l'honoraire d'un curé ou d'un chapelain comme étant de la même nature que les salaires de cet artisan. » (ibidem, **p. 271**.)

231. « ... *gens de-lettres*.... » (ibidem, pp. 275-76.)

231. « ... *étudiant et mendiant*... » (ibidem, pp. 276-77.)

231. « ... dans une même société ou canton, le taux moyen de profits ordinaires dans les différens emplois des capitaux se trouvera bien plus proche du même niveau, que celui des salaires pécuniaires des diverses espèces de travail... » (ibidem, p. 228.)

231. « C'est *l'étendue du marché* qui, offrant de l'emploi à de plus gros capitaux, diminue le profit *apparent* ; mais aussi c'est elle qui, obligeant de se fournir à de plus grandes distances, augmente le premier coût. Cette diminution d'une part, et cette augmentation de l'autre, semblent, en beaucoup de cas, se contre-balancer à peu-près... » (ibidem, p. 232.)

---

[a] In the manuscript: "cent".—*Ed.*
[b] In the manuscript: "Quoique leur métier **exige**".—*Ed.*

231. « Dans de[a] petites petites villes et dans des[b] villages, au moyen du peu
     d'étendue du marché, le commerce ne peut pas s'agrandir à mesure
     que grossit le capital : aussi dans ces endroits-là, quoique le taux
     des profits d'une personne en particulier puisse être très-haut, cependant
     la masse ou la somme totale de ces profits ne peut jamais être très-
     forte, ni par conséquent le montant de son accumulation annuelle. Au
     contraire, dans de grandes villes, on peut étendre son commerce à me-
     sure que le capital augmente, et le crédit d'un homme qui est économe
     et qui fait bien ses affaires, augmente encore bien plus vîte que son
     capital. A proportion de l'augmentation de l'un et de l'autre, il agran-
     dit la sphère de ses opérations... » (ibidem, p. 233.)

231. « ...petit jardin potager, autant d'herbe qu'il en faut pour nourrir une
     vache, et peut-être un acre ou deux de mauvaise terre labourable. »
     (ibidem, p. 241.)

231. « ...le superflu de leur tems à quiconque les voulait employer, et qu'ils
     travaillaient pour de moindres salaires que les autres ouvriers. » (ibi-
     dem, p. 241.)

231. « Cependant plusieurs écrivains qui ont recueilli les prix du travail
     et des denrées dans les tems anciens, et qui se sont plû à les repré-
     senter tous deux prodigieusement bas, ont regardé *cette rétribution acci-
     dentelle* comme *formant tout le salaire de* ces ouvriers. » (ibidem, p.
     242.)

232. « ...cette égalité dans la somme totale des avantages et désavantages
     des divers emplois de travail et de capitaux ne peut avoir lieu que
     dans les emplois qui sont la seule ou la principale occupation de ceux
     qui les exercent. » (ibidem, p. 240.)

232. « Chaque classe, il est vrai, au moyen de ses réglemens, se trouvait
     obligée, pour les marchandises qu'il lui fallait prendre dans la ville,
     chez les marchands et artisans des autres classes, de les acheter
     quelque chose de plus cher qu'elle n'aurait fait sans cela ; mais en
     revanche elle se trouvait aussi à même de vendre les siennes plus cher,
     dans la même proportion, de manière que jusque-là cela devait, comme
     on dit, aller l'un pour l'autre ; et dans les affaires que les classes dif-
     férentes faisaient entr'elles dans la ville, aucune d'elles ne perdait à
     ces réglements. *Mais dans les affaires qu'elles faisaient avec la cam-
     pagne, toutes également trouvaient de gros bénéfices ;* et c'est dans
     ce dernier genre d'affaires que consiste tout le trafic qui soutient et
     qui enrichit les villes. Chaque ville tire de la campagne toute sa sub-
     sistance et tous les matériaux de son industrie. Elle paie ces deux
     objets principalement de deux manières ; la première, en renvoyant
     à la campagne une partie de ces matériaux travaillés et manufacturés,
     dans lequel cas le prix en est augmenté du montant *des salaires des
     ouvriers, et du montant des profits de leurs maîtres ou de ceux qui les
     emploient immédiatement ;* la seconde, en envoyant à la campagne le
     produit tant brut que manufacturé, soit des autres pays, soit des en-
     droits les plus éloignés du même pays, qui s'importe dans la ville, dans

---

a In the manuscript: "les".—*Ed.*
b In the manuscript: "les" instead of "dans des". —*Ed.*

lequel cas aussi le prix originaire de ces marchandises s'accroît *des salaires des voituriers ou matelots, et du profit des marchands qui les emploient.* Ce qui est gagné dans la première de ces deux branches de commerce, compose tout le *bénéfice que la ville retire de ses manufactures.* Ce qui est gagné dans la seconde, compose *tout le bénéfice que lui rapportent son commerce intérieur et son commerce étranger.* La totalité de ce qui est gagné dans l'une et dans l'autre branche, consiste en salaires d'ouvriers et profits de ceux qui les emploient. Ainsi, tous réglemens qui tendent *à faire monter ces salaires et ces profits au dessus de ce qu'ils devraient être naturellement,* tendent à mettre *la ville en état d'acheter, avec une moindre quantité de son travail, le produit d'une plus grande quantité du travail de la campagne.* » (ibidem, pp. 258-59.)

233. « ... au dessus de ce *qu'ils devraient être naturellement...* » (ibidem, p. 259.)

233. « Ils donnent aux marchands et artisans de la ville un avantage sur les propriétaires, fermiers et ouvriers de la campagne, et ils rompent cette égalité naturelle, qui sans cela aurait lieu dans le commerce qui s'établit entre l'une et l'autre. La *totalité du produit annuel du travail de la société se divise* annuellement entre ces deux différentes sections du peuple. L'effet de ces réglemens est de donner aux habitans des villes *une part plus forte* que celle qui leur échoirait sans cela dans ce[a] produit, et d'en donner une moindre aux habitans des campagnes. Le *prix* que paient les villes pour les denrées et matières qui y sont annuellement importées, ce sont tous les objets de manufactures et autres marchandises qui en sont annuellement exportées. *Plus ces dernières sont vendues cher,* plus les autres sont achetées bon marché. L'industrie des villes en devient plus avantageuse, et celle des campagnes vient l'être moins. » (ibidem, pp. 259-60.)

233. « Les habitans d'une ville étant *rassemblés dans un même lieu,* peuvent aisément communiquer et se concerter ensemble. En conséquence les métiers les plus minces qui se soient établis dans les villes, ont été érigés en corporation, dans un lieu ou dans un autre... » (ibidem, p. 261.)

233. « Les habitans de la campagne, qui vivent dispersés et éloignés l'un de[b] l'autre, ne peuvent pas facilement se concerter entr'eux. Non-seulement ils n'ont jamais été réunis en corps de métier, mais même l'esprit de corporation n'a jamais régné parmi eux. On n'a jamais pensé qu'un apprentissage fût nécessaire pour l'agriculture, qui est la grande industrie de la campagne. » (ibidem, p. 262.)

234. « ... il faut bien plus de jugement et de prudence pour diriger des opérations qui doivent varier à chaque changement de saison, ainsi que dans une infinité d'autres circonstances, que pour des travaux qui sont toujours les mêmes ou à peu près les mêmes. » (ibidem, p. 263.)

234. « Ce n'est pas seulement aux corporations et à leurs réglemens qu'il faut attribuer la supériorité que l'industrie des villes a usurpée dans

---

a In the manuscript: "le".—*Ed.*
b In the manuscript: "et".—*Ed.*

toute l'Europe sur celle des campagnes, il y a encore d'autres réglemens qui la maintiennent : *les forts droits* dont sont chargés tous
ouvrages de manufacture étrangère et toutes marchandises importées
par des marchands étrangers, tendent tous au même but. » (ibidem,
p. 265.)

234. «...réglemens les garantissent de celle^a des étrangers. » (ibidem,
p. 265.)

235. « Il paraît qu'anciennement dans la Grande-Bretagne, l'industrie des
villes avait sur celle des campagnes plus de supériorité qu'à présent :
aujourd'hui les salaires du travail de la campagne se rapprochent davantage de ceux du travail des manufactures, et les profits des capitaux employés à la culture, de ceux des capitaux employés au commerce et aux manufactures, qu'ils ne s'en rapprochaient, à ce qu'il
semble, dans le dernier siècle ou dans le commencement de celui-ci.
Ce changement peut être regardé comme la conséquence nécessaire,
quoique très-tardive, de l'encouragement forcé donné à l'industrie des
villes. Le capital qui s'y accumule, devient, avec le tems, si considérable, qu'il ne peut plus y être employé avec le même profit à cette
espèce d'industrie qui est particulière aux villes : cette industrie a ses
limites comme toute autre, et *l'accroissement des capitaux, en augmentant la concurrence,* doit nécessairement réduire les profits. *La baisse
des profits dans la ville force les capitaux à refluer dans les campagnes*
où ils vont créer de nouvelles demandes de travail de culture, et font
hausser par conséquent les salaires de ce dernier travail ; *alors ces
capitaux se répandent,* pour ainsi dire, *sur la surface de la Terre,* et par
l'emploi qu'on en fait en culture, *ils sont en partie rendus à la campagne, aux dépens de laquelle, en grande partie, ils s'étaient originaire-
ment accumulés dans la ville.* » (ibidem, pp. 266-67.)

240. „die Ricardosche Fiktion, als ob der *Vorrat* von Kapital sich nach
dem *Wunsche* seiner Anlegung richte". (Rodbertus, *Sociale Briefe an
von Kirchmann. Dritter Brief,* Berlin, 1851, S. 211.)

342. «...prix payé pour *l'usage de la terre*...» (Adam Smith, *Recherches
sur la nature et les causes de la richesse des nations.* Traduction nouvelle ... par Germain Garnier, t. I, Paris, 1802, p. 299.)

342. «...le capital qui fournit la sémence, paie le travail, achète et entre-
tient les bestiaux et autres *instrumens* de labourage...» (ibidem, p. 299.)

342. « Tout ce qui reste du produit ou de son prix... au-delà de cette portion, quel que puisse être ce reste, le *propriétaire* tâche de se le réserver
comme *rente* de sa terre... » (ibidem, p. 300.)

342. «...et [...] en outre les profits ordinaires...» (ibidem, p. 299.)

342. «...ce *surplus* peut toujours être regardé comme la *rente naturelle*
de la terre... » (ibidem, p. 300.)

343. « Le propriétaire exige une rente même pour la terre non améliorée...»
(ibidem, pp. 300-01.)

---

^a In the manuscript: "de la concurrence des étrangers".—*Ed.*

343. « Il exige quelquefois une rente pour ce qui est tout-à-fait incapable d'être amélioré par la main des hommes. » (ibidem, p. 301.)

343. « La rente de la terre, considérée comme le prix payé pour l'usage de la terre, est donc naturellement un prix de monopole. » (ibidem, p. 302.)

343. « ... *être portée au marché...* » (ibidem, p. 303.)

343. « Si le prix ordinaire est plus que suffisant, le *surplus* en ira naturellement à la rente de la terre. S'il n'est juste que suffisant, la marchandise *pourra* bien être portée au marché, mais elle ne peut fournir à payer une rente au propriétaire. Le prix sera-t-il ou ne sera-t-il pas plus que suffisant? C'est ce qui dépend de la demande. » (ibidem, p. 303.)

343. « Ces trois parties semblent constituer immédiatement ou en définitif la totalité du prix... » (ibidem, p. 101.)

343. « Néanmoins dans les sociétés les plus avancées, il y a toujours quelques marchandises mais en petit nombre, dont *le prix s e r é s o u t en deux parties seulement* ; les *salaires du travail et les profits des fonds*, et d'autres en beaucoup plus petit nombre encore, *dont le prix consiste uniquement en salaires de travail*. Dans le prix du poisson de mer, par exemple, une partie paie le travail des pêcheurs, et l'autre les profits du capital placé dans la pêcherie. Il est rare que la *rente* fasse partie de ce prix... Dans quelques endroits de l'Ecosse, il y a de pauvres gens qui font métier de chercher le long des bords de la mer ces petites pierres tachetées, connues vulgairement sous le nom de *cailloux d'Ecosse*. Le prix que leur paie le *lapidaire* est en entier le *salaire de leur travail ; il n'y entre ni rente ni profit*. Mais la *totalité du prix de chaque marchandise* doit toujours, en dernière analyse, se résoudre en *quelqu'une de ces parties ou en toutes trois...* » (ibidem, pp. 103-04.)

344. « *Des parties constituantes du prix des marchandises.* » (ibidem, p. 94.)

344. « Des parties constituantes du prix des marchandises. » (ibidem, p. 94.)

344. « ...la *totalité du prix de chaque marchandise* doit toujours ... se résoudre *en quelqu'une* de *ces parties* ou *en toutes trois...*» (ibidem, p. 104.)

345. « Quand ces trois différentes sortes de revenus appartiennent à différentes personnes, il est aisé de les distinguer ; mais quand ils appartiennent à la même personne, on les confond quelquefois l'un avec l'autre, au moins dans le langage ordinaire. » (ibidem, p. 106.)

345. « Comme dans un pays civilisé il n'y a que très-peu de marchandises dont *toute la valeur* échangeable procède *du travail seulement,* et que, dans la très-majeure partie d'entr'elles, la *rente et le profit* y contribuent pour de fortes portions, il en résulte que le *produit annuel du travail de ce pays* suffira toujours pour *acheter et commander* une *quantité de travail beaucoup plus grande que celle qu'il a fallu employer pour faire croître ce produit, le préparer et l'amener au marché.* » (ibidem, pp. 108-09.)

345. « Comme dans un pays civilisé il n'y a que très-peu de marchandises dont *toute la valeur* échangeable procède *du travail seulement,* et que, dans la très-majeure partie d'entr'elles, la rente et le profit y *contri-*

buent pour de fortes portions, il en résulte que le produit annuel du travail de ce pays suffira toujours pour acheter et commander *une quantité de travail* beaucoup plus grande que celle qu'*il a fallu employer pour faire croître ce produit, le préparer et l'amener au marché.* » (ibidem, pp. 108-09.)

346. « Il faut observer que la valeur réelle de toutes les différentes parties constituantes du prix se mesure par la *quantité de travail que chacune d'elles peut acheter ou commander.* Le travail mesure la valeur, non-seulement de cette partie du prix qui se *résout* en *travail,* mais encore de celle qui se *résout* en *rente,* et de celle qui se *résout en profit.* › (ibidem, p. 100.)

346. « Un ouvrier indépendant qui a *un petit capital* suffisant pour acheter des matières et pour subsister jusqu'à ce qu'il puisse porter son ouvrage au marché, gagnera à la fois, et *les salaires du journalier* qui travaille sous un *maître,* et le profit que ferait la maître sur l'ouvrage de celui-ci. Cependant la totalité de ce que gagne cet ouvrier se nomme *profit,* et les salaires sont encore ici confondus dans le profit. Un jardinier qui cultive de ses mains son propre jardin, réunit à la fois dans sa personne les *trois différens caractères* de *propriétaire, de fermier et d'ouvrier.* Ainsi le produit de son jardin doit lui payer la rente du premier, le profit du second et le salaire du troisième. Néanmoins le tout est regardé communément comme le *fruit de son travail.* Ici la rente et le profit se confondent dans le salaire. » (ibidem, p. 108.)

347. « . . . le fruit de son travail. » (ibidem, p. 108.)

347. « Salaire, profit et rente sont *les trois sources primitives* de tout *revenu, a u s s i   b i e n* que de *toute valeur échangeable.* » (ibidem, p. 105.)

348. « . . . *parties constituantes du prix des marchandises.* » (ibidem, p. 94.)

348. « Lorsque le prix d'une marchandise n'est ni plus ni moins que ce qu'il faut pour payer suivant leurs taux *naturels,* et la r e n t e   d e   l a   t e r r e et *les salaires du travail,* et *les profits du capital* employé à la produire, la préparer et la conduire au marché, alors cette marchandise est vendue ce qu'on peut appeler *son prix naturel.* La marchandise est alors vendue *précisément ce qu'elle vaut. . .* » (ibidem, p. 111.)

348. « Le *prix de marché* de chaque marchandise particulière est déterminé par la proportion entre la quantité de cette marchandise existante actuellement au marché, et les demandes de ceux qui sont disposés à en payer le *prix naturel* ou la *valeur entière des rente,* profit et salaire *qu'il faut payer pour qu'elle vienne au marché.* » (ibidem, p. 112.)

348. « Quand la quantité d'une marchandise quelconque, amenée au marché, se trouve *au dessous* de la demande effective, tous ceux qui sont disposés à payer *la valeur entière d e s   r e n t e,* salaires et *profits* qu'il en coûte pour amener cette marchandise au marché, ne peuvent se fournir de la quantité qu'il leur faut . . . *le prix de marché* s'élevera plus ou moins *au dessus* du *prix naturel,* suivant que la *grandeur du déficit,* ou suivant que *la richesse* ou la fantaisie des concurrens viendra à animer plus ou moins la chaleur de cette concurrence » (ibidem, p. 113.)

348. « Quand la quantité amenée au marché excède la demande effective, elle ne peut être toute vendue à ceux qui consentent à payer la valeur entière des rente, salaires et profits qu'il en a coûté pour l'y amener ... Le *prix de marché* tombera alors plus ou moins au dessous du *prix naturel,* selon que la quantité de l'excédent augmentera plus ou moins la concurrence des vendeurs, ou suivant qu'il leur importera plus ou moins de se défaire sur-le-champ de la marchandise » (ibidem, p. 114.)

349. « Quand la quantité amenée au marché suffit tout juste pour remplir la demande effective, [...] le *prix de marché* se trouve naturellement être précisément... le même que le *prix naturel* ... La concurrence des différens vendeurs les oblige à accepter ce prix, mais elle ne les oblige pas à accepter moins. » (ibidem, pp. 114-15.)

349. « Si cette quantité excède pendant quelque temps la demande effective, il faut que quelqu'une des parties constituantes de son prix soit payée au dessous de son *prix naturel. S i c'e s t l a r e n t e,* l'interêt des propriétaires les portera sur-le-champ à *retirer une partie de leur terre de cet emploi...* » (ibidem, p. 115.)

349. « Si au contraire la quantité amenée au marché restait, pendant quelque tems, *au dessous de la demande effective,* quelques-unes des parties constituantes de son prix hausseraient nécessairement au dessus de leur taux *nature. S i c'e s t l a r e n t e,* l'intérêt de tous les autres propriétaires les portera naturellement à disposer une plus grande quantité de terre à la production de cette marchandise... » (ibidem, p. 116.)

349. « Les fluctuations accidentelles et momentanées qui surviennent dans le *prix de marche* d'une denrée, tombent principalement sur ces parties de son prix, qui se résolvent en salaires et en profits. La partie que se résout en rente en est moins affectée. » (ibidem, pp. 118-19.)

349. « Le *prix de monopole* est, à tous les momens, le plus haut qu'il soit possible de retirer. Le *prix naturel* ou le prix résultant de la libre concurrence est au contraire le plus bas qu'on puisse accepter, non pas à la vérité à tous les momens, mais pour en tems un peu considérable de suite. » (ibidem, p. 124.)

349. « Quoique le *prix de marché* d'une marchandise particulière puisse continuer long-tems à rester au dessus du *prix naturel,* il est difficile qu'il puisse continuer long-temps à rester au dessous. *Quelle que soit la partie de ce prix qui soit payée au dessous du taux naturel,* les personnes qui y ont intérêt sentiront bientôt le dommage qu'elles éprouvent, et *aussitôt elles retireront, ou tant de terre,* ou tant de travail, ou tant de capitaux *de ce genre d'emploi,* que la quantité de cette marchandise qui sera amenée au marché ne sera bientôt plus que suffisante pour répondre à la demande effective. Ainsi son *prix de marché* remontera bientôt au *prix naturel,* au moins sera-ce le cas partout où règne une entière liberté. » (ibidem, p. 125.)

349. « De la rente de la terre. » (ibidem, p. 299.)

350. « ...*la valeur entière des rente,* profit et salaire *qu'il faut payer pour qu'elle vienne au marché* » (ibidem, p. 112.)

350. « On *ne peut porter ordinairement au marché* que ces parties seulement du produit de la terre dont *le prix ordinaire est* suffisant *pour rempla-*

*cer le capital qu'il faut employer pour les y porter, et les profits ordi-
naires de ce capital »* (ibidem, pp. 302-03.)

350. « ... la valeur entière des rentes. .. » (ibidem, p. 112.)

350. « Si le *prix ordinaire* est *plus que suffisant, le surplus* en ira naturellement à la rente de la terre. S'il n'est juste que suffisant, la *marchandise
pourra bien être portée au marché*, mais elle ne peut fournir à payer
une rente au propriétaire. Le prix sera-t-il ou ne sera-t-il pas plus que
suffisant? C'est ce qui dépend de la demande. » (ibidem, p. 303.)

351. « Il y a quelques parties du produit de la terre dont la demande doit
toujours être telle, qu'elles rapporteront un prix plus fort que ce qui est
suffisant pour les faire venir au marché, et il y en a d'autres dont il
se peut que la demande soit telle, qu'elle rapportent ce prix plus fort
que le *prix suffisant*, et dont il se peut aussi qu'elle soit telle, qu'elles
ne le rapportent pas. Les premières doivent toujours fournir de quoi
payer une rente au propriétaire ; les derniers peuvent quelquefois fournir de quoi en payer une et quelque-fois ne le pas fournir, suivant la
différence des circonstances. » (ibidem, p. 303.)

352. « Il faut donc *observer* que la *rente entre d a n s   l a   c o m p o s i t i o n
du prix des marchandises, d'une   a u t r e   m a n i è r e   q u e   n'y   e n-
t r e n t   l e s   s a l a i r e s   e t   l e s   p r o f i t s* ... Le *taux haut ou bas
des salaires ou des profits* est l a   c a u s e   *du haut ou bas prix des
marchandises: le t a u x   h a u t   o u   b a s   d e   l a   r,e n t e* est *l'e f f e t
du prix* ; le prix d'une *marchandise particulière* est haut ou bas, *parce
qu'il faut, pour la faire venir au marché, payer des salaires et des profits hauts ou bas; mais c'est parce que son prix est haut ou bas, c'est*
parce qu'il est ou beaucoup plus, ou guère plus, ou *point du tout plus
que ce qui est suffisant pour payer ces salaires et ces profits*, que cette
marchandise fournit de quoi payer une forte rente ou une faible rente,
ou ne fournit pas de quoi en payer une. » (ibidem, pp. 303-04.)

354. « *Première section. Du produit qui fournit toujours de quoi payer une*
rente. » (ibidem p. 305.)

354. « Les hommes, comme toutes les autres espèces animales, se *multipliant
naturellement en proportion des moyens de leur subsistance*, il y *a* toujours plus ou moins demande de nourriture. Toujours la nourriture
pourra acheter ou commander une quantité plus ou moins grande de
travail, et toujours il se trouvera quelqu'un disposé à faire quelque chose pour la gagner. » (ibidem, p. 305.)

354. « Or, la *terre*, dans presque toutes les situations possibles, *produit plus
de nourriture* que ce qu'il faut *pour faire subsister tout le travail* qui
concourt à mettre cette nourriture au marché, et même le faire subsister
de la manière la plus libérale qui ait jamais eu lieu pour ce genre de
travail. Le *surplus* de cette nourriture est aussi toujours plus que suffisant *pour remplacer avec profit le capital qui fait mouvoir ce travail.*
Ainsi, il reste toujours quelque chose pour donner une rente au propriétaire. » (ibidem, pp. 305-06.)

354. « La rente varie selon la fertilité de la terre, quel que soit son produit,
et selon sa situation, quelle que soit sa fertilité. » (ibidem, p. 306.)

355. « Il faut donc que ce dernier produit fasse subsister une plus grande quantité de travail ; et par conséquent que le *surplus, dont le profit du fermier* et *la rente du propriétaire sont tirés tous les deux,* en soit d'autant diminuée. » (ibidem, p. 307.)

355. « Une *pièce de blé,* d'une fertilité médiocre, produit une beaucoup *plus grande quantité de nourriture pour l'homme,* que la meilleure prairie d'une pareille étendue. Quoique sa culture exige *plus de travail,* cependant *le surplus* qui reste après le remplacement de la semence et la *subsistance de tout ce travail,* est encore beaucoup plus considérable. Ainsi, en supposant qu'une livre de viande de boucherie ne *valût jamais plus* qu'une livre de pain, cet *excédent plus fort* serait partout d'une *plus grande valeur* et formerait un fonds plus abondant, tant pour le profit du fermier, que pour la *rente* du propriétaire. » (ibidem, pp. 308-09.)

356. « ...les *profits et la rente que cette terre mise en labour aurait pu rapporter au fermier et* au *propriétaire.* Quand les bestiaux sont venus au même marché, ceux qui ont été nourris au milieu des friches les plus incultes, sont, à proportion du poids et de la qualité, vendus au même prix que ceux qui ont été élevés sur la terre la mieux cultivée. Les propriétaires de ces friches en profitent, et ils haussent la rente de leurs terres en *proportion du prix du bétail* qu'elles nourrissent... C'est ainsi que, dans les progrès de l'amélioration des terres, les *rentes et profits des pâtures incultes* viennent à se régler en quelque sorte sur les rentes et profits de celles qui sont cultivées, et *celles-ci, à leur tour, sur les rentes et profits des terres à blé.* » (ibidem, pp. 310-11.)

356. « ... partout où il n'y a pas d'avantage local... , la rente et le profit que donne le blé ou tout autre végétal qui sert à la nourriture générale du peuple, doivent naturellement régler la rente et le profit que donnera une terre propre à cette production, et qui sera mise en nature de pré.
L'usage des prairies artificielles, des turneps, carottes, choux, etc. et *tous les autres expédiens* dont on s'est avisé pour *qu'une même quantité de terre pût nourrir un plus grand nombre de bestiaux que ne faisait la pâture naturelle,* ont dû contribuer, à ce qu'il semble, à diminuer un peu cette supériorité que le prix de la viande a naturellement sur celui du pain, dans un pays bien cultivé. Aussi paraissent-ils avoir produit cette effet... » (ibidem, p. 315.)

356. « Dans tous les grands pays, la majeure partie des terres cultivées est employée à produire, ou de la nourriture pour les hommes, ou de la nourriture pour les bestiaux. La rente et le profit de ces terres règlent les rentes et profits de toutes les autres terres cultivées. Si quelque produit particulier fournissait moins, la terre en serait bientôt remise en blé ou en nature de pré ; et s'il y en avait quelqu'un qui fournît plus, on consacrerait bientôt à ce genre de produit quelque partie des terres qui sont en blé ou en nature de prés. » (ibidem, p. 318.)

356. « ... les rentes et profits de ces productions qui exigent ou de plus fortes avances primitives pour y approprier la terre, ou une plus grande dépense pour leur culture annuelle, quoique souvent fort supérieurs aux rentes et profits des blés et de l'herbe des prés, cependant, dans tous les cas où ils ne font que compenser les avances ou dépenses extraordinai-

res, sont en effet réglés par les rentes et profits de ces deux espèces ordinaires de récoltes. » (ibidem, pp. 323-24.)

357. « C'est ainsi que la rente des terres cultivées pour produire la nourriture des hommes, règle la rente de la plupart des autres terres cultivées. » (ibidem, p. 331.)

357. « En Europe, c'est le blé qui est la principale production de la terre servant immédiatement à la nourriture de l'homme. Ainsi, excepté quelques circonstances particulières, la rente des terres à blé règle en Europe celle de toutes les autres terres cultivées. » (ibidem, pp. 331-32.)

357. « ... alors *la rente* du propriétaire *ou l'excédent de nourriture* qui lui resterait après le paiement du travail et le remboursement du capital et profits ordinaires du fermier, serait nécessairement beaucoup plus considérable. Quel que pût être, dans ce pays-là, le taux de la subsistance ordinaire du travail, ce *plus grand excédent de nourriture en ferait toujours subsister davantage*, et *par conséquent* mettrait le propriétaire en état d'en acheter ou d'en commander une plus grande quantité. » (ibidem, p. 332.)

357. « Dans la[a] Caroline ... les *planteurs sont généralement*, comme dans les autres colonies anglaises, *fermiers et propriétaires à la fois,* et où par conséquent la *rente se confond dans le. profit...* » (ibidem, p. 333.)

357. « ... propre ni au blé, ni au pâturage, ni à la vigne, ni dans le fait à aucune autre production végétale bien utile aux hommes ; et toutes les terres propres à ces diverses culture ne le sont nullement à celle du riz. Ainsi, même dans les pays à riz, la rente des terres qui le produisent, ne peut pas régler la rente des autres terres cultivées qu'il est impossible de mettre dans cette nature de rapports. » (ibidem, p. 334.)

357. « ... il en résulterait que la *même quantité de terres cultivées ferait subsister une bien plus grande quantité de monde*, et que ceux qui travailleraient étant généralement nourris de pommes de terre, il se trouverait un *excédent* bien plus considérable, après le remplacement du capital et la subsistance de tout le travail employé à la culture. Il appartiendrait aussi au propriétaire une plus grande portion dans cet excédent. La population augmenterait, et les rentes s'élèveraient beaucoup au dessus de ce qu'elles sont aujourd'hui. » (ibidem, p. 335.)

358. « Quand la quantité amenée au marché suffit tout juste pour remplir la demande effective, [...] le *prix de marché* se trouve précisément être précisément ... le même que le *prix naturel.* » (ibidem, p. 114.)

358. « *Seconde section. Du produit qui fournit quelquefois de quoi payer une rente, et quelquefois ne le fournit pas.* » (ibidem, p. 337.)

359. « La *nourriture* de l'homme paraît être le seul des produits de la terre qui fournisse *toujours*, et *nécessairement* de quoi payer *une rente quelconque au propriétaire*. Les autres genres de produits peuvent quelquefois en rapporter une, et quelquefois ne le peuvent pas, selon les circonstances. » (ibidem, p. 337.)

359. « Les deux plus grands besoins de l'homme, *après la nourriture*, sont le *vêtement et le logement.* » (ibidem, p. 338.)

---

[a] In the manuscript: "En" instead of "Dans la".—*Ed.*

359. « ... dans son état primitif et inculte... » (ibidem, p. 338.)

359. « ... qu'elle n'en peut *nourrir*. » (ibidem, p. 338.)

359. « ... *surabondance* de ces matériaux... » (ibidem, p. 338.)

359. « ... et le prix de celles dont on fait usage est *regardé comme équivalent seulement au travail et à la dépense de les mettre en état de
servir.* » (ibidem, p. 338.)

359. « ... ne ... aucune rente au propriétaire du sol. » (ibidem, p. 338.)

359. « ... qu'elle serait dans le cas de nourrir... » (ibidem, p. 338.)

359. « ... tels que ces personnes voudraient les avoir et consentiraient à les
payer. » (ibidem, p. 338.)

359. « ... ce qui augmente nécessairement leur valeur. » (ibidem, p. 338.)

359. « ... il y a *souvent demande pour plus qu'on n'en peut avoir.* »
(ibidem, p. 338.)

359. « ... la dépense de les transporter au marché ; ainsi leur prix peut
toujours fournir quelque chose pour *faire une rente* au propriétaire de
la terre. » (ibidem, pp. 338-39.)

359. « ... des plus gros animaux. » (ibidem, p. 339.)

359. « ... chaque homme, *en pourvoyant à sa nourriture, se pourvoit en
même tems de matières de vêtement pour plus qu'il n'en pourra porter.* »
(ibidem, p. 339.)

359. « ... *au-delà de ce que coûte la dépense de les envoyer vendre. Ce prix*
fournit *donc* quelque rente au propriétaire de la terre. » (ibidem,
pp. 339-40.)

359. « ... un peu la rente du pays qui la produisait. » (ibidem, p. 340.)

359. « Les *matières de logement* ne peuvent pas toujours se transporter à
une aussi grande distance que celles de vêtement, et ne deviennent pas
non plus aussi promptement un objet de commerce étranger. Lorsqu'elle
sont *surabondantes* dans le pays qui les produit, il arrive fréquemment,
même dans l'état actuel du commerce du monde, qu'elles ne sont
d'*aucune valeur* pour le *propriétaire de la terre.* » (ibidem, pp. 340-41.)

359. « ... dans un pays bien peuplé et bien cultivé... » (ibidem, p. 341.)

359. « ... dans plusieurs endroits de l'Amérique septentrionale... » (ibidem,
p. 341.)

360. « Quand il y a une telle surabondance dans les matières de logement,
la partie dont on fait usage n'a d'autre valeur que le travail et la dépense qu'on a mis à la rendre propre au service. Elle ne rapporte aucune
rente au propriétaire, qui en général en abandonne l'usage à quiconque
prend seulement la peine de le lui demander. Cependant il peut quelquefois être dans le cas d'en retirer une rente, s'*il y a demande* de la
part de nations plus riches. » (ibidem, p. 341.)

360. « ...n o m b r e que leur produit *peut vêtir et loger*, mais en raison de celui que ce *produit peut nourrir*. Quand la nourriture ne manque pas, il est aisé de trouver les choses nécessaires pour se vêtir et se loger ; mais on peut avoir celles-ci sous sa main, et éprouver souvent de grandes difficultés à se procurer la nourriture. Dans quelques endroits, même du royaume d'Angleterre, le travail d'un seul homme dans une seule journée, peut bâtir ce qu'on y appelle une maison. » (ibidem, p. 342.)

360. « Mais quand, au moyen de la culture et de l'amélioration de la terre, le *travail d'une seule famille peut fournir à la nourriture de deux*, alors le travail d'une moitié de la société suffit pour nourrir le tout. » (ibidem, p. 343.)

360. « ...cherchent toujours à en échanger le surplus... » (ibidem, p. 344.)

360. « ...Les pauvres, *pour obtenir de la nourriture*... » (ibidem, p. 344.)

360. « ...une extrême subdivision de travail... » (ibidem, p. 344.)

360. « De là naît la demande de toute espèce de matières que puisse mettre en oeuvre l'invention des hommes, soit pour l'utilité, soit pour la décoration des bâtimens, de la parure, de l'équipage ou du mobilier : de là la demande, de fossiles et de minéraux renfermés dans les entrailles de la terre : de là la demande de métaux précieux et de pierres précieuses.
   Ainsi, n o n - s e u l e m e n t c'est d e l a *nourriture* q u e l a *r e n t e* tire s a p r e m i è r e o r i g i n e, mais e n c o r e s i q u e l - qu'a u t r e p a r t i e d u p r o d u i t d e l a t e r r e v i e n t a u s s i p a r l a s u i t e à r a p p o r t e r u n e r e n t e, e l l e d o i t c e t t e *addition de valeur à l'accroissement de puissance qu'a acquis le travail pour produire de la nourriture*, au moyen de la culture et de l'amélioration de la terre. » (ibidem, pp. 344-45.)

360. « ...pour que le *prix* qu'elles rendent soit *au-delà de ce qu'exigent le paiement du travail fait pour les amener au marché et le remplacement du capital employé pour le même objet avec ses profits ordinaires. La demande sera ou ne sera pas assez forte pour cela, d'après différentes circonstances.* » (ibidem, p. 345.)

361. « Quoique ces animaux ne multiplient pas dans la même proportion que le blé, *qui est entièrement le fruit de l'industrie humaine*, cependant la propagation de leur espèce est favorisée par les soins et la protection de l'homme... » (ibidem, p. 347.)

362. « ...les profits ordinaires,[a] le capital employé... » (ibidem, p. 346.)

363. « Le *propriétaire n'en permettrait pas l'exploitation à d'autre sans exiger une rente, et personne ne trouverait moyen de lui en payer une.* » (ibidem, p. 346.)

363. « *Le prix le plus bas* auquel le charbon de terre puisse se vendre, pendant un certain tems, est comme celui de toutes les autres marchandises, *le prix qui est simplement suffisant* pour *remplacer, avec ses profits ordinaires, le capital employé à le faire venir au marché.* » (ibidem, p. 350.)

---

a In the manuscript instead of a comma: "sur."—*Ed.*

363. « Ainsi le prix des métaux même grossiers, et plus encore celui des métaux précieux, *aux mines les plus fécondes qui existent*, influe nécessairement sur le prix de ces métaux à toute autre mine du Monde. » (ibidem, p. 352.)

363. « Ainsi le prix de chaque métal à chaque mine étant réglé en quelque sorte par le prix qu'a ce métal à la mine la plus féconde qui soit pour le moment exploitée dans le Monde, il en résulte qu'à la plus grande partie des mines, ce *prix ne doit guère faire plus que payer la dépense de l'exploitation*, et qu'il peut *rarement* fournir une bien forte rente au propriétaire. Aussi à la plupart des mines, la rente ne compose-t-elle qu'une petite part dans le prix du métal, et une bien plus petite encore s'il s'agit de métaux précieux. Le travail et le profit forment la majeure partie de ce prix. » (ibidem, pp. 353-54.)

363. « Le plus bas prix auquel on puisset pendant un certain tems, vendre les métaux précieux ... se règle sur les mêmes principes qui déterminent le plus bas prix ordinaire de toute autre marchandise. Ce qui le détermine, c'est le capital qu'il faut communément employer pour les faire venir de la mine au marché, c'est-à-dire, la quantité de nourriture, vêtement et logement qu'il faut communément consommer pour cela. Il faut que le prix soit tout au moins suffisant pour remplacer ce capital avec les profits ordinaires. » (ibidem, p. 359.)

364. « La *demande de pierres précieuses* vient entièrement de leur beauté. Elles ne servent à rien qu'à l'ornement, et le mérite de leur beauté est *extrêmement rehaussé par leur rareté ou par la difficulté et la dépense de les extraire de la mine*. En conséquence, c'est de salaires et de profits qu'est composée le plus souvent la presque totalité de leur haut prix. La rente n'y entre que pour une très-faible partie, très-souvent elle n'y entre pour rien, et il n'y a que les mines les plus fécondes qui puissent suffire à en payer une un peu considérable. » (ibidem, p. 361.)

364. « Le prix des métaux précieux et des pierres précieuses étant réglé pour le Monde entier, par le prix qu'ils ont à la mine la plus féconde, il s'ensuit que la rente que peut rapporter au propriétaire une mine des uns ou des autres, est en proportion, non de la fécondité *absolue* de la mine, mais de ce qu'on peut appeler sa fécondité *relative*, c'est-à-dire, de sa supériorité sur les autres mines du même genre. Si on découvrait de nouvelles mines qui fussent aussi supérieures à celles du Potosi, que celles-ci se sont trouvées être supérieures aux mines de l'Europe, la valeur de l'argent pourrait par-là se dégrader au point que les mines, même du Potosi, ne vaudraient pas la peine de les exploiter. » (ibidem, p. 362.)

364. « L'abondance dégrade nécessairement la valeur d'un produit, qui ne tire sa principale valeur que de sa rareté. » (ibidem, p. 363.)

364. « Il en est autrement des biens qui existent à la surface de la terre. La valeur, tant de leur produit que de leur rente, est en proportion de leur fertilité *absolue* et non de leur fertilité *relative*. La terre qui produit une certaine quantité de nourriture ou de matériaux de vêtement ou de logement, peut toujours nourrir, vêtir et loger un certain nombre de personnes ; et *quelle que soit la proportion dans laquelle le propriétaire prendra part dans ce produit*, cette part mettra toujours à son com-

mandement une quantité proportionnée du travail de ces personnes, et des commodités que ce travail peut lui procurer. » (ibidem, pp. 363-64.)

364. « La valeur des terres les plus stériles n'éprouve aucune diminution par le voisinage des terres les plus fertiles. Au contraire, elle y gagne en général une augmentation. Le grand nombre de personnes que les terres fertiles font subsister, *procurent à maintes parties du produit des terres stériles un marché* qu'elles n'auraient jamais trouvé parmi les personnes que leur propre produit eût pu faire subsister. » (ibidem, p. 364.)

365. « Tout ce qui tend à rendre la terre plus fertile en subsistances, augmente non-seulement la valeur des terres sur lesquelles se fait l'amélioration, mais encore contribue à augmenter pareillement la valeur de plusieurs autres terres, en faisant naître de nouvelles demandes de leur produit. » (ibidem, p. 364.)

366. « *Troisième section. Des variations dans la proportion entre les valeurs respectives de l'espèce de produit qui fournit toujours une rente, et l'espèce de produit qui quelquefois en rapporte [une et quelquefois n'en rapporte point].* » (Adam Smith, *Recherches sur la nature et les causes de la richesse des nations.* Traduction nouvelle... par Germain Garnier », t. II, Paris, 1802, p. 1.)

366. « Dans un pays naturellement fertile, mais dont la très-majeure partie est tout-à-fait inculte, comme le bétail, la volaille, le gibier de toute espèce, *peuvent s'acquérir au moyen d'une très-petite quantité de travail, il s'ensuit qu'ils ne peuvent en acheter ou en commander qu'une très-petite quantité.* » (ibidem, p. 25.)

366. « Quel que soit l'état de la société, quel que soit son degré de civilisation, *le blé est toujours une production de l'industrie des hommes*[a] : or, le produit moyen de toute espèce d'industrie s'assortit toujours avec plus ou moins de précision à la consommation moyenne, la quantité moyenne de l'approvisionnement à la quantité moyenne de la demande ; d'ailleurs, *dans les différens degrés d'amélioration d'un pays, il faudra toujours,* l'une portant l'autre, des *quantités de travail à peu près égales, o u,* ce qui revient au même, *le prix de quantités à peu près égales,* pour faire croître des quantités égales de blé dans un même sol et un même climat ; l'augmentation continuelle qui a lieu dans les facultés productives du travail, à mesure que la culture va en se perfectionnant, étant plus ou moins contre-balancée par l'accroissement *continuel du prix des bestiaux,* qui sont les *principaux instrumens* de l'agriculture. Nous devons donc, d'après ceci, être bien certain qu'*en tout état possible de la société,* dans tout degré de civilisation, *des quantités égales de blé* seront une *représentation o u* un *équivalent* plus juste de *quantités égales de travail,* que ne le seraient des quantités égales de toute autre partie du produit brut de la terre. En conséquence le blé ... est, dans tous les différens degrés de richesse et d'amélioration de la société, une mesure de valeur plus exacte que toute autre marchandise ou que toute autre classe de marchandises ... En outre, le *blé* ou tout autre végétal faisant la nourriture ordinaire et favorite du peuple, constitue, dans tout pays civilisé, la *principal partie de la subsistance de l'ouvrier...* Ainsi

---

a In the manuscript: "de l'homme".—*Ed.*

le prix du travail en argent dépend beaucoup plus du prix moyen du blé, qui est la subsistance de l'ouvrier, que de celui de la viande ou de toute autre partie du produit brut de la terre ; par conséquent, la valeur réelle de l'or et de l'argent, la quantité réelle de travail qu'ils peuvent acheter ou commander, dépend beaucoup plus de la quantité de blé qu'ils peuvent acheter ou représenter, que de celle de viande ou de toute autre espèce de produit brut dont ils pourraient disposer. » (ibidem, pp. 26-28.)

367. « On peut dire d'une marchandise, qu'elle est *chère* ou à *bon marché,* non-seulement en raison de ce que son prix habituel fait une grosse ou une petite somme, mais aussi en raison de ce que ce prix habituel se trouve plus ou moins au dessus du prix le plus bas, auquel il soit possible de la mettre au marché pendant un certain tems de suite. *Ce prix le plus bas est celui qui remplace purement, avec un profit modique, le capital qu'il faut employer pour mettre cette marchandise au marché. Ce prix est celui qui ne fournit rien pour le propriétaire de la terre, celui dont la rente ne fait pas une partie constituante, et qui se résout tout entier en salaires et en profits.* » (ibidem, p. 81.)

367. « Le prix des diamans et des autres pierres précieuses est peut-être encore plus près que le prix de l'or, du prix le plus bas auquel il soit possible de les mettre au marché » (ibidem, p. 83.)

367. « ... n'a qu'une puissance bornée ou incertaine. » (ibidem, p. 89.)

367. « ... la quantité de ces marchandises restant la même ou à peu près la même, tandis que la concurrence des acheteurs va toujours croissant, leur prix peut monter à tous les degrés possible d'excès... » (ibidem, p. 91.)

367. « ... elle consiste dans ces plantes et ces animaux utiles que la nature produit dans les pays incultes, avec tant de profusion, qu'ils n'ont que peu ou point de valeur, et qui, à mesure que la culture s'étend, sont forcés par elle de céder le terrain à quelque produit plus profitable. Pendant une longue période dans le cours des progrès de l'amélioration, la quantité des produits de cette classe va toujours en diminuant, tandis qu'en même tems la demande qu'on en fait va toujours en augmentant. Ainsi leur valeur réelle, la quantité réelle de travail qu'ils peuvent acheter ou commander, s'élève par degrés jusqu'à ce qu'enfin elle monte assez haut pour en faire un produit aussi avantageux que toute autre production venue à l'aide de l'industrie humaine, sur les terres les plus fertiles et les mieux cultivées. Quand elle est montée jusque-là, elle ne peut plus guère aller pus haut; autrement, pour augmenter la quantité du produit, on y consacrerait bientôt plus de terre et plus d'industrie. » (ibidem, pp. 94-95.)

368. « ... de tous les différens articles qui composent cette seconde classe de produit brut, le bétail est peut-être celui dont le prix s'élève le premier à cette hauteur, dans le cours des progrès de l'amélioration. » (ibidem, pp. 96-97.)

368. « ... si le bétail est une des premières parties qui atteigne ce prix, le *gibier* est peut-être une des dernières. Quelqu'exorbitant que puisse paraître le prix de la venaison en Angleterre, il s'en faut encore qu'il

puisse compenser la dépense d'un parc de bêtes fauves, comme le savent
très-bien tous ceux qui se sont occupés de la conservation de ce genre
de gibier. » (ibidem, p. 104.)

368. « ... dans toutes les fermes, les rebuts de la grange et de l'étable peuvent entretenir un certain nombre de *volailles*. Comme elles sont nour-
ries de ce qui serait perdu sans cela, on les a seulement pour faire
profit de tout ; et comme elles ne coûtent presque rien au fermier, il
peut trouver encore son compte à les vendre pour très-peu de chose. »
(ibidem, pp. 105-06.)

368. « ... il y ait profit à cultiver la terre exprès pour en nourrir. » (ibidem, p. 106.)

368. « ... on a, dans l'origine, [...] pour faire profit de tout. » (ibidem, p.
108.)

368. « Il est évident que les terres d'un pays ne peuvent jamais parvenir
à un état d'amélioration et de culture complète avant que le *prix* de
chaque produit que l'industrie humaine se propose d'y faire croître, ne
soit d'abord monté assez haut pour *payer la dépense d'une amélioration et d'une culture complète*. Pour que les choses en soient là, il faut
que le prix de chaque produit particulier suffise à payer d'abord la
rente d'une bonne terre à blé, qui est celle qui règle la rente de la
plupart des autres terres cultivées, et à payer en second lieu le travail
et la dépense du fermier, aussi bien qu'ils se paient communément
sur une bonne terre à blé, ou bien, en autres termes, à *lui rendre
avec les profits ordinaires, le capital qu'il y emploie*. Cette *hausse dans
le prix* de chaque produit particulier doit évidemment *précéder* l'amélioration et la culture de la terre destinée à faire naître ce produit ...
ces différentes sortes de produit brut [...] sont *venues à valoir*, non
une plus grande somme d'argent, mais une plus grande quantité de
travail et de subsistances qu'auparavant. Comme il en coûte une *plus
grande dose de travail et de subsistances pour les faire venir au marché,* par cela même elles en *représentent* ou *en valent* une plus grande
quantité quand elles y sont venues. » (ibidem, pp. 113-15.)

369. « ... sur la multiplication duquel l'industrie humaine n'a qu'un pou-
voir limité ou incertain. » (ibidem, p. 115.)

369. « Dans les pays mal cultivés, et qui par conséquent ne sont que très-
faiblement peuplés, le prix de la laine et de la peau est toujours beaucoup plus grand, relativement à celui de la bête entière, que dans les
pays qui, étant plus avancés en richesse et en population, ont une
plus grande demande de viande de boucherie. » (ibidem, p. 117.)

369. « Il faut alors, en général, aller chercher le poisson à de plus grandes
distances ; il faut employer de plus grands bâtimens et mettre en
oeuvre des machines plus dispendieuses en tout genre. » (ibidem, p.
130.)

369. « ... ne pourra guère être alors approvisionné à moins d'un travail ... »
(ibidem, p. 130.)

369. « ... travail qu'il fallait pour l'approvisionner dans le premier état. » (ibidem, p. 130.)

369. « Ainsi *le prix réel* de cette denrée doit augmenter naturellement dans les progrès que fait l'amélioration... » (ibidem, p. 130.)

370. « Si l'extension de l'amélioration et de la culture élève *nécessairement le prix de chaque espèce de nourriture animale,* relativement au prix du blé, d'un autre côté elle fait aussi nécessairement *baisser* celui de toute espèce, je crois, de *nourriture végétale.* Elle élève le prix de la nourriture animale, parce qu'une grande partie de la terre qui produit cette nourriture, étant rendue propre à la production du blé, doit rapporter au propriétaire et au fermier la rente et le profit d'une terre à blé. Elle *fait baisser le prix de la nourriture végétale,* parce *qu'en ajoutant à la fertilité de la terre,* elle accroît l'abondance de cette sorte de nourriture. Les améliorations dans la culture introduisent aussi plusieurs espèces de nourriture végétale, qui, exigeant moins de terre que le blé, et pas plus de travail, viennent au marché à beaucoup meilleur compte que le blé. Telles sont les pommes de terre et le maïs ... D'ailleurs, il y a beaucoup d'espèces d'alimens du genre végétal, qui, dans l'état grossier de l'agriculture, sont confinés dans le jardin potager, et ne croissent qu'à l'aide de la bêche mais qui, lorsqu'elle s'est perfectionnée, viennent à se semer en plein champ, et à croître à l'aide de la charrue ; tels sont les turneps, les carottes, les choux, etc. » (ibidem, pp. 145-46.)

370. « ... le prix réel des *matières premières* ne hausse point ou ne hausse pas extrêmement... » (ibidem, p. 149.)

370. « De meilleures machines, une plus grande dextérité et une division et distribution de travail mieux entendues, toutes chose qui sont les effets naturels de l'avancement du pays, sont cause que, pour exécuter *une pièce quelconque, il ne faut qu'une bien moindre quantité de travail ;* et quoique, par suite de *l'état florissant* de la société, le *prix réel du travail doive s'élever* considérablement, cependant *la grande diminution dans la quantité du travail que chaque chose exige,* fait bien plus en général que compenser quelque hausse que ce soit qui puisse survenir dans le prix de ce travail. » (ibidem, p. 148.)

371. « Il en *coûtait une bien plus grande quantité de travail pour mettre la marchandise au marché;* ainsi, quand elle y était venue, il fallait bien qu'elle achetât ou qu'elle obtînt en échange le *prix* d'une plus grande quantité de travail. » (ibidem, p. 156.)

371. « ... toute amélioration qui se fait dans l'état de la société, tend, d'une manière directe ou indirecte, faire monter la rente réelle de la terre... » (ibidem, pp. 157-58.)

371. « L'extension de l'amélioration des terres et de la culture y tend d'une manière directe. La part du propriétaire dans le produit augmente nécessairement à mesure que le produit augmente. » (ibidem, p. 158.)

371. « ... survient dans le prix réel de ces sortes de produits bruts, dont le renchérissement est d'abord l'effet de l'amélioration et de la culture, et devient ensuite la cause de leurs progrès ultérieurs... » (ibidem, p. 158.)

371. « Ce produit, après avoir haussé dans son prix réel, *n'exige pas plus de travail, pour être recueilli, qu'il n'en exigeait auparavant.* Par conséquent il *faudra une moindre portion qu'auparavant de ce produit,* pour suffire à *remplacer le capital qui fait mouvoir ce travail, ensemble les profits ordinaires de ce capital.* La portion restante du produit, qui est la part du propriétaire, sera donc plus grande, relativement au tout, qu'elle ne l'était auparavant. » (ibidem, pp. 158-59.)

372. « Tout ce qui réduit le prix réel de ce premier genre de produit, élève le prix réel du second... » (ibidem, p. 159.)

372. « ... et la rente grossit avec le produit. » (ibidem, p. 160.)

372. « ... intérêt général de la société. » (ibidem, p. 161.)

372. « La classe des propriétaires peut gagner peut-être plus que celle-ci à la prospérité de la société ; mais aucune ne souffre aussi cruellement de son déclin, que la classe des ouvriers. » (ibidem, p. 162.)

372. « ... intérêt général de la société. » (ibidem, p. 163.)

372. « ... l'intérêt particulier de ceux qui exercent une branche particulière de commerce ou de manufacture, est *toujours,* à quelques égards, *différent* et même *contraire* à celui du public. » (ibidem, pp. 164-65.)

372. « ... une classe de gens dont l'intérêt ne saurait jamais être exactement le même que l'intérêt de la société, qui ont en général intérêt à tromper le public et même à le surcharger, et qui en conséquence ont déjà fait l'un et l'autre en beaucoup d'occasions. » (ibidem, p. 165.)

NOTES

[1] In accordance with his plan, Marx should have begun the section on Ricardo after completing the extensive chapter on "Theories of Productive and Unproductive Labour" and three further chapters, which by their nature represent supplements to the section on the Physiocrats (on Necker, on Quesnay's *Tableau économique* and on Linguet). Yet Marx did not immediately tackle this work. Having concluded the chapter on Linguet, he began to write the chapter on Bray. Evidently this was connected with his reference, in the chapter on Linguet, to the "few socialist writers" whom Marx said he would "come to speak of in this survey". (See *Theories of Surplus-Value*, Part I, Moscow, 1963, p. 335.) Accordingly, in the draft of the table of contents on the cover of notebook X, in the heading "(f)" (this heading comes immediately after the heading of chapter "(e) Linguet") Marx struck out the name "Ricardo" which he had originally written down, and replaced it by "Bray". (Ibid., p. 37.) But the chapter on Bray remained unfinished. Subsequently, Marx decided to transfer the analysis of Bray's views into the chapter "Adversaries of the Economists". (See *Theories of Surplus-Value*, Part I, Moscow, 1963, Preface, p. 38.)

When Marx began to write the chapter on Bray, he intended to open up the section on "Ricardo" with chapter "(g)". But once more, Marx struck out the name "Ricardo" in the heading, and chapter "(g)" became the "Digression" entitled "Herr Rodbertus. New Theory of Rent".

Marx began to work on the chapter on Rodbertus in June 1862. Ferdinand Lassalle had reminded Marx in a letter of June 9, 1862: "The books which I lent you (Rodbertus, Roscher, etc.) you must ... send back to me at the *beginning* of October ..." (see: *Aus dem literarischen Nachlass von Karl Marx, Friedrich Engels und Ferdinand Lassalle*. Published by Franz Mehring. Fourth Volume, Stuttgart, 1902, S. 355). This obviously gave Marx the external impetus to take up at once the work of writing the chapter on Rodbertus. But there were also serious inner reasons which made it necessary, before all else, to subject the Rodbertian theory of rent to a critical analysis.

Marx's letters on *Capital* show that already at this time he clearly saw the shortcomings and errors of Ricardo's theory of rent. Marx considered the absence of the concept of absolute rent to be one of the major deficiencies of Ricardo's theory of rent. An attempt to develop this concept was made by Rodbertus in the third of his *Sociale Briefe an von Kirchmann*. Before tackling the specific examination of the Ricardian theory of rent, Marx subjected Rodbertus's work to a detailed critical analysis in the "Digression" now before us.   p. 15

2 Marx means here his work *Misère de la Philosophie* (see *Poverty of Philosophy*, Moscow, paragraph 4 of the second chapter "Property or Ground Rent") which is directed against Proudhon.   p. 18

3 This is a reference to the book by John Wade, *History of the Middle and Working Classes*, which was published in London in 1833.   p. 19

4 By "raw material" in this instance, Marx evidently understands a subject of labour which has not undergone any alteration by means of labour, but which is provided by nature. In all other instances, in his manuscript of 1861-63, Marx uses the term "raw material" in the narrower sense as defined by him in Volume I of *Capital*, seventh chapter, namely, objects which are "already products of labour" (see *Capital*, Vol. I, Moscow, 1965, p. 181). "...not every subject of labour is raw material; it can only become so, after it has undergone some alteration by means of labour" (ibid., p. 179).

   The departure from the normal use of the term "raw material" in this instance is probably due to the fact that, in his critique of Rodbertus, Marx at times uses the Rodbertian terminology for polemic purposes.   p. 21

5 In notebook IV of his manuscript of 1861-63 (page 149 et seq.), Marx describes as the *"first division of labour"*, the division of labour within society, between producers of commodities who are independent of one another, and as the *"second division of labour"*, the division of labour within a capitalist enterprise, in particular within a workshop. (Cf. *Capital*, Vol. I, Moscow, 1965, pp. 350-59.)   p. 23

6 These quotations are taken from the second edition of Thomas Charles Banfield's book, *The Organisation of Industry*, which appeared in 1848 (pp. 40 and 42).   p. 23

7 The term "average price" ("Durchschnittspreis") is here used by Marx in the sense of price of production, i.e., $c+v$ (cost of production)$+$average profit, and it is evidently identical with "the average market-price over a long period, or the central point towards which the market-price gravitates" (see p. 319 of this volume). The term "average price" is first used by Marx on p. 93 of the *Theories of Surplus-Value*, Part I, Moscow, 1963.   p. 25

8 About the difference between *"production period"* and *"labour period"* or *"working period"*, particularly in agriculture, and about the special features of capitalist development in agriculture to which it gives rise, Marx wrote in his manuscript of 1857-58, first published in Moscow in 1939 under the title *Grundrisse der Kritik der politischen Oekonomie* (see pp. 560-62 either of the Moscow edition or of the Berlin edition of

1953). The concept "production period"—i.e., the period which, in addition to working time, also comprises the time "during which the subject of labour is ... subjected to natural processes, and must undergo physical, chemical and physiological changes"—has been expounded by Marx in the second volume of *Capital,* Chapter XIII "The Time of Production".

p. 28

9 In Volume III of *Capital* Marx states that capitalists are at once hostile competitors and "allies". In connection with his investigation into the equalisation of the general rate of profit, in which "in each particular sphere of production the individual capitalist, as well as the capitalists as a whole, take direct part in the exploitation of the total working class by the totality of capital and in the degree of that exploitation ..." he writes: "Here, then, we have a mathematically precise proof why capitalists form a veritable freemason society vis-à-vis the whole working class, while there is little love lost between them in competition among themselves" (*Capital,* Vol. III, Moscow, 1966, pp. 196 and 198.)   p. 29

10 According to Marx's original plan his economic work was to be divided into six books; "this book" refers to *Capital,* the first of these six books. (See the preface to *A Contribution to the Critique of Political Economy* by Karl Marx in K. Marx F. Engels, *Selected Works,* Vol. I, Moscow, 1962, p. 361.)   p. 30

11 See P. J. Stirling, *The Philosophy of Trade; or, Outlines of a Theory of Profits and Prices,* Edinburgh, 1846, pp. 209-10.   p. 33

12 Carey declared that rent is merely the interest on capital sunk into the land. Marx speaks of this vulgar conception of Carey's without actually mentioning him by name, on page 523 of his manuscript (see p. 163 of this volume as well as pp. 595 and 622 of *Capital,* Vol. III, Moscow, 1966).

p. 34

13 Buchanan's conception of the monopoly price of agricultural products, is dealt with by Marx in his manuscript on pages 523 and 644 (see this volume, p. 162 and pp. 386-87). Marx examines Hopkins's views on rent on pages 508 to 510 (see this volume, pp. 136-41).   p. 34

14 See George Opdyke, *A Treatise on Political Economy,* New York, 1851, p. 60.   p. 34

15 This refers to Francis William Newman's book *Lectures on Political Economy,* London, 1851. On page 155 of his book Newman writes: "... looking to the majority of those farmers who are not indigent and who must certainly be called Capitalists, we must judge that the love of a country life makes them (on a permanent average) satisfied with *less* gain than might have been expected in other businesses from the same capital."   p. 37

16 In the manuscript there then follows a rough sketch in which Marx examines the production of a cotton-grower, a spinner and a weaver. Marx starts out from the profit which each of them receives individually and then proceeds to a consideration of the amount of profit that is made when the *weaver is assumed to be also the spinner and the cotton-grower.* But Marx was not happy about what he had written. He broke off the draft which he had begun, struck it out and followed it up with the clearer exposition of his thoughts which is given in the text.   p. 49

[17] Marx has in view his extensive section on John Stuart Mill which is contained in notebooks VII and VIII (pp. 319-45 of his manuscript of 1861-63). In accordance with the table of contents compiled by Marx, and with the references which appear in notebook VII (p. 319), the section on John Stuart Mill is transferred to Part III of the *Theories of Surplus-Value*, into the chapter on the disintegration of the Ricardian School.   p. 49

[18] See Karl Marx, *Theories of Surplus-Value*, Part I, Moscow, 1963, section [10] "Exchange of Revenue and Capital", pp. 224-45.   p. 49

[19] Marx refers here to that part of his inquiry into "capital in general" which eventually grew into Volume III of *Capital*. See Note 12 in Part I of *Theories of Surplus-Value*, Moscow, 1963, p. 460.   p. 49

[20] Marx refers here to his notebook XII of the abstracts on political economy. On the cover of this notebook Marx wrote: "London, July 1851". The passage from Thomas Hopkins's book, *Economical Enquiries relative to the Laws which Regulate Rent, Profit, Wages and the Value of Money* (London, 1822), which Marx has in mind here, is to be found on page 14 of this notebook. He subsequently quotes the passage again on the cover of notebook XIII of his manuscript of 1861-63 (p. 669b). In the present edition this quotation is given in the Addenda on p. 592 of this volume.
          p. 55

[21] Marx deals with the influence which the high or low cost of the raw material exerts on the industry using it, in the section on John Stuart Mill (mentioned in Note 17) which is published in Part III of *Theories of Surplus-Value*.   p. 65

[22] See T. R. Malthus, *Principles of Political Economy*, 2nd edition, London, 1836, p. 268. This passage from Malthus is quoted and analysed by Marx in the chapter on Malthus in *Theories of Surplus-Value*, Part III (pp. 765-66 of the manuscript).   p. 69

[23] Marx refers here to the example given in notebook VIII of his manuscript (pp. 335-36) in his extensive digression on John Stuart Mill published in Part III of the *Theories of Surplus-Value* (see Note 17).   p. 76

[24] See Karl Marx, *Theories of Surplus-Value*, Part I, Moscow, 1963, pp. 224-45.   p. 80

[25] This passage from Rodbertus is quoted here by Marx with the "necessary alterations" which follow from a circumstance which Rodbertus left out of account, namely, that the value of the machines and other means of production necessarily enters into the product of agriculture in just the same way as the value of agricultural raw materials enters into the product of industry. Marx quotes this passage as it was presented by Rodbertus, at an earlier point (see this volume, pp. 58 and 59). The term "machine value" (Maschienenwert) is used by Marx, not without irony, as an analogy with the Rodbertian term "value of the material" (Materialwert). All words inserted by Marx are printed in the text in interspaced roman type.   p. 81

[26] See Karl Marx, *Theories of Surplus-Value*, Part I, Moscow, 1963, pp. 237-43.   p. 83

[27] See Karl Marx, op. cit., pp. 228-37.   p. 84

[28] In the manuscript there follows a short insertion here on capital as "the legalised reflexion of other people's labour". Marx put this into square brackets and indicated that, as it interrupted the continuity of presentation, it should be inserted at another point. We reproduce this passage in the form of a footnote on p. 34 of this volume. p. 96

[29] In this paragraph, with which Marx begins his investigation of the dependence of the aggregate rent (i.e., absolute and differential rent) on the relative fertility of the land, he assumes, to begin with, that the amount of rent is directly proportional to the fertility of the land (in the sense that if any class of land is one-fifth more fertile than another, the amount of rent for this class is one-fifth greater than the rent which is yielded by the less fertile class of land). In the subsequent investigation Marx drops this assumption and gives a more precise formulation of the dependence of the amount of rent on the relative fertility of the land.

If we add up the rents for the classes of land II, III, IV in accordance with these subsequent explanations by Marx, and if, in so doing, we go by the number of quarters which are yielded in these classes and which are sold at a price of £$1/3$ per quarter, then we arrive at £34 for II, £$62^4/_5$ for III and at £$97^9/_{25}$ for IV. The calculation runs as follows: Since class II is more fertile than I by $1/_5$, it produces $360 + 72$, i.e., 432 quarters, which are sold at £$^{432}/_3$, i.e., at £144. Of this £144, £110 represents production costs plus average profit; this leaves £34 for rent (absolute and differential rent). The calculation for classes III and IV follows exactly the same lines.

This method of calculating the amount of rent, which is used extensively by Marx in Chapter XII ("Tables of Differential Rent and Comment"), already appears in the present Chapter VIII. Although on page 98 and again on page 104 Marx writes that £$17^7/_{25}$ is the total rent of class IV and £$7^7/_{25}$ the differential rent of this class, a few lines lower he indicates the correct way of determining the differential rent of class IV: £$207^9/_{25}$ — £120 = £$87^9/_{25}$. If £10 absolute rent is added to this amount, we arrive at £$97^9/_{25}$ for the total rent of class IV, which corresponds perfectly with Marx's subsequent conclusions. p. 98

[30] In his *Cours d'économie politique*, Tome II, St. Petersburg, 1815, pp. 78-79, Storch writes: The rent of the most fertile land determines the rate of rent on all other lands competing with the most fertile land. So long as the produce of the most fertile land is sufficient to satisfy demand, the less fertile lands ... cannot be cultivated, or in any case, they yield no rent. But as soon as demand exceeds the amount of produce that the best land can supply, the price of the products rises and it is then possible to cultivate the less fertile soil and to draw a rent from it." Marx discusses this proposition of Storch's in *Capital*, Vol. III (see *Capital*, Vol. III, Moscow, 1966, pp. 183 and 658). p. 99

[31] In Note 30 to Chapter X of Volume III of *Capital* (Moscow, 1966, p. 182) Marx says that, on the question of the market-value of agricultural products, Ricardo and Storch "are both right and both wrong and that both of them have failed to consider the average case". p. 102

[32] Regarding the two methods of calculation used in this example see Note 29. p. 105

[33] See Karl Marx, *Theories of Surplus-Value*, Part I, Moscow, 1963, pp. 68-83
and pp. 93-95.   p. 106

[34] Marx here disregards the profit accruing to the agricultural capital laid
out in classes I, II, III, and IV. Since the £100 capital laid out in I produces 330 bushels at 6s. 8d. per bushel, the value of the total product of
I amounts to £110, of this £10 falls to rent and consequently there is no
profit. The same applies to the aggregate product of the four classes, which
comes to £500 consisting of £400, replacement of the capital outlay, and
£100, the total rent of classes I, II, III, and IV, that is £10+£20+£30+
+ £40.   p. 108

[35] Marx does not make an exact calculation here. For a general illustration
of the thesis that the production of a product which is more than four
times as great as the product of class I is less costly if it is being produced simultaneously by all four classes than by class I alone, it suffices
that the figures which express the costs in each of these four classes
individually, should form a descending line. For the sake of simplicity,
Marx uses the round figures 100, 90, 80, 70.

If one made an exact calculation, one would arrive at different figures.
Thus, for example, if the amount of product in class I is assumed to be
330 bushels, the product in class II, where the fertility is greater by one-
fifth, would be 396 bushels with an outlay of £100; the production of
330 bushels on land II would then cost $\dfrac{100 \times 330}{396} = £83^{1}/_{3}$.   p. 108

[36] In the manuscript this paragraph, which Marx put into brackets, is to be
found two paragraphs lower down, (on the same page, 494) wedged in
among a short historical discourse on the views of Petty and D'Avenant
on the variability of the magnitude of rent. According to its content, the
paragraph set in brackets follows on from Marx's preceding consideration
of the relationship between productivity in agriculture and productivity
in industry.   p. 112

[37] This is a reference to Anderson's work *An Enquiry into the Nature of the
Corn Laws; with a View to the New Corn-Bill proposed for Scotland,*
Edinburgh, 1777.   p. 114

[38] The reference is to Adam Smith's *An Inquiry into the Nature and Causes
of the Wealth of Nations* published in two volumes in London in 1776.
                                                                      p. 114

[39] This refers to Ricardo's "Preface" to the first edition of his book *On the
Principles of Political Economy, and Taxation*, which was published in
London in 1817.   p. 115

[40] This refers to Malthus's book *An Essay on the Principle of Population* ...
which appeared anonymously in London in 1798.   p. 115

[41] Marx refers to the book by Joseph Townsend, *A Dissertation on the Poor
Laws* ..., which appeared anonymously in London in 1786. He quotes
from it in notebook III of his manuscript of 1861-63 (pp. 112-13) in the
section on "Absolute Surplus-Value". The three passages quoted there can
also be found in Volume I of *Capital*, Chapter XXV (see *Capital*, Vol. I,
Moscow, 1965, pp. 646-47).   p. 115

[42] See Note 40.   p. 119

[43] This refers to Malthus's pamphlets *The Grounds of an Opinion on the Policy of Restricting the Importation of Foreign Corn* ... and *An Inquiry into the Nature and Progress of Rent* ... which appeared in London in 1815. p. 119

[44] An allusion to the Corn Law of 1815, which prohibited the import of corn into Britain so long as the price of corn in the country remained below 80s. per quarter. p. 119

[45] An allusion to the Leipzig University Professor Roscher, the vulgar economist. p. 120

[46] The Austrian preacher and writer known as *Abraham a Santa Clara* (his real name was Hans Ulrich Megerle) sought to propagate Catholicism in a form the general public could easily understand, his sermons and moral tracts were therefore written in a pseudo-popular style. p. 120

[47] In the manuscript there follows a short insertion in which Marx compares Ricardo's views on the level of wages with those of Malthus. This insertion is printed in the form of a footnote on page 120 of this volume. p. 121

[48] Marx refers to the work by John Ramsay McCulloch, *The Literature of Political Economy*, which appeared in London in 1845.

[49] Marx designates Roscher by the name of the outstanding ancient Greek historian Thukydides, because "Professor Roscher" as Marx writes in notebook XV of his manuscript (p. 922) "modestly proclaims himself the Thukydides of political economy". Roscher makes an immodest reference to Thukydides in the preface to his *Grundlagen der Nationalökonomie*.

The designation "Thukydides Roscher" is obviously ironical: Roscher, as Marx shows in the present, ninth chapter and in a number of other places, crudely distorts both the history of economic conditions and the history of economic theory. p. 122

[50] Here Marx has in mind Edward West's work *Essay on the Application of Capital to Land* ... which appeared anonymously in Lonlon in 1815 and also David Ricardo's work *An Essay on the Influence of a low Price of Corn on the Profits of Stock* which was published in London in the same year. p. 124

[51] See W. Roscher, *System der Volkswirtschaft*. Band I, *Die Grundlagen der Nationalökonomie*, Dritte, vermehrte und verbesserte Auflage, Stuttgart und Augsburg, 1858, S. 191. p. 124

[52] This refers to Thomas Hopkins's book *Economical Enquiries relative to the Laws which regulate Rent, Profit, Wages, and the Value of Money* published in London in 1822. Marx quotes the relevant passage from this book at a later stage (see this volume, pp. 140-41). p. 126

[53] Marx does not return to the analysis of these views of Roscher's in the subsequent text of the *Theories of Surplus-Value*. But in Part III of the *Theories* in the chapter on "The Disintegration of the Ricardian School", Marx makes a detailed criticism of similar vulgarised views held by McCulloch who was, like Roscher, strongly influenced by the apologetic concept of the "productive services" which Jean-Baptiste Say had put forward and which Marx mentions in the next paragraph. Marx touches

upon Roscher's views on nature as one of the sources of value, in Note 22, Chapter VIII of Volume I of *Capital* (Moscow, 1965, p. 206). Also see *Capital*, Vol. III, Moscow, 1966, p. 826.   p. 132

[54] Marx writes at greater length about enclosures in Britain in Chapter XXVII of *Capital*, Vol. I.   p. 143

[55] This refers to the Malthusian theory of population.   p. 145

[56] James Anderson quotes here from *Ricordo d'Agricoltura* by Tarello da Lonato which was first published in Venice in 1567. Anderson refers to the first Mantua edition which appeared in 1577 and quotes from the French translation of this, which was published by the Société économique in Bern.   p. 145

[57] McCulloch quotes these passages from Anderson's *An Enquiry into the Nature of the Corn Law*, Edinburgh, 1777, pp. 45-48.   p. 146

[58] See Karl Marx, *Theories of Surplus-Value*, Part I, Moscow, 1963, pp. 95-104.
                                                                            p. 151

[59] See James Mill, *Elements of Political Economy*, London, 1821, p. 198.
                                                                            p. 152

[60] In Volume I of *Capital*, Chapter XXVII, Marx writes that between 1801 and 1831, 3,511,770 acres of common land were stolen from the English agricultural population, "and by parliamentary devices presented to the landlords by the landlords". (See *Capital*, Vol. I, Moscow, 1965, p. 728.)
                                                                            p. 157

[61] See Karl Marx, *The Poverty of Philosophy*, Moscow, 1962, p. 150.   p. 158

[62] Ibid., p. 154.   p. 158

[63] Ibid., pp. 157-58.   p. 158

[64] Ibid., p. 151.   p. 159

[65] By "*agricultural machines*", Rodbertus understands here the various classes of land with different fertility. Rodbertus borrowed this comparison of classes of land with machines of varying efficiency, from Malthus.
                                                                            p. 159

[66] See Jean-Baptiste Say, *Traité d'économie politique...*, Cinquième edition, t. I, Paris, 1826, p. LXXXIII to LXXXIV (or also: sixth edition, Paris, 1841, p. 41).   p. 166

[67] In addition to the 12 chapters (VIII-XVIII and XXIX) of Ricardo's book which are concerned with taxes in the actual sense of the word, Marx also counts Chapter XXII ("Bounties on Exportation and Prohibitions of Importation") and Chapter XXIII ("On Bounties on Production") which also touch upon questions of taxation, since bounties, according to Ricardo's theory, are paid from a fund which is made up of various taxes paid by the population.   p. 167

[68] See Note 19.   p. 169

[69] By "*means of subsistence which enter into consumption in general*" Marx understands here on the one hand the means of subsistence consumed by the workers and on the other hand auxiliary materials (such as coal, lubricating oil, etc.) which are consumed by the machines in the process of production.   p. 173

[70] Regarding the terms *"production period"* and *"labour* period" see Note 8.
p. 178

[71] The average profit amounts to $20^5/_{26}$ per cent only when the capitals laid out by the manufacturer and the farmer are the same. But if we take into consideration the difference in the size of the capitals laid out: £800 by the farmer and £1,300 by the manufacturer (altogether £2,100), then, since the aggregate profit of both comes to 400, the average profit is $\frac{400 \times 100}{2,100} = 19^1/_{21}$ per cent.   p. 187

[72] On the views of Malthus, Torrens, James Mill and McCulloch, see the corresponding sections in Part III of *Theories of Surplus-Value*.   p. 191

[73] A*"quarter"* as a grain measure contains 8 *bushels*.   p. 201

[74] By the "numerical ratio or the proportional size of the categories", Marx understands here the mass of products which each of these categories brings on to the market.   p. 205

[75] Marx refers to Thomas Corbet's book *An Inquiry into the Causes and Modes of the Wealth of Individuals*... published in London in 1841, in which Corbet maintains that in industry, the prices are regulated by those commodities which are being produced under the most favourable conditions and those commodities, in his opinion, represent the majority of all commodities of a given type (see pp. 42-44 of Corbet's book).   p. 205

[76] Cf. above, in the ninth chapter, p. 122 of this volume.   p. 210

[77] It is assumed that the average rate of profit is 10 per cent.   p. 219

[78] The reference is to James Steuart, *An Inquiry into the Principles of Political Economy*, Vol. I, Dublin, 1770, which contains a description of the transition process from the mainly natural economy of the English countryside to capitalist commodity production. This transformation is accompanied by the intensification of labour in agriculture and the expropriation of the rural population. The expression "time becomes precious" is used by Steuart on p. 171 of the above-mentioned volume. It is quoted by Marx together with other passages from Steuart in the economic manuscripts of 1857-58 (see Karl Marx, *Grundrisse der Kritik der politischen Ökonomie*, S. 742).   p. 132

[79] This is a reference to the work by Karl Dietrich Hüllmann, *Städtewesen des Mittelalters*, in 4 parts, Bonn, 1826-29.   p. 234

[80] The proposition, that the whole amount of rent (the absolute rent and the differential rent taken together) equals the difference between the market-value and cost-price, is gone into more fully by Marx at a later stage (see p. 293 of this volume).   p. 257

[81] Marx arrives at the differential rent per ton—$£^{16}/_{65}$—by deducting $£1^3/_5$, the individual value of the ton of coal produced in III, from $£1^{11}/_{13}$, the new market-value.   p. 257

[82] The preceding examples did not refer to agriculture but to the exploitation of coal-mines of varying productivity. But everything that has been said about these mines is also applicable to agricultural land of varying fertility.   p. 259

[83] As Marx explains further on (p. 268 of this volume), he calls *differential value* the difference between market-value and individual value. The differential value is calculated per unit of the product, the differential rent, on the other hand, is worked out for the aggregate product in the given class. If the market-value of a unit of the product is greater than its individual value, the difference is a positive quantity, if, on the other hand, the market-value is smaller than the individual value, this difference is a negative quantity. Hence the signs + and — in the table on page 574 of his manuscript (see the insertion between pages 264 and 265 of this volume).

In tables C, D and E on page 572 of the manuscript (261-62 of this volume) Marx puts the signs + and — before the numbers which express the amount of differential rent in pounds sterling. For instance in Table C in the column "Differential rent", we have the negative quantity "—£9³/₁₃". This means that in the given case the productivity of class I is so low that, with the given market-value, the land of this class not only yields no differential rent, but that even the absolute rent falls considerably below its normal magnitude. In case I C, the absolute rent amounts to only £10/₁₃, i.e., it is £9³/₁₃ less than the normal size of this rent, the normal size in the given example being £10.

In the table on page 574 of the manuscript, Marx expresses this same phenomenon of negative differential rent by negative values in the column "Differential value" and in these cases he simply writes the figure "0" into the column "Differential rent", thus indicating the absence of a *positive* differential rent (moreover *negative* differential rent correspondingly reduces absolute rent, and this reduction is shown in the column "Absolute rent"). The transfer of the negative quantities into the column "Differential value" obviates the difficulty which arose in Table C on page 572, when it was necessary to add up the differential rents of the different classes. Only with the positive differential rents (marked with a + sign) entered into the addition, while the negative quantity "—£9³/₁₃" was simply regarded as nil to avoid duplication. That is why, for the calculation of negative rents, Marx set up a special category in his summary tables, entitled "Differential value per ton", into which he entered the negative differential values as well.   p. 262

[84] Following on directly from this paragraph, on page 573 of his manuscript, Marx sets out the tables A, B, C and D, including in each of them all the categories enumerated here. On the following page of his manuscript (page 574) all the data of tables A, B, C and D are set out once again, in a more orderly fashion, and the corresponding data of Table E are appended. This results in a uniform arrangement which is to be found in this book between pages 264 and 265. Since the scheme drawn up by Marx on page 573 of his manuscript contains no additional data for tables A, B, C and D and was taken over completely in the second compilation it is not reproduced in this volume.   p. 262

[85] This is a reference to Karl Marx, *Zur Kritik der politischen Ökonomie. Erstes Heft*, first published in Berlin in 1859.   p. 264

[86] See Karl Marx, *Theories of Surplus-Value*, Part I, Moscow, 1963, pp.208-12.
                                                                                      p. 265

[87] In the example quoted by Marx, the product whose production depends on landed property, enters into both component parts of the capital advanced, in equal proportions. Marx assumes that, regardless of the increase in the constant capital (88c instead of 80c following upon the increased price of the raw material) and the variable capital (22v instead of 20v following upon the increased price of the means of consumption of the workers), the market-value of the total product continues to be 120. This could only be the case because the surplus-value appropriated by the capitalists has gone down from 20 to 10. Such a reduction in surplus-value has been due to an increase of 10 units in the differential rent, which rose on the more productive sections of the land as the exploitation of less productive sections of land took place. In this way, the newly created value which continues to be 40 (since the same method of production is employed), is redistributed in the following way: 10 units now form the surplus-value which falls to the capitalist, 20 units are used to replace the variable capital, and 10 units serve to increase the differential rent, an increase caused by the rise in the value of the constant capital, by 8 units, and of the variable capital, by 2 units.

At a later stage, on pages 684-86 of the manuscript (454-57 of this volume) Marx considers a similar case.   p. 277

[88] In this instance, and now and again later on in the text, Marx uses the term "Produktionskosten"—"*costs of production*"—in the sense of the cost of production plus the average profit, i.e., in the sense of cost-price. An analogous use of the term "Produktionskosten" is also occasionally to be found in Volume III of *Capital*.   p. 292

[89] See Note 30.   p. 293

[90] On Wakefield's theory of colonisation, see Karl Marx, *Capital*, Vol. I, Chapter XXXIII, Moscow, 1965, pp. 765-74.   p. 301

[91] By "*the market cost-price*" Marx understands the general cost-price, which regulates the market-prices of the commodities in a particular sphere of production. Cf. p. 126 of this volume, where Marx uses the term "average market-price" for the same concept.   p. 320

[92] By "*absolute rent*" in the text on page 327 and in the last column of the tables set in between pages 328 and 329 of this volume Marx means the *rate* of absolute rent.   p. 327

[93] *The Morning Star*—daily paper, organ of the Free Traders, was published in London from 1856 to 1869.   p. 328

[94] Ricardo calls rent "creation of value" in the sense that it enables the landowners to pocket the *increment in the value* of the total social product which, according to Ricardo, results from the increased difficulty of producing a part of the grain. Ricardo calls this increment in the value "nominal" because it adds nothing to the real wealth of the society. In Chapter XXXII of *Principles* Ricardo criticises Malthus's proposition that rent is "a clear gain and a new creation of riches" and states that rent does not increase the wealth of the society as a whole, but merely transfers "a portion of the value of the corn and commodities from their former possessors to the landlords".

A longer excerpt from this passage from Ricardo's *Principles* is given by Marx on pp. 549-50 of this volume. Marx's views regarding the creation

41*

of "a false social value" are set forth in Chapter XXXIX of *Capital,* Vol. III
(cf. Karl Marx, *Capital*, Vol. III, Moscow, 1966, p. 661).   p. 341

[95] This is a reference to the thesis put forward by Rodbertus, that the value
of raw materials does not enter into the costs of production of agricultural products. See this volume, Chapter VIII, Section 4.   p. 342

[96] These words set in brackets were inserted here by Marx at a later stage
after he had written the section dealing with Smith's views on house
rent—on page 641 of his manuscript.   p. 365

[97] This and the following extract from Adam Smith are quoted by Marx in
English—not in Garnier's French translation as most of the other passages from Smith reproduced in this volume. The two quotations are taken
by Marx from Ricardo's *Principles of Political Economy*, London, 1821,
pp. 227 and 229-30.   p. 365

[98] Marx is referring here to the views put forward by Ricardo on page 230
of the third edition of his book *Principles of Political Economy*, London,
1821.   p. 366

[99] In the manuscript there follows a section in which Marx analyses a passage from the *Principles* in which Ricardo writes about his conception
of rent. This section, which is separated by a line from the preceding text,
is a supplement to those chapters in which Marx examines Ricardo's
theory of rent. According to the content it belongs to the thirteenth chapter
and that is where it has been placed in this edition (see p. 317 of this
volume).
    In the manuscript this section is followed by a passage set in round
brackets; this is a supplement to the analysis of the Ricardian theory of
cost-prices, which Marx makes in the tenth chapter. This supplement has
therefore been transferred there (see p. 216 of this volume).   p. 372

[100] In the manuscript (page 641) there follows a section which deals with
Adam Smith's views on house rent. This section has been put into the
fourteenth chapter in this edition (see pp. 365-66 of this volume).   p. 384

[101] In the manuscript there follows a section (pp. 642-43) in which Marx
examines various examples in which the values of constant and variable
capital move in opposite directions. Since the section is a supplement to
the manuscript pages 640-41 it is reproduced in this volume of pages 382-83.
                                                                               p. 385

[102] Ricardo puts forward this definition of monopoly price in Chapter XVII
of his book *Principles of Political Economy* (third edition, London, 1821,
pp. 289-90). An analogous definition of monopoly price put forward by
Adam Smith, is quoted by Marx earlier, see p. 349 of this volume.   p. 387

[103] Marx is referring to sections IV and V of the first chapter of Ricardo's
Principles of Political Economy, where Ricardo investigates the effect of
rising and falling wages on "the relative value" of commodities produced
by capitals of different organic composition. A detailed analysis by Marx
of these sections can be found on pp. 174-99 of this volume.   p. 390

[104] As an example, Marx sets out here one of the ways in which the process
of approximation of the organic composition of agricultural capital to
that of industrial capital can take place. Marx takes as his starting-point:

$60c + 40v$ for the agricultural capital
$80c + 20v$ for the non-agricultural capital

Marx assumes that as a result of the rise in productivity of agricultural labour, the number of workers in agriculture is reduced by one quarter. The organic composition of agricultural capital thus alters: the product which previously demanded an outlay of a capital of 100 units $(60c + 40v)$ now requires an expenditure of a capital of only 90 units $(60c + 30v)$, which if reckoned on 100 units amounts to $66^2/_3c + 33^1/_3v$. In this way, the organic composition of the agricultural capital would approximate to that of the industrial capital.

Marx assumes further, that simultaneously with a reduction in the number of agricultural workers, the wage—due to a lowering in the price of corn—also falls by one quarter. In this case it must certainly be assumed that wages in industry fall in the same proportion. The fall in wages, however, must have a greater effect on the agricultural capital, which has a lower organic composition, than on the non-agricultural capital. This would lead to a further reduction in the difference between the organic composition of agricultural and industrial capital.

With a fall in wages by one quarter, the agricultural capital of $66^2/_3c + 33^1/_3v$ will be transformed into a capital of $66^2/_3c + 25v$, which, when reckoned on 100 units, amounts to $72^8/_{11}c + 27^3/_{11}v$.

With a fall in wages by one quarter, the non-agricultural capital of $80c + 20v$ will be transformed into a capital of $80c + 15v$, which, when reckoned on 100 units, amounts to $84^4/_{19}c + 15^{15}/_{19}v$.

With a further reduction in the number of agricultural workers and with a further fall in wages, the organic composition of agricultural capital will approach even more closely to that of non-agricultural capital.

In his consideration of this hypothetical case used to explain the influence of the growth in the productivity of labour in agriculture on the organic composition of agricultural capital, Marx abstracts from the simultaneous, and often even more rapid growth in the productivity of labour in industry, which causes a further rise in the organic composition of the industrial capital in comparison with the agricultural. On the relation between the organic composition of capital in industry and agriculture, see above, pp. 18-21, 92-93, 103, 105-06, 109-12, 243-44 of this volume.   p. 392

[105] In numbering the pages of the manuscript, Marx left out the figure 649.
p. 395

[106] Marx's last remark regarding Say and a similar one on the following page of the manuscript are based on an error. For in the note to the French translation of Ricardo's *Principles of Political Economy* to which Marx is referring here, Say expresses (malicious) pleasure, not because Ricardo has to invoke the law of supply and demand to determine the "value of labour", but to determine the "value of *money*" (cf. David Ricardo, *Des principes de l'économie politique et de l'impôt*. Traduit de l'anglais par F. S. Constancio, D.M. etc.; avec des notes explicatives et critiques, par M. Jean-Baptiste Say. Tome II, Paris, 1835, pp. 206-07). The relevant passage from Say's annotations to Ricardo's *Principles* is *correctly* quoted by Marx in *Misère de la philosophie* (see Karl Marx, *The Poverty of Philosophy*, Moscow, 1962, p. 84).   p. 399

[107] See Note 106.   p. 400

[108] Marx refers here to the pamphlet by James Deacon Hume, *Thoughts on the Corn-Laws...* (London, 1815). Hume, who discusses there Adam Smith's proposition, that "the price of labour is governed by the price of corn" (p. 59), explains that Adam Smith "in speaking of corn must be understood to be speaking of food, because the value of all agricultural produce... has a natural tendency to equalise itself" (ibid.).   p. 402

[109] Marx refers here to the section which begins on page 95b in notebook III of his manuscript of 1861-63, and is entitled "2. Absolute Surplus-Value". The passage referred to by Marx is to be found in the subsection "Simultaneous working days", on pages 102-04 of this manuscript.   p. 410

[110] Marx refers to the value newly created by the twenty workers: in one hour of labour, a value of £2 is created by these twenty workers and in one working day of 14 hours, a value of £28, which is made up of 10 hours necessary labour equal to £20, plus 4 hours surplus-labour equal to £8.   p. 411

[111] The value of the total product contains the value (c) which has been transferred to the product, and the newly created value ($v + s$). Since in the case quoted here, Marx abstracts from fixed capital, the value transferred consists of the value of the raw materials. In the example under consideration, the value of the raw materials is £$93\frac{1}{3}$ (in one hour, $133\frac{1}{3}$ lbs. cotton are worked up into yarn; in 14 hours, $1,866\frac{2}{3}$ lbs; 1 lb. cotton costs 1s.). This, together with the newly created value (£28), amounts to £$121\frac{1}{3}$.   p. 411

[112] See Note 21.   p. 437

[113] This is a reference to such critics of Ricardo, as Jean-Baptiste Say, who, for example, in the introduction to the fifth edition of his book *Traité d'économie politique...* (Paris, 1826), reproaches Ricardo for "judging, at times, on the basis of abstract principles, which he generalises too much" (*de raisonner quelquefois sur des principes abstraits auxquels il donne trop de généralité*), thus arriving at conclusions that do not correspond to reality. See J. B. Say, op. cit., p. LXXXI.   p. 437

[114] The total number of tons, $51\frac{11}{39}$, is obtained by the following calculation; if $16\frac{2}{3}$ workers in class III of Table *E* (between pages 452 and 453) produce $62\frac{1}{2}$ tons, then with the same productivity of labour, $13\frac{79}{117}$ workers will produce $\dfrac{13\frac{79}{117} \times 62\frac{1}{2}}{16\frac{2}{3}} = 51\frac{11}{39}$ tons.   p. 455

[115] See Note 11.   p. 460

[116] Marx is referring to *Observations on the Effects produced by the Expenditure of Government During the Restriction of Cash Payments,* London, 1823, by William Blake. Excerpts from this book dealing with the subject broached here together with Marx's comments can be found in the economic manuscript of 1857-58 (see Karl Marx, *Grundrisse der Kritik der politischen Ökonomie*, S. 672-73).   p. 460

[117] This refers to the World Exhibition opened in London on the 1st of May, 1862, at which were shown exhibits of agricultural and industrial products, works of art and the newest achievements of science.   p. 460

[118] Here Marx points out for the second time that in the passage he quotes from the *Principles of Political Economy,* Ricardo uses the term *"producer"* in the sense of "worker" (Marx noted it for the first time on p. 421 of this volume). Apart from this passage the word "producer" is used in the sense of "capitalist entrepreneur" in Ricardo's *Principles,* see for instance the extracts quoted on pp. 422, 428 and 550 of this volume. p. 463

[119] Ricardo's comment quoted here, on Say's views regarding the relation between profit and interest, was repeated by Marx on page 736 of his manuscript, but, since it did not appertain to what was written on that page, he set it into square brackets, and to Ricardo's concluding words "it is impossible for *any circumstances* to make them change places" made the following retort: "The latter is definitely wrong 'under certain circumstances'."

In *Capital,* Volume III, Chapter XXII, Marx shows that it is possible for the rate of profit and the rate of interest to move in opposite directions from one another, in certain phases of the capitalist cycle. Marx writes: "If we observe the cycles in which modern industry moves ... we shall find that a low rate of interest generally corresponds to periods of prosperity or extra profit, a rise in interest separates prosperity and its reverse, and a maximum of interest up to a point of extreme usury corresponds to the period of crisis." (*Capital,* Vol. III, Moscow, 1966, p. 360.) p. 469

[120] Here Marx returns to the question considered on page 672 of the manuscript (pp. 375, 436-37 of this volume)—the question of how the average rate of profit and accordingly cost-prices are influenced by the profits derived from colonial and foreign trade in general, for on the whole profits are higher in the colonies than in the metropolis. As Marx shows, Smith's conception of this question was more correct than Ricardo's. See also Karl Marx, *Capital,* Volume III, Chapter XIV, Section V "Foreign Trade" (Moscow, 1966, pp. 237-40). p. 469

[121] See Karl Marx, *Theories of Surplus-Value,* Part I, Moscow, 1963, pp. 122-35 and 228-37. p. 472

[122] Ibid., pp. 135-47, 182-93 and 237-45. p. 472

[123] This example is based on the assumption that with growing productivity of labour, the harvest obtained from 20 quarters of wheat expended as seed, will be 50 per cent larger than before. If the harvest previously amounted to, say, 100 quarters, then with the same expenditure of labour as before, it will now amount to 150 quarters. But these 150 quarters cost just as much as the 100 quarters did previously, that is £300. Previously, the seed made up 20 per cent (both in terms of number of quarters, and in terms of value), whereas now it constitutes only $13^1/_3$ per cent. p. 474

[124] The words "See McCulloch", set in brackets, have been added by Marx subsequently, in pencil. In his letter to Engels, of 24th August, 1867, Marx mentions that previously—in his letter of 20th August, 1862—he had expressed the idea that the *amortisation fund* is used for the purpose of accumulation, and adds that he had *later* found that McCulloch "represented the sinking fund as an accumulation fund". (The reference is to McCulloch's book *The Principles of Political Economy,* pp. 181-82 of the Edinburgh edition of 1825.) Marx returns to this question in Part III of

his *Theories of Surplus-Value* on pages 777 and 781 of his manuscript.
p. 480

[125] See Karl Marx, *Theories of Surplus-Value*, Part I, Moscow, 1963, pp. 135-47, 182-93 and 237-45.
p. 489

[126] Marx refers to this work *Zur Kritik der politischen Ökonomie*.
p. 493

[127] J. B. Say writes in *Traité d'économie politique*. Seconde édition, tome II, Paris, 1814, p. 382, "Products can only be bought with products". This formula is almost literary repeated by Ricardo in his *Principles of Political Economy* (third edition, London, 1821, p. 341). Marx later quotes the passage from Ricardo's *Principles* where the formula occurs and examines it critically (see this volume, pp. 499-502 and the Chapter "Decline of the Ricardian School" in Part III of *Theories of Surplus-Value*, p. 811 of the manuscript).
p. 493

[128] Marx is referring to James Mill's observations on the constant and necessary balance between production and consumption, between supply and demand, between the total amount of sales and the total amount of purchases—observations which are contained in the third section of the fourth chapter of his book *Elements of Political Economy*, on pages 186-95, in the London edition of 1821. Marx examines this view of James Mill's (which the latter first expressed in his pamphlet *Commerce Defended*, published in London in 1808) more fully in the section "Die Metamorphosen der Waren" in his work *Zur Kritik der Politischen Ökonomie*.
p. 493

[129] See S. Bailey, *A Critical Dissertation on the Nature, Measures, and Causes of Value*, London, 1825, pp. 71-93.
p. 495

[130] See W. Roscher, *System der Volkswirthschaft*, Erster Band. *Die Grundlagen der Nationalökonomie*, Dritte Auflage, Stuttgart und Augsburg, 1858, S. 368-70.
p. 498

[131] The term "below or under its price" is explained by Marx in an earlier passage where he writes: "*under* its price, that is to say, for less than the sum of money which represents its value" (i.e., the value of the commodity) (see Karl Marx, *Theories of Surplus-Value*, Part I, p. 308).
p. 504

[132] Marx evidently refers to the weaver, or rather owner of a weaving-mill, discussed on p. 478 et seqq. of this volume. There, it is true, a linen weaver is mentioned and here a calico weaver, but the raw material used makes no difference at all to the question at issue.
p. 507

[133] Marx has in mind here that part of his investigations which subsequently grew into the third volume of *Capital*. See Note 12 on p. 460 of *Theories of Surplus-Value*, Part I, Moscow, 1963.
p. 513

[134] Brief observations on the forms of crisis were not long afterwards jotted down by Marx on the covers of notebook XIII (page 770a of the manuscript) and notebook XIV (pages 771a and 861a). They are printed in this volume in section 11, "On the Forms of Crisis" (see p. 513), in accordance with Marx's note: "Supplement to page 716".
p. 517

[135] In the manuscript there follows a small insertion on Ricardo's views on money and exchange-value. This insertion is set into brackets and annotated

to the effect that it should be inserted elsewhere, since it interrupted the continuity of the subject-matter related there. Accordingly, this insertion is reproduced as a footnote on page 504 of this volume.　　　　　　　　p. 520

[136] The passage in which Ricardo says that "demand is only limited by production" (p. 339 of the *Principles,* third edition) is quoted by Marx at greater length earlier (see page 493 of this volume). "There is no limit to demand—no limit to the employment of capital" occurs in a passage of Ricardo's *Principles* (p. 347 of the third edition), which is quoted on p. 497 of this volume.　　　　　　　　p. 520

[137] This is a reference to notebooks I to V of the manuscript of 1861-63, and in particular to the sections dealing with the production of absolute and of relative surplus-value. The *Theories of Surplus-Value,* which begins with notebook VI, forms the direct continuation of the earlier notebooks.　　　　　　　　p. 521

[138] Marx is alluding to two passages from Ricardo's *Principles,* namely "nothing is required but the means, and nothing can afford the means, but an increase of production" (p. 342 of the third edition which is quoted at greater length on p. 506 of this volume) and "it is not probable that he will continually produce a commodity for which there is no demand" (pp. 339-40 of the third edition, the entire sentence is quoted on pp. 493 and 502 of this volume).　　　　　　　　p. 522

[139] In the manuscript there follows a brief insertion set in brackets, which contains an example of a partial crisis—over-production of yarn called forth by the introduction of the spinning machine. This insertion is reproduced as a footnote on p. 521 of this volume.　　　　　　　　p. 524

[140] Marx is alluding to the views expressed by Say in *Lettres à Malthus,* and quoted in *An Inquiry into those Principles, Respecting the Nature of Demand and the Necessity of Consumption* published anonymously. Compare also Say's proposition that "sluggishness in the sale of some products arises from the scarcity of some others" which is examined by Marx in the *Theories of Surplus-Value,* Part I, p. 260.　　　　　　　　p. 531

[141] Marx refers to Thomas Tooke's *A History of Prices, and of the State of the Circulation,* Volumes I-VI, London, 1839-57. The work contains many references to the influence of the weather on prices. Tooke deals with this subject in particular at the beginning of Volume IV, which was published in 1848.　　　　　　　　p. 533

[142] Sismondi declared that crises are due to "la disproportion croissante entre la production et la consommation" [the growing disproportion between production and consumption] (*Nouveaux principes d'économie politique ou de la richesse dans ses rapports avec la population.* Seconde édition. Tome premier, Paris, 1827, p. 371). In his book *Misère de la Philosophie* Marx says that according to Sismondi's doctrine "diminution in revenue is proportional to the increase in production" (see Moscow edition of 1962, p. 34). Marx returns to the consideration of Sismondi's views on crisis in Part III of *Theories of Surplus-Value,* where he brings out the

valuable elements in Sismondi's conception as well as its fundamental weaknesses (see in particular page 775 of the manuscript).   p. 534

[143] See James Steuart, *An Inquiry into the Principles of Political Economy*, Vol. I, Dublin, 1770, p. 396. Marx quotes the relevant passage in the economic manuscript of 1857-58 (see Karl Marx, *Grundrisse der Kritik der politischen Ökonomie*, S. 666). Also cf. Karl Marx, *Theories of Surplus-Value*, Part I, p. 48 and *Capital*, Vol. III, p. 786.   p. 554

[144] Ricardo is probably alluding to his speech in the House of Commons, of 16th December, 1819, on William De Crespigny's motion that a special commission should be set up to examine Robert Owen's plan for the liquidation of unemployment and for the improvement of the conditions of the lower classes.

In this speech Ricardo said that in general one could not deny that "machinery did not lessen the demand for labour". (See *The Works and Correspondence of David Ricardo*, Edited by Piero Sraffa with the collaboration of M. H. Dobb, Vol. V, Cambridge, 1952, p. 30.)   p. 555

[145] On the term *"real wages"* as used by Ricardo, see pages 401, 404, 417, 423-24, 438 of this volume.   p. 558

[146] *The Standard*—a daily paper founded in London in 1827, since 1857 organ of the Tories.   p. 575

[147] This refers to the article "America in the Exhibition" which was published anonymously on pages 5-6 of *The Standard* of 19th September, 1862. On the World Exhibition, see Note 117.   p. 575

[148] The brief notes presented as addenda to Part II of the *Theories of Surplus-Value* were written by Marx on the covers of notebooks XI, XII and XIII. They contain material supplementary to some of the questions considered in the main text of Part II of the *Theories*.   p. 587

INDEX OF AUTHORITIES

NAME INDEX

A

Abraham a Santa Clara (alias of Hans Ulrich Megerle) (1644-1709) —Austrian Catholic preacher and writer.—120

Anderson, James (1739-1808)—British economist, a forerunner of Ricardo's in the theory of rent. —34, 89, 114-117, 121-125, 129, 131, 144-147, 158, 159, 161, 162, 236-238, 241, 244, 274, 321, 595

Arbuthnot, John (18th century)— British farmer and economist. Author of a work, which appeared anonymously in 1773, on the connection between the price of food and the size of farms.—589

B

Bailey, Samuel (1791-1870)—British philosopher and economist; polemised against Ricardo. Marx calls him a "trite, superficial and sapient critic".—124, 164, 170, 172, 399, 401, 495

Banfield, Thomas Charles (1795-1880)—British economist.—23

Barton, John (end of the 18th to about the middle of the 19th century)—British economist.—547, 550, 561, 562, 576-585

Bastian, Adolf (1826-1905)—German explorer, ethnologist, Professor at the Universitly of Berlin.—124

Blake, William (end of the 18th to about the middle of the 19th century)—British economist, author of several works on the circulation of money.—459, 460

Buchanan, David (1779-1848)—British economist, "great opponent of the Physiocrats" (Marx).—34, 386, 387, 392

C

Carey, Henry Charles (1793-1879)— American economist; opponent of Ricardo's theory of rent; originally a free trader, later a protectionist.—33, 157, 166, 313, 593

Chalmers, Thomas (1780-1847)— Scottish theologian and economist, follower of Malthus.—239, 460

Cobbett, William (1762-1835)—English publicist, forerunner of the Chartists in the battle for universal suffrage and for the improvement of the conditions of the working people. "The greatest political writer of this century" (Marx).—120, 123

Constancio, Francisco Solano (1772-

K

King, Gregory (1648-1712)—British statistician, engraver and genealogist.—584

Kirchmann, Julius Hermann von (1802-1884)—German lawyer, politician and philosopher.—15, 149, 150

L

Louis XIV (1638-1715)—King of France (1643-1715).—137

Louis XV (1710-1774)—King of France (1715-1774).—137

Louis XVI (1754-1793)—King of France (1774-1792), executed in 1793.—137

M

McCormick, Cyrus Hall (1809-1884) —American inventor.—575

McCulloch, John Ramsay (1789-1864)—British economist; vulgarised Ricardo's economic theory. —114, 122, 124, 146, 191, 192, 480

Malthus, Thomas Robert (1766-1834)—English priest, economist; put forward a reactionary theory of population.—31, 34, 69, 114-123, 138, 144, 162, 167, 191, 199, 341, 393, 397, 416, 423, 484, 540, 548, 577, 584, 589, 593, 594

Mill, James (1773-1836)—Scottish historian, philosopher and economist; follower of Ricardo.—152, 191, 493, 503, 504

Mill, John Stuart (1806-1873)—son of James Mill; philosopher and economist; free trader; descendant of classical school of political economy.—49, 123, 502

N

Newman, Francis William (1805-1897)—British philologist and economist; bourgeois radical; wrote a number of works on religious, political and economic problems.—23, 37, 322

O

Opdyke, George (1805-1880)— American economist, banker, Republican; Mayor of New York from 1862 to 1864.—34

Ovid (Publius Ovidius Naso) (43 B.C.-17 A.D.)—Roman poet.—124

P

Petty, Sir William (1623-1687)— English economist and statistician. "Founder of modern political economy, one of the most outstanding and original economists" (Marx).—112, 129

Proudhon, Pierre-Joseph (1809-1865)—French petty-bourgeois socialist; founder of the theory of anarchism.—18, 158

Q

Quesnay, François (1694-1774)— French physician and economist; founder of the Physiocratic school.—45

R

Ramsay, Sir George (1800-1871)— British philosopher and economist.—579

Ricardo, David (1772-1823)— English economist; the last great representative of classical political

REQUEST TO READERS

Progress Publishers would be glad to have your opinion of this book, its translation and design and any suggestions you may have for future publications.

Please send your comments to 21, Zubovsky Boulevard, Moscow, U.S.S.R.